Poetics & Polemics

Poetics & Polemics

1980–2005

JEROME ROTHENBERG

Selected and Edited by
Jerome Rothenberg and Steven Clay

Introduction by Hank Lazer

THE UNIVERSITY OF ALABAMA PRESS
Tuscaloosa

Copyright © 2008 by Jerome Rothenberg
The University of Alabama Press
Tuscaloosa, Alabama 35487-0380
All rights reserved
Manufactured in the United States of America

Typeface: ACaslon

∞

The paper on which this book is printed meets the minimum requirements of
American National Standard for Information Sciences-Permanence of Paper for
Printed Library Materials, ANSI Z39.48-1984.

Library of Congress Cataloging-in-Publication Data

Poetics & polemics, 1980–2005 / selected and edited by Jerome Rothenberg and
Steven Clay ; introduction by Hank Lazer.
p.   cm. — (Modern and contemporary poetics)
Includes bibliographical references and index.
ISBN 978-0-8173-1627-3 (cloth : alk. paper) — ISBN 978-0-8173-5507-4
(pbk. : alk. paper) — ISBN 978-0-8173-8075-5 (electronic) 1. Poetry—History
and criticism. 2. American poetry—20th century. 3. American poetry—19th
century. 4. English poetry. 5. Poetry—Translations into English. I. Rothenberg,
Jerome, 1931– II. Clay, Steven, 1951– III. Title: Poetics and polemics.
PN1111.P62 2008
809.1—dc22

2008019425

for Pierre Joris, nomad & fellow traveler

Contents

A GALLERY OF POETS

DIALOGUES & INTERVIEWS

Introduction

To put it quite simply and directly, this is an absolutely stunning collection of essays, reviews, and interviews. For many years Jerome Rothenberg has been one of our nation's most important poets, translators, and anthologists. Since the publication of *Pre-Faces* (New Directions, 1981), which collects much of Rothenberg's critical writing through 1980, there has not been a volume that collects and displays the richness and range of Rothenberg's thinking. *Poetics & Polemics, 1980–2005* is destined to be a major publication event—the source book for anyone interested in learning more about a range of topics, from ethnopoetics to the making of modern anthologies to Jerome Rothenberg's own poetry and development. It is a large, significant collection of work. It is also a very inspiring collection; it wakes us (poets, critics, readers) up to the possibilities of poetry and to the centrality of poetic activity to human life and to the possibilities that emerge from an insistently global perspective. Rothenberg provides an energetic, intelligent, exemplary path for a life of sustained investigation into the human (language) riches throughout time and throughout the planet.

Rothenberg, as *Poetics & Polemics* demonstrates, thinks about poetry in all-encompassing terms growing out of a modernism that goes far beyond the customary European-based syllabus. Often, it is the making of an anthology that allows Rothenberg to explore what poetry might be. Ultimately, as he states in *Symposium of the Whole,* he is interested in the "dream of a total art," as well as the "recovery of the oral," categories and concepts integral to his notion of an ethnopoetics. But, as Rothenberg notes, there is not "anything final or tidy about such an ethnopoetics." It is this guiding assumption and passion—a rigorous resistance to closure or finality—that makes possible much of Rothenberg's restlessly investigative writing life. As Rothenberg suggests in "The Poet as Native," his range of interest and the scope of his poetry/poetics comes to include "all functionally languaged people." The reading experience of *Poetics & Polemics* is that of a series of gradually evolving ideas—thoughts subject to ongoing skepticism, reconsideration, and modification. In fact, the lack of finality, the lack of recurring fixed doctrines, becomes one of the most inspiring features of the overall collection.

Perhaps Rothenberg's most enduring accomplishment—an activity central to the essays and interviews in *Poetics & Polemics*—is his radical reconception of the anthology. He has collaborated with a number of poet-editors to produce a range of anthologies that quite simply redefine what a poetry anthology might be and what the proper range of such anthologies ought to be. Rothenberg's anthology work began with *Technicians of the Sacred* (1968), followed by *Shaking the Pumpkin* (poetries of the North American Indians, 1972), *America a Prophecy* (with George Quasha, North American poetry from pre-Columbian times to the present, 1973), *Revolution of the Word* (American experimental poetry between the two world wars, 1974), *A Big Jewish Book* (1977), *Symposium of the Whole* (with Diane Rothenberg, selected writings on ethnopoetics, 1983), *Poems for the Millennium* (two volumes, with Pierre Joris, global anthology of modernist and postmodernist experimental poetry, 1995 and 1998), and *A Book of the Book* (with Steve Clay, examining the poetics and ethnopoetics of the book, 2000). As he notes in the *Sibila* interview included in *Poetics & Polemics,* Rothenberg realized with his very first anthology that "an anthology didn't have to be a conservatizing instrument but could be used as a vehicle for transformation." In that same interview Rothenberg thinks of his anthologies as "a manifesto for whatever poetry was still to come" and a reconfiguration of "the poetic past from the point of view of the present." In other words, a Rothenberg anthology constitutes a well-researched, well-thought-out provocation, but one that does not pretend to be final or totally authoritative. A Rothenberg anthology is, in a maximal sense, a large poem and a fundamentally heuristic activity. As Rilke's famous poem "Archaic Torso of Apollo" ends with the startling line, "You must change your life," a sustained experience with a Rothenberg anthology is likely to leave the poet/reader with a changed mind, particularly about what might be the most exciting and generative resources for experimental poetry now. *Poetics & Polemics* manifests the structuring assumptions that make possible the adventurous, ground-breaking anthologies that Rothenberg has assembled during the past four decades.

What comes through loud and clear in *Poetics & Polemics* is Jerome Rothenberg's omnivorous appetite for a sustained, never-to-be-completed exploration of the possibilities for adventurous living-in-language. He is the preeminent ecologist and advocate for the most democratic, loving study, preservation, and active practice of human language play, and this collection will inspire, inform, and challenge generations of readers, writers, and performers.

Hank Lazer

Pre-Face

My published work now spans a period of more than forty years—nearly a hundred books during that time and a range of other writings and publications. The majority of those books are my own poetry, both those in the original English and a number translated into other languages, including five substantial volumes in French, two in Flemish/Dutch, and four in Spanish. I have also been actively engaged as a translator and as a compiler of anthologies, which I have treated as large assemblages of work from areas of composition and performance that have often been neglected in academic circles while linking in many ways to the major trends of experimental and innovative poetry over the last two centuries. In these anthology-assemblages I first used short prose commentaries to bring out critical points about the poets or the works I was including. These in turn became my opening for the construction of a poetics and, in my own terminology, an equally necessary *ethnopoetics*, which I also pursued through a series of essays, written talks and interviews, "prefaces" and introductions to the works of others, and as editor or coeditor of several magazines (*Alcheringa, New Wilderness Letter,* and *some/thing,* among the better known ones). From the publication of my first assemblage, *Technicians of the Sacred,* in 1968, I have thought of these prose works and related projects as forming a continuum with the poetry—an attempt, that is, to build an image of poetry and an image of the world in which I would always be speaking as a poet.

With the poetics as such I have published a single book of selected writings, *Pre-Faces* (from New Directions), which gives a sampling of work up to 1980 but leaves uncollected or unsampled the considerably more prolific work of the next quarter of a century.[1] Readers who know my poetics through that or the seven or eight dispersed anthologies will therefore lack a sense of the full range of what I've been doing and how that work has developed over several decades. For that reason alone I believe that this new collection of my essays—particularly focused on the writings after *Pre-Faces*—can usefully function to put my critical work into perspective. In putting together this collection I have followed a long-standing pattern of poets and writers who reach a point where vagrant volumes, whether of poetry or prose, can no longer take the full measure of their thought's trajectory and its relation to the work of other poets or to "the life of poetry."

For the first twenty years of my work, then, the reader, if interested, can look back to *Pre-Faces*, which still remains in print through New Directions. With its emphases on ethnopoetics and on the poetics of performance, the book served its purpose initially but has obscured the changes in my work over the decades that followed. Foremost among these changes has been an expansion of my poetics and ethnopoetics toward a more explicit exploration of modernism/avant-gardism and renewed speculations on the book and writing. (These interests come across most clearly in my more recent anthologies: *Poems for the Millennium, The Book, Spiritual Instrument,* and *A Book of the Book.*) At the same time, the last quarter of a century has provided me with increased opportunities for the development and dissemination of my poetics—essays and reviews for journals and magazines, prefaces to books by other poets and artists, and numerous talks and interviews, both spoken and written.

To fill the gap since 1980, the work in *Poetics & Polemics* has been selected to carry along and elaborate my earlier concerns with ethnopoetics and performance, while giving new emphasis to questions of modernism and postmodernism and to the work of poets and movements within that framework. As with *Pre-Faces,* the writings include selections from essays, talks, interviews, reviews, pre-faces, and a section of capsule commentaries from collections such as *Revolution of the Word* and *Poems for the Millennium.* For some of the latter I worked in collaboration with Pierre Joris, as I did with Diane Rothenberg on *Symposium of the Whole,* although the essays selected here are those for which I was primarily re-

1. A new collection of prose writings, specifically focused on ethnopoetics, has recently appeared in a Portuguese translation from Azougue Editorial in Rio de Janeiro under the title *Etnopoesia no milênio. The Riverside Interview* (1984), with Eric Mottram and Gavin Selerie, not included here, was in effect a book-length critical work.

sponsible. In the section titled "Dialogues & Interviews" the sense of collaboration and community, as I understand it, is even more pronounced. And on a number of occasions—including the opening of each of the book's three sections—I have included a poem or a section of a poem, hoping in that way to show the continuity of the work or to blur the line between poems and poetics.

While I haven't followed a chronology in any of the sections, it is my hope that the gathering as a whole will still give a sense of both continuities and changes. Looking back on these pages as a reflection of my life and thought, I am aware not only of a gradually evolving series of ideas and practices but of a clash of ideas—with those of others and with my own. In that process I have confirmed—against all self-doubt—that the work of poetry, for myself and many others, goes beyond the writing of poems, to intersect as well with other forms of writing. What follows is, I hope, another aspect of that work—"[to] mix and fuse poetry and prose, inspiration and criticism, the poetry of art and the poetry of nature," as Friedrich Schlegel had it more than two centuries ago. If I haven't carried that off to everyone's satisfaction, I have tried throughout, as David Antin once said in his definition of "the artist," to be someone "who does the best he can."

Jerome Rothenberg
Encinitas, California
August 2007

POETICS & POLEMICS

The Times Are Never Right

Warm days hanging
over San Diego,
where streets
slide into murky
canyons. What
is this but
home & what
is home
but a misnomer?
Pisces has shifted
into Aries.
Aggravated
bumps shadowing
the server's
arms are no
concern to anyone
yet called to our
attention show
a strain, a fearsomeness
hard to conceal.
The times are never right.
A skin of air is over
everything. The sun
flows like a liquid,
all the universe we see

has never happened.
There is no truth to time
except for birthdays.
In a city under siege
a ceremony
gathers, scattering
the birds.
We live forever
in the instant,
in the house we share.
A groom & bride
are figures,
smaller than a thumb
& little reckoning
how short
the passage between
death & life.

20.iii.02
for Diane Rothenberg's birthday

The Poetics of the Sacred

A Range of Topics for a Keynote Speech

Fu Jen Catholic University, Taipei, September 1990.
Others present: Gary Snyder, Wai-lim Yip

> Blessed art thou, O Lord our God, King of the Universe, who per-
> mittest that which is forbidden.
> > —The personal prayer of Sabbatai Zevi, seventeenth-
> > century Jewish messiah and mystic

The strange thing about it, for many of us, is that we so clearly recognize
the origins of poetry in states of mind and in forms of behavior that we
think of as religious in nature. And yet, speaking for myself and for many
like me, our tendency has been to pull away from religion as such. It is a
tension that I feel in whatever I've done as a poet, and it's a tension that
I'd like to address on this occasion: what a concern with the sacred might
mean in a climate of secular thinking and being.

The Sacred

The sacred rather than the transcendent, because the transcendent, however generously defined in the prospectus for the present conference, implies for me too great a denial of the here and now; and the source of poetry, as I understand it, is deeply rooted in the world around us: doesn't
deny it so much as brings it back to life. "Eternity is in love with the productions of time," wrote William Blake, who was our first great poet
of the here and now. It is in *time* that I engage myself, and it is to discover or create the sense of a life that can energize the common world we
share. In that energizing—that first, deceptively simple, act of poesis—
something strange happens, whether to the world at large or to our sense
of it. Remaining here-and-now, the world begins to lure us with a feeling, an intuition, of what the poet Robert Kelly speaks of as the not-
here/not-now. Poetry, like religion, has been filled with such extraordinary manifestations ("coincidence, chance, odd happenings, large rocks,

hailstorms, talking animals, two-headed cows," and so on), but for those of us for whom poetry in some sense takes religion's place (albeit a religion without assurances), they aren't bound or fixed but open-ended, different (we would like to think) each time we go at them.

On God

If this implies a yearning for what the Surrealists, say, called the "marvelous" and "wonderful," I would be careful not to play down the risks involved—the dark side of the picture. "The world is charg'd with the grandeur of God" begins the great sonnet by Gerard Manley Hopkins, not as an image of transcendence but of immanence. I respond still to what he writes, but I can't speak of God without a sense, too, of negation and rejection. For after Auschwitz and Hiroshima the line comes back to me distorted: "The world is charged with the terror of God."

Here I report my intuition, but it is an intuition curiously reinforced by a form of hermeneutic numerology from the tradition of Jewish kabbala. There, since every letter of the Hebrew alphabet was also a number, words whose letters added up to the same sum were treated as being in significant relation to each other. This system was used, not surprisingly, to substantiate accepted "truths," though there were times when the system (called *gematria,* from the Greek) was used by the heretical and the heterodox to call the others into question. In following that system, I found that the letters in the Hebrew god-name *aleph-lamed-vav-hey (eloha)* add up numerically (= 42) to the Hebrew word *bet-hey-lamed-hey (behalah),* "terror, panic, alarm." That they also add up to *kvodi* ("my glory") only intensifies the problematic. In short, a way of making poetry. So, take it any way you choose. Where God breaks into what I write or think, it is the terror that admits Him.

The "Other" Traditions

There is, accordingly, a string of words with which we work with some degree of caution—the sacred, the holy, the numinous, the spiritual, and others that we shy away from even more—the supernatural, the pious, the divine, the transcendent. Even the sacred for me depends on how and why I'm using it and is resonant therefore with its own problematics. When the American poet David Antin, reacting against the easy—and popular—view of the sacred, says, "I reject the idea of a sacred language,"

I understand his objection even before he completes it: "For me, poetry is a mental act, not work which will become the object of a specialized cult." But I also understand the mental as the *spiritual* (another danger word) and that there are times, for Antin as for me, when the language of the mental act of poetry becomes itself what André Breton called "a sacred action."

It is largely a question of where we locate these words—in what context or tradition. Antin's rejection of the "cult" reflects a distrust of institutional and pietistic forms, of orthodoxies and closed systems, wherever found. In our own generation in America and Europe this has meant a turning from a Western and Judeo-Christian view of mores and religion—in contrast, say, to the rush into orthodoxy of the Eliot and Auden generations. What we came to identify with, beyond our own mental acts, was what Snyder speaks of as a subterranean tradition—or series of such—that manifests globally in movements antithetical to established governments and religions. It represents a poetics of the open as against the closed, the free against the fettered, the transgressive and forbidden against the settled. Its shibboleths are terms like *free verse* and *open form;* the Dada cry "to liberate the creative forces from the tutelage of the advocates of power"; the assertion by William Blake that "poetry fetter'd, fetters the human race."

The Spiritual in Art

It is so easy to lose sight of this; so easy, say, for an academic formalism to obscure the understanding of an artist like Kandinsky, that the work in which he was engaged was not merely "modern" but aimed toward a renewal of the "spiritual in art." So too—in its own way—was Apollinaire's call for a "new spirit" in poetry and art. Or Tristan Tzara's insistence that the Dada poetry and art which he was fostering weren't based on a new method or technique but on a profoundly altered state of mind *(esprit),* something like "an ancient Buddhist religion of indifference," as he also called it. It may seem a curious insistence from a man who was also, politically and philosophically, a dialectical materialist, but something like this turns up again and again as a defining issue within the avant-garde. It's there in Breton's contentions (for Surrealism) that "existence is elsewhere" and that at the end of the surrealist search, "the mysteries which are not will give way at last to the Great Mystery." And for the American poet Ezra Pound it's a mark of a yearning that transcends the trap of the

political and that leads at last to the sense of his own (and possibly necessary) failure.

> I have brought the great ball of crystal
>   who can lift it?
> Can you enter the great acorn of light?
>   But the beauty is not the madness
> Tho' my errors and wrecks lie about me.
> And I am not a demigod,
> I cannot make it cohere.
>   —(Canto 116)

There are times, too, when the search and struggle have centered on a
conflict with Western science and materialism (Kandinsky and a multitude of others would be the case in point), but it would be a mistake not
to recognize that religion—Western religion certainly—has also been at
issue. For some this has meant a re-viewing (re-thinking) of Christian
and Jewish ties and sources, some of it extreme, rejectional, embattled,
openly transgressive but unwilling in general to stray far outside what
Robert Kelly has called "the through-the-west-inherited gnosis." This
would range from the foregrounding of metaphysical but recognizably
Christian poets like Donne or Gongora or Angelus Silesius to the fascination in our time with gnostic traditions outside the normative religious
orders. There is already an "othering" at work here—more exactly a sense
that our own singleness is more akin to what was silenced and made other
in an alliance of church and state that may now be coming to an end. Or
that may, conversely, be returning once again to haunt us.

New Archaeologies, etc.

The freedom to think in these terms—a spiritual gift of the Enlightenment, for which religion (even when most rejected) was a central issue—
has allowed us to move radically beyond the Christian and the Western.
The connection of poetry to pre-Christian and pagan sources goes very
deep into Western history, moving into radical new territories and ar-
chaeologies from the eighteenth century on. A form of such a pagan-
Christian linkage is familiar enough from Eliot's use of Frazer and Har-
rison as underpinnings for *The Waste Land*, although his intellectual
conservatism (both in religion and in poetry) kept him from a fuller ex-

ploration of the possibilities that this kind of move had opened up. With others—Pound, say, as one example—the normative Christian gave way substantially to the force of the non-Christian and non-European past and present.

But the alternative past—even where it keeps, roughly, within the boundaries of Europe or of Asia Minor—can take still more extreme forms. I'm thinking here of poets like Robert Graves, whose image of the White Goddess, among others, drew largely from the bardic taxonomies of the pagan North; of Charles Olson, who explored a pre-Hellenic "archaeology of morning" in the Sumerian and Hittite past; of Clayton Eshleman, with his direct entry into the Paleolithic caves and imageries of ancient Europe; of Velimir Khlebnikov, who found a primal "beyond-sense" language among the Slavic peasants and Central Asian shamans; of Edmond Jabès, who reshaped a kabbalistic literature into a new mental landscape of endlessly discoursing rabbis. It is precisely in mappings and remappings of this kind that one begins to sense the ongoing power of any Western-centered modernism that we would still be willing to inherit.

Such a "modernism"—pushing as well into the "post"modern present—has often enough left Europe far behind it. If this connects in some sense to terms like Edward Said's "orientalism," or to "primitivism" as we've often had it thrown at us, it's also, I would insist, a part of what Gary Snyder, echoing Whitman, once called a "passage to more than India." For Europeans and Americans who have used it sensibly, it is a work of the immediate present, not of the exotic and romantic past. And it is a work intended—above all—to question and disrupt the power of the dominant European discourse.

Pound's *Cathay*

Take Pound's *Cathay* as an example, about which Wai-lim Yip has written so brilliantly. Rather than a capsule glimpse at an ancient—and from a Western perspective, exotic—poetry, it represented Pound's sense of what it was to be alive and writing poetry in 1915 (in the midst of the First World War). "Largely a war book," as Hugh Kenner describes it, "its exiled bowmen, deserted women, leveled dynasties, departures for far places, lonely frontier guardsmen, and glories remembered from afar, were selected from the diverse wealth in the Fenollosa notebooks Pound was working from by a sensibility responsive to torn Belgium and disrupted

London." Pound's writing, then, came at a moment in history when a de-based poetry, an unanchored language of transcendence, had separated us from the immediacies of our experience (debilitating as that experi-ence may have been) and when a new sacralization (the renewal of the spiritual-in-art) depended on connecting to the concrete particulars of the world around us. For this, which was the objective of Pound's imag-ism and of that version of it "in motion" that he called vorticism, some-thing in Chinese language and culture served as both a model and a con-firmation.

In his repeated three-point directive for imagism, two of Pound's im-peratives spoke clearly to and from the ways of poetry he thought he found in China: "direct treatment of the 'thing,' whether subjective or ob-jective," and "using absolutely no word that did not contribute to the pre-sentation." The third—"as regarding rhythm: to compose in the sequence of the musical phrase, not in the sequence of a metronome"—was a nec-essary part of this modernist package but with a more ambiguous relation to Chinese practice as such than he might have thought. It is a package, circa 1913, without reference to the sacred or transcendent or religious, but in the aftermath Pound himself found that it would move toward the intellectul worlds of Kung Fu-tze and Tao, say, and would relate them also (as with the poetry of Li Po and of the *Book of Songs*) to contempo-rary circumstance and praxis. All that as a starter for the century at large: a through-the-*East*-inherited gnosis that would, particularly on its Bud-dhist side, have a fundamental impact on poets like Snyder and Ginsberg and a host of others. (Also, although much less often recognized, in the radical experiments with systematic chance that underpin the projects of a Cage and a Mac Low.)[1]

Toward a Primal Poetics

The idea of a concrete language dominated both American experiments with "image" and Surrealist, largely European, explorations of an onei-ropoetics, a poetics of the dream. In either case the orientation was to-ward the *thing*—the object sighted, sensed, "directly" treated—with an insistence on the closeness between thing and word ("signified" and "sig-

1. Snyder's attempt, as I see it, to write an American poetry unencumbered by reference to a traditional Christian and European past, is an immediate example of how such an experi-ment in gnosis can take shape.

nifier," for those who prefer the abstract counterpart). "We have lived [too] long in a generalizing time," Charles Olson wrote as he too turned away from it, aiming (while bound to fail) to heal the break between reality and language. Something like this has been a central project of our work as poets—a key both to our search for a primal poetics and to our search for the sacred. It has led us into the depths of our own cultures and into cultures far distant from our own, this idea that a sacralized view of the world was tied, somehow, to a clear sharp language of names and nouns, dream names included. "Poetry," wrote Gertrude Stein, "is really loving the name of anything. . . . It is knowing and feeling a name." And George Oppen, American "objectivist" poet, based a poetics on "The small nouns / Crying faith / In this in which the wild deer / Startle, and stare out."

It is this, or something very close to it, that I tried to put forward in *Technicians of the Sacred*, a global anthology of tribal and oral poetries that I fashioned as a series of connections between two mythic poles: a "present" and a "past." *Sacred*, of course, was one of the two key words in that title and behind it was Mircea Eliade's description of the shamans (religious figures rooted in our deepest human past) as masters of the techniques of ecstasy and of the means to bring those into language. If this sometimes implies a poetics of transcendence, I would be careful not to place it "beyond experience" but to remember, for example, how Snyder locates the shaman's work in the experience of those who have "seen the glint in the eye of an eagle or the way a lizard's ribs quake when he does pushups"—and from that as a base "have stepped outside the social nexus to make contact with a totally nonhuman other" from which the poem, as inspired voice, arises. The source of a contemporary poetry of similar intensity may shift the area of experience—the place in which it happens, even the object of the search—but can never be wholly separated from it. And the poet's work may, like the shaman's, make its encounter foremost within language—may start with language and use that as the vehicle with which to drive toward meaning, toward a (re)uniting with the world.[2]

The idea that we could learn about such things from a wide range of cultures—some more advanced in them than our own—triggered the

2. It is needless to point out that the etymology of *religion* underscores its denotation as a "reconnecting" or a "binding up." Its use in an expression like "nature religion" may be what's at stake here—as a reconnecting (not a separation) from the world. The binding to an orthodoxy or to a settled version of the real is, of course, another reading.

move in our time to a new poetics grounded in an *ethno*poetics. Such an ethnopoetics—my coinage, in a fairly obvious way, circa 1967—refers to an attempt to investigate on a transcultural scale the range of possible poetries that have not only been imagined but put into practice by other human beings. It was premised on the perception that Western definitions of poetry and art were no longer, indeed had never been, sufficient and that our continued reliance on them was distorting our view both of the larger human experience and of our own possibilities within it. The focus of our ethnopoetics as such was not so much inter*national* as inter*cultural,* with a stress on those stateless and classless societies that an earlier ethnology had classified as "primitive."

A Poetics of the Sacred

Behind this search for origins—for what would allow us to begin again, to break free from the past even as we reclaimed it—was the trauma of the Second World War, when "man" (Charles Olson wrote for all of us) "had been reduced to so much fat for soap, superphosphate for soil, fillings and shoes for sale." It was against the background of this crisis— of the mind, the spirit—that the work we were engaged in first revealed its meaning. So, if Gary Snyder, say, spoke of that work—"the real work of modern man"—as the "uncovering of the inner structure and actual boundaries of the mind," the urgency of his statement related it to the time in which it was spoken. If mind is its own mystery, so are the objects that the mind uncovers or conceals: in short, the world. So is that language which is both mind's vehicle and prison.

In writing of those poetries (traditional/oral/tribal) that filled the first part of *Technicians of the Sacred,* I underscored first off my sense that they were (like the languages in which they were framed) complex rather then simple. This was reinforced by seeing the words as part of larger ritual and mythic wholes and served me further as a way of undermining the notion that complexity and intelligence were all on "our" side, minimalism and a kind of naked energy on theirs. Rather, I suggested, poetry both then and now (there and here) was a juncture of intelligence and energy that I equated with (another poet's codeword) "imagination." And from that juncture—which was what the gathering was really about— emerged the idea, but also the experience, of what we've sometimes called "the sacred."

In Lieu of a Conclusion

With an eye, then, on both the here and there of it, it was my hope that the poems and juxtapositions in *Technicians of the Sacred* would illuminate the ways in which poetry—wherever found—may act as a vehicle for enhancing our sense of the human and other-than-human, their convergence in the sacred. If we don't etherealize or abstract this process, it can of course be read as an equivalent to that definition of transcendence that the organizers of this conference gave us to work with: as "a function or being that transcends [that goes beyond or through] the possibilities of experience and yet is necessary to give meaning to the data of experience." Such a search for meaning will take us into dangerous areas as well as safe ones, "blinding images" (in Wai-lim Yip's formulation) as well as clear ones; and its effectiveness will be proven in some sense by the degree to which it remains problematic and resistant to our attempts to evade or to resolve it.

As a function of our *un*belief, it may resemble that absurdity—that doubting of the sensible and probable—in which Tertullian once rested his *belief.*

The Anthology as a Manifesto & as an Epic Including Poetry, *or* the Gradual Making of *Poems for the Millennium*

Talk first presented at the Modern Language Association,
December 30, 1995, modified for presentation at the Boston
Alternative Poetry Conference, July 18, 1998

I would like to go back over my own relationship to anthologies, and to contrast it to a general discomfort I have with anthologies as such, before entering into a discussion (however it falls out) of *this* anthology or of "the anthology as an epic poem and/or a manifesto." In 1979 I had done five anthologies, the most recent of which *(A Big Jewish Book)* had been published by Doubleday the year before. It was with relation to this that Charles Bernstein, who was then editing the important (poets') journal of poetics, *L=A=N=G=U=A=G=E*, asked me to write a piece on my own work and/or "on anthologies." I began that piece with a quote from Gertrude Stein about the new and the old, since the anthologies I had then made were a conjunction of modernist poems with ancient or culturally distant works of near-poetry that I wanted (in Robert Duncan's words) to "bring into their comparisons." What Stein wrote (words that I've quoted a number of times since, as I have a way of doing with quotations) was "As it is old it is new and as it is new it is old, but now we have come to be in our own way which is a completely different way."

With that as epigraph, I tried to distinguish two, at least two, kinds of anthology (a point that seemed to me self-evident): those that *deceive* me/us by a false sense of closure and authority, as over against those that I had hoped to do with regard to the *past,* and those still more rare and useful ones that opened up and thereby changed the *present.* (Both of the latter I took, rightly or wrongly, as instances of a single impulse.) The canonical anthologies we all know as the great conservatizing force in our literature(s), against which—as artists of an avant-garde—many of us have had to struggle. As gatherings of acceptable/accepted poets their conservatizing thrust is evident; as gatherings of contemporary poets it is to rein in or exclude those moves that challenge too overtly the boundaries of form and meaning or that call into question the boundaries (genre boundaries) of poetry itself.

The other possibility of anthologies is to use the form as a kind of manifesto-assemblage: to present, to bring to light, or to create works that have been excluded or that collectively present a challenge to the dominant system-makers or to the world at large. In my time the great American work of this kind was Donald Allen's (1960) *New American Poetry* (replete with its appended section of poetic statements/manifestos) but also LaMonte Young and Jackson Mac Low's *An Anthology*, as a manifesto of the 1950s/1960s Fluxus movement, and Emmett Williams's *An Anthology of Concrete Poetry*, as a first summary and presentation of the movement of that name. Still earlier works were Pound's Imagiste gathering and later *Active Anthology* or (better yet) Louis Zukofsky's "Objectivists" anthology of the early 1930s (a prime example, that, of the construction of a movement through a book—and little else by way of publication).

From these I sensed the possibility of the anthology as (1) a manifesto; (2) a way of laying out an active poetics—by example and by commentary; and (3) a grand assemblage: a kind of art form in its own right. My first anthology, *Technicians of the Sacred*, grew from premises (theory) *within* experimental modernism rather than from critical authority situated outside it—what Tristan Tzara implies in his (1918) *post*modern divergence, that "Dada is . . . not a *modern* school . . . [nor] a reaction against the schools of today . . . [but] more in the nature of an almost Buddhist religion of indifference." Beginning in that general area I was able to explore an open-ended range of deep cultures, of culturally embedded poetries and related language works, many of them subsumed as poetry by resemblance to contemporary work and in that comparison also opening the range and giving a new depth to the experimentally modern. So, too, I used the last quarter of the book for a section of commentaries that not only gave some ethnographic context to the traditional pieces but allowed the entry and comparison (for better or worse) of a number of more contemporary works (an early revival of Gertrude Stein and a mix of new and old voices, of the modern and the postmodern: André Breton, Diane Wakoski, Tristan Tzara, Gary Snyder, Anne Waldman, Allen Ginsberg, Ian Hamilton Finlay, Simon Ortiz, Hannah Weiner). This was, of course, the hidden (secret) heart of the collection, what made it (I hope) not a book of antiquities or orientalisms or primitivisms but a manifesto for our time: each commentary a pointed statement of a way of poetry long overlooked.

All of the anthologies I've assembled since then—by myself or with others—have shared in this; or, to use a key word of the 1960s European Situationists, who helped so much in the development of a strikingly "appropriative" postmodernism, they have been a *détournement* (a turning or a twist) on the structures and presumptions of those fixed anthologies that continue (like the darkness) to surround us.[1] After claiming it as a right, I later found that I had gotten leverage to continue and to expand this work and (with Pierre Joris as a powerful coworker) to construct an assemblage of the twentieth century that would bring together (on a global scale) works entirely of this time that had been (the greater part of them at least) too often kept beyond the pale or, if present, had been kept from those comparisons, those coexistences that were so real to our generation of poets *throughout the world*. In that sense I would bow also to those many others who have been our companions, even forerunners in this attempt: cultural hunters and gatherers (or, simply, formal and experiential innovators), who recognized that the common work cut across boundaries; that alliances and strategies were international, intercultural, in scope; that it was possible to seek wholeness or completeness while knowing that we never would achieve it; that the explorations and discoveries of a new poetry and art were precisely what made the attempt at wholeness possible.

That work, which Pierre Joris and I called *Poems for the Millennium*, is now complete, and its two volumes and sixteen hundred pages (some twelve years in the making) are generally available. The first volume *(From Fin-de-Siècle to Negritude)* covers the century up to the Second World War and is the first such gathering to put the avant-gardes and movements of that time into a place of principal consideration. With that in mind we were able to devote whole sections to six of those movements (Futurism, Dada, Expressionism, Surrealism, the American "Objectivists," and the African & Caribbean Negritude poets) and to draw on individual voices from a still wider range of languages and cultures. And we were able to show, too—if it needed showing—that multiculturalism

---

1. In *Poems for the Millennium* such détournements extend to the overblown subtitle *(The University of California Book of Modern & Postmodern Poetry)*, the board of advisers (largely themselves experimental poets), the quasi-scholarly commentaries, and the various other accoutrements and paraphernalia of the *official* book.

and avant-gardism were not incompatible but historically, though not inevitably, related. Our last section, in that sense, was devoted to ethnopoetic explorations from throughout the century.

The gathering—insofar as it smacked of "anthology" in the ordinary sense—was replete with problematics and anxieties. This tension intensified, of course, with the second volume, which moved us into the (almost) present, moved us, literally, into a time and poetry in which we shared. The tough thing here—and we knew it from the start—was that as an anthology (and I mean a largely *contemporary* anthology) it had to be a flawed book—a compendium of absences as well as presences; and we also knew that there was no way that it would not be read as an anthology in that sense. For me, though—and I'm sure this holds for Pierre as well—it was conceived, like other gatherings of mine or his, as something else: an *assemblage* or pulling together of poems and people and ideas about poetry (and much else) in the words of others and in our own words. That *imago*—that representation of where we've been and what we've lived through—is something in fact that I would stand by—like any poem. (It's also why we've allowed ourselves to end the book—as epic poem replete with histories and voices—with two poems of our own.)

What is missing from that gathering exists in the still greater gathering we carry with us—as a mental, a spiritual, construct. It is in this sense that every one of us has his or her anthology, that every one of us, given the opportunity, could bring it into some kind of form or structure in the outer world. At the end of a joint interview with Chris Funkhouser, following the publication of volume 1, Pierre suggested that as far as future projects went, the two volumes were (for us at least) "the anthology to end all anthologies." To which I added that the only anthology still left to do was "an anthology of everything." In saying that I suppose there was an echo of Mallarmé's intuition that "everything in the world exists in order to be put into a book." By that measure, of course, Mallarmé continues to be a guardian angel for the work—one of those who led us into the domain of the impossible, which is really where we want to be.

Symposium of the Whole:
A Pre-Face

(with Diane Rothenberg)

1

When the industrial West began to discover—and plunder—"new" and "old" worlds beyond its boundaries, an extraordinary countermovement came into being in the West itself. Alongside the official ideologies that shoved European *man* to the apex of the human pyramid, there were some thinkers and artists who found ways of doing and knowing among other peoples as complex as any in Europe and often virtually erased from European consciousness. Cultures described as "primitive" and "savage"— a stage below "barbarian"—were simultaneously the models for political and social experiments, religious and visionary revivals, and forms of art and poetry so different from European norms as to seem revolutionary from a later Western perspective. It was almost, looking back at it, as if every radical innovation in the West were revealing a counterpart—or series of counterparts—somewhere in the traditional worlds the West was savaging.

The present gathering will center on the poetics of the matter and will map, from the perspective of the editors, a discourse on poetics (really a range of such discourses) that has been a vital aspect of twentieth-century poetry and art—with precedents going back two centuries and more. The poetics in question, which we will speak of as an *"ethnopo-etics,"* reemerged after World War II (with its rampant and murderous

Jerome Rothenberg and Diane Rothenberg, *Symposium of the Whole: A Range of Discourse toward an Ethnopoetics* (Berkeley: University of California Press, 1983).

racism) and the dislocations of the European colonial system during the postwar period.

Whenever it has appeared—and some version of it may be as old as human consciousness itself—it has taken the form of what the anthropologist Stanley Diamond, in a recently renewed "critique of civilization," calls "the search for the primitive" or, more precisely, the "attempt to define a primary human potential." This search is by no means confined to the "modern" world (though our concern with it will be just there) but is felt as well, say, in the words of ancient Heraclitus often cited by Charles Olson: "Man is estranged from that with which he is most familiar." And it is present too in the thought of those the West had cast as ultimate "primitives," as when the Delaware Indians tell us in their *Walum Olum:*

in the beginning of the world
all men had knowledge cheerfully
all had leisure
all thoughts were pleasant

at that time all creatures were friends . . .

The past is what it is—or was—but it is also something we discover and create through a desire to know what it is to be human, anywhere.

Some of the results of that search and its attendant yearnings are obvious by now—so much so that a principal defense against their power to transform us involves an attack on a primitivism debased by the attackers and abstracted thereby from its revolutionary potential. Such a primitivism is not, in any case, the stance of this collection. Nor is our interest directed backward toward a past viewed with feelings of decontextualized nostalgia. We contend, in fact, that the most experimental and future-directed side of romantic and modern poetry, both in the Western world and increasingly outside it, has been the most significantly connected with the attempt to define an ethnopoetics.

There is a politics in all of this and an importance, clearly, beyond the work of poets and artists. The old "primitive" models in particular—of small and integrated, stateless and classless societies—reflect a concern over the last two centuries with new communalistic and antiauthoritarian forms of social life and with alternatives to the environmental disasters accompanying an increasingly abstract relation to what was once a living universe. Our belief in this regard is that a re-viewing of "primitive" ideas of the "sacred" represents an attempt—by poets and others—to preserve and enhance primary human values against a mindless mechanization that has run past any uses it may once have had. (This, rather than the advocacy of some particular system, seems to us the contribution of the "primitive" to whatever world we may yet hope to bring about.) As a matter of history, we would place the model in question both in the surviving, still rapidly vanishing, stateless cultures and in a long subterranean tradition of resistance to the twin authorities of state and organized religion.

What we're involved with here is a complex redefinition of cultural and intellectual values: a new reading of the poetic past and present that Robert Duncan speaks of as "a symposium of the whole." In such a new "totality," he writes, "all the old excluded orders must be included. The female, the proletariat, the foreign; the animal and vegetative; the unconscious and the unknown; the criminal and failure—all that has been outcast and vagabond must return to be admitted in the creation of what we consider we are." If that or some variant thereof is taken as the larger picture, it can provide the context in which to see most clearly the searches and discoveries in what we call "the arts." In painting and sculpture, say, the results of those searches are by now so well known that there's little surprise left in marking the change from Ruskin's late nineteenth-century comment, "There is no art in the whole of Africa, Asia, and America," to Picasso's exclamation on his first sighting of an African sculpture, "It is more beautiful than the Venus de Milo." Yet the obviousness of the change is itself deceptive. The "human" concerns demanded by the Dada poet Tristan Tzara—for an art that "lives first of all for the functions of dance, religion, music, and work"—remain largely submerged in the "aesthetic"; and it's a long way, too, from Picasso's classicizing admiration of the static art object to the reality of a tribal/oral "art in motion" (Robert Farris Thompson's term) that brings all our scattered arts together.

This dream of a total art—and of a life made whole—has meant different things and been given different names throughout this century. *Intermedia* was a word for it in its 1960s manifestation—also "total theater" and "happenings"—behind which was the sense of what the nineteenth-century Wagnerian consciousness had called *Gesamtkunstwerk* and had placed—prefigured—at the imagined beginnings of the human enterprise. The difference in our own time was to smash that imperial and swollen mold, to shift the primary scene from Greece, say, to the barbaric or Paleolithic past, or to the larger, often still existing, tribal world, and to see in that world (however "outcast and vagabond" it had been made to look) a complexity of act and vision practiced by protopoets/protoartists who were true "technicians of the sacred." And along with this shift came the invention and revival of *specific* means: new materials and instruments (plastic and neon, film and tape) alongside old or foreign ones (stones, bones, and skin; drums, didjeridoos, and gamelans); ancient roles and modes of thought that had survived at the Western margins (sacred clowns and dancers, shamanistic ecstasies, old and new works of dream and chance); and a tilt toward ritual, not as "an obsessional concern with repetitive acts" but, as Victor Turner describes it, "an immense orchestration of genres in all available sensory codes: speech, music, singing; the presentation of elaborately worked objects, such as masks; wall-paintings, body-paintings; sculptured forms; complex, many-tiered shrines; costumes; dance forms with complex grammars and vocabularies of bodily movements, gestures, and facial expressions."

The description, which fits both "them" and "us," holds equally true in the language arts—as this book will attempt to show—though by the nature of language itself (and the need to translate ourselves in—always—partial forms) the complexity and the interplay of new and old haven't been as clear there. Taken as a whole, then, the human species presents an extraordinary richness of verbal means—both of languages and poetries—closed to us until now by an unwillingness to think beyond the conventions and boundaries of Western literature. This "literature" goes back in its root meaning to an idea of writing—more narrowly and literally, the idea of alphabetic writing (*littera*, Lat. = letters) as developed in the West. In poetry the result has been to exclude or set apart those oral traditions that together account for the greatest human diversity, an exclusion often covered over by a glorification of the oral past. Thus Marshall McLuhan—defining the words *tribal* and *civilized* on the basis of alphabetic literacy alone—can write: "Tribal cultures like those of the Indian and Chinese [!] may be greatly superior to the Western cultures in the range and delicacy of their expressions and perception," and in the same paragraph: "Tribal cultures cannot entertain the possibility of the individual or of the separate citizen."

If the recovery of the oral is crucial to the present work, it goes hand in hand with a simultaneous expansion of the idea of writing and the text, wherever and whenever found. To summarize rapidly what we elsewhere present in extended form, the oral recovery involves a poetics deeply rooted in the powers of song and speech, breath and body, as brought forward across time by the living presence of poet-performers, with or without the existence of a visible/literal text. The range of such poetries is the range of human culture itself, and the forms they take (different for each culture) run from wordless songs and mantras to the intricacies (imagistic and symbolic) of multileveled oral narratives; from the stand-up performances of individual shamans and bards to the choreographies of massed dancers and singers, extended sometimes over protracted periods of time. From the side of visual and written language—which may, like the oral, be as old as the species itself—a fully human poetics would include all forms of what Jacques Derrida calls *archécriture* (= primal writing): pictographs and hieroglyphs, aboriginal forms of visual and concrete poetry, sand paintings and earth mappings, gestural and sign languages, counting systems and numerologies, divinational signs made by humans or read (as a poetics of natural forms) in the tracks of animals or of stars through the night sky.

Recognizing that practices like these correspond to experimental moves in our own time isn't needed to justify them, but it indicates why we're now able to see them and to begin to understand the ways they differ from our own work. Other areas in which such correspondences hold true may be more involved with "idea" than "structure," though the distinction isn't always easy to maintain. Traditional divination work, for example—the Ifa oracles of Africa, say, or the Chinese *I Ching*—rests on the recognition of a world revealed moment by moment through processes of chance and synchronicity (the interrelatedness of simultaneous events), and these processes in turn inform one major segment of our avant-garde. Similarly, the widespread practice of exploring the "unknown" through the creation of new languages shows a strong sense of the virtual nature of reality (what Senghor speaks of as the traditional surreal) and the linguistic means to get it said. The idea of the surreal—at its most meaningful—also suggests the dreamworks so central to other cultures and so long submerged in ours. And from these, or through them, it's only a short step into a life lived in a state-of-myth ("reality at white heat," Radin called it) and to the recovery of archetypes (as image and/or symbol) that infuse our own work at its most heated: the animal and trickster side of us; the goddess and the feminine; the sense of "earth as a religious form" and of a living, even human, universe; and the commitment to imaginal geographies and journeys that lead into our own lives and minds. These are as old as the human, maybe older, and they come back to us, transformed, not so much when we shut out the immediate world around us as when we choose to work within it.

The twentieth century—and with it the attendant modernisms that have characterized our poetry and art—is by now winding down. It has been a long haul and a sometimes real adventure, but the work is in no way complete, and some of the major points have still to be hammered home. My own choice has been to write from the side of a modernism that sees itself as challenging limits and changing ways of speaking/ thinking/doing that have too long robbed us of the freedom to be human to the full extent of our powers and yearnings. The struggle is immediate, and the objects and attitudes to be destroyed or transformed appear on every side of us. But it isn't a question of our having no sense of history or of the human past—no sense of possibilities besides the most apparent. The clincher, in fact, is the transformation beyond that, of our consciousness of the human in all times and places.

2

By the end of the 1960s, I first introduced the term *ethnopoetics* as a necessary part of a poetics (an idea of poetry) changed by a century of such experimentation and mapping. A number of often previously involved poets, anthropologists, and critics (David Antin, Kofi Awoonor, Ulli Beier, Stanley Diamond, Dell Hymes, Michael McClure, Simon Ortiz, George Quasha, Gary Snyder, William Spanos, Dennis Tedlock, Nathaniel Tarn, et al.) responded immediately to the discourse around the term, while others, who remained aloof, were in their own terms implicit contributors to the issues clustered therein. What this marked wasn't so much a first invention as a recognition that ethnopoetics, once it had entered our work, altered the nature of that work in all its aspects. And behind it was the century itself and a crisis in language and thought not of our making: an international avant-garde on the one hand, an American opening to history and myth on the other, and a de facto but rarely acknowledged collaboration between poets and scholars by whom the attack on the narrow view of literature (the "great" tradition) was simultaneously carried on. Few poets and artists—post–World War II—weren't somehow involved in these new mappings, for what had changed was our paradigm of what poetry was or now could come to be.

The explicit discourse—that around an ethnopoetics per se—involved the magazine *Alcheringa* (founded by Rothenberg and Tedlock in 1970) and included the 1975 gathering, at the Center for Twentieth Century Studies in Milwaukee, of the "first international symposium on ethnopoetics," which drew from many of the principal contributors, as well as from others working in related areas. On the one hand, this discourse explored an ongoing "intersection between poetry and anthropology," in Nathaniel Tarn's words, and on the other hand, it explored the relationship between contemporary poets as the "marginal" defenders of an endangered human diversity and poets of other times and places who represented that diversity itself and many of the values being uncovered and recovered in the new poetic enterprises. The discourse opened, as well, to include what Richard Schechner called the "poetics of performance" across the spectrum of the arts, and it also tied in with movements of self-definition and cultural liberation among ethnic groups in the United States and elsewhere.

The present anthology is an attempt to present some highlights of that discourse—both over the last two decades and in relation to its own history—and to show how ethnographic revelations can change our ideas of poetic form and function. There is otherwise no claim to an ethnopoetics movement per se, and many of the present contributors, in fact, remain largely unaware of each other's work. Nor is there anything final or tidy about such an ethnopoetics, which works instead to churn up a whole range of issues about "art and life" (as those terms are used by practitioners like John Cage and Allan Kaprow)—not as a closed field but as an always shifting series of tendencies in the thought and practice of those who in any sense might be considered participants. And the participants themselves are not only poets but—in an age of intermedia works and genre crossovers—other artists as well, not only anthropologists and folklorists but the indigenous poets and shamans for whom the others often act as conduits to the world of print and text.

We have structured the book to present these issues historically, ethnographically, and from a number of contemporary points of view. Working from our two bases as poet and anthropologist, we are calling our book *Symposium of the Whole* after Robert Duncan's phrase already noted in this pre-face. To this we have added the subtitle, *A Range of Discourse toward an Ethnopoetics*. That means, quite literally, that we are, in spite of the privileges of editorship, trying to remain open to the variety of voices and stances around this subject and, above all, to see the work as a movement toward something that can in no sense be taken as presently achieved.

The Poet as Native: An Aspect of Contemporary Poetry & Art

Written as a talk for the American Folklore Association
conference, "Homo Narrans: Storytelling as Integration of Self,"
University of Southern California, Los Angeles, October 1979

From an interview:

Why do you write? Who do you write for?

Because Indians always tell a story. The only way to continue is to
tell a story and that's what Coyote says. The only way to continue is
to tell a story and there is no other way. Your children will not survive
unless you tell something about them—how they were born, how they
came to this certain place, how they continued.

Who do you write for besides yourself?

For my children, for my wife, for my mother and my father and
my grandparents and then reverse order that way so that I may have a
good journey on my way back home.

—Simon Ortiz, A Good Journey

Opening remarks. In my work I have no life histories but my own . . . in
an ongoing, maybe oblique way . . . and maybe, as another speaker said, "a
life as it might have been."

Gary Snyder says that when he gave up his folklore studies at the University of Indiana in the early 1950s, he changed from being an anthropologist and became an informant. As poets, we are all professional informants.

I wanted to say—in the spirit of the title for this conference—that I can
only speak for myself or as myself: that I will speak, here as elsewhere,
as a poet concerned (in my more self-conscious workings) with the crea-

tion of meaning through language. The creation, the making of meaning, is involved with self-making (or self-invention) and more ambitiously of world-making (or world-invention); and this process, which I have elsewhere called poesis, is not the work (or play) of poets and artists only but of all functionally languaged people. In their acts of poesis, all languaged people are poets, and this has been the intuition of poets who might mistakenly be thought of as "elitist"—William Blake, for example, who translated the biblical text, "Would that all God's people were prophets," into a virtual "All God's people are poets"; or, maybe more surprising, the French Surrealists, quoting Lautréamont on the masthead of their magazine, *The Surrealist Revolution:* "Poetry must be made by all. Not by one." The search, there as here, was for a broadly human approach to creativity, to return with a renewed self-consciousness to what should be the most familiar ground for all of us (our selves, our humanness in place and time) and from which, as the poet Charles Olson wrote in quotation from Heraclitus, we have been (tragically) estranged.

We proceed by telling, and the telling by which a world is told and comes to be is our sense of myth. Myth as telling—storytelling or whatever other form it takes—is the lifework of each languaged person, which he or she may do "well" or "badly"—and who are we to judge? Its thrust is to experience and enact, not to explain the world—or to explain as afterthought, the experience of all that foremost. That experience itself is knowing—religiously as gnosis, otherwise as history, which Olson, after Herodotus this time, etymologized as knowing, going out and seeing for oneself—one's self as witness and as teller in a circumstance, an enactment in which the thing known is the thing said or spoken—for "thought," as Tristan Tzara wrote, "is made in the mouth." The intention of the one who tells that kind of story is to make his or her voice a witness, to put himself and those who hear him into the condition of experiencing—in response to the basic questions of self-identity and world-identity. As in the Iroquois Indian account: "A man who was a crow was traveling. As he walked along he asked himself: 'Who am I? Where did I come from? Where am I going?'" Or again: who are *we*, etc.: the question asked in the voice of the group, the people for whom the individual as poet may think himself or herself to be speaking, giving an account.

Language (voiced or written, verbal or pictorial) creates the answers, the accounting, as an individual act that is also the culmination or recounting of those previous acts and thoughts (cultural traditions, say) of which the individual is aware. If the culture defines the limits of the things spoken of—persons, actions, objects—it is defined by those things in turn. Mythology always carries with it an element of automythology. Mythology as automythology (experience as *mythos*) reaches its extremes in the self-projections and world-creation of tribal shamans and certain post-tribal mystics, and perhaps equally so in the work of contemporary poets/artists as mythmakers, narrating the world and their experience of it as a story. The poet's and the artist's telling is an instance of any person's need to do the same but with a continuing demand for a heightened self-consciousness and, often, a quirkiness and openness to change that casts doubt on its own projections. In the contemporary instance the poet/artist as rebel challenges the idea of a culturally legislated reality and seems, in the aftermath of an internationalizing imperialism, to move beyond the particulars of culture, time, and place.

I will point out very briefly some of the many forms that this automything, self-telling, has taken in twentieth-century poetry—modern and postmodern.

First, in so-called confessional poetry (Plath, Sexton, Lowell, etc.): a widely used but unfortunate term that seems sometimes to limit the work of poetry to its suicidal fringe; that psychologizes too rapidly and escapes (in the work of its interpreters, not necessarily its practitioners) the mythic encounter with what Euripides called "not my story but one my mother told me."

Second, the long mythic poem (Pound's *Cantos*, Williams's *Paterson*, Olson's *Maximus*, Zukofsky's *"A,"* etc.) in which the created/experienced ego intersects with the experience of the past and present as multiple times and/or with a single place as center. This is the poem "including history," as Pound defined the epic. The poem *as* history.

Third, a range of poems in which cultural particulars dominate, as the poet tries to deal with the embattled traditions of American ethnicities: the idea of Acoma Pueblo continuities in the poetry of Simon Ortiz or the struggle with discontinuities in my own *Poland/1931* and *A Seneca Journal.*

Fourth, the poet carrying his work into the public arena: as a performance in which he restores sound to writing or "talks to discover" meanings inherent in his poems or, in the case of David Antin, works through the performance itself to talk his way toward meaning—preeminently by telling a story.

Fifth, the poet's use of collage and assemblage as a rearrangement of

the fullest range of feelings and meanings (myths) available to a culture—
again the basic method of the *Cantos, Maximus,* etc. and, in one form or
other, common to the work of many poets active in the twentieth century and more. (I take this as a contemporary equivalent to the traditions
transmitted orally in other cultures.)

Even so-called lyrics—short poems, etc., personal or "image-"centered—are tellings: the recounting and/or creation of a momentary event,
an experience of an action or perception or dream, or an occasion within
language itself. The poet as reporter narrates/tells "news that stays news"
but (like the newsman in the practice) also makes or shapes the news.
And, where experiment is possible or demanded, he or she makes new
ways of making news: new strategies for language—strategies that are
themselves "another kind of story."

Art and poetry are today permeated with narrative and performance:
extended and full or broken into the fragments of stories told and retold.
If you, as anthropologists or folklorists, and so on, are concerned with
these questions, so are we; and we look to the work that you bring from
the many sources once despised as below "high culture" and set apart as
"folklore." These contain both the wide range of cultures from which we
learn in pursuit of a still illusory ethnopoetics and, for each of us, the still
familiar worlds, the small towns and neighborhoods, the particular cultures from which we come and to which we cannot return because they
are gone or we or they have changed. And that dislocation, like that of
the Iroquois crow-man, causes us to ask and to answer-in-language, as
the basic poetic act, those questions: Who am I? Where did I come from?
Where am I going?

Poets & Tricksters: Innovation & Disruption in Ritual & Myth

For the conference "Standing at the Margins-Crossroads of Culture: Poet as Trickster," Sapporo University Institute of Cultural Studies, May 14, 2004, Sapporo, Japan

1

The larger context in which I want to speak about the trickster figure involves my developing sense of the innovative and disruptive nature of ancient ritual and myth and of how those enter into contemporary work and thought. To say that much at the start already implies a relative disinterest in other forms of myth and ritual—forms in which it would be more difficult to place the trickster figure and that would be outside the range of what most interests me in the work—the art and poetry—of my contemporaries and near-contemporaries. So I will start with what *does* interest me in the ancient worlds of tricksters and sacred clowns and will move from there to an account of how the trickster entered my own work at a crucial point in its development.

Tricksters and clowns are among the elusive (mythopoeic) figures who have appeared increasingly in our poetry and poetics but in so many different ways and with such varying degrees of both affection and suspicion that I hesitate a little, fearing that what I say may confuse as much as clarify. Now I'm not against confusion—really—and, as you'll see, what I think of as most essential to myth and ritual is, in a certain sense, a welcoming of contradictory accounts of who we are and where we came from and where we're going. And more: ritual, which most of us (though not

An earlier version of this essay, "Innovation and Disruption as Ritual Modes," appeared in Gavin Selerie, ed., *The Riverside Interviews 4: Jerome Rothenberg* (London: Binnacle Press, 1984).

most of us in this room) probably think of as a fixed and invariable, mind-lessly repetitive order of (usually religious) events with little room for in-novation, was programmed in certain very traditional cultures/religions to promote or consolidate change and to include activities that were open and formless and threw the established/everyday order of things into confusion. A programmed and fruitful, sometimes terrifying chaos, as the point of departure for the creation of a new order—for the individual, the group, the world.

I'm going to open my presentation, then, by giving some examples of this side of myth and ritual, drawing the examples not from the older classical West (as we sometimes do where I come from) but from mostly American Indian sources—that in itself a matter of some significance as to where many of us as artists position ourselves in relation to the past or the culturally distant. (I will compare freely as one distanced by culture but related by art.)

The Iroquois—of the American Northeast—had a ceremony/ritual that they called *ononharoia:* literally, turning-the-brain-upside-down. This was a large-scale dream feast: a group enactment and fulfillment of individual dreams, often preceded by a variety of dream-guessing cere-monies. Dreams were viewed as secret desires-of-the-soul, which were dangerous/destructive if left unsatisfied, and their fulfillment in the *ononharoia* was like a culturally validated psychodrama, some of which I've summarized in the following "dream events":

DREAM EVENT ONE
After having a dream, let someone else guess what it was. Then have everyone act it out together.

DREAM EVENT TWO
Have participants run around the center of a village, acting out their dreams & demanding that others guess & satisfy them.

The dream itself was the entry to the other world: the dreamworld/mythworld, as reversal of our own: the place of secret longings, sighted upside down. The *ononharoia*—turning-the-mind-upside-down—was an enactment of the dream as myth.

Reversals, then, are a widespread way of getting into, of participating in and enacting, myth—that primordial and still-existing state that the Australian aborigines called by names such as *alcheringa*, "dreamtime."

Among the Huichol Indians of Mexico, the participants in the annual peyote hunt entered into such a dreamtime and themselves became the dreamtime gods and ancestors (Our Father Sun, First Shaman/Fire, Our Mother Maize, Our Elder Brother Deer, and so on), as they journeyed to Wirikuta, mythic center of the gods and the peyote. The *mara'akame*—the shaman/ritual leader—gave them their names and created (literally *dreamt*) a new language for them to speak, its meanings, its names for things, the reverse of what they knew back in their village. Thus, the shaman Ramón Medina Silva explained to the anthropologist Barbara Myerhoff:

> It is the mara'akame who directs everything. He is the one who listens in his dream, with his power and his knowledge. . . . Then he says to his companions, . . . look, now we will change everything, all the meanings, because that is the way it must be with the *hikuritámete* [the peyote pilgrims]. . . . Look, the mara'akame says to them, it is when you say good morning, you mean good evening, everything is backwards. You say goodbye, I'm leaving you, but you are really coming. You do not shake hands, you shake feet. You hold out your right foot to be shaken by the foot of your companion. You say good afternoon, but it is only morning.
>
> So the mara'akame tells them, as he has dreamed it. He dreams it differently each time. Every year they change the names of things differently because every year the mara'akame dreams new names. Even if it is the same mara'akame who leads the journey, he still changes the new names each time differently.

The work of shamans (traditional healers: masters of ecstasy and trance, says Mircea Eliade . . . technicians of the sacred) is to explore and create the extraordinary (the "marvelous" of André Breton and the Surrealists), to explore and to create it by means of trance and by control over language and rhythm, and so on (for he who controls rhythm, wrote someone, *controls*). From the perspective of ordinary consciousness, this shaman work is disorientating, frightening, and the shaman (himself or herself) often experiences it as terror: a terror of death and disease—to cure the terror of death and disease—and madness/psychosis/soul-terror, when it actually afflicts us. "I did cure death when I was young," says the Pomo Indian shaman Essie Parrish, and the Eskimo shaman Sanimuinak describes his fourth vision and psychic death as follows:

I went inland to Tasivsak. Here I cast a stone out into the water, which was thereby thrown into great confusion, like a storm at sea. As the billows dashed together, their crests flattened out on top, and as they opened, a huge bear was disclosed. He had a very great black snout, and, swimming ashore, he rested his chin upon the beach, the land gave way under his weight. He went up on land and circled around me, bit me in the loins, and then ate me. At first it hurt, but afterwards feeling passed from me; but as long as my heart had not been eaten, I retained consciousness. But when he bit me in the heart, I lost consciousness and was dead.

In the curing rituals themselves the terror is renewed, and the regular beat of the shaman's drum (and heart?) is offset by the frenzy of possession—like the Kirgiz-Tatar shaman in Wilhelm Radloff's nineteenth-century description, say, who "runs around the tent, springing, roaring, leaping; he barks like a dog, sniffs at the audience, lows like an ox, bellows, cries, bleats like a lamb, grunts like a pig, whinnies, coos, imitating with remarkable accuracy the cries of animals, the songs of birds, the sound of their flight, and so on, all of which greatly impresses the audience."

At such points of frenzy—frantic dislocation—the shaman closely resembles the traditional sacred clown: a figure both comic and terrifying, who comes into his clown work, like the shaman, through an overwhelming and mind-altering experience. The Sioux clown, the *heyoka*, attains his power through a vision of the Thunder Being: a shapeless, winged form, who "lacks feet but has huge talons and is headless but has a large beak; his voice is the thunderclap, the glance of his eye is lightning." The clown, like the shaman, speaks a language of reversals and has license to break the rigid patterns of the established ceremonies, as anyone knows who has seen Pueblo clowns, say, in their countermovements around the masked kachina dancers, parodying the sacred. The Pueblo Indian anthropologist Alfonso Ortiz describes the clowns as *antiritualists* (a term reminiscent of the antiart of artists in our own world), but they could as easily be described as ritualists of disorder: free and improvisatory in their movements and innovations, at the extremes of a theater a modern ritualist like Artaud once dreamed of. Thus, Bandelier's description of sacred clowns in 1880:

They chased after her, carried her back and threw her down in the center of the plaza; then while one was performing the coitus from behind, another was doing it against her head. Of course all was simulated and not the real act, as the woman was dressed. The naked fellow performed masturbation in the center of the plaza or very near it, alternatively with a black rug and his hand. Everybody laughed.

It is something that the ritual/performative frame makes possible: a (barely) controlled release of wild potential in the human psyche. The ritualized behavior of the Crow Indian Crazy Dog [Warrior Clown] Society is another example:

CRAZY DOG EVENTS

1. Act like a crazy dog. Wear sashes & other fine clothes, carry a rattle, & dance along the roads singing crazy dog songs after everybody else has gone to bed.
2. Talk crosswise: say the opposite of what you mean & make others say the opposite of what they mean in return.
3. Fight like a fool by rushing up to an enemy & offering to be killed. Dig a hole near an enemy, & when the enemy surrounds it, leap out at them & drive them back.
4. Paint yourself white, mount a white horse, cover its eyes & make it jump over a steep & rocky bank, until both of you are crushed.

Now, some of this still exists for us in the reversals of Mardi Gras and, in spite of the temptation to trivialize, in the actions of circus and movie clowns, the actions and words of the really great stand-up comics. And maybe there's an even stronger, certainly more deliberate, reflection in the work of certain poets and artists: those who create an experimental space to challenge and transform . . . what? A limited reality . . . a lying and deceptive sense of order . . . the politics of single vision. From Dada spontaneity and disgust, surrealist invocation of private and collective dreamtimes and black humors, to the avant-gardes of the 1960s and 1970s (and beyond), whose public (and private) rituals took shape as happenings, trance dances, sonic meditations, systematic chance, street provocations, Holy Actors, body art and body music, mantric sound-texts, visions, theaters of "cruelty" and of "hysteria," against the expectations of what was "real" and what was "sane behavior." A programmed chaos, in which the brain turns upside down and lets another order come to birth.

So far, I've stressed rituals of disruption/disorder and of a generally open and innovative form, although these aren't all the rituals there are (most rituals in fact are very low-key: spare and minimal and doggedly, if wildly, repetitive or boring to the point of madness). But let's get over to myth for a little, one view of it sometimes overlooked but which for the myth people among us (as contrasted, say, to the ritual people) may be the heart of the matter.

We have, many of us, a sense of myth as the story (singular) of that-which-happened (also singular) at a time in the remote past (again: the dreamtime, if you're into that). But in oral traditions, word-of-mouth traditions, myths exist in many versions—as the *mouthed*, individuated accounts of—or speculations on—the fundamentals. The telling of the myth—that is, the telling of the *telling*—is itself a ritual, a cultural performance, and the form of the myth, the thrust behind it, is an implied question or a series of questions. Thus the Seneca Indian storyteller begins:

A man who was a crow was traveling. As he walked along he thought: "Who am I? Where did I come from? Where am I going?"[1]

The answer is the myth, which in its first Greek use meant only telling/talking, then came to be the telling of the fundamentals (an old-time telling), and only later, a lesser telling in contrast to a second mode, *logos,* once its synonym. The source is traditional, the recounting individual, from the mouth of each teller; or, as they used to say, some say this, but others say that. It is like biblical *genesis* (the foundation telling for the Western world), which only late in its career gets fixed as single vision, logos, word of God—erasing in that act the other versions, equally true, the record of which hasn't wholly vanished. Or put another way:

Some say Elohim—translate it "God" or "the gods"—created the world and man in seven days: first the animals, then man as male and female in his image
THIS IS THE PRIESTLY GENESIS OF BIBLE

But others say Yahveh [the "name" itself] created man from earth as male before the animals, then made the animals and woman
THIS IS THE YAHVIST GENESIS OF BIBLE

1. See also above, page 26.

And others say Yahveh, like Babylonian Marduk, stirred the sea called YAM, then in his cunning crushed Rahab [female serpent], by his wind set YAM in net, his hand made holes in the twisty snake

THIS IS THE BOOK OF JOB

Still others say that El created Wisdom as a goddess, in her words
"I came out of El's mouth   first
     flooded across the earth
  then built my home high
        my seat in cloud pillar
He made me   starting   before the world"

THIS IS ECCLESIASTICUS, THE BOOK OF WISDOM,
THE WISDOM OF BEN SIRA

And others say, in God's own words:
I conceived the thought of creation / putting a floor under it / letting everyone see / what I had done / the bottom of the dark // I called down to the deep below / "come from the unseen dark / all that eye can see / Ado-il—come"—he came hauling so large / a stone of light it made / his belly a great ball / "explode - Ado-il / push the light out / give it birth" // he blew the stone / light gaping from his belly womb / opening all I willed for shape // light the mother of light / bore a great age / the star heaven / which I saw was good

THIS IS THE BOOK OF THE SECRETS OF ENOCH

And others say the creation came through laughter:

the 7 Laughs of God
Hha   Hha   Hha   Hha   Hha   Hha   Hha
Each laugh he gave
engendered the seven
god   god   god   god   god   god   god
the Fore-Appearers
who clasp everything one

THIS IS THE HIDDEN SACRED BOOK OF MOSES
CALLED "EIGHTH" OR "HOLY"[2]

2. Most of the preceding examples are from Charles Doria and Harris Lenowitz, eds., *Origins: Creation Texts from the Ancient Mediterranean* (Garden City, NY: Anchor, 1976).

Something of this Lévi-Strauss senses, writing of the versions of Oedipus in "The Structural Study of Myth":

> Our method . . . eliminates a problem which has, so far, been one of the main obstacles in the progress of mythological studies, namely, the quest for the true version or the earlier one. On the contrary, we define myth as consisting of all its versions; or, to put it otherwise, a myth remains the same as long as it is felt as such. . . . Therefore, not only Sophocles but Freud himself should be included among the recorded versions of the Oedipus myth on a par with earlier or seemingly more "authentic versions."[3]

And, once that process is grasped (not necessarily in Lévi-Strauss's terms), the mythical past and present open up in a great kaleidoscope of images: a "clash of symbols" (in the words of Paul Ricoeur) which is both natural to mind and forms its one sure hedge against idolatry.

Every *old* culture (*authentic* culture, I wanted to say) had such a treasury of images—concrete/realized speculations, mirrors of the mind—which together projected the imaginal world for the individual and the community. The experience of such a mythic world is overwhelming: "not an allegory," wrote Jung, "not just another way of talking (the description of one thing under the image of another) but an image presented by the world itself." Myth here is the expression/projection of such an image, such a world of images: imaginal geographies, apologies, theologies, whose beings appeared in dream and again and again in ritual . . . in ritual and again in dream . . . a constant interplay between them.

Those dreamtime beings that illuminated the old myths and rituals (not static *objects* but images in motion) live now in our museums: object/ified. That is: the response to a ritual mask hanging on a museum wall—or on a wall in my living room—will doubtless be to a "beautiful thing" or even (by projection to its original meaning or context) to a powerful or awesome *thing*. But all such objects remain stationary, frozen, in contrast to their dynamism, their movement in ritual—when set into motion or brought into contact with moving, dancing bodies, chanting voices, the

---

3. I will be asserting this later when I speak of my own poem, "Cokboy," as well as poems by other of my contemporaries, as an "authentic version" of the trickster myth.

actuality of drums and bells that truly *sound.* And it is at such moments—as anyone who has experienced it will know—that myth comes alive in its enacted beings: like a theater played out for keeps or a theater through which we move also as participants.

I have most vividly experienced something of this order—what it is to be in a state-of-myth and how ritual (performance and enactment) assists with this—in traditional Yaqui Indian ceremonies in Tucson, Arizona. I will describe this, not because the ritual, the enactment in question, opened me to something culturally Yaqui (I would feel foolish to make any such claim) but because a coincidence of shared images (and myths) and their emergence in actual ritual time allowed a response on my part that was clearly outside the immediate Yaqui experience though triggered by it.

The ceremonies—like so much in ritual and religion—are syncretistic: in art terms, a *collage* of disparate elements fused into a new configuration. The principal religious images are both Catholic and Yaqui, along with numerous symbols, textures, and sounds drawn from Mexican, European, and popular American sources. In Yaqui terms—as I understood those from conversations with the anthropologist Edward Spicer and with the Yaqui ceremonial and political leader, Anselmo Valencia—the basic intercut is between the world of the village (itself Catholic and sacred) and the Flower World or Enchanted/Etheric World *(sea aniya, huya aniya)* outside the village: the wilderness from which come the old Yaqui mythic beings, the great Deer Dancer and the sacred clowns. In the forty-day Easter ceremony the curious emphasis/displacement in the collage is that the costumed and impersonated figures of the passion play aren't Jesus and the holy family but only the persecutors and stalkers of Jesus: Roman soldiers and black-veiled Pharisees and those weirdly masked nonsacred clowns called *chapayekas.* Jesus is a wooden statue or later (in his rebirth) a plastic baby-doll, and the Yaqui catholic maestros who defend the church lead a strict, text-oriented ceremony; but the Pharisees and especially the chapayeka clowns bring the mythic to life and engage in often open, often improvisatory rituals, including a comic mock scourging of Jesus as an eggheaded old man and a zany clown orchestra getting "drunk" and celebrating the crucifixion on the midnight of Good Friday.

The myth of Jesus is, of course, our shared myth, and the divergences from "my own" version are quickly apparent and comprehensible—

sometimes themselves astonishing. Similarly the chapayeka clowns—the
principal stalkers of Jesus—tie in by their actions and by their other Yaqui
name *(fariseos)* to the biblical antagonists of Jesus. They are therefore the
"jews" of the story—though scarcely named as such—and their actual
appearance is flower worldish, even surreal, with many of the masks representing animals and birds but the human ones including feathered Indians, pirates, Negroes, Arabs, college professors, and so on. They play
their roles persistently, and over the ritual period (for the culminating
four or five days of which we were witnesses) they become very real, very
familiar, before the climactic battle on Saturday morning: the storming
of the church and the defeat of the chapayeka-Pharisees in a highly animated ritual drama: both rehearsed (preplanned) and improvised. At the
end the current masks are burned, and the masks of the following year
will never be precisely the same.

For me the syncretistic/collaged nature of the chapayeka masks became in their enlivening the embodiment of the fantasized Jews of my
own poetry as they had come to me through language in *Poland/1931*. I
had often tried to realize those images in performance, but in 1982 and
again in 1983 the curious displacements of the Yaqui ritual opened that to
me as never before. And it was clear to me that the force of the ritual was
less in its repetitive, mechanical side (the Latin chanting of the Yaqui-
Catholic maestros, though I would scarcely disregard that) than in the
generous and quirky and largely unpredictable (but increasingly real) behavior of the chapayekas and the strange meeting of worlds that their
presence came to represent.

This is the poem that came from that—in three sections, including a
final one addressed to Anselmo Valencia, in which the (ideological) assertion on my part is that both art and ritual/myth (Dada and Yaqui in my
terms) are part of the same human experience:

[reads the opening section of "Yaqui 1982"]

> the jews of ceremony
> dance in the thin sand of
> pascua pueblo   in their pinhole
> eyes new fires start
> watched by ourselves & others
> the bright memory of days to come

tomorrow   but the face
back of the mask
is fathomless
the jews march through the night
clack-clack their sticks
speak for them
red & white
the tips like dagger points
& voiceless
they are the purveyors of the death of jesus
yaqui-style
they stomp & whip each other
Thursdays   the master jew
baldheaded man with droopy eyes
& half-a-beard
fresh crown of thorns over his ears
squats by the cross
black coated
in white jodhpurs
he is the man without the belt
(el viejito)
who seeks the heart of jesus
in a box
white-covered
with lines of green above
the flat red heart
& silver rays
he looks into & sees
a crucifix   a water bottle
flowers & candles
then bangs his sticks
together   in a trance
they lead him with a silky rope
pinned to his shoulders
jews & clowns
how beautifully they walk
the stations of the cross
in yaqui

the plaza stretches to infinity
where the smallest freak is jesus
& the angels sing

2

It is from this world of disruptions and reversals, of dreams, of sacred
clowns and shamans, of the marvelous and surreal, as well as from an
old and new understanding of the maximally human, that the trickster
emerges for us. He (or she, for I have also noted female tricksters) is the
mythic counterpart of the sacred clown and the bearer of energies that
trigger transformation of old worlds and the creation of the new. But he
is all of this in the context of absurdity and perversity, maintaining the
clown's reality in an always comic, sometimes terrifying world. As I wrote
of him some years ago, in one of his American Indian manifestations—
that of Old Man Coyote:

> Coyote appears throughout the Americas in the familiar role of pri-
> mordial shit-thrower, cock-erupter, etc., to satisfy the need for all
> that in the full pantheon of essential beings. . . . No merely horny
> version of a Disney character, he is like other tricksters in tribal
> America (Rabbit, Raven, Spider, Bluejay, Mink, Flint, Glooscap,
> Saynday, etc.) the product of a profound and comic imagination
> playing upon the realities of man and nature. . . . Among the Crow,
> as in other Indian religions, he appears as the Supreme Trickster but
> also as the first maker of the earth and all living things. . . . Thus
> Old Man Coyote [called elsewhere: "mad Coyote"] is the imper-
> fect (= dangerous) creator of an imperfect (= dangerous) universe—
> a view which, being more empirical and rational in the first place,
> presents fewer problems to rationalize than the Christian view, say,
> of a perfect God and universe, etc. [Writes the Acoma Indian poet
> Simon Ortiz]: "Existential man. Dostoyevsky coyote."

Like many of my generation I had first come to Trickster—or, more
accurately, to something like Trickster—through the diluted and sanitized images in comic strips and animated movies: Daffy Duck, Bugs
Bunny, Krazy Kat, and the later but strikingly derivative figure of Wile
E. Coyote (among many others). Those were images and characters from
childhood—"myths" I was tempted to say (and didn't)—but what came to

some of us later and with considerable astonishment was the full-blown figure of the Trickster. The initial purveyors were the hunter-gatherers of an earlier academic anthropology: Paul Radin foremost with his classic work *The Trickster* but notable texts as well from Melville Jacobs, Herbert Spinden, Knud Rasmussen, and others. These were at my disposal by the time I put together my own first ethnopoetic gatherings—*Technicians of the Sacred* and *Shaking the Pumpkin*—and as I carried on with this it became clear that the myth of Trickster (the image and the personage) went beyond Coyote and American Indian sources. For Trickster was, if anything, a near universal figure, resident on every continent in some form or other—so much so that some came to see him as an archetype, a mask, embedded in every human psyche.

On one of those occasions (there have been several) when I entered into a life of poetry, I felt myself a part of a lineage that included older poets—forerunners—whose lives and acts resembled those of ancient clowns and tricksters or whose written works, whose texts, incorporated some of them. In the former instances—the worlds of the *poètes maudits* and the radical transformers and self-transformers ("chameleon poets" in John Keats's earlier words)—many of the poets of my time were under the spell of certain key predecessors: Shelley and Keats, Hölderlin and Whitman, Rimbaud and Jarry, Dadas and Surrealists, Artaud and Duchamp, and many others. (Nakahara Chuya in Japan might be another such example—if we want to bring it closer to where we are, *right here*.) Their work, if we took it seriously (and we did), was one of transformation and transgression (sometimes comic, though often not)—renewing or challenging the worlds and selves we think we know or creating new worlds beyond our former knowing. That they weren't Trickster in any strict sense didn't matter, only that we could see them in that guise—and more to our convenience than to theirs. It was clear as well—and central to their meaning—that if their personas and works resembled those of sacred clowns and tricksters, they operated without the sanction of the larger society, toward which they acted (often but not always) as an avant-garde in opposition.

Getting closer to our own time, at the end of the Second World War, an oppositional avant-garde again came into prominence, something I've described elsewhere as the second great awakening of poetry in the century just ended. If we connect such an avant-garde with the disruptive work of traditional clowns and tricksters, we can see it as a dominant trend for art and poetry in the times through which we've lived. The

goal at its extreme was to turn the mind upside down and to call everything into question—a program that showed up, to one degree or another, in movements and practitioners of poetry on a nearly global scale.
It was something of this kind that I tried to summarize a few years ago
in a large two-volume assemblage or anthology of the twentieth-century
avant-garde called *Poems for the Millennium*. To give you an idea of where
my coeditor and I felt the presence of such an oppositional and transformative counterpoetics, I will mention only the movements and groupings to which we gave special attention: the Vienna Group in Austria, the
Tammuzi poets in Lebanon and Syria, concrete poetry worldwide, Cobra
in western Europe [*C*openhagen/*B*russels/*A*msterdam], the Beat Poets
in the United States, and branching out, the Postwar Poets in Japan, the
Misty Poets in China, the Language Poets in the United States, and un-
specified cyberpoets *everywhere* and *nowhere*. (To these, of course, we
could have added a number of others, both international and regionally
specific—from the widely dispersed Situationists and Fluxus artists and
poets to the early and germinal Gutai Group in Japan.)

In most instances the Trickster comparison is at best suggestive or
metaphorical, but for others, like myself, he or she manifests quite explicitly as a being-in-the-poem. For American poets he comes up most frequently in the guise of Coyote, and certainly this is the case for American
Indian poets such as Simon Ortiz or for a non-Indian poet like Gary
Snyder in his essay "The Incredible Survival of Coyote" or in the German
artist Joseph Beuys's performance work "I Love America and America
Loves Me" (a week spent locked in a cage with a coyote). Aside from
these, other Trickster-related poems include such major works as Ed
Dorn's *Gunslinger*, David Meltzer's *Hero/Lil*, Michael McClure's *Coyote
in Chains*, and Diane DiPrima's female-centered *Loba*.

For myself, then, my work in the late 1960s and early 1970s had included the anthologizing of translations from traditional Trickster narratives. (These appeared with attendant commentaries in assemblages
such as *Technicians of the Sacred* and *Shaking the Pumpkin*.) I was simultaneously "exploring ancestral sources of my own in a world of Jewish
mystics, thieves, and madmen"—a description of my work that I hoped
would call attention to its deliberately transgressive qualities. From 1972
to 1974 I was living at a Seneca Indian reservation in western New York
State, where I finished writing *Poland/1931* and began the writing of *A
Seneca Journal*. The immediate national or international context for this
was the war in Vietnam, which was moving into its final phases and had

already created public protests, many of which involved actions that resembled those rituals of disorder and disruption that had been a central aspect of many traditional cultures.

The culminating poem of *Poland/1931* was a short mock epic called "Cokboy," and it's this poem that I want to read from as the final part of my presentation here. The title when pronounced in English means something like penis-boy, although the spelling (c-o-k-b-o-y) is aberrant—something I picked up from a misspelling or typographical error in a poem by the Chilean poet Vicente Huidobro, circa 1913, for what he intended as the English word "cowboy." Still, from the time I first saw it, it played in my mind as the possible name of an *ithyphallic* new world trickster.

There is of course no mention of this in the poem, only the spelling of the word itself, which would strike an English reader as rather aberrant. Also aberrant is the yiddish accent that I use near the opening of the poem—exaggerated and very far from accurate. It is one of several voices that I allow myself, the poem shifting unannounced from one voice to another: my own voice (perhaps) as narrator, the voice of a mythopoeic trickster, the voice of a fictitious explorer/conqueror, the voices of ancestral Jews and Indians, and so on. In the course of it other figures—both historical and contemporary—are called into play: the eighteenth-century Baal Shem (founder of the ecstatic Hasidic cult of orthodox Judaism, wearing a traditional broad-brimmed hat called a *shtraimel*); William Blake, the great English poet and visionary; and iconic American figures such as General Custer, Buffalo Bill Cody, and the conservative American senator Barry Goldwater, referred to only as "the senator from Arizona."

Having said this much by way of introduction I will go to a reading from "Cokboy." It is my contention in doing so, that Cokboy, like Freud's Oedipus as viewed by Lévi-Strauss, or like Dorn's Gunslinger and Ortiz's Coyote, should be included now among the bona fide versions of the Trickster myth we've been discussing.

But if not, then not.

[Reads from "Cokboy," beginning:]

saddlesore I came
a jew among
the indians

vot em I doink in dis strange place
mit deez pipple mit strange eyes
could be it's trouble
could be   could be
(he says) a shadow
ariseth from his buckwheat
has tomahawk in hand
shadow of an axe inside his right eye
of a fountain pen inside his left
vot em I doink here
how vass I lost tzu get here
am a hundred men
a hundred fifty different shadows
jews & gentiles
who bring the Law to Wilderness
(he says) this man
is me   my grandfather
& other men-of-letters
men with letters carrying the mail
lithuanian pony-express riders
the financially crazed Buffalo Bill
still riding in the lead
hours before avenging the death of Custer
making the first 3-D movie of those wars
or years before it
the numbers vanishing in kabbalistic time
that brings all men together

. . . .

The Poetics & Ethnopoetics of
the Book & Writing

The following was written for the First Annual Conference in
Memoriam Eric Mottram, London, September 19, 1997,
and has been revised several times since.

It is strange to begin—as indeed we have to begin—in Eric Mottram's
absence. For myself this is the first time that I've been in London since his
death and the first time that I'll be speaking to his interests and not have
him here to listen and respond. Eric was for me one of the great listeners
and responders—a quality that entered into his own work as a poet and
as a writer on poetry and on the larger world of which poetry is a part—a
small part maybe but crucial for those of us for whom it's been an entry to
that world at large. With Eric, as with few others, I could speak at length,
because he gave the sense that what we said between ourselves could matter and that he was there to hear.

My intention today is to return to an interrupted part of a longer conversation that we had back in 1981. I can do that because Gavin Selerie
was there with a tape recorder and with the intention, which he soon carried out, of transcribing the talk and publishing it in what was then his
series of Riverside Interviews.[1] I had been very much connected until
then—through the anthologies I was assembling and through my own
readings and performances—with a re-exploration of the oral bases / the
oral sources of our poetry. And what Eric took as an opening for our talk
was a statement of mine that I was (or thought I was) "much more honest as a writer than a speaker." The reference was back to an earlier "dia-
logue" with William Spanos in *boundary 2*, which Eric described as having to do "with this whole problem of the relation between oral poetry

1. See Gavin Selerie, ed., *The Riverside Interviews 4: Jerome Rothenberg* (London: Binnacle
Press, 1984).

and the text." Having raised a question about what had been and became
even more fertile ground for me—the idea, I mean, of writing and the
book, which I had been exploring in some sense since *Technicians of the
Sacred*—both of us passed it by in favor of a discussion of various aspects
of oral poetry "past and present [and to come]." And when the conversation got around—as it later did—to matters of ethnopoetics and ethnicities, there was a passing suggestion of a concern with books (or with the
idea of "the book") in relation to the Jewish sources I had been exploring in *Poland/1931* and elsewhere, but mostly to point out that the Jews,
while founding much of their mystic tradition in oral law and a poetics of
the voice, were preeminently a people-of-the-book. So the book, again,
was a point of contrast rather than departure.

Eric, in other words, had given me an opening, and I had let it pass
without making it clear (as Eric was perhaps pushing me to do at the
beginning) that the book and writing had always been part of my poetics and even my ethnopoetics and was at that moment becoming—
if anything—still more overt. To begin with, I was at the time of the
Riverside interview the author of some twenty-seven books of my own
poetry, eight other books of translations, and seven (mostly very large)
anthologies and assemblages. And it was alongside these—and not apart
from them—that I had, like most of us, been entering deeply (I thought)
into *performance* as a strategy of voice and body. With that came what I
described to Eric as an attempt to "desanctify and demystify the written word"—initially by finding ways to present or re-present those vast
areas of language art that seemed—everywhere—to precede or (often)
supersede the act of writing. At the same time I began—but possibly
more slowly—to recognize the similarly diverse origins and possibilities of writing and that a "symposium of the whole" (in Robert Duncan's phrase) would also involve a mix and *possibly* a clash of writings. It
was as if, in place of the Bible, say, as a singularly fixed text, we were to
view it now as the multiple books (the *biblia*, plural) that it actually was.
And all this, in the contemporary context, against the resurgence of those
(fundamentalists and others) who pretend to a single book, not in Mallarmé's sense but in that of the tyrannies from which they've descended
and which they threaten to restore.

Still, for me, the central impulse in *Technicians of the Sacred*, the first
of the big assemblages that I've continued to construct, was to bring together a display of those ("oral") poetries that seemed to exist apart from

writing and the book. This was the start of my ethnopoetics as such, but even within that there were spaces, inevitably, in which the source poems were themselves in written form—the Egyptian Book of the Dead, say, or the Chinese Book of Changes, among the works that were the most immediately familiar. And there was also an intuition, a sense that began to play itself out, of writing like speech as some kind of universal (human) constant. So, in *Technicians*, there was, among other entries, a section early in the book called "The Pictures," with examples of pictographs and glyphs from a number of diverse cultures (largely American Indian and South Pacific), paired in the commentaries with works by visual and concrete poets of our own place and time. And elsewhere in the book I was able to include *Midē* healing songs and picture-songs from the Ojibwa Indians, *nsibidi* secret writings from the Ekoi in Africa, and pictorial songs and narratives from the Na-Khi "tribe" in China. Accompanying commentaries—as later also in *Shaking the Pumpkin*—called attention to the thin line between "writing" and "drawing" that made it "hard"—as I said there—"to keep the functions separate or to assert with any confidence that writing is a late development rather than indigenous, in some form, to the human situation everywhere."

When Dennis Tedlock and I founded *Alcheringa* in 1971 as "a first magazine of ethnopoetics" (of the world's tribal poetries), the emphasis, again, was on "poetry made in the mouth," but our pages were open as well to a range of traditional and early written art: Paleolithic calendar notations, Egyptian and Mayan hieroglyphs, recastings of Bible and other Jewish book works, Old Norse runes, and Navajo pictographs (among others). I was also working by the middle 1970s on *A Big Jewish Book* (later revised as *Exiled in the Word*), where I could focus on the written alongside—and drawing from—the oral, and with a strong awareness of how central the "book" was in that highly charged, sometimes overdetermined context. (Earlier anthologies of the 1970s like *America a Prophecy* and *Revolution of the Word* also put a high emphasis on the written, including—most surprisingly I thought—instances of both traditional and modern [experimental] alternatives to our normative ideas of books and writing.) This was still before the 1981 discussions with Eric and with Gavin Selerie, as was the founding, after my separation from *Alcheringa*, of a successor magazine, *New Wilderness Letter*, in which I promised as editor ("a poet by inclination and practice") to pursue *poesis* "in all arts and sciences . . . [and] not [to] be specialized and limited by culture or profession" but to enlarge the context of poetry as "a report, largely through the creative work itself, of where that process [of poesis] takes us."

That in brief was the situation in June 1981, a year before the appearance of the book issue of *New Wilderness Letter* (about which, more later) and during the preparation of *Symposium of the Whole* as an anthology of writings (by poets, anthropologists, and others) "toward an ethnopoetics." In the latter work Diane Rothenberg and I were attempting as co-editors to open from the more specialized emphasis on oral poetry to a still wider view that would encompass writing and the book as well, along with other forms of visual poetry and language (those from the cultures of the deaf a prime example) for which there was as yet no actual poetics. By the time, then, that I returned to London in December 1982 and was interviewed by Gavin Selerie alone, the concern with writing and the book took up (for me) a significant part of the conversation. And since I certainly saw Eric then, I feel quite certain that these concerns were also part of what was further said between us.

Looking back at the conversation with Selerie, I'm aware that the point of departure for me—the emblematic point at least—was in the poetry, the shamanistic *veladas*, of the Mazatec shamaness María Sabina. For her—and this was a matter that had been made clear to us by her American translator, Henry Munn—there was no actual practice of writing (or reading) but the words of her extraordinary chants were opened to her in the form of a great Book of Language that was given to her in her first empowering visions and which, although she remained unlettered, she was (in her own mind) fully able to read and to give back as song. In light of this and of my own meeting with her a few years before, I went on to speak of myself as a writer and of writing as a primal human function:

> Increasingly [I said to Gavin] I've had to assert that what I'm involved in is not a denial of the powers of a written language, because that—the written language, writing—would be a part of the exploration also. Over the last couple of years, in fact, I've been trying to explore the uses of writing in cultures that we usually speak of as oral, non-literate, pre-literate, & so on. And the conclusion I'm drawn toward is that writing in some sense is also universal & shared among all peoples. Therefore, when human beings developed as human beings at some point in the far past—at the point

where we became human beings we were probably already using some form of speech—& along with that, I would think, some form of writing, art-making, & so on.

And I added (by way of conclusion): "It's *all* very old."

In that sense, as Eric clearly knew, the book (taken as the "scene," the place in which the writing comes together) was the hidden side of my ethnopoetics, as the city was (for me) the scene of the "new wilderness" named as my project of that time. And as the talk with Eric and Gavin and others helped all of that develop, I found a number of ways over the next two or three years to let it surface. *Symposium of the Whole* had appeared by mid-1982, and in the aftermath of that we were organizing (through the University of Southern California) a second international symposium on ethnopoetics for the spring of 1983 in Los Angeles.[2] With that, as with the book from which we took the conference's name, the idea was not simply to recapitulate what had been said before but to bring the discourse on ethnopoetics into areas from which it seemed to have been set apart. Writing and the book clearly marked off one such territory—aided in this instance by the visit of Edmond Jabès, whom I had brought to San Diego as a visiting Regents scholar. (Others who were there were Robert Duncan, David Antin, Marjorie Perloff, Michael McClure, Roger Abrahams, Wai-lim Yip, Hugh Kenner, Paula Gunn Allen, Nathaniel Mackey, J. Stephen Lansing, Clayton Eshleman, Wendy Rose, David Guss, and Barbara Tedlock.) By this time I had already lifted for my own uses Jabès's aphorism that "the book is as old as fire and water" and had juxtaposed it with Tristan Tzara's contention that "thought is made in the mouth." So those two were now, in *my* mind at least, the axes for our discussions of an expanded ethnopoetics.

In the year preceding the symposium, then, I had opened the concern with writing and the book in a still more deliberate way—coediting with David Guss a book issue of our magazine *New Wilderness Letter*. The work had by then accumulated—including preliminary work for the international symposium—and had been accelerated by Michael Gibbs's retranslation and visual commentary on Mallarmé's *Le livre, instrument spirituel*. The push provided by the Mallarmé (as I later wrote) "not only brought us back to the first modernist breakthroughs but also provided a

2. The first one, more restricted in scope, had taken place eight years before at the Center for Twentieth-Century Studies in Milwaukee.

context in which those breakthroughs corresponded to an ancient sense
of book as sacred object." All of this—for me—was now no longer hidden but brought to surface—abetted also by the California visit earlier
that year of the Peruvian *curandero* Eduardo Calderón Palomino, whom
David Guss had led into a useful discussion of his *mesa* (his healing al-
tar) as an assemblage of objects that could be read the way one reads a
book. The rhyming with Mallarmé was perfect—like that of Mallarmé
with María Sabina—and suggested a series of links, a web of ancient and
modern possibilities that could be woven into a new display or book. And
the gathering itself—a small anthology of works immediately to hand—
ranged between new and old (deeply traditional and startlingly avant-
garde) in such a way (I thought) that we could "grasp the actual potentialities of writing (as with any other form of language or culture) [and by
so doing] could extend the meaning of literacy beyond a system of (pho-
netic) letters to the practice of writing itself."[3] In concluding my "editor's
note," I wrote:

> It is our growing belief (more apparent now than at the start of the
> ethnopoetics project) that the cultural dichotomies between writing
> & speech—the "written" & the "oral"—disappear the closer we get
> to the source. To say again what seems so hard to get across: there is
> a primal book as there is a primal voice, & it is the task of our po-
> etry & art to recover it—in our minds & in the world at large.

That recovery, of course, is also a matter of demonstration and of coming to understand the implications of where such a view might lead us. As

---

3. The work in the book issue, broken along the lines of modern and traditional, included
on its experimental side Karl Young's sculptural "bookforms"; Alison Knowles's *The Book of
Bean,* a monumental walk-through work with accompanying remarks and "auto-dialogue"
[reflections] by her and by George Quasha; and assorted writings and commentaries by
Jabès, Dick Higgins, Jed Rasula, David Meltzer, Gershom Scholem, and Herbert Blau;
and *on its ethnopoetic side,* it included the Eduardo Calderón *mesa;* an essay by J. Stephen
Lansing, "The Aesthetics of the Sounding of the [written] Text," on Balinese performance;
excerpts from Dennis Tedlock's translation of the Mayan *Popol Vuh* that spoke specifically
of books and writing; Tina Oldknow's offering of a Muslim practice using written (sacred) words removed from their material base and decocted in an herbal mixture ("Muslim
Soup"); and Karl Young's speculative analysis of the Mixtec *Codex Vienna,* one of the surviving illuminated books from ancient Mexico. Along with this, there was a series of striking photo portraits by Becky Cohen, in which a number of American poets are shown in
the act of reading, making of the book (as it were) "an instrument of performance."

such it is a process that those like Eric or myself or any of us here might help to start but without the real hope or even the desire to bring it to conclusion.

A decade and a half has passed since then, during which time the books have multiplied for all of us. For myself I have been lucky not only in the normal run of book publication but to have joined with book artists like Ian Tyson (a longtime companion in this work) and Barbara Fahrner, Walter Hamady, Steven Clay, and others in the making of particular works that correspond to their ideas of where the art of books might take us. I have also worked with Pierre Joris on two volumes of an end-of-century assemblage, *Poems for the Millennium*, as a work drawing from the writings of the last one hundred years and more—both those that work from a demotic spoken base and those that draw on visible language and the written word. (That there is often no clear division between the two—both the works and the makers of the works—is likely an obvious point but still a point worth making.) With regard to the book and writing (at their "limits") the work that opens the century for us is Mallarmé's—both the notes for his *Le livre* and his promethean *Coup de dés* of 1897. (A page from William Blake's *Milton: Book the Second* is the actual first volume opener in a section called "Forerunners.") This focus—most of it book-referential—is followed up in the experiments of Futurists and Dadaists but also in exemplary works by those like the "outsider" writer/artist Adolf Wölfli and the master of the collage book, Max Ernst, as well as in an ethnopoetic final section that draws from a range of works—both oral and written, ancient and modern.

The second volume is dedicated to Eric Mottram and attempts—with probably "unpardonable" omissions—to bring the work into the (almost) present.[4] The volume, at more than 850 pages, is both long and complex, but one of the dominant thrusts is to deliver the sense—as far as can be done within anthology constraints—that poets will often write not only for the single (visible) *page* but with an idea of the poem as an extended work or *book*. (Jabès, with his lifelong *Book of Questions*, would be a case in point but only one among many.) On its strongly visual side, however, the *Millennium Two* book includes works by Michaux, Cage, Mac Low, Cobra artists Christian Dotremont and Asger Jorn (but also other Cobra

4. The dedication reads: "For Eric Mottram poet, friend, & teacher" and follows with a quote extracted from a poem of his: "that creative life be rescued / from tyranny decay sloughed for a share / in magnificence hoof thunder silence of / pines & birches across the taiga."

artist-poets such as Appel, Kouwenaar, and Alechinsky), Robert Fil-
liou, a whole range of concretists (Gomringer, Finlay, Williams, Seiichi
Nikuni, Ilse and Pierre Garnier, Haroldo and Augusto de Campos, and
Karl Young, whose "bookforms" had earlier appeared in *New Wilder-
ness Letter*), Hannah Weiner, Kamau Brathwaite, George Maciunas, Bob
Cobbing, Steve McCaffery, Carolee Schneemann, Tom Phillips, Clark
Coolidge (in collaboration with Philip Guston), Cecilia Vicuña, and
Theresa Hak Kyung Cha. Along with these come chapter-length ex-
cerpts from text-centered works composed as books and not compen-
dia by poets such as Alice Notley, Anne Waldman, Jacques Roubaud, and
Lyn Hejinian, among many others. And there is also a section, "Toward a
Cyberpoetics," going back to visual/verbal machine works by Duchamp
and Abraham Lincoln Gillespie and up to computer-generated texts by
Jim Rosenberg and John Cayley—as a starter.

I have no theory as to where all of this may lead us, though some sense
of theory (neither "critical" nor "French" but very much, I hope, my own)
must underlie all that I'm saying. Still I feel it's close to whatever basis for
a poetics Eric Mottram was pursuing in his art and thought. The work
continues of course, as it has to, and over the last year—but no longer able
to share with Eric—I've supervised the republication (by Steven Clay and
Granary Books) of the *New Wilderness Letter* book issue—now an independent volume called *The Book, Spiritual Instrument.* And looking ahead
(and very much at Clay's instigation), I've embarked with him on another
anthology project: a wide-ranging book of writings on "the book," taken
in some sense as an extension of what *The Book, Spiritual Instrument* was
attempting with those materials that were then immediately to hand.[5]
(This is the difference, then, between a magazine and an anthology.) It is
in this context that we hope to explore more fully the points at which a
poetics and an ethnopoetics of the book and writing come together or illuminate each other. And we want at the same time to expose the material bases (ink and paper, manufacture and dissemination) of those ends
to which the work of Mallarmé was leading.

There will be no limits here to what we might include—of books that
have been made and books that have still to be imagined. I believe in this
regard that there is also a *future* of the book—as an extended and self-

---

5. It should be noted that this larger collection was published by Granary Books in 2000 as
A Book of the Book: Some Works & Projections about the Book & Writing, coedited with Steven
Clay and including the present essay as a kind of secondary introduction.

contained compendium of (visible) language—and that the emergence of new technologies—new *cyberworks* I meant to say—is not a threat to our identity as poets and book people but a new aspect of it that can and will enhance all that poesis is or ever has been. In much the same way, I no longer believe, if I ever did, that the book or writing had—in some earlier time—destroyed orality or made the human voice obsolete. The book *is* as old as fire and water, and thought *is* made in the mouth—as it is also in the hands and lungs and with the inner body. If that was our condition at the beginning, it will be also in the end.

"Secular Jewish Culture / Radical Poetic Practice"

Notes for a conference with that title, organized by
Charles Bernstein, in 2004

1

Every time I appear in a Jewish anthology—except those of my own devising—something goes wrong. Lines are omitted or placed out of sequence, prose is set as verse or verse as prose, and footnotes are used that represent an editor's imagining of what a word might mean or a place-name represent. I believe that the God of the Jews has something to do with this—a punishment for my deliberate withdrawal from Him or Her or It. Or else, to be more Jewish about it in the manner of a writer whom I admire and have sometimes drawn from, it is as if one of Isaac Bashevis Singer's imps or demons had been there to gum up my works—not when I'm being a Jew on my own terms but when I give in to temptation and let myself be part of somebody else's order or communion.[1]

I will speak, then, *in my own terms* (on my own grounds), though with continuing doubts as to whether there is any particular "*radical* poetic practice" that can be viewed as distinctively Jewish. That isn't to say that there aren't plenty of Jews (however defined) who have been active in avant-garde (or twentieth- and twenty-first-century) poetics, still less to deny that by this time many—perhaps too many—Jewish poets have actively engaged in a Jewish version of identity writing, though I don't think that that's what "radical practice" is intended to mean in the present con-

1. See made-up footnotes in *Jewish American Literature: A Norton Anthology;* prose changed to verse in *Princeton University Library Chronicle* (Jewish-American issue, gathered by C. K. Williams); poem truncated and missing part added to another poem, in Steven J. Rubin, *Telling and Remembering: A Century of American Jewish Poetry.*

text. I would also say, in my own case at least, that I would be willing to construct a connection between aspects of traditional Jewish linguistic practice (much of it religious or mystical rather than secular) and current forms of poetic (i.e., language) experimentation. I have in fact done this at some length, along with a proposition that Jewish history has been marked as well by an ongoing and more obvious resistance, by *the Great Refusal,* as I once put it, *to the lie of church and state.* (I would include here synagogue as well—at least for some of us.) That resistance may not have been secular in the first instance, but it carried the mark of outsider or *outrider* traditions (to use Anne Waldman's word); or that was how it felt to me when I first turned to it.

It was in the sense of such an outsiderness—and placing it clearly in "this most Christian of worlds"—that Marina Tsvetayeva spoke of *all poets* as *Jews*—much like Norman Mailer's "White Negro" of the 1950s. That was in her poem "Poem of the End," later quoted by Paul Celan in the Cyrillic epigraph to his own poem "Und mit dem Buch aus Tarussa" and by me in *A Big Jewish Book,* where it became a central proposition of the stand I was then taking.[2] My argument here wasn't for some kind of Jewish exclusiveness but for a recognition that such resistances existed both there and elsewhere and that my address, in Tsvetayeva's sense, was to "all poets" or to all poets who share the outrider stance or to all, poets and others, who resist the rule of totalizing states and constrictive religions. I saw myself—then as now—not writing in a specifically Jewish context for a Jewish audience, as such, but opening the Jewish mysteries to all who wanted them. And I dramatized some of that in the dream that opens *A Big Jewish Book:*

> There was a dream that came before the book, & I might as well tell it. I was in a house identified by someone as THE HOUSE OF JEWS, where there were many friends gathered, maybe everyone I knew. Whether they were Jews or not was unimportant: I was & because I was I had to lead them through it. But we were halted at the entrance to a room, not a room really, more like a great black hole in space. I was frightened & exhilarated, both at once, but like the others I held back before that darkness. The question came to be the room's name, as if to give the room a *name* would open it. I knew that, & I strained my eyes & body to get near the room, where

2. Right here, in an aside, I pointed out: "Of course—conversely—all Jews aren't poets."

I could feel, as though a voice was whispering to me, creation going on inside it. And I said that it was called CREATION.

I now recognize that dream as central to my life, an event & mystery that has dogged me from the start. I know that there are other mysteries—for others, or for myself at other times, more central—& that they may or may not be the same. But CREATION—*poesis* writ large—appeared to me first in that house, for I was aware then, & even more so now, that there are Jewish mysteries that one confronts in a place no less dangerous or real than that abyss of the Aztecs:

   ... *a difficult, a dangerous place, a deathly place: it is dark, it is light* ...

& with a sense too that this space must be bridged, this door opened as well—the door made just for you, says the guardian in Kafka's story. Yet Kafka, like so many of us, poses the other question also: "What have I in common with Jews? I have hardly anything in common with myself."

That last, of course, is an extraordinarily Jewish statement.

2

Having gotten this far by way of introduction, I want to say something of how I came to be here and to launch a few other comments, in no particular order but as they came to me while writing.

Like Louis Zukofsky and Charles Reznikoff, among other children of Jewish immigrants, my first language (to the age of three or four) was Yiddish. (I learned later from reading T. S. Eliot, who I know had *me* in mind, that this disqualified me as a poet within the English mainstream [and probably out of it as well], and I came to take that as a challenge and an opportunity.) My parents (unlike Zukofsky's) were avowedly secular, from late adolescence on, but my mother's mother, who lived with us from a month or two before my birth, was an orthodox Jew, though the relations between her and them were never less than cordial. The outside world—in street and school—was emphatically secular, extending even to the Jewish school where I would go most afternoons for Yiddish lessons. I had no problem with my grandmother's love of God, though as the terror of the Holocaust came back to her—two of her sons and their families having vanished by then—I heard it rather as an argument—an interrogation and rebuke—that came into her nightly prayers. For myself the experience of the war—viewed fitfully but at an easy childhood distance—brought out, with regard to that, my first poetic stirrings and what Tristan Tzara, in an earlier war, had spoken of "not [as] the beginnings of an art, but of a disgust." Such in a nutshell was the story of my early turn to poetry.

I grew up knowing a little about Jewish religion and lore but almost nothing about Jewish mysticism (the richest source for a poetics, as I later found). What came to me at some time in my teens was what I felt to be a need for poetry and for the intensities and disgust that brought the poetry I knew to life. At a still later point—I don't know just when—I was surprised to find something like that intensity in the language of religion—more likely in pagan and Christian sources than in Jewish ones. It soon seemed to me that I wanted to steal that language and to make it my own.[3] In doing so I meant to shift the field from religion to poetry, while not denying but even emphasizing the origins of what I took as poetry in areas of religious languaging and ritual. The transfer here, as the Dada poet Richard Huelsenbeck once pointed out for his own borrowings and deformations, was from the *mis*believers to the *dis*believers of religion. *I wanted to stand here firmly with the disbelievers.*

The involvement with Jewish materials as such came about when it had to, coterminous with *Technicians of the Sacred* (in 1968) and with a need I felt then "to explore ancestral sources of my own," most specifically and deliberately (I wrote & would write again) "in the world of Jewish mystics, thieves, & madmen." That project—experimental through & through—began for me with *Poland/1931,* continued with *A Big Jewish Book* (as Jewish anthology or assemblage), and returned in *Khurbn, Gematria,* and *14 Stations* (holocaust poems using modified aleatoric procedures). (Even so, I would remind you, I was producing a still larger body of poetry and poetry gatherings that wasn't part of my Jewish experiment *as such.*) The intention throughout was not so much to discover or exploit identity (in the ethnic/tribal sense) as to put identity into doubt or question.

3. Thus William Carlos Williams, when, as a student at City College, I met him: "*Seize the language! Smash it to hell! You have a right to it!*"

For this I applied or meant to apply the full range of modernist techniques and procedures to identity thematics, taking the resultant work, if it's right to say so, as itself a form of romantic/modernist *irony*.[4] In that sense, too, I saw what I was doing as the continuation of an aborted Jewish/Yiddish poetry in another language (American or English rather than Yiddish) and by every means at my disposal. Once into it I also found that I could draw from procedures and imageries embedded in traditional Jewish sources. This was true in particular with gematria (mystical Jewish numerology), which I adapted and *secularized* as a processual form of composition, culminating in the book-length poem *Gematria* (from Sun & Moon Press) and *14 Stations* (gematria turned to memorialization of the Holocaust). But *Poland/1931*, my first experiment with a constructed Jewish poetry, is also full of fragments (verbal and visual) appropriated from traditional sources.[5]

I've been involved, then, with a secularization of the mystical and supernatural, a project that I share with others going back to at least the eighteenth century, but with twists and turns of my own and reflective also of the times in which we've lived. What this involves is the transfer of a body of work and language from religion to poetry and from poetry to the domain of Huelsenbeck's *dis*believers. My effort— but hardly mine alone—has been to open the field of poetry into areas of *poesis* (oral *and* written, sacred *and* secular) that have not had an adequate accounting. In so doing, it was *our* intention to hold onto the energy and ferocity/intensity that we found there but without the "mind-forg'd manacles" of orthodox religious thought.

For me the process went beyond my engagement with Jewish sources, and before I assembled *A Big Jewish Book* I had already assembled "a big Indian book" *(Shaking the Pumpkin)* and before that "a big human book"

4. My first deliberate attempt at writing "the Jewish poem" was a mix I created by bringing together structures from Gertrude Stein's serial poem "Dates" with mystically loaded and sexually charged vocabulary from Isaac Bashevis Singer's novel *Satan in Goray*.
5. And even here, let me add, I was not alone but entered a discourse with poets I had known or was soon to meet, like David Meltzer, Nathaniel Tarn, Jack Hirschman, Edmond Jabès, and even (from our one meeting) Paul Celan; or others, important to me at different times, like Robert Kelly and Robert Duncan. In addition the totalizing impulse of *Technicians of the Sacred* and, later, *Poems for the Millennium* may itself have been part of a secular Jewish thrust, something, as Charles Bernstein has suggested, that could even have influenced a similar tendency in Ezra Pound and others still more obviously outside the Jewish context.

(Technicians of the Sacred). [I would, still later, do the same in my own poetry with Christian and Buddhist imageries.] In those non-Jewish gatherings the act of assemblage or construction was similar, but my position
was different in that I couldn't be thought of as writing from *within* the
subject or with myself identified *as* subject. *A Big Jewish Book,* then, was
an experiment along the lines of the other anthologies but with myself
as a participatory subject in a shared subjectivity. With an awareness of
all of that, I set out to explore what was possible in extremis and with no
holds barred. I thought of myself as operating through a secular/poetic
consciousness that set the content and form of the sacred against that of
the not-so-sacred, the heretical, the heterodox, the blasphemous, and certainly the secular as such.

But even in *A Big Jewish Book* or *Poland/1931*—a plunge into a constructed world based on real witnessings and documents as "data-clusters"
(Ed Sanders's term in his argument for an "investigative poetry")—if I
were to play it from within, I had to perform some part of it in costume,
which I did in fact with the additional aid of photographs and films, something I would never have done in the Indian instance. Similarly, when I
was writing, or rather performing, *That Dada Strain,* I costumed myself again—in imitation this time of Hugo Ball and Tristan Tzara (a.k.a.
Sammy Rosenstock)—but that was still another kind of identity poetics
that would get us too far afield if I stopped to speak about it here.

There was a time, then, when I became concerned with "the jewish poem" as such and even wondered—in light of Tsvetayeva—where
I might, if I continued, place its final boundaries. ("Jewish American"
was of far less concern to me than "Jewish," which in itself was international in scope.) In the Pre-Face to *A Big Jewish Book* I even made a list
of Jewish "topics & conflicts/tensions," with the caveat that many of these
were not unique to Jews although the history of the Jews might—up to a
point—offer an exemplary instance. I presented these, as characteristics
that still held me to the Jewish work, as follows:

• a sense of exile both as cosmic principle (exile of God from God, etc.)
  & as the Jewish fate, experienced as the alienation of group & individual, so that the myth (gnostic or orthodox) is never only symbol but
  history, experience, as well;
• from which there comes a distancing from nature & from God (infi-
  nite, ineffable), but countered in turn by a *poesis* older than the Jews,

still based on namings, on an imaging of faces, bodies, powers, a working out of possibilities (but principally, the female side of God—
Shekinah/Shekhina—as herself in exile) evaded by orthodoxy, now
returning to astound us;

- or, projected into language, a sense (in Edmond Jabès's phrase) of being "exiled in the word"—a conflict, as I read it, with a text, a web of
letters, that can capture, captivate, can force the mind toward abstract
pattern or, conversely, toward the framing, raising, of an endless, truly
Jewish "book of questions";
- &, finally, the Jews identified as mental rebels, who refuse consensus,
thus become—even when bound to their own Law, or in the face of
"holocaust," etc.—the model for the Great Refusal to the lie of Church
& State.
- [And I concluded]: . . . it's from such a model—however obscured by
intervening degradations from *poesis,* impulse to conform, etc.—that I
would understand the Russian poet Marina Tsvetayeva's dictum that
"all poets are Jews."

Two points to end it, and then, if I may, a poem.

There is also a curious way in which Jewish writers—contrary to
Harold Bloom, say—have had an advantage, a leg up, *as poets* and as long
as they maintained their sense of *otherness,* even as a counterpoint to the
at-homeness they may have sought in the language that surrounds them
and is nevertheless, for all of us, a place of exile. As my brother-in-arms
Pierre Joris has written, in defense of a "nomadic poetics": "It is only when
constantly aware that the writer is not 'at home' in language (or anywhere
else, for that matter) that any real and critical engagement with the enemy
forces is possible." It is then, too, that the strongest engagements with language *qua poetry* take place.

The context for such remarks is of course diasporic/dispersed, and it's
in the condition of diaspora—not exclusively but largely—that our poetics (Jewish & not so Jewish) has been constructed. That has led me, in the
course of preparing this talk, to wonder about the *state* of Israel and the
emergence of a Jewish *home*land—whether the connection between Jews
and an exilic/nomadic/diasporic poetics isn't by now distressingly anachronistic. To say "all poets are Jews" in an Israeli-Palestinian context, in
which Jews are the privileged insiders, is something quite different from
Tsvetayeva's 1926 context "in this most Christian of worlds" and gives me
the acute sense that history has somehow overwhelmed us.

I think that I may pursue this at a later point, but for now it seems to me enough simply to have said it.

To conclude, then, I'll read a poem from *Poland/1931* that speaks both to the persistence of Jews in history and to my bewilderment at being called on as an expert in this kind of forum. (The irony is even more obvious today than when I wrote it.)

[reads:]

THE CONNOISSEUR OF JEWS

if there were locomotives to ride home on
& no jews
there would still be jews & locomotives
just as there are jews & oranges
& jews & jars
there would still be someone to write the jewish poem
others to write their mothers' names in light—
just as others, born angry
have the moon's face burnt onto their arms
& don't complain
my love, my lady, be a connoisseur of jews
the fur across your lap
was shedding
on the sheet were hairs
the first jew to come to you is mad
the train pulls into lodz
he calls you
by your polish name
then he tells the other passengers a story
there are jews & there are alphabets
he tells them
but there are also jewish alphabets
just as there are jewish locomotives
& jewish hair
& just as there are some with jewish fingers
such men are jews
just as other men are not jews
not mad

don't call you by your polish name
or ride the train to lodz
if there are men who ride the train to lodz
there are still jews
just as there are still oranges
& jars
there is still someone to write the jewish poem
others to write their mothers' names in light

Harold Bloom: The Critic as Exterminating Angel

Among the uglier images making up what will emerge as the myth of the twentieth century is that of Dr. Josef Mengele—exterminating angel of Auschwitz—who separated the victims bound directly for the gas chambers from those healthy enough to be spared for terminal labor assignments. His characteristic gesture, at least in my own vision of it, was a flick of either wrist and the laconic words, "You to the right" or "You to the left." One variant of the myth would have us believe further that Mengele, being a man of some "culture" or pretensions thereto, found the task sad but otherwise inevitable.

As goodness, we have been told ad infinitum, may sometimes spring from evil, I would have hoped that the image of Mengele's judgment (or its innumerable counterparts) might have helped us pull away from the model of man casting himself in the role of a judgmental god. At least I would have hoped so in the domain of art: an experimental ground on which such human possibilities can be played out as images. "Pour en finir avec le jugement de Dieu"—Artaud's great verbal act of exorcism—followed the savageries of Auschwitz by a couple of years, and a characteristic if milder stance of some later avant-gardists aimed to create for art and poetry a function that allowed discovery while avoiding the pretense to judgment characteristic of most critical and literary traditions.

1

I'm reminded of all this in going over the critical writings of Harold Bloom—a task I set myself after reading a particularly indulgent piece

Originally published in *Sulfur*, no. 2 (1981).

of his exclusionary criticism that I'll discuss below. In Bloom, more blatantly than elsewhere, the idea of the critic as exterminating angel appears with characteristic regrets, etc., but in no uncertain terms. "However diffidently I give the answer," he writes in *Kabbalah and Criticism*, "I am engaged in canon-formation, in trying to help decide a question that is ultimately of a sad importance: 'Which poet shall live?'"

I'm aware of the hyperbole, even the absurdity involved in setting Bloom beside Mengele, but I can't help feeling that he himself must have had some such comparison in mind when presenting his work in those terms. The play of much of his criticism (and by far its most interesting aspect) involves his incorporation of Jewish mysticism and myth into a description of "post-Enlightenment poetry"; and this includes, beyond a reinforcement of Bloom's six rhetorical tropes or of his "revisionist" poetics in general, the use of such a solidly traditional figure as the Malakh ha-Mavat = Angel of Death = Satan = (by a common gnostic and Blakean inversion) god as Jehovah. His criticism seems obsessed, as well, with the killing off of poets—largely, of course, with poets killing other poets, both forerunners and contemporaries, in a veritable battle-to-the-death. Given all that, it seems unlikely to me that as "Jewish" a critic as Bloom would not, in making his assertion of a "you live / you die" function for criticism, have been struck by the image of Mengele, in much the same way that as "Jewish" a poet as myself immediately felt its presence.

I will get back to the "Jewish question" shortly—as well as the not unrelated questions of poetic struggle and canon formation. For the moment I would like to play with (and even "*mis*read") some of the key terms in Bloom's criticism, which together form a coherent if spiritually stingy view of reality and one that seems aimed (for whatever we might want to salvage from it) against much of what I take to be of most value in the poetry and art of this century.

2

Much of Bloom's energy as a critic has gone into the exposure of the blindness of poets about their origins in other poets—a blindness and an attempt at concealment that involves, most crucially, those poets Bloom professes most strongly to admire. This work of exposure is more than critic's busywork, whether as simple source-study or as what Geoffrey Hartman calls, using some of Bloom's own terms, "a type of 'mis-reading' which helps poets to overcome the influence of previous poets"—or, as

Bloom more accurately puts it, a "deadly encouragement that never ceases to remind them of how heavy their inheritance is." Bloom's involvement is intense, even personal, and what it finally reveals is his own blindness about the motives of his enterprise and its origins in what may be a deep struggle with, and antagonism toward, the very objects of his admiration. The work, in other words, is highly deceptive (to himself and others)—at least if one misses certain key confessions sprinkled through it, or if one is diverted by the radical nature of Bloom's great predecessor poets (Milton, Blake, Shelley, Emerson, Whitman, and so on) into thinking that Bloom is dealing in the present—as they in the past—with a true poetics of liberation. The approach through Bloom is in fact the reverse of any such position.

To begin with—and this shouldn't surprise anyone out there—Bloom's poetics, as he presents it, is militantly "literary." (This doesn't mean that it may not have other ends in view—political, social, etc.—but more of that later.) He is by self-proclamation an "academic critic," who presents the history of Western poetry as the work of a succession of academically based canon makers, from the time when "Alexandria, which . . . founded our scholarship, permanently set the literary tradition of the school, and introduced the secularized notion of the canon"—a process that modernism (= "the Romantic psychology of belatedness") has challenged or confused but never, presumably, replaced. "Nothing in the literary world," writes Bloom in *A Map of Misreading*, "sounds quite so silly to me as the passionate declarations that poetry must be liberated from the academy, declarations that would be absurd at any time, but peculiarly so some twenty-five hundred years after Homer and the academy first became indistinguishable." (How the assembled ghosts of Blake, Shelley, and Whitman would have handled that one boggles the mind—though no doubt it provides Harold with a chuckle as well.)

What holds for the critic-as-academic-reader must also hold for the poets. That most poets who read are readers isn't the point at issue nor that poets are "desperately obsessed with poetic origins"—and with other origins as well: personal, linguistic, cosmic, and so forth. For Bloom it must be tighter than that, so he writes, in *Poetry and Repression:* "Even the strongest poet must take up his stance within literary language. If he stands outside it, he cannot begin to write poetry. For poetry lives always under the shadow of poetry." (Thus Bloom's favoring of rhetoric and so on over Wordsworth's "selection of the real language of men" or its more precise, therefore more threatening, contemporary equivalents.) Or again, in *A Map of Misreading:* "Poems, I am saying, are neither about 'subjects' nor about 'themselves.' They are necessarily about other poems; a poem is a response to a poem, as a poet is a response to a poet, or a person to his parent." And the response, in Bloom's terms, is always a misreading, a misinterpretation, the outgrowth of a struggle oedipally conceived: "To live, the poet must *misinterpret* the father, by the crucial act of misprision, which is the re-writing of the father." (Such misprision, in Bloom's account, may also involve the critic as reader, though the struggle there seems muted—not presented, for all of Bloom's exterminating passion, as a battle-to-the-death.)

In all of this, as I see it, the problem is not that Bloom takes a literary or textual approach but that he leaves us room for almost nothing else: an occasional nod toward the "reading" of nature or of experience, or a passing hint that precursors, even literary ones, may be other than poets or that the struggle may be with forces other than literary ones. Such one-sidedness is the price of obsession—his own, self-acknowledged, with the idea of influence and its attendant anxieties—and it leaves him often and inevitably at odds with his poets, their poetics and self-interpretations, their views of their own and others' struggles where those contradict the needs of Bloom's particular "misprision." While Bloom is certainly aware of this, he "take(s) the resistance shown to the theory by many poets, in particular, to be likely evidence for its validity, for poets rightly idealize their activity; and all poets, weak and strong, agree in denying any share in the anxiety of influence."

The finesse of that last shot is absolutely breathtaking: an assertion of the critic's hegemony against all odds and certainly "all poets"—like Bloom's comment elsewhere that "the true poem is the critic's mind." It is as if Claude Lévi-Strauss had inadvertently confessed to Russell Means's worst suspicions about anthropologists; and seen in the larger frame of Bloom's intentions and assumptions, it drives home a separation between poet and (academic) critic, not as many of us have long felt it but toward ends that Bloom announces here and there with great forthrightness. So, he tells us in *A Map of Misreading,* "No strong poet can deign to be a good reader of his own works," nor should the critic speak for him exactly, because "this is not the critic's proper work, to take up the poet's stance." And having said that much, he goes on to question—from the critic's perspective—the term most central to the poetics of nearly all his targeted "strong poets" and to that romantic tradition one might have thought he was defending:

Perhaps there *is* a power or faculty of the Imagination, and certainly all poets *must* go on believing in its existence, but a critic makes a better start by agreeing with Hobbes that imagination is 'decaying sense' and that poetry is written by the same natural man or woman who suffers daily all the inescapable anxieties of competition.

The key word here—since Bloom has pulled us back into the "light of common day"—is *competition*. Few poets would deny their identity as natural men or women (it is, if anything, part of the inheritance of the romantic); but the discovery that competition—not imagination!—is the central definition of the natural and human (and, ultimately, the poetic) is a point that wouldn't escape the readers of *Commentary*, say, whatever effect, or non-effect, it may have on the readers of *Sulfur*.

We are approaching the crucial split between two human possibilities that marks Bloom's doleful "deconstruction," the moral choice behind his poet-critic cleavage, whose implications, since his position isn't timeless, become much clearer, more specific and more contemporary, elsewhere in his work. Thus, he writes in the introduction to *Figures of Capable Imagination* (1976):

Poets lie, both to themselves and to everyone else, about their indebtedness to one another, and most critics and literary scholars tend to follow poets by hopelessly idealizing all interpoetic relations. Now that the tides of aggressive ignorance, or the counterculture, are ebbing, many of the absurd hopes that the young and their middle-aged followers placed in an apocalypse of society are coming to rest in the arts, particularly literature, in the belief that there at least the repressed can return, a belief much encouraged by such false prophets as Marcuse and Norman O. Brown.

If this isn't Bloom at his best—and it isn't—it's Bloom giving an unequivocal context for his present disturbance. The identity of the "false prophets" isn't worth an argument, though the question of the other poets/prophets, who "lie . . . to themselves and to everyone else" (but from whom Bloom derives his livelihood), should at least give one pause—the relation of Blake, say, to "counter-culture" and "apocalypse" and "art" and the "return of the repressed." A notable "misreading," I'd have thought, to go from Blake's dream of liberation to this hostility toward those who would presume to carry it into the present. Knowingly or not (but no critic should "deign to be a good reader of his own works"), Bloom is here playing out the archetypal role of Blake's "Devourer": the antithesis of the "Prolific," who thinks he has the Prolific/the "producer" in his chains ("but it is not so, he only takes portions of existence and fancies that the whole"). In this, Blake writes as a (true? false?) prophet, pointing to the continuing existence of "these two classes of men . . . [who are and] should be enemies," for "whoever tries to reconcile them seeks to destroy existence."

If Bloom is the Devourer—the diluter of energy, the reductive agent— "revisionism" is no longer the poet's (prolific) revisioning but an attempt to turn the unqualified "freedom" of the romantics and their successors into a qualified and "repressed freedom": itself a product of anxiety. The Devourer, then, swallows the Prolific's "excess of delights" but seems to choke on them; or, as Devourer-turned-teacher, he laments: "How is he [am I] to teach a tradition now grown so wealthy and so heavy that to accommodate it demands more strength than any single consciousness can provide?" Unlike the Prolific—the producer—who revels in his own and others' excesses, the teacher/Devourer/critic is driven to despair and to canon formation to relieve the stress.

As mere "academic criticism," the Bloom dilemma seems a little sad and silly. But it's never more than a short step from literature to those other areas where ideas like "freedom" and "repression" affect the actual ways we think and act as human beings. Given Bloom's own time frame and his sense already quoted of the counterrevolutionary nature of the middle 1970s and beyond, I will allow myself a political reading of one of his statements vis-à-vis "strong" poets and "strong" poetry in *Poetry and Repression,* that "it is only by repressing creative 'freedom,' through the initial fixation of influence, that a person can be reborn as a poet." The terms are slippery and may at first be taken as purely self-repressive and/or psychological; but while Bloom relates his work to Freudian ideas of sublimation ("Geoffrey Hartman . . . calls the poetic will 'sublimated compulsion' . . . [while] I would call it 'repressed freedom'"), he himself tells us that his aim isn't "so much to apply Freud (or even revise Freud) as to arrive at an Oedipal interpretation of poetic history." Nor is it simply a question of poetic restraints as a matter of technique or method. The issue for Bloom increasingly involves a response to a contemporary condition of yearning for which Bloom's own precursor poets had acted as prime movers. That response—at least the part of it that concerns me here—is threefold.

He is, to begin with, scornful of the ambitions of "post-Enlightenment poets," although the scorn is sometimes hidden behind a mask of "melancholy." "Unfortunately," he tells us in *Kabbalah and Criticism*, "we have all of us arrived too late in the day to take on such a flamboyance" as that of Emerson and Whitman "chanting . . . that a large consciousness contradicts itself because it contains multitudes." But this late-in-the-day, therefore absurd, flamboyance extends, we find out in *A Map of Misreading*, from "all of us" to all American poets whatsoever, "the most consciously belated in the history of Western poetry," who, "rather more than other Western poets, at least since the Enlightenment, are astonishing in their ambitions. Each wants to be the whole of which all other poets are only parts." Applied to Emerson and Whitman themselves (but also Dickinson, Thoreau, Hawthorne, and Melville), the Bloomian misreading moves from muted mockery to a diffident paternalism that only a true Devourer could master.

From such a defensive-aggressive posture Bloom can put into question the stand of any of his great poet-precursors against repression itself. Such a strategy is at the heart of Bloom's mis-readings, in line with which he proposes, in *Poetry and Repression*, to revise "all reasonings, including my own," of such a poem as Blake's "London," since said readings "are wholly mistaken in seeing ['London'] primarily as a protest against repression, whether societal or individual." Here a cautious adverb ("primarily") keeps him from the archrevisionist statement he seems really to be aiming at, but later he crosses the line and tells us that "Blake's poem is not a protest, not a prophetic outcry, not a vision of judgment. It is a revisionist's self-condemnation, a Jonah's outcry at knowing he is not an Ezekiel." All of which is a crazy "academic" view of a poet who shivers the boundaries of literature; who is Blake rather than Ezekiel (and no less important for that); and whose prophetic outcry coexists with whatever "negative and self-destructive" elements Bloom may rightly or wrongly see in him.[1] We have here passed from misreading to decep-

---

1. Before being misled by the contrast between Blake and, say, the Hebrew prophets, the reader can check out, e.g., the self-doubt of Ezekiel 20.49: "Ah Lord God, they are saying of me: Is he not a maker of allegories?" Or Jeremiah 20.9: "There is something in my heart like a burning fire / Shut up in my bones / & I am weary of holding it in / & I cannot." Or Abraham J. Heschel in *The Prophets:* "The prophet is human, yet he employs notes one octave too high for our ears. He experiences moments that defy our understanding. He is neither 'a singing saint' nor a 'moralizing poet,' but an assaulter of the mind." [All quoted by J. R. in *A Big Jewish Book*.]

tion: the attempt to reduce Blake's fine frenzy to that "failure of nerve" that, if I remember it correctly, underpinned the new conservatism of the critics of my childhood. (Bloom's teachers, too—to whom he once again succumbs.) The process from here on in begins to read like critic's self-projection.

The third response I have in mind is something more than that, though clearly tied to Bloom's own situation. For what Bloom does at the extreme of his deconstruction is virtually to reject the idea of "freedom" in favor of that of "repression"—terms he has already revealed to have a "social" as well as "individual" dimension (i.e., not merely "literary"). Emblematically Bloom phrases this rejection as his turning from Milton's Satan (as interpreted by Blake): a poetic creation whose influence had extended into the work of such American poetic "revisionists" as Ralph Waldo Emerson and, even, Emily Dickinson. In his characteristic manner he describes the turning not only as a matter of regret but something deeper. "I am temperamentally a natural revisionist," he writes in *A Map of Misreading,* "and I respond to Satan's speeches more strongly than to any other poetry I know, so it causes some anguish in me to counsel that currently we need Milton's sense of tradition much more than Emerson's revisionary tradition. Indeed, the counsel of necessity must be taken further: most simply, we need Milton, and not the Romantic return of the repressed Milton but the Milton who made his great poem identical with the process of repression that is vital to literary tradition.")

In the light of current New Conservative and Moral Majority maneuvers, the invocation of the language of repression and of Milton the Puritan (or a parody thereof) as counselor-on-tradition cannot be confined to the world of literary studies. The "we" who need the Milton of Repression is ultimately a "we" that can't be narrowed down, Bloom tells us, by "sex, race, social class," and so forth. "If we are human," he writes, "then we depend upon a Scene of Instruction, which is necessarily also a scene of authority and of priority." And no matter how he tries to modify this into a middle-ground accommodation with the authoritative fathers, the stance remains contemporary with Bob Dylan's recent need "to serve somebody"—as Bloom's competition-as-creation might make a fit with the revivalist side of Milton (Friedman)'s economics.

⌒

I'm not refuting Bloom here so much as indicating his obvious and admitted deviations from the line of poets (the nineteenth-century ones at least) foregrounded in his work. The spirit of that work, it seems to me, isn't revisionist but, as he himself renames it, "antithetical": almost a full turn from the revisioning—the actual return to vision—that has marked our poetry from Blake until the present. I've found Bloom useful in clarifying some of this, and I sympathize with some larger part of what he attends to: romanticism, kabbala, gnosticism, and so on. At the same time I'm distressed by the reductiveness of his work, by his unwillingness to revise or revision a narrowly conservative idea of tradition and "priority." There is, in other words, no questioning of "tradition" at its roots, only a reductive assertion "that everyone who now reads and writes in the West, of whatever racial background, sex or ideological camp, is still a son or daughter of Homer." No Coyotes or Taras appear in his mythologies, no Milarepas or Li Pos among his canonized poets. Kabbala and gnosticism gain entry as maps for criticism, but otherwise his "canon" is still European and his specialization post-Enlightenment and English. So it remains only those poets devoted to the idea of the prolific, exuberant, and flamboyant who have made the move to let the greater world into our work.

Bloom's narrowness helps him turn any new or liberating sense of the past into a species of "belatedness," and it allows him to disregard the forwardness that has again and again defined an avant-garde over the last two centuries. It is against such forwardness in particular that his rage seems directed—and even more particularly against the forwardness that surrounds him here and now. The poets wandering past the Bloomian woods should at least be warned of this. "A map of misreading" may sound like a step toward the openings of indeterminacy or chance or toward a free experiment with word and thought, but it isn't. Similarly, his selection of John Ashbery (Bloom's one candidate for canonization among the old "New American poets" and the New York School) may feel like a leftward tilt but is, if anything, the scorning of poetic "movements" (the attempt to draw multiple voices into the work of poesis) in favor of the single poet winnowed from his peers.

While obscuring his own critical precursors in the anti-Blakean, anti-Miltonic New Critics, Bloom's aim—against the whole thrust of visionary and revolutionary poetics—has been to maintain the process of canon formation and the mastery of critic over poet, Devourer over Prolific, system maker over "Inspired Man." To keep poetry within the domain of academic literature—to maintain, that is, the separation between art and life—he has devised a system that has both limited his own ability to read and to create and has allowed him to be arbitrary in his selection of "strong" poets and "strong" poems. More than his method, it is his intention that seems so wrong and devious: a deliberate obfuscation that would reject (at least in his own time) the strong and bold in favor of those he sees, rightly or wrongly, as candidates for the purveyors of a "repressed freedom."

3

The arrogance of criticism prospers, even fattens, on the silence of the poets whom it means to tyrannize. It is an illusory fatness, anyway, and there does come a time when some of us who make poetry are moved, for one reason or another, to break the silence and to respond in kind. For if critics are instructors, as in Bloom's view of it they are, so are poets; and it isn't always possible or useful to save ourselves the effort of that clash of instructions by surrendering the field.

What finally pushed me to a reading and a response to Bloom was his second attempt at dealing with, and dismissing, a generalized entity called "the American-Jewish poet." Since I'm a particularized version of that entity, I can be seen to have a personal stake in the matter. As a poet, of course, I'm supposed to thrive on personal stakes, while Bloom as a critic may be thought to have a need for more objective standards. But what's attractive to me in Bloom's work is that such "objectivity" is almost never there—and surely not when dealing with an entity so close to home as this one.

Bloom himself is a marvelous example of "belated" Jewish culture. It colors a large part of his criticism, and it is, as I said earlier, its most interesting aspect (at least for me). This isn't a question of a down-home feeling shared by Jews but that in dealing with certain areas of Jewish tradition, Bloom allows himself access to the kind of uncanonized traditional material for which, by a curious display of willful ignorance, he seems otherwise to have so little use. The result, in a work like *Kabbalah and Criticism,* is sometimes very useful, and similar insights turn up in his other works and intersect with a referential network that touches as well on Jewish orthodoxy and gnostic heterodoxy—noncanonical also from a Western/Christian point of view. If Bloom had only allowed this network to expand, he could have made an extraordinary synthesizing contribution to our concepts of poesis. But he would also have been poaching incredibly on the poet's terrain, where "all ages are contemporaneous in the mind" and everything is possible.[2]

Bloom on the Jewish poets is something very different. The two pieces that raise that issue are "The Sorrows of American-Jewish Poetry," which appeared in *Commentary* about ten years ago and was reprinted in *Figures of Capable Imagination,* and "The Heavy Burden of the Past," from the January 4, 1981, issue of the *New York Times Book Review.* The first piece seems to have come out of nowhere—or out of nothing more than Bloom's suspicion of, discomfort with, or hostility to the idea of (American) Jewish poets—while the second is a review of a specific book, *Voices within the Ark,* that presents twelve hundred pages, worldwide in scope, of what the editors, Anthony Rudolph and Howard Schwartz, call "The Modern Jewish Poets." The "simple" question, raised in the first essay but covering both, is "Why isn't modern Jewish poetry better?" since, Bloom assures us, of the ninety American Jewish poets in the Rudolph-Schwartz book, "only about a dozen have written authentic poems, true artifacts, and none of these alas has yet earned a place in the canon, though one or two yet may." And of those ninety American Jews (the Europeans end up only a little better at Bloom's hands, but it's clearly the Americans he's after), Bloom further assures us that "no single figure [is included] who so far matters urgently or overwhelmingly in the poetry of our country."[3]

2. Bloom backs off from any such wide-spectrum synthesizing, which I assume is something he identifies, too exclusively, with the mythical "school of Pound." He is reticent as well about his relation to kabbalists and mystics, writing in *Kabbalah and Criticism:* "I myself am no Kabbalist, and hold no theosophical beliefs of any kind. I am merely a skeptic." While this is fair enough, his view of kabbala as "an interpretive and mythical tradition [rather] than a mystical one" also plays down its creative & performative side—in spite of his perception, e.g., "that the Sefirot are like poems in that they are names implying complex commentaries that make them into texts." Interestingly, too, his dismissal of himself as kabbalist is coupled with a repetition of his hostility to poets who make a conscious use of precursors: "Only weak poems, or the weaker elements in strong poems, immediately echo precursor poems, or directly allude to them." (I take this as one of the most symptomatic and debilitating attitudes in all of Bloom's writings—a damning result of his critic-poet cleavage and the surest guarantee that poets will be trapped in the past rather than free it up toward future uses.)

3. In the earlier piece he writes, under the categories of "melancholy phenomenon" & "sorrowful conclusion," that no "single American-Jewish poet of undoubted major status has established himself in a century now more than two-thirds gone." (Here, of course, his field isn't even restricted by the previous editors' choices.) The response—by a citation of poets—is obvious, though it would involve the literary equivalent of naming all-time "dream teams" without having first agreed on what game we're playing.

Since this is Bloom writing, I take it, in the language of "natural man and woman"—or what we used to call "the man in the street" or "average *N.Y. Times* reader"—I assume we can go by the ordinary meanings of those sentences. Bloom in fact makes it a little difficult to test his proposition, since he names not one American Jewish poet in the course of his review—unlike the earlier *Commentary* piece, where he may have exposed himself by doing precisely that. Still, a casual glance at the Rudolph-Schwartz book shows that among the ninety canonless Jews are Louis Zukofsky, Allen Ginsberg, and George Oppen; among those missing, Gertrude Stein. Of these, Zukofsky and Oppen (along with Charles Reznikoff) had been dismissed ten years before by Bloom for ties to Pound and Williams; Ginsberg had been tagged "Mock bardic" and had really blown it by being "beyond the reach of *criticism*" (italics mine); and Stein, as always among "academic" critics and anthologizers, had again been left unmentioned. While I'm not one to get that easily into reputations and achievements, it seems inconceivable that in the ordinary sense in which a "figure . . . matters urgently or overwhelmingly in the poetry of our country," the aforementioned poets (or a dozen more if we really started naming names) could be said not to matter or that some of those others Bloom does mention—Elizabeth Bishop or James Merrill or A. R. Ammons—could be said to matter more.

But we know already—don't we?—that Bloom is into something else: a devourer's need for reduction; a myth of poetry as a response to poetry and of person as a response to parent; and with that as the preset pattern, a decision by fiat as to who best fits it. So, the reduction and the claim for what matters proceed—here as elsewhere in Bloom—by a definition of "strong" poets as those who "tend to achieve an individualized voice by first all-but-merging with a precursor and then by pulling away from him, usually by way of a complex process of fault-finding and actual misinterpretation of the precursor." (This is the famous path-of-poetry-through-ignorance—as if to prove that Harold likes his poets blond and dumb.) And if we ask, before we swallow that, is that the mark of every "strong" poet, the answer from Bloom is every-strong-poet-since-the-Enlightenment. (He exempts Shakespeare and Co. as "antediluvians" and can't conceive of primal sources like Homer and the Bible as themselves "belated.")[4]

---

4. Consider the cover-up of Mesopotamian and Canaanite influence, etc. on the Bible—as part of the true enterprise of Western canon making up to the present.

It is Bloom's handle par excellence, and since it is, he wields it as he chooses—this one "strong" and that one "weak"—and if the parent-precursor gambit doesn't work (or if it works too well where he doesn't want it), he comes up with the "authentic poem" as the "true artifact." And so on.

As for the Jews, they fall, well, like Jews before the critic-executioner, who informs us:

> All post-Enlightenment poetry in English tends to be a displaced Protestantism anyway, so that the faith in a Person easily enough is displaced into an initial devotion to the god-like precursor poet. This, to undertake it, is hardly a very Jewish process, and yet something like it seems necessary if poets are to continue to be incarnated. However far from Jewish tradition they may be, something recalcitrant in the spirit of young Jewish poets prevents them from so initially wholehearted a surrender to a Gentile precursor, and indeed makes them nervous about the process itself.

The statement looks so crazy as I read it over that I wonder if Bloom isn't out to prove that critics are the real madmen in the critic-poet cleavage. All of it could, of course, be argued—from any number of directions—but to accept the premises to start with is, I fear, to walk into Bloom's language trap. Its mechanism is the standard double bind: if Jews appear too Jewish they're in trouble, and if they don't appear so, they're in possibly worse trouble. "The dilemma," he writes, "seems to be either too much tradition or too little, and while such a dilemma typifies all 'modern' poetry, it assumes acute and crippling manifestations in most verse that intends somehow to be Jewish." Still, the Jews "work on under peculiarly internalized disadvantages"—a statement, in spite of its racist implications, never spelled out more clearly than in what I've already quoted. But then, he tells us, "Jewish history [was] almost always catastrophic"—or, as they said, in my family and probably in his, "OY OY OY it's hard to be a Jew."

⤺

I have been asked by friends—both Jew and Gentile—who have watched me tussling with the Bloomian angel, to conjecture on the root problem. Although speculation of that sort—dealing, as it would have to, with questions of literary and psychological "priority"—would turn the tables

on a critic devoted to a probing of such origins, it feels uncomfortably far
from my previous poetics. I can, however, speculate on some of the reasons, explicit and implicit, that appear in his own writings, and can see
where my comments on those will lead us.

In *Poetry and Repression,* for example, there's a discussion of Giambattista Vico's "new science," an eighteenth-century enterprise that involved
a return to what Vico took as the oldest strata of human thought and language: a hieroglyphics of "mute signs and physical objects" followed by a
figurative "poetic" language or "poetic wisdom"—much like that "science
of the concrete" (C. Lévi-Strauss) later ascribed to "primitive" peoples
by the strangers who came to study them.[5] The true poets for Vico were
the first peoples (= "gentes" or "gentiles"), "who spoke in poetic characters" and whose language, theology, and social institutions he contrasted
not only with those of Jew and Christian (as Bloom presents it) but of all
peoples (Chaldeans, Scythians, Egyptians, Germans, Greeks, and Lat-
ins) who had gone through a development from family or tribe (= gens)
to a "civilization" that brings a separation from "poetic wisdom" and the
creation of a "human language" of "common uses" that he identified with
"prose."

Since the Jews had also undergone such changes, it is curious how
often in Bloom's discussion the distinction becomes that of Jew and Gentile, with the Christian given entry as a kind of adjunct to the Jew. (That
last point, however, I find truly ambiguous.) Thus he writes in *Poetry
and Repression:* "In Vico's absolute distinction between gentile and Jew,
the gentile is linked both to poetry and history, through the revisionary
medium of language, while the Jew (and subsequently the Christian) is
linked to a sacred origin transcending language, and so has no relation to
human history or to the arts." And again: "A strong poet, for Vico or for
us, is precisely like a gentile nation; he must divine or invent himself, and
so attempt the impossibility of originating himself. . . . Since poetry, unlike the Jewish religion, does not go back to a truly divine origin, poetry is
always at work imagining its own origin, or telling a persuasive lie about

5. "In devoting half his book to poetic wisdom, Vico exhibits scientific and religious
wisdom seeking to know itself by recovering its own origins in vulgar or poetic or creative wisdom. In doing this, it becomes itself creative, or recreative . . . re-creates itself
by re-creating the first science, that of augury or divination, out of which all the others
grew" (Thomas Goddard Bergin and Max Harold Fisch, *The New Science of Giambattista Vico*).

itself, to itself."[6] It is as if Bloom had taken one of the terms in Vico's universalizing version of a primitive-civilized dichotomy—"with our civilized natures we cannot at all imagine and can understand only by great toil the poetic nature of these first men [= gentiles]" (thus: Vico)—and had fixated on the Jewish-Gentile distinction the term implies in common usage. By so doing he can advance the standard view of the Jews as a people set against divination, graven images, and so forth and can contrast "the link between poetry and pagan theology" with the "[perpetual] war between poetry and Hebrew-Christian theology." In this the Christians are somehow let off the hook by Bloom, but the Jews, himself among them, are made to live forever beyond the pale of poetry.

I can only sense that Bloom, as Jew, feels himself cut off from poetry and that he projects this deprivation onto other Jews as if to explain and even justify this loss of poetry. In doing so he invokes the horrors of the Holocaust and the "burdens" of Jewish history:

> If one adds to the indescribable horrors of Jewish history the strength and power of Jewish religious traditions, from which most contemporary Jews are now so largely estranged, then the force of the past becomes so great as to inhibit imaginative consciousness and to stifle inventiveness. Who could be adequate to thematic concerns so annihilating, to losses so painful, so fresh, and so irreparable? (*New York Times Book Review,* Jan. 4, 1981)

Bloom is here echoing Adorno's famous comment on the impossibility of writing poems after Auschwitz, pushing it further than Adorno, and placing the curse on those Jews—whether they write as Jews or not—who can imagine the possibility of a survival into the present. This self-projection—and I have no other way of describing it—is then translated into a "double belatedness" for modern Jewish poets, "coming after the

---

6. That poetry—"unlike the Jewish religion"—doesn't go back to a divine origin would seem to be Bloom's opinion or his misreading of Vico. In *The New Science,* in fact, Vico has it that the first language—hieroglyphic & poetic—was from an "age of the gods in which the gentiles believed they lived under divine government." It was only the later ages, then, that brought a "human" view of poetry and language. Accordingly, the "gentile poets" must share with the "Jewish religion" a sense of divine origins—or, in my own terms, a sense of the "sacred" underlying all acts of poesis. Unless one argues that the Jewish revelation is "true" and all the others "false," as Bloom may in fact be doing, the Jewish-Gentile distinction is canceled at this level.

virtues and sufferings of their ancestors, and also after the main sequence
of Western poetry has worked itself through and perhaps out." It would
thus seem that if American poets are "the most consciously belated in
the history of Western poetry" and Jewish poets are "doubly belated," the
combination of the two is absolutely "catastrophic."

∽

"A strong poet," then, "originates himself"; and in this rereading of old
Whitman, the possibility of all our poetry opens itself again. Such self-
origination ("soul-making" in Keats's phrase, world-making elsewhere)
takes many forms—including a "collaging" from the (literary and non-
literary) past and present. Its constructions of identity are individual or
broadly human or set in the framework of a special culture or tradition.
In the Jewish instance it has involved the work of rewriting ourselves
within a real but collapsed tradition of language-centeredness and resistance to oppression. As such the collapse is more an opportunity than a
threat, which Bloom, had he survived the struggles with a crippling orthodoxy ("the hand of jealousy among the flaming hair"), should have
been the first to see.

But this "Jewish instance" itself, for all its particularities, is part of a
larger work of human striving. The Jews, like others, have a history that
moves from tribe to state and in that movement sets up a struggle between
new vision and the literalisms of the canon-making mind. In *A Big Jewish Book* I had to make this clear because the Jewish distinction was a trap
that robbed us—even as Bloom would—of much of our power as poets.

If Jewish history is a "burden," so is all human history—I take it this
is the final message of what Bloom calls his "Gospel of Gloom"—and no
poet's voice should now be possible. But this is nonsense and a neurotic
distortion of what the real work is all about. When Maria Tsvetayeva,
herself not Jewish, tells us that "all poets are Jews," I would hope it's in
this sense that she means it.

The manifestos have been writing themselves for eighty years, and
Bloom has still not learned to read them.

4

In *The Anxiety of Influence* Bloom conjures up the Covering Cherub, a
figure from Jewish mythology incarnated anew through Blake's imagination. The Cherub—who in one tradition may be the Exterminating Angel himself, the Malakh ha-Mavat—guards the Tree of Life and blocks the

return of fallen man to Paradise. The same figure appears in the Jerusalem temple, where the two carved cherubs over the ark (the Edenic cherub is also double) "cover" the mercy seat with their wings; and in Ezekiel the Covering Cherub represents the "Prince of Tyre," a type of the earthly city whom "I will destroy . . . from the midst of the stones of fire" (28:16).

Like any genuinely multiphasic image, the Cherub's surface meanings continually shift, no less so in Blake than in his biblical predecessors. (Singular meanings—or "allegoric delusions and woe"—would in fact be an aspect of the Covering Cherub's threats to the "Inspired Man.") With Bloom, working after Blake, we get a number of set and sometimes contradictory readings, and at least one major omission, of what seems, curiously, a most obvious use of the image in Blake. The occasion for Bloom is his attempt to drive home the "anxiety of influence" as the central fact of poetic composition—of which the "struggle" between Blake and Milton provides the clearest instance. And since Milton—or "Miltons Shadow," to be more precise about it than Bloom is—is at times identified, in Blake's *Milton* and *Jerusalem,* as the "Covering Cherub," it isn't surprising that Bloom calls up the identification and generalizes the process to poets after Blake: "For Collins, for Cowper, for many a Bard of Sensibility, Milton was the Tyger, the Covering Cherub blocking a new voice from entering the Poet's Paradise. . . . In Blake he is fallen Tharmas, and the Spectre of Milton; in Yeats he is the Spectre of Blake." But elsewhere in *The Anxiety of Influence* Bloom tells us that "the Covering Cherub stands between the achieved Man who is at once Milton, Blake, and Los, and the emanation or beloved"—in which case the poets aren't pitted against each other, and the covering Cherub, who threatens Blake and Milton both, may in fact not be a poet. There are a number of such nonpoetic readings in Blake, and one of the ideologically crucial ones— as interpreted by S. Foster Damon in *A Blake Dictionary* and here omitted by Bloom—is that "the Covering Cherub sums up the twenty-seven Christian heavens which shut out man from eternity" and by which "the truth becomes petrified into dogma and relegated to ritual":

> And these the names of the Twenty-seven Heavens and their
>   Churches . . .
> All these are seen in Miltons Shadow who is the Covering
>   Cherub . . .
> The Heavens are the Cherub, the Twelve Gods are Satan . . .
>   —(W. B., *Milton* 37:35, 44, 60)

Here, of course, is the ideological kingpin of Blake's argument with Milton—the puritanical side of him (his "Shadow") that "wrote in fetters when he wrote of Angels and God" and thereby "entered into the Covering Cherub." But Bloom prefers his own psychological and literary struggles to the struggles of his "post-Enlightenment" poets against repression, authority, and dogma—that is, against the total apparatus of canon formation both as a religious and secular phenomenon.

In place of Blake's anti-Christian/anticanonical view, Bloom chooses to put forward the idea of the Covering Cherub as a "demon of continuity"—the enemy therefore of that "discontinuity" from the past that was "freedom" for the romantics. By doing so, he can present the romantics and moderns as narrowly future-directed and hostile to ideas of poetic lineage that would—at least in Bloom's terms—psychologically diminish them and threaten their survival after death. The concept that he needs to pull this off is that of an established and unchanging past—just the kind of fixed tradition (= canon) challenged by those poets who have sought a true revisioning of the larger human past and present. To misread in this way is to conceal the "strong" (experimental) poet's simultaneous regard for lineage and the "academic" critic's desire to obstruct it.

The Covering Cherub—to pull Bloom's reading further—keeps the poet not only from the paradise of poetry but from a natural relationship to all those poets who inhabit it. It's a pretty rotten business all around, and the Cherub in this sense begins to lose his resemblance to anything like a "strong" precursor poet—even for Bloom, who writes:

> In this discussion he is a poor demon of many names (as many names as there are strong poets) but I summon him first namelessly, as a final name is not yet devised by men for the anxiety that blocks their creativeness. He is that something that makes men victims and not poets, a demon of discursiveness and shady continuities, a pseudo-exegete who makes writings into Scriptures.

But the weariness and weakness of Bloom's "poor demon" is such that Blake's words from another occasion leap to mind: "Those who restrain desire, do so because theirs is weak enough to be restrained; and the restrainer or reason usurps its place and governs the unwilling." Who, then, is the Covering Cherub? If we accept Bloom's version of him—and in fact we don't—are we to see him as Milton's specter or as Blake's, or as any poet's who still speaks to us from the past? How turn Shelley or

Whitman into victimizers of future poets, except on the level of a trivial psychological competition? Is it a poet who tries to keep us from our poems or someone else: "a demon of discursiveness and shady continuities, a pseudo-exegete who makes writings into Scriptures"?

But we know, after all, who threatens us. We know who reminds us of how "heavy" our "inheritance" is; who tells us not to deign to be good readers of our own poems or to think that we can write at all "after the deluge"; who enters into Milton's Shadow—and "not the Romantic return of the repressed Milton" but the Puritan Milton of repression. And we know who proposes the discontinuities between poets and rejects those who might know their lineage too well. We know who thinks that he "can block a new voice from entering the Poet's Paradise" or who would presume "to help decide a question that is ultimately of a sad importance: 'Who shall live?'"

The game, in short, is up. The Cherub's wing droops and reveals a face a little rounder and a little softer than we might have thought: the melancholy sweet face of those "cherubs" of our childhood. That much, it seems to me, is clear. And clear also is Bloom's summation, his confession in *The Anxiety of Influence,* of the Cherub's fate: "He cannot strangle the imagination, for nothing can do that, and he in any case is too weak to strangle anything."

Poems for the Millennium:
Two Pre-Faces

(with Pierre Joris)

Know this:
the only game I play is the millennium
the only game I play is the Great
Fear

Put up with me. I won't put up with you!
—Aimé Césaire

Pre-Face One: From Fin-de-Siècle to Negritude

1 To pick up at the turning . . .

The book began under far different conditions—in the middle 1980s, with the reality of the "cold war" and of the "specter of communism" (K. Marx) still haunting Europe and the world. These were among the defining circumstances of our time, and while they continued it seemed that the twentieth century as we knew it would never end—that it would outlast its final decade and that the context of the life from which our poems arise would remain, largely, the way it was for us. With the changes of the 1990s came the strange sense of a return to the century's beginnings: a time dominated by nationalism and ethnic conflict, when totalitarian ideologies were still in their early stages and science and technology were on the move toward new and ever faster transformations. It was circumstances like these to which the century's first modernists were responding politically and artistically. The difference was in their sense that the norms of the culture were—like its politics—open to unprecedented changes, which they accepted exuberantly or from which they recoiled with equal passion. For most of those represented in these pages, such changes were centered in the conditions of their work as poets and

From Jerome Rothenberg and Pierre Joris, *Poems for the Millennium: The University of California Book of Modern & Postmodern Poetry* (Berkeley: University of California Press, 1996, 1998).

artists—an intuition or prophecy, as William Blake had put it in the century before, that "poetry fetter'd, fetters the human race," or, by extension, that poetry set free, can free or open up the human mind.

The intention of this gathering is to trace the history of that intuition—and its attendant poetry—from *then* to *now*. From its earliest emergence—out of the eighteenth-century Enlightenment and into the seedbed of a radical romanticism—it reflected a tension between the growth of totalizing nation-states and repeated declarations of the rights of "man." In the ensuing conflicts poets were not only "unacknowledged legislators" in the ideas they projected (Shelley) but transformers of and through the language in which the work was written. What began to take shape, then, was the idea of poetry as an instrument of change—a change that would take place foremost in the poem itself, both as a question of language and structure and of a related, all-connecting vision. Such a change—deep-seated, not cosmetic—was felt to be a virtual reinvention of poetry (or any other art), even (for some of its practitioners) of language itself. So Tristan Tzara, as spokesman for postrational Dada, would quote Descartes as an informing slogan: "I would like to believe there were no other men before me." And yet, as we will say again and again in these pages, a new past was also being fashioned in the process—many new pasts in fact.

The form of the work we have assembled is that of a synthesizing and global anthology of twentieth-century modernism with an emphasis on those international and national movements that have tried to change the direction of poetry and art as a necessary condition for changing the ways in which we think and act as human beings. While the first volume of the anthology runs—historically—from the beginnings of modernism to the middle 1940s, its emphases come largely from concerns of the later twentieth century as the editors and their contemporaries have experienced them. These emphases include

- an overall sense that what has characterized the century's poetry has been an exploration of new forms of language, consciousness, and social/biological relationships, both by deliberate experimentation in the present and by the reinterpretation of the "entire" human past;
- poetry-art intersections, in which conventional boundaries between arts break down, sometimes involving generalized art movements (Futurism, Dada, Surrealism, Fluxus, etc.) led by poets and with the presence of a poetics at their centers;
- experiments with dreamwork and altered forms of consciousness (from

the outburst of Surrealist dream experiments in the 1920s to the psy-
chedelic experiments of the 1960s, the meditative experiments of the
1970s, and beyond) in which language itself becomes an instrument
of vision;

- a return to a concept of poetry as a performative genre, from Futurist and Dada soirées, sound-poems and simultaneities to the "new
orality" and the expanded performances and textsound works of the
"post"modern (post–World War II) decades;

- language experiments, including the sound poetry and textsound works
mentioned above, as well as experiments with visual and typographical
forms, attempts to develop a nonsyntactic (abstract) poetry, and explorations of new languages and those sublanguages that had long been at
the fringes of accepted literature;

- ethnopoetics and related reassessments of the past and of alternative
poetries in the present: a general enlargement of cultural terrains directed by the sense of an ancient and continuing "subterranean tradition" with the poetic impulse at its center: a widespread attack on the
dominance in art and life of "high" European culture, leading in the late
twentieth century to a proliferation of movements stressing an exploration and expansion of ethnic and gender, as well as class, identities;

- an ongoing if shifting connection to related political and social movements ("surrealism at the service of the revolution," etc.) during what
became heroically, sometimes disastrously, an age of ideologies;

- an overall sense of excitement and play ("to work in the excitedness of
pure being . . . to get back that intensity into the language"—G. Stein)
that must be brought across to show the work of the century in all its
color and as the poetry "that might be fantastic life" (R. Duncan).

It has been our hope throughout that we could accomplish all of these
ends without turning the selection of authors into the projection of a new
canon of famous names—rather to have the anthology serve a more useful function as a mapping of the possibilities that have come down to us
by the century's turning.

Finally, by way of starters, it should be clear that we have not been
looking for any more certainty regarding form or content than what the
work itself allows us. In that sense we've welcomed the problematic, even
the contradictory, into the poetry that we've brought together here. Thus,
if an awareness of the "new," say, seems central to these projects, it is
often balanced, sometimes overbalanced, by an obsession with the "old"

and "ancient." This represents a problematic and an issue, as do polarities of high and low (in language, diction), of symbolism and realism, lyric exuberance and "objective" precision, hermetic condensations and epic expansions, minimals and maximals, verses and proses, sacreds and seculars, maleness and femaleness. While the predilection of the work is to push things to their limits, even those limits (and that predilection) may be called into question—as in the Dada poet's turning on the Dada work: "The true Dadas are against Dada." Or put another way: at the core of every true "modernism" is the germ of a "*post*modernism."

2 Of what makes a history and what it is . . .

It is the persistence of such issues (political and cultural as much as formal) that makes a history of the "modern" and the "avant-garde." For the better part of two centuries, the Western World and then the world in general have been witness to a revolution of the word that's simultaneously a revolution of the mind and (consistently or not) a revolution in the (political, material, and social) world itself. Much of that is already implicit in "romanticism," but it's "modernism" (at least the experimental modernism projected in these pages) that takes it all the way—through a sometimes unrestrained attempt to change both word and thought. On the simplest level, the romantic poet carries along a still traditional, if increasingly shaky, image of the poem—its formal structure or poetic "line"—as in that side of William Blake that writes (but noticeably minus all punctuation)

Mock on Mock on Voltaire Rousseau
Mock on Mock on tis all in vain
You throw the sand against the wind
And the wind blows it back again

while the emergent new poet (Blake again) blasts the line apart, casts off "the bondage of Rhyming" and "Monotonous Cadence," to produce "a variety in every line, both of cadences & number of syllables." Thus:

To cast off Bacon, Locke & Newton from Albions covering
To take off his filthy garments, & clothe him with Imagination
To cast aside from Poetry, all that is not Inspiration
That it no longer shall dare to mock with the aspersion of
    Madness

Cast on the Inspired, by the tame high finisher of paltry Blots,
Indefinite or paltry Rhymes: or paltry Harmonies.

The difference here is what Rimbaud will later call us to, writing in the
final quarter of the nineteenth century that "the invention of the unknown demands new forms," or, again along those lines, "one must be absolutely modern."

The story of the modernism that characterized the twentieth century
goes back at least to Blake or to Hölderlin at the start of the nineteenth—
poets who took traditional verse to its limits and then stepped across the
line into unprecedented "freedom." With Baudelaire (another key figure)
the old verse was more persistent, however much he was (in Rimbaud's
view of him) the first "*voyant*" or "seer," and was, with Novalis or with
Edgar Poe in his extraordinary *Eureka,* an early master of the (so-called)
prose poem—a form that Lautréamont and Rimbaud, somewhat later,
brought to a first fulfillment. In their positioning between the old and
new, most of the nineteenth-century forerunners resembled Emily Dickinson, whose recognizable metric was accompanied by a revolutionary
sense of off- or near-rhyme and by the use of hyphens/dashes to call
her own set rhythms into question. Only with Whitman do we see the
work turning irreversibly to free or open rhythms (and to the realization of Wordsworth's earlier prophecy of a demotic poetry written in "the
language really spoken by men")—equaled, in a sometimes more radical
and quirky way, by the sprung rhythms and soundscapes (= instress) of
Gerard Manley Hopkins. Often unrecognized, unpublished, or scorned
in their own time, these would become the major forerunners for the century ahead. And with them as a master innovator was Stéphane Mallarmé, whose extraordinary *Coup de dés* of 1895 both finished the nineteenth century's fade-out into symbolism and marked the beginning of
the twentieth's relentless transformations.

It is with Mallarmé, then, that our view begins. In the works that followed his, barrier after barrier began to crumble, toward the construction
of new forms, the exploration of new behaviors, and the opening of new
possibilities. Early in the twentieth century this development expressed
itself in movements (some tightly organized, some hardly so) across the
arts, as well as in the work of individual poets, acting off a new permission to write a poetry freshly invented—reinvented—in each succeed-
ing poem. The first decade of the century was already filled with this

new breed of creative innovator—in poetry as in the other arts. Stein, Apollinaire, Cendrars, Reverdy, Jacob among the cubists of Paris are obvious examples of poet-experimentalists interacting with other experimentalists. This interaction accounts also for the visual edge in Apollinaire, the verbal edge in Picasso's collages (always present, heretofore overlooked).[1] Elsewhere, too, the push against boundaries and restrictive definitions of poetry and language can be felt: Darío's *modernismo;* Blok's late symbolism; Huidobro's interactions with the Parisians and self-generated creationism; the multiple names (personae, "others") created by Pessoa; Rilke's breakthrough into angelic visions (prodded in part by the emergence of Expressionism and rediscovery of Hölderlin as forerunner); Pound's declarations favoring a new poetic image (or, later on, the image set in motion).

The movements of those first two decades functioned also as collaborative *vortices* (Pound's term), bringing together many individualities in a common push toward a new dispensation, aimed at a drastic change of poem and mind. Of those movements, Futurism was both the first and the first to have a poetry and a poetics at its center. Based in Italy, it was paralleled by Expressionism in Germany, the other Futurism in Russia and in central Europe, Vorticism in the Anglo world, the various new -*isms* coming out of Paris, and a culmination (circa World War I) in Dada, which was also the first (*post*modern) turning against movements and against modernism as such. The highly individuated poets working from within these movements included Marinetti, Trakl, Benn, Khlebnikov, Mayakovsky, Pound, and Tzara, along with boundary-breaking artist-poets such as Arp, Kandinsky, Klee, and Schwitters.

This energy—first sighted in a time of war and revolution—continued into the century's third decade and beyond, as typified, perhaps, in what Clayton Eshleman has described as the banner year of 1922. In that year Europe and America saw the publication of Eliot's *Waste Land* and Joyce's *Ulysses* but also Rilke's completed *Duino Elegies* and Vallejo's incredibly knotty, thwarted *Trilce.* It was the decade, too, of the birth of Surrealism (1924), led by poets like Breton, Soupault, Aragon, Péret, Eluard, Desnos, and culminating in a poet-artist like Artaud, who turned against it with unprecedented inner violence. In its central focus on the

---

1. A much more detailed approach to Picasso as an *actual* poet appears below (pages 156–166).

dreamwork (S. Freud) and in its call for a strategy of moral and artistic transgression that it only (very) partially began to realize, Surrealism has colored a major area of post-Surrealist writing. At the same time it was countered, largely from the American side, by a push from "Objectivists" and others toward a poetry that would focus on the "luminous detail" and would allow thereby a reperception of the here and now—the familiar world from which (Charles Olson later wrote) we were the most *estranged*. A result—in Pound, Zukofsky, others—was to set history alongside myth and dream as areas of mind and practice to be newly rediscovered. . . .

3 A poetics in advance of a poetics . . .

The history of twentieth-century poetry is as rich and varied as that of the century's painting and sculpture, its music and theater, but the academic strategy has been to cover up that richness. Imagine—now—a history of modern art that left out abstract painting or collage or Cubism or Surrealism and Dada, and you have a sense of what the literary histories (in America for certain) look like to those of us who know that similar things exist in poetry and that many of the earlier moves and movements—but Futurism, Dada, and Surrealism in particular—were essentially the work of poets. It is this realization—so obvious and so deliberately concealed—that the first of our two volumes is intending to express.

A characteristic of modern art (and poetry) so defined—but this carries into the "postmodern" as well—has been the questioning of art itself as a discrete and bounded category. Some such radical questioning of art and of its boundaries is what defines our sense of an "avant-garde" and of some form of "deconstruction" as a strategy for coping with the inherited (authoritative) past. (Both of the terms in quotes are themselves now under question—the result of two centuries of abuse in the former case, of two decades in the latter; or as David Antin puts it elsewhere: "When I hear the word 'deconstruction,' I reach for my pillow.") In an essay on Robert Wilson's "theater of images," Robert Stearns writes (in a configuration we would share with him): "The avant-garde might be characterized as those creators who do not take their environment and its traditions at face value. They separate and view its elements and realign them according to their own needs."

This description (while devoid as yet of social/revolutionary purpose) is general enough to include the great range of strategies and stances in experimental poetry and art. Since nothing around us is (ideally) taken for granted and the conclusion or intention of the work (again ideally) arises or emerges from the work itself, the work by definition is experimental: its outcome unknown, its process crucial. Such experiments/re-definitions/reconstructions may work with and on structures, ideologies (contexts and contents), materials, and technologies or (in any instance) combinations of all of the above. From our shared perspective as poets of a certain place and time, we see the coming together of these possibilities as (still) the great opportunity of art and poetry as these cross into a new millennium. We would want to go so far as to suggest that the experiments of the twentieth-century avant-gardes can be viewed as prolegomena to the realized workings of the century to come.

While the basis for most of these new poetries has been a drive toward social—even spiritual—transformation, the experimental moves on their structural/compositional side have involved a range of procedures that bring out the opaque materiality of language as a medium, disrupting the "romantic" view of language as purely a transparent window toward an ideal reality beyond itself. These moves have included developments (from Mallarmé and Marinetti on) in visual, typographic, and concrete poetry; in primarily English language experiments (from Pound and Williams to Charles Olson and beyond) with "projective verse" and composition-by-field; in systematic chance operations (Duchamp and Arp the early prompters, Mac Low and Cage the leading latter-day practitioners); in variations, foremost, of montage and collage from throughout the century. Along with such quasi-formalist moves, more strictly ideological/ideational experiments permeated Dada and Surrealism during and after World War I, Negritude (broadly defined) by the start of World War II, Beat and Beat-related poetry in the 1950s and 1960s, Situationist street poetics in the 1960s, and aspects of feminism and other liberationist movements over the last three decades. Equally extreme but often less recognized experiments involved the materials and media of poetry—from the obvious return to poetry as an art of live performance to the creation of a new electronic poetry (soundtext, *poésie sonore*, etc., grounded in its Futurist beginnings), the rudiments of a computer poetry (leading to recent hypertext and cyberpunk experiments, etc.), and the beginnings (toward the other end of the technological spectrum) of a poetry without sound in the culture of the deaf. And along with these developments there have been persistent thrusts to raise demotic, collo-quial, common speech as the language of a new poetry and culture. Tak-ing many different forms and challenging many long-standing prejudices and language barriers, these experiments mark a key point at which lan-guage experiments and politics meet.

This terrain is a much larger field of experiment and change than has been brought forward, say, in recent controversies about "the death of the author" or "nonreferential writing" and similar textual/intertextual modes of conceiving writing and the world. The field is still larger in that the old rules and basic definitions within each art have increasingly and deliberately been set aside or reversed. The imageless (nonrepresen-tational) art that characterized the American and European midcentury has been matched (in deed if not in prominence) by a wordless poetry: the *Lautgedichte* (sound poems) of Hugo Ball (early) or the *poésie sonore* of Henri Chopin (late). Other moves from within language have included those as obvious as the development of a *free* verse (an oxymoron, as William Carlos Williams taught us) and the *parole in libertà* (free words) of Marinetti; experiments in the prose poem and the aphorism and their questioning of the boundaries between prose and poetry; nonsyntactic, antisyntactic, and "totally syntactic" poetry from Gertrude Stein to the Language Poets of the 1980s; and a poetry of elementary forms—letters and numbers—that works with reduced alphabets (Otto Nebel in the 1920s) or extended ones (Isidore Isou in the 1950s) or that reads num-bers as words (Kurt Schwitters) or words as numbers (neogematria and beyond).

Similarly, the boundaries between the arts have been dissolving into an age of blended media (intermedia) and hybrid forms of poetry and art. The distinctions between word and picture, action and text, have bro-ken down. Definitions of high and low art have fallen away: the primi-tive chant, the pop song have become parts of the poet's arsenal—new in-struments at our disposal. The language of everyday speech collides with or expels the exalted language of an older poetry—like the art that seeks to break the boundaries between itself and everyday life, to reenter the mundane world or to elevate the mundane into art. At the same time that some poets have reclaimed prophetic and visionary functions (the most expansive claim of all), they or their contemporaries have been altering the physical nature and location of the poem: new shapes of books (the Cendrars/Delaunay "Prose of the Transsiberian" a prime example); new materials to print on (metal, acetate, film, and videotape); poetry as sculpture in the early works of Kurt Schwitters (*merzbau,* etc.) or the later ones of Ian Hamilton Finlay; the poetry reading and performance, moving poetry off the page and into the cabaret, the theater, the lecture hall, the gallery, the coffee shop, the loft, the prison, and the street. Writes Michael Davidson of a postmodernism that extends one thrust of the modern presented in these pages: "The boundary to what is possible in writing is a fiction created by and within writing. Only when the boundary is recognized as moveable can it become a regenerative element in art, rather than an obstacle to its growth."

The twentieth century may be remembered for its push against the boundaries. Where once the definitions were apparent and the frame known, we have now come into the open, have taken up a stance outside the walls. The most interesting works of poetry and art are those that question their own shapes and forms and, by implication, the shapes and forms of whatever preceded them. But it is possible for one to become a master of poetry (or even a doctor of poetry) and still be ignorant of all this. (It may even not be possible to do so without that kind of ignorance!)

It is our intention in this book to bring that much to light.

Pre-face Two: From Postwar to Millennium

If the first book was an opening, the second is a continuation and a movement into future works. It is the celebration of a coming into fullness— the realization in some sense of beginnings from still earlier in the century. Yet the poetry like the time itself marks a sharp break from what went before, with World War II and the events of Auschwitz and Hiroshima creating a chasm, a true aporia between then and now. It is on the near side of that paradoxical break that our own lives first come in—not outside history this time but living in and through it. The years the book covers are those of the cold war and its aftermath and, viewed from where we are, the time, too, of the second great awakening of poetry in the century now fading out. The story told is one that we have lived in and have found never to have been truly told, neither in its triumphs nor its failures (with an affection for the failures sometimes as great as for the triumphs). If ideas like that guided our first book, they will more strongly dominate our second, where we can no longer act as distant and objective viewers but as witnesses and even partisans for the works at hand.

1 A work resuming "in the dark" . . .

The gathering (to use the title of one of Robert Duncan's last books) begins "in the dark": a midcentury of molten cities and scorched earth, of
chimneys blowing human ashes through the air, of slaves in labor camps
and gulags, of nations enslaved to other nations, of racism and apart-
heid rampant.[2] In that darkness the brilliant, often strident, promise of an
earlier avant-garde was no longer visible or viable. The surge of totalizing governments and the resultant state of war had decimated the former
avant-gardes—in Germany and Russia, Italy and Japan, as in the conquered lands of Europe, Africa, and Asia. The stakes for some were death
or exile, for others an underground resistance and continued struggle,
for still others (all too often) a collaboration with the very advocates of
power and repression that their work had set out to oppose.

If that began it, the half century that followed witnessed a continuous
wave of wars and repressions, interspersed with rebellions and occasional
luminous victories that for the moment seemed to light the darkness.[3]
Sometimes claimed as the longest "peaceful" period in memory—a virtual *pax americana*—it could be felt (and was by those who lived it) as
a continuation of the midcentury war by other means: a diffuse but unrelenting form of World War III.[4] The wars of the time included not only
the U.S. conflicts in Korea and Vietnam—and the forty-year-long cold
war—but hundreds of other regional conflicts, wars of independence,
revolutionary guerrilla wars and uprisings, genocides, mass slaughters,
and cultural wars fueled by ideology and, increasingly, by ethnicity and
religion. And with this, too, was the sense of a natural world under continuing attack or lashing back with new plagues and hitherto undreamed-
of biological disasters.

2. "I lived in the first century of world wars. / Most mornings I would be more or less insane" (Muriel Rukeyser).
3. "The dark world that is illumined is the very thing that leads poetry toward an even
darker world" (Adonis).
4. "Pound, Lawrence, Joyce, H.D., Eliot, have a black voice when speaking of the contemporary scene, an enduring memory of the First World War that has revealed the deep-
going falsehood and evil of the modern state. . . . Their threshold remains ours. The time
of war and exploitation, the infamy and lies of the new capitalist war-state, continue. And
the answering intensity of the imagination to hold its own values must continue" (Robert
Duncan, as quoted by Nathaniel Mackey).
    And William Carlos Williams: "Poetry is a rival government always in opposition to
its cruder replicas."

This was the darkness that came through, along with whatever other forms of darkness—and of light—that moved within the cosmos or the individual psyche. "Poetry therefore as opposition," Nanni Balestrini wrote, within a neomodernist, experimental framework. "Opposition to the dogma and conformity that overlays us, that hardens the tracks behind us, that entangles our feet, seeking to halt our steps. Today more than ever is the reason to write poetry." And Pierre Guyotat, as a further marker of the poet's relation to the art as such and to the sense of earlier betrayals: "The very origin of the whole system of literature has to be attacked."

In the United States, where experimental modernism had yet to make its ineluctable breakthrough, the first postwar decade was marked by an ascendant literary "modernism"—hostile to experiment and reduced in consequence to a vapid, often stuffy, middle-ground approximation. It was in that sense the Age of Eliot (T. S.) and of the *new* critics, as they were then called—not as an extension of Eliot's collage-work in *The Waste Land,* say, but as a dominant and retrograde poetics in which the *old* ways of the English "great tradition" were trotted out and given privilege. The mark of that time, revived in every decade since, was a return to prescriptive rhyme and meter: a rejection thereby of the uncertainties of *free verse* and the barely remembered *freed words* of a Mallarmé or Marinetti. Wrote the poet Delmore Schwartz, as one of those then in ascendance: "The poetic revolution, the revolution in poetic taste which was inspired by the criticism of T. S. Eliot . . . has established itself in power." And he gave as an example of new poets writing in "a style which takes as its starting point the poetic idiom and literary taste of the generation of Pound and Eliot," the following from W. D. Snodgrass:

The green catalpa tree has turned
All white; the cherry blooms once more.
In one whole year I haven't learned
A blessed thing they pay you for

—at which David Antin looked back and commented (circa 1972): "The comparison of this updated version of *A Shropshire Lad* . . . and the poetry of the *Cantos* or *The Waste Land* seems so aberrant as to verge on the pathological."

Yet it was typical, inevitable in fact, for those who couldn't distinguish between "the poetic revolution" and a "revolution in taste" or who still thought of taste as an issue. Even an attempt at such distinctions was then unlikely, for the careers of the inheritors were too often literary, resting like the idea of literature itself on a fixed notion of poetry and poem, which might be improved on but never questioned *at the root.* And behind it, too, there was a strange fear of "freedom" as that had been articulated by earlier, truly radical ("experimental") moderns—whether as "free verse" or "free love" or the abandonment of judgment as a bind on the intelligence or of taste as a determinant of value.[5] So if the taste and judgment they still clung to (and which made them critics "inspired by the criticism of T. S. Eliot") demanded "modern" as an article of twentieth-century faith, they retained it, but they pulled back into traditional and institutional securities, "picking up again the meters" (Schwartz) as a moral, even a political buttress against their own midcentury despair. And this itself, qua ideology, was made a part of a *modern* dilemma, which came to define their rapidly evaporating modern-ism—not as a promise of a new consciousness but as a glorified "failure of nerve."

Against which a counterpoetics was quickly starting to develop—a push, foremost, to find new beginnings (or to retrieve old ones) appropriate to the time.

2 The work in all its fullness . . .

The *postwar* when it came, then, came from all directions. In that coming it faced both a modernism stuck dead in its tracks and a resurgence of much of what that modernism *at its fullest* had set out to challenge. The new turning in America—in full motion by the middle 1950s—was central to our own perception but only a part (a large part but a part) of a much greater global whole. The *war,* which William Carlos Williams called "the first and only thing in the world today," was of course the great dividing line—and with it the *bomb* that put an end, he also reminded us, to much that was past, while

          all suppressions,
     from the witchcraft trials at Salem
        to the latest
           book burnings

---

5. "My eyes are erotic. My intelligence is erotic. / All combinations are possible" (Göran Sonnevi).

are confessions
>   that the bomb
>   has entered our lives
>   to destroy us.

By which he meant that the stakes were now raised and would remain
raised to the present millennium's end and the next millennium's beginning. It was from here—*everywhere*—that the new generations were to
take their start.

The nature of that start was not so much post*modern*—as it would
come to be called—as it was post-bomb and post-holocaust. Or it was
postmodern in the sense that Tristan Tzara had spoken of Dada three decades before, naming a resistance that called both past and present into
question, including all those "modern schools" that still obeyed the rule
of empire. It was this rebellion and rejection, this "great refusal" at its extreme, that marked all that was best in what was then beginning to take
shape. As such its extremes, which typified it as the stance of a new avant-
garde, represented a diverse development and a series of departures from
what had come before. Alongside the revival of the full range of modern
[modernist] moves, more notable expansions and divergences were taking
place—from critiques as correctives of a poetry mislabeled "modern" to
more far-reaching departures from Renaissance-derived modernities and
the reclaiming of old powers in the name of what Charles Olson early
called "*postmodern* man." Rightly or wrongly named, the term and the issues raised thereby (but never resolved or capable as such of resolution)
came to define the time and poetics in question.

The following, then, are some aspects of that time, which to a great
extent is still the time we live in.

There was a breakdown, first, of the more tyrannical aspects of the earlier
literary and art movements and a turning away with that from totalizing/
authoritarian ideologies and individuals. Such a stance—"against all *isms,*
against all that implied a system" (C. Dotremont)—was in that sense
a matter of both life *and* art.[6] On its political and social sides, it was
marked by a generally leftward tilt—rarely the fascist and totalitarian

---

6. "Art's obscured the difference between art and life. Now let life obscure the difference
between life and art" (John Cage).

temptations of many of the prewar poets, though not entirely immune to a seductive—and repressive—totalitarianism of the left from time to time. The result was the appearance by the 1960s of a new "dialectics of liberation," political and personal, marked by a sense of resistance, of breaking free (in word and act, mind and body), while retaining a more-than-formalist conception of the poem as vehicle-for-transformation. Wrote Allen Ginsberg, drawing from an older source: "When the mode of the music changes, the walls of the city shake." And the Japanese "postwar poets" (in a "demand" voiced by Ooka Makoto): "Bring back totality through poetry."[7]

The "liberation" saw a resurgence, along with more stabilized forms of poem-making, of old and new varieties of *free* verse and *freed* words ("concrete," "projective," "open," "variable," and so on). Along with this came the assertion—and practice—of other freedoms in the poem and, by implication *and* assertion, in the world beyond.[8] Thus the poem was again and decisively opened to the full range of the demotic (spoken) language, but with the freedom also to move between demotic and hieratic (= "literary") modes or into other areas of discourse long out of bounds for poetry. For a number of the poets in these pages this meant an opening to popular modes and voices—a breakdown of distinctions that both prefigured the "pop art" soon to come and later merged with it. At a deeper or older ("folk") level this was matched by the appearance of submerged languages (dialects and idiolects) as new/old vehicles for poetry: the Viennese of H. C. Artmann and others, the Friulian of Pier Paolo Pasolini, the Jamaican "nation language" in oral works by Michael Smith or Miss Queenie (and the written variations by Kamau Brathwaite), the appropriations of "black speech" in the work of African American writers (and others) too numerous to mention, the pidgin writings of Pacific poets in a range of *topoi* from New Guinea to Hawaii. *And so on.* Wrote the American poet John Ashbery of his own very real and very different aspirations in that direction: "My idea is to democratize all forms of expression . . . the idea that both the most demotic and the most elegant forms of expression deserve equally to be taken into account."

---

7. And from another direction the Nigerian poet/novelist Chinua Achebe: "New forms must stand ready to be called into being as often as new (threatening) forces appear on the scene. It is like 'earthing' an electrical charge to ensure communal safety."
8. "Today freedom is more in need of inventors than defenders" (André Breton).

This, then, is fulfillment. It is a wedge, among many, by which *all* words will enter into presence—as in Whitman's prophecy (circa 1860) of a total poetry that would (like "the Real Dictionary" he also envisioned) incorporate "all words that exist in use, the bad words as well as any.... [Like language itself] an enormous treasure-house, or range of treasure-houses ... full of ease, definiteness and power—full of sustenance." In such a poetry, with its open and unlimited vocabulary, all subjects/themes were also possible—from the most demeaned to the most exalted, from the most commonplace to the most learned, from myth to history and back, from present into past and future.[9] While the first round of breakthroughs had occurred in the earlier twentieth century, the realizations and divagations now were coming helter-skelter— and with them a persistent questioning (experimental and [soon to be] "post"modern) of language's relation to any experience whatever, to any reality, even that of language itself.[10]

The results are contradictory and often *self*-contradictory, yet one senses behind them a commonness of purpose: to throw down *and* restore. And with this comes a necessary reassertion of the role of the poet as seer and chronicler. The former guise, which an earlier neoclassic tilt had covered over, was the image that vibrated through the Beat poetics (and much else) from the mid-1950s on, and in its assertion across the globe included an exploration of different forms of postsurrealist writing and an alliance for some with previously suppressed religious and cultural forms: shamanism, tantrism, sufism, kabbala, peyotism, and so on. It also saw the reappearance of what Allen Ginsberg spoke of as a *heroic* poetics: a renewed willingness to thrust the poet forward as a heroic, even sacrificial, figure in defense of self and tribe, of human and mammal life (M. McClure)—and with that, of poetry itself.[11] (The moments of public breakthrough—for Ginsberg and others—were notable in early

9. "The gift is that you are forced to put much more of the world into the poem. Sometimes it feels as though the poem is carrying you along. You have access to a universe that begins to carry you ... into something that you would never have been able to see or write" (Inger Christensen).

10. Again Adonis: "The poem will be transgression. And yet, like the head of Orpheus, the poem will navigate on the river Universe, completely contained in the body of language."

11. "If anybody wants a statement of values—it is this, that I am ready to die for Poetry & for the truth that inspires poetry—and will do so in any case—as all men, whether they like it or no—." (A. G., 1961).

resistance to the Vietnam War, in *samizdat* and underground publication in the crumbling Soviet orb, and in the many independence movements of the postcolonial "third world.") In more literary terms the second half of the twentieth century was marked by the reassertion, in the persistent (and false) divide between classicism and romanticism, of the romantic impulse—with a spiritual and material force that dominated the early postwar period and has remained a presence thereafter.

While what was at issue here was a poetry of displacements and dreamings, it was accompanied (sometimes in the same work) by a new "objectism": an imagism of the familiar ("here-and-now") and an unprecedented *poetry of fact*. In the formulation by the Nicaraguan poet Ernesto Cardenal, the call was for a new "*exteriorismo* . . . [an] objective poetry . . . made with elements of real life and concrete things, with proper names and precise details and exact data, statistics, facts, and quotations." Behind it was a half-century of explorations, from those that focused on "minute particulars" (the poems of Francis Ponge and Marianne Moore are eminent examples) to variations on Ezra Pound's recasting of the epic ("long poem") as "a poem including history." That definition—or something close to it—prefigured "maximal" works by poets like William Carlos Williams, Louis Zukofsky, Melvin Tolson, Muriel Rukeyser, Robert Duncan, Charles Olson, Theodore Enslin, Robert Kelly, and Anne Waldman in the United States, and elsewhere by poets like Pablo Neruda, Vladimir Holan, Anna Akhmatova, Ernesto Cardenal, Hugh MacDiarmid, and René Depestre. With an eye toward the contemporary political implications of "history," the push was later extended by Ed Sanders to an "investigative poetry" in which "lines of lyric beauty descend from . . . data clusters [:] . . . a form of historical writing . . . using *every* bardic skill and meter and method of the last 5 or 6 generations, in order to describe *every* aspect (no more secret governments!) of the historical present."[12]

Such an effort, as (re)visioning, was tied as well to the reinvestigation and reconfiguration of the entire *poetic* past and present—a major subtext, surely, of the present volumes. In a "postcolonial" world it became one way—again among many—for poets to come forward as voices for "nation" or "tribe" or "community" (as elsewhere for "nature" and "world"),

---

12. "The twentieth century, in its violence, has brought about the marriage of Poetry and History" (Hélène Cixous).

or to explore, increasingly, the specifics of ethnicity and gender as they entered into thought and word.[13] Here, as elsewhere in the art of the postwar, the work laid claim to a renewed permission and validity, both as "investigative poetry" and as a vehicle for *direct* political resistance— a contrast thereby to the outright dismissal of such political poetry by "new critics" and "high" modernists on the one hand and by Surrealists in the mode of Breton on the other. Concurrently, and contrastively as well, there was a renewed sense of history as *personal* history: the inner life, including the deepest areas of sexuality and hitherto covert desires, (again) laid bare.[14] In this the resultant work went far beyond the psychological limits and distress of the so-called confessional poets of the 1960s, edging toward what Clayton Eshleman, with the likes of Antonin Artaud among the forerunners, spoke of as the "construction of the underworld" and traced back, as a form of "grotesque realism," to its (painted) sources in the cave art of the late Paleolithic.

Here is a tension, then, between extremes of the personal and communal—the "unspeakable visions of the individual" (J. Kerouac) and the reconstructed "tale of the tribe" (E. Pound). (It is from a number of such "tensions" or "oppositions" that our work as a whole has been constructed.) In the working out of those extremes, both formal and historical explorations came up against what Alfredo Giuliani, writing for the Italian *Novissimi*, demanded as "a genuine 'reduction of the I' as producer of meaning," or what Olson, in a famous act of condemnation (more exactly, of realignment and questioning), called "the getting rid of the lyrical interference of the individual as ego." But alongside the continuing "inwardness" of Olson's developing poetics (= "projective verse"),[15] there were other attempts at still more objective, non-"expressionistic" methods

---

13. "It is inconceivable that any Caribbean poet writing today is not going to be influenced by [the] submerged [Caribbean] culture, which is, in fact, an emerging culture. . . . At last our poets today are recognizing that it is essential that they use the resources that have always been there, but which have been denied to them—which they have sometimes themselves denied" (Kamau Brathwaite).

"To write directly and overtly as a woman, out of a woman's body and experience, to take woman's existence seriously as theme and source for art" (Adrienne Rich).

14. Note, for example, the important assertion within a new feminist poetry and art (circa 1970) that the "personal" is in fact the "political."

15. "But if he stays inside himself, if he is contained within his nature as he is participant in the larger force, he will be able to listen, and his hearing through himself will give him secrets objects share" (Charles Olson).

of composition. These included not only experiments with systematic (objective) chance operations—a tension (post-Dada) between "chance" and "choice," as notable in the works, for example, of Jackson Mac Low and John Cage—but a concern with other procedural, even mechanical (machine-derived) methods that seemed, momentarily at least, to put the will in suspension, to allow the poem "to write itself," and, by so doing, to invite still more of the world to enter the poem.[16] There is in this approach—in Europe, the United States, and elsewhere—something like Wittgenstein's sense of philosophy as "a struggle with the fascination that forms of expression have upon us." (Both the poignancy and force of such a dictum, when transferred to poetry, are here worth noting.)

This interrogation of language, or of the language-reality nexus as such, was from the late 1940s (and continuing, increasingly, into the present) the second great arena for what came to be called the "postmodern." Here the experiencing *self,* while never disappearing, was superseded by processes of language and by the appropriation and redirection of texts and utterances already present in the language. The outcome was a number of versions of what the Cobra poets, say, or the European "Situationists" spoke of as a *détournement*—not merely a "diversion" or "deflection" of an inherited text but, as stated elsewhere by Ken Knabb, "a turning aside from the normal course or purpose (often with an illicit connotation)." Such a turning, twist, or "torque" (G. Quasha) was deeply sourced in earlier workings with collage and in the language-centered experiments of predecessors like Gertrude Stein, Velimir Khlebnikov, and Kurt Schwitters, among others. But what had been the scattered, sometimes casual, breakthroughs of that earlier time now took new directions and became the central work of poets in many different places. Such foregroundings of language had also influenced a number of key figures in areas like philosophy or ethnology, and these in turn would come to influence or interact with the postwar generations of poets, particularly in the reconceptualization of poetry as a function of language and, inversely, language as a function of *poesis.*

At work here was a renewed focus on language's role in shaping our perception of reality, with the poets' experimental work vindicated and enriched, for example, by linguistic investigations like those of Benjamin

16. "All of these are ways to let in forces other than yourself . . . possibilities that one's habitual associations—what we usually draw on in the course of spontaneous or intuitive composition—would have precluded" (Jackson Mac Low).

Lee Whorf on the nature of non-Indo-European languages such as Hopi and Maya.[17] Similarly, many of the old questions on "the nature of representation" received new formulations and thought, both in the practice of the poets (articulated as *poetics* by, for example, the Italian Neoavanguardia, the U.S.-centered Language Poets, and, maybe primarily, the French *Tel Quel* group) and in the developing "science" of semiotics (from Ferdinand de Saussure early in the twentieth century to various poststructuralisms in the [almost] present). If such metapoetic concerns could open a window on alternative language possibilities, they also pointed to the trap inherent in a language-dominated universe—a trap of language through which the poet would have to break, Artaud had warned us, "in order to touch life."[18] Given the allure and danger of that situation, the response was either to investigate the laws and limits (= rules) of language or to break those rules deliberately; to devise new ways of "making language" (thereby making—or denying—meaning) or to play variations on language as discovered in a range of cultural/linguistic contexts.

Related to all that—and a point of reference, often, in poet-directed discussions of poetics—was the sense that the poet, like all humans, is a vehicle through or by which language speaks. Outside the immediate poetry nexus, the point revealed itself in Heidegger's insistence, say, that it is language that thinks rather than man; in Wittgenstein's related meditations ("the limits of my language mean the limits of my world"); or in Lacan's formulation that "the unconscious is structured like language." While such views triggered active responses from poets, they were less a revelation than a confirmation of what had long been known—that language has always been both familiar *and* uncanny, and that there is a point at which one can say with Rimbaud, e.g.: "I do not think but I am thought." What was news for critics and theorists, then, was a familiar realization (and practice) for poets, those in particular who were conversant with shamanic and other forms of mediumship, with Western/romantic ideas of inspiration and numinosity, with zeitgeists and collective unconsciouses. In its more extreme formulations (early Roland Barthes, say, and the later post-everything critical establishment, especially in U.S. academia), the autonomy of language devolved into the canard of "the death

17. "We are thus introduced to a new principle of relativity which holds that all observers are not led by the same physical evidence to the same picture of the universe, unless their linguistic backgrounds are similar or can in some way be calibrated" (Benjamin Lee Whorf).
18. "Reality is not simply there, it must be searched and won" (Paul Celan).

of the author."[19] Yet news of the latter's death has been much exaggerated: the authors are alive and writing, in full awareness (both ludic and serious) of language's ambiguous and sometimes awesome nature—as we hope this volume shows.

Under such circumstances—historical and intellectual—the period witnessed the full panoply of modernist/postmodernist projections, increased in number and pursued with a precision and thoroughness that elevated some areas to the status of a new art, even (though one speaks of this now with caution) of a new life.[20]

3 The work from all directions . . .

That the early "postwar" corresponded with the great American moment (the "American century") is quite clear. Its impact on our poetry as such appeared most convincingly in *The New American Poetry,* edited by Donald Allen in 1960: a summary of experimental work over the previous decade and a half and the most public challenge till then to the entrenched middle-ground poetry and poetics of the 1950s. Concerning the poets gathered therein, Allen wrote: "They are our avant-garde, the true continuers of the modern movement in American poetry. Through their work many are closely allied to modern jazz and abstract expressionist painting, today recognized throughout the world to be America's greatest achievements in contemporary culture. This anthology makes the same claim for the new American poetry, now becoming the dominant movement in the second phase of our twentieth-century literature and already exerting strong influence abroad." Yet what was less apparent for many of those participating in or being drawn to it was that what was happening in American poetry was part of a larger *global* awakening, some of it occurring before or apart from the American influence and some of it in collaboration with or influencing other young Americans in turn. (That other avant-gardes were active in the United States should also be considered.)

19. "[We] can no longer abide the scaleless world in which theory and its prose disciplines dislocate us" (Don Byrd).
20. "What, then, is the postmodern? . . . It is undoubtedly a part of the modern. All that has been received, if only yesterday (modo, modo, Petronius used to say), must be suspected. . . . A work can become modern only if it is first postmodern. Postmodernism thus understood is not modernism at its end but in the nascent state, and this state is constant" (J.-F. Lyotard, *The Postmodern Condition*). And Jackson Mac Low: "post-nuttin'."

We are saying this, of course, with more than forty years of hindsight. What was then revealing itself from outside the United States was from an earlier generation that poets in America were (and, to some extent, still are) in the process of (re)discovering. Just as word was coming back about the older American "Objectivists" (themselves becoming visible again as makers of a transitional "new American poetry"), the poets recovered from elsewhere included the likes of Neruda and Vallejo (poet heroes of the other "America"), of Surrealist masters like Breton and Artaud (disregarded by the American middle-grounders in favor of less "convulsive" practitioners like Eluard and Desnos), of Dadaists like Tzara and Ball or like Kurt Schwitters, whose work was hinted at—but only hinted at—in Robert Motherwell's great *Dada Artists and Poets* (1951), another generative, albeit historical, anthology appearing in the postwar time. And there were glimmerings, too, of an older but still obscure generation of Negritude poets in Africa and the Caribbean—a whole world, in fact, to reassemble.

What was known then, much of it obscured by the antimodernist turn at the beginning of the decade, was imperative to know. What was not known—obscured here by a heady breakthrough as *American* poets [pre-Vietnam]—was how much else was coming into presence then or had emerged, even in this most American of centuries and moments, without our blessings. Over the last few years the two editors have had a chance to go over the terrain of the immediate postwar decades (1945 to 1960, the years of the New American Poetry per se) and to carry that exploration into the still less charted places that define the boundaries of the present gathering. This journey has been fired in some sense by our own nomadism[21] and our sense of a community/a commonality of poets that both of us have known (and continue to know) across whatever boundaries. Being far enough away from inception now to have a wider view of that terrain, we see the "new American poetry" as itself a part (a key part, sure, but still a part) of a worldwide series of moves and movements that took the political, visionary, and formal remnants of an earlier modernism and reshaped and reinvented them in the only time allowed to us on Earth.

21. "A nomadic poetics will cross languages, not just translate, but write in all or any of them. If Pound, Joyce, & others have shown the way, it is essential now to push this matter further, again, not as 'collage' but as a material flux of language matter, moving in & out of semantic & non-semantic spaces, moving around & through the features accreting as a poem, a lingo-cubism that is no longer an 'explosante fixe,' as Breton defined the poem, but an 'explosante mouvante'" (Pierre Joris).

It is our hope, then, that what we have done here will have some resonance in the century and millennium now emerging. Looking backward at the same time we are aware of the distance even now between ourselves and most of the century in which we're writing: a time of two great avant-garde awakenings, when much seemed possible and poetry held out a still untested promise as an instrument of transformation, even of redemption. We are at the moment in a possibly less threatening but curiously less hopeful state, caught between a rapidly developing technology and a resurgent economic conservatism threatening to become a cultural and social conservatism as well. In that sense the core conflicts are very much like those at the old century's beginning. And yet with all of that the idea of millennium still draws us on, allures us again with the hope of a poetics pointed firmly toward the future. We began our assemblage with Whitman's words "for poets to come":

Indeed, if it were not for you, what would I be?
What is the little I have done, except to arouse you?

and we resume it now with those of Paul Celan, two years before his death:

THREADSUNS
above the grayblack wastes,
A tree-
high thought
grasps the lighttone: there are
still songs to sing beyond
mankind.

Three Modernist Movements:
Dadaism, Futurism, Surrealism

(with Pierre Joris)

Prologue to Futurism (I)

The "Futurist moment" was the brief utopian phase of early Modernism when artists felt themselves to be on the verge of a new age that would be more exciting, more promising, more inspiring than any preceding one. Both the Italian and Russian versions of Futurism found their roots in economically backward countries that were experiencing rapid industrialization—the faith in dynamism and national expansion associated with capitalism in its early phase. In the prewar years, political and aesthetic decisions seemed, for however brief a time, to be, so to speak, in synch—hence, no doubt, the extraordinarily rich artistic production.

> —Marjorie Perloff, *The Futurist Moment*

But it is the movements that survive, oddly, here where we live & work as poets, artists: or, if not the movements, then their sense of art as an extension, by other means, of the life around us—as coextensive, then, with life itself. All of which, as *futurism,* had come sharply into focus by the start of "the world war"—a first radical mix of art & life—the epitome in the popular mind of an avant-garde. It was, on both its Russian & Italian sides, the first great "art" movement led by poets; & if its means now

Jerome Rothenberg and Pierre Joris, *Poems for the Millennium: The University of California Book of Modern & Postmodern Poetry,* 2 vols. (Berkeley: University of California Press, 1995, 1998).

sometimes seem exaggerated, unripe in retrospect, they carry with them the seeds of all that we were later to become.

While Marinetti's opening manifesto for Italian Futurism bristled with a polemical stance in favor of the transformed present (1909), the later manifestos of Futurist poets & artists offered formal/"technical" projections of the works then getting under way. The key term—still resonant—was *parole in libertà* (= words set free), by which poetry was to become "an uninterrupted sequence of new images . . . [a] strict net of images or analogies, to be cast into the mysterious sea of phenomena." This freedom-of-the-word, while it resembled other forms of collage & of image juxtaposition, more fully explored the use of innovative & expressive typography toward the visual presentation of language set in motion by forerunners like Mallarmé. But the verbal liberation didn't end with the page—moved rather toward a new performance art & a poetry that "scurried off the page in all directions at once," as Emmett Williams phrased it for the "language happenings" of a later decade. Outrageous & aggressive, the Futurists' performances mixed declamation & gesture, events & soundings, indifference & engagement, to break the barriers between themselves & those who came to jeer or cheer them. Wrote Marinetti *selbst* (circa 1915): "EVERYTHING OF ANY VALUE IS THEATRICAL."

But their impact on the future showed up in other ways as well. In their manifestos—as a leading instance—they created a radical form of poesis in which theory & practice—like their poetry & politics—were inexorably tied together. Their call for speed—improvisation—as spirit of the present, moved via Dada toward Surrealism's stress on automatic writing & the later cry of Olson (1950)—in setting forth a new "projective verse"—that "always one perception must must must MOVE, INSTANTER, ON ANOTHER!" Their experiments with typography—like those with performance—were picked up by other European movements & artists &, in somewhat altered form, by Americans like Ezra Pound & e. e. cummings—&, through them, by post–World War II groupings from Fluxus to Black Mountain. Marinetti's call for "the total destruction of syntax," while it didn't match the works, say, of a Gertrude Stein in practice, did foreshadow the experiments, post World War II, of artists like Mac Low & Cage or the 1980s innovations of the American "language" poets. Nor is there any question that the Futurists' glorification of the machine was a first step toward what would later emerge as a fusion of art & technology through computers, videos, & synthesizers—in the work, for example, of poets like Henri Chopin or Bernard Heidsieck. In their ability to set such things in motion—if not to complete them on their own—the Futurists extended their "moment" from the century's beginning to its end.

With all of that, too, came a fearful, destructive masculinity: an enthusiasm for war ("the world's only hygiene") & (not uniquely, alas) for fascism; & a railing against presumptive forms of social "weakness" (e.g., feminism) & "passéist" institutions (libraries, museums, etc.)—well past the leveling strategies (in the latter instance) of most other avant-gardes. The result has been to obscure—even now—the memory of what the Futurists accomplished in their own right or helped to open up for others.

Prologue to Futurism (II)

I have destroyed the ring of the horizon and got out of the circle of objects.

—Kasimir Malevich, 1915

The afterlife of Russian Futurism extended into the post–World War II period, where it was mediated—in the absence of workable translations— by the writings of formalist critics such as Roman Jakobson & Viktor Shklovsky. Around it, too, was the glamour of revolution, or of a revolution that later swallowed up its children & defenders. The political side of Futurism was early felt through Mayakovsky, who moved—larger than life, from all accounts—through postwar Europe & America & whose suicide in 1929 coincided with the early years of the Stalinist terror. As such a self-proclaimed political force, the *Futuristy* sought, along with other movements of the time, to bring the energies of (transformed) art into all facets of life—to change that life thereby in body & in spirit. The response that ground them down was itself political in nature.

In the "formalist" interpretation, the dominant thrust of the *Futuristy* compresses to an idea of "defamiliarization" or "estrangement" (*ostranenie* = "making strange"). Thus, by what Shklovsky calls a "semantic shift," our habitual way of knowing the world (= "automatism") is disrupted, turned on its head, as "the poet . . . wrests the concept from the conceptual set in which it stood and transfers it, with the help of a word or a trope, to another conceptual set." In the words of the poet Alexei Kruchenykh, the process emerges as "the world turned backwards";[1] or again—more as a matter of inclusion or expansion than of strangeness: "A common language is binding [restrictive]; a free one allows more complete expression." Toward those ends, the *Futuristy* proposed, like other avant-garde movements, a transformation of language down to its roots, entering—in their case—into the place where words *sound,* to create a new "transrational" language (*za/um* = [literally] "beyondsense") "that undermines or ignores the conventional meanings of a given word, thus allowing its sound to generate its own range of significations, or, in its more extreme form, the invention of new words based purely on sound" (M. Perloff).

If such a poetics of sound was one side of the futurist coinage, the other was a renewed emphasis on the visible word—both printed & written. The most remarkable experiments here were with handwritten books that often involved the collaboration of futurist poets & artists (Larionov, Goncharova, Malevich, et al.) but were otherwise the work of the poets themselves, many of whom had come into poetry by way of painting. Crude in appearance, the books remind us also that the *Futuristy,* unlike their Italian counterparts, pursued a primitivist program, connecting their own experiments with *zaum,* say, to native Russian forms of glossolalia, spiritualism, & so forth, their books & writings to a form of popular broadsheet called a *lubok.* While they were part of a still larger "futurist moment" & pursued many of the same innovations as other movements of their time, the depths of their populism—both visual & linguistic—were beyond those of any other avant-garde.

As with other movements of their time & after, that of the *Futuristy* left openings for a range of individual gestures. Its two major figures—Khlebnikov & Mayakovsky—are indicative, in that sense, of its parameters: the former with a deep investment in both the poetics/antipoetics of *zaum* & in a science & mathematics that he believed revealed the fundamental Laws of Time—"the [cosmic] equations that . . . govern natural and historical events" (Paul Schmidt); the latter (who was also an artist, playwright, filmmaker, & virtual performance artist) turning his cutup strophes & stepped verses—with their apparent later influence on William Carlos Williams—to the service of the Revolution & the emerging SuperState. Of the others presented here, Kruchenykh (too little translated until now) was probably the dominant *zaum* poet,

---

1. A good comparison here would be to the Seneca Indian *ononharoia* ceremony—"turning-the-brain-upside-down"—for which see page 30, above.

Kamensky the maker of "ferroconcrete poems" that went beyond the other *Futuristy* on the visual/graphic side. Important, too, was the movement's push outside of Russia—as in the work of Polish poets such as Anatol Stern & Alexander Wat. The direction throughout was persistently leftward.

↢

everything is good that
has a good beginning
and doesn't have an end
the world will die but for us there is no
end!
—(Alexei Kruchenykh,
"Victory over the Sun")

Prologue to Dada

You are mistaken if you take Dada for a modern school, or as a reaction against the schools of today. . . . Dada is not at all modern. It is more in the nature of an almost Buddhist religion of indifference. . . . The true Dadas are against Dada.

—Tristan Tzara, *Lecture on Dada*

Which was Tzara's way of proclaiming Dada's *post*modernity—not as chronology but as an irritation (a *disgust*) with solutions altogether ("no more solutions! no more words!") & with prescriptions (old or new) for making art. It is important to remember: that at the heart of Dada was a pullback from the absolute: from closed solutions based on single means: not a question of technique, then, but of a way of being, a state-of-mind (of "spirit"), "a stance" (Charles Olson, decades later) "toward reality." For which the only technique was the suppression of technique, the only sense of form was to deny form as a value. And for all of that, Dada drew from means that were common to its time & to its predecessors in Futurism & Expressionism: a series of projects it would work on until its own (predicted) self-destruction as a movement. Collage. Performance. New typographies. Chance operations. And a high devouring humor.

At the same time Dada had its myth(s) of origin. Its time was one of war, its place the neutral heart of Europe. In Zürich, then, a group of artists/poets, brought together by a flight from war & time, set up a venue of their own (the Cabaret Voltaire) & took a name at total variance with the names that came before (expressionism, futurism, constructivism, orphism, etc.). Their strategy was what a later poet (E. Sanders) would call "a total assault on the culture"—or in the words of one of their own (R. Huelsenbeck) "the liberation of the creative forces from the tutelage of the advocates of power." From Zürich the movement dispersed to Germany & France & elsewhere: a first international & generational outcry, by means of art & at the same time making Art (with capitals) its central target. The "official" German version lurched toward a leftist politics, while the French, holding the center of European modernism, turned Dada into Surrealism (1924) & brought the movement to an end. With that turning came a realignment with Art or an attempt to conquer Art's domain: a sense that Dada-qua-Surrealism—like Dada-qua-Bolshevism in Berlin—was itself a solution rather than a challenge to all possible solutions, Dada included. But the Surrealist accommodation—if it was that—was mild compared to other attempts to rein in the revolutionary nature of the new poetry & art, in favor of a middle-ground & fashionable modernism. Through all of which, Dada remained a lurking presence, erupting in a battery of neo-Dadaisms, from then to now.

Like other such "movements" before and after, Dada was largely the work of poets or of those who saw in poetry a liberating gesture setting it apart from that of Art. Of the poets in the Zürich group, Hugo Ball was the founder of the Cabaret Voltaire & of the first Dada magazine, with which it shared its name; he claimed—in a Dada act that turned into a kind of mystic seizure—to have invented a new "poetry without words" but fled Zürich shortly thereafter to live out his life in the Swiss mountains, as a kind of Catholic Dada saint. Tristan Tzara (b. Sammi Rosenstock in Rumania) was—at nineteen—the movement's principal publicist & its link to the Dada poets of Paris (Breton, Soupault, Péret, Picabia, et al.), some of whom would be, in turn, the founding fathers of Surrealism. In a similar vein Richard Huelsenbeck brought Dada to Berlin & a new life at the edge of postwar German politics. Less overtly political, the work of a number of other German & Dutch Dadas (Kurt Schwitters, who changed his movement's name to Merz; Hans Arp; Max Ernst; Theo van Doesburg, working through the Dutch De Stijl) crossed notably into poetry, with Schwitters & Arp approaching major status as new language artists. Finally, New York Dada (so-called) virtually preceded that of Zürich & focused, oddly, on such European expatriates—

circa World War I & early 1920s—as Duchamp, Francis Picabia, & Else von Freytag-Loringhoven. Like Futurism & Surrealism, the movement also had worldwide implications.

Prologue to Surrealism

Language has been given to man so that he may make Surrealist use of it.

—André Breton, *Manifesto of Surrealism*

(1) With the dust long cleared by now, André Breton remains the consummate poet of Surrealism, Antonin Artaud its most authentic renegade expression. As a movement, Surrealism's way had been prepared in the preceding century—a romanticism it would never shake off—& its actual birthing came with the self-destruction of Paris Dada. As much Descartian (& thereby French) as Freudian, Breton & company (like the founders, e.g., of "scientific" Marxism vis-à-vis earlier Utopians) broke from the utopian/dystopian Dadas—circa 1924—to form a movement based on principles of consciousness & politics: a "surrealist revolution" that changed within five years to a "surrealism at the service of the revolution" (the words in quotes the names of their two magazines). If their goal—like that of Dada—was to challenge & overturn "logic," to make "the poem . . . a debacle of the intellect" (P. Eluard), they claimed to do it with a scientific-like precision—a research project centered on poesis; its subject: the hidden dimensions of the mind &, therefore, of reality.

Like Dada, too, the Surrealists' goal was to transform the world—in attempting which, they left their mark down to the present, but foundered on internal struggles; clashes over left-wing ideologies (Eluard & Aragon to Stalin, Breton to quirky dialogues with Trotsky); schisms & Breton-led excommunications as pope or party chairman. At issue, too, were unresolved contradictions between the poet/artist as gifted genius/medium & an egalitarian view of a poetry "made by all, not one." While they did in fact open art's domain to include the work of nonpoets/nonartists, the Surrealists (artists & poets both) remained a breed apart; the movement became increasingly given to hermeticism & occultism; & art continued to tyrannize the life the practitioners pursued. Exiled or underground in World War II, the Surrealists barely survived its aftermath & Breton's death in 1964.

(2) In their poetic practice the Surrealists shared a collage aesthetic with other modernisms & (to a lesser degree than Dada) a complementary poetics of ("objective") chance. In Max Ernst's paraphrase & generalization of Lautréamont's playful dictum on the poetic image,[2] collage was defined as *the chance encounter of two distant realities on an unfamiliar plane . . .* or, in short, the cultivation of the effects of a *systematic displacement . . . a function of our will to the complete displacement of everything.*" As such, collage was closely linked to "dreamwork" (Freud) & (in an unfortunate conjunction) to the mental processes of the insane & "primitive"—with "automatic writing" as its driving mechanism. Putting such writing at the heart of his project, Breton described it further as "a monologue spoken as rapidly as possible without any intervention on the part of the critical faculties, a monologue consequently unencumbered by the slightest inhibition and which was, as closely as possible, akin to *spoken thought.*"

For all of which, Surrealism maintained a genuine aestheticism: a dedication to "beauty" under code words like "the marvelous," "the wonderful," etc. Wrote Lucy Lippard, within the decade after Breton's death: "The Surrealists hoped eventually to draw from the juxtaposition of those dislocated fragments a new super-reality, rather than a mere destruction of the old." If so, it was a reality infused, infected, with fierce desires for "transgression" (G. Bataille); or, as Breton had it in his novel, *Nadja* (1928): "Beauty will be convulsive, or it will not be."

(3) The initial roster of Surrealist poets—most later "excommunicated" by the authoritarian Breton—included some of the major practitioners of French poetry between the wars: Philippe Soupault, who with Breton coauthored the first book of "automatic writing," *Les champs magnétiques* (1920); Paul Eluard & Louis Aragon, who broke with Breton over Communist politics & won post–World War II prominence beyond the bounds of poetry as such; Robert Desnos, credited by the others with clairvoyant powers, who died as a political prisoner in the German concentration camp at Terezine [Teresienstadt]; Benjamin Péret, first editor of *La révolution surréaliste* & early compiler of ethnopoetic anthologies; & Tristan Tzara, whose late-Dada conflicts with Breton led directly to the onset of Surrealism, with which he later had an intermittent but significant connection. In addition, the idea of the poem as "an imponderable that can

2. "[A]s beautiful as the chance encounter of an umbrella and a sewing machine on a dissecting table."

be found in any genre" (H. Michaux) drew in artists & sometime writers like Max Ernst &—later—Salvador Dalí, whose presence & "paranoiac critical method" dominated the public perception of the movement from the 1930s on. The roster of participants also included such powerful figures as René Char & Antonin Artaud, along with discoveries of Breton's like the fifteen-year-old Gisèle Prassinos or the American poet Philip Lamantia, first published as an adolescent during Breton's wartime exile in New York. Surrealism's impact on African & Caribbean Negritude is a final legacy worth noting.

The History/Prehistory of the Poetry Project

Opening remarks to 20th Year Symposium of Saint Marks
Poetry Project, May 1987, with Allen Ginsberg,
Kenneth Koch, Ed Sanders, and Anne Waldman

I want to welcome you all as the moderator of this session, although I don't think that moderation (in the sense of the safe or middle position) is what this quasi institution has been (or should be) about. Chronologically—in terms of age—I'm in the middle position between Koch and Ginsberg (as my almost elders) and Sanders and Waldman (as my juniors). So much for chronology. I think we're otherwise in it together.

But the key word in the symposium title is *prehistory*. It is a knockout word, and we're of course free to take it any way we want. I'll make a couple of suggestions (my five-minute presentation written down this morning) and pass them along.

As it might relate to the circumstances immediately leading to the Poetry Project at St. Mark's Church in-the-Bowery, I find myself the only one here who was part of the original/founding committee of the Saint Mark's readings circa 1965 and 1966 that preceded the Poetry Project as such. The dominant figure in that proto-Project was Paul Blackburn, who was not only a magnificent and influential poet but a tireless organizer of readings (at the Caffe Borgia, at the Tenth Street Coffee Shop, at the Deux Magots and Le Metro, at Saint Mark's Church, and after Saint Mark's at Doctor Generosity's and other venues north and south in Manhattan). Those early Saint Mark's readings (after a pitched battle broke things up at Le Metro [coffee shop] around the corner) were done without funds and set up the pattern of Monday and Wednesday readings that has remained in place thereafter. Among the other committee members—if I remember right—were Carol Berge, Allen Plantz, Carol Rubenstein, and Diane Wakoski. Ted Berrigan was invited too but couldn't yet make it.

It was in 1967 that those looser and unfunded readings became the Poetry Project, and as such the Project developed (particularly under Anne Waldman's directorship) into the closest thing we have to an ongoing, venerable center for poetry, run by poets and open foremost to the full range of visionary, revolutionary, language-centered, spirit-centered arts that poets have both invented and discovered in the newest and oldest possibilities of our human (and animal) natures. In that sense the prehistory is more than local, more than only of-this-place. It is what Ezra Pound called a vortex—the Poetry Project vortex: a point of concentration for accumulated human energies: past and present shaped by the place of its occurrence and the needs and yearnings of its participants. "All experience rushes into this vortex," Pound wrote in 1914. "All the energized past, all the past that is living and worthy to live. ALL MOMENTUM . . ., instinct charging the PLACID, NON-ENERGIZED FUTURE. . . . All the past that is vital, all the past that is capable of living into the future, is present in the vortex, now." The Poetry Project as a vortex has drawn its energies from surrounding New York and the larger world, as also from each of us who has worked within it. The works and movements of poets and artists in the twentieth century created many new vortexes/configurations, many pasts and presents / energies old and new. The Poetry Project vortex circa 1967—to which I was witness—included Beat poets, New York School poets, San Francisco poets, Black Mountain poets, Deep Image poets, Midwest and Southwest regional poets, Fluxus poets, Umbra poets, and so on. And from then on: African American poets, Latino poets, feminist poets, gay poets, Indian poets, Language poets, anti-Language poets, sound poets, silent poets, mumbling poets; even—in this usually most generous of vortexes—academic poets.

But the pre-history goes even further.

Gertrude Stein is of the Poetry Project vortex and has been from the start.

So are Pound and Williams and Wallace Stevens.

The Dada fathers are not forgotten here, and there is a lingering resonance of old Surrealists once in exile in New York.

Koch's New York School—transmitted through Berrigan, Padgett, Waldman, and others—brought in the energies of (American) painters from abstract expressionism to pop to present manifesters.

Performance poetry and art grew naturally from the readings and were foregrounded some years ago through director Ed Friedman's kindly efforts.

But PREHISTORY: this is something older still. Beyond romantic and metaphysical ghosts it summons up Provençal poets who came in early with Paul Blackburn; Chinese poets, the work of Pound but also Mac Low's and Cage's mining of the *I Ching* as a guide to poetry; Sumerian poets via Olson and Schwerner; Egyptian poets via Ed Sanders; American Indian shaman poets; Mayan and Aztec poets; ancient Hebrew poets; Sufi poets; and whole lineages and traditions of Buddhist poets— all of these are part of what we are.

It is a history/prehistory of poetry reaching back into Paleolithic times: our true prehistory as human beings: in a configuration that has surfaced elsewhere—to be sure—but nowhere more tenaciously than here, more continuously than here. It is in these ways that the Poetry Project, now more than ever, is a dependable haven for a tradition of poem-making whose loss would incredibly diminish us. It is very much about prehistory and history, because it is very much about a present in which (Ezra Pound again) "all ages are contemporaneous in the mind."

A Secret Location on the
Lower East Side

Pre-Face to Catalogue for New York Public Library Exhibit,
January 1998

Since everyone loves a paradox, let me start off with this now familiar one: the mainstream of American poetry, the part by which it has been and will be known, has long been in the margins, nurtured in the margins, carried forward, vibrant, in the margins. As mainstream and margin both, it represents our underground economy as poets, the gray market for our spiritual/corporeal exchanges. It is the creation as such of those poets who have seized or often have invented their own means of production and of distribution. The autonomy of the poets is of singular importance here—not something we've been stuck with *faute de mieux* but something we've demanded as a value that must (repeat: *must*) remain first and foremost under each poet's own control. And this is because poetry as we know and want it is the language of those precisely at the margins—born there or, more often still, self-situated: a strategic position from which to struggle with the center of the culture and with a language that we no longer choose to bear. Poetry is another language, as it is another orientation, from that of the other, more familiar mainstream, which has, in Paul Blackburn's words, "wracked all passion from the sound of speech." For many of us, so positioned, it is the one true counterlanguage we possess—even, to paraphrase Alfred Jarry (and to be almost serious about it), our language (and our science) of exceptions.

The model figure here—a hundred years before the Lower East Side works presented in these pages—was surely Walt Whitman, whose 1855 *Leaves of Grass*, self-published, was the work of his own hands, as well as mind, from manuscript to printed book to first reviews ghostwritten by the man himself. And contemporaneous with that, our second found-

ing work was that of Emily Dickinson, who never would be published
in her lifetime but, more secretly and privately than any, handwrote and
stitched together a series of single-copy booklets/(fascicles) as testimony
to her own experiments with voice and line. Along with William Blake
before them, Dickinson and Whitman are the poets of our language
who first brought inspiration and production back together as related, un-
divided acts.

The work of the twentieth century is the continuation and expansion of those acts. In Europe the years immediately before and after the
World War I—what Marjorie Perloff calls and chronicles as "the futurist moment"—saw a proliferation of poet- and artist-driven publications,
from the collaborative "prose of the transsiberian" of Blaise Cendrars and
Sonia Delaunay (a powerful multicolored foldout extravaganza) to the
rough-hewn books of the Russian constructivists and the movement-
centered magazines and books (Expressionist, Futurist, Dada, Surrealist)
under the command, nearly always, of their poet/founders. The American
equivalent was the first (golden) age of "little" magazines and presses—
central publications for what was emerging as a bona fide American
avant-garde. Writers who sought new ways and languages took charge of
their own publication—Gertrude Stein, a case in point, whose works for
years were published by herself and Alice Toklas, while others (Pound,
Loy, Williams, among many) drew from a network (noncommercial,
often poet-run) that ranged from Robert McAlmon's Contact Editions
to Harry and Caresse Crosby's Black Sun offerings to the important publications by George and Mary Oppen's To Publishers, linking imagist(e)s
to "Objectivists" and both to the new poetries that would emerge post–
World War II. James Laughlin's New Directions—alive and vital to the
present day—came from the same fertile source, which also included
magazines and reviews like Margaret Anderson's and Jane Heap's *Little
Review* and Eugene Jolas's *Transition* as first publishers respectively of
works like Joyce's *Ulysses* and *Finnegans Wake* (the latter then known as
"Work in Progress").

The disruption of all that came with the new midcentury war and holocaust, preliminary to the cold war that defined the next four decades.
The great European movements were long since gone or—notably in
the case of Surrealism—had splintered into warring factions. A number
of once marginal poets had received more general recognition (Eliot,
Moore, Stevens, among the Americans) and with it access to the commercial literary networks. Others, like the American "Objectivists" (Zu-

kofsky, Oppen, Reznikoff, Rakosi), had fallen between the cracks and into a life of near nonpublication. And the climate, in the decade following the war, seemed unremittingly reactionary, both on its "new critical" literary side and its McCarthyite political retrenchments.

The story by now is well known, but it is also true—that it was against this background that the second great awakening of twentieth-century poetry was starting up, not only in the United States but in Europe, in Latin America, and in much of what was becoming, increasingly, the postcolonial world. Its two American centers—as everybody also knows—were New York and San Francisco, with links to other places large and small. If San Francisco was the great "refuge city" overall (I think that's Robert Duncan's term), New York was where a counterpoetics flourished in what Richard Schechner spoke of—for theater and related arts—as "a resistance and alternative to the conglomerate . . . [that] exist[s] only in the creases of contemporary society, and off leavings, like cockroaches . . . not marginal [he adds, but] . . . run[ning] through the actual and conceptual center of society, like faults in the earth's crust." But the actual topography of the new poetry (circa 1960) was at a necessary distance from the commercial hub of American publishing (the concentration of media power in mid-Manhattan). Its terrain included not only the old bohemia of Greenwich Village but moved increasingly, significantly, into surrounding regions—eastward and southward into the tenement and loft areas of the Lower East Side, or into what came to be called the East Village, Soho, Tribeca, and so on. Rents then were cheap, and the cheapness, the economic advantage of life in the creases, was one of the attractions for the writers and artists who entered that territory. It was also—at least at the start—a time that was favorable for producing works on the cheap, either printing abroad (the dollar was still at its postwar high) or utilizing new and inexpensive means for the setting and manufacture of magazines and books: increasingly available photo offset technologies, but also more rough and ready means such as mimeo, ditto, and (somewhat later) Xerox and other photocopying processes.

The result is what this show and book are all about: the emergence on the Lower East Side and environs (stretching all the way to Highlands, North Carolina, and Kyoto, Japan)[1] of that kind of intellectual and spiritual energy that Pound, in the context of an earlier independent magazine and movement, had called a *vortex:* a place of cultural inter-

---

1. Highlands = Jonathan Williams & Jargon Society; Kyoto = Cid Corman & *Origin.*

sections and fusions, into which "all experience rushes," to make the past
and the present into something *new*. The publishers and publications included here represent the vortex, the vital center, of their own time and
place. At its beginnings it was also part of that wave of liberations and
resistances, still largely self-generated and unfinanced, that marked the
1960s and 1970s in fact as well as in the popular imagination. The activity, with its spin-offs into readings and performances, was intense and
(in its size and scope) unprecedented. The movements or groupings then
active included the kingpins of the New American Poetry from the time
of its 1960 emergence: Black Mountain poets, Beats, New York School,
along with Fluxus, concrete poetry, Black Arts, deep image, ethnopoetics, L=A=N=G=U=A=G=E. Under such headings—or in some fertile
space between—the poets directly involved in the work of publication
included the likes of Robert Creeley, Jonathan Williams, Cid Corman,
Amiri Baraka, Lawrence Ferlinghetti, James Laughlin, Jack Spicer, Ed
Sanders, Diane Di Prima, Vito Acconci, Bernadette Mayer, Ted Berrigan, Ron Padgett, Anne Waldman, John Ashbery, Clark Coolidge, Aram
Saroyan, Ron Silliman, Charles Bernstein, Bruce Andrews, Bob Perel-
man, James Sherry, Lyn Hejinian, Margaret Randall, James Koller, Dick
Higgins, Emmett Williams, Jackson Mac Low, Dennis Tedlock, David
Antin, Robert Kelly, David Henderson, Ishmael Reed, Nathaniel Mackey,
even (at several points) the present writer. Yet even so large a list—limited
as it is to poets who doubled as publishers—fails to catch the full breadth
and force of what was happening there and throughout the world.

By 1980—the terminal date for this presentation—the situation was
no longer as clear as it had been earlier. The Vietnam War had shattered
the image of American hegemony, and the cold war had begun to sim-
mer down. And while the Reagan years might have brought about a new
resistance (and sometimes did), they also brought a new defensiveness
in what became increasingly a culture war directed *against* the avant-
garde rather than *by* it. The secret locations of this exhibit's title were no
longer secret but had come into a new and far less focused visibility and
a fusion/confusion, often, with the commercial and cultural conglomer-
ates of the American center. Increasingly, too, there had developed a de-
pendence on support from institutional and governmental sources—the
National Endowment for the Arts, say, as the major case in point. The result was to impose both a gloss of professionalism on the alternative publications and to make obsolete the rough-and-ready book works of the
previous two decades. But the still greater danger of patronage was that

the denial of that patronage, once threatened, became an issue that would override most others.

At the present time, then, the lesson of the works presented here is the reminder of what is possible when the makers of the works seek out the means to maintain and fortify their independence. It seems possible with the new technologies now opening—computer-generated publications and the still-wide-open possibilities of Internet and Web—that the great tradition of an independent American poetry will stay alive and well. Toward that end the contents of the present exhibition with its attendant book may prove to be a guideline and an inspiration.

How We Came into Performance: A Personal Accounting

For KriKri 2005 Polypoetry Festival and Conference,
Ghent, Belgium

By sometime in the 1970s it had become clear to me that poetry, as we in my generation knew and practiced it, had either discovered or invented its origins in performance. More precisely the discovery or invention was *ours*, first on our own grounds and then, as our awareness developed, in the practice of our predecessors, both those from the near past and others in remote or distant times and places. I can think back to a time when none of this was clear or pressing for me and for the poets I grew up with, as well as to a time, only a few years later, when performance/orality/improvisation became the central issue for many of us—myself, at various times, included.

The relation of poetry to performance had long been implicit. The words we were given to speak about it shared a vocabulary with music, so that John Cage—a poet in his own way as well as a musician—could define poetry in the simplest terms "not . . . by reason of its content or ambiguity but by reason of its allowing musical elements (time, sound) to be introduced into the world of words." Traditional formulas, even in ages dominated by writing, spoke of the poet as a singer and the poem as a song—a rhythmic flow of words transmitted by the voice or the breath—by the voice *and* the breath. There was, in other words, a fiction of performance long after poetry had come to be read in silence as a form, primarily, of writing—or, put another way, there was a memory of origins, of a time prior to writing, when the poem was truly carried by the voice and *only* by the voice.

When I was first coming into poetry—more than fifty years ago by now—the opportunities for readings, much less "performances," were very few. That isn't to say that poetry was never read or performed in public—in traditional verse plays and early modernist theater, in readings by actors, in *lieder* and operas and other musical settings, and sometimes (but not then so often) by established poets on what was still a limited lecture circuit, with readings few and far between. What changed, as we then entered into it, were the venues and the participation of increasingly large numbers of poets as readers (later, for some, as performers) of their own work. Once readings could exist and find an audience—as they did—in noninstitutional settings, the possibility of readings opened for poets of all ages and with or without established reputations. (I take readings as such to be a modest but primary form of performance.) At the same time more poets began to compose their poems with performance in mind, some of it close to the older ways of "reading [from] writing" but others with a new freedom and openness to unprecedented mixtures and fusions.

The new arenas for poetry performance—like those for simultaneously emerging performance art in the form of "events" and "happenings"— were outside of familiar and restricted institutional settings, a fact that in itself allowed the entry of the alternative, the unrecognized, and the largely unfunded. I remember readings from that time taking place (famously) in coffee shops, but also in bars, in art galleries and artists' lofts, in church basements, in bookstores, in public parks, in little theaters that were themselves living a vagabond or gypsy existence. Surprisingly too (at least I remember my own surprise), there was an audience for the alternative readers and performers, expanded further in the context of the great be-ins and love-ins of the 1960s and a few years later in the antiwar rallies of the 1970s.

Once the opening to perform and the desire to perform were there, new forms of performing (a step and more beyond the solo reading) began to appear. From the vantage point of what was called the "New American Poetry"—and this was where I was perched as well—the first extensions of performance came for many of us through poetry and jazz. I took it at first hearing as a kind of parody of classical *lieder* or of the kitschy reading of sentimental poetry (still occasionally heard) to a background of sentimental (pop classical) music. That poetry and jazz moment was in the late 1950s and early 1960s, and the poets who stood out at first were mostly white (Rexroth, Patchen, Kerouac, Ferlinghetti the ones I most remember); the better situated black poets would enter later. I also took a shot at it, most memorably an evening or two of "medieval poetry and jazz" with Paul Blackburn, Armand Schwerner, Robert Kelly, as the other poets in the mix.

It was the solo reading, however, that remained the principal performance mode for the New American Poetry. At the same time there were still other, more complex, forms of language-based performance taking shape on both sides of the Atlantic (and beyond)—performances to which we soon had access (particularly those of us in larger cities) and in which we could often play a part. These I thought had their roots largely in Dada, by then a half century or so in the past, and the name that I've come to use for them in retrospect is Fluxus, although Fluxus as an actual name and movement was only a part of what was happening. (World War I Dada was in fact slim pickings when compared to post–World War II performance.) In all of this the boundary between poetry and the other arts "blurred"—was intentionally "blurred" or "erased," in a well-known slogan of that time—yet there were those, poets and others, for whom language (even language qua poetry) was a principal vehicle for the work (or play) at hand.

For me—for many of us—the decisive linking figure was Jackson Mac Low, a poet and sometime musician, who like John Cage brought systematic chance and randomization into the composition and performance of poetry, along with a strong sense of intermedia (Dick Higgins's word), simultaneity, the use of conventional and unconventional instrumentation, and early explorations of computerized and digitalized technologies. With Mac Low and on my own I came to know a number of Fluxus poets and artists who were either living in or passing through New York—Dick Higgins, already mentioned, who would be my publisher for two or three books and pamphlets through his Something Else Press, but also Emmett Williams, Alison Knowles, Philip Corner, Cage himself, and others with whom my connection was more fleeting but always of interest and with performance among the key elements holding things together. Allan Kaprow, whose name was then synonymous with Happenings, was increasingly available, and Carolee Schneemann made an extraordinary entry into New York in the early 1960s. As I recollect it now, in fact, the amount and level of avant-garde performance activity seems both incredible and early enough into it so that any performer, any artist, might have the illusion of being a first discoverer of the work at hand. (I take it that this is a marked difference between *then* and *now*.)

I would like to pause here and mention some of the others who were into forms of performance that involved poetry or the manipulation of language in ways resembling poetry. In doing so, I will largely limit my-self to the 1960s and 1970s (with some spillover into the 1980s), realiz-ing, even so, that I barely scratch the surface.

—In theater, Julian Beck's and Judith Malina's Living Theater was rooted in poetry from its early repertory days to epic or monumental works like *Frankenstein* and *Paradise Now,* and a similar poetic presence in-formed groups like Joseph Chaikin's Open Theater and Richard Fore-man's Ontological-Hysteric Theater. Also a number of poets close to us—Michael McClure, Rochelle Owens, Amiri Baraka—were for a number of years known as much for their theater work as for their poetry.

—Language-centered musical works, as a near approach to poetry, were composed by musicians such as Cage, Charles Amirkhanian, Robert Ashley, Steve Reich, and Charlie Morrow. Later jazz poetry and jazz-related poetry came from poets like Amiri Baraka and Jayne Cortez, and still later rock and pop crossovers included Patti Smith and Jim Carroll, supplementing in that sense those like Bob Dylan and Tom Waits, whose lyrics, taken as poetry, came from outside the poetry nexus *as such.*

—Others who were near and available to me include, in no particular order, poetry ensemble performers such as the Four Horsemen and the Fugs, or solo performers such as Allen Ginsberg, John Giorno, Richard Kostelanetz, Armand Schwerner, or Anne Waldman, whose performances went beyond solo performance as such.

—Finally, it should be remembered that the 1960s and 1970s saw the beginnings of a network of international poetry gatherings, many of them dedicated to performance or to experimental/avant-garde cate-gories such as sound poetry or textsound. Situated in cities like Lon-don, Paris, Stockholm, Amsterdam, and Toronto, as well as New York and San Francisco, these offered the chance of exchange and col-laboration with poets such as Henri Chopin, Bob Cobbing, Bernard Heidsieck, Ernst Jandl, Gerhard Rühm, Sten Hanson, Julien Blaine, and Franco Beltrammetti.

The opportunities for performance were thus immense, and for poets like me they opened into an exploration of what our poetry could be—

what we could make it be—as an art of sound and gesture. By the early 1960s I came to my own first realizations with music, generally with musician-composers who were looking in turn for new ways to bring music and language back together. My most sustained efforts—from then till now—were with Charlie Morrow, who composed works for and with me and with whom I often performed in close collaboration, and Bertram Turetzky, who accompanied me on contrabass and on a number of digitally enhanced sound works. The Fluxus composer Philip Corner provided music for a group performance I directed at the Judson Church (Judson Dance Theater) in New York, and composer Pauline Oliveros was part of a klezmer ensemble I put together—some years before the klezmer revival—as part of a multimedia performance of *Poland/1931*. Some years later the Living Theater would also do a (staged) performance of *Poland/1931,* and an offshoot of theirs (the Center for Theater Science and Research, directed by Luke Theodore Morrison) staged a version of *That Dada Strain,* in which I performed with Turetzky and other musicians and actors. (I also directed, with the assistance of Klaus Schöning, a radio version of *That Dada Strain* [*Der Dada Ton*] for Westdeutscher Rundfunk in Cologne.)

This omnipresence of performance, as I came to think of it, colored my presentation of the tribal and oral in *Technicians of the Sacred* and other gatherings of traditional poetries—and of avant-garde poetry as well. Some of what I found I incorporated into my own practice, and both there and elsewhere I began to write about performance and orality wherever and whenever I found them. I also lived for two years at a Seneca Indian (Iroquois) reservation, where I became a part of the local Indian "singing society"—a performance artwork in itself, if I had ever thought of framing it as such. It was in this way—in all these ways—that performance came to represent for me both the oldest and the newest ways of making poetry.

My own strongest statement along these lines—a kind of manifesto at the time toward both a poetics of performance and a new *ethnopoetics*—came in 1977 in a short essay called "New Models, New Visions." I would like to return to that now and to see, with your help, if it still holds true. On my own grounds since then, I have had to open up anew—or with renewed emphasis—to the force of writing and the visual word in my work and in that of others, but I remain embedded still in the domain of body and breath, voice and gesture, time and place, as I tried to express them in what follows.

⌒

[August 1977, condensed from "New Models, New Visions"][1]

The fact of performance now runs through all our arts, and the arts themselves begin to merge and lose their distinctions, till it's apparent that we're no longer where we were to start with. The Renaissance is over, or it begins again with us. Yet the origins we seek—the frame that bounds our past, that's set against an open-ended future—are no longer Greek, nor even Indo-European, but take in all times and places. . . . The model—or better, the vision—has shifted, away from a "great tradition" centered in a single stream of art and literature in the West, to a greater *tradition that includes, sometimes as its central fact, preliterate and oral cultures throughout the world, with a sense of their connection to subterranean but literate traditions in civilizations, both East and West. "Thought is made in the mouth," said Tristan Tzara, and Edmond Jabès: "The book is as old as fire and water"—and both, we know, are right."*

When Tzara, as arch Dadaist, called circa 1917 for "a great negative work of destruction" against a late, overly textualized derivation from the Renaissance paradigm of culture and history . . . the other side of [his] work—and increasingly that of other artists within the several avant-gardes, the different, often conflicted sides of "modernism"—was, we now see clearly, a great positive work of construction/synthesis. . . . [Ninety years] after Dada, a wide range of artists has been making deliberate and increasing use of ritual models for performance, has swept up arts like painting, sculpture, poetry (if those terms still apply) long separated from their origins in performance. . . . The performance/ritual impulse seems clear throughout: in "happenings" and related event pieces (particularly those that involve participatory performance), in meditative works (often on an explicitly mantric model), in earthworks (derived from monumental American Indian structures), in dreamworks that play off trance and ecstasy, in bodyworks (including acts of self-mutilation and endurance that seem to test the model), in a range of healing events as literal explorations of the shamanistic premise, in animal language pieces related to the new ethology, and so on.

While a likely characteristic of the new paradigm is an overt disdain

1. Originally published in Jerome Rothenberg, *Pre-Faces & Other Writings* (New York: New Directions, 1981).

for paradigms per se, it seems altogether possible to state a number of go-
ing assumptions as these relate to performance. . . .

> *(1) There is a strong sense of continuities, already alluded to, within*
> *the total range of human cultures and arts, and a sense as well*
> *that the drive toward performance goes back to our pre-human*
> *biological inheritance—that performance and culture, even lan-*
> *guage, precede the actual emergence of the species: hence an etho-*
> *logical continuity as well. . . .*
>
> *(2) There is an unquestionable and far-reaching breakdown of*
> *boundaries and genres: between "art" and "life" (Cage, Kaprow),*
> *between various conventionally defined arts (intermedia and*
> *performance art, concrete poetry), and between arts and non-*
> *arts (musique concrete, found art, found poetry, etc.). The con-*
> *sequences here are immense, and I'll only give a few, perhaps too-*
> *obvious, examples . . . :*

>> *— that social conflicts are a form of theater (V. Turner) and that*
>> *organized theater may be an arena for the projection and/or*
>> *stimulation of social conflict;*
>> *— that art has again recognized itself as visionary, and that there*
>> *may be no useful distinction between vision-as-vision and*
>> *vision-as-art (thus, too, the idea in common between Freud*
>> *and the Surrealists that the dream is a dream-work, i.e., a*
>> *work-of-art);*
>> *— that there is a continuum, rather than a barrier, between music*
>> *and noise; between poetry and prose; . . . between dance and*
>> *normal locomotion (walking, running, jumping, etc.);*
>> *— that there is no hierarchy of media in the visual arts, no hier-*
>> *archy of instrumentation in music, and that qualitative dis-*
>> *tinctions between high and low genres and modes (opera and*
>> *vaudeville, high rhetoric and slang) are no longer operational;*
>> *— that neither advanced technology (electronically produced*
>> *sound and image, etc.) nor hypothetically primitive devices*
>> *(pulse and breath, the sound of rock on rock, of hand on water)*
>> *are closed to the artist willing to employ them. . . .*

> *(3) There is a move away from the idea of "masterpiece" to one of*
> *the transientness and self-obsolescence of the poem or artwork as*

performed. The work past its moment becomes a document (mere history), and the artist [the poet in particular] *becomes, increasingly, the surviving nonspecialist in an age of technocracy.*

(4) From this there follows a new sense of function in art, in which the value of a work isn't inherent in its formal or aesthetic characteristics—its shape or its complexity or simplicity as an object—but in what it does, or what the artist/poet or his surrogate does with it, how he or she performs it in a given context. . . .

(5) There follows further, in the contemporary instance, a stress on action and/or process. Accordingly the performance or ritual model includes the act of composition itself. . . . Signs of the artist's or poet's presence are demanded in the published work, and in our own time this has come increasingly to take the form of his or her performance of that work, unfolding it or testifying to it in a public place. . . .

(6) Along with the artist, the audience enters the performance arena as participant—or, the audience "disappears" as the distinction between doer and viewer, like the other distinctions just mentioned, begins to blur. For this the tribal/oral is a particularly clear model, often referred to by the creators of 1960s happenings and the theatrical pieces that invited, even coerced, audience participation toward an ultimate democratizing of the arts. . . .

(7) There is an increasing use of real time, extended time, etc., and/or a blurring of the distinction between those and theatrical time, in line with the transformative view of the "work" as a process that's really happening. . . .

For all of this recognition of the cultural origins and particularities [as I try to show it in greater detail in the uncut version of this text], *the crunch, the paradox, is that the place, if not the stance of the poet and artist is increasingly beyond culture—a characteristic, inevitably, of biospheric [global] societies. Imperialistic in their earlier forms and based on a paradigm of "the dominant culture" (principally the noble/imperial myths of "Western civilization" and of "progress" on a Western or European model), these have in their avant-garde phase been turning to the "symposium of the whole" projected by Robert Duncan. More strongly felt in the industrial and capitalist West, this may be the last move of its kind still to be initiated by the Euro-Americans: a recognition of the*

new/old order in which the whole is equal to but no greater than the
works of all its parts.

~

That was in 1977, and now that we're more than thirty years beyond it, there are a few things I would like to add.

That much of this has been brought into question in the new century—today—in a time of renewed ethnic and religious conflicts, calls perhaps for a still greater effort toward what poetry and art—as our experimental ground—may allow to happen, as the new model/new vision for a world still far beyond our reach. It is no easier now than it was then, and the very success, however tentative, of some of what I've been describing may make it more difficult to assert its alterity, its difference from what we once set out to overturn. For myself I can only hope, as always, to begin again or, failing that, to encourage others into a new beginning. A wise poet from the time in question—though one who spoke out memorably "against wisdom as such"—wrote that "what does not change / is the will to change." It's not for me to decide whether what Charles Olson asserted then still holds at present, but I can only act and urge you to act as if it does.

Ethnopoetics & (Human) Poetics

Keynote for "Symposium of the Whole: Toward a Human Poetics," a conference in March 1983 at the Center for the Humanities, University of Southern California, Los Angeles

A few words, first, as one of the makers of the plot for the present gathering.

The underlying theme is what we've elsewhere called *ethnopoetics* and the question of its possible expansions, but we didn't (deliberately didn't) use the term in the conference announcement except in the title of my own presentation. This is, therefore, not (strictly speaking) a conference on ethnopoetics as discussed on other occasions by many of those gathered here.

Nor is it limited to "non-Western" traditions.

This is not from any lack of devotion to ethnopoetics on the part of the organizers—the present one in particular—but an ethnopoetics conference or more specifically a non-Western conference would have had to focus on other energies than we could presently assemble and wouldn't be true (without a great deal of stretch) to a "symposium of the *whole*," which is meant to be what it literally says. Not that we're that symposium of THE WHOLE either, but we're here to talk about what such a symposium, such a configuration of energies, might possibly mean.

We have therefore decided to let it spill over, while starting (from my own perch) with a sense of ethnopoetics as a necessary part of whatever new poetics we may now hope to develop . . . and a necessary part of a search not for "the primitive" (as Stanley Diamond would have it) but for a primary poetics, an idea of poetry based on the interplay and clash of cultures that may now be a part—for better or worse—of our human possibility.

I would like to begin my own contribution with the preface to the book *Symposium of the Whole: A Range of Discourse toward an Ethnopoetics*, which Diane Rothenberg and I assembled and which is published by the University of California Press, and to add to that, in particular, my sense of some still unresolved questions, some new proposals, and some (to my mind) necessary cautions as we begin the present work.

[Here follows the first section of the Pre-Face to *Symposium of the Whole* (above, page 18), beginning "When the industrial West began to discover—and plunder—'new' and 'old' worlds beyond its boundaries, an extraordinary countermovement came into being in the West itself," and ending with the sentence, "The clincher, in fact, is the transformation, beyond that, of our consciousness of the human in all times and places."]

That ends the opening section of the pre-face and in reading through it, it occurred to me, first of all, that there were already many different kinds of ethnopoetics at work among us. I will list some of these without in any sense pretending to exhaust the approaches and with the certainty that any ethnopoetics, my own included, would necessarily involve some fusion among them. I'm not trying to be precise here—rather to give some idea of how we've sometimes gone at it.

Nathaniel Tarn has spoken of ethnopoetics as "the intersection of poetry and anthropology in our time." Conceivably any culturally based approach to poetry or any poet's poaching on the anthropological territory would make it under this "definition."

A second approach centers on the idea of the "primitive" or of a primitive/civilized dichotomy. Diamond in anthropology, Snyder in poetry as two primary examples—with a strong emphasis in Snyder's work on poetry's roots in the Paleolithic and its projection of ecological and communal/tribal alternatives.

Closely related to the "primitive" is the approach that focuses on the idea of oral poetry—though the dominance of the oral clearly continues in cultures that could by no stretch of the imagination be thought of as technologically "primitive." The approach through "performance" over a wide range of cultures might almost be synonymous with that through the oral, while spilling over as well into cultures with a fixed system of writing.

The equating of ethnopoetics with non-Western or with third-world cultures is common enough—and, again, the divergence from a purely oral circumstance should be apparent.

Ethnic poetry, in an American context, sometimes dovetails with ethnopoetics, sometimes not. I sense/acknowledge the relation, though I suspect it can lead to as much confusion as clarity.

Yet another approach identifies certain traditional forms of poetry and performance with certain "experimental" moves in our own time. Richard Schechner was explicit about this in an earlier ethnopoetics conference, including the "avant-garde" in the "category" of traditional ritual theater viewed as "transformational"; and I suppose my own use of analogues to experimental work in *Technicians of the Sacred* and *Shaking the Pumpkin* is an implicit gesture in this direction. As is the attempt—whether by a Simon Ortiz or a Gary Snyder (or by any of us, in short)—to incorporate some aspect of the ethnopoetic into our own work.

And, finally, there's a more technical, usually translative, approach practiced by anthropologists like Dell Hymes, Dennis Tedlock, and Allan Burns—another very useful approach that would reveal or present whole poetic systems from within particular cultures.

What I see all these approaches having in common is, negatively, a rejection of the supremacy of Western ideas of high art (not by any means the art itself) and, positively, an intention to encompass all those art forms and gestures excluded by that Western and European hierarchy. In that sense, too, ethnopoetics can be seen as a strategy—one of many—aimed against closure and the "authoritative" version—allowing the individual voice to emerge and to free itself (in Richard Huelsenbeck's old Dada prophecy) "from the tutelage of the advocates of power."

All such ethnopoetics tie in also—at least for the poets involved—with an idea that has been strong among us at least since the time of the romantics: a sense of poetry engaged with the exploration of beginnings: a new start toward an art in which (in Duncan's words or my own) "everything was possible." Eliade used much the same words to describe the art of the traditional shaman, and William Carlos Williams, speaking in the name of a "new localism" (ethnopoetics is in a certain sense an interweaving of such localisms), identified the new poetry as "a movement, first and last to clear the GROUND . . . a strong impulse to begin at the beginning." And the beginning, he made clear, involved a rediscovery/recovery, a reconsideration of origins, in the past and as developed in the present.

I find something like this wherever ethnopoetics has become a part of our present concerns rather than a study of the remote and exotic to which we can have no vital relation. This seems to me equally true in the work of our predecessors, poets and thinkers like those Diane Rothenberg and I chose to present in *Symposium of the Whole:*

VICO, who gave us an ethnopoetics of the age of the gods and of the gentile nations;

HERDER, who gave us an ethnopoetics of the nature-people (as the German language has it);

BLAKE, who gave us an ethnopoetics of Albion and of our antediluvian energies (a gnostic ethnopoetics);

MARX AND ENGELS, who gave us an ethnopoetics of the communal;

THOREAU, who gave us an ethnopoetics of wilderness;

RIMBAUD, who gave us an ethnopoetics of the seer and of the internal "nigger";

FENOLLOSA, who gave us an ethnopoetics of the ideogram as "a splendid flash of concrete poetry";

POUND, who gave us an ethnopoetics of the tale of the tribe and as the new vortex;

TZARA, who gave us a DADA ethnopoetics;

CÉSAIRE, who gave us an ethnopoetics as negritude;

LORCA, who gave us an ethnopoetics as duende and black sounds and the blood culture of Manuel Torre;

GRAVES, who gave us an ethnopoetics of the goddess and the muse;

ELIADE, who gave us an ethnopoetics of a universal shamanism;

OLSON, who gave us an ethnopoetics of myth and history, and a projective ethnopoetics of voice;

SNYDER, who gave us ethnopoetics as a new ecology/a buddhist ethnopoetics;

DUNCAN, who gave us title to an ethnopoetics of the whole.

౿

From the time of the First International Symposium on Ethnopoetics (1975 at the Center for Twentieth-Century Studies in Milwaukee) it became clear—at least to me—that our ethnopoetics could no longer be easily contained within set boundaries—that it had already expanded beyond the "primitive," the "archaic," the "non-Western," even the "oral" (that great cornerstone of a new poetics we had taken such efforts to give its rightful place). My own work—I was then assembling *A Big Jewish Book*—was also struggling with such boundaries, as limiting as all boundaries are, however strong the need to bring forward that which has been too long suppressed. And from the time when I had done *Technicians of the Sacred* as a "range of poetries from Africa, America, Asia, and Oceania," I was concerned, say, by the absence of the Western, the European, from that configuration. As I had presented it there, the Western/non-Western dichotomy seemed too sharp, excluding as it did a whole range of (largely) subterranean traditions still active into the present and emerging often in those contemporary poetries to which I felt the closest. What was wanted, I came to feel, was an expansion of the discourse to include the European and Western—despite the fears I had (and still have) about the distortions and political uses of mythology and folklore in the context of nineteenth- and twentieth-century European nationalism. This "European project," so to speak, is a work I've now set for myself in undertaking a revised edition of *Technicians of the Sacred*—along with attempts to make clear a number of points about the old poetries (the *ur*-poetries) that seem to need more insistence than I've yet been able to give them.

These ur-poetries, on their Western side, would link the present to what Snyder calls the Great Subculture and George Quasha "the Other Tradition," suggesting a link "from what (Frances) Yates terms 'The Rosicrucian Enlightenment,' through Blake, Goethe, and Nerval, on to Alfred Jarry, Erik Satie, certain Dadaists and Surrealists, unclassifiable poets like René Daumal and Harry Crosby, and into the present." (Something like that, since the lines are complicated and would vary greatly from poet to poet. Snyder, e.g., on its Western/European side: "a powerful undercurrent in all higher civilizations . . . which runs . . . without break from Paleo-Siberian Shamanism and Magdalenian cave-painting; through megaliths and Mysteries, astronomers, ritualists, alchemists and Albigensians, gnostics and Vagantes, right down to Golden Gate Park.") As fundamental poetic process—still alive among us—the ways presented (not as systems but ways!) would help heal the split between self and other: to locate in the West (as Sylvia Wynter pointed out in the earlier Milwaukee conference) "alternate modes of cognition ideologically suppressed in ourselves, yet still a living force amidst large majorities of the third-world peoples."

The call I felt at that Milwaukee symposium was to integrate ethnopoetics into a fuller human/(pan)human poetics. The term *human poet-ics* was David Antin's, and as someone asked me the other day, what po-etry isn't "human"? As Antin used it, anyway, the discussion ran (in part) like this:

> Among (the) grab-bag of human language activities are a number of more or less well-defined universal discourse genres, whose ex-pectation structures are the source of all poetic activity. If there is any place that we should look for an ETHNOPOETICS it is here, among these universal genres, where all linguistic invention begins. For by an ETHNOPOETICS I mean Human Poetics. I suppose *ethnos* = people, and therefore ETHNOPOETICS = People's Po-etics or the poetics of natural language. [And again:] What I was afraid of in the term ETHNOPOETICS was the historical legacy of the term *ethnos*, a kind of anthropological commitment to ex-oticism, to whatever is remote from us and somehow different— tribal if we are not tribal, religious if we are secular, dark if we are light, etc. Here *ethnos* = other, so not Human Poetics but the Poet-ics of the Other.

I take this as an attempt to understand poetry over the fullest human range, including (for Antin centrally) the neglected everyday use of lan-guage to discover and transform. A search for "universal genres" and for continuities between the language of poetry and all human language, con-tinuities that can, at the same time, honor distinctions and differences/ potentials as a way of undercutting that most arrogant assertion of a dif-ference *in kind* between one's self and any less privileged other.

The project, so stated, probably sounds more magnanimous than it really is—because it's clearly, like all such projects, involved above all with our own benefit, our own enhanced understanding or participation. The "we" in this case refers, of course, not merely to Westerners or Euro-peans but to all contemporaries, wherever situated, who live with a sense of a larger world than that of their own locality and culture. For those the possibilities of learning and acting can proliferate—unavoidably, I would think, as in the very nature of the lives we live. The question, then, isn't whether we should formulate an approach to the "other" (and therefore to ourselves) or enlarge our discourse and practice by so doing—but whether we do it well or badly.

That question of the "well" or "badly" is crucial and thorny—probably the central issue for any such meeting as the present one. It is late in the game by now, and it seems to me (given whatever experience I've had with it) that we're still overwhelmed by preconceptions as we enter on this work. I have tried, myself, to argue against certain of these preconceptions that I find questionable or disproven by the actual investigation. And again and again I find that part of my work the hardest to get across. A few explicit warnings, therefore:

— that we must, above all, avoid too-obvious assumptions about the poetics/ethnopoetics of technologically simpler cultures—which led me to begin *Technicians* with an emphasis on the complexity of tribal/ oral language and (ritual) arts
— that we must question—by investigation—the idea that traditional art is collective rather than individual, when it is reflective in fact, as Paul Radin wrote, of "an individualism run riot";
— that we must not assume that it is our culture alone (or those cultures most like our own) that has introduced reflexivity/self-reflection into the creative process, when scholars like Victor Turner have taken such pains to demonstrate the reflexive nature of ritual and art throughout the full range of human cultures;
— that we can no longer assume that the poetry and ritual of traditional cultures aim at stasis rather than change—transformation, that is, not only in a mystical sense but in a social sense as well. (In brief, human nature/culture, where and whenever, is *neophiliac* in the ethological sense, or in Olson's paraphrasing of Heraclitus: "What does not change / is the will to change.")

And we must be careful not to assume:

— that orality totally defines "them" or that writing totally defines "us" (an expanded ethnopoetics would include an ethnopoetics of writing/ of the book);

nor should we overlook:

— that people have thought long and hard, everywhere, about language and performance;
— that a poetics (a generalized "idea of poetry") has arisen again and again in the total human story, no more nor less "universal" than the

Athenian poetics that gave a start to one such line of thought in the
West;

— that even this one line of thought is threatened;

— that poets in our world remain a threatened culture;

— that the poeticide envisioned by a Rimbaud or an Apollinaire is a real
and present danger;

— that the weapon of annihilation is indifference—a loss of spirit—but
also repression and orthodoxy, wherever found;

— that what threatens the other threatens us as well . . . again, as Sylvia Wynter had had it in the 1975 symposium: "There can be no
concept of a liberal mission to save 'primitive poetics' for 'primitive'
peoples. The salvaging of vast areas of our being is dialectically related to the destruction of those conditions which block the free development of the human potentialities of the majority peoples of the
(third) world."

And we must remember, to our own good:

— that a poetry of the mind (spirit) / a visionary poetry is not only to be
found apart from us; that while it permeates many old cultures, it has,
since the nineteenth century at least become a dominant mode among
our own poets (and in some sense has probably always been that, as a
kind of crypto [hidden] vision). And knowing that, we have the advantage of discovering among the traditional cultures how such modes
have permeated whole populations and how they've been carried forward over millennia.

By doing this we can also discover forms we've barely dreamed of, or
we can ignore them to our own loss and hardly (as far as I can see) to *their*
advantage. One result of a continuing ethnopoetics will be that our own
poetry will cease to be "modern" (as Tzara, a major forerunner in the work
of ethnopoetics, had long ago predicted) and will emerge, with the dissolution of modernism, as what it was all along: "a state of mind (esprit),"
not an interest in a "new technique" but "in the spirit."

If we can do all of this, while maintaining/fostering a respect both
for distant traditions and cultures (with their own localisms and particularities) and for the displaced and estranged and pervasive aspects of our
own, we will have served both the poetic and the human.

A GALLERY OF POETS

I Come into the New World

Voices are dumb until
I speak for them.
Knowing the sound
I find myself between
two fires. One
is dark green, one
the color of my mind
asleep. I come into
the new world
where the thought of death
no longer rankles.
It will be good to be
a stranger always
to know the terms by which
we visit back & forth
& sideways.
In the morning I will wear
a suit with shoulders
big as boards. My clothes are
silver plastic.
When I step into the car
it starts to fly.
I play games with
children
where I make

a nose
into an ear.
Like a clock my heart
moves closer
to the burning babe
& stays there.
I will now count
the century
by ones & twos.
This morning
all the voices in my dream
spoke with one voice.
I feel privileged to be here
among you.
From now on
we will live
on borrowed time.

January 1, 2000

A Range of Commentaries

From *Poems for the Millennium* and *Revolution of the Word*

William Blake's Visionary Forms Dramatic

And they conversed together in Visionary forms dramatic which bright /
Redounded from their Tongues in thunderous majesty, in Visions / In
new Expanses, creating exemplars of Memory and of Intellect / Creating
Space, Creating Time according to the wonders Divine / Of Human
Imagination . . . / & every Word & Every Character / Was Human.
—W. B., from *Jerusalem*, 1804

"Poetry Fetter'd, Fetters the Human Race!" wrote Blake (1801), in whom
we find, then, a first act of mental liberation & a recall to the oldest function of poetry & of the poet as inspired "prophet"; later as a shamanistic
"seer" (Rimbaud) & "technician of the sacred." And it's Blake who also
turns transmitted Wisdom on its head, working out a poetics of oppositions, a new dialectic in which desire [= "energy"] can have a central place
alongside "reason." At the same time it's just that thrust into embodiment that literally changes the face & voice of poetry—gets to the heart
of the poem as structure/form, thus setting out the paradigm for much
of what's to follow. Here Blake's line swings wide & opens, leaves the
"bondage of rhyming" & "monotonous cadence" behind, & demands new
forms of shape & color to present the visible poem by "a method of print-

While *Poems for the Millennium* was a collaborative work with Pierre Joris throughout, the
commentaries presented here have been chosen from those for which I was primarily responsible.

ing which combines the painter and poet." Representing Blake's intended total work—as painter, poet, printer—such "visionary forms dramatic" have been suppressed too often in favor of cold type & print.

Friedrich Hölderlin's Palimpsests

I believe in the forthcoming revolution of attitudes and conceptions which will make everything that has gone before turn red with shame.

—F. H., 1807

A veil of madness lies over the vision . . . as it will with others. But its first results, before its isolation overtakes him, is to allow silences—shown as blank spaces—an entry to the poem, by which the poem-as-fragment becomes a field of energies, a kind of palimpsest or map, the process of his thinking/searching rendered on the page. It is something of this sort—a form of action writing that translator Richard Sieburth describes as "the pace at which verbal relations come to be perceived"—that Hölderlin spoke of as the "rhythm of representation," to be rendered through a "configuration of gaps and breaches." Within that configuration—at its extreme in the later notebooks—the levels of language swing from distortions of Greek-based syntax & high-flown biblical intonations to the gutsier voice of his Swabian dialect. And with it all, he sees himself in a space in which the history of poetry & thought, of mythology & religion, is reconsidered from its most archaic roots, as what Giambattista Vico, writing some eighty years before him, called "the language of the gods." While there is also a legacy of completed works (the early poems, his play *Empedocles,* his novel *Hyperion*), the palimpsestic versions of certain of the poems, like many of Hölderlin's "hymns & fragments," are derived from notebook sketches, written & overwritten during his years of confinement. Their recovery a hundred years later thrust Hölderlin's romanticism into the twentieth century—as a poet, in effect, of the new movements & poetries emerging then.

Walt Whitman's New Line & Lineage

*I sometimes think the Leaves is only a language experiment—that is,
an attempt to give the spirit, the body, the man, new potentialities of
speech . . .*

—(W. W.)

Or again, in a Chomskyan frame: *"As humanity is one under its amaz-
ing diversities, language is one under its."*

Like Blake & Christopher Smart before him, Whitman cast aside the re-
strictions of the old line, to set the standard for the century to come, both
in America & outside it—a natural measure, he shows us, "like the invisible influence [of the sea] in my composition . . . perpetually, grandly,
rolling in upon [the shore], with slow-measured sweep, with rustle and
hiss and foam, and many a thump as of low bass drums." His task beyond
that was to use the new means to revive the vatic function, to employ
the total language & range of human identities—body *and* soul, evil *and*
good—toward a poetry that would be actualized only after his own time,
by "poets [yet] to come." In doing this his aim was to bring "self" and
"world"—but also self & selves—into a new alignment—the singular
pronoun of his poetry—its "I"—used with a new freedom, to summon
up a range of real & fictive selves: "All identities that have existed or may
exist on this globe, or any globe." And along with that, a radical opening
of the poet's vocabulary to "all words that exist in use," for "All words are
spiritual—nothing is more spiritual than words" *(An American Primer).*
The political aspect of the "democratic vistas" he thus opened in both poetry & life was also central to his vision—as it still may be to ours.

   In line with such ambitions, here and elsewhere, Whitman invested
the Poet with a consciousness of Earth & of a mind-&-body continuum
that points back to old shamanic functions & forward to the degradation, as we have come to know it, of Earth & of its sentient beings. It is
in this sense both a culmination of nineteenth-century Nature poetry &
a premonition of a later view—in Gary Snyder's words—of "poetry as an
ecological survival technique" & the "shaman-poet" as the one "whose
mind reaches easily out into all manners of shapes and other lives, and
gives song to dreams." But even here the range & depth of Whitman's
recoveries—political, social, sexual, as well as poetic—are far from ex-

hausted. The result, as Japanese poet Ooka Makoto had it for his own post–World War II generation: "To bring totality back into poetry."

Gerard Manley Hopkins's Inscapes

Poetry is in fact speech only employed to carry the inscape of speech for the inscape's sake—and therefore the inscape must be dwelt on.
—G. M. H., c. 1873–74

Like the work of others during & before his time—Blake, Hölderlin, Dickinson, Lautréamont—Hopkins's work was virtually unpublished or uncirculated during his lifetime. No matter. His conversion to Catholicism & life as a Jesuit priest concealed within it a second conversion—as a seeker for ways to foster a new & "inner" vision in the world at large, believing as he wrote "that the poetical language of an age shd. be the current language heightened, to any degree heightened and unlike itself, but not (I mean normally; passing freaks and graces are another thing) an obsolete one" (1879). The visionary work proceeded through startling effects of word & sound: heightened alliterations, consonances, dissonances, words drawn from dialect or newly coined, new names for new moves: chiming, vowelling, oftening, over-and-overing, aftering; & so on. And with that came a systematic push to a new measure, a "sprung rhythm . . . less to be read than heard" & that would—for all the strangeness ("queerness") it might seem to have—be "nearest to the rhythm of prose, that is the native and natural language of speech, the least forced, the most rhetorical and emphatic of all possible rhythms" (1877). In the terminology he made for it, "sprung rhythm" is the praxis of an "instress," & instress is the force that brings & binds to language that defining pattern of a thing or person, their deep identity, that he called "inscape." In this light he writes, "poetry is speech which afters and oftens its inscape, speech couched in a repeating figure, and verse is spoken sound having a repeated figure." As Cézanne with *land*scape, the simple intention of Hopkins's *in*scape led to a work of complex surface—at which he persisted—& to a radical, beautifully tangled poetics.

Gertrude Stein's Cubism

This woman who speaks without breath has opened the ring for me.
                                                            —J. R., 1968

Her own appraisal of her work ("the most serious thinking about the nature of literature in the 20th century has been done by a woman") seems reasonable enough compared to the intervening neglect of that work, but particularly the poetry, in established literary circles. She came early to a root investigation of language and form ("going systematically to work smashing every connotation that words ever had, in order to get them back clean"—William Carlos Williams) and to a poetry that brought "cubism" into language (here as an altered concept of time, the "continuous present") & otherwise set the stage for much that was to follow. Her materials were simple enough to be easily misunderstood, & her declared intention was to "work in the excitedness of pure being . . . to get back that intensity into the language." She could produce work that was literally abstract, the end of a process of experiment by subtraction, or, as she would write later when looking back at her early *Tender Buttons:* "It was my first conscious struggle with the problem of correlating sight, sound and sense, and eliminating rhythm—now I am trying grammar and eliminating sight and sound." And it was, at the same time, a struggle to reorder thought & to explore what her teacher William James called "other forms of consciousness"—that process recognized by Mabel Dodge, who wrote in the special issue of Stieglitz's *Camera Work* (1913): "Nearly every thinking person nowadays is in revolt against something, because the craving of the individual is for further consciousness and because consciousness is expanding and is bursting through the moulds that have held it up to now. And so let every man whose private truth is too great for his existing conditions pause before he turn away from Picasso's painting or from Gertrude Stein's writing, for their case is his case."

Rainer Maria Rilke's In-Seeing

Work of the eyes is done, now / go and do heart-work / on all the images
imprisoned within you; for you / overpowered them: but even now you
don't know them. / Learn, inner man, to look on your inner woman, / the
one attained from a thousand / natures, the merely attained but / not yet
beloved form.

> —R. M. R., from "Wendung" [Turning-Point], 1912,
> translated by Stephen Mitchell

The push in his work was toward "the task of transformation"—of the
poet as "transformer of the earth"—or, as in "Wendung," toward a "heart-
work," liberating "all the images imprisoned within you," that he also
called "in-seeing." If that made him—as the story goes—the last &
greatest symbolist poet, it connects him also to the most far-reaching ambitions of radical modernists like Kandinsky & other German expression-
ists from whom he otherwise lived in separation. Like theirs, his work
exists at the extremes (of terror, exaltation) & becomes "that unexampled
act of violence . . . [that] sought among visible things equivalents for the
vision within." As he went on with it, it brought him to a struggle with &
within language as such; or, as he described it further, "One often finds
oneself at variance with the external behavior of a language and intent
on its innermost life, or on an innermost language, without terminations,
if possible—a language of word-kernels, a language that's not gathered,
up above, on stalks, but grasped in the speech-seed." Following a breakthrough into what he called *Ding-Gedichte* (thing-poems; object-poems)
in the period before, this view carried him by 1912 into the beginning of
The Duino Elegies, one of the benchmarks—at every level—of twentieth-
century poetic (= spiritual) practice. Here the epitome of "in-seeing" is
centered in the "Angel"—not "the Angel of the Christian heaven" but
more like "the angelic figures of Islam"—"in whom the transformation
of the visible into the invisible we are performing already appears complete . . . therefore 'terrible' to us, because we, its lovers and transformers,
still depend on the visible." The experience, then, is overwhelming, comparable in its intensity ("an indescribable storm, a mental and spiritual
hurricane") to Lorca's vision of the "duende," or, again in Rilke's words:
"Everywhere appearance and vision came, as it were, together in the object, in every one of them a whole inner world was exhibited, as though
an angel, in whom space was included, were blind and looking into him-

self. This world, regarded no longer from the human point of view, but as it is within the angel, is perhaps my real task, one, at any rate, in which all my previous attempts would converge." It is the key, too, to the reading of the work—at which point everything stands in the open.

Marcel Duchamp's Ready-Mades

A major force in the reinvestigation of artistic and poetic categories, Duchamp "opened the era of poetic experience in which chance and the concrete thing constitute a poetry that you can pick up in your hand or repulse with a kick" (thus: Georges Hugnet). As a progenitor of what would later be known as chance composition, found-poetry & -art (*vide* his "ready-mades," etc.), intermedia, and conceptual art ("to put painting once again at the service of mind"), his work early showed a strong verbal side. Wordplay & punning appear both in his titles & in writings under the name Rrose Sélavy *(eros c'est la vie)*. Although he did give up painting after 1920 (& became a chess & proto-Zen master, as the legend goes), he remained an artist & poet, contributed important service to Surrealism, & began after 1940 to have a new influence on many areas of creativity throughout the world. His two great erotic works, the early "Large Glass" (The Bride Stripped Bare by Her Bachelors Even) & the posthumously shown *étant données,* are bridged by the verbal materials & notes that he began to write in 1912. Duchamp first came to N.Y.C. in 1915, two years after his "Nude Descending a Staircase" rocked the Armory Show, where he was the principal proponent of an emerging New York Dada. But it was with his "ready-mades," principally, that he disrupted the long-standing separation between art & other forms, however debased, of human creativity.

Mina Loy's Futurism

Energized by meetings with Marinetti & other Futurist poets, her work started to appear circa 1913, & by 1918 Pound (probably unaware that she was an Englishwoman) reviewed her & Marianne Moore as "a distinctively national product . . . something which could not have come out of any other country" & which, he said, typified the process he called *logopoeia* or "poetry that is akin to nothing but language, which is a dance of the intelligence among words and ideas and modification of ideas and characters." His further description of it, "the utterance of clever people in despair, or hovering upon the brink of the precipice," now seems more true of Loy than Moore; & what he fails to observe on Loy's side is that her work by 1918 had taken on a largeness of theme & an energy of sound & image that few in her generation could match. By then, too, or soon thereafter, she had come through her Futurist time & was into a private mythology, *Anglo-Mongrels & the Rose,* comparable to, & probably not chronologically behind, Pound's early *Cantos* & Eliot's *Waste Land.* But the parts ended up scattered like the limbs of Osiris, & by the time a few fragments turned up under other titles in Jargon's expanded reprint of her selected poems, *Lunar Baedeker* (1958), none of the three poets introducing the book (William Carlos Williams, Kenneth Rexroth, & Denise Levertov) could recall the larger work from which they came. A quarter of a century later, the efforts of editor Roger L. Conover in *A Last Lunar Baedeker* helped to piece together (at least in part) one of the lost master-poems of the twentieth century—to which the reader's attention is hereby called.

Ezra Pound's Vortices

Our only measure of truth is . . . our own perception of truth. The undeniable tradition of metamorphosis teaches us that things do not remain always the same. They become other things by swift and unanalysable process. It was only when men began to mistrust the myths and tell nasty lies about the Gods for a moral purpose that these matters became hopelessly confused.

—E. P., *Pavannes and Divagations,* 1918

On the way from conventional to modern modes, his breakthrough into "imagism(e)" came in 1912, cut almost out of whole cloth & still restrained by classicist notions of *good* writing, but it produced the influential three dicta: "1. Direct treatment of the 'thing' whether subjective or objective; 2. To use absolutely no word that does not contribute to the presentation; 3. As regarding rhythm, to compose in the sequence of the musical phrase, not in the sequence of the metronome." By 1914 the association with painter/writer Wyndham Lewis (two issues of *Blast,* etc.) & a strong whiff of Cubism & Futurism brought the earlier definition of "image" ("that which presents an intellectual and emotional complex in an instant of time") into the high energy of vorticist theory & the onset soon thereafter of the *Cantos.* The poem appeared in history, in time;

the image became a "moving image"; both image & cubist collage were subsumed (along with translation & tradition = "make it new") under the proposition of mind as a vortex, where "all times are contemporaneous," & the poem as a "knot of patterned energies" (H. Kenner) & a process of making it "cohere." [See above, page 8.] As entry to the work, then, Canto One (first version: 1917) recasts the Odyssey's underworld section (Ulysses' meeting with the dead) in the alliterative language of Anglo-Saxon verse, while adding to the voices of Homer's ghosts those of Andreus Divus, a Renaissance translator of Homer into Latin, & of the anonymous Greek authors of the hymns to Aphrodite. In doing which, Pound lays out Vortex upon Vortex—not least his own—thus putting modernist collage at the service of his search for origins.

William Carlos Williams's New Measure

Only the imagination / is real!
       —W. C. W., 1955

Of the first generation of dominant American moderns, he was the most open to the full range of new forms & possibilities, to the actual scope of what had to be done. Along with his Ezra Pound association—going back to his student days at the University of Pennsylvania—he engaged directly during World War I with poets & artists around the Others group & the N.Y. Dadaists & wrote of that time: "There had been a break somewhere: we were streaming through, each thinking his own thoughts, driving his own designs toward his self's objectives. Whether the Armory Show in painting did it or whether that also was no more than a facet—the poetic line, the way the image was to lie on the page, was our immediate concern. For myself all that implied in the materials, respecting the place I knew best, was finding a local assertion—to my everlasting relief." With poets over the next two decades—but most significantly with the "Objectivists" group (Zukofsky, Reznikoff, Oppen, Rakosi, et al.)—his ongoing concerns were with the relation of poetry to the given state of the language & to the details & particulars of experience: the materials de facto through which the imagination could act. In the 1950s the pattern of his sympathies—his exploration in particular of a "new measure" & the "poem as a field of action," along with the need to transform the idea of tradition & the social ground of poetry—brought his work to the center of a number of poetic "movements": projectivists, Beats, and so forth. An overview of his early breakthroughs would focus on the "improvisations" & nonsequential arrangements of *Spring & All*, with its interplay of prose & verse, leading in effect to the concept & structure of *Paterson*, the complex long poem whose appearance, initiated in a preliminary sketch of the mid-1920s, was being eagerly awaited by the end of World War II.

Federico García Lorca's Duende

The true struggle is with the Duende.
                    —F. G. L., 1930

One of the century's poet-martyrs, he was born in Granada & executed there by fascist gunmen in the early days of the Spanish Civil War: hardly political himself but fusing old & new—gypsy "deep song" & modern *deeper* image—in a poetry that brought Surrealist moves (or variants thereon) into a quasi-populist framework. In both early & later works he used traditional forms (both "high" & "low") in ways that carried forward a poetics of collage & synchronicity, while retaining (William Carlos Williams wrote of him) "the singing quality of Spanish poetry and at the same time the touch of that monotony which is in all primitive song—so well modernized here." An important playwright & popular figure, Lorca moved freely throughout Spain, visited Latin America on at least two occasions, & spent a year in New York City (1931), from which time *A Poet in New York* came, to place him squarely at the center of a radical, experimental poetics. At its base, however, was a traditional demonic "earth-force" (drawn from gypsy/flamenco singer-heroes) that Lorca called *duende*—opening like Antonin Artaud's theater-of-cruelty to ideas of possession, of struggle, of those "black sounds" that make of art "a power, not a construct." It was this—more than his "style" as such—that linked him to poets of the 1950s & beyond—in North America specifically to what Paul Blackburn later called "an American duende." But poems like the early (but posthumously published) *Suites*[1]—structured as what Robin Blaser & Jack Spicer came to designate as "serial poetry"—show a characteristic coolness & sometimes quirkiness, a playfulness of

1. Translated into English by J. R. and published in 2001 by Green Integer Books in Los Angeles.

mind & music, that place him among the most graceful & elegant of twentieth-century poets.

Laura Riding's Breaking of the Spell

I have written that which I believe breaks the spell of poetry.
—L. R., 1970

If poetry is a questioning of poetry—as one modern/"post"modern proposition might have it—Riding can well be looked at as a central player toward that end. Her "renunciation of poetry" came soon after publication of her *Collected Poems* (1938), when she found poetic serious-ness "irremediably compromised . . . by its subjecting linguistic integri-ties to aesthetic requirements, as if there were no resultant linguistic loss." The break in her case appeared to be absolute. Or, as she wrote in retro-spect (1971): "When . . . after pressing the linguistic possibilities of po-etic utterance to further and further limits, I comprehended that poetry had no provision in it for ultimate practical attainment of that rightness of word that is truth . . . I *stopped*." Yet poetry, which had been the "center" of all her other writing (criticism, stories, a novel, etc.), remained the point of contention & departure. Her later work—most notably *The Tell-ing* (1973)—concentrated her attention on language, "its intrinsic provi-sions," & on what might be achieved "in 'trueness of word,' beyond the qualified truth-potential of poetry, or any other literarily verbal style." An independent writer of & about poetry until 1938, she was both ex-perimental in her poetry & influential (in her critical & antimodernist poetics) on directions like those of the American "new criticism" of the 1940s, with its deterrent effect on the radical modernism that came be-fore it.

Riding's renunciation of poetry echoes curiously with Duchamp's well-known abandonment of painting—with the proviso that both are understood as meaningful in a context defined by essential notions of poetry & art. Such moves—to be a poet, say, *in spite of poetry*—relate to later conceptual approaches to art making or to the decision by a poet like David Antin to turn to "talk" and "discourse" as a form of poetry cut loose from "the poetic." While Riding left no room for her later work to be subsumed as poetry, her defense of her earlier writings remained equally strong.

Edmond Jabès's Return to the Book

*I talked to you about the difficulty of being Jewish, which is the same as the
difficulty of writing. For Judaism and writing are but the same waiting,
the same hope, the same wearing out.*

—E. J., 1963

It is in this sense, too, that Jabès's concern with the word *Jew* ("an obsession for me . . . like the word 'God'") connects to Marina Tsvetayeva's
well-known dictum cited elsewhere in these pages: *In this most Christian
of worlds / all poets are Jews.*

Descended from generations of Cairo Jews, Jabès's meditations on
Jews and God, the Book and Exile/Desert/Wilderness (among his central themes) came with the 1956 banishment of Jews from Egypt: a
forced immersion in his Jewishness, to learn diaspora in his own flesh.
It took him from the lyrical surrealism of his early poems to a newly recovered form of dialogic writing, in which the voices of imagined rabbis comment (in the manner of the Talmud or more mystical Zohar) on
the world in aftermath of holocaust or with the sense of holocaust as constant (even where unspoken) presence. The grand scheme of that work
called for a seven-volume *Book of Questions* & a three-volume *Book of
Resemblances*—twenty related books in the final counting—in which the
underlying text, the story of two lovers, Yukel & Sarah, victims of geno-
cide & (subsequent) madness, is told in fits & starts or, like the holocaust itself, is never fully spoken, never *there*. It is this "absent, nonexistent
Book . . . [this] pre-text"—holocaust or absent God—"that engenders
the rabbinical commentaries, the reflections that oscillate between poetry and aphorism, the open, 'exploded,' nonlinear form of Jabès's work"
(R. Waldrop).

In the course of telling & concealing, then, Jabès not only links up
with ancient traditions of the Book, but with Mallarmé's idea of *Livre* as
a worldbook or María Sabina's more mystical (shamanistic) Book of Language (below, page 180) & Olson's *mappemunde*, whether or not the latter two were known to him.

John Cage's Silence & Nothing

*Art's obscured the difference between / art and life. Now let life obscure /
the difference between life and art.*

—J. C., 1965

His well-known definition of poetry—"I have nothing to say and I am
saying it, and that is poetry"—belies his ability to bring meaning *fully*
into the body of the work. It is a statement, for all of that, of what he
helped to translate from early modernism & to give an immediately useful form in his own time. With his base solidly in music, he sought an *in-
terpenetration* with the world at large, to blur thereby the boundaries between art & life (A. Kaprow). But he also made it clear from early in his
work, that the strongly verbal/conceptual edge of his lectures and appropriated "songs" came not from an urge to teach or even "to surprise
people" but from "a need for poetry." As a poet his work paralleled & in
some sense followed that of Jackson Mac Low, whom he had earlier introduced to the use in music and art of systematic chance operations as a
form of buddhist/anarchist *noninterference* and "a means . . . of silencing
the ego so that the rest of the world has a chance to enter into the ego's
own experience." (In this context his other well-known "epiphany" concerning silence: "There is no such thing as an empty space or an empty
time. There is always something to see, something to hear. In fact, try as
we may to make silence, we cannot. . . . Until I die there will be sounds.
And they will continue following my death. One need not fear about the
future of music.")

But it was from the 1960s on that he emerged fully as a poet—a maker
& performer of verbal texts in some sense as formalized as music, whose
surfaces ranged from sound-based, lettristic abstractions to information-
ally loaded works of utmost, even *didactic* clarity. Among these were texts
derived by fixed but often randomized procedures from the works of
other authors and, as a personally invented or developed form, the mesos-
tic, resembling the biblical acrostic, in which the vertically spelled message (& pivot of the poem) is set along the poem's central axis. Or again,
in response to Daniel Charles's question, "Why do you insist on that word
poetry?": [answer] *There is poetry when we realize that we possess nothing*
(J. C., 1968).

Pablo Picasso:
A Pre-Face

I abandon sculpture engraving and painting to dedicate myself entirely to song.

—Picasso to Jaime Sabartés, April 1936

When we were compiling *Poems for the Millennium,* we sensed that Picasso, if he wasn't *fully* a poet, was incredibly close to the neighboring poets of his time, and when he brought language into his cubist works, the words collaged from newspapers were there as something really to be read. What only appeared to us later was the body of work that emerged from 1935 on and that showed him to have been a poet *in the fullest sense* and possibly, as Michel Leiris points out, "an insatiable player with words . . . [who, like] James Joyce . . . in his *Finnegans Wake,* . . . displayed an equal capacity to promote language as a real thing (one might say) . . . and to use it with as much dazzling liberty."

It was in early 1935, then, that Picasso (then fifty-four years old) began to write what we will present here as his poetry—a writing that continued, sometimes as a daily offering, until the summer of 1959. In the now standard Picasso myth, the onset of the poetry is said to have coincided with a devastating marital crisis (a financially risky divorce, to be more exact), because of which his output as a painter halted for the first time in his life. Writing—as a form of poetry using, largely, the medium of prose—became his alternative outlet. The flow of words begins abruptly ("privately," his biographer Patrick O'Brian tells us) on 18 april XXXV while in retreat at Boisgeloup. (He would lose the country place the next year in a legal settlement.) The pace is rapid, violent, pushing and twisting from one image to another, not bothering with punctuation,

Largely my introduction to *The Burial of the Count of Orgaz & Other Poems* (Cambridge, MA: Exact Change, 2004), which was followed by Pierre Joris's own introductory essay as coeditor, "The Nomadism of Picasso."

often defying syntax, expressive of a way of writing/languaging that he had never tried before:

if I should go outside the wolves would come to eat out of my hand
just as my room would seem to be outside of me my other earnings
would go off around the world smashed into smithereens

as one of us has tried to phrase it in translation.

Yet if the poems begin with a sense of personal discomfort and malaise, there is a world beyond the personal that enters soon thereafter. For Picasso, like any poet of consequence, is a man fully into his time and into the terrors that his time presents. Read in that way, "the world smashed into smithereens" is a reflection also of the state of things between the two world wars—the first one still fresh in mind and the rumblings of the second starting up. *That's the way the world goes at this time or any other,* Picasso writes a little further on, not as the stricken husband or the discombobulated lover merely but as a man, like the aforementioned Joyce, caught in the "nightmare of history" from which he tries repeatedly to waken.[1] It is the time and place where poetry becomes—for him as for us—the only language that makes sense.

That anyway is where we position Picasso and how we read him.

As with his work as a painter, such a reading can take off in multiple directions. The poetry is centered, first and foremost, on this person writing day by day—no titles for most poems but dates only and occasional markers of the times and places where the poems are being written (Paris, Juan-les-Pins, Cannes, Boisgeloup, Mougins, or, still more specifically: the Café de la Régence or the Antibes train). But the field of the present is further expanded by a sense of history and of events unraveling around him. It is our contention in fact that the writings throughout are set against a ground of present terror—implicit always but sometimes wholly foregrounded as in his *Dream and Lie of Franco.* Written in the same year as his memorialization of the bombing of Guernica and accompanied by an extraordinary suite of images in comic-strip mode (the personal/political theme of the "weeping woman" is also first introduced here), this poem ends with a catalog of people, animals, and things in dissolution:

1. Or Picasso himself: *"history's bottom of the heart which has us by the throat neither more nor less"* (10.2.37). And again: *"That death could fall from heaven on so many, right in the middle of rushed life, had a great meaning for me"* (interview with Simone Gauthier, 1967).

cries of children cries of women cries of birds cries of flowers cries of wood
and stone cries of bricks cries of furniture of beds of chairs of curtains of
casseroles of cats and papers cries of smells that claw themselves of smoke
that gnaws the neck of cries that boil in cauldron and the rain of birds
that floods the sea that eats into the bone and breaks the teeth biting the
cotton that the sun wipes on its plate that bourse and bank hide in the
footprint left imbedded in the rock.

If this is the shadow voice of great events, there are also the smaller ones gleaned from reports he reads or hears: *in the papers everyday misleading pictures of the families who beat their kids so that they can be copied by the likes of me who paint and sing.* And finally, in recollection of the pasted papers of his early cubist days, collages from the newspapers themselves:

Paris 14-12-35 ("Le Journal" 8-12-35, page 2)
Maxima: on the ground—under shelter—minima—under shelter—
maxima under shelter 755 millimeters (1.007) maximum + 5
. . . .
—Salon d'Automne, Grand Palais—French association for the De-
fense of Animals—Pasteur's precursors—martyrized or kidnapped
children . . . and the Christmas message—A.C of 35 and 285 R.A.L.
artistic matinée at 2 p.m.—after the call of the war dead and the min-
ute of silence

Since we are dealing here with what Robert Duncan liked to call a "multiphasic" poetry, the private and public worlds within the poems play off against deep images embedded in the mind or, still more likely, in the seedbed of a culture. The tauromachian (bull fighting) symbols—as in the paintings also—are obvious and persistent, but along with them comes a range of other images drawn from folk memories and recollections (Spanish, Catalan) or echoing a still more distant or occulted past.[2] The tone throughout is raw, *transgressive*—a concept and mode later explored in the fiction and poetics of his acquaintance Georges Bataille. If it is sometimes (but rarely) sentimental and often (comically or tragically) self-disparaging, it strikes us with a Rabelaisian—or, maybe better yet, Artaudian—ferocity; with secrets of the body: food and sex and all the lower human drives. And, like others in the French tradition he adopts,

---

2. *"Critics have said that I was affected by Surrealist poetry as well as by family problems. Absolute nonsense! Basically I've always written the same way. . . . Poems about the postman or the priest"* (Picasso to Roberto Otero, in John Richardson, *A Life of Picasso*, 1:107).

the work hums with new inversions (invocations, blasphemies) of catholic
images and dogmas:

> *the festival of wheat there on the altar cloth the sepulchre the joyjoy por-*
> *trait pissing the whole globe away with smells of fat cigars or playing*
> *ball beneath black curtains dribbling out its clear white egg wax daub-*
> *ing the glass windows of the wondrous reliquary's chest of drawers the*
> *lacy porker liquefied between the almond sheets. [6.7.40]*

These intensities and densities come into the poetry before—at the
time of Guernica and into "the war years"—they inform the paintings,
and they mark a transition in his work in general. They enter there with
a fullness and kaleidoscopic richness that language now allows him. As
with other poets, there is a sense in which language is itself a part of
the work he makes—the ways in which it can be made to reveal and
equally to mask the life from which it issues. And as with other poets
also, the thoughts on language and poesis aren't his alone but are shared
visions. For Picasso, since his first entry to Paris and the larger art world,
was in close contact with poets who were exploring language's limits in
a way that paralleled his own workings with pictorial form and image.
(He was also—it is now quite evident—a heavily engaged reader.)[3] His
relations with Stein, Apollinaire, Jacob, and Reverdy remain a part of
the cubist myth a hundred or so years after the events themselves. The
chalked sign over his studio door read AU RENDEZ-VOUS DES POÈTES, and
the exchanges with poet friends would have been not only about the new
painting but the new poetry as well. (The "new spirit" or "new mind,"
Apollinaire would call it in a famous essay.) Writes his principal biographer, John Richardson, about the ambience of what he calls Picasso's
"think tank": "It enabled the artist to become vicariously a poet—a poet
in paint, not yet a poet in words." And even so, the verbally dense newspaper collages and isolated stenciled words that marked his cubist can-
vases give us a measure of how far he had already gone in opening his art
to language.

3. "There were many books in his home . . . Detective or adventure novels side by side
with our best poets: Sherlock Holmes and the publications of Nick Carter or Buffalo Bill
with Verlaine, Rimbaud, and Mallarmé. The French eighteenth century, which he liked
very much, was represented by Diderot, Rousseau, and Rétif de la Bretonne. . . . Thanks
to Rimbaud and Mallarmé, it is certain that Picasso's work owes something to literature"
(Maurice Reynal, 1922). And Christine Piot, citing this and much else adds: "As we see,
his literary culture was most eclectic."

Through all his work, in fact, there was a "need for poetry"[4] (the phrase here is John Cage's, in relation to his own writings), and that need brought Picasso to an alignment—in the 1920s and 1930s—with the younger poets who made up the core of Paris-based Surrealism. Prior to the 1924 Manifesto of Surrealism and the founding that December of *La révolution surréaliste*, members of the about-to-be Surrealist group countersigned Breton's essay "Hommage à Picasso," which appeared in the June 20 issue of *Paris-Journal*. From 1924 to 1929 works by Picasso were reproduced in eight of the eleven issues of *La révolution surréaliste*, and he was often cited by Breton and other poets as an exemplary Surrealist figure—"their prophet," Patrick O'Brian writes, with sufficient quotations to back it up. Or Breton, who had "claim[ed] him" as "one of us": "If Surrealism is to adopt a line of conduct, it has only to pass where Picasso has already passed and where he will pass again."

In all of this—from Apollinaire and Stein to Breton and Paul Eluard—Picasso must have been fully into, fully aware of, the poetry around him, and when he let it rip in April 1935, it wasn't as an isolated or naive voice but as a participant in what was then a verbal art in transformation. The poetry through much of 1936 was probably his dominant activity (the painting by most accounts had then been put aside), and he would often pursue it on an almost daily basis. It is hard to guess how much stock he put in it; Roland Penrose, who was close to him, speaks about "[his] reticence in showing his poems" and his "[lack of] pretensions about the quality of his poetry."[5] And yet when Stein dismissed the poems he read to her (and those of *all* other painters and Breton's as well), it probably marked the low point of a friendship that by then was almost over. "The egotism of a painter," she wrote and lectured him in explanation, "is an entirely different egotism than the egotism of a writer." And again: "This was his life for two years, of course he who could write, write so well with drawings and with colours, knew very well that to write with words was, for him, not to write at all."

---

4. "Picasso, after reading from a sketchbook containing poems in Spanish, says to me: *'Poetry—but everything you find in these poems one can also find in my paintings. So many painters today have forgotten poetry in their paintings—and it's the most important thing: poetry'"* (Daniel-Henry Kahnweiler, 1959).

5. But another account, decades later: "Picasso once told a friend that long after his death his writing would gain recognition and encyclopedias would say: 'Picasso, Pablo Ruiz—Spanish poet who dabbled in painting, drawing and sculpture'" (Miguel Acoca, "Picasso Turns a Busy 90 Today," *International Herald Tribune*, Oct. 25, 1971).

By contrast the response of the younger French poets was immediate and strongly in Picasso's favor. Like Stein they recognized in Picasso's art a mode akin to writing, but where she would draw a line between the genres, they were open—enthusiastic even—to his crossing over into poetry. Because of that the first publication of the poems came shortly after he started writing—a curiosity since, for all his reputation, he published only rarely after that. By the end of 1935, then, Breton had arranged a special issue of *Cahiers d'art,* with a number of Picasso's poems translated into French or shown in Spanish typescript, accompanied by Breton's own introduction ("Picasso poète") and shorter pieces by Eluard and Georges Hugnet. Of the poems' impact (bright, mysterious), Breton writes:

> The play of light and shadow has never been observed more tenderly or interpreted more subtly and lucidly; it keeps the poem within the bounds of the present moment, of the breath of eternity which that moment at its most fugitive contains within itself. Nothing is more characteristic of this than the care Picasso has taken to indicate in the text of several of these verse or prose poems the place, day and hour in which they were composed. We have the impression of being in the presence of an intimate journal, both of the feelings and of the senses, such as has never been kept before.

In writing this, Breton was aware as well—or seems to have been—that the actual process of the poems wasn't linear—all moving in the same direction—but that the written—the handwritten—works were circular or else, like palimpsests, were reaching out in all directions. If we're unable to show that hand-play, that concrete writing in these pages, we would direct the reader of Picasso to those handwritten poems that consist—at least in part—"of words that appear to have been thrown onto the page without any preconceived links and that Picasso has joined together by red, yellow and blue lines in such a way that they can be read in various directions [so] that the handwritten page looks like a dew-laden spider's web under the first rays of the morning sun."[6]

6. "After a swim, on the beach at Golfe-Juan, we are talking about Chinese characters *(écriture).* A Chinese friend is drawing Chinese characters on the sand. Picasso had amused himself before by drawing his own ideograms in the sand: bulls, goats, faces of peace. He is fascinated by the interplay of Chinese characters, the strengths and economy of their construction. '*If I were born Chinese,*' says he, '*I would not be a painter but a writer. I'd write my pictures*'" (Claude Roy, 1956).

Poetry in this sense remains a fiercely formal undertaking, or else an interplay, forever shifting, of form *and* content. In admitting Picasso to his company of poets, Breton, whose 1924 manifesto had announced a new surrealist poetry that would be "psychic" at its core ("psychic automatism in its pure state"), still could not evade its other, "formal" features. For Picasso, as for Breton in his actual practice as a poet, the work of poetry wasn't restricted to unmediated psychic acts or automatic writing, but subject, in its workings—however rapid—to a flux of changes, scratch marks, and erasures. *"I am intent on resemblance,"* he said, *"and resemblance more real than the real. . . . For me surreality is nothing else, never has been anything else, than that deep likeness far beyond the shapes and colors of immediate appearance"* (Picasso to the photographer Brassai). For this, from Picasso's perspective, the issue was not "pure" automatism but something more impure, more unapologetically deliberate and artful:

> *"Poems?"* he said to me, *"when I began to write them I wanted to prepare myself a palette of words, as if I were dealing with colors. All these words were weighed, filtered and appraised. I don't put much stock in spontaneous expressions of the unconscious and it would be stupid to think that one can provoke them at will."* (Picasso to Louis Parrot, 1948)[7]

If this represents a kind of *faux*-surrealism—and it does—it puts him closer to later practitioners, not unrelated to their Surrealist or Dada forerunners but clearly divergent as well. He is willing also, like poets of all persuasions, to sometimes move the oral or the auditory into the central position—*"not to tell stories or describe sensations, but to suggest them by the sounds of words"* (Picasso to Sabartés, 1946). It is clear, too—here as elsewhere—that *Picasso poète*, like other poets worth a backward glance, makes his own moves, the total configuration of which marks the achievement of his writing and, thereby, his vision. And if we trust him here— or trust those others who report his words—we must look to the music of his poems, both in their *melos* and in what Pound otherwise spoke

---

7. And further: *"'The work of madmen' he told me, 'is always based on a law that has ceased to operate. Madmen are men who have lost their imagination. Their manual memory belongs to a realm of rigid mechanism. It is an infernal machine that breaks down and not an intelligence that progresses and constantly creates in order to progress. One cannot compare poems resulting from automatic writing with those of the insane. The work of a madman is a dead work; the poetry it contains is like the ghost which refuses to give up its corpse.'"*

of as "the dance of the intelligence among words." With Picasso, suggests his French editor Marie-Laure Bernadac, that dance is "in the incantatory and monotone manner of flamenco or in the staccato rhythm of *taconeo* . . . the deep and disturbing chant of *cante hondo.*"

His way is persistent—both sound and meaning—from its onset in 1935 to the culminating work *(The Burial of the Count of Orgaz)* in 1959. As with some other—but surely not all—early avant-gardists, punctuation is set aside, allowing thereby a play between the apparent rush of writing and the ways that meaning comes into the works when read. Such unpunctuated prose blocks—coming at the time they do—are almost uniquely his and bring with them a number of other moves, exploring the varied possibilities of what Bernadac calls "this new 'plastic material' [of language] . . . chipping, pulverizing, modeling this 'verbal clay,' varying combinations of phrases, combining words, either by phonic opposition, repetition, or by an audacious metaphorical system, the seeming absurdity of which corresponds in fact to an internal and personal logic. . . . Lawless writing, disregardful of syntax or rationality, but which follows the incessant string of images and sensations that passed through his head." (The lack of titles and their replacement by the dates of composition is another marker of his work, as are various rearrangements of words and phrases from one text to another, "as if he were moving paper cutouts in a painting or drawing" [Christine Piot].)

In all of this there are two languages through which he writes—the Spanish of his youth and the French to which he came by incremental stages—and possibly a third, unwritten one as well, the Catalan he spoke with friends and that may be a hidden stream beneath the others. It is however the Spanish that dominates the early poems, that never leaves him, and that emerges again in the final poem. But most of the work in between—including the two full-length plays *Desire Caught by the Tail* and *The Four Little Girls*—is written in his characteristic and idiosyncratic French. (Sometimes also he translates himself from one language into the other.) Picasso's writing is—in that sense, and in others as well— what one of us has called a rhizomatic or nomadic art, that is a writing not at home (i.e., settled and at rest in some convention or other) but always "*unterwegs*"—on the way—as Paul Celan put it.

It is curious now—moving out of Picasso's own century—to find how close the written work is to what would later become a postmodernism working through and struggling with the more "experimental" and "lawless" sides of modernism. For this, Picasso's poetry stands without further comment on his part. It is at points prolific—when he seems to work it as a day-by-day endeavor—and it plays out as a denser and often more intimate complement to his even more prolific art. (It has a resemblance in this sense to the Minotaur engravings *[Minotauromachy]*—in which the painter/sculptor also plays a role—first issued like the poems in 1935 and carried forward like them in the later work.) There are also the two plays among his writings, one of which, *Desire Caught by the Tail* (1941), became his best-known written work, translated often (including a venture into German by Paul Celan) and performed by experimental groups throughout the world.[8] Still there's very little publication overall and virtually no poetics or written statements about poetry (or art—his own or others'—for that matter). This leaves us dependent for such statements on his biographers or on the numerous witnesses reporting "conversations with Picasso." Some of those we've presented here as footnotes—radical insights sometimes and always with that sense of poetry's centrality and presence that was a given for the artists and the poets (even the "anti-poets") of his time.[9]

Our own work here is derived from *Picasso: Ecrits,* a massive and heavily illustrated volume (some 340 dated texts in all) edited by Marie-Laure Bernadac and Christine Piot and published by Gallimard in 1989. We have accordingly been dependent on the *Ecrits* for transcriptions of the work, which retain many—but certainly not all—of the manuscripts' particularities. While we have made do with what we were given, we might have preferred to work with the poems in their more rough-and-ready forms or, of still more interest, to attempt translations that would show the way Picasso positioned his words in the act of composition. At the same time, however, we recognize that too visual a representation—at least at this juncture—would likely detract from our contention that Picasso as a poet of words—even a "language poet," if we can use that term—is a force and a presence not to be ignored.

For the time being, then, it's worth noting Picasso's own comments about the irregularities of grammar and spelling in his written work: *"If I begin correcting the mistakes you speak of according to rules with no rela-*

8. The initial performance/reading took place (March 19, 1944) at Michel Leiris's place in Paris, with "actors" who included the Leirises (Michel and Louise), Jean-Paul Sartre, Simone de Beauvoir, Raymond Queneau, Jean Aubier, and Dora Maar. The director was Albert Camus, and the musical accompaniment was by Georges Hugnet.
9. *"Painting is never prose,"* he declared to Françoise Gilot; *"it is poetry, it is written in verse with plastic rhymes. . . . [P]ainting is poetry."*

tion to me, I will lose my individuality to grammar I have not incorporated. I prefer to create myself as I see fit than to bend my words to rules that don't belong to me" (Picasso quoted by Sabartés, 1946). There is an assertiveness here, a playfulness reminiscent of Fluxus artists and Beat poets of a later generation—even more so in the account (again by Sabartés) of Picasso's truly innovative projection of a work—like William Blake's perhaps, or Mallarmé's—that broke new and outrageous ground for the presentation of language:

> The book Picasso would like to create would be a perfect reflection of his personality and the most faithful portrait of the artist. In its spontaneity, we would see his own disorder. Each page would be a true "potpourri," without the slightest hint of organization or composition. There would be letters and numbers, aligned and non-aligned, sometimes parallel, sometimes perfectly horizontal, now ascending, now descending, as if written by one unaccustomed to script, or driven by enthusiasm or impatience. There would be notes, scribbles and splotches, additions between the lines, arrows pointing to sentences in the margins, figures and objects, sometimes entirely comprehensible, sometimes less easy and readable.[10] Simplicity and complexity would be united as in his paintings, his drawings or his texts, as in a room in his apartment or his studio, as in himself. . . . Picasso confided this layout to me, or better, this image of his dream book, one morning in the month of July (1939).

Unrealized as most such schemes have been, this brings us to the boundaries nonetheless of what Maurice Blanchot would later call "the book to come."

In the actual books, then—the writings left behind—something similar prevails. Some of the writing was in a little notebook that he carried with him;[11] also, we're told, "[on] drawing paper, letter paper, backs of envelopes, backs of invitations, pieces of newspaper and even sheets of toilet paper" (M.-L. Bernadac and C. Piot). His instruments were "black or colored pencils . . . , blue-black ink (in 1939–1940), ballpoint pens or

---

10. "A few attempts at illegible writing or writings with 'unknown words' appeared in 1938 and 1949" (Christine Piot).

11. *"[W]riting in his small notebook—elbows sticking out one more than the other over the table's edge—the left hand holding the already written page the other on the paper—the point of the pencil here—where I press it"* (Picasso, 3 november XXXV).

markers (in 1951 and 1959)." From 1935 to 1939 poems (in highly calligraphic, highly visual form) "were directly written or recopied in India ink on sheets of Arches paper" and were then gathered together in portfolios. Others were written in larger notebooks, a couple of which give titles to the poem cycles in our book. In addition some of the manuscripts— most of those on Arches paper, for example—were typed by Sabartés, the visual elements stripped away, as if in preparation for reading and/or publication of the texts.

As editors of the present work we have been constrained—as stated above—to work with such typed versions and with the texts transposed further into the uniform typography of printers' fonts. In the resultant Gallimard edition the poems appeared in their original Spanish or French (the French outnumbering the Spanish by some 200 to 140 texts) and with the Spanish ones further translated, usually by the Gallimard editors, into French. For our own division of labor, Joris concentrated on the French writings and Rothenberg on the Spanish, and we also invited contributions by a range of contemporary poets/translators as a mark of Picasso's entry into our own time. Of these the most radical translator is Paul Blackburn, who shifts Picasso's medium from prose to verse. (He was also of course the first important American poet to bring Picasso into English.) With the others who joined us here, the invitation was to translate a small selection each and otherwise to make their own decisions as to form and voice. In both our own work and in theirs, the choice was to stay with the text while creating, in various ways, a work that speaks in a demotic, largely American, English and that stresses exuberance over a probably futile "literalism." We have remembered, too, that in this kind of writing—as in much of our own—meaning is slippery and has like our desires to be caught (again and again) by the tail.[12]

The result is a reflection of the past that is also, we would urge, a beacon for our workings in the present.

12. The guest translators, for the record, were David Ball, Paul Blackburn, Anselm Hollo, Robert Kelly, Suzanne Jill Levine, Ricardo Nirenberg, Diane Rothenberg, Cole Swenson, Anne Waldman, Jason Weiss, Mark Weiss, and Laura Wright, with a special assistance in my own case from Manuel Brito.

Kurt Schwitters:
A Pre-Face

(with Pierre Joris)

The Man in the Myth

he who walks with his house on
his head is heaven he
who walks with his house
on his head is heaven he who walks
with his house on his head
—Charles Olson, *Maximus* 11

In the myth we see him as the Dada artist, founding his own movement
in the world of art, lugging his art from place to place, victim of a politics
and life he can't control. His center is Hannover, and the center's center
is his house, inside of which he builds a column, a sculptural collage he
calls "a monument to Dada" or, again, "cathedral of erotic misery." The
column's growing; it's pushing through the ceiling; it spreads in all directions, grafting itself on adjacent rooms, breaking through walls and
partitions, until it seems to fill the world. But it's not enough; the world
is bigger. In 1936 he leaves it—his first flight from the terror of the total state—and makes his way to Norway, where he starts to build again.
And again in 1940—now he's Olson's Man-with-His-House-on-His-

Kurt Schwitters, *Poems Performance Pieces Proses Plays Poetics (PPPPPP)*, translated and
edited by Jerome Rothenberg and Pierre Joris (Philadelphia: Temple University Press,
1993; Cambridge, MA: Exact Change, 2002).

Head—the darkness surrounds him, and he sails for England, only to get thrown in prison there, a German alien in wartime. He stops writing, even stops speaking, German. Given some food, a place to sleep, and lots of garbage for his art (he says), he stays in prison for a year—then on release, out in the British countryside, starts building it again. At his death in 1947, the house in Hannover has been destroyed by bombs, the one in England stands unfinished. In 1951 the house in Norway disappears in flames.

The Man in the Poems

My aim is the total Merz art work, which combines all genres into an artistic unity. First, I married off single genres. I pasted words and sentences together into poems in such a way that their rhythmic composition created a kind of drawing. The other way around, I pasted together pictures and drawings containing sentences that demand to be read. I drove nails into pictures in such a way that besides the pictorial effect a plastic relief effect arose. I did this in order to erase the boundaries between the arts.

—(K. S.)

Although Kurt Schwitters is increasingly recognized as one of the great visual artists of the twentieth century—a recognition reconfirmed in 1985 by a highly acclaimed retrospective at New York's Museum of Modern Art and by a large exhibition that same year at the Centre Pompidou in Paris—his achievement as one of the major poets and theorists of modernism has so far not received the same degree of attention, at least not in the English-speaking world. Art critics and museum curators, perhaps because of their own professional leanings, tend with few exceptions to consider his language-oriented work as a curious by-product of his art or even as a minor phase of his early, Dada-associated career. While such an appraisal may be true for an artist and occasional writer like Picasso, in this case it is more than an unfortunate oversight—it is a major distortion of Schwitters's accomplishment, especially because he himself never saw his various art and literary activities according to some such hierarchical model. On the contrary, Schwitters's push was toward an ever greater integration and equivalence of the various facets of his artistic oeuvre. In this sense—in that extension of Dada experimentation that he personalized with the coined word *Merz*—his attempt "to erase the boundaries between the arts" resembles and predicts the work of such later artists as

John Cage, Claes Oldenburg, and Allan Kaprow, indeed of a significant portion of the "postmodern" generation.

Schwitters wrote prolifically throughout his life. His earliest poems date from his student days in pre–World War I Germany, his last writings from 1947, the year before his death in England. It is in his poetry, he tells us, that he made his initial breakthrough as an artist, and it is in the fusion of the poetry and painting that he made his entry into Merz. Besides the poetry, the boundaries of which he stretched as much if not more than any of his contemporaries, he wrote essays and manifestos, plays and fictions. Although most of his writing was in his native German, he also wrote in English and Norwegian (he renounced the German language during his exile in World War II). The true extent of his written opus has only become apparent more recently, thanks to the five volumes of his collected writings, *Das literarische Werk*, published by DuMont Verlag in Cologne.

Kurt Schwitters's continual inventiveness is revealed by even a cursory glance at his collected writings. He ranks squarely among the protean writers of the first part of the twentieth century, along with figures such as Apollinaire, Stein, Tzara, Marinetti, Pound, and so on. The professed sweep and aim of his poems (no contemporary poet worked with or developed more new forms and genres) are truly Poundian or even Wagnerian, though without Pound's or Wagner's mythohistorical ambitions or ideological strictures. Schwitters worked all his life toward a *Gesamtkunstwerk*, a total work of art, as an amalgamation of elements from all artistic genres assembled through the common synthesizing principle of radical collage. His famous *Merzbau* (Merz tower) was "an extraordinary architectural sculptural column, or assemblage," as Lucy Lippard describes it, or Schwitters himself in a letter from 1946: "My Merz tower was not confined to a single room, but spread over the whole house. . . . Parts of it were in the adjoining rooms, on the balcony, in 2 rooms of the cellar, on the 2nd floor, in the attic." And again: "I am building an abstract sculpture into which people can go."

Schwitters also conceived but never brought into full play the idea of a Robert Wilson–like total theater, as what he called "the ultimate, total Merz work, distinguished by the fusion of all factors; even people can be included into a total work of art." While unable to put his ideas for the Merz stage into practice, Schwitters wrote tirelessly about how he imagined it to be, this final incarnation of his dream of art. Thus, in his 1920 essay "Merz":

The Merz stage knows only the fusion of all the parts into the total work. Materials for the stage set are all solid, liquid, and gaseous bodies such as white wall, man, barbed-wire fence, water stream, blue distance, light cone. Use surfaces that can become solid or dissolve into gossamer meshes, surfaces that can fold like curtains, shrink or expand. Let things turn on themselves and move; let lines broaden into surfaces. Parts will be inserted into the set while other parts will be removed. The materials for the score consist of all sounds and noises that can be created by violin, drum, trumpet, sewing machine, ticking clack water stream, and etcetera. The materials for the text are all experiences that excite the brain and the emotions. These materials are not to be used logically in their objective relationships, but only within the logic of the work of art. The more intensively the work of art destroys rational objective logic, the greater the possibility of artistic form. Just as in poetry word is played off against word, so in this instance one will play off factor against factor, material against material.

But even in his smaller visual collages, words invaded the world of paint and form, not only as detritus from the commercial/banal worlds around him, but speaking to the issues of his time—signs of a democratizing politics and of a poetics of everyday life: "the search for an artistic complex in an artless world . . . and from that complex the creation of works of art through acts of framing." This highly conscious quest to use everyday objects and language shards—"banalities" he calls them—is foregrounded by Schwitters in a number of theoretical texts. In "Banalities (4)" he writes:

Not all banalities are totally dada, but every banality hides a load of dadaistic nonsense. I have merzed banalities, i.e., made works of art by juxtaposing and evaluating sentences that, taken by themselves, are banal. I am also conscious of the fact that not all the sentences I used are banalities. The reader has to decide for himself. For "there is an essence in us able to explode greenly" (Theodor Däubler). I do not dare to decide if "Lord, Lord, give me strength" is banal, given the quantity of explosive force stored in this sentence; it is probably expressionism. Lordy Lord, give me your Sturm! It is, to say the least, a direct order from a man who frets powerless and is essentially not different from me saying: "Mrs. Meier, give me two

ounces of coffee!" At which Mrs. Meier is likely to explode greenly.
And thus we have also managed to reduce expressionism to its simplest formula: "An exchange of spiritual goods," where the spirit
consists of the fact that one cannot check the weight of the strength
as easily as that of the coffee.

In all of these enterprises the relation between language and art is continuous and all-pervasive, and Schwitters is at all times both an artist and
a poet.

Viewed in the narrower sense, Schwitters's poetry-as-such displays
a similar sweep and inventiveness. It includes early expressionistic lyrics (the most radical of which—strongly influenced by the experimental
expressionism of August Stramm—already move him toward his kind
of asyntactical poetry) and their later, often hilarious, reworkings ("An
Anna Blume" is the primary example); Dada and protosurrealist poems;
and vocovisual experiments, often taking the shape of what would later
be called sound texts and concrete poetry. While he is best known for the
latter works (his "Ur Sonata" foremost here), his language experiments
led him also into other areas of what he called "abstract poetry," where
syntax was dissolved or transformed, isolating words or placing them in
untried combinations, as an exploration of the problematics of referentiality and nonreferentiality in language:

Desire
And
Without
Have
Sing
Earthworm
    Strut
Lyric
Tradition
The beggar
    Of
Hollow
Green
Of about
Of abutments
The grass.

Of such works he writes: "In poetry, words are torn from their former context, dissociated, and, brought into a new artistic context, they become formal parts of the poem, nothing else." His central methods here, as with his best-known paintings, are those of collage and assemblage, or, as he describes it: "[The poetry] is analogous to Merz painting in making use of given elements such as sentences cut out of newspapers or taken down from catalogues, posters, etc., with or without alteration." Along the same lines he remains as open to voices as to written words—attentive as a Gertrude Stein would also be to the sounds of fractured conversations, which he makes into the building blocks of a number of his early poems.

In the grand scheme, too, Schwitters's Merz poetry may be seen to include prose works along the lines of what Ron Silliman, writing in the 1980s, called "the new sentence." There is also that in Schwitters which reminds us of work like the 1950s "cut-ups" and "fold-ins" of Brion Gysin and William Burroughs. Gysin, who came in fact from painting to writing, where work of this sort has had such little play, made the reasonable observation that "writing is fifty years behind painting." Yet, if Gysin's remark reflects on the late reception of earlier experimental poetry, it also points to the degree to which Schwitters's workings as a poet preceded or paralleled his workings as a painter.

In looking at those workings, then, it is impossible to keep a sharp division between the poetry and painting. The pursuit of diverse forms, Schwitters wrote, "was an artistic necessity for me . . . [and] the reason for it was not so much a desire for a widening of the scope of my work, but rather the endeavor to be an artist and not a specialist in one genre." The key term in either case was *abstraction,* not as a formal device but toward a recovery of the spiritual in art (Kandinsky's term) and as a reflection of, and comment on, the time in which he lived. In both instances he employed collage as a procedure by which to bring the world of nonart (= "life") into his frame; in both he sought for elementary forms (as letters, consonants and vowels, numbers, primal sounds) to act as building blocks for something older, newer. The intermingling was everywhere, inseparable. As John Elderfield describes it:

> In Schwitters' case, the arts he practiced not only share a common structure, the principle of collage, but are interrelated and mixable. Painting and poetry come together in the pasted words and phrases of his collages; the ready-found phrases of the poems are joined

in collage-like word-chains; the Dadaist and rubber-stamp drawings juxtapose literary and graphic forms in one structure, while the
imagery of these drawings is also found in Schwitters' poems and
prose, and in some of the early Dadaist sculptures as well. Schwitters emphasized the reciprocal relationship of his visual and literary
work, saying he made poems that could be looked at as drawings,
collages that could be partly read, and pictures that contained elements of collage, of poetry, and indeed of sculpture too.

Even the titles of his workings and paintings sometimes were, he said, "a
poem about the picture."

But for all of his radical language experiments, Schwitters, during his
most active period on native ground, was the author of what was possibly
the best known and most popular German poem of the 1920s, "An Anna
Blume" [For Anna Blossom]; and his almost equally popular "Ur Sonata," a wordless thirty-five-minute performance poem, is to sound poetry what Joyce's *Ulysses* is to the twentieth-century novel. If the success
of "An Anna Blume"—"both a Dadaist poem . . . and a sentimentalized
Expressionist one," as Elderfield describes it—came easily, the success of
the "Ur Sonata" was more equivocal and depended in large measure on
Schwitters's own personality and presence as a performer. This involved
not only his performance tours with avant-garde colleagues like Theo van
Doesburg and Raoul Hausmann but appearances like the one described
in almost mythic terms by the Dada artist and filmmaker Hans Richter,
which took place in Potsdam in 1924 or 1925 in a private house and before an audience made up largely of the local gentry—retired generals
and other people of rank from the old Prussian nobility:

> Schwitters stood on the podium, drew himself up to his full six feet
> plus, and began to perform the Ursonate, complete with hisses, roars
> and crowing, before an audience who had no experience whatever
> of anything modern. At first they were completely baffled, but after
> a couple of minutes the shock began to wear off. For another five
> minutes, protest was held in check by the respect due Frau Kiepen-
> hauer's house. But this restraint served only to increase the inner
> tension. I watched delightedly as two generals in front of me pursed
> their lips as hard as they could to stop themselves laughing. Their
> faces, above their upright collars, turned first red, then slightly blu-
> ish. And then they lost control. They burst out laughing and the

whole audience, freed from the pressure that had been building up inside them, exploded in an orgy of laughter. The dignified old ladies, the stiff generals, shrieked with laughter, gasped for breath, slapped their thighs, choked themselves.

Kurtchen was not in the least bit put out by this. He turned up the volume of his enormous voice to Force Ten and simply swamped the storm of laughter in the audience, so that the latter seemed almost to be an accompaniment to the Ursonate. . . . The hurricane blew itself out as rapidly as it had arisen. Schwitters spoke the rest of his Ursonate without further interruption. The result was fantastic. The same generals, the same rich ladies, who had previously laughed until they cried, now came to Schwitters, again with tears in their eyes, almost stuttering with admiration and gratitude. Something had been opened up within them, something they had never expected to feel: a great joy.

There is no anonymous or absent author here, but a remarkable, self-defined, and often misunderstood artist.

The Man in the Book

The word Merz *had no meaning when I found it. Now it has the meaning which I gave it. The meaning of the concept Merz changes with the change in insight of those who continue to work with it.*

—(K. S.)

In bringing Schwitters into the present we were aware—increasingly— of how much his work resembled and impacted our own. There is clearly more than a single Schwitters moving through his writings, and we've tried accordingly to show some of his range, while acknowledging that his principal pull for us was in the area of the experimental and avant-garde viewed as the continuing struggle with a form and content. In this sense the work crescendos in the early Merz years, moves toward the more conventional and obvious in the 1930s, and enters into a new problematic and invigoration during his final exile. In those last years, too, he makes a remarkable shift to a quirky, collagist's use of English, not as a native language but as an instrument, a new material or pigment, so to speak, for that central work of assemblage in which he remained engaged.

⟳

Finally, while we were reading, translating, and assembling Schwitters, we came again to realize how alive his work remains for poets writing here and now. His idea of a work of art—a Merz work—that would change in time with the perceptions of those who might embrace it, plays itself out in such an enterprise as Jackson Mac Low's "*Merzgedichte* in Memoriam Kurt Schwitters," which has continued to appear during the time of our working. There have been others as well, including one of the present editors, who have sought in their own poetry to address and celebrate the "dada strain" in Schwitters's work. The latent power of that work in the present is perhaps best exemplified by an event recorded by the British jazz musician George Melly. Late one night he decided to take a break between two sets in a London jazz club. As he stepped into the alleyway behind the club for a breath of fresh air, a menacing figure suddenly loomed before him, wielding a knife and demanding his money. Melly's spontaneous response was to start reciting the "Ur Sonata" at the top of his voice—which baffled and scared his assailant so much that he dropped the knife and ran. No matter how apocryphal this anecdote may turn out to be, Schwitters would have loved it, for, as he put it in one of the last poems he wrote:

> The gazelle trembles,
> As the lions roar.
> The hyena shambles,
> But ART GIVES MORE.
> —(Trans. Pierre Joris)

María Sabina:
A Pre-Face

In Mazatec, María Sabina's calling was, literally, that of "wise woman"—
a term that we may choose to translate as "shaman" or, by a further twist,
as "poet." But that's to bring it and her into our own generalized kind of
reckoning and naming. In much the same way, the book containing her oral
autobiography or *vida*, which first appeared in Spanish in 1977 and which
makes up a large part of the present volume, translated her from the particularities of local Mazatec culture to the generalities of a book and media
technology that can travel almost anywhere. (Or so we like to think.)

When I visited Mexico in the summer of 1979 to arrange for publication and translation of the Vida into English, the film, *María Sabina:
Mujer Espíritu*, a documentary by Nicolás Echevarría, was playing under
government sponsorship at the large Cine Régis in downtown Mexico
City. María Sabina herself had been brought to Mexico City the previous
month—a small, elderly Indian woman, dressed in the traditional bird
and flower *huipil*, and with only a touch of Spanish at her service—and
had been much patronized (even lionized I think the word is) before her
return to native Huautla de Jiménez, a small and remote hill town in the
mountains of Oaxaca. (All this in contrast to the attempt, a dozen years
before, to arrest her for practice of the sacred mushroom ceremonies that
existed in the Mazatecan sierras long before the first conquerors set foot
there.)

I hope, in calling attention to the degree of fame that she has, that I

From *María Sabina: Selections* (Berkeley: University of California Press, 2003)—one of
the two opening works (the other from André Breton) in the series Poets for the Millennium, for which Pierre Joris and I were the series editors.

don't frustrate the reader's enthusiasm for things Indian and remote. She was certainly aware of being famous ("the Judge knows me, the Governor knows me," she sings), though by our standards her fame had little effect on her life per se. She continued to live in her old tin-roofed house—even while a new prefabricated home supplied by the government was going up nearby. She continued to walk barefoot up the hillside, to speak Mazatec not Spanish, to cure and to shamanize, to smoke cigarettes and drink beer from the bottle, to celebrate her own life of labor and her ability to make a clean bed, along with those other powers, language foremost among them, that had won her local and international repute. A poet, in short, with a sense of both a real physical world and a world beyond what the mind may sense or the mouth proclaim.

Before her name reached us clearly, her image and words had already come into our world. By the late 1950s, R. Gordon Wasson's recording, *The Mushroom Ceremony of the Mazatec Indians of Mexico*, was in circulation, and even before, *Life* magazine had run a feature (part of a "Great Adventures Series") on Wasson's "discovery of mushrooms that cause strange visions."[1] Soon thereafter one heard from travelers in Mexico of side-trips to see and be illumined by the "mushroom woman" of Oaxaca. (Her own view of these matters awaits the reader in the pages of her *Vida*.) And in the strange way in which ideas about language may travel in advance of the language itself, the Spanish Nobel poet Camilo José Cela constructed, early along, a highly fantastical opera about her, *María Sabina y el carro de heno, o el inventor de la guillotina*—a takeoff in part on what he took, from what was then available, to be her style of languaging.[2] In Mexico she became the subject of at least one comic book and of other forms of popular diffusion, and the American poet Anne Waldman, having come across the liner notes to Wasson's *Ceremony*, used them, circa 1970, to model a work called *Fast Speaking Woman*, which she performed in poetry readings and even, if memory doesn't fail me, as part of Bob Dylan's short-lived Rolling Thunder review or of his film *Renaldo and Clara:*

1. *Life*, May 13, 1957. The cover, which mentions the Wasson piece as one of its headlines, also shows a photo of comedian Bert Lahr ("as a bumbling lover") peering through tropical fronds—a curious example, so to speak, of cultural synchronism.
2. "I'm a woman who cries / I'm a woman who spits / I'm a woman who pisses / I'm a woman who gives milk no longer / I'm a woman who speaks / I'm a woman who shouts / I'm a woman who vomits / I'm an unrefined woman but I know how to fight against death and the grass that brought forth its venom" (Camilo José Cela).

I'm a shouting woman
I'm a speech woman
I'm an atmosphere woman
I'm an airtight woman

in distinct reflection of the other's:

I am a spirit woman, says
I am a lord eagle woman, says

—which the North American poet acknowledges formally as her "in-debtedness to the Mazatec Indian Shamaness in Mexico." Yet she fails at that point to name her—with a sense, one guesses, that the "shaman-ess" is of the anonymous tribal/oral sort. But María Sabina was already in "the world" by then—beyond the boundaries of her own place, to be given a measure of fame and the Western trappings of immortality-through-written-language that she herself could hardly have sought.

The confusion is easy enough to understand. María Sabina is Mazatec without question, and the mode of her chants (the way the words go, etc.) isn't merely personal but common to other Mazatec shamans. Among them she stands out—not alone but sharing a language with the other great ones, including those "tiger shamans" we hear of in the hills, who rarely make themselves visible in the town environs of Huautla.

This book, then, is centrally hers.

But it is as well a book of transmissions, of which Waldman's (like my own) is a curious and distant instance. The songs, the words, come to María Sabina through the agency of what her American translator, Henry Munn, has elsewhere called "the mushrooms of language." (Her qualification of each line with the word *tzo* [says] is a testimony to that: that it isn't María Sabina but the unspoken he/she/it whose words these are.) Then, sometime past the middle of her life, R. Gordon Wasson be-gins the other transmission that carries her words over great distances: an offshoot of his studies of mushroom history and lore but one that con-tinued to affect him for the rest of his life.

The transmission most crucial to this book is that between María Sabina and Álvaro Estrada. A Mazatec speaker and fellow townsman, Estrada engaged her in a series of recorded conversations, which he trans-lated into Spanish and made the basis of her "oral autobiography." To this he added a new translation of Wasson's 1956 recording and a series of footnotes and commentaries, not as an outside observer but with a native feel for Mazatec particulars and with testimony from older members of his own family and from other Mazatecs, local shamans among them, still deeply involved in the native religion. He is in that sense no innocent Carlos Castaneda, nor is María Sabina a shadowy Don Juan, but both stand open before us.[3] The poetry and the vision are nonetheless intense.

It was on the basis of Estrada's work that I was able to arrange for the publication, in 1981, of *María Sabina: Her Life and Chants*. That book was part of an unrealized series of books, New Wilderness Poetics, that I had intended as a bringing together of ethnopoetic and experimental poetries under the imprint of Ross-Erikson Publishers in Santa Barbara, California. With the death of publisher Roy "Buzz" Erikson and the suspension of the press, the book, while published, had only a very limited circulation.

In the Ross-Erikson version the active translator and commentator was Henry Munn, who was also my own contact to María Sabina and the Mazatec ritual world. Continuing the process begun by Estrada, Munn added a second chanting session (the only recorded one in which only Mazatecs were present), along with additional observations from both "inside" and "outside" points of view. Munn's connection was itself a part of the recent history of Huautla. His entry there, circa 1965, was as one of those "oddballs"—visitors to Huautla in the 1960s—cited by Wasson in an accompanying "retrospective essay"; but Munn was a genuine seeker as well, and after the "great bust of 1967," he returned to Huautla, married into the Estrada family, and has since become his own witness and a devoted student of Mazatec culture. His early essay "The Mushrooms of Language" is a brilliant introduction to the verbal side of Mazatec shamanism: a first recognition of the shaman's work as an essentially poetic act and, in the Surrealist master André Breton's definition of *poesis* quoted therein, "a sacred action." Munn's translations (drawing on both Mazatec and Spanish) are equally attentive, and his commentaries there and elsewhere direct us to a range of mythopoeic connections (local and universal) informing the Mazatec chants.

The presence, alongside María Sabina, of Estrada, Munn, and Wasson made of this work a multileveled book of testimony—and something more: a book of exiles and losses. This will seem surprising only if

3. The reference is to Castaneda's 1968 classic, *The Teachings of Don Juan: A Yaqui Way of Knowledge* (Berkeley: University of California Press).

one sentimentalizes or primitivizes the Mazatec present, for the present is perennially a time of loss and change. Viewed in this way, Estrada may appear as the acculturated Mazatec, whose adolescence coincided with the arrival in Huautla of anonymous hippies and world-famous superstars in search of God, and who early withdrew to work in Mexico as a writer and engineer. However, Estrada's yearning here (as it came across to me in conversation with him) is for something that draws him backward, fascinates and troubles him, and that he cannot possess; he honors it but mostly lives apart from it. With Munn, the stance—of exile and escape—seemed different from the start: a flight-from-time in search of mysteries/illuminations that brought him to the place left vacant by Estrada: the town, the family, and so on.

But overshadowing them both is the culturally authentic, strangely marginal figure of María Sabina, whose personal history (never "erased" in the Castanedian sense) is always precarious and whose spiritual universe begins to change (she tells us) with the coming of the blond strangers, a few at first, then in great waves in the 1960s. It was with a sense of what was at stake and of his own role in the subsequent engulfment of Mazatec culture that Wasson, accused, responded as poignant witness: "[Her] words make me wince. I, Gordon Wasson, am held responsible for the end of a religious practice in Mesoamerica that goes back far, for millennia. 'The little mushrooms won't work any more. There is no helping it.' I fear she spoke the truth, exemplifying her *sabiduría.*" And, still more striking, the words of another shaman count the losses for Estrada: "What is terrible, listen, is that the divine mushroom no longer belongs to us. Its sacred language has been profaned. The language has been spoiled and it is indecipherable for us."

The word *language* hits here with tremendous force; for this is crucially a book of language, a reflection of the great Book of Language that María Sabina saw in her initiatory vision:

> On the Principal Ones' table a book appeared, an open book that went on growing until it was the size of a person. In its pages there were letters. It was a white book, so white it was resplendent.
>
> One of the Principal Ones spoke to me and said: "María Sabina, this is the Book of Wisdom. It is the Book of Language. Everything that is written in it is for you. The Book is yours, take it so that you can work." I exclaimed with emotion: "That is for me. I receive it."

And she did and was thereafter a woman of language—what we would dare to translate, by a comparison to those most deeply into it among us, as "poet."

Her own words and her highly tuned chants (the improvised and collaged "sessions" that function like long, driving poems) make this clear. Wasson's account of her actual performance and its impact on the first enthralled outsiders brings the message home, as do appraisals by poets (Waldman, Homero Aridjis) from outside her time and place. And hearing her voice on tape or reading her here in translation, we catch the presence of a great oral poet, one whom we can now see working and changing over the course of time—in three recorded sessions, 1956, 1958, and 1970. The Language revealed is awesome, not because it allows her to control the world around her (it doesn't) but because it lets her survive the sufferings of a world in which the spirit of Language itself has been "profaned," in which "it wanders without direction in the atmosphere . . . not only the divine spirit . . . but our own spirit, the spirit of the Mazatecs, as well."

A devastatingly human book and testimony, hers is an appropriate inclusion for a series on millennial poetics over a broad human range. This broadening and expansion was the motive for those of us who entered some years ago into the pursuit of an actual "ethnopoetics"—a term that the poet David Antin expanded still further to mean "Human Poetics . . . People's Poetics or the poetics of natural language" [see above, page 136]. And other-than-human as well, if we take her word for it: "Language belongs to the saint children"—the sacred mushrooms—"They speak and I have the power to translate." Or Antin further: "What I take the 'poetics' part of ETHNOPOETICS to be is the structure of those linguistic acts of invention and discovery through which the mind explores the transformational power of language and discovers and invents the world and itself."

In that sense we aren't dealing with something merely alien/exotic, but we are all potential witnesses and transmitters, all suffering exiles and losses, are all in an encounter with language and vision. María Sabina's Language bears the traces of such an encounter and presents them in a form in no way incomplete: a language-centered poetics and a guide that encompasses even that art or act of *writing*, which we would still speak of, in our arrogance, as the final instrument of language that separates her and us. But she has seen the book as well—the Book of Language—and that makes of her own work and Estrada's a Book about the Book. And, if we let it, it is also a book of healing: a language directed against that *sparagmos*—that classic split in consciousness—that tears us all asunder. The wounds are deep and are probably irremediable, but the dream, while we're alive, is that of wholeness. Here is language as a medicine, its ancient function; for, as she puts it elsewhere, "with words we live and grow," and (again speaking of the mushrooms with a familiar Mazatec word): "I cured them with the Language of the *children*."

Vitezslav Nezval:
A Post-Face

(with Milos Sovak)

An Opening Image. In the half-light of the century from which we're just escaping, Nezval is standing with a band of poets from its early years. The image shows him volatile and round, a mass of energy just waiting to explode, as one of us remembers him from childhood. He plays with oranges and draws the juice from them like magic. At night his fingers run along the keys of an accordion while studying the stars. In the light he squeezes paint on canvas. Among the poets of his time he is an equal force—even while writing in that language that the others do not understand. Picasso is the small man to his right. Teige, Styrsky, Toyen are his cohorts. In the doorway at his left Breton and Eluard are wrestling. There are other shadow images that only some can see: Neruda, Lorca, Tzara, Hikmet, Césaire. These are the poets of the Surrealist left; they occupy a corner of this paradise of poets, and from there he looks across a space and through a window where a square like Vaclavske namesti opens up to him. He calls for neon lights to fill it in the shape of poems. They flash out in the darkness, make a place like that where "poetry erects its lantern in the woods." He says, "I am a poet and a child" and falls back with the others.

Vitezslav Nezval was born on May 16, 1900, into the family of a village teacher in Samikovice in southern Moravia. His father had cultivated an interest in the arts and had traveled long distances to see important exhibitions. He was especially involved with music, and his teacher

Vitezslav Nezval, *Antilyrik & Other Poems*, translated and edited by Jerome Rothenberg and Milos Sovak (Los Angeles: Green Integer Books, 2001).

was the composer Leos Janacek. Nezval's grand-uncle was an eccentric toolmaker and telegraph clerk, a man who knew the world, spoke several languages—"half scientist, half poet," Nezval would later say of him. The young boy's life was profoundly marked by these two men but also by the village culture, close to nature and the vocabulary of those who worked the soil. In 1911 Nezval entered the gymnasium in Trebic, where he also learned piano and tried his hand at composing music. From 1916 on he was systematically reading and writing his first poetry. This was during the First World War, and in March 1918 he was drafted but was sent home soon thereafter for partly real and partly simulated illnesses.

With the war over, Nezval came to Prague in the fall of 1919 and started studying philosophy at Charles University. This was the time when a newly formed Czechoslovakia (under its philosopher-president Thomas Masaryk) was emerging as the first real and socially oriented democracy in central Europe, and the question of its further political and economic direction was then in contention. Like most other Czech artists and intellectuals, Nezval veered toward the left and in 1924 became a member of the Communist Party. As with others also—not only in Prague but throughout Europe—political revolution had its artistic counterpart, and from 1922 on, Nezval allied himself with the "Nine Powers" *(Devetsil)*—a collective of poets and artists that included among its core figures: Jindrich Styrsky, Jaroslav Seifert, Karel Teige, Frantisek Halas, and Toyen (Marie Cerminova). Written before his twenty-second birthday, Nezval's long poem, *The Remarkable Magician,* was included in the group's "Revolutionary Collections," a series of books of essays, poems, and manifestos, that accompanied the founding of a new "poetism" as the principal Czech avant-garde movement.

Nezval dated his own "discovery of Poetism" from 1923. As a program and a poetics—developed by Nezval and Teige in the latter's 1924 *Poetist Manifesto* (contemporary with André Breton's *Manifesto of Surrealism*)— Poetism set itself against "literary poetry" and proposed "a new art which will cease to be art" (Nezval's words) and will become "the art of life, the art of being alive and living life" (thus: Teige). In a tension shared by other movements then and after, their poetism tilted between a rejection of "art" in the name of "a pure poetry . . . [within] a life [turned] into a magnificent entertainment" (Teige) and a commitment to political and social struggle taking shape around a nascent and, for them, a still admired Soviet Union. Nezval would later rename the movement "realism" and later still would ally it for several years with the Surrealists of Paris.[1]

In this way Nezval's public career—like that of many of his contemporaries—moved between political and literary commitments and alliances. With the onset of the Great Depression of the 1920s and 1930s he engaged directly in labor struggles—those in particular of striking Czech coal miners. In 1932 he attended the first Congress of Soviet Writers in Moscow, and in the same year he made an extensive and for him a transformative trip to Italy and to France, where he met with the leaders of the French avant-garde: Breton, Eluard, Péret, Aragon. At the same time his recognition as a poet—the central figure of the new Czech poetry—continued to grow. He received the prestigious State Prize for poetry in 1934 and donated the entire sum to a fund for helping refugees from Nazi Germany.

Nezval's meeting with the French poets and his continuing involvement with Surrealism had a kind of inevitability about it. As early as 1924 the event and content of Breton's *Surrealist Manifesto* of that year (along with that of Yvan Goll) had been disseminated in Prague. From the early 1920s on, Nezval's connection as writer and dramaturge with Jindrich Honzl's Liberated Theater involved him in the presentation and translation of works by Apollinaire, Jarry, Soupault, and Breton, among others. The painters Styrsky and Toyen, both close to him, emigrated to France and entered actively into the Paris art scene. From 1928 to 1931 Styrsky, along with Karel Teige, published a number of key articles concerning French Surrealism, and in 1931 three important shows of French avant-garde painting were organized in Prague (an internationally based *Poetry '32* exhibition came shortly thereafter), with Nezval intimately involved in their planning and presentation.

It was only after Nezval's 1932 meeting with Breton, however, that a more formal collaboration was set in motion. Nezval came to the Surrealists' defense against attacks by the Russian writer Ilya Ehrenburg, and in 1934 eleven writers, poets, and painters in Prague published a manifesto,

---

1. Of this "realism" Nezval would write: "Logically the glass belongs to the table, the star to the sky, the door to the staircase. That is why they go unnoticed. It was necessary to set the star near the table; the glass hard by the piano and the angels; the door beside the ocean. The idea was to unveil reality, to give it back its shining image, as on the first day of existence. If I did this at the expense of logic, it was an attempt at realism raised to a higher power."

written largely by Nezval and Teige, in which they presented themselves ("hand in hand with the revolutionary proletariat") as a part of the international surrealist movement.[2] Along with this came a proclamation "to the Central Committee Agitprop of the Communist Party," announcing the decision to found a "Surrealist Group in Czechoslovakia . . . to test and develop in the broadest, most revolutionary way, in the spirit of dialectical materialism, the human condition in all its expressions, whether writing, speech, drawing, painting, sculpture, theater, and/or life itself."

The alliance between Prague and Paris led to a period of heightened activity on the Czech side: new books and magazines; art exhibitions; visits from Breton, Eluard, and others; the establishment of the Surrealist-oriented New Theater with its productions of Breton and Aragon's *The Treasury of Jesuits* and Nezval's *The Oracle of Delphi*. With its balancing act of poetic and political absolutes, however, the Czech group, much like its Parisian prototype, began quickly to come apart. In 1938, while Europe was heading into a new war, Nezval issued a proclamation dissolving the movement, which for a year or so continued a shadow existence under Teige.

For Nezval the war period was a time of withdrawal and holding back. Before the Germans invaded in March of 1939, he had declined to leave the country, although arrangements had been made for him to do so. His books became unpublishable, and he turned his attention to painting and

---

2. The manifesto reads in part:

A CALL TO ARMS that doesn't have to wait for real wheels under it, a decision that resists inertia, the depression over a jammed pistol, and first and foremost our own instinct not to be hemmed in by any artifice but panting after that reality from which it seemed to be excluded by historic fictions—the Supreme Being, say, or Look into Your Heart and Write—deceived by all those understuffed *pirozhky*, beginning with mandated prayer and ending with deflated art, it has convened us at the graveside of these gas-bags, spouting out the best we can remember to the open air, until we light the very last balloon, so late returning to the primrose path without that famous fire exit at our service.

We are Surrealists . . .

And you will either get enthused by this expression of our will to tear ourselves away at any cost from literature and from moronic sensibilities of every kind, or you'll end up siding with those steady self-improving bunglers of good writing.

And you will either be turned off by that old glory-comb that made our head-hairs stand on end or else you'll join us all the way in following Surrealism's never dying lamp, whichever way it takes you, and in light of which our isolation will be only make-believe, a pure illusion once we've set foot on the soil of surreality, and moving freely into all your secret alcoves, shut inside them by so many useless locks.

to the writing and production of plays, most notably *Manon Lescaut,* a work based on l'Abbé Prévost's famous eighteenth-century novel. More lyrical and conventional than his earlier work, it slipped past the German censors and became (in the popular mind at least) a celebration of poetry and human values in an age of terror. In 1944 Nezval was arrested by the Germans but was released soon thereafter.

After the liberation in 1945, Nezval returned to poetry and to increasingly recognized publication, though rarely with the avant-garde thrust of his earlier work. For a while he was the director of the film section of the Information and Culture Ministry in Prague, and after the Communist takeover in 1948 he received a number of official prizes and considerable governmental support. His political affinities and international stature made him a prominent member of that network of tolerated avant-gardists/poet-heroes that included Neruda, Brecht, Picasso, Hikmet, Eluard, and Tzara, with some of whom he shared pro forma hymns to Stalin in the early postwar years. In 1954 he traveled again to France, this time to meet with Picasso and to see the French premiere of his play *Today the Sun Is Setting on Atlantis.* But by then he had already experienced his first heart attack and with it the sense that death was closing in on him.

The last years of Nezval's life were a time of frenetic activity—publishing poems, essays, memoirs, and copious translations of world literature, but especially of poetry. On a trip to Italy in 1958 he felt his heart condition worsen, and he returned to die at home, precisely on the day the stars predicted to him. For him it was, as he had written earlier, a return "to my most ancient ancestors—metal, plants and stones / . . . and what mankind, in baby babble, labels elements."

Nezval died on April 6, 1958.

⌐

What remains, then—in the aftermath of war and cold war—is the work of a poet who stands alongside his Czech contemporary Vladimir Holan as one of the major writers of mid-twentieth-century modernism. In Nezval's case the range of the work and the apparent ease of its execution are the first matters to be noted. He was, when we look at him closely, a protean poet for whom everything seemed possible. His language was simple, where simplicity was needed, while the linkages, by which the mind enters more deeply into its own domain, were gnarled and multiphasic. Like his counterparts elsewhere, he rejected the generalized or symbolic ("allegorical") word in favor of a vocabulary and a poetics of concrete particulars—the "antilyrik" that a poem of his once named. Of this he wrote: "It is surprising how many a person of quality . . . fails to comprehend the modern poem which is simple, because he is searching for allegories. . . . Such people would introduce into poems something that isn't there. . . . If, for example, one says a rose, they do not see a rose; they are searching for an allegory."[3] If this concurs with Pound's contention that "the natural object is always the *adequate* symbol" or Blake's that "Eternity is in love with the Productions of Time," its privileging of the particular made of Nezval a poet of Prague—a specific place—and himself a man talking and thinking within it. Yet his thoughts, once released, could not stand still. They led him into his dreams, and the dreams—reinforced by a studied mysticism: kabbala, astrology, alchemy, etc.—came into the poetry as well. That along with the ability of language to present him with new and previously unexplored areas of meaning—of a new reality in short.

3. And again: "I am more touched by a lily that I accidentally broke one morning in my childhood than by a lily that is a general symbol of purity."

Louis Zukofsky:
A Reminiscence

For the Louis Zukofsky Centennial Celebration,
Columbia University, 2004

Louis Zukofsky wasn't as old as my father—or my mother for all of that—
but he was the first poet of their generation who offered friendship and a
particular model of what it meant to be a poet *against the odds* and with a
persistence approaching the *heroic*. If Pound was, as Louie and he had it
in various letters, "papa" to Louie's "sonny," Zukofsky wasn't that for me
or for the poets close to me (Antin, Kelly, Schwerner, Economou, Blackburn) who enjoyed his company back in the early 1960s. He was, however, a remarkable and delightfully graceful poet and a link to a time before ours and to other (older) poets of that time still largely out of reach.
That interested me a lot as I tried to imagine the pathways of poetry and
what came before us or what was likely to follow. I knew him to be older
than me but I had little use for a hierarchical or reverential view based on
age or gifts or anything else for that matter. I thought we were a generation that believed in an equalizing of all such relationships, though I may
shortly have been proved wrong in that assumption.

My initial contact with Louie was in June of 1959. I had sent him a
copy of my first little magazine—*Poems from the Floating World*—and he
had responded (as was his custom) with a brief and courteous note, handwritten on a postcard and starting off "Dear Sir." George Economou
thinks it was Paul Blackburn who brought a few of us to the Zukofskys'
Brooklyn Heights apartment on Willow Street, probably not long after. I
knew of him, of course, as one of the lost "Objectivists" and a collaborator
in that sense with the generation before his, most specifically with Pound
and Williams. The first edition of *"A" 1–12* had come out from Cid Corman's Origin Press in 1959 and was a featured book when a number of

us opened a short-lived East Village bookstore, The Blue Yak, in 1960 or 1961. A year or two later, Economou and Robert Kelly published *I's (Pronounced Eyes)* [a.k.a. *Ryokan's Scroll*] under their Trobar imprint, and by then Louie was, in some sense, part of our circle or network or cabal, or at least we thought he was. Diane Rothenberg and I saw him and Celia at their place (I can't remember if at ours), at some readings and other public events (one of his in Brooklyn at which he introduced me to Marianne Moore), at an occasional concert of Paul Zukofsky's, and at at least one glorious excursion out of town. From Louie's side it seemed clear that he welcomed the attentions shown him by younger poets, earlier contact with Duncan and Creeley being cited as events of particular importance.

For me the Pound connection at that point (it would be different for me a few years later) mattered less than it did for some of the others, since I saw my main derivations from other aspects of the international avant-garde. It's also likely that the interaction with Zukofsky was one of the circumstances that allowed me to expand my poetics to include and draw from the American line of vorticists and "Objectivists," though I may not be the best judge of how that came about. I knew that Louie had his long essay on Apollinaire, but it was also clear to me that his focus—like so many at that time—was on American [Poundian] modernism as the dominant center of poetic interest.

By autumn of 1961 I had taken on a teaching position at the Mannes College of Music in Manhattan, where I was a one-person English or literature department, though I was able to hire part-time assistance from people like Antin, Diane Wakoski, Jackson Mac Low, and Frank Kuenstler. I was also given a small budget to set up a poetry reading series, for which I had a vast ambition but not much money to support it. My memory fails me here, and I can remember only two of those who read in the series during its only year of operation: Paul Blackburn and Zukofsky. (Charles Olson also accepted—or seemed to—but finally backed off.) At Louie's reading, as I led him to the reader's podium, we managed to spill a pitcher of water between us, which allowed me to make some inane apology and Louie (who was being a little nervous otherwise) to shrug it off with a pun about making a splash, or words to that effect. The reading went off very well, though, and it's his voice from that evening that mostly sticks with me in memory: a very musical voice with a very refined overlay on what was otherwise a very healthy New York accent—nothing of Pound's or Yeats's oldfangled bardic raptures but a gently anachronistic cadence that bested both of those, at least to my New Yorker's ear. And

then, when the reading was over, we took a cab downtown, where someone was hosting a party for Louie, and the cab driver, who overheard us
talking about it, allowed that he was a great fan of Zukofsky's and joined
us for the celebration. (That—for me at least—was the beginning of "the
sixties," as we soon came to know and love them.) At the party itself I remember Louie, clearly pumped up by the event, interrogating a number
of listeners still new to his work, about the structure of "A"-7, which he
had read that evening, and delighted (I think) that no one had *heard* it as
a sequence of seven sonnets, though in the written text the form was evident. ("As I love: / My poetics," I thought out loud, in a phrase of his that
I even then remembered.)

   We were most of us barely in our thirties then—or even our mid-
twenties—and Louie was getting on to sixty, so there was room enough
to be reverential, if you chose to do that. Nor was he young-looking for
his age—a thin body and a kind of gray frailty that he exaggerated by
the way he would protect himself against the elements—a shawl wrapped
around himself when he felt a lack of warmth in their Seventh Avenue
apartment. He smoked a lot and drank a lot of coffee, but so did we, so all
that came out even. I don't think there were any physical problems at the
time, though those who knew him better spoke affectionately about his
hypochondria and let it go at that.

   There was some concern about Louie's health when a number of us
decided—in the spring of 1964 it must have been—that we would go for
a couple of days to the Amish (Pennsylvania Dutch) Fair in Kutztown,
Pennsylvania, and would ask the Zukofskys to join us. It was, I believe,
at the height of our friendship, and Louie and Celia were eager to be a
part of the expedition. The other couples, since we were definitely into
couples, were Paul and Sarah Blackburn, Armand and Dolores Schwerner, and George Economou and Rochelle Owens. We stayed at a hotel
an easy distance from the fair and found lots of time for talk—mostly
swapping stories and once (I remember) getting into a discussion about
e. e. cummings, among other key poets, in which Louie and I were cummings's big defenders. On our second afternoon, as a break from the fair,
we went over to the house or farm of someone whom one of us knew,
where most of the time was spent batting a baseball around. (George
Economou reminds me that he always carried a ball and bat in his car.) At
one point, Louie and Celia were standing with Sarah Blackburn in what
passed for the outfield and weren't paying much attention to what was going on, when someone fungoed a hard line drive and struck Sarah on the

back [on the head, someone else corrects me], knocking her down. When we came rushing up, she was still on the ground, and Louie said (jestingly of course): "You almost hit the *poet.*"

I think, although his timing here was somewhat off, that this was Louie's self-mocking (ironic) reference to his position in the little world around him—like Williams asking, "Who shall say I am not / the happy genius of my household?" There was a kind of wistfulness in all of that— a regret, let's say, about the lack of recognition in the larger world, that some of us were seeking to redress. For me it added to the fondness that I felt for him, though I would take our friendship (over all and look- ing back at it) as rather *shallow* in affect—not in any invidious sense, you understand, but never really reaching to the depths. On the level of ideas, my own poetics were shared more easily with poets closer to my age, those who engaged with me in what David Antin would later call "tuning," talking to each other, seeking, plotting, looking back at him and others of his age for clues to our own futures. In retrospect now—and approaching the age at which he died—I have a sense of lost opportunities and obvious omissions, along with which, a blanking out of memory or else a memory of things that weren't said, of absences perhaps, perhaps evasions.

Louie, by his own witness, wasn't one to talk about himself or about his works, and though he wrote at length about poetry (in very specific ways), I remember his pushing me, at the time I was assembling *Techni- cians of the Sacred,* to play down the "commentaries," which I was mak- ing an intrinsic part of the mix. That he had been involved with poli- tics (Marxist, even Communist) in the preceding decades is clear from his published correspondence, but (unlike my experience with Oppen, say) I don't recall it coming into conversation. I also don't remember, though it would have been a shared area of our experience, that there was any talk about our both having had Yiddish as our primary early child- hood language. In retrospect it seems like something we would have gone into or that we would have exchanged some talk in that language, which Louie appears to have known better than I did, but if we did, I have no memory of it. I was still, at our time of greatest contact, some years away from *Poland/1931* and *A Big Jewish Book,* both of which were for me experiments—*real* experiments—in writing (or constructing or assem- bling) "an ancestral poetry." It was in that way a little like my meeting with Paul Celan—also in the 1960s—in which, as I've described it else- where, we spent several hours in a café near the École Normale in Paris (where Celan taught), talking in a mix of hesitant German (mine) and hesitant English (his), and only at the end acknowledging that other language, common to us both, which we could have spoken and yet didn't. (A few years later I would have pressed Louie on that and related matters—particularly when I was assembling *A Big Jewish Book*—but by then he was out of New York and we had very little contact.)

We did talk some about Pound, however, and the question of antisemitism was clearly a part of that. There was no real defense of Pound—nor did I have any reason to expect one—beyond some observations—quite understandable on Louie's part—that Pound was less vehemently antisemitic than some of the other American modernists. At the time I hadn't seen transcripts of Pound's World War II broadcasts—and Louie probably hadn't either—nor was I aware of the depth of their relationship or their curious dance of the nonintelligence in social and political matters, antisemitism no small part of it. When I finally read their letters, a decade or so after Louie's death, I felt a pang of regret, of sympathy too, for Louie caught up in the other's madness (*mishigass,* I meant to say) and feeling forced to account for the cardboard Jews of Pound's (banal) imagination. At the same time I tried to think myself into Louie's place—and (with more difficulty) into Pound's—and got no further than the pain of it, and stopped.

Theirs was a strange relationship all in all and very different from how the other "Objectivists" related to Pound (or failed to). For it seems to me that it's in the letters—the correspondence—far more than in the poetry, that Louie takes on the master's voice: the pseudofolksiness, the free orthography, the portmanteaus and punnings, even the mock-yiddish accents of Pound's *Der Yiddisher Charleston Band* parody and Louie's occasional declarations of his own "antisemitism" (possibly ironic, possibly not). In the course of the letters, Louie argues (from a Marxist and Communist perspective) against Pound's fascism and his embrace of Major Clifford Douglas's social credit theories, but with the antisemitism he seems more often than not to play along with the joke or to deflect Pound's absolutism with regard to Jews—*all* Jews. The most egregious example of the latter is the commission that Pound gives him (circa 1936) to get a reading from his father Pinchos on whether prohibitions on usury in Leviticus 25 apply equally to Jews and Gentiles—"whether the jew IF he enters a community of nations proposes to treat the goyim as his own law tells him to treat his own people." It is a curious mission, this, from poppa to poppa, a curious notion that the older Jew, as informant, will speak in this regard for *all* Jews (much as the American Indian informant is sometimes thought to speak for *all* Indians). The result, to say the least, is ambiguous, another well lost cause.

If Pound was the master here—the FATHER—Louie was in many ways his equal and in some ways (dare I say it?) his superior. Where it came to Louie's "music," say—a tempting but elusive word applied to poetry— it wasn't that he was better than Pound (that would be a spurious distinction) but that he was more radical in certain ways, more removed from the Victorian lyric voice qua *music*, as Williams was also, and Olson later— all of them operating like Pound on strategies of long poem composition, though nowhere more musically conceived or constructed/composed than by Zukofsky, "specifically," as he said of himself, "a writer of music." (I would refer here to Cage's contention that poetry, if it isn't music as such, is most readily defined by the formal and rhythmic elements it *shares* with music—all of which, like other Cage "definitions," seems fairly obvious but no less true.)

On still another level of language—both its sound *and* meaning— there was in Louie's work (at least as I heard it) an idiom of New York and of a portion of the early twentieth-century immigrant world that created a demand for a new or altered dynamic in poetry (in Louie's case the sound of Yiddish pulsing beneath the surface of "Poem beginning 'The'"—and elsewhere—as a deliberately inserted presence). This was an opening of language that Williams would specifically have encouraged, Pound less so, and that someone like Eliot would have (and did) hold up to scorn—a fancy British overlay obscuring his own Missouri base. None of this of course is absolute, and much of it may be open to question, but it was something that seemed fresh to me when I first read and heard Zukofsky, and even more so now.

What also seemed fresh—and the degree of its freshness only became clear to me later—was the entry into Louie's mix (his grand collage of cultures, times, and places) of the deep tradition of Jewish lore and mysticism—even against its dismissal or erasure by his masters. Here was something different from Reznikoff's judaica and from that of many far lesser poets, something that set him apart also from the other *big* writers of his time, both Jew and Gentile. I can't say that it was a direct influence on my own work—much less on that of Meltzer or Tarn or Hirschman or others: Robert Kelly, who was so good at it, and Robert Duncan, who knew "that lute of Zukofsky" and its airs as well as anyone. What Zukofsky gave us, then, wasn't so much ethnic writing in the ordinary sense (though Louie, like others of us, could do that too) as an addition to an ethnopoetics on a grand scale, diving into the poetic and near-poetic past with the charge to make-it-new ("contemporaneous in the mind") and to carry it freshly into the present. In doing so, he found a place for himself (and for all of us), where he could hunker down and leave his masters well behind.

What we have in common, I would suggest, is a matter of source that needn't comment on itself as source.

Robert Duncan:
A Memorial

I first met Robert Duncan in 1959. San Francisco was and remained his city, but he was then living in Stinson Beach, a short ways up the coast. We had been corresponding for maybe a year before that, although I was a dozen years younger and very little published. Ferlinghetti's City Lights was bringing out my first book, *New Young German Poets* (a book of translations), and that summer Diane and I had come to San Francisco for the first time. We ran into him at the City Lights Bookstore—there was a kind of photo session going on—and a few days later Diane and I drove to Stinson Beach, picking up Robert, who was hitchhiking, somewhere along the way. He was at that rare moment bearded, as was Jess, and looked to my naive eye a little like the forty-year-old Whitman. (Jess then looked oddly like a youthful D. H. Lawrence.) There was a feeling of enchantment about it all: themselves, their house and garden, the books they read, the paintings and collages Jess was making, the grunion running that night along the shore, the meteorites that flashed across the night sky, and a meal (Diane reminds me) replete with sorrel and lemons and nasturtiums from their garden. I felt myself led, by a kind of magic, into a world suggested by his poems.

It was, I now realize, a moment of change for me, even in some sense of transformation, to which those two were among the singular contributors. I had like others been wavering about my location as a person and a poet, and Robert showed me in his own terms the possibility of relating to a vast and uncharted domain of poetry—and something more. With

From *American Poetry* (fall 1988).

an incredible lightness and cheerfulness he announced himself as "book-ish" and "derivative," freeing those words suddenly from the academic bounds in which I had then placed them. He spoke impassionedly, for he was then most into it, of Williams and of a poetic line determined by the breath. More singularly, he brought "romance" and "gnosis" back into a world of common things—a merging, in David Antin's later, clearly too flippant, terms, of Anaheim and Disneyland. In exchange for Paul Celan, whom I first gave him then, he led me into Gershom Scholem's vision of kabbala and the lore of the "old Jews," and he sensed, before anyone else and least of all myself, that I would move in that direction.

What he offered then and later—in spite of any shifting moods and weathers—was a generosity of spirit or, more immediately, a poetics *of* the spirit, even where the generosity might seem to falter. It was an ac-knowledgment of, and an insistence on, the spiritual-in-art, as Kandinsky might have known it: an inspired reminder of what art and poetry still could be and a vision—through Whitman and/or Dante and/or others—of a totalizing universality that included and surpassed all separate indi-viduals and species.

All of this he spoke in what sometimes seemed like a language of pure parataxis, a leapfrogging speech that was constantly on the lookout for connections—like a rare form of collage brought into the world of con-versation. If his rap included camp, as Jonathan Williams has elsewhere pointed out, that was good also and an essential part of who he was. But the language of the poems and essays was, above all, a noble and enno-bling language—a stance that he was willing to project as few others among us:

> Often I am permitted to return to a meadow
> as if it were a given property of the mind
> that certain bounds hold against chaos,
>
> that is a place of first permission,
> everlasting omen of what is.

An ennobling language and one striving at the same time (through what he called "courage in daily act") toward the creation of a new and "natu-ral" measure.

Robert Duncan was in the end a poet of enormous means and complexity—one of the last to assay a cosmological poetics, to be "the model of the poet," as Michael Davidson described him, "for whom all of reality can enter the poem." As such he was (he made himself) a man and poet open to multiple influences, accepting and announcing a sense of his own *derivations* that freed others to do the same. One has only to think of the remarkable lists of predecessors—and contemporaries— that filled his essays or, by collage and paraphrase, came into his poems: "Ezra Pound, Gertrude Stein, James Joyce, Virginia Woolf, Dorothy Richardson, Wallace Stevens, D. H. Lawrence, Edith Sitwell, Cocteau, Mallarmé, Marlowe, St. John of the Cross, Yeats, Jonathan Swift, Jack Spicer, Celine, Charles Henri Ford, Rilke, Lorca, Kafka, Arp, Max Ernst, St. John Perse, Prevert, Laura Riding, Apollinaire, Brecht, Shakespeare, Ibsen, Strindberg, Joyce Cary, Mary Butts, Freud, Dalí, Spenser, Stravinsky, William Carlos Williams, John Gay . . . [and] Higglety-pigglety: Euripides and Gilbert. The Strawhat Reviewers, Goethe (of the *Autobiography.* I have never read *Faust*) and H.D."

So goes one list in his 1953 essay, "Pages from a Notebook," the same piece in which he also tells us, memorably: "I make poetry as other men make war or make love or make states or revolutions: to exercise my faculties at large." It is the kind of statement by which one knew and loved him—the kind of statement that placed him, by its bravado and because the poetry itself had also proved it, among that visionary company of which he knew he was a part. And that company could then be extended in every direction—noble and lowly—toward the greater symposium of the whole that he prophesied in his later "Rites of Participation" and that he saw already forming in our time.

He was, then, a poet (even a *great* poet) who created—like Whitman before him—his own life as a poet. Toward that creation he was aware, and he made us aware, of the stages (the grand design) by which a life like his might grow. His retreat from publication, a fifteen-year hiatus that he announced in 1969, was an aspect of that, as was the prophecy for his later years, which he foretold as a delirious and creative senility and in which he was (alas) to be thwarted by several years of debilitating illness. The relative lack of critical response to *Ground Work I: Before the War* was also, I suppose, unforeseen—to place him among those great poets whose own lifetimes were not sufficient to receive the acclaim that a posterity would give them. Yet that nonrecognition itself became the occasion for an outpouring of devotion by dozens of outstanding contemporaries who joined together in creating for him a national poetry award for *Ground Work I* and for a lifetime of achievement.

For one who thinks in terms of patterned lives, of grand designs, an artist's later work takes on a special meaning. With Robert Duncan the final book of his lifetime—*Ground Work II: In the Dark*—is, we now can see, one of those culminating works: his creation of an *altenstil* marked not by a mere quiescence but by ominous premonitions/confrontations with sickness and pain—he who had once thought himself the master of a charmed life, for whom a mighty hand was always ready to appear (he told me once), to pluck him from disaster. So, in a great dark section of the "passages" sequence, "In Blood's Domain," he contemplates the death by illness of poets before him:

The Angel Syphilis in the circle of Signators   looses its hosts   to swarm
     mounting the stem of being   to the head
                        Baudelaire, Nietzsche, Swift

are not eased into Death
                the undoing of mind's rule in the brain.

That same poem ends:

What Angel   what Gift of the Poem,   has brought into my body
     this sickness of living?   Into the very Gloria of Life's theme and variations
     my own counterpart of Baudelaire's terrible Ennuie?

Ground Work II ends—for he lived to achieve it—with the single poem written after the final illness struck his body and with the contemplation also of the devastation it had already carried to his mind and spirit. He read it to us shortly after it was written—the hope implicit in it that he would be spared to write still more. He never did, as if Death's angel had to rebuke the beautiful optimism of his life and his desire to leave it intact. But the last time I saw him—a month before his death—with my wife, Diane, and Jess, and Michael Palmer, the two hours at the bedside were mostly spent in laughing, joking, as if to show us that he had entered the outrageous and hilarious "senility" of his earlier prediction. And I thought (for my own part and likely not for his) that that was right—that on this occasion we could laugh Death and God to scorn. That God and that Death who are the same.

Reading Celan:
1959, 1995

At the International Paul Celan Symposium,
Maison des Ecrivains, Paris, 1995

Paul Celan was for me and others the great poet of what we later came to call the Holocaust. I was (I think) the first to translate him into English (or to translate him publicly), and I was fortunate enough to meet and talk with him in Paris three years before his death. When I was assembling *A Big Jewish Book* in the late 1970s (later called *Exiled in the Word*, from Edmond Jabès's phrase), I used a poem of Celan's as that gathering's concluding work; and I would like to start with it now, as a way to come into speaking about what I want to say about him today and in the reading I will do later in these sessions. He has been present for me since I first heard about him and long before I came myself to a kind of writing that I had put off for many years, although what propelled it had also propelled my life as a poet from the very beginning. I would like to suggest in doing this that Paul Celan was, for me and many others, the exemplary poet in pointing to the possibility that such a poetry could still be written—and that it could, in any instance, be written as if written for the first time.

Celan's poem is called *Zürich, zum Storchen*. It is dedicated to Nelly Sachs and translated here by Joachim Neugroschel:

[Reads the poem beginning *"The talk was of too much, / too little. Of Thou / and Thou again, of / the dimming through light, of / Jewishness, of / your God. // Of / that."* And ending: *"We / simply do not know, you know, / we / simply do not know / what / counts."*]

With Celan, who was a poet of the human—not only Jewish—disaster of the Second World War, I would like to address a theme or presence to which until several years ago my own work only barely alluded but which has been an ongoing subtext in most of my poetry and in that of much of my generation. In a period of barely half a dozen years (from 1939 to 1945), there were more than forty million state-directed murders of human beings and at least that many sufferings, maimings, and tortures: a disaster so large as to be almost incomprehensible and itself only a part of the disasters and conflagrations of the century and millennium from which we're now emerging. Auschwitz and Hiroshima came to be the two events by which we spoke of it—signs of an enormity that turned myth into history, metaphor into fact. The horror of those events encompassed hundreds and thousands of like disasters, joined (as we began to realize) to other, not unrelated violence against the environment/the earth and the other-than-human world. By the mid-twentieth century, in Charles Olson's words [cited above, page 12], "man" had been "reduced to so much fat for soap, superphosphate for soil, fillings and shoes for sale," an enormity that had robbed language (one of our "proudest acts" he said) of the power to respond meaningfully, had thus created a crisis of expression (no, of meaning, of reality), for which a poetics must be devised if we were to rise, again, beyond the level of a scream or of a silence more terrible than any scream.

The ground against which Olson, writing in the late 1940s, set his own poetry of "resistance" was the too-familiar ground of Auschwitz—in his most specific reference: Buchenwald—and the death camps of World War II. Even now, when that ground has been sanitized and turned into a museum (a museum more than a shrine), the presence as exhibits of hair, shoes, fillings, glasses, prayer shawls, toys, can still bring an immediate, uncontrollable sense of the reduction, the degradation that the modern world allows. When I first came to Paul Celan's poetry—in 1957 or 1958—the war and the *Holocaust* (though I still didn't call it that) seemed very close to hand. I cannot remember how central that was to my reading of Celan then, although *Death Fugue (Todesfuge)*—his most overt poem about the death camps—was one of the poems that I translated. But I want to be quite clear about that opening attraction to Celan, for what allured me those thirty-seven years ago was not simply his relation to the Holocaust as subject but that I felt a renewal in his work of energies and gestures that the war—if anything—seemed to have set aside, called into question. A renewal and the beginnings—there and elsewhere—of a new twist on those older moves and stances (Surrealist and Dada) in which the war, the Holocaust, could also find a voice.

Since that was 1959, the bulk of the poems I translated (as part of a small anthology of mine called *New Young German Poets*) were from *Mohn und Gedächtnis* and *Von Schwelle zu Schwelle*, in which the fear or terror, rarely overt in its references (*Death Fugue* is in that sense an exception), was carried forward by a music of (almost) songlike rhythms and (not only in *Death Fugue* but throughout) quasi-formal repetitions. But it was only with the last poem I translated—*Schneebett* (Snowbed) from his (then) new book *Sprachgitter*—that the language began to show that convulsiveness—that disassembling and reassembling of language—that would later be the hallmark of his work. Looking back at *New Young German Poets,* I see the page with "Snowbed" sitting next to a page with Helmut Heissenbüttel's "Combination II," and I note (as it struck me then, too) that both (I stress *both*) have the marks of a consciously experimental deconstruction of ordinary verse and language. (I use the word *deconstruction* advisedly.) The first numbered section of Heissenbüttel's poem consists of the single word *blackness* hyphenated and broken into two lines, and the first line of his second section (written entirely as capital letters) reads as a single linked word AFTERNOONSSLEEP-REMINISCENCE . . . both of these being gestures described far too quickly as "uniquely" Celan's. And yet already at that time, while I spoke of Heissenbüttel in my introduction as "the most consistent verse experimenter" of the poets presented, I said of Celan (in a very brief contributor's note): "Paul Celan (b. 1920, Czernowitz/Bukowina, Rumania, now living in Paris) is regarded by many as the greatest of the post-war poets in Germany, perhaps in Europe. Because of his Jewish background, he grew up apart from the German world whose language he shared. Surviving, he has transformed that language into a unique personal instrument for assaulting a reality that has wounded him but that he still desires to address as 'Thou.'"

Looking back at it in that context I am curious as to what I meant by Celan's "uniqueness." It is as if there were already an inkling of the extremity of the later work, the shape it would take (in extremis) as he moved it further through his life and toward his death. For it suddenly occurs to me that to speak of Celan's 1959 work as *unique*—sitting as it does here next to Heissenbüttel's, with whom it shares certain (less-than-unique) characteristics—is already to assume, as I did, something *personal* (particular to him)—the use of language (a specific language) as "a personally unique instrument" (meaning a tool, or possibly a weapon): the voice in German of a Jew who had survived the German-led Holocaust and was about to become the greatest poet of the German language after Rilke, say, or after Hölderlin, or what? His was, then, an act of subversion and defiance, clear enough even at that early point, although I had no way of knowing how deep, how, specifically, deep into language, that defiance, that mastery on every level of the German tongue, would go.

By the time I met Celan—in 1967—his reputation had certainly begun to grow, and his work had touched the extremes of a post-Holocaust poetics. (It was still, however, four years before a first volume of his poems would appear in English.) By then his own work had developed through the 1963 publication of *Die Niemandsrose* (The Nomansrose) and the publication—just that year (1967)—of an even greater breakthrough volume, *Atemwende* (Breathturn). My own work then was heavily involved with experimental processes—of sound, of image, of metaphor, of visual presentation, of heightened oral performance, of ethnopoetic delvings into a multiplicity of human pasts. I was also acutely aware of my own contemporaries in English, to a lesser degree of his in German; and it seemed to me, among other things, that Celan's most recent verse (as in the poem I read at opening and in works with titles such as *Breathturn* and *Breathcrystal*) was as close as that of any European writer to the desired poetics of the breath (and body) that was forming the basis of what was then the most germinal side of the new American poetics. In Celan's words, which were so pregnant for us then and will be repeated often, I believe, in the sessions here: "Poetry is perhaps this: an *Atemwende*, a turning of our breath . . . [and] it is perhaps this turn, this *Atemwende*, which can sort out the strange from the strange." And still further, as the call for a new poetics to meet a new reality, or to mine into our deepest layers (of history, of thought), he showed in his work the model for a poetry stripped down, compressed, exploring unavoidable "difficulties of vocabulary, [a] faster flow of syntax, [and] a more awakened sense of ellipsis" that connect (however "indirectly," he tells us) to "[the poem's] strong tendency toward silence."

He is, in this sense, one of those in the postmodern (post-Holocaust) period who came to realize and extend the innovations of the modern—not as a matter, simply, of his formal practice but of that practice turned into a process of salvation/salvaging driven by the poet/seeker's desperation. We all have that to some degree, but there are certain poets—like Celan, Artaud, Vallejo, Hölderlin—whose lives (whose sufferings perhaps) invade the work and thereby dramatize the human fate the form addresses. In Celan's case—not uniquely perhaps but *astonishingly*—the suffering seems so closely tied to "holocaust," to that ultimate disaster of a people and a culture (that ultimate reduction of the human that brought about Olson's cry for a resistance through the breath, the body of both man and poem)—the suffering seems so closely tied to "holocaust" that the central issue of his work (the pursuit of a "reality [that] is not simply there [but] must be sought for and won") becomes alive for him and us: the dramatic example of what the revolution of language/revolution of the word might mean in our time. If something like this is inherent in the work of many, in his work and life it was brought to an unavoidable realization; for what sets him apart even here is that the language itself seems shaken to its foundations—disassembled and reassembled in such a way that the act of language becomes (for the moment) a believable act of redemption. It is reminiscent in that sense of William Blake's prophecy from nearly two hundred years ago:

Obey thou the Words of the Inspired Man
All that can be annihilated must be annihilated
That the Children of Jerusalem may be saved from slavery

and again:

. . . Till Generation is swallowed up in Regeneration.

This has been noted often enough as it appears in Celan: a work of re-demption carried on as a struggle against the horrors inherent in everyday language and act—more specifically the ways in which the dominant lan-guage (German in his case) is shaped and distorted by those whom the Dada poet Richard Huelsenbeck had called "the advocates of power" and had contrasted to the "creative forces" that it was Dada's goal to free. In that light, I would say, Celan's struggle with language—like ours—should not be viewed as his *malaise* so much as a sane, *totally* sane, ef-fort to get rid of what still another Dada poet, Hugo Ball, in the midst of World War I, had called "the filth that clings to language," and by that very act of poetry—again I'm quoting Ball—"to get rid of language it-self." Of the realization in Celan's work and life of that most profound and moving of avant-garde incitements (and of its relation to a specific language, German), our American colleague Jed Rasula has written:

Very few writers have so openly allowed the language of their po-ems to be helpless, to be written from a condition of abrupt syntactic disintegration *consciously* attended to. The great difficulty—and thus his greatest example for later poets—is in practicing a craft on material that disappears in proportion to the success of the poet. . . . With Celan, the German language itself becomes the means of its own disembodiment. In his hands, more and more of the language simply goes up in smoke. There is nothing like it in any other language that I know of.

A language that goes up in smoke is symptomatically, inherently, a language "after Auschwitz"—after the death camps and crematoria and deaths by fire of World War II. As poetry—as an assertion that such an act of language is only possible *as* poetry—it is a rejection or a radical and ironic reinterpretation of Adorno's pronouncement about the barbarity or immorality of writing *lyrik* after Auschwitz. By his work and by his life, then, Celan stands as a beacon for all of us who came to poetry as a means of resistance—a necessary counterlanguage to the other languages—the languages of power. I would therefore want to end this praise of Celan with a poem of my own wherein I address the question of poetry after Auschwitz. In 1970 I dedicated to him the first installment of a series of poems called *Poland/1931,* in which I invoked an imagined ancestral Poland as the place from which my Jewish parents had come and where their parents and parents' parents had lived before them—as far back as we can remember. Nearly twenty years later I went to Poland for the first time and found myself haunted by the ghosts of that place and driven toward a poetry that spoke—in my own words—of what we in my family had called, not "holocaust" but (using a familiar Hebrew-Yiddish word) *khurbn.* In the poem that I'll read I address the spirits of the dead as *dibbikim/dibbiks:* those numbering in the tens of millions who had died before their time. And in the same breath I invoke Adorno's familiar words about Auschwitz.

[reads *Dibbikim*]

> spirits of the dead   lights
> flickering (he said) their ruakh
> will never leave the earth
> instead they crowd the forests the fields
> around the privies the hapless spirits
> wait millions of souls
> turned into ghosts at once
> the air is full of them

they are standing each one beside a tree
under its shadows or the moon's
but they cast no shadows of their own
this moment & the next they are pretending
to be rocks   but who is fooled
who is fooled here   by the dead   the jews
the gypsies   the leadeyed polish patriot
living beings reduced to symbols
of what it had been to be alive
"o do not touch them" the mother cries
fitful, as almost in a dream
she draws the child's hand to her heart
in terror   but the innocent dead
grow furious they break down doors
drop slime onto your tables
they tear their tongues out by the roots
& smear your lamps your children's lips
with blood a hole drilled in the wall
will not deter them
from stolen homes stone architectures
they hate they are the convoys of the dead
the ghostly drivers still searching
the roads to malkin   ghost carts overturned
ghost autos in blue ditches
if only our eyes were wild enough
to see them our hearts to know their terror
the terror of the man who walks alone
their victim whose house whose skin
they crawl in   incubus & succubus
a dibbik leaping from a cow to lodge inside
his throat   clusters of jews
who swarm here mothers without hair
blackbearded fathers
they lap up fire   water   slime
entangle the hairs of brides
or mourn their clothing hovering
over a field of rags   half-rotted shoes
& tablecloths   old thermos bottles   rings
lost tribes in empty synagogues

at night their voices
carrying across the fields
to rot your kasha your barley
stricken beneath their acid rains
no holocaust because no sacrifice
no sacrifice to give the lie
of meaning   & no meaning   after auschwitz
there is only poetry   no hope
no other language left to heal
no language   & no faces
because no faces left   no names
no sudden recognitions on the street
only the dead still swarming   only khurbn
a dead man in a rabbi's clothes
who squats   outside the mortuary house
who guards their privies who is called
master of shit   an old alarm clock
hung around his neck   who holds
a wreathe of leaves under his nose
from eden   *to drive out*
the stinking odor of this world

Jackson Mac Low:
A Pre-Face

Mac Low stands with John Cage as one of the two major artists bringing systematic chance operations into our poetic and musical practice since the Second World War. The resulting work raises fundamental questions about the nature of poetry and the function of the poet as creator. For raising such and other questions, Mac Low like Cage has sometimes met with strong rejection and, being primarily a poet, has found less public recognition for a work that's often sensed as "abstract" and that seems, by setting "chance" over "choice" in the making of poems, to act against the projection of personality usually associated with "the poet." Still, he's widely influential and recognized by many (Cage among them) as the principal experimental poet of his time.

My own first response to Mac Low was one of resistance, which (since I was still inexperienced) I didn't recognize as a sign that something important and new was going on. The occasion I now remember was in 1961, a performance of his play, *Verdurous Sanguinaria*, at Yoko Ono's loft in what would later be New York's Tribeca district. Diane Wakoski, Simone Forti, LaMonte Young, and Mac Low were "acting" in it, and Wakoski was the one who had coaxed some of us to come along. We just couldn't get with it that night—although it touched off the obvious comparisons to things we said we admired: Dada or the works of Gertrude Stein: the great traditions of twentieth-century experimental poetry and art. But it's one thing to carry the torch for events already historical—

From Jackson Mac Low, *Representative Works, 1938–1985* (New York: Roof Books, 1986).

another to tune in to the work of a contemporary moving in what (at the time) seemed like a bewildering, even a "self-indulgent," direction.

There followed a period in which one heard Mac Low perform his work more often than one read it. And a period in which one (I mean myself and others like me) began to push our own work past the initial breakthroughs of the 1950s—in our case expressionistic and imaginal— toward the even more open and unexplored terrain of the 1960s. For this, Mac Low—his work, I mean—began to appear more and more as a challenge and incentive. Then, very suddenly it seems in retrospect, it came to be something still more: an achievement of the first order.

I want to be clear about all this because I know that from then to now my own experience has been repeated by others—that it will he repeated, I'm sure, by still others for whom this book is a first encounter with Mac Low. The great block to Mac Low's work, as I observed earlier, lies with his use of random and chance methods of composition and performance—the very heart of his achievement and his challenge to our inherited ideas of authorship and authority in the work of art.

For myself I can recall three points of entry to his work. The first was through a series of poems from the early to the mid-1960s, in which "chance" and "choice" were both operative—notably *The Pronouns,* the early *Light Poems,* and *The Presidents of the United States of America.* The most chance-determined of these, *The Pronouns,* definitively answered my own lingering questions about Mac Low's "accessibility"; they were nothing but stunning—as I later wrote: "a masterpiece of language and a total joy." And once being stunned—and thereby vulnerable and open— the range of his contributions became clear, still clearer as more of his work appeared, to show him without limit.

In addition to numerous ways of making chance do the poem's work, what we were seeing were continuing experiments—both beautiful and outrageous—with a range of compositional and performance modes: simultaneities and other group forms, music and language intersections, phonemic sound poems, collage and assemblage, intermedia, high-tech computer work, concrete and visual poetry, acrostics and syllabics. If that sounds overly formal, the corpus viewed differently runs the gamut from the "abstract"/impersonal *Stanzas for Iris Lezak* to the "expressionistic" but still highly structured *Odes:* "a work of personal history that (in some of its sections at least) out-confesses the 'confessionals.'" And there are still other magnificent choice-determined segments and whole poems: Mac Low, say, writing to a friend:

The traitorous light turns as the
whirling earth
turns.
The traitorous light turns from pale
blue to grey.

My traitorous heart turns from one to the other loyally.
Faithfully my traitorous heart
turns
trying to make no promises or none it cannot keep
or none that cannot keep it
or none that cannot keep it keeping them . . .

or addressing a lover (he is in fact an incredible love poet), while simultaneously tracking the operations of chance that bring key words into the
poem and his actual life:

I know when I've fallen in love I start to write love songs
Love's actinism turns nineteens to words & thoughts in love songs
as your "A" & the date made "actinism" enter this love song . . .

or celebrating chance itself:

And chance—what else can I call it?—has opened my life now
    again
And again beautiful life opening up and blossoming when it seems
    to have died to the roots
Nothing but rotting at the roots . . .

that "blessed chance" to which he would again and again turn, to summon poems whole:

Asymmetry 205

silence,
        island.
                Lordship eyes no
        cable eyes
island.
        silence,

                              Lordship anchor no
                    descended
          Lordship oars rapidly descended silence,
                    hand island.

                              praying

—which is, well, simply beautiful.

But nothing, come to think of it, is *simply* beautiful, and everything
gets back (crucially in Mac Low) to what Charles Olson spoke of as the
poet's "stance toward reality." This was, for me, the second point of entry
to Mac Low's work—the recognition, through what he himself revealed,
of how that work was placed in relation to the world, even to "reality" itself. And the fact was that it really was so placed, that he was (even in his
most chance-determined work—or especially there) reporting the world
to us with a cranky accuracy. Poems like those already quoted literally
spelled out the poetics of which they were a part, and where that wasn't
enough, he wrote in prose to clarify his methods and to show their link to
ideology.

The basis of that ideology is anarchist and pacifist on its political side,
Taoist and Buddhist in its reflection of what he calls "the world 'in general.'" The offering throughout is of a "synchronous" view of the world, in
which coincidences of occurrence ("acausal connections" in Jung's writing about the *I Ching*—or, more simply, things happening together) are
never meaningless but allow the mind to experience the most diverse relations, "*across* any present, between any two things co-existing." And it's
the turning to "chance"—"to produce a kind of art that is not egoic"—
that lets things happen in this way. Speaking of all that, in 1975, he said:

> That's the main motive for "letting in" other things than oneself,
> randomizing means or other people or the environment, as when
> performances include long silences: during silences when you, as
> a performer, don't do anything for a while, other things that are
> happening become part of the piece. All of these are ways to let
> in other forces than oneself. At first one thinks one can avoid the
> ego, make works that are egoless, by chance. This illusion passes
> after you work this way a while. You realize that making a chance
> system is as egoic, in some ways, or even as emotional, as writing a
> poem spontaneously. But at the same time you realize there is some-
> thing more than just yourself doing it, & by interacting in that way

with chance or the world or the environment or other people, one
sees and produces possibilities that one's habitual associations—
what we usually draw on in the course of spontaneous or intuitive
composition—would have precluded, for our so-called intuition or
taste is always involved with our biographies & habits, & you know
that in Buddhism, the ego includes the Unconscious, in the Freudian sense; all the layers of the mind as dealt with in modern psychology are still within the bounds of the ego, & this includes the
deep Unconscious.

Beyond that, he tells us, he travels with those like Duchamp and Cage into
something that "has to do with what in Zen is called the 'No Mind'":

that layer of mind below the Unconscious, the impulses, the instincts, the Id, the deepest layer, which is common to all people: the
No Mind (Sunyata viewed as an aspect of mentality). From the No
Mind, or from emptiness, everything arises, & if one can step aside
a little bit, one can allow it to manifest itself.

The politics ("I've been a serious pacifist most of my life, & since
about '45, I've also identified myself as an anarchist") are in some sense
an extension of those other concerns—what he calls "the political side
of Dharma." They move him, in other words, toward a "society without
a coercive force pushing everybody around"—in which the world can be
accepted with least interference; in which "the poet does not wish to be a
dictator but a loyal co-initiator of action"; and in which performance together establishes a new social bond or serves as model for "the free society of equals" that it is hoped the work will help to bring about. Put
this way, Mac Low's art returns to something like the stance of an earlier
avant-garde (Russian Futurism, Dada, etc.) for which artistic, spiritual,
and political renewals were all part of a single impulse. In no contemporary does it show through as clearly, movingly, this vision of experimental/
language-centered art as social action.

An ideal of egolessness, then, which he pursues and never reaches,
the failure itself, like the failure of all great art, a goad to more reflection; thus:

Despite the fact that the ego is going to make up these systems &
pride itself on becoming "Jackson Mac Low, the great poet who

makes up chance systems," nevertheless, there is something or other happening, though now I'm not sure what it is.

Or again:

> I think it is rather hard to think concretely about anarchist politics. In the 60s, many people went through semi-anarchic situations in communes & so on, & all of the theories of government were probably born again in people's minds as they went through those experiences, when the communes fell completely to pieces because no one would take responsibility, or some guy took over, or a small clique took over: nearly every possibility worked itself out.

The disappointment shows through; it underlies the great fervor and yearning with which he continues to give himself to projects like those David Antin describes: "Jackson the modernist at an avant-garde festival in the early '60s, treating us to a formalized prophecy of the death of our cities; . . . Jackson the concrete poet at Bryant Park, where we had been expressly forbidden to read 'sexual or political poetry,' reading his 'nonpolitical poem,' which he explained 'expressed no attitudes or opinions or ideas of a political nature,' and nearly causing a riot with a single litany of names."

And it's all the more moving, to me, because the stance is so devoid of fanaticism—is, rather, generous and open to "the world 'in general'" and to other poets, rejecting few in his own thought, whatever crankiness he may show as a matter of style or instinct. ("How can I reject anyone who's risked this much?" he said to me with respect to my own work with anthologies and the need to exclude therefrom, etc.) An inclusive rather than an exclusive avant-garde, then—and that's a pretty rare bird in itself.

The third entry I found into Mac Low's work was through performing it. He's undoubtedly one of those who have contributed most to reviving a poetics of performance—from the side of music in his case, since he's a composer and sometime pianist himself, who tends to conceive performance works in musical terms. For myself—as for other poets and artists in the vicinity—the invitation to perform with Mac Low became the occasion for hearing the work from within it. If this made us part of "a free society of equals," then it was as well a society in which one figure exercised a curious and quirky leadership, to bring us toward our own experience and understanding; for, along with the anarchist commitment, was a desire that the others act as real "co-initiators," in an atmosphere of mutual attention.

I got the "idea" early along, but I really got the idea sometime mid-1960s in a performance of one of the "gathas," scores and instructions for which appear in these "representative works." The text, as I remember, was the Japanese Buddhist prayer or mantra, *namu amida butsu* ("praise Amitabha Buddha"), a repetitious, quite familiar formula of Pure Land Buddhism. Mac Low's directive, as it would be thereafter, was to *listen! listen! listen!* and to observe and interact while "listening intensely to everything in the performance & in the environment"—though our inclination back then was more likely to take his "anarchism" in the colloquial sense as each man or woman for him- or herself. It didn't matter that night. The old Japanese words, resonant from earlier readings, and the recognizable *aum* as mantric axis line that held the piece together, appeared and disappeared as phonemes and syllables began to move around the space in which we had dispersed ourselves. I had never so clearly heard or felt my own voice or Voice Herself as carried by the others—the separation and recombination of sounds that related back to a fixed string of sounds and to a meaning that I didn't reach but that I knew was there. It was something very old and very new: Jackson's arrangement and invention but vibrant with the source itself.

Part of the intention of the series in which *Representative Works* was originally intended to figure as the second book—its principal intention— was to place the poetry of our time in relation to other times and places.[1] Mac Low, who is one of our true inventors, creates new modes and brings us back to the oldest possibilities of sound and language as they enter poetry and music and performance. If it's possible to see that here "objectively" and through a silent reading of the work presented, it's also possible, through what he offers, to follow his directions for composition and performance into one's own creation or into one's own realization of the work. The more one does that—treats the book not only as a text but as a score and manual—the more one realizes the service of this work, its lasting power. It is in this sense that the book becomes, in Ezra Pound's words, "a ball of light in one's hands."

1. A project of the early 1980s under the imprint of Ross-Erikson Publishers in Santa Barbara, California, suspended on the death of publisher Roy Erikson. The two books that did appear were María Sabina's *Life and Chants* and Howard Norman's *Wishing Bone Cycle.*

A Pre-Face for Paul Blackburn

He remains a young man in my mind; young to the year of his dying, a young-looking forty-four. In his face a kid even, with a kid's wisp of beard or mustache when he had it: oriental Fu Manchu–like face we kidded about often. And the youngness got into his manner, too, the way he held himself, walked or ran down the street, drove bike, held hand of wife while strolling, laughed, got tangled in his own relentless stories that sooner or later betrayed his age through details no kid could know. The maturity was in the words and poems, his language, out of a rich stock of languages—or outside of language as such, in a kind of pained sigh he sometimes had, likewise the way he clicked his tongue against his cheek when thoughtful (a habit I picked up from him qua influence, or in fulfillment of the text: *not what the rebbe says but how he ties his shoes*).

So I find it hard to trace the changes from when I first saw him, busy about his work of 1958, at one of the many poetry series he would initiate then and later. This one was in the Café Borgia—Bleecker and MacDougal, if you remember, across from the legendary San Remo and Figaro, which latter I had frequently inhabited from college years: a gathering place for tourists and others until its transformation into ice-cream parlor circa 1970 and resurrection some years later. The Borgia readings were ephemeral (like so many others), but the poetry was solid, and on the day I sighted Paul there, Denise Levertov was reading (my first hearing of her work), over which Paul officiated: clean-shaven, boyish, aloof (I thought),

Revised from an earlier version for inclusion in Carol Bergé's projected *Light Years: An Anthology of Artists' Memoirs from NY's East Village Avant-Garde Arts in the 1960s.*

and serious under heavy-rimmed glasses, showing his customary attention to the enterprise at hand. There was something he was fussing about that day, something that seemed to agitate him, but what it was I can't remember, or can't be certain if it wasn't already the business of getting it down on tape, say, as he always did later. But I know he was counting the house and was making sure, if the hat was passed around, that the right words would be spoken: to make things well.

No one I knew could match him in that regard: in the easy professionalism of his gestures, his devotion to phantom benevolent organizations of poets, his vagabond teaching and learning among peers: a trick he may have borrowed from the old troubadours and would restore to us. That was the first thing to be learned or shared: that urge of a generation to set up a new life in which poetry became a likely occupation and the extension of a gentle lifestyle among friends. For myself, too, I learned from him (and no one before had so convinced me) that natural speech and attention to line and line-breaks (heard as movement of the voice) were possible poetic ventures; and at the same time, at a more profoundly human level, his was the model of a poet who, Octavio Paz admiringly told me in a taxi ride from Paul's place early in the 1960s, spoke of his contemporaries with great generosity and (except for one point of deep disappointment) with less rancor than any I would ever meet. ("The mark of a wonderful poet," Octavio said, or words to that effect: "the way that the wonderful poets must be" and too often weren't.)

It was in that manner that he continued to travel through the world and, in particular, through New York: the city he had come to as a young kid from Vermont and where he had grown up to become a reigning poet—though without the title in that "New York school" as such. He was differently tuned to New York from the "school" poets, traveled in it further: to the bridges and compromised outskirts of Brooklyn via BMT; or the good unfashionable bakery at Twenty-fourth and Third, where we used to meet for lunch; or riding the Staten Island Ferry a century past Whitman, where he would have myopic "visions" of the moon, before returning home to Fifteenth Street, or Spring Street, or Seventh Street above McSorley's Ale House. I wouldn't even try to catalog his places and his people, American and European both, and the other times and places that his mind, by contrast, set them up against with so much intelligence and grace: Provence and Barcelona and terrible Toulouse: a sense of time that saw the history of alphabets scrawled on the sides of industrial cranes and caterpillar tractors:

>   earth / debris / & schist, the stud/stuff of the island
>   is moved by this
>   PASCO
>   CAT-933
>   Oregon 6-
>   it does not rain   .   smoke, the
>   alpha-beta tau.

Who could be more the New York poet than he who knew the three or four taverns of Manhattan, circa 1960, where Ballantine's ale was served on tap, or could lead you to every Lower East Side bar that had Ukrainian music on the jukebox? For us who were also urban-bred he was our final, fateful connoisseur of cities.

And part of that concern, I think, was to find a place for the poet to take a stand within the city: an arena in which the friends could gather and where they wouldn't have to keep apart but could share in the rhythm of the surrounding world. The entry of poetry into new places pleased him—but particularly places for other uses: a bar at best, although a coffee shop was also reasonable or *(faute de mieux)* a church. He was always on the lookout: got mixed into the group that started circa 1960, at Mickey Ruskin's Tenth Street Coffee Shop, moved to the Deux Megots on Seventh Street, the Metro on Second Avenue, and later to St. Mark's Church just up the block. Each stop on the way was important in the creation of a nexus: a subtle network of poets too diverse in their explorations to ever make a "school"—although the Church would later be the center for a younger "New York School" or lend itself, for better or worse, to such a designation. But by then circumstances had intervened and had separated him from that enterprise, which the initial heavy funding (from HEW, etc.) had turned overnight into a large-scale "poetry project." To the organization created thereby, although his energies had set it in motion, he afterwards remained a stranger: often passing by but never really moved to enter in-the-spirit.

His own attentions in that sense turned to a number of bars around the city, in which the enterprise as he knew it could continue: first to Max's Kansas City (for readings on Sundays) and Doctor Generosity's (Saturdays), and later (though he may have been away from NYC by then, a visitor on weekends) to St. Adrian's Company on Lower Broadway. A string of reading places he didn't live to complete, they were his final gift to us—although he preferred even more than in the late Metro, early

St. Mark's days, to stand back and oversee the operation without making himself too frontal. But as long as he remained in New York (before the last gig at SUNY-Cortland, where the cancer overtook him), he couldn't truly keep himself hidden but went always through old familiar motions: checking the sound levels, recording and amassing that incredible collection of tapes, taking his turn with introductions, drinking with friends, and so on.

The last time I saw him at a New York reading was at Dr. Generosity's: his own on a trip to the city, winter of 70/71, when I was myself ready to leave for a quarter of teaching out in San Diego. Not only in retrospect, but at that time too, there was a sense that something different was happening. Maybe that he mentioned not feeling too well, that he drank as heavily as he did even while reading, apologized to us for poems that "weren't poems" (though speaking hopefully about a turn the work was taking, toward a greater sense of earth and totem beings), seemed about to cry (I thought), and when we parted, in that crowded room, hugged me and asked about *my* health and future, but so strangely that I spoke about it later: as if he wasn't asking about me but a whole world (I now think) that was turning sick and fading.

"Not a bad year on the whole though," he wrote in a letter he sent a few months later to tell about the cancer. He wanted to keep on and didn't take lightly to dying and leaving it behind. When we saw him early that summer at the Michigan poetry festival, he had grown skeletal and could barely keep his food down—although he managed somehow with the Spanish brandy and the defiant Picayunes he kept on smoking. The big tape recorder seemed an almost impossible burden, but he lugged it around as ever and went about the business he set for himself how many years before. (That and the ping-pong match he beat us all at were the two main facts that I remember.) And when I came to visit for the first time during the last weeks at Cortland, it was my own voice I heard from upstairs, singing a horse-song on a tape he'd made in Michigan and still was into cataloging. You don't fuse your life with that of the old troubadours and easily forget those acts of *cortesia*—even dying.

But generosity was the name of the place, as it was truly of the game he played. His poems will all be published someday, and the achievement (which his own strange diffidence would often hide) will loom large in retrospect, while the other accomplishments, because they don't exist on paper, will fade with time. Where other poets made their after-hours contributions as "editors" and "critics," Paul's way was to organize the oral part of the enterprise, over that remarkable and terribly short span of years. And it's to that side of his career that I would want these words to be a homage.

Gary Snyder:
The Poet Was Always Foremost

For me the poet was always foremost and the legend of the poet secondary. The person is there in any case, but where I continue to see him best is as he emerges from his poems. It was Robert Kelly, I think, who first turned my attention to the work—around the time that LeRoi Jones's Totem Press was bringing out the edition of *Myths and Texts* with the Will Petersen calligraphic cover—and it was Robert Bly who made the contact. I had been seeing poems signed "Gary Snyder" for maybe a year or two before that and had by then formed a small sense of what he did. The Donald Allen anthology (published the same year) gave us some more of it, but otherwise, for me, there was no Snyder myth as yet. Only the poetry.

Its beginning and its end—among the stars—brought Dante to mind, or Thoreau in its claims to wilderness and a kind of ecstasy through wilderness, but mostly that here, in the territory he had chosen (of a poetry like Pound's, say, that drew from many times and places), there was a new space in which to work, with a link to the illustrious predecessors but opening old Whitman's democratic vistas in a way that most of those before him had failed to do. ("If Snyder hadn't been there," Richard Schechner said later, "we would have had to invent him.") It was a time, for poets, of rediscovery and extension, in which the modernist past (and all the premodernist pasts it laid claim to) were again there as resources to be used and to be addressed—to a new and, so we thought, a very different

From John Halper, ed., *Gary Snyder: Dimensions of a Life* (San Francisco: Sierra Club Books, 1991).

generation. In this Gary had a line—both as verse and program—and it was that which we sighted and seized on in a reading of his work.

The time itself was still postwar—or what I've come increasingly to think of as post-Holocaust—even for those of us who were too young for it. I can't get at the heart of it even now, but something about that war, that point in history, had turned the great American modernists on their heads or, put another way, had infused the kind of work they left for us with what George Oppen pointed to as a new populism. With a new openness too—or generosity with regard to who might be thought to belong. What Snyder gave us, then, was a kind of Wobbly modernism (even before the Zen): regional and specific, gritty, disciplined; true to his own voice, surely, but opening as well to larger worlds, as that sort of thing, that largeness, was happening also in Olson's work, say, or in Duncan's. It was a time, as I saw it, to reclaim and to expand—transform—the century's beginnings, and what he did, while it felt different from my own concerns then, seemed true and proven in the work. Alongside Duchamp's project ("to put art again at the service of mind") or Breton's ("the critical investigation of the notions of reality and unreality, of reason and unreason, of reflection and impulse, of knowing and fatally not knowing, of utility and uselessness"), it was soon possible to join and to relate Snyder's articulation of "the real work of modern man: to uncover the inner structure and actual boundaries of the mind."

The primary means for that uncovering is the actual work we do as poets—and *work* is a better, bigger word for it than *poem*—but it is or can be more than what that seems to say. To uncover or discover is to open to a search for sources—in the human past and in the greater world beyond the human. In this sense Snyder was then and was to become still more a leading figure. There is no poet I know with a surer sense of that possibility of staring our animal natures in the eye that he attributes to the shaman-poet—in any and all cultures, and all times and places. It is no small thing that he does here: To open poetry again to the possibilities of a genuine engagement with nature and to know that to write of a tree is not a sin in our time, as Brecht would have had it, but an exploration of matters central to our survival in this world. So, in his poem, "The Humpbacked Flute Player," a landmark work for me, the poet is left in Canyon de Chelly, having invoked a world of Buddhist saints and American Indian ghost dancers, with no sense of guilt about the work itself, but letting the poem come to him, the old communion restored/redeemed, where

Up in the mountains that edge the Great Basin

    it was whispered to me
    by the oldest of trees.

    By the Oldest of Beings
    the Oldest of Trees

    Bristlecone Pine.

    And all night long sung on
        by a young throng

    of Pinyon Pine.

It is survival that he celebrates here, and survival comes also into his sense of poetry over all, and with that a truly contemporary, truly meaningful, approach to what I have elsewhere (and using the wrong word maybe) spoken of as an "ethnopoetics." It is part of Snyder's premise as a poet opening to larger worlds—that one moves from the regional (the bioregional at that) into a regard for other times and places. It was this, beyond the visions of those who preceded us, that he first knew how to make meaningful for our own time and place. For myself: Though I had come with others to the common store of ethnopoetics, it needed his impetus, his insight, to sense poetry not only as a work of mind in search of worlds and meanings but as the "ecological survival tool" that he set forth in his essay on "poetry and the primitive." In a letter that he wrote me when I was already deep into the work, he spoke of poetry in this sense as "a vehicle to ease us into the future." The bridging effect of that statement was tremendous—as if something vital, missing from our Great Collage, had there been set in place.

In retrospect I want to say at least that much in tribute.

David Antin:
The Works before *Talking*

But maybe—as I said to the well-read questioner at a recent California reading—the most important poets today are the ones you haven't heard of. While I don't usually come on like that, the question does keep getting asked, and the communications gap it represents is something awful. Poetry, after all, is still in a corner, which means (for those of us who live by it) that the occasions for talking it through with anyone outside that corner are very rare. But, then, the corner itself may be an issue, and the poets who are most aware of it (as a crisis of thought, I mean, and not a body-count of readers) may prove to be the most important ones among us, whether my well-read questioner had heard about them yet or not.

To begin with Antin, he's possibly as important a poet as we've got in America—or one of a dozen such operating today, if I may be allowed the estimate. His only problem, so to speak—and here I'm referring to the language of publishing acquaintances in the environs of zip code 10017 in Manhattan—is that he hasn't "surfaced," that is, hasn't appeared in books published by business establishments whose lack of interest in poetry or vague sense of its cultural prestigiousness somehow makes their judgments more objective than those of the (specifically) poetry presses and makes their books worthy of attention by equally disinterested institutions like the *New York Times Book Review* or *New York Review of Books*. The result is that my questioner, whose depth of reading depends on a network made up of just such institutions, hadn't heard of Antin or most of the other poets I might mention and who (for reasons often ideo-

From *Sumac* (fall/winter 1971); reprinted in *Vort*, no. 7 (spring 1975).

logical) have chosen to channel their major works through an alternative communications network my publishing acquaintances call the "underground."

Antin's ideology—as it has influenced his choice of publishers—was apparent from the opening of his first book, *Definitions,* which he published with Black Sparrow Press back in 1967. That book's title poem (on one level, a lament for a dead friend) begins with a definition of "loss" from an insurance manual, namely

> loss is an unintentional decline in or disappearance of a value arising from a contingency

and the poems that follow go on to explore the central image of entropy (loss or degradation of energy and order in any closed system) as it defines the issues of our lives on Earth. But why do I mention this in the context of where a man chooses to publish his poems? Because it seems to me that for Antin as for others of us, there has been a strong sense that what we do as poets (more simply: as people responsible for keeping language and reality together) is in danger of an inescapable, premature reduction as it's forced to enter the unique entropy machine of the modern communications nexus. All of which Antin (whose real outside reputation is as an art "critic") has shown in his model of a Jean Tinguely–type "self-stabilizing data processing machine," the blueprint of which strongly resembles the ground plan of the Museum of Modern Art. Put any kind of input into this machine, and it will process it in such a way that the output will be "indistinguishable from the pre-input or initial state of the said machine": a product called "art" there or "poetry" elsewhere, but with its specific features degraded to the level of what we were expecting all along. Whatever. The danger to what it's really about must be obvious.

So much, then, for the literary framework, which the poet has continually to challenge, even as he or she must more and more frustrate and disappoint our expectations—a crucial development in Antin's work that I'll get to later. That work itself neither begins nor ends there but somewhere in the middle, a point where we may find ourselves at any given moment. In the first book, then, a man has died, and the poet asking questions (he is as much a philosopher as a poet) challenges the reality of all our lives where such losses are certain. So far—except for that opening definition of loss with its insurance manual language—the ground is elegiac and familiar. What begins to distinguish it is that Antin won't let himself drift into a "poetic" softness: a refusal that grows fiercer with each successive work. Instead his reiterated refrain becomes "it is a fact," and his choice of reference isn't to older poetic or mythological extravagances but to the "cooler" terrors of scientific data. (If you understood what they were really saying, wouldn't you go mad?)

Let me give some explanation of how the theme and its treatment have developed in the four books seen thus far.[1] In the first of these, *Definitions* (1967), Antin is emerging from a formative period as neosurrealist (his translations of Breton are still the best I know of) and carries the surrealism along in images like that of

a waterbird standing on one leg
shifting the time from one hand to another

or of

skinless divers
diving past flowers and sea urchins
their own pink petals of flesh flowering.

But he's also been into the cooler ambience of Cage, Mac Low, and Stein (also of newer artists like Robert Morris, say, and Warhol), which has brought him closer to his own predilections as poet. Thus the central concern of the lament for his dead friend, the inability to hand a glass of water across barriers that include the glass and the water themselves, goes from surreal spookiness to the terror of a world of bodies and physical laws in which

a glass of water falling
is a falling body of water
and obeys the laws of falling bodies
according to which
all bodies fall
at a rate that increases uniformly

1. Circa 1971, just before the publication of *Talking* (New York: Kulchur Foundation, 1972). More recently these were included with other early poems in Antin's *Selected Poems, 1963–1973* (Los Angeles: Sun & Moon Classics, 1991).

> regardless of their form or weight
> at the same altitude and latitude

even light, say, which

> is heavy and falls
> three hundred and sixty tons of light fall
> from the sun on the earth every day

in case you hadn't heard.

Through the three long poems that make up *Definitions,* the imagery swings between that kind of hard data and the "language," as we used to call it, "of dreams." Only in the last two sections of the final poem (a long, presumably ongoing work called *The Black Plague* and triggered by the murders in Mississippi of the civil rights workers Chaney, Goodman, and Schwerner) does the temperature go all the way to "cool." Where the poem's opening was a detailed taxonomy of the human body scored as a sacerdotal lament, his strategy by the third section is to lift (and modify) materials from Wittgenstein's *Philosophical Investigations,* incorporating the logician's words and rhythms into a maddening discussion of how we "feel" emotions and pain, our own or others'. (He will reveal in one of the comparatively rare "personal" sections of *autobiography* that there was a turning point in his own life, when the terror of not being able to "feel" was brought home to him in an angst-vision of late adolescence.) But in a poem that began with the political murders of three young men, it's startling to hear the nearly affectless voice that tells us how impossible it is to know the suffering of others, since "we might as well imagine a number in pain" or a stone. A far cry from the poem as catharsis—an ennobling, therefore cheap way out (meaning: I *feel* bad, therefore I share your suffering).

Unfortunately *Definitions* is now out of print, which deprives any new reader of a sense of buildup to the present cool, almost "antipoetic" phase of Antin's writing. The middle book, *Code of Flag Behavior* (1968), retains visible traces of the fury behind the work (such traces are disturbingly nonvisible thereafter), while pursuing questions of linguistic and moral deterioration with increasingly objective finesse. A masterpiece from *Code*—and one that shows how a poet can deliver the goods and circumvent the need for explanations and other prose fillers—is "the delusions of the insane," where he produces (reproduces, in fact) a typical list of "what they are afraid of," from

the police
being poisoned
being killed
being alone
being attacked at night
being poor

through a series of more and less exotic instances, to the sense that

... they are in hell
that they hear people screaming
that they smell burnt flesh
. . . .
that houses are burning around them
that people are burning around them
that children are burning around them
that houses are burning
that they have committed suicide of the soul

until we realize that *they* haven't made it up at all. How are "we" different from "them," then? In our capacity, probably, to sidestep suffering and that obvious "suicide of the soul"—unless we commit a more subtle form of same in the process.

Delusions, then, is one way in which Antin questions the "legislated reality" presented to us by the tried-and-true process of enculturation. It's also an example of how he uses "found materials" (collaging, he would say, from the language of the culture itself) to sort out reality from delusions: a salvaging job, in brief, but one carried on with more surprises and true ironies of perspective than is common in our poetry. Where do the "objective" materials end and the "personal" ones begin? It's as hard to say in these poems as it might be in your life or mine. The series called *autobiography* (1967) is made up largely of anecdotes decked out as prose poems (or vice versa), but are they about him or about someone he knows, or did he lift them from a novel or a textbook? A key question, too, since, as one of the poems states in its entirety:

the terrible thing Gedalish said would be if all our ideas of reality were based on the evidence of 200 years of experimentation and measurement and the constitution of the universe was changing all this time.

It's this question of disorientation—of who-we-are and what-we-know—that also generates the songs and music of his "novel-poems" (a recasting of lines and passages by a man who "liked whatever was recorded at 33 that sounded good at 78"), like this one:

you must wait till spring
March would be all right perhaps
April certainly
but November
December
have you ever been to a lonely part of Austria in December

or at its coolest/coldest, again, in the "12th meditation" (complete):

if we slowly approach a surface of water with our finger we often deceive ourselves about when we are wet. a patient may feel the surgeon's scalpel while it is still a slight distance away.

This is poetry with a vengeance—not because it sounds like what we were expecting all along (obviously it doesn't) but because he's deeply into it and challenging the language on its own ground. Don't fret that Antin has left "emotion" and "imagination" to the businessmen who care about such things (that's what he says he's done and I believe him), but watch him move deliberately toward that rementalization of reality he hopes will spring us from the trap of the Tinguely Machine. Which is probably what "meditation" means to him in the most recent of his works (*Meditations*, 1971): a discipline more Western than Eastern I'd guess, that reaches its peak (the point, I mean, where it's hardest for us to follow) in the long series of "separation meditations" based on phrases drawn and recast from the classical Stoic philosopher Epictetus. Not any old Epictetus either, but a scholarly nineteenth-century translation and dilution of what were the actual in-process meditations of a Hellenistic slave trying like mad to escape the web of life and thought. From the footnotes at that, as if to emphasize the distance between a mentation that's real and

one that's merely faithful to some prescriptive past. And in response to
the process, the oracle comes through and says:

> avoid
> authority

> take what comes
> what is given
> is used
> the extreme
> is used

> express
> its sense

and lots else besides—toward changing matter back to energy.

A moral oracle, too (as Brother Epictetus's was before him), and probably accounts for the awe and suspicion with which less focused avant-
gardniks sometimes view him. The choice, anyway, isn't surprising: Antin's choice of Epictetus, I mean, and the hardness, maybe aloofness, of
that last work. For it's the whacked-out moralist who recognizes (finally
and at long last) that at the bottom of our misdoings is the evasion of our
own responsibility to express the reality of things at all costs. I think he's
getting there, by every means a rementalized avant-garde can put at his
disposal. At least I mean to say I'm grateful.

David Meltzer:
A Pre-Face

I first became aware of David Meltzer—as many of us did—with the publication in 1960 of Donald Allen's anthology, *The New American Poetry*, which celebrated the emergence over the previous decade of a new and radical generation of American poets. Those included ranged in age from Charles Olson, already fifty, to David Meltzer, then in his early twenties. Meltzer's four poems were all short, filling up most of three pages, and displayed a surefooted use of the kind of demotic language and pop referentiality that was cooking up in poetry as much as it was in painting. His lead-off poem mixed traditional Japanese references with more contemporary ones to Kirin Beer and Havatampa cigars, but there was otherwise no indication of a wider or deeper field of reference—as in the work, say, of older contemporaries such as Olson and Robert Duncan or of Ezra Pound or William Carlos Williams or Louis Zukofsky before them. Like many of our generation, his aim was not to appear too literary; as in the conclusion of his biographical note: "I have decided to work my way thru poetry & find my voice & the stance I must take in order to continue my journey. Poetry is NOT my life. It is an essential PART of my life."

It took another decade of journeying for Meltzer to emerge as a poet with a "special view" and with a hoard of sources and resources that he would mine tenaciously and would transform into unique poetic configurations. For me the sense of him had changed and deepened some years before I got to know him as a friend and fellow traveler.

From David Meltzer, *David's Copy: The Selected Poems of David Meltzer* (New York: Penguin Poets, 2005).

The realization—as happens with poets—came to me through the books that he was writing and publishing and that I was getting to read—on the run, so to speak, like so many others. In *The Dark Continent,* a gathering of poems from 1967, I found him moving in a direction that few had moved in—or that few had moved in as he did. The "transformation," as I thought of it, appeared about a quarter of the way into the book—a subset of poems called *The Golem Wheel,* in which the idiom and setting remained beautifully vernacular but the frame of reference opened, authoritatively I thought, into new or untried worlds.

The most striking of those worlds was that of Jewish lore and mysticism, starting with the Prague-based legend of Rabbi Judah Loew and his Frankensteinian creation (the "golem" as such), incorporating a panoply of specific Hebrew words and names along with kabbalistic and talmudic references and their counterparts in a variety of popular contexts (Frankenstein, the Mummy, Harry Bauer in the 1930s *Golem* movie, language here and there from comic strips, etc.). It was clear, too, that the judaizing here—to call it that—was something that went well beyond any kind of ethnic nostalgia, that he was tapping, in fact, into an ancient and sometimes occulted stream of poetry, while moving backward and forward between "then" and "now." In an accompanying subset, *Chthonic Fragments,* a part of it presented in *David's Copy,* he expanded his view into gnostic, apocryphal Christian, and pagan areas that left their mark, as a kind of catalyst, even when he swung back to the mundane 1960s world: the "dark continent" of wars and riots, the funky sounds of blues and rock and roll, the domestic pull of family and home.

I mention this as a recollection of my own very personal coming to Meltzer and to the recognition that he was, like any major artist, building a special world: a meltzer-universe in this case that spoke to some of us in terms of our own works and aspirations. ("The Jew in me is the ghost of me," began one stanza in *The Golem Wheel,* and I was smitten.) His pursuit of origins of all sorts was otherwise relentless—not only in his poems but with a magazine and a press that also took as their point of departure or entry the hidden worlds of Jewish kabbalists and mystics. The magazine was called *Tree (etz hayyim,* the tree of life, in Hebrew) and was connected as well to a series of anthologies of his devising *(Birth; Death; The Secret Garden: An Anthology of the Kabbalah),* alongside chronicles of jazz writing and jazz reading and of poetry—Beat and other—that had emerged or was emerging from the place in California where he lived and worked.

What was extraordinary here was the lighthearted seriousness of the project—a freewheeling scholarship in the service of poetry—and his ability to cast an esoteric content in a nonacademic format and language. In this he shared ideas and influences with a range of contemporary artists and poets—notably the great West Coast collagist Wallace Berman, whose appropriations of the Hebrew alphabet as magic signs and symbols led directly to what Meltzer, borrowing a phrase from Allen Ginsberg's *Howl*, called Bop Kabbalah. It was also in that California ambience that he made contact with older poets like Robert Duncan, Jack Spicer, and Kenneth Rexroth, and with younger ones like Jack Hirschman, engaged like him in the search for old and new beginnings. In circumstances where everything suddenly seemed possible, he joined with his wife, Tina (as singer), and with fellow poet Clark Coolidge (as drummer) to form a rock performance group called Serpent Power—the name itself an echo of ancient yogic and tantric practice.

The totality of Meltzer's work will wait for another occasion—a Meltzer Reader perhaps or a collected Meltzer—in which all of it can be mirrored. For now—and not for the first time—he has condensed his nearly half century of poetry into the pages of this book. As such it is a reflection of where he has worked and lived, often with great intensity—first in polyglot New York (Brooklyn, to be exact) and later (most of his life, in fact) in California. He has never been a great traveler, in the literal sense, but his mind has traveled, metaphorically, into multiple worlds. In the process he has drawn from a multiplicity of times and places and set them against his own immediate experience. His attitude is that of a born collagist, a poet with a taste for "pilfering," he tells us, or, paraphrasing Robert Duncan: "Poets are like magpies: they grab at anything bright, and they take it back to their nest, and they'll use it sooner or later." And he adds, speaking for himself: "I use everything, everything that shone for me."

The range of the work itself follows from another dictum: "Poems come from everywhere." As such, the focus moves from the quotidian to the historical and, where it fits, the transcendental. The mundane stands out, for example, in a poem like "It's Simple," though not without its underlying "mystery." Thus, in its opening stanza:

It's simple.
One morning
Wake up ready
For new work.

Pet the dog,
Dog's not there.
Rise and shine
Sun's not there.
Take a deep breath.
No air.

If the presentation here gives the appearance of simplicity—something like what Meltzer calls "the casual poem"—we can also remember his warning, that "art clarifies, it doesn't simplify," that his intent as a poet is, further, "to write of mysteries in language as translucent and inviting as a mirror."

Mystery or "the potential of mystery" turns up often in Meltzer's *poetics*—his talking about the poetry he and others make. It is no less so where the poem is family chronicle than where it draws on ancient myth or lore: the fearful presence in "The Golem Wheel"

. . . returning home to a hovel
to find table & chair
wrecked by the Golem's fist

or the celebration and lamenting of the parents in "The Eyes, the Blood":

my father was a clown,
my mother a harpist . . .

There is a twofold process in much of what he does here: a *demythologizing* and a *remythologizing*, to use his words for it. In this sense what is imagined or fabulous is brought into the mundane present, while what is mundane is shown to possess that portion of the marvelous that many of us have been seeking from Blake's time to our own.[1]

David's Copy is full of such wonders, many of them excerpts from longer works that show a kind of *epic* disposition—in the sense at least of the *long poem* as a gathering of fragments/segments/image-and-data

---

1. Writes Meltzer further, in our talking through of it: "To demythologize means countering that person or product or event made mythic, somehow emptied of complexity; to re-mythologize is to pick up castoff debris from the assemblyline & rework (like assemblage & collage) into new & more problematic relationships—I do take the 2 words as 2 distinct actions, intrusions, or interventions."

clusters. Watch him at work, full blast, in *Chthonic Fragments* or in his long poem, *Hero/Lil*, in which he draws the Lil of the poem (= Lilith, Adam's first wife; later: the mother of demon babes) into the depths of postexilic life:

> She-demon deity
> lies on the sofa
> stretching like a cat.
> Small hot breasts.
> Miles breathes *Blackbird.*
> She accepts
> the hash and grass joint.
> Cool fingers
> Dive under my pants
> *ka! ka! ka!*
> Screech of all
> Lil's hungry babies
> caged-up next door.

Or again:

> She wants words only at dawn.
> I touch her mouth with language
> then afterwards move against her.

In other serial works the touch is lighter, where he observes or playfully takes the role—totemlike—of magical yet ordinary animal beings: the dog in *Bark: A Polemic,* say:

> Bark is what us dogs do here in Dogtown
> also shit on sidewalks door mats porches trails
> wherever new shoes walk fearless.
> Bark is what us dogs do here in Dogtown
> it's a dog's life
> we can't live without you.
> Mirror you we are you.
> Beneath your foot or on the garage roof.
> You teach us speech bark bark
> for biscuits we dance for you.

You push us thru hoops
& see our eyes as your eyes
but you got the guns the gas the poison
all of it.
Bark is what us dogs do here in Dogtown.

Or the Monkey in the singular poem of that name—both pseudo-orthodox ("bruised before Yahweh") and quasi-stylish ("suave in my tux").

These are the marks of a poet who has worked over a span of time, to pursue interests near and dear to him. To cite another instance, *music*—the full range of it for Meltzer—comes into a large portion of the poems, a reflection of his own musical strivings inherited in part from his harpist mother and cellist father, celebrated in the long poem or poem series, *Harps*, itself a section from a much longer ongoing work called *Asaph*, one intention of which is to use music, he tells us, "as a form of autobiography." Of such musically engaged works the great example is his book-length poem for Lester Young, *No Eyes*, to which can be added another big work, *Bolero* (again a part of *Asaph*), and short poems or references to Hank Williams (the "lamentation" for him), Billie Holiday ("Darn That Dream"), and Thelonious Monk, among recurrent others. Later, too, when he becomes a chronicler (*Beat Thing* the most recent and most telling example), the music of the time, like its poetry and loads of pop debris and rubble, has a place at center.

I would cite *Beat Thing* in particular as both his newest book as of this writing and as something more and special: a harbinger perhaps of things to come. As recollection and politics, it is Meltzer's truly epic poem—an engagement with once recent history (the 1950s) and his own participatory and witnessing presence. If the title at first suggests a nostalgic romp through a 1950s-style "beat scene," it doesn't take long before mid-twentieth-century America's urban pastoralism comes apart in all its phases and merges with the final solutions of death camps and death bombs from the preceding decade. This is collage raised to a higher power—a tough-grained and meticulously detailed poetry—"without check with original energy," as Whitman wrote—and very much what's needed now.

The reader of *David's Copy* will find in the more recent poems that end it a sense of timeliness amidst the timelessness that poetry is often said to offer—*Beat Thing* clearly but also *Feds v Reds*, *Tech*, or even *Shema 2*, with its linking of Judaic supplications and Koranic language in the wake, I would imagine, of the ongoing Israeli-Palestinian conflict. The political engagement—embedded in the poetry itself—is both real and heedful of his earlier remarks that looked down at the "onedimensionalizing" of so much political poetry ("a tendency to supply people with conclusions, but you don't give them process") in contrast to which "a certain kind of pornography was what I wanted to do as politics." And that in fact was something that he also did—a genre of novel writing that he called "agit-smut" and described as "a way for me to vent my rage and politicize . . . a way of talking about power."

Elsewhere, in speaking about himself, he tells us that when he was very young, he wanted to write a long poem called *The History of Everything*. It was an ambition shared, maybe unknowingly, with a number of other young poets—the sense of what Clayton Eshleman called "a poetry that attempts to become responsible for all the poet knows about himself and his world." Then as now it ran into a contrary directive: to think small or to write in ignorance of what had come before or in deference to critic-masters who were themselves, most often, nonpractitioners and nonseekers. By contrast, as is evident throughout this book, Meltzer allied himself with those poets of his time and place (Beats and San Francisco Renaissance and others) who were both international in their range and the true carriers or creators of traditions new and old.

It was at this juncture that I met him, and his companionship added immeasurably to my own work as a poet. I continue not only to prize him but to read his poems with the greatest pleasure.

Alison Knowles's *Footnotes:*
A Pre-Face

*Once upon a time Jim Tenney and I went walking in the woods. We came
to a clearing and there under a tree was an arrangement of toy locomotives
in the middle of nowhere. Pausing we mused, where are they going, where
have they been?*

—(A. K.)

The work that Alison Knowles has given us here is a personal *kunstkammer*—a treasure-house of words and images that underlie an art that she
has made and taken with her on a journey through and over many worlds.
That journey now covers a span of thirty years and more. As such it links
with a history of what has been—in the time that she and we share—an
adventure in making and extending art as it was understood before her. In
the early years the locus of her engagement was with Fluxus and Something Else Press—performances and installations in New York and in
the streets and fields of America and Europe, along with books crafted
by silk-screen techniques that she had taught herself and that offered us
a full range of innovations and surprises. Her monumentally scaled *Big
Book* from the 1960s—a pioneer example of installation art—remains
vivid in the minds of those who saw and *walked* in it. And this was followed in turn by her "computer instigated dwelling," *The House of Dust,*
and by her second walk-in book, *The Book of Bean* from 1983. Then and
after she has worked at home and while traveling—an honored member
of what one, perhaps mutual, friend called the avant-garde that cannot be
defeated. It is a work (and play) that goes on now as it did yesterday—but
richer by each increment she adds to it.

Footnotes, presented here, is the accounting of where her feet (and
hands and mind) have taken her. On its physical side it consists of bits
and pieces from a series of red Windsor and Newton 5-×-7-inch notebooks, whose blank pages she inscribed or filled with cutouts in the manner of collage; all of these have references to real performances and places

From Alison Knowles, *Footnotes: Collage Journal 30 Years* (New York: Granary Books, 2000).

visited, combined with things she overheard or that she saw and thought herself. The pages, which date from the mid-1970s to the mid-1990s, are torn out of the original notebooks and attached with scotch tape to clean sheets of paper. The content of each resultant page of collage in *Footnotes* remains exactly as it was on the original page but "enhanced," Knowles writes, "by drawing around the scotch tape that affixes the scraps to the new page . . . [as an] artistic artifice as well as an homage to Diter Rot and his Something Else Press book *246 Little Clouds*." A still further enhancement is the addition, on the facing page of each collage, of a range of new materials—road signs, directions, recipes—that were collected largely on a recent trip to Europe, "when I was thinking of how to put this book together and to give the pages breathing space." Also, at the bottom of many of the facing pages, are the "footnotes" that give the book its title and provide a time and context for the events recorded. The matter of the book in its final form consists of a multitude of texts and images— some dreams, some anecdotes, some quotes (contemporary and ancient), some illustrations and rubbings, some traveler's notes, some bits of flowers (lilies, dried), some labels from wine bottles, some references to her researches in the botany and history of beans.

In addition to all the foregoing, the book brims with a number of independent creations or works in series. The most striking of these derives from a group of photographic works she calls embedments. These go back to her early days in New York's SoHo, circa 1970—a former factory area that left behind it "objects and items from the garment trade imbedded in the tar by the wheels of the trucks transporting fabric." From the photographic slides she took of these, a copy turns up here along with drawings made from it by "drawing blind"—either with eyes closed or otherwise "not looking at the paper . . . or extremely rapidly or slowly according to clock time." It is all symptomatic of the ongoing theme of presence and absence—of perception right now and memory long after— that so defines this book with its array of works and personalities and things in situ.

So, I take it that this is Alison's testament, her testimony, and so much richer than I can convey in this brief space. Besides which, the book speaks for itself and through the simple/not-so-simple things through which she dreams and meditates. But she knows this far better than most of us, of course, and says it too: "It is important to remember that we are free to make art and poetry out of anything: a loaf of bread, some beans, a hasty jotting on the train."

Carolee Schneemann:
A Tribute

I had heard about her first from Robert Kelly and other poets of my New York acquaintance, circa 1962 or 1963, and in the typical way of the talk of that time the report of an artistic intelligence was almost obscured by description of her physical presence: a young and beautiful woman who does art and is interested as well in the work of poets.

All of that made a friendly combination but told me little except the name, which stuck in mind, and then the face, too, and the voice met at readings of poetry she attended; maybe parties also. So I wouldn't say that I really knew her—and surely not her work—until the New York/Judson performance of *Meat Joy* very nearly turned my head around, and she became for me one of the germinal masters of a new art that I had only dreamed before.

I want to stick with the memory of that as it exists for me now, some one or more decades beyond it. There had been "happenings" before it and other possibilities of "new performance" and "environmental art," and so forth. But I was unprepared, even so, for the sensual/kinetic intensity of her work ("I work towards metaphors of sensation," she wrote: "an intensification of all faculties simultaneously"): the remarkable sense not only that things could be juxtaposed (which we had learned before) but that the juxtaposition ("the images are realized by a process that unites visual obsessions & precise physical action") could be organized and moved toward particular ends, in the service of both mind and body.

From Carolee Schneemann, *More Than Meat Joy: Complete Performance Works & Selected Writings* (New Paltz, NY: Documentext, 1979).

There is an image I carry of coming into a room of sounds, a large room in which the performers were already present, working their way into the picture, while a double-barreled tape shot words at us in different languages. The room is very cool (a coolness of the air that I remember also from her other works) and the bodies of the "dancers" are only shadows now that once were visible and held attention in that first near-nakedness of early 1960s. (She had managed the nakedness in Paris; New York had still a way to go.) But the bodies were central to all those acts: living bodies upon which materials were sent to work, beautiful or shocking/painful. Bodies among rolls of paper, packaged, papers pressed against their legs, their hips; or bodies under plastic sheets, a play of flashlights over them; or bodies painting bodies, dripping sponges of wet paint; or bodies moving, tying bodies; or bodies living, holding the remains of other bodies: chicken, fish, and sausages, the raw meat that we all become. But it was beautiful for all of that, almost austere and not an imposition, an exploitation of dead flesh, like a "mere cruelty"—but tender (I mean joyful and forlorn at once) in its proposition "that we become what we see what we touch" and what she elsewhere wrote: "A certain tenderness or empathy is pervasive even to the most violent action." And to the perception that a body under plastic is a body under plastic, in a theater or on the white counter of the supermarket butcher—for "we are a part of nature & of all visible & invisible forms."

It was not only that it confirmed my own vision, circa 1960, of "white butcher shops" and such but that she had rightly brought it into ritual: down to the very reverence and terror of the enactment of our dreams, and to a degree I hadn't seen it done before. Body is beautiful and fragile/powerful, and body dies and forms another beauty we can barely reach. The work is celebration: therefore it transforms us. That much was evident, and if it was, it was an art that was no longer art but the precision born of art directed now toward life. With that "precision" and that "direction" nothing proves "too much" but the "total sensibility" is in fact "alerted"—as she would then have said. And as she was (in setting the parameters of a new performance that would truly be performance) indeed the first to show us.

Ian & Me—A Collaboration

> I have tried an *altenstil*
> & dropped it.
> —J. R., *A Book of Witness*, 2003

"Ian Tyson reads us"—or so I wrote a number of years ago when the question first came up. He is illustrator of the work not as subject or as mood per se but as structure. The rest comes out of that, a play between the poet and the artist, where the poet's words are taken not for what they say at surface but for the *directions* they imply—the rules or inner structures that are there for him to read and follow, or evade. I am a poet with some feel for content, for signification, that may sometimes act to hide the structure. I began to come alive in poetry with a series of polemics arguing the primacy of image ("deep" or "surreal" or otherwise) as a concern to be explored anew in the awakening of the late 1950s. That part, the image part, had no need for picture as a form of illustration. And even later, when I used photos and other images to let the physical eye catch a glimpse of a *mythical* Poland disclosed through words, said photos were sparing and personal, my additions, often ironic, to a work that was proceeding as a whole by means of an already evident collage.

I was working in the middle 1960s on a group of poems called *Sightings*—a form of poetry that challenged continuity and organic flow in favor of a rigid demarcation between the fragments or perceptions that composed the poem. If my images remained "soft," the structure was no longer flowing but sharply cut (by visual "bullets," aural silences). In that sense I was already approaching Tyson's world, coming to a first meeting circa 1967 and a friendship and sometime collaboration down to the

Introduction to catalog for the exhibition *Ian Tyson and Jerome Rothenberg: Collaborations,* Eric Linard Gallerie, La Garde Adhenar, France, 2003.

present. The result for me was an immediate recognition of the structural side of my own work.

The poems of mine to which he first turned his attention were those in *Sightings*. As I conceived them, they made up a single poem divided into nine numbered sections, and each section subdivided into smaller "fragments." His translation into abstract visual images bore a close but by no means slavish relation to the structure of the poems, less evidently to their content, tone, and so forth. For this, his first move was to generalize the numbers in the subsets—or as he later wrote about it:

> Carefully considering the text I found that each section had an average of nine lines so I devised a grid of 3 × 3 large squares subdivided into 12 × 12 alternating black to color. I used the grid to form the pulse or ground base of the images & as a structure for the typography [*the poems printed* en face]. The colored squares were thematic relating to each part of the text but once having established it I improvised freely until I arrived at what I felt to be a satisfactory counterpoint of typographically correct text & page.

From that reading—the best in any sense that my work had had up to that point—and from a feeling for his work, which was then new for me, I made another poem, "Red Easy A Color," that followed Gertrude Stein's steps into a common meeting. And this one he translated into a rich and glowing, almost monumental, image that sealed up that book.

I had begun by then a work in *ethnopoetics* that would bring me into the experimental translation of American Indian poetry, largely but not exclusively derived from song texts. The first collaborative piece to emerge from that was a large pamphlet/broadsheet derived from an Aztec description (a lexical definition, in fact) of the ceremonial and private uses of flowers. The verbal piece, which I in turn had mined from Bernardino de Sahagún's sixteenth-century *Florentine Codex*, was a cataloging of repetitive and parallel declarative sentences that rose at times to crescendo. In the resultant piece, *Offering Flowers*, the words on the left are pulled toward the image on the right by cross-bars of a large *F* taken from the title; and the image itself (in orange, black, and white), while it's still composed on the grid, is allowed dramatic bursts, like clusters of squared-off flowers, pathways, stairs, in a manner reminiscent of pre-Columbian design or, as he writes of it, "*rather like an embroidery pattern.*"

From the "more explicitly illustrated," almost fluid, flower image, he went in *The 17 Horse Songs of Frank Mitchell* to a group of much more austere, more minimal pieces. The poems here were "total translations" of four of the seventeen Navajo songs, which I took as sound-poems and to which his images related in a more general way than before—an accompaniment rather than a mapping of the infrastructures. The principal response to the structure (this time of the songs overall) was in the choice of color (white and blue) suggested by the alternation of blue and white objects (turquoise, whiteshell [abalone], etc.) in the systematically paired horse songs themselves. Tyson's designs kept an American Indian feeling, akin to Navajo sand painting and even closer—as with the Aztec flowers—to native weavings. And along with this there was also a sense in which the form of his images might be thought to represent, in line with the underlying mythological narrative, "a 'going through' portals to the sky, to obtain and bring back the horses."

A more extended and more collaborative work was *Songs for the Society of the Mystic Animals,* a series of poems derived from Seneca Indian ceremonial sources. I had already translated these into "concrete poems," transformed them in that instance since the originals were purely oral. What I now sensed, along with Tyson, was the possibility of driving them still further, incorporating color and significant typography, plus (in line with Tyson's vision) a greater adherence to the structure of the grid. This would take us, I thought, toward the creation of a meditative visual field—as the tantrist *yantra* is the classic visualization of the chanted *mantra.* At the heart of that linkage was the fact that the songs—qua mantra—contained not only words but vocables ("meaningless," nonlexical sounds: *highyohoweyehhey,* etc.) to which the words related as with figure and ground. Color and position could both reveal and conceal such distinctions, however we chose to handle them, and this became the basis of much of the collaboration between us. His own words cover this far better—the care given to each work as an event, an action triggered by the field, the way the words are set before us:

> The choice of color was determined subjectively where appropriate to the elements described; e.g., earth, smoke, fire, water, etc., or objectively to separate out the textual changes between the sensible & chant elements & to punctuate any accents as they occurred. The shape of each song was indicative of its subject matter ["but in a non-illustrative way," he points out earlier] so that in the *Song about a Mole, or Was It a Dead Person?* the shape became long to support

the idea of burrowing or traveling through whereas in the songs about *Acting like a Crow* I kept the format to an approximate square to engender the notion of performing within a limited sphere.

The Mystic Animals series was done by 1982, and since then we've engaged in a range of individual publications, something like half of which involve a process of composition based on a form of traditional Jewish numerology called *gematria*. While the texts for these works resemble my earlier *Sightings*, the process by which they're composed is much cooler, more hard-edged than what I had allowed myself in the 1960s. As a form of process-generated poetry, the gematria poems play off the fact that every letter of the Hebrew alphabet is also a number and that words or phrases the sums of whose letters/numbers are equal are at some level meaningfully connected. For myself—as for Tyson—these coincidences/synchronicities function not as hermeneutic substantiations for religious and ethical doctrines but as an entry into the kinds of correspondences/constellations that have been central to modernist and postmodernist experiments over the last century and a half.

Where *Mystic Animals* had brought us to a place in which the components of the visual image were themselves letters and words, the works thereafter were, as he describes them, "typographically *[un]*interpretable other than the choice of type face and the careful placing on the page, i.e. they are not translatable into visual poetry." What moves the work forward, then, is a mutual interest in numbers ("as opposed," he points out, "to mathematics") that can function for both of us as an opening for "specific compositional doors . . . less as systems than as philosophical speculations." In the most complex of these collaborations, the book-length *Delight/Délices* (1998), five gematria-derived poems are set in units that include the English text, a translation into French by Nicole Peyrafitte, and a visual extension that places strikingly colored squares on a black ground, disposed according to their numerical position—determined by the gematria number—on an imagined grid. In another collaboration, *Six Gematria* (1992), my selection of poems assures that each will include reference to a primary or secondary color, and Tyson follows with a single image made up of twenty-six "lozenges" (for the twenty-six letters of the alphabet), which changes color as he moves from poem to poem.

In other, still more recent, work the strategy varies from piece to piece, with a tendency for the visual image to attenuate by stages: a series of thin, variously dispersed lines in *A Case for Memory* (2001), or an arrangement

Two songs about a Mole, or Was It a Dead Person? (From *The 17 Horse Songs of Frank Mitchell*) of colorless intaglio squares, embossed so lightly as to hint at their own disappearance, in *The Times Are Never Right* (2003). Here, if I read him rightly (and I think I do), he follows my own struggle with time, both personal and cosmic, and with the sense of "loss and desolation" that the struggle implies. "In making the visual corollary to these," he tells me, "I put forward my own image of time, gained and lost. A very abstracted conception which I tied together in the general design."

It is something of this kind that informs our most recent work together: *In Memory of Paul Celan: Three Death Poems* (2003). My own contribution to this was to pull together a series of words and phrases drawn from Celan's poems or reminiscent of his texts or textures:

Death (1)   **Death (2)**

greyblack   Metastasized.
of waters   God emptied.
                                              Broken light.
& the eye
impaled.

                    Death (3)

                    The bone
                    over my door.

                    False angel.

To meet these, Tyson turns to an image, he writes, that "comes from a gradually developing structure first encountered when I took another (very oblique) look at cubism and started to deconstruct the grids in [a series of his] drawings." Working for the first time with computer, he transferred the ideas into QuarkXPress, "where I could cross reference the text and image on the screen." The result, as he saw it, was "a gradual seeping away of the colour filigree—there and only just there—paraphrasing the *Three Death Poems*. . . . Perhaps a metaphor for my state of mind although the possibilities it opens up for me are immense."

For me, as well, the openings are now extraordinary. We may have entered—both of us—into an *altenstil* or a series of such as a place of reflection—not, I would stress, of rest—that neither of us could earlier have imagined. Here all possibilities are equal and we can *descant,* like the ancient figures evoked by Yeats or Duncan, on *art and song,* or on Stevens's presentiment, maybe, of "a colossal sun . . . like / a new knowledge of reality." (If only the world allows it . . . and of course it never does.)

For this I will let Tyson have the final word, glancing back like me at our long-shared musings: "John Christie has said that my work 'seems to withstand the vicissitudes of daily life.' This may be but I can't help thinking that of late there are some undertones of angst creeping in and reflecting themselves, however subtly, in our recent works, which only seems natural given the times. As for the future, we haven't even started talking of it."

DIALOGUES & INTERVIEWS

In the Way Words Rhyme

In the way words
rhyme
or fail to
I found my truth.
I walked through little parks
elated   crooning.
In the parade of angels
I was first to start.
My life bled through
my skin.
I was connected to the moon
by sonar.
What I couldn't
get a grip on
I discarded.
Sooner than slip back
I let the wranglers
ride me.
I felt my jaw
disgorging
every word
I spoke.
The smell of
mackerel
was the greatest

poem. America was
promises.
I thrust my hand in yours
& yammered.
Miracles came cheap
& fast. I beat myself
with nettles
until the flesh
fell off.
I made a rhyme
of womb
& slaughter,
filling in
the empty sounds.

Performance Artists Talking: Ritual/Death

(with Linda Montano)

MONTANO: What do you remember from your childhood that you would now consider ritual activity? How old were you when those things occurred?

ROTHENBERG: The ritual things that I remember I wasn't terribly interested in. Or maybe I was. But if I was, I was resistant to them also. There was a regular pattern around religious rituals, especially around Jewish holidays, many of which took place, largely, in the home. There were also occasional visits to the synagogue in which my grandmother was a member of the congregation. My parents were atheists and didn't, except as a matter of courtesy, participate in those synagogue occasions, but since my grandmother lived with us, we carried out most of the traditional household rituals. I had a very close relationship with my grandmother, so maybe there was a kind of feeling, a resonance around that and, up to a point, a desire to please her. But after a while I was following my parents' way rather than my grandmother's, so there was a period in adolescence when I more and more distanced myself from the traditional forms. I don't remember creating alternative rituals, as such, although there was an interest in doing theater and setting that up with some friends in a more or less formal way. We wrote plays, acted out plays, and maybe there are ritual qualities in doing that. Maybe some of that underlies the writing of poetry—formalizing and ritualizing language.

From Linda Montano, ed., *Performance Artists Talking in the Eighties: Sex, Food, Money/ Fame, Ritual/Death* (Berkeley: University of California Press, 2000).

MONTANO: So there was a double aspect—the fact that you had access to it via your grandmother and then not having to do it because of your parents. You had permission to go your own way.

ROTHENBERG: Yes, but you should remember, too, that neither of my parents took a really strong antireligious stand, even though they were atheists and had separated from the religion as such. In some larger sense they were against it, but there was also a mixture of respect for it, so it was never a question of putting down or knocking those people like my grandmother who were involved in the religion. Later, in fact, I found that they were actually hostile to the more religious and outwardly costumed Jews of the ultra-Orthodox and Hasidic sects. And when I became attracted to Hasidism as a historical phenomenon, they assured me that the Hasidim were narrow and even vicious people, and that I shouldn't be taken in by the exoticism of the outer trappings or by Martin Buber's sentimental accounts. What attracted me about the Hasidim was the mysticism and a glimmer of the poetry. I have never otherwise had much sense that they were necessarily *good* people.

MONTANO: Were their reasons political, and was it a brave gesture for them at that time?

ROTHENBERG: At the point that they broke from the religion—and this held particularly for my father—it was a brave and painful gesture, because he had been raised in an ultrareligious Hasidic family. In other words, what he was saying about the Hasidim was really with reference to the world of his own father. My father was the oldest son in his family and had been sent from where they lived in Poland to the city of Vilna [Vilnius] in Lithuania, to study and to become a rabbi. Then, as the story goes, when he got to the Slabodka Yeshiva, he found a group of young students there who were secretly reading Dostoyevsky and Tolstoy and French writers like Rolland and Zola. Yiddish writers also, lots of those, and Marxists, socialists, and Leninists. Kropotkin. Darwin. That's how it was told to me. And within a year, he had left the yeshiva, cut off his earlocks—shaved off all of his hair in fact—and returned home, a bald ultra-German type in a short jacket, wearing city clothes. Gentile clothes. All of this very much to the dismay of his own father. And shortly thereafter, he and my mother ran off to Warsaw to get married in secret and for him to set off for America the day after the wedding. Apparently on that same day—the day of the wedding—his father died, but word wasn't sent to him until he arrived in America, so as not to distress him or discourage him from going. After that he was socialistically oriented, although less aggressively leftist, less active than other members of the family who were further to the left. Politically he remained a moderate socialist in his beliefs. Later on he became disillusioned and disappointed, attitudes common to his generation.

So traditions form a part of my mental and physical memory—physical because of the sensuous recollections of the interior of synagogues and the sound of the singing, the chanting, when you're inside them. Also a kind of olfactory memory, particularly from the extreme holidays like Yom Kippur, when people would stay in the synagogue, in their seats for hours, and you could literally smell their presence. I remember my grandmother's first synagogue, which was in a loft in a building on Webster Avenue in the Bronx, where it crosses Gun Hill Road, and the Third Avenue El would go past there. And I remember very clearly the collage of sounds—voices in the synagogue, the words and music, and the El train making a turn as it goes from Webster Avenue and then cuts onto Gun Hill Road.

MONTANO: When did sound, word, thought, and ritual correspond for you in your work?

ROTHENBERG: The impulses of what we do as poets and artists go back to ancient sources in religion and ritual. I've known that for a long time, but in the beginning I had a conflict with it because I felt a strong need also to break from all of that. What I chose to do, I think, was to accept it as one of the givens of being a poet or an artist, and then to try to see what that could possibly mean in the basically secular and deritualized world in which we live. At some point, particularly in the late 1950s and early 1960s, I found myself drawn toward the inclusion and acceptance of more and more ritual elements in my work, and more understanding of those in the work of others. Poetry, art, and music have taken over some part of the function that religious ritual once had—true for me as well, but with a great ongoing distrust of institutionalized, formalized religion. But once I was able to deal with a sense of ritual in my own work, I was as happy to spend time going to a religious celebration as going to a movie or an art performance. Even more so with religions where I felt no sense of conflict or of kitsch—or felt a rawer, even a harsher, power.

Montano: What do you mean by *ritual?*

Rothenberg: *Ritual* is a tough word, and my tendency, as I've been saying, is to see it in a religious or quasi-religious context. *Performance,* on the other hand, is a very neutral word, and when you speak about something as performance, there is no question of having to think about religion. It's like the distinction I feel between mind and spirit—different words in English, but not in other languages—where the one word almost always has a religious sense and the other almost always doesn't. When we speak of ritual, then, there is some kind of religious implication intended, unless we're talking like animal behaviorists—insect rituals and all of that—which usually we aren't. What many of us have wanted is to have a poetry and art that are as powerful and meaningful for us as religious and ritual poetry was for those who practiced that.

Montano: Your strength is that you are grounded in both. You are incredibly secure in your analytical processes as well as your right brain! Did you have to develop the thinking side of your work before you could let go into the trance of poetry?

Rothenberg: Both aspects came with a certain amount of difficulty and with some insecurity about my ability either to analyze or to take off and fly. If I've learned to do any of it, it's because of diligence. Persistence. Part of the process for me has been to make myself as informed as possible about what others have been doing, either now or in the past, ritual and art both. At first, as a young artist, I was a little concerned about exposing myself to too much outside influence, too much other art, with the typical fear that it would stifle me. But then I found, at least for me, that that was not the case, that the more I came to know, the more in fact I was able to do. In the German language—and in Yiddish, too—the words for knowing and for being able are virtually the same. So knowing something is an enhancement of one's abilities. Ability and knowledge go together. I don't mind that at all and am not hurt or repressed by knowing more.

Montano: You made a real effort to spend time with the American Indians. Do you feel that you have to take time to do different kinds of study?

ROTHENBERG: You get to know certain things by doing them, and in the process of doing, you find out what it is that you're doing. There is a sense of uncertainty to begin with, and then all kinds of clarifications come with persistence and experimentation. You can contrast this to another kind of knowing that comes from a distance—either from books or from some equivalent medium: movies, television, even word of mouth. All of those are different from placing yourself in a position and observing or doing or participating. That kind of knowing—to put myself someplace in order to see for myself at firsthand—opened up for me, really, around the late 1960s. By that time I had already become interested in ritual poetry as a worldwide phenomenon and had researched it through books and the works and observations and experiences of others. I was then sent out—through Stanley Diamond's good offices—to the Allegany Seneca Reservation in western New York, and from that point on a lot of things began to open up for me. That first going-out was very significant because suddenly I really knew the value of doing that, of going to the place where it was happening and placing myself there. In the decade that followed I was able to do that more frequently—to go into other situations and to learn in the process—without, I hope, doing damage to the people I found myself among.

MONTANO: Was your trip to see María Sabina a similar placing of yourself at a source?

ROTHENBERG: With María Sabina it was a much more casual, much briefer encounter. Others had gone to visit her long before us, so by the time I went down there, I knew a lot about her as a famous Oaxacan Mazatec shaman. Also, things had come together in a way that made it possible to see her under very good circumstances—with our friend Henry Munn, who had spent a lot of time there and had married into a Mazatec family. Since I was already aware of the glamour surrounding her—although in truth she continued to live in a very third-world kind of poverty—it was like going to visit any famous person. The experience, in other words, was like that of finally meeting a fellow poet or artist whose work you have long known and honored. We also participated in a Mazatec mushroom ceremony at that time, but not with María Sabina. Not mushroom tourism or anything like that, but a very sweet family occasion in Henry Munn's in-laws' house in Huautla. They were very nice people, and the part of the world they live in is very beautiful. María Sabina is a great ritual poet of that place, and what I wanted to see—and did see—is the way in which she's a contemporary of ours, a living human being who inhabits the same world and time that we do. Otherwise the books turn her into something too much "other."[1]

On the Seneca Reservation I was interested in the ceremonies and how they persisted into the contemporary world: both what was old and what had changed with regard to materials and behavior as the lifestyle of the Senecas had changed. Obviously, I was an outsider to all of that, although I was invited to sit in with the secular Singing Society and, much more rarely, to trot around in a few of the larger public dances that were religious—ritualistic—in nature. I couldn't say to what degree I was personally involved in that, although the poems in *A Seneca Journal* can be read as an attempt to place myself in relation to it.

My most personal experience of Indian ritual happened a number of years later through an immersion in the long, extended Easter ceremonies of the Yaqui Indians of Arizona. We were there for four, five days at a clip, in a ritual space filled with a large number of masked figures—chapayeka clowns—who finally became very real, very much the defining figures of that landscape, that imaginal world. And what tied it immediately to my own imaginal life was that the principal masked figures for the Yaqui Easter were the Jews of the ceremony, who wear crazy and unbelievable masks that are really a whole collage of masking types. There are animal beings, pirates, white businessmen and entrepreneurs, blackface clowns with big red lips and fat stogies in their mouths, masked figures who look like Arabs or like Hebrew patriarchs, or other masked figures who look like stereotypical caricatured American Indians. And, after a while, it was for me as if the imaginal beings of *Poland/1931*, Jews who did and didn't exist in time and history, were all around me. They were faces that I hadn't made up but that I recognized, and by the end, when the ceremony ended and the masks were burned, it was with a real sense of loss, a real kind of emptying. What was special here was that my world and theirs shared the same images, the same beings, that they had brought to life for me.

MONTANO: What is nourishing your performances now?

ROTHENBERG: Most of the performance work now is coming out of the poetry-music collaborations with Bertram Turetzky. Turetzky's presence

1. For more on María Sabina see above, page 176.

on the bass keeps the work charged for me. As I go around doing more and more poetry readings, there is a problem I run into because the act of reading becomes repetitive after a point. It's the sort of thing that David Antin says drove him from doing poetry readings into improvising "talk-poems." Turetzky has a freedom of improvisation that I don't have as a text performer, but with him I'm encouraged into readings of the poems in which my rhythms and phrasings are pushed and colored in new ways and new directions. He forces me to surprise myself with my own work, with work with which I'm otherwise very, very familiar.

And then last year, just before I left California to come to teach in Albany, I became involved, along with Bert and Luke Theodore [Morrison] (an old hand from the Living Theater), in a theatrical production of my Dada poems *(That Dada Strain),* in the course of which (a little bit like the Yaqui ceremony) I was able to immerse myself in a living, moving fantasy world—another imaginal world of images that were here embodied. It is quite different when a work is fleshed out and you walk among the beings that inhabit and empower the poetry as a part of them yourself. I'm aware, of course, that this is a theater and that the people around me are acting and performing. But it's a very personal theater for me, and it offers the possibility of a different presentation to those who come as audience, a visual way of projecting language and image to the outside world. Projecting that and then entering into it deeper and deeper is what ritual is about for me.

The *Samizdat* Interview

(with Robert Archambeau)

In looking over Harry Polkinhorn's Jerome Rothenberg: A Descriptive Bib-
liography, *and in looking over your career as a writer of various kinds of literature, one cannot help but be impressed by the volume of different ways in
which you've presented your work and ideas. This may be even more striking
in this "Age of the Academy," where the poetry world seems greatly dependent
on "legitimate" publishing houses to validate itself and to decide who will staff
the English departments. And yet you've remained steadfast in your efforts to
retain a sense of process, a true sense of improvisation and collaboration in the
way your work has been "published."*

*Could you first talk about where your sense of "publication" (for lack of a
better term here), or presentation, comes from? From what sort of aesthetics?
How do you keep a sense of "art" in your work?*

*And then could you talk about how collaborations with people like Pierre
Joris (one of MANY collaborators) fit into that aesthetic?*

Collaboration and publication work together in my mind, although I've
hardly been as persistent with these things as I had started out to be. The
context that I imagined—that "we" imagined, I would like to say—was
one in which poets took over the means of production for their works—
a network of books and journals, broadsheets and painted images, set in
type or written by hand, then printed and bound by whatever means available. By the late 1950s, when I first got started, some of us had learned
the finer arts of book production, while for others like myself the postwar

From *Samizdat*, no. 7 (winter 2001).

allowed the luxury of printing cheaply overseas or, absent that, a change in attitude made even the humblest processes—mimeo or ditto, say—adequate for the task of putting work in multiples and ready to be placed in circulation. The actual distribution, of course, was trickier, but by the time I got to it, there was already a small network in place—bookstores and other outlets dotting the country and with growing connections overseas. And public readings had grown up simultaneously, in places often as casual as the books themselves.

I've written about this elsewhere—most recently in the pre-face to *A Secret Location on the Lower East Side* (a history of American little presses from the 1950s through the 1970s)[1]—so I don't think I have to go into it now in any detail. The main thrust here was that from Blake and Whitman on, poets had often been their own best presenters—not only operating from outside the commercial publishing nexus but often placing themselves there deliberately and with good reason. (*Samizdat,* as name of the present publication, is of course a testament to that.) I tried to point out further that this favoring of independent publication—not only in the States but throughout the world—was itself a principal mark of the avant-garde in poetry and art. [To this I should have added, but don't know if I did, that as independent publication falls away, so does the avant-garde's position as a force for transformation. In place of which the Internet, perhaps, takes up the slack.]

To talk of an avant-garde at this point in time is somehow to mythologize, but I'll do so anyway and won't bother, either, to spell out my misgivings.

The avant-garde, as I conceive it, is—or was—the work of individuals acting together—an effort somehow in common, even if performed one by one. There are times of course when an individual proclaims himself (or herself, need I say?) to be an avant-garde, but I don't believe that there are, strictly speaking, avant-gardes of one. (There are great and unique experimentalists who operate in isolation, but that I think is something different—referential sometimes to an avant-garde but different.) And there are individuals also—Bretons or Marinettis—who dominate their avant-gardes, probably to nobody's advantage. Strong individuals like that, I now believe, were not only influential in forging their avant-gardes but were responsible, as well, for the ephemeral nature of what they had created. In that sense it's also possible that avant-gardes are destined for

1. See above, page 117.

short lives, hell-bound for self-destruction—or an aspect, maybe, of what Tzara might have had in mind when he told us that "the true Dadas are against Dada."

I think that I came to believe early that poetry and art could make a difference—for myself certainly but for others as well—for the world-at-large at our most ambitious. I remember Auden's line that "poetry makes nothing happen" but feeling it then as an irony—an incitement—where making nothing happen was itself an act of transformation in a world of misdirected politics and systems. In retrospect this ties up in my mind with a sense of desperation in the aftermath of "world war" and the start of "cold war"—the desire opening from that for a different, *other* language. That desire affected many—not all who would be poets but many who would—and led them into new languages and forms of verbal happenings. Against this—after the hiatus of war and the dispersal of the former avant-gardes—there was, in what we came to think of as "academy" and "establishment," a pullback from the earlier experiments (linguistic *and* experiential) of revolutionary modernism. As a kid I suffered through this, as did almost everyone I knew. That was something that we had in common—the need for poetry as we would make it and the rejection of that ambition by what seemed to us to be the culture brokers.

When I finished with army service in 1955, I felt incredibly isolated as a writer. I came back to New York and teamed up with David Antin—my oldest companion in poetry (we had been together at City College from '49 to '52). David had already met Robert Kelly (also at City), and Kelly, while still very young, was founding a magazine called *Chelsea* or *Chelsea Review* with George Economou, Venable Herndon, and Ursule Molinaro. That was a start for us, but there were more things in the air and a coming to fulfillment of feelings generated by the two wars of the previous decade (World War II and Korea) and the repressive and clearly hostile spirit of 1950s McCarthyism. The emergence of the Beats at the same time was the first public signal that we weren't alone in the desire to assert or reassert what we thought of as a new revolution-of-the-word and a second awakening of a radical and unfettered modernism.

What's to be noted here—for purposes of answering your question—is that we were aware that there were others before us who had seen poetry and art as vehicles for transformation. We were also aware that there were contemporaries who shared our need for transformation—not only the publicly visible Beat poets but others far more radical or experimental in the range of their poetry and poetics—and that our own needs and explorations might also be a part—a meaningful part—of the present world in which we moved and acted. For this we needed a platform—a springboard—and it became clear that to have it, we would have to construct it on our own. So the first move—for us—was to take charge of our own publication and, as far as possible, to utilize whatever means of production were then available.

In 1957 or 1958 Antin and I launched—with Diane Rothenberg as an unnamed but key collaborator—a publishing venture called Hawk's Well Press. We were uncertain at the start, but as things got moving and we did, too, I began to sense it as a vehicle for matters long suppressed—a way to bring out first books of poems by myself, by Robert Kelly *(Armed Descent)*, Armand Schwerner *(The Lightfall)*, Diane Wakoski *(Coins and Coffins)*, Rochelle Owens (her first play, *Futz*), and a collage classic by Jess *(O!)* with Robert Duncan's "pre-face." Still more pointedly, I published a very small magazine, *Poems from the Floating World*, which took off from my own (postsurrealist) proposals about what I labeled as "deep image" but expanded as I came to realize that the possibilities of poetry went beyond any such single program. At much the same time Kelly and Economou had left *Chelsea* and had started a much more avant-garde, more poetry-linked magazine and press, *Trobar*. We worked together and copublished, and this was also a part of the process of mutual discovery that we were into.

The time, anyway, was dynamic, and the links and connections arose very quickly, toward what we came increasingly to see as a project in common. For me a turning point was when Lawrence Ferlinghetti approached me to do a book of "new young German poets" that he published in 1959 in his City Lights Pocket Poets series. This was my first international connection, my first link with other experimental poets, my first anthology, and above all, my first chance to see the larger compass of what I was doing and to see it as something beyond myself and my immediate company. So, while American poetry was turning in on itself, I felt more strongly an opening outward (this was what later tied me to someone like Kenneth Rexroth, say, and propelled my explorations in cultural space and time [*Technicians of the Sacred*, etc.]).

The American postwar moment—the economic accompaniment to what came to be called "the new *American* poetry"—allowed us access to cheap printing abroad, and we made use of it. Along with this, new means

of book production—by offset and by Xerox—were relatively easy to
come by, and, where all else was lacking, we joined together in assembling
and binding our books, as well as in getting them to a growing network
of bookstores and other outlets around the country. We also established
a bookstore of our own—The Blue Yak on east Tenth Street—and ran it
as an outlet for our work and as a kind of meeting place from 1960 into
1961. Again, collectively, we set up or joined others in readings and performances at bookstores, galleries, coffee shops and bars—before schools
or universities became an easy venue for our readings. (The St. Mark's
Poetry Project—a brainchild of Paul Blackburn's—was an offshoot of
those efforts and has expanded and persisted to the present day.) In all of
this, of course, there was no NEA (National Endowment for the Arts),
no government or private sector we could turn to.

*It seems these smaller collaborations and joint publication efforts of the 1950s
and early 1960s gave you the credibility and creative energy to begin "larger"
projects, perhaps stemming from others' recognition of your success working in
this kind of spirit. How, then, did these earlier ventures work their way into
your own sense of things, broaden your sense of what could be in the world of
poetry?*

What we had here was not so much a movement as a merge of movements, and the sense of something like that carried over as well into my
own work and ventures. From the 1960s through the 1980s there were a
number of books and magazines that I worked on by myself and others
that were totally collaborations—Hawk's Well Press (with Antin early
on and Schwerner toward the end), *some/thing* (with Antin), *Alcheringa*
(with Dennis Tedlock), and *New Wilderness Letter* (established with the
composer Charlie Morrow, carried forward with the help of David Guss
and Barbara Einzig, and in the last two issues as a merger with *Wch Way*,
the magazine Jed Rasula and Donald Byrd were editing). By the middle
1960s I was also being drawn toward the big assemblages like *Technicians of the Sacred* and *Shaking the Pumpkin*. *Technicians* in fact originated
from a series of readings (from "primitive" and "archaic" poetry) in which
I was joined by Antin, Jackson Mac Low, and Rochelle Owens—another
work (at least in its performance) made in common. While I could manage some of these on my own, I found it useful—even stimulating—to
extend the range of the work through an active collaboration with others.
The big American anthology, *America, a Prophecy*, was a straight collabo-

ration with George Quasha; *A Big Jewish Book* needed Harris Lenowitz to translate from Hebrew and related languages, Charles Doria to work from Greek and Latin; while with *Symposium of the Whole* [above, page 18], Diane Rothenberg provided—as she did in other projects before and after—the anthropological and intellectual grounding for a historically centered "range of discourse toward an ethnopoetics." If editorial collaboration came into the books as a whole, the same spirit was functioning within each volume, where poets and others both advised and gave consent to use their poems and their translations—often as free gifts to help the work along. For me this was more than a financial question, rather a need I felt to think of the work as something shared—a reflection of a "will to change" (in Olson's phrase) affecting others of my time and place.

In addition I thought of the big books not so much as anthologies but as assemblages or collages, which fulfilled for me the primary function of collage—to bring the words of others into the work at hand. It was the recognition of something like that, I think, that freed my own poetry to be more than it had been to start with. It also energized me in the direction of translation—an activity that I've pursued into the present. Even working as a solitary translator I felt myself in an interaction with whomever I was then translating, and I came to believe that all translation—of poetry at least—was inherently a matter of collaboration. (I've called such processes—both of translation and collage—"othering" and have spoken about them elsewhere.) But to carry on the translation work in particular, I often had to call on the help of others—either because the task at hand was too big or too foreign or needed more than my own voice to make it stick.

With the ethnopoetic books I thought that all of this was obvious. *Technicians* and *Shaking the Pumpkin* were assemblages of (mostly) translations, generally as I found them but sometimes with interventions of my own. The range of languages was vast, and my own competence outside of the European sphere was nonexistent. On two principal occasions I came more properly into the translator's role—both times with a collaborator. In the one instance (Seneca Indian) my coworker was a native speaker and song maker, Richard Johnny John, and in the other (Navajo) the work was made possible by the great American ethnomusicologist David McAllester. Aside from that—and apart from the ethnopoetic experiments—there were the Hebrew translations with Lenowitz and a recent book of poems from the Czech modernist poet Vitezslav Nezval

(Milos Sovak my cotranslator here) that is now awaiting publication by Douglas Messerli's Sun and Moon Press (Green Integer).[2]

And yet there is still another landscape of collaboration in your history that we haven't covered—that which steps into other fields of art, such as music, performance, and the visuals.

For years I've worked in close association with two extraordinary musicians—the contrabassist Bertram Turetzky and the composer and performer Charlie Morrow. With Morrow, in fact, the collaboration went well beyond the confines of one-on-one performance, taking in a number of ventures in publication (print and audio) and an elaboration of performance leading into theater. I feel comfortable with these collaborations and where they've pulled me, as I do also with the work I've done (over a thirty-year span) with the British artist Ian Tyson and more recently on the *14 Stations* project with the American artist Arie Galles and a heavily illustrated French edition of *A Book of Witness* (Un livre de temoignage) with the French artist Arman.[3] A push into theater and related performance forms was also possible—some with Turetzky, some with Morrow, some with the Living Theater *(Poland/1931)* and with an offshoot of Living Theater through the late actor and director Luke Theodore Morrison and his Center for Theater Science and Research *(That Dada Strain)*. In the last of these I worked on the music with Turetzky, on the staging with Morrison, and on its transfer as a *hörspiel* (radio sound-play) with Klaus Schöning of Westdeutscher Rundfunk in Cologne.

During all this I believe you had also been working with Pierre Joris. Can you say something about the differences in working with him and how that collaboration has lasted so long?

The later work with Pierre Joris is, as I see it, a culmination for me of what came before and an indication of how fruitful collaboration can be in the kind of world we share. For all of that I'm a little hard pressed to remember the steps by which we came to work together. I had known Pierre since the late 1960s, when he was a student at Bard College and

2. Vitezslav Nezval, *Antilyrik & Other Poems* (Los Angeles: Green Integer, 2001).
3. A still more recent work, as a collaboration with the artist Susan Bee, is *The Burning Babe & Other Poems,* published in an illuminated and limited edition by Granary Books in 2005.

was living in New York City for a year or two after graduation. After he moved back to Europe, we saw each other on and off in London and Paris, and in 1986, when I started a brief tenure at SUNY-Binghamton, we got the bright idea of bringing him over as a graduate student. I had already floated a proposal for a big twentieth-century book but was very uncertain about it as a one-man proposition. Once into conversation with Pierre, however, it became clear that we were both close enough and different enough to consider this as, simultaneously, a singular and dual venture. The key, in fact, was in the interplay that it allowed us—the possibility, as with other collaborations, of opening it up beyond what either of us was capable of doing on his own. And right from the start—and over the years that followed—the work proceeded, minus all acrimony, as a process that energized us in the work at hand and in our other workings.

Both of us had made anthologies before and both of us were devoted to the idea of the anthology as a kind of manifesto. We were also, both of us, devoted to the idea of poetry—the kind of poetry we needed— as a radical enterprise that cut across nations and cultures, and we both felt the absence of a gathering reflecting the history of modern (and "post"modern) poetry as we knew it. Over the years we had been engaged in acts of translation, and *Poems for the Millennium,* we knew, would be heavily dependent on translation. And when Larry Venuti, in affiliation with Temple University Press, raised the possibility of commissioning a work of translation in a new series he was starting, we sensed the chance to create a selected writings of the German artist and poet Kurt Schwitters. The Schwitters project—later published as *PPPPPP: Poems Performance Pieces Proses Plays Poetics*—became a kind of testing ground for the collaboration, and a work also that we felt long overdue in English.

Here, however, I would like to digress for a little and call some attention to the process of publication around the anthologies and the other big books. My first such assemblage was *Technicians of the Sacred* in 1968. As I indicated earlier, this had started out as a series of readings at the Hardware Poets Theater in New York, along with some related publication in *Poems from the Floating World* and in *some/thing.* When I first began to consider the possibility of a full-scale version, I approached James Laughlin at New Directions (I wasn't yet a New Directions author), and Laughlin, for whom it was also too big a venture, passed me along to Anne Freedgood at Doubleday. (My actual introduction there was through Sara Blackburn—Paul Blackburn's wife—who was then an editor at Pantheon.) And because this was still in the 1960s—a time in which commercial publishers, however atypically, had an ear open to new or experimental approaches—Doubleday gave me a free hand to proceed, and over the next several years they published not only *Technicians* but two more assemblages, *Shaking the Pumpkin* and *A Big Jewish Book*. In the years that followed I also published with Random House *(America a Prophecy)* and with a couple of university presses (University of California and University of New Mexico) for new books and for reissues of a couple of the earlier ones. (To this list I would also add four "alternative" presses—Exact Change, Copper Canyon, Granary Books, and Station Hill—just to keep the record straight.)

That I made such publishing connections seems to me—after all this time—to have been curiously fortuitous. It was also, I believe, something that I needed for a kind of publication that wanted resources for production and distribution that were difficult or impossible in the alternative press world to which I continue to feel most strongly connected. But I have also felt compelled to further the workings of that world by any and all means at my disposal.

Joris's background and intentions, then, were in most ways very similar to my own. At the very least we felt a kinship as poets that made the work of collaboration a consistently meaningful process and reinforced a sense that our dual input strengthened our ability to create an image of poetic worlds more diverse (and therefore "truer") than what either of us might have done in isolation. We could also call on a significant number of others to add to that diversity and to the necessary sense of creating a big work in common. In doing this we were aware that the immediate model for what we were doing was the otherwise debased form of the university anthology. We willingly accepted the subtitle *The University of California Book of Modern & Postmodern Poetry* as a kind of riposte to Oxford- and Harvard-sponsored compendia (among others) that perpetuated a tediously canonical poetry and poetics of which we (a larger "we" than just the two of us) no longer chose to be a part. We supplied commentaries—sometimes as minimanifestos—in much the way I had done in the earlier assemblages (themselves a send-up on academic practices), and we enlisted a distinguished board of "advisers" that spoke to our overriding sense of kinships and alliances.[4] We were careful in doing so that such a

4. Chinua Achebe, Adonis, Nani Ballestrini, Charles Bernstein, Mary Ann Caws, Andrei Codrescu, Michel Deguy, Rachel Blau DuPlessis, Allen Ginsberg, Lyn Hejinian, Hiromi Ito, Ernst Jandl, Nathaniel Mackey, Eric Mottram, Marjorie Perloff, Quincy Troupe, Cecilia Vicuña, Anne Waldman, Rosmarie Waldrop, and Eliot Weinberger.

board would be dominated by poets rather than academics and would be international in scope.

The structure of the book was otherwise of our own devising and different in kind and intention from more conventional assemblages. We chose in the first volume to highlight a number of the movements that characterized the early twentieth century and had been ignored or diminished in most academic gatherings. Accordingly we gave a separate section of the book to each of six of them—Futurism, Expressionism, Dada, Surrealism, Negritude, and the American "Objectivist" poets. The rest of the poets were grouped in three large "galleries" following a rather loose chronological sequence, and we opened the book with a section of nineteenth-century "forerunners" and ended with a section ("A Book of Origins") that gave a glimpse into historical and ethnopoetic recoveries across the whole preceding century. In the second volume we limited ourselves to two galleries and incorporated a number of movements or quasi movements as "corridors" or "clusters" within the galleries— many of them still more local or regional than those in the previous volume. And—as a kind of musical or compositional gesture—we began with a section that was pure prelude ("In the Dark") and closed with a short codalike section ("At the Turning") in which we joined two of our own poems with Robert Duncan's final, *altenstil* poem, "After a Long Illness."

In all of this we were trying to present a range of realized possibilities while hoping that the work wouldn't be read canonically in terms *only* of its inclusions and exclusions. To avoid that, I suppose, we also put what was probably a greater than needed emphasis on the personal nature of what we were doing—in Olson's words again, our "special view of history." Going still further, I would describe the book as a *construct* or even, if it comes to it, a *fiction*—but the kind of fiction ("supreme" or otherwise) that all such works must surely be.

With that said, however, *Poems for the Millennium* remains for me a meaningful if not necessarily "true" accounting of an adventure in poetry in which we ourselves were small but for the moment active players.[5]

A FINAL NOTE. My most recent anthology and, simultaneously, my most recent collaboration is *A Book of the Book: Some Works & Projections about*

5. Two later collaborations worth mentioning are the translation and editing with Pierre Joris of Picasso's *The Burial of the Count of Orgaz & Other Poems* (Cambridge, MA: Exact Change, 2004), discussed above; and the third volume of *Poems for the Millennium (The University of California Book of Romantic & Postromantic Poetry)* with Jeffrey Robinson.

the Book & Writing, which I gathered and coedited with Steven Clay. Here, through Clay's generosity as a publisher, we accomplished the work without recourse to larger publishers or institutions—indeed without financial backing from any outside source. I don't know if this will either pay its way or reach the audience that we would like to reach, but it is, like all the books I've mentioned, a project that we thought was needed—for both ourselves and others. The desire to fill such gaps or absences has been the driving force—in one way or another—for all the poets and the artists to whom I've felt the closest.

The *Medusa* Interview

(with Rodrigo Garcia Lopes)

The connection between language and reality has been a major focus of your poetry and poetics. It seems that we've crossed a long way from Blake's "doors of perception" to Bill Gates's "Windows 98." I'd like to start our interview with this provocation, as well as pointing out the medium by which this interview is being taken: the e-mail. How do you think that this Media Age— of TV, Internet, consumerism, and rapid technological advances—is affecting the language of poetry written today (and specifically in the United States)? How do you think poets are responding to this so-called globalization? Retaking the anxiety posed by Marjorie Perloff in Radical Artifice, "given the particular options (and nonoptions) of writing at the turn of the twenty-first century, what significant role can poetic language play"?

The question has a special relevance for me, I suppose, since I've long been engaged in a project that involves an interplay of very new and very old forms of languaging and representation. I think that one of the principal allures of poetry—even or (maybe) especially for many of our most "experimental" poets—has been the sense of engaging in a process—a way of thinking and of saying—that has until very recently been universal both in space and time. The time factor is a measure of its oldness, and the emergence of a "new" poetry over the last hundred or two hundred years has almost always been accompanied by declarations of "re"covery/"re"discovery at the heart of every new invention. This is clear

From *Medusa*, no. 1, Curitiba, Brazil, 1999.

enough in U.S. poetry, where someone like Ezra Pound, whom we take as radical—structurally radical—from *The Cantos* on, insists on pushing the time frame back and expanding it horizontally or culturally to a range of earlier initiating moments: first Anglo-Saxon rhythms merged with Homeric shaman journeys down among the shades in Canto One; then in his other and his later writings with the Chinese Book of Songs, the African "Gassire's Lute" as given by Frobenius, erotic poems of ancient Egypt, recastings of neglected Provencal and Roman poets. This was what put him in conflict with Marinetti and the Futurists—a "tale of the tribe," as he named it, but curiously—in that fascist mind—a greater tribe than privileged race and nation might have led us to expect.

The same spirit of newness and transformation with relation to the past and present (what I used to speak of as "an ongoing attempt to re-interpret the poetic past from the point of view of the present") infused the work of many of us in post–World War II America—Olson, Duncan, Snyder, Kelly, Waldman, Schwerner, among the major ones from my per-spective. And there were others, too, outside of the United States—Tzara, with his projected gathering of African and South Pacific poems; the Surrealists, who set up a bureau (under Artaud!) of research aimed in that direction; and the French Negritude poets and their counterparts in the Spanish "new world." (The Portuguese, too, since that's the ground on which we're speaking.)

The Russian Futurists are possibly exemplary here. Unlike the Italians with whom they shared that name, they dug enthusiastically into their own prehistories—the past a necessary part of all that future. Malevich was a kind of folk artist before he made himself a suprematist, and their rough and very lovely handmade books had sources in an old, popular, very low-tech form of bookmaking. And Khlebnikov and Kruchenykh are a mix throughout of science fiction laced with *zaum* as futuristic glos-solalia. (Khlebnikov makes the connection back to religious chants with undecipherable word-sounds.)

I would, I think, want to suggest a pendulum moving for many of us between those same poles. In my own experience I remember a time—the 1960s, a part of the 1950s—when an antitechnological impulse was very strong. It wasn't a Luddite, machine-wrecking thing for most of those I knew who shared some part of it. There was, in fact, an ongoing interest in machines, a use of machinery for traveling, writing, publishing and making images, or even (in the old wilderness of mountains and rivers or the new urban wilderness of cities) cutting logs and building houses; and by the 1970s there was an acknowledgment (within the art world certainly) of a new territory that brought art and technology together. What we've come into today—what you're asking about directly—is an extraordinary immersion in the world of high technology—even for most of us for whom the past is also opening and deepening.

More specifically the question comes up about "this Media Age," beginning with the fact that we're conducting this interview by e-mail. I find this no more surprising or threatening in itself than were the telephone, say, or the typewriter early in the twentieth century. Quite the contrary. The first thing that strikes me about our situation is that we're communicating between California and Brazil—that we're doing it rapidly and with the luxury of setting it in writing—as we could as well by voice, although the costs of doing that in detail would clearly be prohibitive. With some more effort, too, we could deliver what we're doing through the Internet, could publish it, so to speak, without relying for approval on an intervening publisher who might be hostile or at least indifferent to our project. In this one week—in January 1999—I've been in touch with France and Germany and Mexico and Greece and Yugoslavia and England—most of it by e-mail, some of it by fax and phone. And you and I might also—through a network or community of which we're a part—meet together before too long in any of a number of places to which poets like ourselves can be transported across borders that are meant to keep us separate.

What this does is to further a globalism—the kind of globalism (not "globalization") that I've always wanted and that I would not shy away from. It also insulates us—in our cybergiddiness—from problematics that some of the other instances you cite still hold for us. The problem with most technologies—including poetry at the low-tech end—is that they're double-edged. Like other means (or *media*) they can be used in good or bad ways—even *evil* ways, or what we used to think of à la Hannah Arendt as the ultimate "*banality* of evil." If the magic of the old sorcerers and shamans could be used—as "white" or "black," for good or evil purposes—it's true in much the same way for all that we class as "media." In this way the Internet tempts us as poets with the sudden ability to publish and disseminate over a wider network than older means afforded us *as individuals*. But it acts as a similar conduit for an ever-expanding commercialism and—still more distressing—for the ugliest forms of racial and gender hatred (among other matters), with consequences still to be determined. Or maybe it's a balance—what we want on one side and an ongoing banalization of word and thought on the other. Also I recognize—as we all do—the further encroachment of a monoculture, which I suppose is felt outside the United States in the growing hegemony of English and in the Americanization of the popular media, with whatever consequences those may have. For us up here it may make the globalism question seem much less threatening, may make the opening of new lines of communication seem an out-and-out gain with scant sense of the losses.

Going back, however, to my own awakenings post–World War II, I recall being driven by a sense of unease—a feeling about a language that had been corrupted by propaganda and mindless sloganeering—and more insidiously, because more omnipresent in the time that followed, by the vacuities of (well-made) advertising and the developing role of news[reality]-as-entertainment. That made some of us look toward poetry as the "other" language—a language for calling language into question—the banality of language as underpinning for the banality of evil. The new technologies give us a bigger opening—or seem to—to let that otherness emerge. It is still a language and a process I prefer—a way of "othering" that brings a range of poetries together in my mind. But the greater push, I must admit, is overwhelmingly in the opposite direction.

In the last years, several anthologies of contemporary American poetry have appeared. From the Other Side of the Century: A New American Poetry, 1960–1990; Postmodern Poetry: A Norton Anthology; The Heath Anthology of American Literature; American Poetry since 1950: Innovators and Outsiders: An Anthology; *as well as your (and Pierre Joris's)* Poems for the Millennium: The University of California Book of Modern & Postmodern Poetry. *(1) Why is there this urge to anthologize at this end-of-the-century? (2) In a recent interview, Brazilian poet Haroldo de Campos rejected the term* postmodern *as applied to poetry: "We are still in modernity," he says, "only if we accept that Mallarmé is already post-modern in relation to Baudelaire." To critics such as Jameson, postmodernism points to an emerging and different cultural logic. Do you believe in a postmodernism in terms of poetry and poetics? (3) How would you place* Poems for the Millennium *within the context of this debate?*

There's "*this* urge to anthologize," as you put it, and then there's *my* urge to anthologize, which has been going on for some time now. (Since the

1960s, to be exact.) And one can easily say that the end of one century and the beginning of another—in this case a millennium as well—is always a retrospective occasion. But three of the anthologies you mention in particular—Messerli's, Hoover's, and mine and Joris's—also represent the public (re)appearance of a certain kind of work after a period of time in which that work was grossly underrepresented. Earlier—in the 1960s and 1970s—there had been a blossoming of experimental and avant-garde gatherings—what I've spoken of elsewhere as manifesto-anthologies. [See above, page 14.] The accomplishment of Donald Allen's *The New American Poetry* in particular encouraged larger publishers to open up to the new poetries—in my own case Doubleday and Random House, who were the publishers of *Technicians of the Sacred, Shaking the Pumpkin, A Big Jewish Book,* and *America a Prophecy,* all of them works within a single ten-year period. All of these books, of course, had a range outside the present, but the pasts that they represented were heavily colored by a sense of radical transformations of poetry and poetics and were presented along with later and very experimental contemporary works. And in the 1980s—even as the larger publishers were pulling back from manifesto-anthologies—the so-called Language Poets were able to use the anthology as a means for manifesting and displaying their own new departures.

By the 1990s—against a backdrop of cautious instructional anthologies—an underground constituency had built up—a relatively large group of writers and readers in search of works to represent and to update the changes since the 1960s. While middle-ground poetry asserted itself, the takeover was far from complete, and many of us who had come into some form of public place found that we were able to act—Douglas Messerli through his own Sun and Moon Press, Paul Hoover through convincing the arch–middle stream publisher Norton that a big "postmodern" anthology was needed, and Pierre Joris and myself through an arrangement with a major university press. (To these I would also add Eliot Weinberger's *American Poetry since 1950,* which appeared in both a North American and a Mexican [Spanish] edition.)

Let me say a little, then, about *Poems for the Millennium* before responding to your question on postmodernism.

Both Pierre and I had been living with a sense that what we valued most in the poetry of our time—what we shared with many others—had been almost systematically omitted from, or marginalized in, the anthologies and literary histories then current. This was true not only for the immediate present but for the near past—in shorthand terms, not only for "post"modernism but for the modernism that came before it, the great movements from the early part of the twentieth century, for example. While we cherished the work of individual, even solitary, poets, we wanted to bring the larger movements back into the picture: Dada and Surrealism, Futurism, African and Caribbean Negritude, and the work of the North American "Objectivists." These we felt were missing elsewhere, and with their absence, there was also missing a sense of poets engaged with their own self-definition as artists and as the makers of their own poetics. The mix of poetry and poetics was something we worked to bring out—and the sense of poetry being the center of a program, a proposition or a set of propositions working in the public sphere. And writing in the United States—now, at the turning of the century and the millennium—we also thought it vital to insist (again) on the global dimensions of modern and "post"modern poetry—following several decades of insistence on the centrality and hegemony of a presumed "American moment."

In doing this we brought the distinction between "modernism" and "postmodernism" into the subtitle of our book. Here there was an advantage—chronologically—in distinguishing one half of the twentieth century from the other. But we made it clear—as I have always done, I think—that we saw a continuity between the two halves—sometimes oppositional, at other times developmental. My own first encounter with postmodernism (I will now leave out the quote marks around *post*) came in the mid-1970s—a written interview, much like this, with the critic and editor William Spanos. At that point, certainly, I felt myself to be a part of an ongoing poetic revolution—"post-nuttin" as Jackson Mac Low once put it—and felt postmodernism to be a critic's term and not a poet's. (None of the poets I knew at that time spoke of themselves in any such way.) So I insisted—and would continue to insist—that postmodernism was an ill-defined term because it depended on a prior definition of modernism, and that such a prior definition was still up for grabs. Over the years—as postmodernism became a part of our time and, still undefined, a part of our vocabulary—I became more prone to use it and to use it as an extension in particular of one form of early modernism—the more experimental and overtly revolutionary—that was often in conflict with the institutionalized version still current then and now. And I came to believe that modernism and postmodernism were like some kind of twin birth— closely related and ready, always, to call each other's birthright into question. For this I would frequently cite Tristan Tzara's statement in the days of Dada: "You are mistaken if you take Dada for a modern school, or as a reaction against the schools of today. . . . Dada is not at all modern. It is more in the nature of an almost Buddhist religion of indifference. . . . The true Dadas are against Dada."[1]

That was postmodernism as I could use it, and that was postmodernism too in relation to your previous question. I believe that something like that was what Haroldo had in mind when citing Mallarmé and Baudelaire; and I would want to extend it, say, to Tzara and Mallarmé, and then to the work of my own generation in relation to Tzara's, and that of some further generation in relation to ours. Still, it would be better to do without those terms.

With a global and wide-range focus, Poems for the Millennium *aims at tracing the international history of poetry since the nineteenth century. What thoughts come to you when you look at this anthology together with* Technicians of the Sacred *and* Shaking the Pumpkin? *What parallels more immediately come to your mind between primal and contemporary poetical procedures?*

I've answered some of this already, so I think this answer will be brief.

One point that I didn't mention about *Poems for the Millennium* is that while it aims, in your words, "at tracing the international history of poetry since the nineteenth century," it sees (or we see) that history as including most of the poetry in *Technicians of the Sacred* and *Shaking the Pumpkin.* In both volumes of *Millennium,* to start with, we have sections of ethnopoetic workings, taking these as something that came to light along with experimental modernism (or even earlier, when romanticism was still dominant) and aware, too, that many of the traditional practitioners—those, in particular, grouped together in an oral poetry section in volume 2—have been contemporaries of ours in the century now ending. (Others, of course, are from a past that's truly past.) The ethnopoetics section of volume 1 ("A Book of Origins") is the concluding section of that volume—a mix of ancient, deeply rooted works and related discoveries among ourselves. "It is impossible," we say in a prologue to that section, "to present the work of a radical or innovative modernism without mapping at the same time some features of the old worlds, brought newly into the present & viewed there as if for the first time, to help to show us where we are."

1. See also pages 15 and 109, above.

In the "pre-face" to *Technicians of the Sacred*—the first of the big anthologies and the one that launched me into ethnopoetics—I set out a
number of parallels between (as you put it) "primal and contemporary poetical procedures." What stands out most clearly is the relation of traditional oral poetry to the modern reinvention of poetry—both sung and
spoken—as a vocal and performative art. The "new American poetry" of
several decades ago—fueled by the energies of Olson and Ginsberg and
others—emphasized the role of voice and breath as the physical/bodily
basis for composition and for poetry as a liberating/spiritual act. The
"dark" side of that comes up in what a poet-companion of mine, Clayton
Eshleman, speaks of as "grotesque realism" and an "American grotesque":
"an immersion in the lower body; not the body of the individual, the
'bourgeois ego,' but the body of all: the 'brimming over abundance' of decay, fertility, birth, growth, death . . . unfinished, exaggerated; . . . protu-
berances and apertures prominent" (interpreted thus by Eliot Weinberger
in *Poems for the Millennium*). From such a vantage point connections are
made—beyond Rabelais and De Sade among the earlier Europeans—to
a world of primal tricksters and sacred clowns or—following the lead of
our Surrealist predecessors and others—in the dreams and visions that are
our common patrimony as human beings. And with this I can also connect
the concern with chance-determined (or *undetermined/indeterminate*)
art—in the Chinese *I Ching*, in various African forms of divination, in
the poetry and related art of Jackson Mac Low and John Cage—coming
to a focus where Cage, defining *indeterminacy*, declares:

IF THERE WERE A PART OF LIFE DARK ENOUGH TO KEEP OUT OF IT A
LIGHT FROM ART, I WOULD WANT TO BE IN THAT DARKNESS, FUM-
BLING AROUND IF NECESSARY, BUT ALIVE.

In all of this I see a questioning of God and World—crucial to our own
work as I understand it and necessary to any final acceptance (or rejection)
of a world and god bound up with death and suffering. And I also find
in this a point where "primary" and "contemporary"—as you call them—
come together; like the words of the old Crow Indian song, "addressed"—
in Robert Creeley's words—"to emptiness":

we want what is real
we want what is real
don't deceive us.

(In all of this I'm also writing in a very personal way, and I'm trying to construct the anthology as a book or as a long poem or narrative. But the problem with anthologies is that everyone takes them as attempts to be definitive and neglects that you're really just telling another kind of story.)

You lived in an Indian reservation in the 1970s, devoting yourself to experimental translations of American Indian poetry. How was this experience? What have you learned from the close contact with those other cultures and poetics? And, in a more general sense, what do you think contemporary poets and readers can learn from them?

Living where I lived was something that came to me without any advance sense that it ever would. I was driven by poetry—to me an *other* language that was constantly in a process of being created and recreated—driven by poetry to seek it in its different manifestations and, through means that I discovered elsewhere and through related means of my own making, to take it beyond what it was when I first felt drawn to it. The first seeking— as with many of my contemporaries—was through books and other forms of transcription that were already there. I craved translations and wanted to know poetry in all its languages and times and places. That was the push behind *Technicians of the Sacred,* and it had moved me for many years before the book arrived for me. I found resemblances to every sort of poetry I knew—the experimental and the visionary foremost—and I found, as well, a range of poetries I never knew existed. I was astonished, too, to come on poetry in places, cultures, where we least expected it to be—so overwhelmed by it that I began to see it everywhere among the so-called primitives and tribal peoples.

I was already well into all of that—most of the *Technicians* book completed—when I corresponded with and then met Gary Snyder. Through Snyder I was led to Stanley Diamond, an anthropologist and poet with an extraordinarily unified and radical view of what intellectual and poetic energies lay behind what had been called "the primitive." And it was Diamond who sent me out to the Seneca Indian Reservation—an Iroquois tribe or nation in the western corner of New York State—to find myself, as Charles Olson often put it, participating in history as an act of "seeing for oneself." We went to the reservation at the end of 1967 and returned for the Midwinter ceremonies a few weeks later—events that I brought into the final version of *Technicians of the Sacred.* It was a moment in my life that I had never anticipated, for which I had never planned, and it had consequences that went on for a decade and more thereafter.

Shaking the Pumpkin—the traditional American Indian anthology—came together over frequent visits to the reservation, and the most experimental parts of it in consultation with traditional song makers like Richard Johnny John and Avery Jimerson. During the time I lived there—from 1972 to 1974—I finished *Poland/1931* (the concluding poem, "Cokboy," an ironic send-up [takeoff] on all of that) and began *A Seneca Journal,* which needed some greater distance for completion. I joined in singing (secular) Seneca songs with the local Singing Society, which brought my sense and experience of performance into a whole new arena. I was moved, even awed, by the rituals to which I was admitted, though I was clearly not admitted to them all. The masked Midwinter doings are still vivid in my mind, and the Dark Dance—with its women singers/dancers in near total darkness—hence invisible—is something that has not been matched for me, no matter where. And along with that—if I can say this rightly—there was an entry, however tentative, into a world I hadn't known before—and people, most of them now dead, who showed me how the work we do can shape and even change our lives and minds. All of that—not only the high ceremonials but the day-to-day living as well—encouraged me to ground my work—at least to try to do so—on the living side of that art and life continuum so many of my artist friends had called to our attention.

That was of course a major thrust in books like *Technicians of the Sacred* and *Shaking the Pumpkin*—that the moves we make from what we think of as an avant-garde perspective have had their counterparts in cultures everywhere. That meant for me that we could think of our work—even at its most innovative and outrageous—as an act of recovery—a reclaiming, somehow, of our rights as poets and of a life of poetry in which we all could share. If the Surrealist poets, say, could blazon Lautréamont's words—that poetry was made by *all*, not one—on the masthead of their journal, that much was still possible for us to say and to explore more fully in our own time.

So, yes, in answer to your final question, I would say that this is something that can still be learned today—this along with the numerous ways of thinking and speaking that the old cultures knew and practiced—a richness of means that we can still search at their source. For my own generation and for many of the poets in *Poems for the Millennium,* both past and present, this has been a necessary proposition. But there have been times too—today not excepted—when I have felt it slipping away, replaced by the idea that poetry can *only* exist at the margins. Inherently realistic from a contemporary perspective, this obscures nonetheless that by doing what we're doing, we're connecting to the great poetic *mainstream*—to position a *real* poetry at the center of our lives.

It is frequent to hear claims about the impossibility of an avant-garde today, as well as complaints about the scarcity and poorness of contemporary poetical production. I feel that Poems for the Millennium *brings a more positive stance, emphasizing the possibilities, the "revolutions of the word" still to come, not their closure. Thinking specifically of the international experimental traditions you gather in* Poems for the Millennium, *do you see that poe(lit)ical movements are possible or desirable today? If they exist, where would they be occurring?*

It's my belief that those "revolutions" are inherent to poetry as we've made it and will continue to be so into the foreseeable future—as long, at least, as ideas of freedom and transformation (change) remain a part of our outlook overall. I don't say that with any certainty, however, because revolutions are an area in which authority—the wisdom or the will to get it done—is, unlike some other things, a matter for the very young. So while I feel, as ever, ready for those kinds of revolution, it's not for me to say.

Revolution—if that's still the going word—is something more than a change of style or fashion. So when you're playing with the words and come up with a portmanteau like *poe(lit)ical,* you're hitting on the dual characteristics (poetical and political) of what was once the avant-garde and certainly the avant-garde of art and poetry that formed itself as *movements.* For those in the early days of experimental modernism—Futurists and Surrealists and Dadas—the ambition was to transform society and consciousness together, and it was only when the social transformation was separated from the poetic one (under the pressures of communism on the left and fascism on the right) that the avant-garde project put itself in question. In the post–World War II time, the poets of the avant-garde—whatever avant-garde there was—were no longer so quick to place their art, as the Surrealists once had it, "at the service of the revolution." The general tone, as in words from the Cobra poet Christian Dotremont that we cite in *Poems for the Millennium,* was "against all *isms,* against all that implied a system." This meant—for many—a politics against a politics but with a leftward tilt and keeping, overall, a freedom of occasion—where and when to act. And the occasions included a wide-spread opposition to war and to resurgent forms of nationalism and racism, but also a reawakened sense of the poet as a spokesperson for peoples and species under siege.

That, anyway, was where I found poetry—in the days in particular of the postwar and the cold war. Even in a movement, say, like that of the American "language poets"—the emphasis falling on that key word, *language*—the underlying issues remained political and existential. Indeed, as Charles Bernstein put it, "In order to fully develop the meaning of a formal rupture or extension, we need a synoptic, multilevel, interactive response that accounts, in hopefully unconventional antiauthoritative ways, for sexual, class, local-historical, biographical, and structural dimensions of a poem." Or, in Ron Silliman's words, which still ring true to me: "[A] critique of reference and normative syntax . . . situated within the larger question of what, in the last part of the twentieth century, it means to be human."

Other movements, like those grouped around ethnic and gender identity, were and remain more overtly agenda-driven and sometimes, from my perspective at least, lose the sense of how a "revolution of the word" relates to those other revolutions. But even here, as I've stated above, there are language questions at issue—black voices/white voices, female voices/male voices, dialects and dialectics, written word and shouted word. Such language issues—the whole slew of them and more—are still the heart of our poetics, though what the future holds is never amenable to easy guessing or glib prophecy. Certainly, as I see it, the work is far from done, and the challenge of a poetry and a counterpoetics is as much needed as ever. That in the end it may be a largely losing proposition is also possible, but I can only act as if it isn't.

POSTSCRIPT. On the matter of revolutions of the word and how they might exist today, that brings me back to your first question—the future of poetry in the computer age. (The survival of "imagination" can wait until your final question.) I would urge—but with some limitations placed upon that urging—that the globalism of the Internet opens up the possibility of a worldwide avant-garde. The limitations, given the dominance of English and other hegemonic languages, involve the threat to cultural and regional particulars. Against this, perhaps, the Internet, the Web, offers a new arena for visual, performative, and interactive modes, moving (sometimes at least) in multiple cultural directions. The number of such Web sites and displays is enormous, so that watching the experimental work already triggered—the technical ease in its construction—there's a sense, isn't there, of a futurism that has come into its future.

You have defined Imagination *(the blend of "energy + intelligence") as being important and constant in poetical production through times, and your poetry invests highly in this power of the image. On the other hand, Italo Calvino, in his "Six Proposals for the Next Millennium," argues that in contemporary media society we've lost the power of imagination. As a poet, how do you see the question of Imagination in this increasingly and massifying Image Culture? Can poetic language still function today as an "instrument of vision," of change, of "seedings"?*

The imagination question is for me a matter of the intention of poetry—as much a matter of that as of the means employed. For many years I had a running argument with David Antin—my oldest and closest companion in poetry—about "imagination." For David—sometimes for me as well—imagination appeared as the dregs of a discourse that were left for poetry after other forms of thought and language broke away and made the greater claim to what was real. He chose strategically to call imagination into question—much as he denied that he ever dreamed, at least until the time came when he chose, for his own reasons, to again affirm his dreaming. He wanted the poetic lineage of Socrates and Diderot—and said so—and he wanted it to lead through Wittgenstein—and said so, too. For me the lineage went through those like Blake ("Imagination is Eternity") and William Carlos Williams ("Only the imagination is real") and Breton ("The imagination is perhaps on the point of reasserting itself, of reclaiming its rights"). More recently, too, I felt it in the work of my own contemporaries, as when Joris and I reproduced most of Diane di Prima's "Rant" in the manifesto section of *Poems for the Millennium,* the poem with the terrific refrain line: THE ONLY WAR THAT MATTERS IS THE WAR AGAINST THE IMAGINATION.

Unlike David and others, I haven't seen this as an inferior reality or as an evasion of reality but as a greater, more complex, even more problematic engagement with the real. When I was publishing a magazine called *some/thing*—again with Antin—we asserted that the question—for our generation, for all of us—was *reality,* meaning by that that we have to look and think beyond what's given to us at any moment. Therefore we have to question ourselves as well and, in that questioning, not be drowned out by the surrounding white noise. The "contemporary media society" (as you and Calvino call it) is omnipresent and alluring, dense with images that sometimes masquerade as the imagination but, better, might be seen as holding the imagination captive. Our early call for a *deep* image—something that I've now almost forgotten—meant that poetry should be ready to be changing rapidly—or that *we* should. I remain mindful—close to a hundred years later—of Joyce's dedication (novelistic but real) to a life of "silence, exile, and cunning" in the face of "that in which I no longer believe." And it seems to me that that's the chance or choice we still have—by all means at our disposal—to not be ground down by what's given but to turn a word against a word, a thought against a thought, an image against an image.

And am I hopeful, then, that this can still change many minds?

Not really, or not more than when Robert Kelly and I, a long time ago, set out to make what even then we thought of as "a poetry of desperation."

The *Sibila* Interview

(with Charles Bernstein, Regis Bonvicino,
Marjorie Perloff, Cecilia Vicuña)

CHARLES BERNSTEIN. Transnational poetry affiliations (imaginary and real), both in Brazil and in the U.S., have more often been east-west than north-south. Can you talk about your own perception of this dynamic and if you see a chance for change, if not in our midst, then on the horizon?

For "us" in general, both in Brazil and in the United States, the outward look has largely been toward Europe and the languages and cultures that dominated much of our earlier poetry. In the United States, England was both the source of the language and the power against which our own literary rebellions came to be directed. The same held true for the Spanish American countries in relation to Spain, and I would imagine, though I'm less secure here, that Brazilian attitudes to Portugal followed a similar path. That, anyway, would be a first east-west dynamic—the new world drawing from the old to begin with, but increasingly the interchange moving in the other direction—liberating ourselves from the old European powers and beginning to influence them in turn.

The second east-west dynamic, as I see it, related to the dominance of France (and to a lesser degree other European countries) in the early modernist project, an inescapable impact on poets in the two (or three) Americas. In the area of the U.S.-France interchange, about which I can speak most easily, a couple of points should be noted. In the first decades

From *Sibila*, no. 6, São Paulo, Brazil, 2004.

of the twentieth century, European modernism (French, German, Italian) represented the limits of formal innovation, felt most strongly (and more strongly resisted than otherwise) in the visual arts, but the U.S. poets who were open to experiment (Williams, Pound, Stein, cummings) also left themselves open to the impact and influence of the overseas innovators. And increasingly U.S. fiction—and certainly U.S. film—began to leave a mark by the 1920s, not only east-west but north-south and various directions in between. At the same time the "great tradition," as we used to speak of it, was essentially European—the "great tradition" of "classical" works that were being rethought by some but that maintained their influence overall as the "western canon."

The other east-west pull—and I think this was true for both Americas—was transpacific: the Far West that we continued, in European mode, to speak of as the Far East. Something of the sort was already there in Whitman's "passage to India," and the chinoiserie of America's first homegrown poetry movement, "imagism," was evident in Pound's "invention of China" as in the work of other of his key contemporaries. Unlike the European connection, however, there was no thrust of the new and innovative from that direction, though new poets in China and Japan were soon to feel the impact of the same radical innovators who were reshaping Western poetry with their ideas, among others, of open verse and demotic language.

My own experience with these directionalities was somewhat different. The circumstances of my coming into poetry were post–World War II—a decade or so beyond it—and U.S. poetry (the Beat eruption in particular) was about to break through and to assert a copresence with the contemporary European—even in places a dominance. The situation, however, was more complex than that might suggest. In the United States, for example, I was part of a movement of poets that looked both outward and inward in "national" terms, and one of the important gestures for us was a crucial turning to the preceding generation of South American poets and some of the more contemporary ones as well. That meant a new focus—late 1950s and early 1960s—on poets such as Vallejo, Neruda, Huidobro, Parra, Paz, and many others—an opening to their experiments and an accelerated work of translation to bring those experiments across. I fell under that spell along with a range of U.S. poets such as Clayton Eshleman, Robert Bly, Nathaniel Tarn, James Wright, Paul Blackburn, Ed Dorn, and others like Eliot Weinberger or David Guss, better known for their translations than for their poetry as such. At the same time there was a swell of interest in Afro-Caribbean writers such as Aimé Césaire and René Depestre, and, at least for those touched by the move toward a new visual and concrete poetry, the absolutely central position of the Brazilian *noigandres* poets.

For the first time, too, our idea of a "transnational poetry" began to dig deep into the "American grain" for a new "classical poetry" drawing on Native American sources, along with a belated recognition of both literary and extraliterary possibilities in African American culture. It was my opportunity with *Technicians of the Sacred* (1968), to open the field in all directions: east-west, north-south, third-world and fourth-world—the last two a part of the north-south distinction that you may have been driving at in your question. If my search focused on *origins*—transhuman origins, as I understood them—there were others better positioned and qualified to explore the *contemporary* possibilities and destinations of such an ethnopoetics. (In recent years, too, living as I do on the Mexico-U.S. border, there has been the possibility of exploring a transnationalism by crossing back and forth, as Mark Weiss has it in the title of a new bilingual anthology of Baja California poetry, *al otro lado*.)

East and west, and north and south, this "transnationalism" and/or "transculturalism" (more far-reaching words than *internationalism* and less negatively loaded than globalism) has been carried forward since the 1960s by a number of multilingual or translation-heavy magazines and poetry publishers (*El corno emplumado* [in Mexico], Stefan Hyner's *Gatē* [in Germany]; *Change* and *Action poétique* [in Paris]; Eshleman's *Sulfur* and *Caterpillar;* Nate Mackey's *Hambone; Sibila* and *Medusa* [in Brazil]); as well as by numerous poetry festivals and gatherings and, more recently, by renewed transnational activity via the Internet. All of these point to a porosity of borders, even at a time when a counterpressure toward cultural isolation and ethnic/religious conflict is again running amok in the world-at-large.

A number of years ago, Donald Allen, who had recently been assembling his pivotal anthology, *The New American Poetry*, described me, in a personal communication, as adhering to the idea of an "international poetry" in contrast, I believe, to what he was then doing. I was a little uncomfortable with it at the time, but in subsequent years I've come to accept it as what I really am and want to be. I have tried in my address to reach across borders and times, while remaining firmly implanted in where I live and work. My most recent poetry anthology, *Poems for the Millennium*, is a celebration of such a stance.

CECILIA VICUÑA. Please speak of the root of your performance art. How did it begin? You have spoken of the connection between your early work in ethnopoetics and performance. Would you describe first attempts, failures, and/or discoveries in the process? Place it in time if you can.

My sense of performance comes directly out of the poetry—the idea, grasped early along, that the shaped and manipulated language of the poem couldn't be held to the page, stripped thereby of half its power, by a tradition of silent reading. I liked to speak the words out loud—both poetry and the words in plays, which I used to read and perform with great pleasure as a kid. I wanted very much to be an actor, but I realized after a while that I was too inhibited for that, that I shied away from playing a role, presenting myself in public as someone I knew I wasn't.

Reading poetry or performing it was different, something more akin to music, and while I didn't play an instrument or join easily in singing, I found increasing pleasure in reading from a text. In adolescence I spoke poems out loud with friends or locked myself away to perform whole Shakespeare plays in solitude, taking on different voices (I thought). When the first wire recorders came around, I remember the shock of hearing my voice reading Whitman or, even more so, poems of my own making. And a few years later, in graduate school in Michigan, I gave Austin Warren, a then well-known "new critic," a tape-recorded "reading from Walt Whitman" as a term paper—my selection and my voice, along with imitations (written) of Emily Dickinson—and we agreed, I think, that that was how it had to be.

There were other things, too, more evident as the outside world began to reach me. I remember a recording of the actor John Gielgud reading poetry (old and new) that an older friend presented to me, Edith Sitwell's *Façade* and Gertrude Stein's *Four Saints* a little later, and from the time I was sixteen or seventeen, a series of readings by poets in New York—Dylan Thomas, T. S. Eliot, e. e. cummings, and others. Sometimes I imitated their voices, concerned about my own New York sound before I began to value that as something dear to me. All of those were preliminary to what was later possible.

The ethnopoetics came gradually and didn't begin to take shape until the late 1950s or early 1960s. What I remember from still earlier were the cantillations in neighborhood synagogues and my own participation at the time of my bar mitzvah. There was a resistance there, as well as an attraction, and I'm hard pressed to make too much of it. But it was clearly a different way of presenting language, as were a number of other things that came to me: the voices of black preachers on the radio, the talking blues of singers like Woody Guthrie and Pete Seeger, the wordless lyrics of jazz and scat before I knew anything about sound poetry and Dada, the sound of chanted Latin and Greek in Catholic and Orthodox churches into which we also ventured. I remember early recordings that were made available through Folkways Records and the Library of Congress—not least the accompanying inserts in which the words were written out.

Even so, it was the texts that really got to me—those in particular that led me into the wonders of oral and mystical traditions that they were representing through writing and translation. When college gave me access to libraries and to a greater range of such works—the late 1940s in New York, the early 1950s at the University of Michigan—the idea of an ethnopoetics started taking shape for me. Those glimmerings coincided with an outburst over the following decade of public readings and performances—in alternative venues, let me stress, that brought the work in from the bottom up. There was also by then the presence of poetry and jazz performances to spur me on and, more so maybe, my own first meetings with Jackson Mac Low and other Fluxus poets and artists for whom John Cage was certainly the central presence.

That was some of what was "in the air"—our own paideuma, as Pound and Frobenius called it—and it let me consider how the oral and tribal works could be fitted into the new configuration that was then emerging. I arranged a couple of readings of "primitive and archaic poetry" in New York, and by 1966 or 1967 I was working on *Technicians of the Sacred*. Before the book was actually out, I met the anthropologist Stanley Diamond, who led me to what would be a long association with the Seneca Indians in western New York State. And more of interest to you, Cecilia, I also met the great American ethnomusicologist David McAllester, who had worked for several decades on the songs and rituals of the Navajos. What those opened up for me was a series of experimental translations, both as a form of text art derived from oral sources in the Seneca instance and as a translation of sound-into-sound and music-into-music with the Navajo "horse songs."

None of this happened in isolation but was accompanied by performances of my own poetry in which I came to engage with composers and musicians (Charlie Morrow and Bertram Turetzky principally, but also Pauline Oliveros, Philip Corner, and George Lewis, among others).

I began to add Dada works and my own extension of Dada works to my performance repertory, I wrote and performed sound-plays for (mostly German) radio, and I worked with the Living Theater and its offshoots on more extended works of poetry performance.

In that way performance—fired by the ethnopoetic experience—took up much of my energy, while I continued to explore the semantic dimensions of poetry and to return finally to the book as the other primary place of composition and performance. It was my intention—in the time I was given—to try to be a poet in every way that was open to me.

RÉGIS BONVICINO. What do you think about "anthologies"? Do you think they take the risk of being superficial? I'm saying that while aware that I'm the editor of an anthology of Brazilian poetry recently launched in the United States by Green Integer. In this sense, what is, in your opinion, the destiny of written poetry nowadays?

Sometime in the middle 1960s I was given the opportunity to do a big anthology of an area of poetry that had rarely been anthologized before. In the vocabulary of the time the words that covered that area were *primitive* and *archaic,* but I turned these around, I thought, with my opening statement: "Primitive means complex." (I later dispensed with those words entirely.) In composing that book, *Technicians of the Sacred,* I realized that an anthology didn't have to be a conservatizing instrument but could be used as a vehicle for transformation. My intention with *Technicians* was to explore oral poetry and its deep cultural traditions on a global scale. This led me also to alternative forms of writing and other visual presentations of language, along with an attention to visionary and shamanistic contexts for poetry and for constructed forms of language that resembled what we had come to think of as poetry. I introduced a section of "commentaries" in which I could specify those contexts and connect the traditional, often ritualized, works to our own experimental poetry— as we knew it or were trying to invent it.

As my idea of anthologies changed, I began to think of them as both a kind of epic-sized assemblage—a highly composed and constructed work—and a manifesto for whatever poetry was still to come. Superficiality, since you raise the question, didn't enter the picture here. Rather my proposition for the historical and ethnopoetic anthologies was "to reconfigure the poetic past from the point of view of the present," and for the modern and postmodern ones it was simply: "I will change your mind." (The wordplay in this is probably not apparent in any language but English.)

How this applies to "the destiny of written poetry" I find it hard to say. If anything, works like these assemblages, which take the form of necessarily big books, would seem to enlarge the sphere of writing—where even what was once oral seems, like the everything else in Mallarmé's formulation, to end up in a book. The future of the book isn't something that worries me, much more the question of what goes into the book. I feel justified in my own efforts if I'm able to cover new ground or to cover old ground in new ways. I also hope, from a personal perspective, that the anthologies, the big books that I've assembled, will be read along with my own poetry and translations (some of it contained within them) as a single multiplex but unified project. Above all I would like to think of them as a gift for and from the poets and others who have lived—far more than me—a life of poetry.

MARJORIE PERLOFF. How has translation of German Dada and concrete poetry—Schwitters, Ball, Jandl, etc.—influenced your own poetry? Does it seem more congenial to you than French Dada?

Among the Dadas, Schwitters was clearly the one with whom I had the most extended encounter through translation, while the concrete poet on whom I worked extensively wasn't Jandl so much as Gomringer. With Ball the only kind of translation I attempted was a performance of his sound-work, *Karawane,* which I slipped into my own performance of *That Dada Strain.* The translations also included a smaller group from French-language poets such as Tzara and Picabia, but it was *That Dada Strain,* the whole series of poems, that was as much my response as the translations.

Back in the late 1950s or early 1960s, when Robert Motherwell's big Dada book opened me up to Dada, I thought that what was needed was a gathering of actual poems. Motherwell had presented very few of those, so I announced that I was preparing an anthology to be called *That Dada Strain* and to be published by my press, Hawk's Well. I translated a handful from Tzara, Arp, Schwitters, Huelsenbeck, and Picabia, but the press didn't last, and I got otherwise diverted. I didn't really come back to anything like that until sometime in the 1970s, and *That Dada Strain,* as it emerged then, was a series of poems addressed to the Dada poets—*transcreations* of a sort, to use Haroldo de Campos's term. Translations and appropriations were embedded or collaged in some of the poems, and sound poems and actual translations were sometimes included in performance versions.

In doing that I don't think I was so much favoring German Dada as Zürich Dada—not least of all because the antiwar and transnational stance of the Zürich exiles corresponded to my own feelings about Vietnam and the Vietnam aftermath—about the whole twentieth-century experience of war and repression if it came to it. Even so, Paris is very much there in the two opening poems, as well as Schwitters's Germany in the poem addressed to him. It was Schwitters, too, on whom I focused later—by way of translation—because I saw him as an experimental extremist whose work coincided with much in our own time but had never been translated and carried over into English. (Except by him, of course, when he was in exile in England.) That Schwitters was himself a victim of war and fascism also had an appeal to me.

What I did with Schwitters was both to translate him and to follow him into performance. I also tried to bring him forward as a precursor of concrete poetry, but his concrete poems like his sound poems and his poems in English needed no translation. Where I got into the translation of concrete poetry was with Gomringer—a whole book of poems translated into English as a kind of primer, I thought, not only of Gomringer's poetry but of the fundamentals of translation, operating in an area of minimal poetry that seemed to eschew translation. Even more of a transcreation for me was a series of ritual songs that I translated from the Seneca Indian "society of the mystic animals." I had collected these in a collaboration with the Seneca singer and ritualist, Richard Johnny John, and I wanted a way to show the sophistication of the apparently minimal use of words and vocables ("meaningless" sounds) in Seneca chanting. Instead of setting up a song poem like this

A POEM FOR THE MYSTIC ANIMALS

The animals are coming
He-eh-eh-heh

I set it up like this:

	H E H E H H E H
	H E H E H H E H
The animals are coming	H E H **U H** H E H
	H E H E H H E H
	H E H E H H E H

The results, I thought, followed along the lines of what Ernest Fenollosa, early in the game and speaking of something quite different, had called "a brilliant flash of concrete poetry."

MARJORIE PERLOFF. In translating, do you try to recreate the rhythms of the original or adapt the work to an American idiom?

I would have to say that both approaches are possible and maybe something else that's a little different from either. It depends on how close the two languages or poetry traditions are, and what features I'm trying to bring out or what point I'm interested in making. In general I favor an American and contemporary idiom, but if there's a crucial element in the original that acts against that, I try to bring it out, even, if it's important enough, in a grossly exaggerated way. With Lorca, for example, when I translate his *Suites*, I want them to read in American but with echoes of Spanish lyricism that would otherwise be foreign to me, or with suggestions of rhyme and song, where those seem naturally to happen. (Paul Blackburn's translations from Provencal are a model here—much more contemporary and interestingly musical than Pound's nearly Victorian versions.) In *The Lorca Variations*, however, which are probably my best shot at transcreation or what I speak of elsewhere as "othering," I hold on to elements of Lorca's vocabulary from my straight translation of his *Suites* and fashion poems that I can think of as essentially my own.

I don't often translate older European poetry, but when I do it's more akin, I think, to Pound's or to Blackburn's "making it new." That's the case, say, with San Juan de la Cruz's "En una noche oscura":

> On a dark night, afraid
> to love you, burning
> Then this joy
> to find the door
> (unseen)
> the house so quiet

or throughout the Hebrew and Aramaic translations in *A Big Jewish Book*, except where I'm bringing across forms such as acrostics (rare in English) or numerically derived *gematria*. (I can't stay consistent with any of this ... and don't intend to.) But I've also done the contemporary remaking with older English poems—some instances in which I'm practicing a deliberate form of translation by paraphrase. So, for example, for a re-

cent book of poems around the European babe-god that Susan Bee will
be illustrating, I take Southwell's [seventeenth-century] "Burning Babe"
that starts like this:

> As I in hoary winter's night stood shivering in the snow,
> Surprised I was with sudden heat which made my heart to glow;
> And lifting up a fearful eye to view what fire was near,
> A pretty Babe all burning bright did in the air appear . . .

and "translate" it like this:

> a pretty babe
> in air
> aglow and glittering
>
> his skin split
> from the heat, his tears
> a flood
>
> but useless
> cannot quench the flames
> but feeds them . . .

With the Navajo horse songs, which I've spoken about elsewhere, I go off
in a different direction, and what emerges is dictated by my perception of
what's happening in the original, particularly the sounds and word distortions, that can't be covered by a partial translation. On the other hand,
I'm also being responsive to my sense of contemporary sound poetry and
that I'm adding to it—in the same way that my translation from the Society of the Mystic Animals relates to contemporary concrete poetry.

There are lots of other approaches, but I'll just mention one more,
where I think you once took issue with me. When translating Schwitters,
I would sometimes (not always) deliberately model myself on the erratic
English of his English-language poems and self-translations, I suppose
with a sense that I was putting myself into his place as a self-translator. I
also found a degree of irregularity, equally deliberate, in his German, so
I reckoned that we came out even.

MARJORIE PERLOFF. Is there a poet you've always wanted to translate but
haven't yet? If so, who?

There are several poets whom I've wanted to translate in the past—generally for a single big work of theirs or what I might think to put together as a single work.

The first one who comes to mind is Hölderlin, and those notebooks in particular where the poems are layered-in like palimpsests. They would in that sense be a little like Mallarmé's *Anatol* or *Le livre,* although the palimpsests, I think, are of a still different order—more a kind of "action writing" or something that I could translate or transcreate as such.

A second work, which I briefly thought of translating with Pierre Joris, is Adolf Wölfli's monumental *art brut* novel, visuals and all. And a third one, from which Harris Lenowitz and I translated excerpts for *A Big Jewish Book* but that we never finished, is a medieval Hebrew work by Abraham Abulafia to which I gave the title "Abulafia's Circles."

Also, since I'm talking about "big works" in a Brazilian context, there's Haroldo de Campos's *Galáxias,* although I'm sure that someone else will get it into English soon—an overwhelming work, for certain, but very challenging and therefore very sweet.

With all of those, translation would bring something truly new into our poetics—or share it between cultures—and what more than that could we ever want?

CHARLES BERNSTEIN. Many of the poems in *A Book of Witness,* your new book from New Directions, are centered on the possibilities of the "I" and, by extension, personal expression. Yet much of your work, as editor, poet, and translator, has worked to decenter conventionally self-expressive verse. Can you talk about the tension between expression and construction in your work?

That was certainly one of the driving ideas in *A Book of Witness,* something that I had had in mind before but on which I had never acted so deliberately. The question of self-expression had come to dominate many of the conventional approaches to poetry, to make poetry almost exclusively an arena for the lyric, first-person voice. Like most of us, I came out of that mind-set, and like many of us, I resisted it. My idea for poetry was that, even where we worked in shorter forms, the range of voice accessible to us, like the range of subject or vocabulary, should be unlimited. At the same time I was fascinated by certain works—largely but not exclusively ethnopoetic—in which the first person ("I" and "me") was used in ways that went far beyond the personal. I gave a number of examples in *Technicians of the Sacred* and the other anthologies, but the one that I took as

template came from the María Sabina *veladas*—wall-to-wall first person
but every utterance attributed to a mythic other voice:

> I am a little launch woman, says
> I am a little shooting star woman, says
> I am the Morning Star woman, says
> I am the First Star woman, says
> I am a woman who goes through the water, says
> I am a woman who goes through the ocean, says
> I am the great Woman of the Flowing Water, says
> I am the sacred Woman of the Flowing Water, says

But even before I knew about María Sabina, I was using the first person in that way—maybe derived from African praise-poems, maybe on
my own:

> I am the man who held the keys.
> I asked you to forgive me.
> I was the first to be insistent and the last to leave.

> I vomited.
> I didn't come there often.
> I was eager and alive.

> I was not the least among them.
> Once I was.
> Once I remember being in a poor position.

> I applied for membership.
> I was sad.
> Then I thought no longer to go on living.

> I turned from you and offered you my keys.
> You turned beside me and offered your position.
> I had turned against them.

All of that, as you point out, is a compositional as well as an expressive
matter, and I'm not sure if expression or self-expression is anything but
misleading when we talk about it. Looking back now, I see that I was

using the "I" pronoun to set up a series of repetitions, more for the sake of contradiction than agreement. I could switch, of course, to third person ("he" or "she" or "they") with similar results, but the power of the "I" and a certain fluctuation in its use—between fact and fiction—had a different meaning. It was clear that language allowed the "I" to testify, but to what was it testifying and who in any instance was the person, the "I," who was speaking? I began to feel, in that way, that an unfettered use of "I" wouldn't so much lock in identity as put it into question.

Regarding composition or construction, there was another work that helped me to launch *A Book of Witness* and to which it has some necessary reference. I had been reading a little book by Jenny Holzer—*Laments*—and finding in it a still more complicated weaving of "I" utterances. For Holzer these seemed to function as narratives that formed a kind of postmodern version of Edgar Lee Masters's *Spoon River Anthology*—twelve individuated "voices of the dead" she called them, but I read each one instead as a series of overlapping voices and identities. I also had a number of other things in mind—compositionally, I mean, as well as intellectually: that the utterances would be separate from each other as I wrote them and would form a unity only later, or however it fell out; that they would include brief "I" utterances from other poets, most of whom I would identify in the margins; and that they would constitute a long series (a hundred poems in total) where the reiteration of the form affected and changed the reading of the individual poems.

Here's one, as a sampler, that starts with a line from the Brazilian poet Jorge de Lima:

I BELIEVE IN THE MAGIC OF GOD

I believe in the magic of god   (J. de Lima)
& in fire. Somebody
dangles a key on the steps.
From a hole in my chest
eyes stare out.
I run into a circle
of friends
little men with pale lips
& soft fingers.
I signal new forms of expression.
The way sand shapes hills
& water shapes fountains.

I am in their hands completely
helpless as a babe
unless the babe command the world
sending a stream of
feathers
back to earth.
A prince he is & dances
between rivers
then rides a shining rocket
to the upper air.
It brings the wolves to me
to eat out of my hand.
The streets of Rome
signal a fresh
disaster. I am one
a pope would deign to speak to
when I wave my arms.

Cecilia Vicuña. In the pre-face to the *New Selected Poems, 1970–1985,* you speak of yourself as a witness, as I understand it, not just to the world but to your own process, which leads us to the old question of "el des-doblaje," being in and out of yourself at the same time while performing. Would you care to explore this further?

This is a different question from Charles's, although it touches on similar ground and on the word *witness,* which is, I suppose, central to my idea of what the aim of my poetry may be. In the pre-face you mention, the dec-laration about witnessing goes as follows: "I am a witness like everyone else to [the world, the present, as it comes and goes], and all the experi-ments [the poems] for me . . . are steps toward the recovery/discovery of a language for that witnessing." At the same time I find myself shying away from such a claim, because it seems to me I've seen and felt so little. I keep coming back to it, however, with a sense that a little may be enough and that I can use the means at my disposal to be a conduit for others—at its most intense for others who have seen and felt a lot.

    In *Khurbn,* the cycle of poems I wrote about the Holocaust, I opened myself to other voices, witnesses to those events, by composing, con-structing, texts—my own words interlaced (collaged) with theirs. *A Book of Witness* is much more constructed, much less constrained by its thematic. Here I take the first person ("I") as voice of witness and follow wherever it leads me, while at the same time I confront the problematics of witnessing and the possible lie of speaking in the first person—in the witness's voice. I am aware here, too, of the degradation of the first person, both by poets close to me who disparage it and by others who restrict it to a narrow, "confessional" perspective. In the Postface to *A Book of Witness* I speak of it as "the instrument—in language—for all acts of witnessing, the key with which we open up to voices other than our own."

When it comes to performance, however, I appear as who I am—as the presenter of my own works or of works like Hugo Ball's *Karawane* or Schwitters's *London Onion* that I've appropriated for myself. I'm not aware of acting a role other than myself; that is to say, I don't have to get into character to perform, as an actor would, but have only to work myself into the performance as a musician might. In doing that I'm aware as well that "myself" in the act of performance feels different for me than "myself" does otherwise. I like your word *desdoblaje,* which I take as a splitting apart or a breaking in two, and I think that what I've said just now may be my version of it.

Or put more simply: I hear myself speak and in that moment of performance I am both subject and object: the one who listens and the one who speaks.

CECILIA VICUÑA. When I hear your story (even though I am reading it) of growing up in the Bronx, in 1948, "behind the times" in a place where the news had not yet arrived of the end of "the age of the modern, the experimental and visionary," I picture your experience as parallel to ours, in Latin America, living even further "behind the times." I wonder, when you finally came across some Latin American poets, did you feel a sense of kinship/difference, with them? and how this compares with your encounter with María Sabina?

As David Antin says in one of his talk-poems: "we are all from Chula Vista." The reference for us Californians is to a small town near San Diego—in somewhat the same relation to San Diego or Los Angeles as the Bronx to Manhattan. To come from such a place—"growing up . . . behind the times"—is in some sense the shared experience of most of us, whether it's a question of location or of moment or of both. We come belatedly into the world that came before us, and we have to wrest from that world and to create in spite of it that which may be meaningful in our own terms. In turn we can anticipate that others will come after us (behind the times that *we* make), like those "other horrible workers" of Rimbaud's imagination who "will begin from the horizons where [we have] succumbed."

The "news" that had arrived to me in 1950 was different from the real news of poetry and was therefore unusable—a widespread assumption that "the age of the modern, the experimental and visionary" was over and that we were doomed, as a generation, to return to the premodernist past. But the true past of modernism was precisely what we needed to construct a new "post"modernism—at least the way I understood it. In that sense my task was to dig my way out of my own Chula Vista, to lay claim to what came before me, and to look for fellow "workers" wherever I could find them. That brought me first into the "vortex" of New York, to use Pound's term, and in an age of rapid communication, I was able soon after to connect with poets from around the world.

My first contact with Latin American poets was in 1960, when I traveled to Mexico City and met Homero Aridjis and a number of other poets my age or younger. A few years later Paul Blackburn introduced me to Octavio Paz, whom I knew first in New York and later in Paris and Mexico, as well as to Julio Cortázar. By the early 1960s, Sergio Mondragón and Margaret Randall were publishing *El corno emplumado* in Mexico, where I must first have seen your own early writings, Cecilia, and to which I was myself a regular contributor. At the same time, as I explained to Charles Bernstein in a previous answer, I was one of a number of U.S. poets who had immersed ourselves in the writing of our Latin American predecessors—Vallejo, Neruda, Huidobro among the many we were reading and translating. What that did for us was to push open the boundaries of twentieth-century modernism in ways that an exclusive focus on European and U.S. modernism would have failed to do. With the older Latin American poets I felt a necessary but productive difference, while the younger ones appeared to me as contemporaries with whom I shared a common "postwar" world and discourse.

My encounter with María Sabina was markedly different, but how could it not be? With the American poets, north and south, and with the European poets as well, there was a common culture of poetry and the shared discourse that I just referred to. Modernism and postmodernism were the names of the game, and even when I turned to the living poets of Japan or China, say, the differences of language and culture had already been weakened enough to allow a lot of play for what was, after all, our common contemporaneity. María Sabina lived in a narrower if possibly more intense world but with no interest in what I or you or our fellow poets were into or concerned with. Nor was poetry itself an issue at any point, although Language clearly was. And it was her sense of Language as a restorative force that was of extraordinary interest to me, though I knew that my Language and poetry didn't have the slightest interest for her. When we met in Huautla in 1979, through the good offices of Henry Munn and of Álvaro Estrada's family, I found our differences confirmed. The English translation of her *Vida*, which I was helping to publish in English, appeared in 1981, and more recently I edited a larger version of the *Vida* and the chants, with commentaries by myself and a number of fellow poets.[1] Nothing was bridged in the course of that, but I hope that the differences were honored.

CHARLES BERNSTEIN. What's the difference between translation and composition?

The glib answer would be that there is no difference. But that would be to overlook what it is that's being translated and, less significantly perhaps, what's being composed. I will therefore try to answer your question as I do in my new book, *Writing Through: Translations and Variations*, for which you wrote the foreword. That comes, of course, from my own perspective, and even so it only covers a portion of my work.

I came to believe that composition and translation form a continuum in my work—that when I translate I feel myself, often, to be simultaneously composing, and when I compose—certain works more than others—I find that I'm drawing on other voices or on the work of significant others who are my predecessors or my contemporaries. Some of my most experimental work has taken the form of translation—the experiments in particular with tribal and oral poetry that I spoke about in an answer to Marjorie. In my own compositions the "othering" comes largely through collage and through modified chance operations (in *Gematria* and *The Lorca Variations*, say). But at another extreme, I'd be ready to say that *all* language is a form of othering—the use of a vital instrument for poetry that is never exclusively my own but has been built up, constructed, over millennia and by countless generations of speakers and writers.

1. See *María Sabina: Selections* (Berkeley: University of California Press, 2003).

That was the reason, in part, for my strongly positive response when you and a number of other poets, a decade or two my juniors, announced the beginnings of a new *language* poetry. I knew, of course, that there were differences between us, but they've faded into insignificance in the years that followed. At least for me . . .

Index of Names

✦ Northern Lights Series ✦

THE JOURNEY OF
Eleven Moons

⊰ A NOVEL ⊱

BONNIE LEON

THOMAS NELSON PUBLISHERS
Nashville • Atlanta • London • Vancouver

Published in Nashville, Tennessee, by Thomas Nelson, Inc., Publishers, and distributed in Canada by Word Communications, Ltd., Richmond, British Columbia, and in the United Kingdom by Word (UK), Ltd., Milton Keynes, England.

Scripture quotations are from the NEW KING JAMES VERSION of the Bible. Copyright © 1979, 1980, 1982, Thomas Nelson, Inc., Publishers.

Library of Congress Cataloging-in-Publication Data

Leon, Bonnie.
    The journey of eleven moons : a novel / Bonnie Leon.
      p. cm.
    ISBN 0–7852–7974–1 (pb)
    I. Title. II. Title: Journey of 11 moons.
PS3562.E533J68   1995   94–18375
813′.54—dc20   CIP

Printed in the United States of America

1 2 3 4 5 6 7 - 01 00 99 98 97 96 95

ACKNOWLEDGMENTS

I am indebted to my mother, Elsa, and her sister, Vera. The stories you shared over the years inspired this book and your eagerness to dig for the facts supplied me with the knowledge to tell this tale. Thank you for believing in me. I love you both very much.

And thank you Jean, Patty, and Sam for laboring through each chapter with me. It is your expert critique and encouragement that have seen me through.

INTRODUCTION

The tall Norwegian knelt at the edge of the cliff and hoped the dense grass along the bluff would hide him from the villagers below. He had been thinking of breaking camp for several days but had been unable to bring himself to leave. As he watched the natives, he wondered why he hesitated. It was time to go.

The Aleuts on the beach below chatted as they worked. Some women fleshed hides while others skillfully weaved the tough Aleutian grasses into beautiful and useful baskets. As the men prepared their lances for hunting, they shared tales of previous expeditions, using grand gestures to demonstrate their successes and near disasters as they sought the great whales, walrus, and sea lions of the Bering Sea.

Peals of laughter came from the children who frolicked along the shoreline. One brave youngster clambered across the sheer cliff wall that rose from the beach.

Instead of finding comfort in the happiness he saw, the quiet observer felt melancholy settle over him. *If they knew about the coming changes,* he thought, *they wouldn't be so content. I guess it's just as well they don't know. Now that Alaska is a United States territory, maybe things will improve. Mr. Seward knows this is an untapped treasure.* But even as he thought of this, he realized that soon everyone would know about Alaska's natural riches. And they would come. It would not be better for the native Alaskans.

The man's attention was drawn back to the beach. Family and friends said their farewells as the hunters pushed off in their kayaks. They headed their boats out to sea, plunging through the surf, and finally disappeared over the horizon.

For some reason, the man tasted death in the air. He tried to shake the feeling but could not. He whispered a prayer. "Father, why is my heart so heavy? Please tell me what you want of me. Help me to be obedient. If you say wait, I will wait."

As he watched a child lightly race across the black sand, he knew something was coming. He wondered what. Had God called him to some purpose greater than exploring the world? But what?

He whispered, "Amen."

Chapter 1

*A*nna's hands stopped their rhythmic work and lay still in her lap as she gazed out at the cold Bering Sea. Kinauquak had gone with the men, and this time he would be allowed to make the kill. Unable to concentrate on her weaving, she looked back at the circle of women. Her eyes met those of Alulak. Anna lowered her gaze, suddenly bashful under the old woman's scrutiny.

Alulak laughed. Her eyes became half-moons, nearly disappearing into the folds of her wrinkled brown skin, which had toughened from years of cold and wind. With a toothless grin, she boasted, "My grandson, Kinauquak, will return with a great walrus. Of this I am certain." Her eyes bright with anticipation, she continued, "Tonight we will feast."

The other Aleut women grinned and nodded their heads; their hands never ceased weaving the stiff Aleutian grasses. They too looked forward to the celebration. Each occasionally looked up from her work to scan the empty sea. As always, they waited, anxious for the men's return, not knowing if they would come back successful hunters, or even at all.

This hunt was special. Custom dictated that when Kinauquak made his first kill, he would be counted among the men and ready to take a wife. Anna and Kinauquak had been promised to each other while still children. Once they had played together. That time was past. And, as was customary and acceptable, they loved each other now as adults.

However, Anna could not dwell in Kinauquak's hut until he came for her.

Anna looked at Luba, her mother, and asked, "The men should come soon?"

Luba smiled knowingly and nodded.

Anna stared at the vast ocean, hoping to see bobbing splotches of brown on the horizon, telling of the men's return. She sighed when she found none. With her mind preoccupied, she accidentally ran the sharp, stiff grass across her finger. "Ouch!" she exclaimed and looked down to find blood oozing from a small cut. She watched as a droplet fell upon the partially finished basket then put her finger to her mouth to stop the flow. With satisfaction, she studied the basket she had marked with a dark stain. This basket would be the first she would bring into her new home, and it seemed fitting that it should contain her lifeblood.

Sixteen summers had passed since her birth, and Anna was ready to take her place as mate and mother. To have been chosen as Kinauquak's partner was an honor. He was a brave and noble man. Her heart swelled with pride as she thought of him and how his eyes lit up when he looked at her. She only hoped she would be worthy of such a man.

Anna had worked hard to learn the skill of fleshing and softening hides, and her baskets were admired even by the old ones. She lay her hand across her abdomen and prayed the gods would favor them with many children. Already she carried Kinauquak's child—the first of many, she hoped. She would not tell him until the time of their joining, but delighted in her certainty of his joy when he heard of it.

Anna's thoughts were interrupted by her young sister Iya and brother Inoki as they raced through the circle of women. Iya squealed with delight as Inoki sprinted behind her. Although the younger of the two, Iya was swifter and more agile and easily avoided her brother's pursuit.

Alulak, the eldest of the women, stood. Stretching her four-foot, eleven-inch frame as tall as possible, she planted her hands on her hips and tried to look intimidating. "You children go and play where you are not a nuisance," she scolded. "You have thrown sand over all our work!"

With no more than a glance, the children scurried off. The women grinned at one another and shook their heads, clucking their tongues. Their irritation was more show than true annoyance. They tolerated the childish behavior, knowing that all too soon the children would have to shoulder the burden of survival. The older ones cherished the joy and freedom of the young.

Anna's attention was drawn back to the beach, and her eyes darted across the vast expanse of water. She twisted a strand of grass, bending it and flawing the design of her basket. Oblivious to her mistake, she wondered, *When will they come?*

The other women giggled knowingly.

Anna glanced about the circle and felt the blood rush to her face. She quickly looked down at her work. *I wonder if he has killed the creature yet?* she thought. *I do not think I can stand to wait much longer. Will I be his wife today?*

Again, she studied the sea, but it gave her no answers. The bay remained empty except for the birds who squalled as they fought over tidbits in the surf and the ever-present kelp that floated aimlessly in the currents. In the small cove the sun reflected off the still water, but beyond it, wind-whipped whitecaps danced across the tops of the waves.

Anna closed her eyes and lifted her chin to catch more of the precious sun, relishing its warmth. Its rare appearance made it something of great value. The wind and rain were often relentless. Many times Anna had complained about the lack of sun, certain she could find more joy in life if the weather were only brighter and warmer.

Luba had often gently corrected her. "Life does not always give you what you want. You must cherish each day, no matter what it brings."

Anna tried to do as her mother said, but some days were just too bleak. She took a slow, deep breath, drawing in the pungent odor of the sea, and sighed as she returned to her work. It felt good to be accepted by the circle of women although she sometimes felt like a child looking in from the outside. She tried to listen to what they said, but her mind was too full of Kinauquak to really take in much. Her mother watched her. Anna smiled, and Luba returned the gesture, but her smile didn't touch her eyes.

"Is all well?" Anna asked.

Luba didn't answer at first. Her chocolate-colored eyes settled squarely on Anna as she quietly spoke. "Life is good. The sea provides and our family is well."

The women quieted as Luba spoke.

"I am well, but I feel your absence from our home, even before you have gone. Soon, you will no longer share our hut, but that of your husband."

Tears pricked Anna's eyes, and she managed a weak smile. *When she learns of the baby, she will forget her sorrow,* Anna thought, but she knew a gap would remain when she left her family hut.

Anna and her mother had always shared a special bond. Luba had named her child after a great Russian princess and she had told Anna, "Your name will be a symbol of your heritage. You will always be special among our people."

Her father had been a visiting Russian sailor who had come and gone before knowing of her existence, so she had never known him.

Instead of the usual straight, coal-black hair, she had dark brown waves, and her eyes, though almond in shape, were a vibrant gold rather than chocolate brown. But her disposition, more than any other characteristic, set her apart. She was bold and determined, sometimes even argumentative, a trait considered unattractive among her people. The elders often chastised her for her stubbornness. Anna tried to follow the dictates of the village leaders but frequently failed, finding herself in trouble time and again. Still, they considered her one of them and loved her.

Anna fidgeted with her basket, then held it up and studied her work. She frowned at the piece of twisted grass and considered removing it.

"The hunters are coming!" Inoki announced.

Dropping her basket, Anna turned her head about to look for the approaching boats. The other women set their work aside and rushed to the water's edge. They shaded their eyes as they looked out over the sea at the boats on the horizon.

Anna shook as she pushed herself to her feet. She stood frozen, unable to move. Her heart raced in her chest, and she held her breath as the kayaks sliced through the water. *What if Kinauquak has failed?* she wondered, almost afraid to consider the possibility. *He will feel disgraced. Please, I pray to you, god of the sea, do not bring disgrace upon Kinauquak.*

The villagers crowded about the boats as they came ashore. As the small sealskin vessels scraped against the sand, the men leapt into the shallow water and, with the help of the excited observers, dragged their crafts up the rocky beach.

Anna stood outside her hut with her hands clasped tightly together and searched for Kinauquak. Then she saw him. He smiled broadly as he emerged from his kayak. He stood erect, spear in hand, and searched the landscape. As his eyes met Anna's, he held his spear high in the air, a look of pride confirming his success.

Grinning, Anna ran to join him. As she approached, she suddenly felt shy and slowed her pace. With her eyes lowered, she quietly stood next to him. But Kinauquak could not contain his elation. With a shout of triumph, he placed his hands around her small waist and lifted her into the air, spinning her about.

Unrestrained energy flowed from Kinauquak to Anna. Suddenly everything was laughter and joy. Trembling with excitement, she wrapped her arms about his neck, looked into his eyes, and, with her voice shaking, said, "It is our time." Kinauquak answered by embracing her. Anna threw her head back and laughed before hugging him tight.

Alulak shuffled through the loose sand and embraced the couple. Finally, she stood back, turned to Kinauquak, and said with a voice full of pride, "As your mother would have done, if her spirit had not departed this world, I will take this beast and prepare it for the feast." With a wide, toothless smile, she added jubilantly, "Come, there is to be a joining!"

With the help of the other hunters, Kinauquak hauled the great walrus onto the shore. Like a strutting cock, he walked about the bloated animal, chanting a tune of triumph. He stopped, placed his spear squarely upon it, and pierced it once more before allowing the men to drag it to Alulak's hut.

As Anna turned to follow Alulak, an ominous rumbling emanated from deep within the earth, and the ground began to shudder and tremble. She turned to Kinauquak. The earth's violent pitching threw her to the ground. She scrambled to regain her footing, but the land rose beneath her. Helplessly sprawled on the writhing sand, she screamed, "Kinauquak!"

Kinauquak looked at Anna and battled the quaking ground as he tried to run toward her. A hut of mud and rocks collapsed, nearly burying him.

All about them others fell. Helpless against the powerful convulsing beach, they cried out in fear. Bushes and scrub trees were swallowed by the earth then spewed out as though bitter to the taste.

Anna tried to stand, but the ground continued to heave, and she could only watch as much of the village crumbled. A rack, draped with drying salmon, toppled over, sending fish sprawling across the vibrating sand. A kayak tumbled from its stand, crushing one side.

Anna's heart raced, and, starved for oxygen, she gulped for air. Although the ground had trembled many times before, she had never felt it move with such power. She couldn't fight the undulating motion any longer, so sat with her hands clasped tight about her legs, pulled herself into a small ball, tucked her head close into her knees, and waited, praying the earth would stop its violent pitching.

Kinauquak tried to make his way to Anna, but was thrown to the ground.

The roar from the earth increased. Anna covered her ears and felt she could stand it no longer. She squeezed her eyes closed, trying to shut out the nightmarish scene. It could not be banished.

As quickly as it had started, the rumbling ceased, and the land ended its distorted dance. All was silent.

Her heart still pounding, Anna hesitantly lifted her head and looked about, afraid of what she would find. The village was askew. Rocks, mud, and grass were mounded where homes had stood only minutes before. Other huts were tipped at odd angles. Trees and bushes no longer stood erect but were now tilted; some still swayed.

Whimpering came from those about her. Anna tried to stand, but her legs would not hold her. For a few minutes, she remained huddled on the ground. She wanted to weep, needed to weep, but there was no time for that now. She blinked back her tears and tried to compose herself.

Kinauquak suddenly appeared beside her. He took her hands in his and quickly looked her over. "Are you all right?" he asked, his voice strained and tight.

Anna hadn't even thought of injuries, and she quickly scanned herself. Finding no problems, she nodded mechanically and looked about as Kinauquak pulled her to her feet.

"It is so still," she whispered. "Even the birds have stopped complaining." She noticed Kinauquak's arm. Blood trickled down his wrist and dripped from his hand. "You are hurt!" Anna exclaimed as she took his hand in hers.

Kinauquak glanced at his wound. "It is nothing," he said and casually brushed at the blood.

Anna ignored his indifference and led him to the surf. She knelt, pulling Kinauquak down next to her and cleaned out the deep gash on his arm. She waded a little way into the surf, fished out a piece of seaweed, and wrapped it about his wound. "This will help," she said as she patted it gently.

"Iya! I can't find Iya!" Anna's mother wailed.

Anna scanned the beach. She saw no sign of her sister.

"Help me!" Luba pleaded, her voice on the edge of hysteria.

Anna rushed to her mother and asked, "Where was she before the ground shook?"

Luba looked about frantically and finally answered, "I do not know."

"We will find her," Anna said with a confidence she didn't feel. The people of the village quickly set out to search for the missing girl. As she scanned the village, her eyes fell upon the family's partially destroyed home. *Iya might be inside,* she thought as she plowed through the sand toward the tilted structure. She fought the impulse to rush inside. Instead, she peered through the door, then patted the walls to make certain it was sturdy. Once she had assured herself of its safety, she stepped inside.

As her eyes adjusted to the half-light she was appalled at what she found. The hut was in shambles, nearly unrecognizable. Everything had fallen from the walls and lay scattered about the dirt floor. A table was tipped on its side, and their furs looked as if someone had tossed them about. A seal-oil lamp had landed on the floor, its light extinguished. The morning fire still smoldered beneath the debris.

Anna initially found nothing and turned to leave but then heard soft sobs coming from beneath a pile of skins. She hurried across the room and searched through the hides. Under the heap she found Iya, hiding from her unseen foe. Her eyes shut tight and her face streaked with tears, she shivered convulsively. Anna gently lifted the little girl and held her close.

"Iya, all is well. The earth has stopped moving. You do not need to be afraid," she comforted. She kissed the little girl's cheek, stroked her straight black hair, and carried the clinging child out of the hut and placed her in her mother's grateful arms.

Oovie Dunnak, Anna's stepfather, assembled the family outside the damaged hut. The stocky, powerfully built man quickly took command, barking orders at Anna and her brothers. He instructed the two older boys to rebuild the fish rack and told a younger brother to clean the partially dried fish and rehang them. The oldest son joined his father, and the two began repairs on the damaged hut. Anna worked inside with her mother. Iya was told to stay out of trouble.

Anna carefully set the seal pelts, used for bedding, back in place while her mother removed the debris from the firepit. Luba hummed an ancient chant of good fortune as they worked inside the dark, musty hut. Anna's sweet, clear voice blended with her mother's. They smiled at each other. Singing had always brought them comfort.

The tiny, brown-skinned woman tried to lift the driftwood table, but it was too heavy. "Anna, could you help me?" Luba asked. Anna quickly grabbed the other side of the table, and together they managed to lift it and set it against the back wall.

Anna considered the promised joining, and with a sharp pang of disappointment realized it would not take place. There will be no celebration tonight, she thought as she tried to swallow her grief. Then she chided herself for such selfish thoughts. Now was not the time to think of her own needs. There would be plenty of time for Kinauquak and her. They had a lifetime.

Luba surveyed the room. It looked much as it had before the quake except for the partially crumbled wall. She placed her arm about Anna's shoulders and pulled her close. "That is better." She stopped and faced her oldest child. "You have always been a faithful daughter, bringing me great joy." She reached out and took a strand of Anna's silky brown hair between her fingers then tenderly smoothed it back. She leveled tear-filled eyes on Anna, and her voice quivered as she said, "I will miss you."

Anna lay her hand over her mother's and said quietly, "There will be no joining today."

"No," Luba answered, "but tomorrow, or the next. Your time is soon."

Anna nodded and sighed, "I know I will be Kinauquak's wife, but not today." Wishing to change the subject, she asked, "What more can I do to help?"

Luba thought for a moment. A smile suddenly brightened her face. "There are blueberries ripening on the bluff. Your father enjoys berries very much. Would you take Iya and pick some to celebrate our good fortune?"

Anna's eyes opened wide and she said, "Good fortune? Everything has fallen down around us."

Luba cupped Anna's face between her hands and explained gently, "The ground shook in a way I have never known, yet we live." She stopped, looked toward heaven, and continued almost in a whisper, "God has protected us. Tomorrow will come."

Anna said nothing and glanced at the ground. She had never trusted the God the Russian priest, Father Ermelov, had spoken of. She believed in the ancient gods of her people. Not wishing to speak of it, she said, "There are not many berries ripe yet, but I think there are enough for one meal."

Luba said nothing more about God, instead she reminded Anna, "Do not forget Iya."

Anna was tempted to protest. She would rather go by herself. She loved to spend time on the high bluffs that overlooked the beach. It was the perfect place to be alone. But she smiled and said, "I will not forget. We will bring back many berries." She slipped a leather pouch over her shoulder, picked up two baskets, and went to look for her sister.

It wasn't difficult to find Iya. She sat on a rock, watching her father and brothers work; Anna could hear her chatter even before she rounded the house.

"It was dark inside the hut," Iya was saying. "I heard a great roar and the world tipped from side to side. Is that how it always is when the earth shakes? Do you think it will come again?"

Anna cut into the little girl's prattle. "No, Iya, it has gone. I am going to pick berries. Would you like to come?"

Iya jumped to her feet and cheered, "Yes!" then raced across the sand toward her sister.

Anna took her hand and led her to the trail that led up the steep cliffs above the beach. After helping Iya over the large rocks at the bottom of the winding path, Anna stopped and looked out over the village. A cloud moved across the sun, casting a shadow on the beach, and a vague sense of unease fell over Anna. Unable to explain her feelings, she shrugged them off as foolishness and followed Iya up the cliffs.

Chapter 2

*A*nna and Iya reached the top of the cliffs. The land opened up before them, reaching out to the base of a volcanic peak, which stood like a sentinel wearing a helmet of white. Fields of tough Aleutian grasses and berry bushes decorated with delicate pink and lavender flowers grew across the bluffs.

Anna gazed at the beautiful tapestry of color and texture that crowned her island. The contrast between this place and her beach home never failed to inspire her. For a moment, she soaked in the artistry, trying to remember every detail so she could take it back to the beach with her.

Iya fidgeted and tugged on Anna's hand.

Anna ignored her sister and took a long, deep breath, inhaling the fresh scent of grass and sweet fragrance of blueberries and wildflowers. "This is where I wish I lived," Anna said as she looked over the landscape.

"Me too," Iya agreed, then asked, "Why do we not live here?"

Anna looked at her younger sister's sweet face and answered, "It is beautiful now, but when the wind blows there is no protection. We would have to continually rebuild our homes and climb the cliffs to hunt and gather food. Our wood also comes from the beach. It would be impossible," she said with a sigh of resignation. "To visit will have to be enough. I love it here during the long summer days."

A sudden urge to romp swept over Anna, and she dashed across the open ground. "Catch me if you can," she called playfully over her shoulder.

A big smile spread across Iya's face as she charged after her sister. Anna darted back and forth through the bushes, trying to avoid Iya's grasp. Though Anna was older, Iya was a fleet-footed five-year-old, and she soon clasped her hands about Anna's waist. They both tumbled to the ground, giggling in delight.

Breathlessly, Anna conceded, "You have won." She rolled to her back, looked up at the brilliant blue sky, and ruffled her sister's hair, saying, "You are too fast for me."

Iya grinned impishly and replied, "You are getting too old and . . ." She stopped and the smile on her face was replaced by a look of fear. She raised up on her arms, as if ready to flee, and peered at something beyond Anna.

"What is it?" Anna asked as she turned to look. She drew in a sharp breath and pushed herself to her feet.

On the ridge behind them stood a man, an outsider. He was watching them. Anna wondered where he had come from. She hadn't seen anyone from the outside for a long while and had heard nothing from the people in her village about such a visitor.

The man was very tall with a full beard and wavy blonde hair that blew wildly in the wind. He held his slender frame stiff and straight, his legs slightly parted. A rifle was slung carelessly across his shoulder. Silently he watched them, but he made no threats.

Anna placed herself between Iya and the stranger and slowly backed away. "Say nothing and stay close to me," she whispered. She was frightened but forced herself not to flee. This man was an uninvited visitor and could not be trusted.

Outsiders had traveled through their village many times before and rarely brought anything of value with them. On the contrary, they were often cruel and treated Anna's people with less respect than they would afford animals.

First the Russians came, ruthless in their desire for furs and riches. They enslaved her people, using them to hunt the sea otter and great whales. If any resisted, they were simply killed. Men were forced to leave their households and serve the fur-greedy Russians. Without hunters, families and whole villages perished.

The intruders brought diseases with them, and many Aleuts died. Anna had heard stories of a time when there were many thousands of her people, but now only small bands survived.

Others brought strange ways and new religions. Anna shunned their God. The intruders reminded her of devils; therefore, their God must be evil.

As she studied the man, her mouth went dry and her heart leapt in her chest. The urge to flee overpowered her resolve to hold her ground; she took Iya's hand and bolted through the brush as though pursued by demons. She glanced over her shoulder to see if the man followed. But he had turned and gone the other way. Anna stopped, pulled Iya close to her, and watched as the stranger disappeared behind a small rise.

"He is not interested in us," Anna panted. "Good." She watched for a few minutes to assure herself he would not sneak back and seize them unexpectedly. When he didn't return, Anna dropped to the soft earth. She patted the ground next to her and motioned for Iya to join her.

The bushes had scratched their unprotected calves and ankles. Anna doctored hers with leaves and dirt, wiping away the blood that trickled down her ankles, then did the same for Iya.

She leaned back on her elbows, closed her eyes, and tilted her head back, allowing the breeze and warm sun to calm her anxiety. "We can rest for a while before we pick berries," she said.

Iya glanced nervously in the direction the stranger had gone and asked, "What about the man?"

"He is gone and is no danger to us," Anna assured her sister.

Iya's face was still tense with fear, and she shivered against the cool breeze as she snuggled close to Anna. "Where did he come from?" she asked softly.

"I do not know. He is an outsider. He comes from places I have not seen." She stared at the sky, her expression hard, and continued, "We cannot trust those from the outside. They care only about themselves and bring nothing but pain and suffering to us."

"Father Ermelov is not from here, and he is always kind," Iya said, coming to the defense of the Russian priest who had visited their village many times.

"He is different. He is a priest. I do not believe in his God, but it is true he has always been kind. I think he hates evil and mistrusts the outsiders as we do."

"Where do you think he came from?"

"Father Ermelov? He is from Unalaska. He has a meeting house there."

"No, I mean the stranger," Iya explained crossly.

"I said I do not know. There are many lands far from here, so I cannot say where he comes from." Wishing to change the subject, she said, "It is too beautiful a day to worry about this man. He is gone."

Anna smiled at Iya, then rolled to her side, closed her eyes, and rested her head in the crook of her arm. Iya leaned her body against Anna's back, and the two relaxed in the summer sun a little longer. The cliffs muffled the rhythmic pounding of the sea, and the cry of irritable seabirds seemed far away. Listening to the wind rustling through the sharp, stiff grasses gave Anna a sense of peace. Even the pungent odor of the nearby ocean seemed less potent. Anna's eyelids drooped and she was tempted to stretch out on the soft earth to nap in the afternoon sun, but she yawned and forced herself to her feet. The gentle breeze blew her hair into a soft tangle. She brushed at it with her hands, trying to keep the wisps of hair out of her eyes, but the warm strands eluded her efforts. She finally gave up and allowed it to do as it wanted.

"I wish we could lie here all day, but Mother is expecting berries. Come on, they are waiting to be picked," she said as she handed a basket to Iya. Still feeling drowsy, they strolled across the field to the berry bushes.

Berry season had just begun, and there was not much ripe fruit. The baskets filled slowly, and as Iya looked into hers she complained, "It will take forever to fill this basket. I wish I had made a smaller one."

"If more berries went into your basket instead of your mouth, it would not take so long," Anna replied with a grin. "And if you had made a smaller one, you would need to carry two."

Iya held up her basket, proudly displaying her work and said, "It is beautiful, is it not?"

"Yes, you did well. It is very pretty. When you are grown, you will make fine baskets like our mother's."

Iya grinned broadly, but as she examined her work, a pout replaced her smile. "Do you think it is crooked? Inoki said it was, and he said I would never be a good weaver—that no one would marry someone who made crooked baskets."

Annoyed with her brother, Anna knelt down and looked squarely into Iya's eyes and told her, "You are a good weaver. Your basket is only a little crooked, but you will learn to make them straight. This is your first, and you can be proud of your work. When Inoki teases, you must not listen."

Iya nodded, comforted by Anna's words.

They returned to their work, and gradually the berries mounded up. Anna glanced at Iya just as she was ready to drop another berry into her mouth. "Iya, no more!" she scolded.

Iya quickly rerouted the fruit and dropped it into her basket.

But Anna was tempted by the juicy fruit as well, and a while later, just as she was placing a berry on her tongue, Iya glanced up. "Anna, do not eat any berries! They go into your basket," she said with a smile, imitating her sister.

They laughed and each purposely popped a small tangy berry into her mouth.

After Anna filled her basket, she helped Iya finish hers. She held a berry up to the sunlight and said, "They are beautiful."

Iya nodded, popped another into her mouth, and said, "They taste even better."

"I think we have enough," Anna said. "Our father will be happy to have so many." She smiled as she thought of the praise he would bestow upon them when they returned with their precious bounty. She was certain her mother would be pleased and would reward them each with an extra portion.

Without warning, a low rumble came from beneath their feet, and the ground shook again for a moment. It was a small aftershock, but it reminded Anna they might be needed at home.

Iya gripped Anna's arm in fear. "Is it going to happen again?" she asked through clenched teeth.

"This is normal after the earth moves. The ground will shake but not so bad as before," Anna reassured her.

Iya looked at her with suspicion, but didn't argue.

Her high spirits deflated, Anna said, "Time to go," and turned back toward the bluffs.

When they reached the trail that led to the beach, they sat in the deep grass. Anna loved the view from this spot and often stopped here when she visited the cliffs. "We can rest here before we climb down," she said as she set her basket on the ground beside her.

For a while, they watched the activity on the beach below. People were busy repairing their homes and other damaged possessions. Anna could see that many huts were beyond repair and would have to be rebuilt. Others would welcome those people without shelter into their homes.

"Look, there," Anna said and pointed at Inoki as he dashed across the sand.

One of his favorite games was to tease the waves. He tramped carefully toward the breaking surf as the sea washed up the beach, then raced ahead of the water, just out of reach of the white foam. The object was to remain dry, although he rarely did. Inoki enjoyed the surf and often gave in to the temptation to dive into the frothy breakers.

Abruptly, he stopped and stared down at the sand. He bent and picked something up. He'd found a large shell, and after examining it carefully, called to his mother. Anna couldn't hear him, but as he raised his prize above his head, it was clear he was proud of his find. Luba looked up from her work and, with a smile, waved at her son.

As Anna watched the scene below, she felt compelled to return. "We'd better get back," she said as she stood and brushed the sand from her skirt.

Iya picked up her basket and started down the path. Anna scanned the beach once more. Something was wrong. The cove looked odd. Trying to clear her vision, she blinked her eyes.

The water in the small bay rushed out to sea! Fish flopped on the wet sand, their large ugly mouths gasping for air. Long submerged rocks and boats covered with barnacles and other crustaceans, were suddenly exposed to the air.

Anna watched with horror. "The sea withdraws from the land!" she cried.

Iya stopped and edged back toward Anna, her eyes trained on the beach. She fumbled for her sister's hand and clutched it tight.

Anna watched Inoki, who only moments earlier had frolicked in the surf, flee toward the village, terror etched across his boyish features. In his haste, he fell and peered over his shoulder at the apparition. Anna willed Inoki back to his feet. "Run!" she screamed. There was nothing she could do.

The villagers wailed in fright. The old ones cried an alarm, urging everyone to run for the cliffs. They knew what was coming. Horror was written upon their faces.

The bay had emptied. It was as though a large plug had been pulled, allowing the sea to drain away. Anna couldn't believe what her eyes told her. She squeezed Iya's hand hard and pulled her close. *I must help!* her mind screamed, but she could only stand and watch as the scene unfolded before her.

A thunderous sound came from the ocean, and Anna looked to see a monstrous swell join the receding water. With terrifying speed and power, it approached the beach, growing larger as it advanced. The merciless mountain of water viciously bore down on the small village.

Panicked natives screamed and scrambled for safety, but the wave was too swift. Mothers picked up crying infants and dragged older children behind, while the old hobbled to promised safety. Alulak didn't run but stood facing the coming water.

"Kinauquak! Where is Kinauquak?" Anna cried as she searched the beach. Then she saw him. He had turned back to his grandmother and now tugged on her arm. But she wouldn't take her eyes from sea, and finally he fled, leaving the old woman to face the ocean's wrath.

But they could not escape its fury. As it hit the beach, the wall of water one hundred feet high scooped up Inoki, tossed him effortlessly into the air, then pulled the helpless young boy into the seething flood. Next the umiaks and kayaks on the beach vanished in the tide. Relentlessly, the churning mass of sea water, sand, and vegetation moved up the beach. It slammed into the village, and Alulak disappeared. She never moved, but met her death honorably.

Anna watched in horror as the water engulfed her home then swooped down upon her family. A scream wrenched itself from her throat as she watched her mother perish beneath the rogue wave. She couldn't bear to watch but was unable to look away.

It moved inland and unbelievably grew in size and intensity as it advanced. It was not selective but destroyed everything in its path. Villagers scrambling for the rocks, trying to escape the giant wall of water, disappeared one by one into the foaming, muddy flood. Kinauquak was swept away as he reached to pull himself up onto the cliffs.

The wave rammed into the sheer rock face and threatened to reach beyond the cliffs, to snatch Anna and Iya from their perch. Unable to move, they watched in fear as the mountain of water smashed against the cliffs with a thunderous roar, hungering for more victims. It took no more.

Its energy spent, the water receded and slowly returned to the sea. It left quietly as though it had never visited, but the spectators on the bluff were not deceived. They knew it had come, devouring their home, their people, their life.

Anna's legs crumpled beneath her, and she slumped to the ground. Iya mutely climbed into her arms. Once safely tucked within her sister's embrace, she whimpered quietly. Anna clung to Iya, comforting and seeking comfort. Her eyes were unseeing as she rocked the little girl and chanted a mournful tune.

There were no tears as dusk settled over the island. The two orphans silently held each other tight, then finally slept. But even in sleep, they could not escape the nightmare of the giant wave. Distorted images and pictures of death filled their dreams. There was no one else to bring comfort; they had only each other.

Chapter 3

*A*s Jarvis rolled to his side, his head exploded with pain and his stomach churned. He moaned and clutched his skull between his hands. "Knew I should've stayed away from that hooch," he complained as he peered through the dim light of the hut. Frank was still sprawled beneath a pelt; his snoring rattled through the room. Jarvis grimaced at the sight of his rotund partner. "I could have done better," he muttered as he slowly stood up, guarding against the crushing pain in his head.

As his eyes adjusted to the dim light, he surveyed the room. It was strewn with besotted natives. Ignoring the fact that he'd been in the same state only moments before, Jarvis found the sight disgusting and went outdoors for fresh air.

The sun filtered through the last layers of morning fog, and Jarvis squinted as he glanced about the village. The mud and grass huts looked old and tattered to him. He was sick of Alaska and its people. There had never been any love lost between Jarvis and the natives or, for that matter, between Jarvis and anyone.

He longed for a hot bath and a good game of cards. *I'll be glad to be rid of this place,* he thought as he scanned the harbor, looking for the ship that would take him back to civilization. The bay was empty. The ship was gone. He looked beyond the cove but still found no sign of the clipper's sails. He spewed a barrage of unsavory words and threw his hat to the ground.

"Frank!" he bellowed and stomped back inside the hut. He stood over his partner's inert form and nudged him hard with the toe of his boot. "Frank, wake up," he ordered.

Frank groaned and blinked his eyes, trying to focus on Jarvis's face. He rubbed his scraggly beard and said, "Com'n, can't a man get some sleep? What do ya want?"

"The ship. It's gone!" Jarvis yelled.

Frank pulled a pelt over his face and mumbled, "You're dreamin'. They wouldn't leave without us. Take another look."

"I've already looked, and I'm not dreaming!"

Frank forced himself into a sitting position and brushed his long hair out of his eyes. "You serious?"

Jarvis growled, "Take a look for yourself."

"Nah, I believe ya, but why would they leave us?"

"How should I know?" Jarvis stormed.

"What're we gonna do now? We're stuck."

Jarvis thought a moment. "We ain't stuck. I don't intend to spend one more day with these stinkin' savages. We'll hoof it out of here and meet old Captain James and his cutter in Kenai."

"Are you crazy? We'll never make it. I think we oughta stay put until another ship comes along. And I don't remember you finding the company of that little maiden so repulsive last night," Frank said with a smirk.

"I was drunk," Jarvis said as he sat on the floor and rested his arms on his knees. "Seems I'm always getting left," he said almost to himself.

"What'd you say?"

"Nothin' just thinkin' about my old man." He glanced in the direction of the bay. "It could be months before another ship comes. You can stay if you want, but, I'm movin' on."

Frank forced himself to his feet. "All right, all right, I know once you've got your mind set, there's no changin' it. I might as well go. Don't feel much like being the only white man around." He scratched his beard and asked, "You got a plan?"

Jarvis took out his tobacco and papers and rolled a cigarette as he thought. "If we move hard and steady, we oughta make Cook Inlet before winter. We can find someone to take us across to Kenai. It'll be worth it to see the look on Mr. James's face when he sees us." He lit the cigarette and took a long drag. "I can't wait to get my hands around his scrawny chicken neck."

○ ○ ○ ○ ○ ○ ○ ○ ○ ○ ○

Anna's skin itched from the moist grass and coarse sand, and she rubbed at her face as she began to rouse from a restless sleep. Brushing aside her damp hair, she rolled onto her back and struggled to open her eyes. Unwilling to reenter the world of reality, she snuggled back into the hidden place of slumber.

In her half-conscious state, she felt wrapped in a heavy blanket of grief and despair—a blanket bound so tight, it smothered her. Distorted images tumbled through her mind: Kinauquak, Inoki, the sea . . . She fought to free herself from the nightmare. Suddenly, she remembered. The wave! Squeezing her eyes tight, she tried to banish the picture from her mind, pushing her fists against her eyelids, willing it to leave. But the image remained. She clenched her jaw, fighting her tears. *It must have been a dream,* she reasoned. But she looked about and knew it was real.

As she raised herself up on one elbow, her breathing became shallow, and her heart beat rapidly, pounding hard against her chest. Carefully she slid away from Iya's sleeping form and slowly stood on shaking legs. She shuffled toward the cliff edge, and a shudder swept through her body as she looked down on the beach. The village was gone! She felt a wave of nausea, and she swayed as unconsciousness threatened to envelop her. She knelt, closed her eyes, and took slow, deep breaths until the ominous blackness subsided.

Then she forced herself to look once more and moaned. No laughing children or chatting women, no hunters sharpening their spears or fishermen repairing nets; there was nothing. The steady rhythmic surf marched endlessly ashore. But the cry of the seabirds sounded empty and lonely, for no one else heard their clamoring chorus.

Dark angry clouds hovered over the top of the steep cliffs that rose sharply from the beach, shrouding the orphaned Aleut girl who stood atop the bluffs. Anna shivered. The cold, damp air, driven by a brisk wind, pierced her clothing. She wrapped her arms about herself and slumped back to the soft earth. She'd never felt so alone. *Everything is gone,* she thought bleakly.

Her chest felt tight and her throat ached as she looked down at her sleeping sister. Iya would never again know the love of their mother and father or have the companionship of the family. *We have only each other,* she thought. Tears burned her eyes, but she blinked them back.

Her empty stomach rumbled. She looked out over the lush fields and knew the warm summer season would be followed by one of darkness and frigid cold when the grasses would die and the withered berries would fall to the ground. *How will we live?* she wondered. *With only two of us, we will perish. The sea holds all we need, but I am not a hunter. Women have always been forbidden to hunt. I know only how to flesh hides, make baskets, and prepare food. The ways of the fishermen and hunters are a mystery to me.*

Defeat washed over her, tempting her to surrender to its call. But as she sat there, an innate desire to survive, forbidding her to give up, stirred deep within her. She grabbed hold of the instinctive summons, as one would a lifeline, and decided they would live.

I will learn what I do not know, she thought with resolve.

Iya began to stir. She blinked her eyes and rubbed them as she sat up. Still drowsy, she yawned and looked about. Her face looked tense and confused, and she trembled slightly as she looked up at Anna. Her eyes filled with anxiety, she whispered, "Was there really a wave?"

Anna couldn't bring herself to speak of it. She only nodded.

Iya fidgeted and her eyes flickered in the direction of the cliff wall. A mixture of fear and grief filled her innocent face. Silently, she climbed into Anna's lap.

Anna wrapped her arms about Iya and stroked her hair as she rocked the little girl. *This is too much for a child,* she thought bitterly. She sang a comforting lullaby and for several minutes held Iya as she would an infant.

Knowing she could not avoid the inevitable, she took a deep breath and said in a rush, "We must return to the beach. . . ."

"No!" Iya interrupted, pushing herself free of Anna's embrace, her usual light brown complexion now a sickly pallor.

Anna understood Iya's panic, for she fought the same fear. Gently, she said, "Iya, we have no choice. We cannot stay here. The sea gives us life."

"No, sea takes life," Iya murmured.

Not knowing how to answer, Anna ignored the comment. She stood up, took Iya firmly by the hand, and walked toward the trail with an assurance she didn't feel.

Her voice shaking, Iya pleaded, "Why can't we stay here? What if the wave returns?"

Anna shook her head, "It will not come again. See how calm the sea is. The gods are no longer angry, and we have broken no taboos."

"Taboos?" Iya asked, clearly frightened even at the mention of the possibility.

"A taboo is never broken willingly, unless someone wishes to anger the gods. I do not know anyone who is so foolish. I have not angered them, and you are too young to know of such things," Anna said, hoping her feigned assurance masked her fear. "We cannot live upon the bluffs," she continued. "We must return."

The sea had always given life. Anna's people had always respected the ocean with its formidable power and constant provision even though many had perished in the great expanse of water. Anna had never feared it until now. She knew she must learn to trust again, to be bonded in a partnership, with the sea as provider.

Anna stopped and stared down the steep track leading to the beach, trying to summon the courage to start down. She scanned the ocean. It looked calm. Gripping Iya's hand, she took a deep breath and began the climb down the winding path. At the end of the trail, she reached out and lifted Iya over several large boulders at the foot of the cliffs. She was surprised to find they hadn't changed but looked just as they always had.

Before stepping onto the beach, Anna stopped, looked up and down the shore, then studied the uniform waves, ready to retreat if given reason. Still leading Iya, she forced herself to move cautiously across the sand.

Uncertain what she was looking for, and afraid of what she might discover, Anna carefully scanned the beach. Would she find anything of her people? Something that would connect her with them?

Occasionally she scanned the ocean, and with each approaching swell, willed her legs not to flee. She could not erase the picture of the great wave from her mind—the ocean slipping away, only to return as a giant mountain of water that crushed out the lives of those she loved. The scene played over and over in her mind. She pushed it away, but each time it returned to viciously taunt her.

Preoccupied, Anna stumbled over something in the sand and found herself lying face down.

Iya crouched next to her and gently touched Anna's shoulder. "Are you all right?" she asked anxiously.

Anna nodded, pushing herself up and brushing at the sand on her hands and face. "What did I trip over?" she asked, as she glanced back at what looked like a stick protruding from the damp soil. She grasped the end of it and with a quick tug, pulled it free.

"A spear!" Iya yelled, excited by the find.

Anna turned the lance over and ran her hand lovingly across the shaft. The shaman's charms hung from the top of the pole. *Even the shaman had no power against the sea,* she thought sullenly. *He had claimed the gods would protect him. What God is so powerful that even the shaman can be destroyed?*

She held the spear close to her, clutching it tight, as she remembered the stranger. *He has brought the white man's God to my home! This God destroyed my people.*

Now she had someone to blame for her pain. She raised her fist into the air and shouted, "What kind of God kills women and children? My mother loved you, and you betrayed her. I hate you!" It felt good to vent her anger.

Frightened by Anna's outburst, Iya cowered by a nearby log and whimpered.

Her crying brought Anna up short. She knelt next to Iya, and wrapped the little girl in her arms. "I am sorry. I did not wish to frighten you. I was angry, that is all. It will be all right."

She tried to pull Iya close to her, but the little girl wiggled free, and asked, "Will God hurt us too?"

Sorry now for her outburst, Anna was unsure how to answer. She hesitated, then asked, "Did he destroy us when the great wave came?"

Iya shook her head.

"I do not believe he wants to hurt us. If so, he would have," Anna said, although she had no confidence he wouldn't slay them at any moment. After all, her mother had believed in this God, and he had not protected her. Luba had always told Anna he was a God who loved them.

So this is a God of love? Where is my mother now? Anna fumed, as she stood defiantly with the spear resting in her hands, her hatred for this God blossoming with each passing moment.

Iya watched Anna closely but said no more.

The anger and hatred that clutched at Anna's heart would remain for some time. Through clenched teeth, she said, "We cannot trust the outsiders and must never trust their God. He is cruel and vengeful." She stooped before the small girl, clasped her shoulders tightly, and, looking straight into her eyes, said, "Iya, always remember, we can believe only in each other. We need no one else."

Iya frowned as she followed Anna down the beach.

When they reached the spot where their hut had stood only hours earlier, they stopped. An indentation in the sand was all that remained. Nothing more. Everything they owned was gone, swept into the sea.

A small tree, partially uprooted, clung precariously to life. A portion of a net was entangled in its branches. Careful not to tear the netting, Anna meticulously unraveled it, knowing it would be useful in the days ahead. Flinging it over her shoulder, she said with confidence, "With this we will catch many fish."

They moved on, scouring the beach for other usable objects, but the few bits and pieces they found were too damaged to use. The cruel wave had taken everything. Anna was thankful she had remembered to take her leather pouch when she had gone to pick berries. At least she had her flints and a good sharp knife.

"There is a cave in the cliff wall that we can use for shelter. It is small but will protect us from the rain and wind," she said as she headed toward it.

"What is that?" Iya asked, pointing down the beach at a large mound in the sand.

Anna stopped and stared hard at the suspicious bulge. "I do not know. You stay here. I will look," Anna said, her mouth dry with fear as she approached the mysterious pile of sand. As she drew near, she saw some kind of animal. She cautiously dropped to her knees near the mound and scooped away the sand concealing the creature. Her efforts revealed a recently killed walrus.

Kinauquak's walrus! Anna sucked in her breath and pushed herself away from the animal. Scrambling to her feet, she lost her footing and fell back into the damp sand. There she sat, unmoving and mute as forbidden tears spilled down her cheeks. She buried her face in her hands and sobbed.

"Everyone is gone—Kinauquak, our mother and father; everyone—gone," she wailed. Sorrow and pain engulfed her. She felt as though her life spirit had been crushed. Her weeping gradually became an empty, monotone song of grief, a chant of death. She cradled her abdomen and her unborn child—all she had left of Kinauquak.

As Anna crouched there on the sand, she heard a sound behind her. She whirled about, wiping at her wet cheeks. The stranger she had seen on the bluffs walked toward her with long, even strides, crossing the sand with ease and rapidly closing the gap between them.

Anna looked for Iya and found her huddled close to a rock. She was trapped. Where could she go? She assessed the man and knew she could never outrun him. She decided to stand her ground. Standing up, she planted her feet firmly in the sand and gripped the shaman's spear in front of her.

The man approached with confidence. He was tall and lean and wore the soft clothing Anna had seen on other outsiders. His full beard gave him the appearance of a fierce and dangerous man, but as he came closer Anna could detect no cruelty in his piercing blue eyes. His leather coat hung loosely across his broad shoulders and he had no hat to cover his light windblown hair.

Anna grasped the spear more firmly, hoping to draw strength from the shaman's powerful possession.

The outsider stopped only a few yards from her. He stroked his beard and stared at her for a moment, then slowly lowered his arms to his sides and said in a low, soft voice, "You can put down your spear. I'm not going to hurt you."

Anna understood what the man had said but didn't trust him and remained silent. She stared at him and did her best to look intimidating. With a sense of satisfaction, she saw a momentary look of confusion and frustration cross the stranger's face.

"I know you can understand me. All you natives speak some English."

Anna still did not respond.

The outsider shrugged his shoulders. "I only wanted to help. I saw what happened to your people. I was on that far bluff," he said, pointing to a cliff on the other side of the inlet. "It was a tsunami. The wave, I mean. It was a tsunami," he repeated.

Still no response.

"I've heard about them but never thought I'd see one. I didn't know they could be so bad. I'm real sorry about your village."

He sounded sincere. Anna felt confused. She knew she couldn't trust this man, but he wasn't what she had expected.

All outsiders are treacherous, she reminded herself.

In a sharp, venomous voice, she finally replied in English, "We not need help." Crossing to Iya, she took the little girl's hand and led her down the beach away from the stranger, heading for the cave. She wanted to look back to see if he was following but forced herself to keep her eyes on the ground in front of her.

"When he leaves, we will return for the walrus," Anna told Iya in a hushed tone. "It will feed us for many days."

The cave was small and the two girls huddled inside, glad for the protective walls. They sat and waited for the outsider to leave their beach.

Iya shivered and asked, "Can we make a fire?"

Tipping her head toward the place they had encountered the stranger, Anna answered, "When he is gone we will gather grass and driftwood."

Iya crawled to the entrance of the cave and peeked toward the beach. "I do not see him," she said and darted out of the shelter.

Anna glanced quickly down the shoreline and, finding it empty, followed Iya.

The two gathered leaves, grasses, and small bits of wood for their fire from the cliff walls and shore. Then they used the fronts of their skirts to carry the larger pieces of driftwood back to their shelter.

Kneeling in the center of the cave, Anna arranged the dried leaves into a small pile, took the flints from her pouch, and struck them against one another until a spark ignited the leaves. When a small puff of smoke rose from the pile, she leaned over, cupped her hands around the smoking foliage, and gently blew into it until a small flame flickered to life. She added more dry grass and bits of wood. Iya then handed her some of the larger chunks of driftwood, which she placed in the flames. Soon a warm fire burned, and the two snuggled together, quietly staring into the flickering light.

Iya fidgeted and finally broke the silence. "If we cannot hunt, how will we live?" she asked quietly.

Anna had been thinking on this and answered confidently, "We have the walrus, and there are mussels in the bay and berries on the bluffs. There are many eggs to collect, and we will learn to hunt and fish."

"But to hunt is taboo," Iya said in a hushed voice.

Anna licked her lips nervously before answering. "I have thought on that. I do not think it is taboo if there is no man to hunt. I do not believe the gods will punish us for doing what we must."

Iya said nothing more, but her eyes darted about, probing the dark corners of the cave.

We will survive, Anna thought with determination as she crept around the corner of the cave and peered down the beach. The cold wind whipped across her face. "We have warmed ourselves long enough. It is time to butcher the walrus." She stepped outside and strode across the wet sand to the half-buried animal.

Kneeling next to the beast, she scooped away more of the soil, trying to expose most of the creature. Iya did her best to help, tossing handfuls of sand aside. Occasionally Anna looked about to reassure herself that they were alone.

Once the animal was free, Anna reached into her pouch and retrieved her prized steel knife. She had worked very hard, fleshing many hides, to trade for the blade.

She plunged the knife into the walrus, sliced along the middle of its abdomen, and exposed the inner cavity. Carefully she removed the precious organ meats and handed them to Iya. The little girl cradled them in her skirt and took them to their camp.

When she returned, Anna was skinning the hide back from the thick layer of fat that covered the animal and carefully slicing this away from the flesh.

Weary, she sat back on her heels and wiped the sweat from her brow, unaware of the bloody imprint she left on her face. She rested a few minutes, allowing the breeze to cool her before resuming her work. Next, she cut the meat away from the bone and into manageable chunks. Later, she would slice these into thin slabs for drying.

She lay the skin out on the ground, set some of the meat on it, and said, "Iya, you take one side. Together, we can carry the meat to our shelter." With the makeshift litter swinging between them, they slowly made their way back to the cave. It took several trips to move and store most of the walrus near their new home.

Tired from their labor, they sat for a few minutes. Anna sliced off a piece of blubber and handed it to Iya, then took one for herself. They smiled at each other while they contentedly chewed. It felt good to have accomplished so much, but Anna knew there was still a considerable amount to do.

She forced herself back to her feet and said, "We will need wood for a drying rack and some hollow rocks to store the rendered fat." They headed for the beach once more.

It wasn't difficult to find the wood; the beach was littered with it. The stones were another matter. It took them some time to find large rocks with carved-out centers that could hold the rendered walrus blubber they would use for candles and to preserve meats and berries.

Anna's stomach grumbled. Exhausted, she picked up one last stone and said, "Enough for today. It is time to eat and rest." She was almost too weary to make another trip back to the cave, but the promise of food and a warm fire hurried her steps.

She sliced another piece of blubber for each of them. Iya took the offered fat and greedily bit into it. Anna speared a chunk of meat with a willow shoot and placed it over the fire. Drops of fat fell from it, sizzling as they splattered on the hot rocks. The aroma of cooking meat filled the air, and Anna's mouth watered in anticipation. Iya's hungry eyes told of her impatience. Unable to wait, Anna removed the meat from the flames long before it had finished cooking. Oblivious to its half-raw state, the girls sat back and ate until they curbed the gnawing pain in their bellies. Nothing went to waste. They even licked their fingers clean.

Her hunger satisfied, Anna felt more optimistic and shared her plans with Iya. "Tomorrow we will go up to the meadows and gather more grass for baskets and bedding. If we weave our baskets very tight, we can keep our berries and meat in them during the winter. But we will have to work very hard. If we find many berries, we can preserve some in oil and dry the rest." She stopped to gather her thoughts. "We will learn to hunt. There are many fish in the shallow waters and with the net we can catch all we need. And there is always seagrass," Anna said, winking at Iya, for she knew seagrass wasn't one of Iya's favorite foods.

Iya wrinkled up her nose. A shadow fell across her face, and she asked, "What about the stranger?"

"He is gone. Do not think of him anymore," Anna said as she lay down and pulled Iya close to her. She rested her head on her hands. "It is time to sleep. Tomorrow there is much work to do."

They huddled close in the soft sand, trying to push aside their fears and feelings of isolation. Anna felt empty and was thankful for her weariness. Exhausted, they soon fell asleep, their sorrow temporarily replaced by their need for rest.

Chapter 4

*S*hivering against the cold, damp air, Erik Eng-strom hunkered deeper into his coat. He leaned close to the fire, stretched out his hands to catch more of the heat, and rubbed them together. The dampness and pervasive cold penetrated his clothing.

He pulled an old cast-iron skillet from the hot coals and, with the expertise born of practice, turned a piece of sizzling, pink salmon with an old worn spatula. He closed his eyes, breathed in the aroma of the frying fish, and said to himself, "There's nothing better than fried salmon." His mouth watered as he settled back and waited for his meal to cook.

He was unable to stifle a cold shudder as he held his coffee mug between chilled hands. Raising the cup to his face, he let the steam bathe his cheeks with warmth. He sipped the hot liquid and relished the feel of it as it slipped down his throat, warming its way to his stomach.

Why did I come to this land? he asked himself. *I should have stayed put. Minnesota's cold, but at least it's dry.*

Erik had set up camp above the cliffs in a small hollow, but the relentless wind found its way across the land and into every niche. It seemed there was no protection from nature's onslaught on this island.

He pulled his coat tight under his chin and looked out over the treeless landscape. His eyes settled on the lone peak that stood guard over the island. As the wind whipped clouds about the pinnacle, it looked oppressive. He scanned the fields that spread out from the volcano. The greenery and brightly colored flowers he had admired only yesterday now looked dull and dreary beneath the gray skies.

If the wind doesn't let up soon, I'll have to move down to the beach caves, he thought. *I've never been any place as dismal as this. Wind and rain, rain and wind, the sun comes out so seldom.*

His mind wandered back to his home. *It's hard to believe I left Minnesota nearly six years ago.* Memories of his parents and their unexpected deaths from small-pox assaulted him. It was still so fresh. After the Civil War, he'd returned home only to watch them die. He had done everything he knew to save them and had prayed for God's intervention. When it didn't come, his faith wavered. He'd asked why many times but had received no simple answer. After much soul searching and prayer, he finally accepted God's plan as one of greater wisdom . . . a wisdom not always comprehensible to him.

With no immediate family to hold him, Erik had decided to strike out on his own. He'd lived in the small community of Clearbrook since the age of five and was known as a man of his word, someone who could be trusted. Friends and neighbors tried to convince him to stay, but he felt compelled to move on.

Erik had since traveled through twenty different territories and states. Always something of a loner, he found that the drifter's life suited him. Having the freedom to pick up and move on when he desired appealed to his nature. He was accountable to no one but himself and God and felt content to live the life of a traveler.

Erik's eyes filled with tears as he thought of his parents. He looked up at the sky and said, "I always feel you're with me." Over time, the pain had lessened, but Erik knew he would never be completely free of it. Memories of their devotion flooded his mind. *Someday I'll have a family of my own,* he thought. *But first I've got more of the world to see.*

He tested the fish to see if it was done. The center was still a little raw so he set it back over the flames and gulped down the remainder of his coffee.

He studied the landscape and remembered how impressed he'd been with the north country he'd seen so far. The stark reality of life on the Aleutian Islands had taken him by surprise. The harsh environment, though beautiful in its own way, was something he'd never encountered. During the summer months, the islands were often blanketed by fog and pelted by rain, leaving everything in an endless state of sogginess. The sun rarely made an appearance, and the wind seemed endlessly present, intensifying the effects of the persistent cold and wet.

In winter, he'd heard, sunlight made even briefer appearances. Darkness lay over the land much of the time. The winds battered the coast, snow replaced the rain, and, along the Bering Sea, the ocean was gripped in a frigid world of ice.

Erik ached for the forest. There was little vegetation on many of the islands where layers of volcanic flows remained from past eruptions. Many of the mountains still spewed ash and steam into the air, reminding those who lived nearby of their tenuous security. Trees could find little rich soil to set down roots, and the persistent wind discouraged those that tried.

Erik grinned as he remembered his first encounter with Alaskan natives. They had greeted him in an open and friendly way—too friendly, in fact. As the tribal leader had embraced him, Erik had struggled not to pull away as the odor of his garments assaulted him. But Erik had been impressed with the people. Their attitude in the midst of their brutal surroundings had inspired him. They were surprisingly happy and hopeful people, accepting what life gave them without complaint. They were generous and kind. Dissent was unheard of. It was imperative that they work together as they faced the constant onslaught of nature.

Since that time, he had encountered others. Most had treated him pleasantly, but some didn't welcome outsiders, and Erik sensed their lack of trust. "Can't say I blame them," he said aloud. "We haven't treated them with much decency."

He refilled his cup as he thought back to the tales of seal and otter hunting that had drawn him to the islands. He had heard that any hard-working man could get rich. However, the waters of the Bering Sea had been overhunted by the Russians and Americans for years, resulting in drastic declines in the numbers of animals. Now a lone man could only make a meager living. This made little difference to Erik; riches had never been his motivation. The excitement of exploration, the challenge of conquering the most difficult conditions, and his desire to know Alaska had brought him to the unknown country.

He had not been disappointed. Alaska was a land of mystery and unimaginable beauty. It was more than he'd expected—a place of contrasts, dangerous but enticing. Even the Aleutian Islands held an appeal, a haunting beauty. The mists clinging to the rocks, when swirled about by wind and surf, brought a soft, alluring quality to the indifferent terrain. Alaska had become a part of Erik, though he was still unaware of its hold.

Others had come to this magnificent land, like Erik, searching for something, something deeper than they could express. Many returned to their homes, while some remained, unable to free themselves from Alaska's spell.

Erik flipped the frying salmon and said aloud, "One thing about this country, the fishing is good. I've never seen better." The wind carried his words across the empty bluffs. Enjoying the solitude, he rested back on his elbows and stared into the fire.

Thoughts of the tsunami returned, though he tried to push them aside. "Never seen anything like it," he said in a whisper. "Those poor devils on the beach didn't have a chance."

His hunger and the smell of the cooking fish pried the image of the wave from his mind. He flipped the salmon one more time, opened a can of beans with his knife, and poured them into the pan, careful not to mix the two. He stirred the beans until they were warm. Sitting cross-legged, he draped an extra blanket over his lap and cradled the hot skillet. He thanked the Lord for the food, then took a large chunk of the sizzling pink meat, blew on it to cool it, and filled his mouth. Chewing slowly, he savored the juicy sweet flavor of the fish, then, urged on by his hunger, wolfed down the remainder of his meal. After refilling his cup with strong black coffee, he sat back and gazed at the fire.

He thought over the last couple of days. His encounter with the native girls was not what he'd expected. *I knew some of them didn't trust outsiders, but I can't believe she threatened to kill me. What does she think she's going to do here on the island alone? Those two will never make it.* For reasons he couldn't understand, he felt responsible for them but tried to convince himself otherwise. *I have no obligation toward those two.* But his prayer on the bluffs only days before nagged at him. He'd felt there was something God had called him to do. *It can't have anything to do with this,* he told himself.

In irritation, he tossed the remainder of his coffee over the hot coals. He was ready to move on. Winter loomed on the horizon and it was time to put these islands behind him. *I've got no time to worry about two native girls,* he reasoned. But no matter how hard he tried to convince himself, he knew he couldn't leave them alone. The tsunami had forced him to take on a role he didn't want to play. Hadn't he promised God he would obey God's will?

He remembered the horror he'd felt as he had watched the great wave sweep down on the beach like an eagle descending upon its unsuspecting prey. Even as he thought of it, his heart beat rapidly. At the time he had wondered about the two he had encountered earlier and had been unable to put them from his mind. Finally he searched the island, hoping to find them alive and discovered them sleeping near the edge of a bluff. He had wanted to let them know of his presence but decided it would be better to wait. After a night's rest, he had set out to speak to them.

Erik grinned as he recalled how the young native woman stood with her spear ready, her face a mask of fierce defiance. *I wonder if she'd have stabbed me with that thing.* His grin softened as he remembered her unexpected beauty. Her flawless light brown face set off her almond-shaped, golden eyes that glinted with fear and fire. She was small but not stocky like many natives. Her long, lean arms were well muscled; her hair was dark brown with a soft wave, unlike the blue-black hair of most natives.

She must be of mixed blood, he thought. *I doubt she'd let me help if I tried.* Aloud, he said, "God, if you have a plan, tell me what it is and how to go about it." He stood and brushed the sand from his wool pants. "Well, I'm going to have to do something. I don't intend to spend my life on this island, and it's clear I can't leave those two here."

With resolve, he strode to the small spring nearby and rinsed out his pan and spoon. The salty wind filled his senses as he stood looking out over the sea. The sun was low in the sky but would disappear beneath the horizon for only a short time.

Darned midnight sun! I swear I'll never get used to it. He closed his eyes, thinking of his home in Minnesota. "It would be nice to live where it gets dark when it's supposed to and light when it's supposed to." He considered returning but quickly dismissed the thought. The pull of Alaska had become stronger than that of his home.

He stooped and picked a handful of blueberries and popped them into his mouth. He enjoyed the berries' sweetness. He gathered several more as he made his way back to the fire, careful to eat only one at a time to make them last.

He lay back and looked up at the sky. Through a break in the clouds, he could make out a faint sprinkling of stars in the semidark canopy. He was overwhelmed by the immensity of the universe and found it hard to comprehend a God who cared about the lives of simple people. Surely to him they must seem small and insignificant. But he recalled the verse that spoke of a God who cared so much for his people that he even knew the number of hairs on each head.

Feeling safe and content, he let out a long, slow sigh and let his mind wander. Before long, his thoughts returned to the young native woman and child, *What am I going to do with those two? I wonder if another tribe would take them in.* "That's it!" he exclaimed. "I'll find them another village." He thought for a moment and wondered how he would convince them to listen to him.

Knowing only one place to go for direction, he turned to God. "Father, you said if we trust you more than ourselves, you will make our paths straight. I know you have a plan, and I'm asking you for guidance. Tell me what to do." He hesitated a moment, then added, "Thank you for being my God. Amen."

Feeling some measure of peace, he climbed under his blankets, rested his head on his hands, and soon fell asleep.

The next morning Erik awakened early. He sat up and looked about, ran his hands through his hair, and rubbed his face, trying to dislodge his drowsiness. The long days of the late summer brightness made it almost impossible to gauge the time, but he guessed it to be about 6:00. Trying to work out his morning stiffness, he hobbled the few feet to his woodpile, grabbed some kindling, and placed it on last night's hot coals. Soon a small blaze flickered to life, and he fed it with larger pieces of driftwood.

The morning air was cool, and he warmed himself near the flames before filling his coffeepot with fresh water. He placed the pot on the hot stones and blew into his cupped hands to warm them. While the coffee cooked, he reached into his knapsack for some pieces of hardtack and jerky. Regarding the hard biscuit with disdain, but resigned to his morning fare, he bit into it, then tore off a chunk of dried meat for flavor. *Boy, what I'd give for some eggs and bacon right now,* he thought, as he chewed. *And some sourdough bread would be heaven.* He considered making some for later in the day, but tossed the idea aside, knowing he wouldn't have the time. He looked up toward the sky and said, "Mom, some of your flapjacks covered with maple syrup would sure hit the spot." He could almost smell the hot maple syrup. Memories of syrup gatherings from previous falls filled his mind. He smiled as pictures of family and friends working together to tap the precious sap danced through his mind. *Maybe a trip back would be a good idea.* His thoughts were interrupted by the sound of perking coffee. He poured himself a cup of the rich, dark liquid and tried to decide what he would say to the native girls.

Maybe if I take some food as a peace offering, they'll listen to me. Natives like fish as much as anything, and there's plenty of salmon to be caught. He stroked his beard. *It's worth a try.* He took his fishing pole and headed toward the beach.

Erik cast his line into the bay and dug his feet into the sand, bracing himself for a strike. The wind whipped his hair across his face, and he tossed his head back, trying to keep his eyes clear. The heavy breeze picked up the mist and sprayed it into the air. Erik could taste the salt as he moistened his lips.

It didn't take long before he felt a sharp tug on the end of the line. He pulled up hard on the pole to set the hook, then began to reel with a steady pressure, patiently playing the fish, tiring it as he pulled it closer to the beach. After fighting with the salmon for several minutes, he was confident he had won. Suddenly, with an unexpected burst of energy, it charged back toward the sea, taking much of Erik's line with it. "So, that's how it's going to be," said Erik between clenched teeth. He pulled on the pole. The rod bent as he reeled, slowly dragging the salmon back into the shallows.

Sweat beaded up on Erik's forehead from the effort and his arms ached. Finally, he caught a glimpse of the silver body of the fish as it darted through the water. With a final quick tug on his pole, he tossed it onto the sand where it lay flopping, its mouth yawning in a gruesome death. Quickly

Erik grabbed hold of a piece of driftwood and clubbed the dying salmon over the head, ending its life.

He slit the fish down the middle and washed the entrails into the surf, then scraped away the slimy scales. Determined to make peace with the two Aleut girls, he slipped his pole under his arm, slid his hand inside the salmon's mouth, and, with the lifeless body hanging from his callused hand, headed down the beach. This time he felt confident that they would accept him and listen to what he had to say.

Chapter 5

*A*nna clamped the tips of her fingers about the rough shell of the mussel and pulled, but the teardrop-shaped creature refused to loosen its grip and clung stubbornly to the rock. She tugged harder but still had no success. Gingerly, she slid her jagged fingernails under the edge of the blue-black shell. It came free in her hand unexpectedly, and Anna lost her balance, falling backward into the shallow, icy water. She sat there for a moment, ignoring the cold and wet, and studied the small animal in her hand, then dropped it into her half-empty basket. She frowned and wondered if all this was worth the effort. The answer was yes. These small creatures would help keep her and Iya from starving during the long winter.

Anna had gathered mussels many times, but always with the help of others. The tedious, often painful work required diligence, but the reward was delicious, succulent meat.

Anna staggered to her feet and stood with her arms extended from her sides. Water dripped from her clothing. Iya watched and tried to keep from laughing as Anna squeezed the excess moisture from her tunic and said, "It is not funny."

With little success, Iya stifled a laugh.

Anna looked at her and shook her head as a smile emerged on her face as well. She glanced down at herself and realized just how funny she must look and finally gave in to laughter. Soon both stood ankle deep in the bay and giggled until they were out of breath. It felt good.

Anna examined her cracked and bloodied hands. They stung. "I need some oil for these," she said as she held them up for Iya to see. She shook her basket. "These creatures are straight from hell I think," she added with disgust. "Father Ermelov used to speak of hell. These must be the demons he spoke of."

Iya's eyes grew large with fright as she peered cautiously into her basket.

"I am teasing," Anna quickly reassured her. "But if we did not need the food, I would not spend a minute more gathering the little beasts."

Iya cringed.

Realizing she was frightening the child, Anna added cheerfully, "They will taste good. I think tonight we will have some."

Iya shivered against the cold. She held her damaged hands up for Anna's inspection, but didn't complain. The laughter gone now, her shoulders sagged, and her inconceivable loss showed on her young face.

As Anna looked at the sad figure of her sister, she longed to hold her and remove all her pain. Sorrow welled up within her, but she swallowed her own anguish and asked gently, "Iya, are you all right?"

Iya's face was a mask of gloom as she slowly moved her head from side to side.

Anna pushed her way through the water and pulled the small child close to her. "You know, we are not alone. Our family is here. They will always be with us."

Iya looked up at Anna, her chin quivering. She wiped away the remnant of a tear and, with a faint smile, said, "My basket fills too slowly. I do not think these mussels wish to be my supper."

Anna chuckled softly and ruffled her sister's hair. Lightheartedly, she said, "Any creature that gives its life is worthy of our respect. Even if it is stubborn, we should be grateful for its sacrifice." She looked inside her basket and added, "We will steam these when we return to the cave. They will slide easily down our throats and fill our empty bellies. We can gather more, and those we can preserve for the months to come."

With renewed interest, Anna returned to her tedious work, trying to ignore the pain in her hands and fingers. She considered using her knife to pry the creatures free but knew it was not worth the risk of damaging or losing the precious tool. Her thoughts returned to Iya, and she wished there were something that she could do to help the little girl. *It is so hard,* she thought, feeling alone and helpless. Iya joined her, and the two worked in companionable silence.

The wind stopped and the air became still—a mixed blessing during the summer months. It felt warmer without the wind, but less breeze meant more pests, especially mosquitos. Anna swatted at the persistent insects, but there were too many, and they zealously persisted in their assault.

Iya was also preoccupied by the insects' onslaught, and her basket remained nearly empty while she swatted and jumped under the bugs' merciless attack.

Soon both girls were covered with welts. "If the wind does not return soon, we will have to cover ourselves with mud," Anna said as she studied a creature that had landed on her arm. She watched until it was still then swiftly swung her hand down and crushed it. With the tip of her finger, she flicked it away.

Iya scratched at a welt on her face. Abruptly, she moved close to Anna and gripped her arm. Her voice shook with fear as she pointed down the beach and whispered, "Look!"

Anna looked in the direction Iya pointed, and drew in a sharp breath.

With long strides, the outsider came swiftly toward them. He looked determined and moved with an air of confidence as he closed the distance. Something dangled from his hand, but he was still too far away for Anna to make out what. Bracing for whatever might come, she drew herself up tall and lifted her chin slightly. Her restless hands remained at her sides.

As the man drew closer, Anna could see he was carrying a large salmon in one hand and something resembling a stick in the other. *A spear!* she thought in alarm. She was frightened but determined not to show it; she forced herself to relax. It became clear that he carried not a spear but something more like a slender stick.

The man's face looked stern and unyielding. Anna swallowed hard and tried to add height to her five-foot frame.

"Anna, what can we do?" Iya asked in a squeaky voice.

"I do not think he will hurt us. We will see what he wants, then send him away," Anna answered, trying to sound confident. "Now, be still."

The two native girls stood bravely and waited.

The stranger stopped only fifteen feet from them. He held out the salmon and nodded as though they would understand his meaning.

Anna maintained her stance. "What you want?" she asked in English with cold hostility.

"I brought this for you and the child," Erik answered in a strong and steady voice.

"We not need help," Anna said stubbornly as she pulled Iya closer to her. "We care for selves." She raised her chin a little higher.

"Look, I'm just trying to help. What do you think I'm going to do?"

"You from outside," Anna answered, as though that was a reasonable explanation.

Erik tried to reason with her. "I'm not going to hurt you. I thought I could help."

"How?" Anna challenged him.

"Well, this will make several meals," he explained, extending the fish to her.

Unintentionally, Anna's voice softened as she replied, "We catch own fish."

Erik looked about, raised his hands in frustration, and countered, "I don't see any. How do you plan to catch them?"

Anna didn't reply at first, then said feebly, "We have net." Unable to maintain her hard stare, her eyes slid away from his, but only for a moment.

"I have a fishing pole," Erik said, and raised it in the air. "It makes catching fish easy."

Anna just stared at him and didn't reply.

They said nothing for a minute, then Erik shook his head and mumbled, "I'll leave this here for you." He laid the salmon on the sand in front of him. "It's yours if you want it." He stared at Anna for a minute, then turned abruptly and marched down the beach the way he had come.

Confused, Anna stood and silently watched him go.

Once he was out of hearing range, Iya asked innocently, "Why can't we eat the fish?"

"We do not need his help," Anna answered stubbornly. "We can care for ourselves."

"Please, could we eat the fish? I am hungry," Iya pleaded.

Anna thought for a minute and admitted it would be senseless to leave it for the gulls. "We will take it when he is gone," she finally answered.

Iya smiled.

As Erik disappeared into the mist, Iya reached for the salmon. It was so large that she had to hoist it onto her shoulder to carry it. Staggering a little, she headed up the beach toward their shelter. A moment later, she set the fish down and stopped to catch her breath. Looking back at Anna, she said enthusiastically, "This is a very big fish!"

Anna only nodded, her thoughts preoccupied by the stranger. Why was he here, and what did he want from them?

Iya groaned as she tried to lift the salmon again, recapturing Anna's attention. "Iya, you carry the baskets," Anna said as she relieved the girl of her burden. Lifting the fish into the air to inspect it, she proclaimed with a smile, "This will quiet the rumbling in our bellies."

Anna cooked a portion of the fish briefly over the open fire then sliced off a piece for Iya and one for herself. She sat with her legs crossed and devoured the mild-tasting pink flesh while juice dripped from her hands.

"Mmm, good," Iya said after finishing her portion. She patted her stomach and smiled. This time, her dark brown eyes smiled too.

"We will dry the rest with the walrus meat," Anna said, and held up the remainder of the salmon. "This will feed us for many days."

As she sliced the fish into thin strips, she contemplated what she knew of the stranger. *He has not harmed us. Still, he is an outsider and cannot be trusted. He must want something,* she thought suspiciously. *The elders always taught us that those from the outside could not understand our ways and would bring only trouble.*

She set the slices of fish aside and looked up to find Iya drawing a picture in the sand with a stick. She watched the little girl for a minute before returning to her work. Her mind was still filled with thoughts of the blond visitor. *Why does he want to help us? And why does he share his food with strangers? In this he is like us.*

She remembered his countenance. He seemed to be a man of courage and strength. A man of his size could have easily overpowered them, but he hadn't. Thoughts tumbled through her mind, and she was unable to stop her evaluation.

She hung the sliced fish up to dry and stoked the fading fire. Iya had fallen asleep, so Anna moved about quietly, careful not to waken her.

She sat for a long time and considered what she should do. *I must talk to him,* she decided. *When the sun is low in the sky and Iya sleeps, I will find this stranger.* As she considered this, she struggled against a suffocating fear. Still, she knew she must go to him.

The woodpile had dwindled, and Anna quietly left the shelter in search of more. While she gathered driftwood, she occasionally stopped and studied the bluffs, wondering where she would find the outsider.

After a while, a sleepy-looking Iya joined her. At first she only followed along while Anna worked. She watched the gulls and puffins as they glided above the waves, squawking and squalling as they competed for food. After a while, she helped Anna.

With enough wood to last awhile, Anna rested outside the small cave. As she looked out across the wet sand, she said, "We must build a larger house. The weather will grow cold soon and this small place will not protect us from the winter storms. We can make mud from the heavy dirt on the bluffs and bind it with rocks and grass. We will have a very strong *barabara* of our own. It will take many days to build. First we can gather the stones we will need." She headed down the beach.

Once more they used the fronts of their skirts as pouches, filling them with stones. They had decided to build their new home near the cliffs, so they carried their heavy loads back to the cliff wall, shuffling through the sand, their backs arched to offset the weight of the rocks. Tiring, Anna set her load down, wiped her brow, and, bracing the small of her back in her hands, said, "I am thirsty." She sat and leaned against the cliff wall, motioning for Iya to join her. Removing a water pouch from her belt, she handed it to her younger sister. Gratefully, Iya gulped down the water. After Iya drank her fill, Anna took her share.

"We will rest awhile. Tomorrow we can collect more stones, but no more today. Instead we can gather grass for our baskets. It has to dry several days before we can use it, so we must cut it now while the weather is good."

After a short break Anna pushed herself to her feet and pulled Iya up after her. They walked down the beach to the trail that led to the cliffs and ascended the familiar path with Anna in the lead. She scanned the open fields but found no sign of the stranger.

Taking a knife from her bag, she grasped a handful of the stiff island grass and sliced it off close to the earth. Iya took the green shoots and laid them in a pile. Soon there were two large mounds of fresh grass. Anna took four long strips of hide and tied two of them tightly around one bundle then did the same with the other. Taking the largest of the piles, she raised it to her shoulder and waited while Iya hefted the other.

"This is all today," Anna said. "We can come back tomorrow for more." She sighed heavily and added, "There is much to do before the dark days come." She looked around hoping to see some sign of the stranger. Finding none, she started back.

Iya fell into step beside her and asked, "What will we do when the darkness comes? What will we eat?

"We will have dried meat and will preserve the berries we pick in the fat from the walrus. The mussels will also stay fresh in the oil. Fish and sea grass can be dried and stored. We will not go hungry, Iya. I promise," Anna assured her sister and wished she could dispel her own doubts. It was all so overwhelming. She preferred not to think about it.

After returning to the beach, they laid out some of the grass in the sun to dry. The rest they spread inside their shelter for bedding. Anna plopped down on the soft grass and took a deep breath. "Mmm, it smells so good. Iya, smell it!"

Iya happily obeyed and lay down beside Anna. She sniffed deeply of the fresh cut grass, closed her eyes, and said, "It is like being on the bluff."

Anna nodded and forced herself to her feet. She stoked up their fire and cut off a chunk of walrus blubber for Iya. Anna took one for herself and the two sat silently enjoying the life-giving food and their soft beds. After finishing, Anna carefully doled out a handful of berries for each.

Iya quickly popped the fruit into her mouth and said, "My stomach is still rumbling. Can I have more?"

"No, that is all. We must eat only what we need. No more. Go to sleep and you will not feel the pain in your belly."

She helped Iya snuggle down into her bed of fresh grass and stroked her hair until the child's eyes closed and her rhythmic breathing attested to her slumber.

Then Anna grasped the shaman's spear and quietly left the cave. She crept down the beach, mulling over what she would say to the stranger when she found him—not certain even why she sought him out.

She knew she must locate him quickly and return to the cave before Iya awakened. She walked up the steep path away from the beach as quickly as safety would allow and, once atop the cliffs, scanned the fields of tall swaying grasses. To Anna's disappointment, patches of fog had settled over the island. In frustration she peered into the haze, but could find no sign of the stranger. Quietly she made her way across the knolls, stopping occasionally to look for anything unusual and listen for any sound that would give away his location. Only the sound of the rushing wind and the continuous pounding of the distant surf greeted her.

Anna searched the entire bluff. Nearly ready to give up, she sat on a large rock to rest. The sun was low in the sky and dusk had settled over the land, although it would never become completely dark. The semidarkness made it more difficult to see. Anna worried that Iya would awaken while she was gone but continued her search, telling herself that she would find him soon.

A slight scent of smoke hung in the air, and Anna stopped to determine which direction it came from. *It must be the stranger,* she thought. She walked toward the smell and soon saw a small plume of smoke rising from a hollow before her.

Cautiously, every sense alert, Anna crept toward the smoke. Her heart raced and her breath became rapid. She stopped to calm herself before entering the stranger's camp. She was small and surefooted, capable of moving silently through the brush, and felt confident of surprising him. What concerned her was what she would do once she got there. She crept to the edge of the embankment. She'd found him. For a moment she quietly studied the tall, blond man as he calmly leaned over, picked up a piece of wood, and added it to his fire. Then he sat back against a rock and sipped some sort of hot liquid from a cup. He seemed completely unaware of her presence.

Anna's mouth watered. The smell of frying fish still lingered in the air. She reprimanded herself for listening to her stomach instead of keeping her mind on her objective, and, taking a deep breath, she walked straight into the man's camp.

With resolve, she stepped into the light of his fire. She stood directly in front of the outsider and planted the tip of the spear in the ground with her right hand while she placed her left hand firmly on her hip. Tipping her chin up defiantly, Anna demanded in English, "What you want from us?"

The look of shock on the man's face pleased her, and she fought to keep her smile hidden.

The man's amazement was quickly replaced by a roguish smile, which unsettled Anna's feeling of confidence. He said nothing for a minute but sipped his drink. When he did speak, it was slow and deliberate. "Well, you are a surprise. Please, have a seat," he said and gestured for her to sit opposite him.

Anna didn't move.

The man ignored her silence and continued, "To answer your question, I don't want anything." He hesitated before continuing. "I didn't plan on you and the girl. It seems we've been thrown together. You two can't survive here on your own, and I can't stay. Winter will be setting in, and I've got to move on." He lowered his gaze and studied Anna closely. "I'll take you and the little one with me."

Anna still said nothing.

Erik continued, "I thought another village might take you in."

Anna considered what he had said and, with her voice sharp and hard, replied, "This our home. We stay."

"Be reasonable. You have no home. There's nobody left. The tsunami took care of that." He stopped for a moment and said with a hint of compassion, "I'm sorry about your family." Quickly he resumed his businesslike tone and continued, "Look, facts are facts. You two are alone. There's no one left to help you."

"We not need help," Anna answered stubbornly.

A muscle twitched in Erik's jaw, and he clenched his fists. He stopped for a moment to regain his composure and said firmly, "I know you think you can take care of yourselves, but have you thought of the girl? What if something happens to you?"

Anna sucked in her breath. The possibility had occurred to her, but she had always pushed it from her mind, unwilling to consider the unthinkable. She tried to hide her confusion and said nothing.

"Well, I asked you a question," the man persisted.

Anna squirmed under his scrutiny. She didn't have an answer. "I not know," she said, almost in a whisper. Unwilling to be mastered by this man, she set her jaw and announced, "Nothing happen me. I not let. Gods protect."

"Gods! Where were your gods when the wave swept away your family?"

Anna winced against the cruel words.

Compassion flickered in the man's eyes as he said more kindly, "You can't be sure of anything. You could fall into the sea or slip while going down the trail. You can't know for certain you'll always be here for that little girl."

Grudgingly, Anna had to agree. She glared at him and finally asked, "What plan?"

Erik leaned back and once more motioned for Anna to sit across the fire from him.

Reluctantly, she sank to the ground and waited for him to speak.

"Well, I thought I could take you with me and find another village for you two. All the Indians I've met have been fairly hospitable, and it seems to me that you and the girl would be happier with others of your own kind."

"How go to other village? We not have umiak or *badarka*."

Erik grinned, "On the other side of the island I've got an umiak. I pulled it up into a cave in the cliffs, so it was protected from the flood."

Anna thought for a moment. She placed her arms across her chest and carefully studied the face of the stranger. Could she trust him? *He speaks the truth. If something happens to me, Iya will be alone. I cannot put her in such danger.* She finally concluded, *I have no choice but to rely on this man.*

Abruptly she said, "My name Anna. What I call you?"

Erik grinned broadly and reached across the fire to shake Anna's hand. "My name is Erik Engstrom. It's a pleasure to meet you."

Anna felt uncomfortable with the gesture and pulled her hand free.

Erik chuckled. "It's just a handshake. It means . . ." he hesitated, looking for the right word, and finally said, "It means we're partners."

"When we leave?" Anna asked.

"In a day or two. The rain will come again soon, and we need to be gone before winter sets in."

"Not enough time. I dry walrus and fish. Only few berries. We need more."

"There's plenty of fresh game. We can take everything we've got with us. I've got lots of supplies, and there will be plants and berries along the way. Plus I'll do lots of fishing."

Anna understood most of what he said and nodded her head in agreement. "I go now," she said, afraid she had been gone too long already. "We talk later." She turned and was gone without another word.

After having set for only a short time, the sun was already beginning to rise when Anna made it back to the cave. She fed the fire and quietly settled into her bed. She enjoyed the sweet fragrance of the summer grass. Iya still slept peacefully, unaware that her life was about to take another incredible turn.

Anna lay on her bed of grass and thought about her conversation with Erik. *What a strange name. Erik. He is not like any outsider I have known. I do not understand why he wishes to help us. Am I doing the right thing? My mother would know what to do.* Her eyes filled with tears as she thought of her family. Kinauquak's memory was so powerful that he almost seemed present. The smell of him filled Anna's nostrils. "You were so brave and strong, you would have cared for us," she whispered to his presence. His spirit suddenly departed, and emptiness invaded the small room. Tears slipped down her cheeks. She didn't bother to wipe them away.

Anna rested her hand on her abdomen. "I will always have a part of you, Kinauquak," she said into the gloom before closing her eyes.

Chapter 6

$\mathcal{A}$ nna awoke to thoughts of the strange man named Erik and his unusual proposition. She felt trapped.

"I do not wish to leave," she moaned, "but there is no choice." She sighed and rolled out of bed. Overwhelmed by a mixture of sorrow, fury, and fear, her face took on the look of an old, embittered woman. "It is your fault. I hate you," she whispered through clenched teeth as she looked skyward.

Iya began to stir and whimpered in her sleep. Anna looked at the innocent child and asked herself, *How can I tell her she must leave her home?*

A knot had settled in the pit of Anna's stomach. She searched for another option but could find none. Trying to sound cheerful, she said, "Time to wake up, sleepy one. There is much to be done."

Iya sat up slowly, blinked her eyes, and rubbed the sleep from them. "It is still early," she whined, then yawned and stretched her arms above her head.

"Do not be so lazy!" Anna snapped, allowing herself to vent her frustration on Iya. Immediately sorry for her ill temper, she patted Iya on the head and said more kindly, "I am sorry. I did not mean that." She handed Iya a piece of blubber and a cup of fresh water and added, "Today we will pick more berries. It will be fun." Iya smiled and shoved a bite of walrus in her mouth.

While Iya ate, Anna mentally calculated what they would need for the journey and what had to be done in the next two days to prepare. *There is no time to make more baskets,* she thought. *What can I use to hold our food?* Her eyes came to rest upon the walrus hide. She lifted it in her hands and turned it from side to side. *This would make several watertight pouches.*

Iya had finished her meager breakfast. She looked at Anna expectantly and asked, "Can we pick berries now?"

Anna took a deep breath, turned to the little girl, and placed her hands squarely on her shoulders. Looking into the child's eyes, she said gently, "First I have news. Good news." She hesitated before continuing. "Iya, I have decided we must leave this place."

Iya started to protest, but Anna shushed her and continued, "Please let me explain. Last night while you slept, I met with the stranger."

Iya's eyes grew wide with astonishment.

"He said he wants to help us. He has a boat and can take us to another village. I think we can trust him." With conviction, she added, "We must trust him."

Iya frowned, looking unconvinced, and said in a tiny voice, "I do not want to go."

Anna continued, "I have thought on it very much, and it is a good thing, Iya. What if something happens to me? You will be alone. How will you survive?"

Iya didn't answer but looked at the ground, as if in thought.

"I cannot risk leaving you alone."

"Nothing will happen to you," Iya argued. "I do not want to leave." As tears welled up in her eyes, she pleaded "Please, can we stay?"

Anna swallowed hard and answered firmly, "No. We must go."

"But he is an outsider. We cannot trust him. You said we could not trust anyone from the outside."

Anna glanced about the room as she searched for an answer. "I know, I did say that. But that was before I met him. It is true we cannot completely rely on anyone from the outside. We must always be careful and alert. But this man is our only hope. We have no other choice."

Iya squared her shoulders, much like her older sister did when she struggled with fear, then, with her chin quivering, she choked back her tears and climbed into Anna's lap. She huddled there for several minutes, but said no more.

After a while, Anna gently loosened Iya's hold and said, "No time for tears now. There is much to do. We leave in two days."

"Two days!" Iya exclaimed, her eyes wide with panic.

"We cannot wait longer. Winter will come, and we must find a home before the days of darkness."

Anna stood, reached down, and gently wiped Iya's tear-stained face, then said brightly, "First, I will make pouches from the walrus hide. I will show you how. Then you can help."

She set to work with determination while Iya watched. It didn't take long before she had divided the hide into squares. With this done, Anna took her blade and pierced several holes along the edges of each. Iya threaded them with long, sturdy strands of braided grass so each pouch could be drawn closed at the top.

They filled several bags with their meager food stores. Each was drawn closed and tied. Iya placed the pouches in a pile in the back corner of the cave.

Anna sat back on her heels, wiped the perspiration from her brow, and said with satisfaction, "Good. That is done. Now we will gather more berries."

She picked up their baskets, handed one to Iya, and set off for the bluffs. Iya had to run to keep up with Anna's determined stride. Now that the decision had been made to go, she wished to complete her tasks as quickly as possible and move on, to put the painful departure behind her.

They hadn't gone far when Iya asked, "Anna, what was the stranger like?" She scrambled over some large rocks at the bottom of the trail and nearly fell. Anna had to catch her and fought the impulse to reprimand the little girl for her carelessness.

She sat on one of the boulders and thought for a moment. "Well, he is like us, but he is not. When he brought the fish, he acted like one of us. When he wishes to help, he is like our people. That is all. Nothing else is the same. His talk is strange, like other outsiders, and he drinks the dark, foul-smelling liquid." She stopped and contemplated the man himself. "His voice is quiet, but strong, and his eyes hold no evil, but I think he hides what he thinks. He told me he wants to help, but I think he does not. I am not sure what is within him. He will be hard to know."

"What is his name?"

Anna thought for a moment, "He calls himself Erik, I think. I have not heard this name before, but he says it with pride."

After climbing the cliff trail, they sat for a moment to catch their breath and watched the sea. The sun peeked through the clouds and warmed their faces while the wind caught their hair and blew it about wildly.

They gazed out over the beach, their faces lined with sorrow. Anna draped her arm about Iya's shoulder. Memories of happier times played through her mind, and tears stung her eyes. She tried to capture each sound and every smell, to feel her surroundings and store the sensations and pictures in her mind—to never forget.

"Anna," Iya broke the silence, "where is Momma?"

Taken off guard by the question, Anna didn't answer right away. "She is in heaven," she finally responded. "You remember Father Ermelov used to tell us about heaven. It is a good place. Momma and the others are happy there. They no longer know pain or sorrow."

She didn't tell Iya how she really felt—that she didn't know where their family was, that she didn't believe in the heaven Father Ermelov had spoken of or in a God of love. How could a God of love kill her people? If he was such a God, he would have cared for the villagers. Instead, he destroyed them.

Father Ermelov had been deceived, as had the shaman. The holy man of her people had trusted in the many gods of their ancestors, yet where had his great gods been when the wave crashed upon their beach?

Anna didn't know what she believed. Was there anything she could trust in? Confused and angry, her doubts so disturbed and frightened her that she was unable to think on them longer. She pushed them from her mind and stood up saying, "There are many berries to be picked." She tucked her basket under her arm and headed for the nearby bushes. They picked till their baskets were full. This time they didn't eat any of the precious fruit. It was too important to keep all they could for their trip.

After they had finished, Iya tried to convince Anna to allow her the pleasure. "Please, can I eat just one?"

Unable to refuse, Anna smiled and nodded permission.

But before Iya could eat one, Erik's voice greeted them from across the field. "Hello," he called, as he approached with his relaxed stride.

Iya stood rigid, clearly afraid of the tall man. She grabbed Anna's hand and clasped it so tight that Anna was forced to loosen her sister's grip. She bent down and quietly said, "It is safe."

"Looks like you two are busy." Erik said as he approached, smiling.

"I told you, there is much to do," Anna answered stiffly.

"What is your name?" Erik asked as he knelt in front of Iya.

Iya stared at him, her face frozen with fear, and edged around behind Anna.

Erik looked at Anna and asked with a chuckle, "Do I have two heads or something?"

In his language, she replied, "You stranger. She not understand talk."

"I didn't mean to scare her. I hope we become friends in the next few weeks." He moved away from Iya. "I saw to the boat. It's seaworthy and ready to go. I thought I'd see if there was anything I could do to help you."

"We need water," Anna answered.

"I've got a container of fresh water stored on the boat already. I figured we could catch rain water to refill it, and I'm sure there will be ample streams inland to replenish our supply."

"This hold water," Anna said as she lifted her basket. "Skins hold berries and meat."

Erik nodded in answer to Anna's statement, but his gaze was fixed on her basket. "Can I have a look at that?" he asked.

Anna handed him the grass container. He examined it carefully, turning it one way then the other, admiring the fine, tight weave and the intricate designs. He gave a low whistle, and asked, "Did you say these hold water?"

"Yes."

"I've never seen anything like it. Did you make this one?"

Anna nodded.

"It's very unusual and beautiful," Erik said as he handed it back to her.

Anna could feel the blood rush to her face at the compliment, and she quickly changed the subject. "We need fish. You catch."

"Don't mind a little fishing," Erik answered. He tipped his hat and grinned at Iya before he headed back in the direction of his camp and disappeared behind a rise. He had come and gone so quickly that it almost seemed he had never really been there.

"My stomach is empty," Anna said as she set her basket on the ground and picked a handful of berries.

Iya grinned and gratefully followed suit.

With their hands full of berries, they sat on the soft grass. "I hope there will be berries in our new home," Iya said as she dropped one of the sweet fruits into her mouth.

Anna smiled but didn't answer. She ate the fruit slowly, one berry at a time, savoring the juicy, sweet flavor.

Unable to restrain herself, Iya shoved a handful of the sweet orbs into her mouth. With her cheeks bulging, she mumbled, "When will we leave?"

"If the sea remains quiet, Erik said we will leave soon," Anna answered as she scanned the ocean. "He said his boat is sturdy and will take us safely across the big water to a new home."

"Where will that be? What will the people be like? Do you think they are like us?"

Anna smiled, "You ask too many questions. I do not know where we will go, but I have heard there are many villages like ours where the people are kind. We will have a new home soon, I think. Father Ermelov traveled and taught many people of the islands. Do you remember how angry he would get when he talked of slaves?"

Iya nodded.

"I do not think we will have to be slaves."

Iya grinned a blueberry smile and cocked her head to one side. "I will be happy to have a family again." Her grin faded and her eyes misted over. "I miss ours," she said almost in a whisper. She looked up at Anna, and as tears cascaded down her cheeks, asked, "We will never see them again, will we?"

"No, Iya, we will not see them again," Anna answered honestly as she pulled the little girl close to her. Silence fell over them as they contemplated their frightening, unknown future and the unbelievable turns their lives had taken.

Anna's voice broke into the silence. "We need to take these berries and put them in a pouch." She stood and brushed the loose grass and dirt from her skirt, then helped Iya to her feet.

Slowly they made their way down the trail and back to the beach. Neither of them spoke as they crossed the empty stretch of sand.

Erik had been true to his word. Two large salmon were waiting for them when they entered their small cave. Erik had gutted and cleaned the fish, so Anna lay them across a cutting stone and sliced each of them into thin strips. She lay the meat across the rack to dry. There wasn't enough time for them to dry thoroughly, but the meat would still last for several days.

Anna stood back, examined the salmon, and said with satisfaction, "We will not go hungry." But when she added the fresh berries to the other supplies, the small pile of goods looked inadequate. She studied the provisions and was uncertain there would be enough to feed them in the days ahead. *Erik seems confident there will be plenty,* she reminded herself and pushed away her doubts.

The next day passed quickly as Anna and Iya made final preparations. Erik came late in the afternoon and seemed eager to begin their trip.

"We'll spend the night at the beach where I've kept the boat," he explained, making it clear he was in charge and would be giving the orders. "That way we can leave first thing in the morning. I've already moved all my gear down. We'll have to haul these provisions over tonight."

Anna and Iya glanced at each other. Without argument, they followed his instructions, although it ruffled Anna's feelings a little to have no say in the plans. After all, it was her life too.

"It's going to take a couple of trips, so we'd better get started," Erik said as he reached for the pouches. He filled his pack, swung it over his shoulder, and waited for the girls.

Anna and Iya gathered as many of the small bags as they could carry in their skirts and followed Erik as he led the way down the beach and up the steep path. He took long strides, and as the three crossed the plateau, Anna and Iya found it hard to follow. The weight of their loads threw them off balance, and their short legs couldn't begin to keep up with Erik's long, graceful gait. They stumbled down a winding path that led to another beach and a small inlet.

Iya stayed close to Anna, keeping as much distance between herself and Erik as possible. It took three trips to pack all their provisions to the new beach. On the final crossing, Erik forged ahead, anxious to get the supplies to the boat.

Anna and Iya held back. They stopped at the edge of the bluff that overlooked their beach. Neither of them uttered a sound; their good-byes were silent. Abruptly Anna turned away from the sea, took Iya's hand in hers, and followed the stranger who had promised them hope.

Erik built a large open fire on the sand. He fried some fresh salmon and warmed a can of beans and some coffee. After dishing up a plate for each of the girls, he said, "Hope you don't mind my cooking. It's probably not what you're used to."

Anna and Iya were hungry after the day's work and gratefully accepted the meal. The fish quickly disappeared, but when Anna tried the beans, the starchy food felt unfamiliar in her mouth and insulted her taste buds. She didn't want to offend Erik, so she said nothing and forced herself to eat the strange food, hoping it was something she would grow accustomed to. Iya, on the other hand, pushed the beans to the side of her plate and refused to eat them.

"Iya, try it. It is rude to refuse food when offered."

"I'm not sure what you're saying, but I can tell by the little one's face that she's not too fond of those beans," Erik cut in. "Don't worry about it. I'm not all that crazy about them myself." He poured himself a cup of coffee and offered some to Anna.

She glanced at the dark liquid and caught a whiff of the foreign drink and quickly refused. "I like water," she said.

Erik downed his coffee, fidgeted with his rifle, and stirred the embers of the fire. He seemed restless. After a while, he stood up and looked out over the sea. Without a word, he sauntered down the beach and out of sight.

Anna sat silently staring into the fire while Iya was slowly lulled to sleep by its warmth. She peered in the direction Erik had gone. *He is worried,* she thought. *I can see it in his face. I do not think he wishes to take us with him.* Once more she questioned her wisdom in trusting their lives to a stranger. After all, he was an outsider, and she knew nothing about him. But she also knew there was no other choice.

Her eyes roamed over the swells beyond the breakers and fear welled up in her as she thought of being on the open sea. It was dangerous and always unpredictable. She had heard the men speak of the treacherous and changeable currents that moved through the islands. It would take an excellent seaman to maneuver through the channels and hidden obstacles that lay in wait for them. *Is he a good boatman?* she wondered then thought, *I am probably sending us to our deaths.* Realizing the futility of worrying, she forced that idea from her mind. They had no alternative but to challenge the sea.

The wind whipped across the beach and raised goose bumps on Anna's arms. She pulled her cloak tighter about her shoulders and placed an additional sealskin over Iya to keep out the chill. She lay down next to her and cuddled close, more for reassurance than warmth.

Anna was unable to quiet her thoughts, and sleep eluded her. Her mind was filled with questions without answers.

Erik had still not returned when sleep mercifully came.

○○○○○○○○○○○

Erik stroked his beard as he moved across the rocky beach. He searched the horizon. *What do I think I'm doing? How am I going to take care of those two? I convinced them to trust me, and I'm not even sure I can help. I might even make things worse.*

He stopped and glanced up at the gray sky and spoke as if to a trusted friend. "Father, it wasn't so bad when I only had to think about myself. But it's not just me anymore. What if I make a mistake? They're depending on me."

He stopped and waited, listening for the quiet voice of his Lord. When it didn't come, he continued. "Where are you? I'm scared. I need your help." He hesitated. "Who do I think I am? I could dump us all into the sea. I don't even know where to take them." The wind howled in his ears and blew his blond hair wildly about his face.

The cold air helped to clear his thoughts. He listened, again, looking for the peace only God could give. Abruptly the big Norwegian fell to his knees. There on the deserted beach, he raised his eyes toward heaven. He was solely dependent upon a God he knew he could rely on, a God who could see the bigger picture and who understood far more than Erik could even begin to comprehend, a God Erik trusted.

"You said you would never leave us nor forsake us. I believe that. I'm asking you to help me now. Help me navigate the umiak and to read the currents correctly. Be my guide. Please help me to follow and not lead."

He stopped and searched the sky, his eyes following the rapidly moving clouds that were pushed along by the wind. "Lord, I'm not worthy of your trust. I don't even want to take care of those two Indians. I mean, I'm a loner. You know that. I don't know anything about them. They aren't even my kind."

Erik knew he was fighting God. He quieted himself before the Lord and said, "Not my will, but yours." He waited a moment more before continuing. "I believe you put us together for a reason, and I'm asking you now to give me a heart for them. Help me to love them. I know you do." The peace he had searched for finally came. Erik added confidently, "Father, I put our lives in your hands. This journey belongs to you."

He moved slowly down the beach and back to the fire, back to the two who had been placed in his care. The burden he had felt a short while before was gone.

He smiled as he thought, *The little one's pretty cute. I bet when she smiles, the world lights up. I wonder how old her sister is. Actually, she's kind of pretty in an Indian sort of way. Maybe in time, she won't be so hostile.* He grinned. *A bath wouldn't hurt either one of them.*

The steady, even breathing of both girls reassured him they were sleeping. He stood over them for a moment, no longer resentful about what he had been asked to do. Instead he was moved by compassion as he looked upon the two native girls and felt a sense of excitement stir as he considered what adventures might lie ahead.

He moved toward his bed. It was late. He realized he had better get some sleep or he'd be worthless the next day. He climbed beneath his blankets, and sleep quickly overtook him.

Chapter 7

*A*s Anna opened her eyes, she was greeted by the crackle and sweet aroma of burning wood. Erik crouched next to the fire, poking at it with a stick. Sparks rose into the air as he pitched a large chunk of wood into the flames.

He tossed a handful of dark granules into an old burnt coffeepot, then went to the spring to fill it with fresh water. When he returned, he set the pot on the hot stones along the edge of the fire. Reaching into his duffel bag, he retrieved a large tin, removed the lid, and dumped a white powdery substance into a pan. He then added lard and water and stirred the mixture thoroughly.

Anna thought this was curious behavior for a man. Fascinated, she watched in silence.

Erik divided the dough into balls, then patted them flat. He glanced up from his work at Anna.

"Morning. I thought I'd make us a real breakfast before we headed out. It'll be a while before we have hot food again." He placed two of the flattened pieces of dough in a pan of hot fat. "Do you like fried bread?"

Anna tried to look uninterested and shrugged her shoulders. "I never taste."

"Well, there's a first time for everything, I guess. I figured we could have some dried venison with it."

Anna felt wide awake now. Today was the day. She shook Iya by the shoulder and said, "Time to wake up."

Iya rolled over. Still sleepy, she squinted at Anna. As her eyes fell upon Erik she sat up and scooted close to her sister.

Anna gave her a quick hug and tried to sound cheerful as she said, "Today we begin our journey."

The July air felt cool, even for the Aleutian Islands, and the sisters shivered as they climbed from beneath their furs. Iya plopped down in front of Anna who quickly combed out the child's tangled hair and braided it. Then she did the same with hers.

"Would you like some coffee?" Erik asked.

Anna shook her head no.

"It's hot. It'll warm your insides. Like I said, it might be a while before we have anything hot to eat or drink. There's a lot of water and wind between us and where we're heading. It'll do you good. The little one too," he added, nodding toward Iya.

Anna conceded he might be right and accepted the offered cup. She sipped it gingerly. As the bitter liquid touched her tongue, she curled her lip back and quickly withdrew the tin. Coffee spilled down the front of her tunic. She tried to return the cup to Erik.

"Give it another try," he said. "You'll get used to it. I remember my first taste. I swore I'd never like it, but it grows on you. Really."

She forced herself to take another sip, this time prepared for the sharp flavor. She had to admit it felt pleasantly warm as it flowed down her throat and into her empty belly. She forced herself to drink half of it, then held the remainder out to Iya.

"It tastes awful, but it does make your insides warm," she said.

Iya looked at the cup suspiciously, then grudgingly relented to Anna's encouragement and accepted the warm drink. She sipped it cautiously. Just as Anna had done, she recoiled from the bitter flavor but tried again and managed to finish most of it.

"What you call?" Anna asked.

"It's coffee. Kind of gives you a kick in the morning, and it's great for warming a person's insides," Erik answered with a smile as he took the nearly empty cup from Iya. "Would you like some more?"

"No," Anna answered. "Enough."

Saying no more, Erik handed Iya and Anna each a piece of fried bread and jerky.

Iya examined the bread carefully. She turned it from side to side, sniffed it, then warily took a small bite. Her eyes lit up. "Good," she said as she took another bite.

Unable to understand the native language, Erik asked, "What did she say?"

"She like it," Anna answered and nibbled at her own. She chewed it slowly, smiled and said, "I like. What you call it?"

"It's just fried bread. My momma used to make it. We always smothered it in honey." He smiled at the memory, then stated matter-of-factly, "It'll fill your belly, that's for sure."

Anna tore off a chunk of the dried meat and asked, "This like our meat but different. Why?"

"It's deer meat."

Anna was puzzled. She had never heard of this animal before. "Deer? What deer?" she asked.

"That's right, you've never seen a deer before." Erik thought for a moment, before explaining. "Venison," he said, holding up the dried meat, "comes from deer. They are animals that live on the land. They aren't big like a moose."

Anna tilted her head to the side and asked, "Moose?"

With a look of frustration, Erik stopped. "You've never seen a moose either." He stroked his beard thoughtfully. "They have long legs and antlers," he said, as he held his hands over his head and wiggled his fingers.

Anna looked puzzled, shook her head and shrugged her shoulders.

Iya giggled.

Erik looked frustrated. "Have you ever *heard* of a moose?"

"I hear name. Men from outside speak of. I not see."

Erik reached for a small stick lying in the sand and drew in the wet soil. "A deer is like a moose. Just smaller." Soon a rough sketch of a deer emerged. "That's a deer," Erik said proudly as he pointed at the drawing.

Anna studied the picture for a moment, then nodded her head. "Now I know." She almost smiled as she asked for the canteen. After gulping down a portion of the water, she handed the remainder to Iya, who happily finished the rest.

Erik took it and said, "I'll refill this. Then we'll load the boat." He ambled up the beach toward the stream.

"He does not seem bad," Iya commented.

"No, not so bad," Anna answered quietly, as she studied the unusual man. She watched him until he disappeared into the underbrush.

Forcing her mind back to the practical tasks at hand, she took several of the hides and laid them out on the ground. "We can set our belongings in the center of the skins," she said to Iya. The little girl quickly stood and helped Anna gather their possessions. After everything had been placed in the pelts, they pulled each into a tight bundle and tied it off with a piece of rope.

With this done, Anna stood and looked out over the sea. *What will it be like in the middle of such a vast ocean?* she wondered. Fear rippled through her as she considered how vulnerable they would be. She took a deep breath, closed her eyes, and forced the frightening thought from her mind.

The sea had always been an unknown and mysterious entity to Anna. The women had never been allowed to hunt with the men. None had even been beyond the small cove near her village. She knew the ocean could be a dangerous and frightening place, unpredictable and often cruel. But it also represented life to her people. It had always provided everything they needed. She feared it now, but still it was a part of who she was.

Determined not to dwell on the dangers, she inspected the contents of her pouch, making certain her flints were in good condition. Carefully she replaced them then tied the small pouch to the inside of her tunic. It was imperative she keep her flints in a safe place. Without them, there could be no fires.

Everything was ready to be loaded when Erik returned. He smiled and said, "You two have been busy. You didn't leave any of the work for me." He dumped out the remaining coffee, dropped the empty pot in a bag, and tied it closed. He looked at Anna and Iya and explained, "We'll push the umiak halfway into the water before we load it. I want both of you to hold the boat steady while I stow the supplies. It needs to be packed just right. Everything has to be kept balanced or we could tip and lose the entire lot."

He grabbed his bag and set it in the back of the small craft. He carefully placed the remainder of their supplies in the vessel, setting each item in just the right location in order to keep an equal balance.

After he finished, he studied his work, then climbed inside the boat and rocked it to check the balance. He seemed satisfied as he jumped back onto the sand. "Well, it looks like we're ready," he said as he glanced self-consciously at the two native girls. Instead of climbing back inside the boat, he removed his hat, knelt in the sand, bowed his head, and spoke quietly to himself.

Anna had seen Father Ermelov do this. *He is praying!* she thought. *He believes in Father Ermelov's God!* She wanted to say something to stop him, but instead she stood and watched.

Abruptly Erik stood up, replaced his hat, and said, "Anna, I want you in the front and Iya in the center. It's important we keep the umiak stable all the time. These things are made for moving through the water with ease, not for steadiness. The only reason I use the darn thing is it's fast. We should be able to make pretty good time."

Anna lifted Iya into the small boat. The little girl tried to look brave, but as she sat on her knees in the center of the craft, her hands went white from gripping the side and her eyes were wide with fear.

Anna took her place in the front as instructed. She was afraid, too, but tried to hide it. With a confidence she didn't feel, she said, "Iya, do not worry. This is a strong boat and will take us to a new life. Do not be afraid. Nothing bad will happen to us."

Erik placed his shoulder against the boat, dug his feet into the sand, and pushed until it floated free. He bounded through the frigid water, then easily pulled himself over the side.

He took his place at the rear, grasped a paddle, and thrust it through the waves and into the sand, pushing the boat into deeper water. The surf crashed over the bow of the small craft as Erik paddled toward the open sea. He pulled hard with the oar, skillfully steering them safely through the water. Anna and Iya clutched the sides of the craft until they were free of the beach swells.

As they entered the calmer seas beyond the breakers, Anna slowly unclenched her jaws and began to relax a little. *He is very strong and a skilled oarsman,* she thought as she quietly observed Erik.

Erik turned the boat eastward and propelled the umiak forward with strong, steady strokes.

Anna looked back at the island. She'd never seen it from the sea. It looked different. The bluffs and hillsides, hemmed in on all sides by jagged gray cliffs, appeared to be covered with green fur. A single towering peak rose high above the bluffs, like a guard, watching over its domain.

Anna felt empty as she gazed upon her home. The familiar land steadily grew smaller as they moved away. Tears filled her eyes as she watched the island fade into the mist. She fought against the pain, biting back her sorrow, and tried to blink away her tears. As her thoughts turned to her family and the life she had lost forever, she was unable to stop the flood that spilled down her cheeks.

She suddenly felt a need to leap from the boat and swim ashore, to yell for Erik to stop, to tell him she had changed her mind.

Instead she sat very still and rigid and silently said good-bye.

Chapter 8

*O*nce under way, Erik paddled with determination. Anna was certain his desire to be free of his extra passengers urged him on.

Without taking his eyes off the sea, Erik said, "I need you to watch for rocks, floating logs, or anything else that could damage the umiak."

Anna nodded and asked, "Where we go?"

"We'll keep the shoreline in sight as much as possible and follow it northeast, keeping a lookout for any villages. Once we find a home for you and Iya, I'll head on up to Cook Inlet. After that, I don't know," he shrugged.

Anna felt uneasy as she thought of trying to fit in to a new village. This time, they would be the strangers, and there was no guarantee of a warm welcome. She knew every tribe was different. Some were much like hers, but others were warriors and cruel to those from outside their own tribe. *What if we end up in such a place?* she asked herself. *Or cannot find anyone who will take us?* She sat straighter and threw her shoulders back a little. *Worrying will do no good,* she reminded herself, and she forced her mind back to watching for obstacles.

The sea was calm, the swells small with long shallow troughs. The water rose and fell gently, lapping at the sides of the boat. Anna began to enjoy the gentle rocking and the feeling of solitude. As she gazed out across the great expanse of water, a feeling of peace settled over her. *It is not so scary,* she thought, and would have been lulled to sleep if she hadn't forced herself to remain alert.

Seaweed and logs floated on the surface, carried gracefully along by the currents, carefree passengers with no specific destination. Anna felt a kinship with these sea gypsies, for her own future was as uncertain as theirs. Like them, she was also a wanderer.

Sea otters became familiar companions. They looked to Anna and Iya like little old men with long whiskers and sad brown eyes. As the otters floated on their backs balancing flat rocks on their chests, they patiently chipped away at abalone until the shell was broken then feasted on the tender meat.

"I think we should call them the old men of the sea," Erik said as he watched one of the comical little animals dive below the surface. Anna explained the name to Iya. The little girl grinned and nodded her approval. She especially enjoyed the little animals and squealed with delight when they approached one.

One time she leaned out and tried to touch one of the animals. In her excitement, she forgot the danger of tipping the boat and falling in. With her arm outstretched, she teetered over the water, nearly plunging over the side while the umiak dipped dangerously close to the water. Erik grabbed hold of the back of her tunic and quickly pulled her back inside the boat. The otter dove beneath the surface, out of the little girl's reach, as the craft rocked violently.

Erik scolded Iya, but when he met her blank stare he remembered she could not understand much of what he said. He turned to Anna. "Please tell her not to lean over the side again," he said, alarm still in his voice. "She could have fallen in or dumped us all overboard."

Anna turned to Iya and relayed Erik's reprimand. The little girl's eyes filled with tears as she quietly returned to her place in the center of the boat. She made no more moves to explore her surroundings that day.

Hours passed without further mishap. Iya had dropped off to sleep, but as she began to stir, a soft moan escaped her lips. Her face had taken on a sickly color, and in a whisper she said, "Anna, I do not feel good. My belly moves with the sea."

Erik asked, "Is something wrong?"

"Her stomach moves," Anna explained.

"She's probably seasick. Poor thing," Erik said sympathetically.

"Seasick?" Anna questioned.

"Yeah, sometimes the movement of the waves will make you sick. You know sick," he said holding his stomach and moaning.

Anna nodded.

"Iya," Erik said gently, "look at the horizon. It will help."

Unable to understand Erik's instructions, Iya looked at Anna for an explanation. But Anna turned to Erik and asked, "Horizon? What horizon?"

Erik took his hat from his head, smoothed back his hair, and looked out over the waves before he said, "It means to look out over the water, to the place where the sun meets the sea."

Anna explained this to Iya, who was more than happy to oblige. After a while the youngster's color improved, and she even managed a weak smile for Erik.

The hours passed and the occupants of the small craft became stiff and weary, but there was little they could do to relieve their discomfort. Music had always played an important role in Anna's life, and she often sang to lighten her burden. A quiet chant rose from her lips, at first so soft, she could barely be heard. She sang of the sea and sky, and, as Iya joined her, their voices grew louder. Soon they were lost in the joy of singing, seemingly unaware of Erik's presence.

The big man's face softened as he listened. He didn't know what they sang, but the words were unimportant, for the natural beauty and intensity of emotion that poured from the two girls told what was in their hearts.

Finally the song quieted, and as it ended, Anna and Iya exchanged smiles before returning to scanning the waters. The music had fulfilled its purpose, making bearable what had seemed unbearable.

"That was a beautiful song," Erik whispered, as if not wishing to break the spell it had cast.

Anna's eyes momentarily met his and a smile played at the corners of her mouth, then she turned her attention back to watching the waves.

The sea remained calm the first day and night. The morning of the second day brought a gentle, intermittent rain and a cold, sharp wind that formed whitecaps on the tops of the waves. Before long, the raindrops grew larger and more plentiful, until they fell in sheets driven by the wind.

Trying to protect themselves from the onslaught, the travelers huddled beneath animal hides. Despite their efforts to remain dry, they were soon soaked.

Anna shivered uncontrollably but continued her vigilant watch while Erik fought to keep the boat steady. It seemed a hopeless battle as the storm intensified and the sea washed over the sides of the umiak. The waves were no longer wide and gentle but had grown tall with deep valleys between them. The small craft with its three passengers plunged down into a deep trough and nearly swamped, then rose to the top of the next wave, and for a moment balanced atop the rampaging sea before being thrown back into the next trench.

Erik yelled at Anna over the wind and rain. "Bail!"

Anna looked at him, not understanding the command.

He picked up a pail from the bottom of the boat, filled it with water from the inside of the craft, and as he dumped it over the side repeated, "Bail."

Her hands shaking, Anna took the pail and immediately began the endless task of scooping water back into the sea.

Iya's face was pale and drawn tight with fear. She gripped the side of the boat and cried out, "Anna!"

Anna could only look at her. She had no time to comfort the little girl now. The water flowed into the small craft so quickly that she was afraid they would sink beneath the wild angry sea if she stopped.

"It's getting worse. We'll have to find a place to put in, or we'll never make it," Erik shouted over the roar of the storm. He squinted, struggling to see through the rain and mist, and scanned the nearby shore, but there were only cliffs. There was no place to beach the boat. Ignoring the rain and seawater dripping down his face and into his eyes, he continued to paddle, intent only on the battle for their lives.

The wind and rain pelted Anna, but she continued to bail, while frantically looking for a safe harbor. Her hair hung in wet tendrils over her eyes, but each time she brushed them out of her face, the wind and rain only washed them back. Her eyes burned from the salty bite of the sea water, yet she continued to bail—she must bail or die.

The wind grew stronger and the waves larger. Anna fought paralyzing fear. Her arms and back ached from her never-ending labor, but she was thankful for the distracting pain. If she had time to consider their situation, she would give in to the fear. Still, the picture of a great wave taunted her. She tried to shut it out but could see it swamping the boat and pulling them beneath the sea. She shook her head and yelled, "No!" forcing the image from her mind.

Erik heard her yell and with a look of concern called, "You all right?"

Anna nodded and kept bailing as the cold wet rain penetrated to her skin. She clenched her teeth, trying to keep them from chattering, while she bailed mechanically, one bucketful after another. Her fatigue and pain grew worse, until it seemed she could bail no more. She would have to stop.

"Look!" Erik shouted and pointed at the shoreline.

Anna turned and peered through the driving rain. Relief washed over her as she saw what looked like a small bay.

Erik pulled hard with the paddle, turned the craft's nose toward the beach and, with renewed strength, propelled them toward safety. As the surf drove the boat into the shallow water and the bottom of the umiak scraped against the sandy beach, a whoop of joy escaped Anna's lips. She had never been so happy to be on solid ground!

Erik leapt out of the craft into the shallow water and pulled the boat up onto the shore. Without hesitation, Anna jumped in alongside him, grabbed hold, and helped pull the boat onto the beach.

With the umiak safely on shore Erik's and Anna's eyes met briefly. Both were aware that for a time they had forgotten they were strangers and had worked together, their differences momentarily forgotten. They quickly looked away and turned to other tasks.

Iya remained in the boat. Thoroughly wet, she hugged herself and shivered uncontrollably. Anna lifted her out and carried her up the beach. She took off Iya's wet tunic, slipped the little girl beneath her own, and held Iya close to her body, trying to warm her against her flesh. Anna was nearly as cold as Iya and could provide little heat, yet there was nothing more she could do. They huddled together and tried to control their convulsive shivering.

Reaching into one of the bags, Erik pulled out the two fairly dry skins and tossed them toward Anna. "Here, use these," he said and guided his two charges toward the umiak. "This will work as a windbreak," he said as he pushed them down behind the boat. Then he walked up the beach.

Anna and Iya clung to each other as they watched Erik scour the beach for usable firewood. Anna felt guilty as she watched him. He was as cold and wet as she, but there was nothing she could do. If she moved to help him, she would have to leave Iya. And as the little girl was hit by another spasm of chills, Anna quickly dismissed the thought.

After gathering enough wood, Erik crossed the beach to the cliff wall and pulled some of the dead grasses and moss from the rock face. He brought these back to where the girls huddled, made a small pile, and, using his body to block the wind, struck a fire stick.

Anna watched, fascinated, but the cold squelched any desire to investigate.

Soon a puff of smoke rose from the vegetation. Erik cupped his hands around the smoldering lichen and blew into it gently until it ignited. Quickly he placed more grass and small bits of wood on the fledgling fire. Before long, he had enough flame to add larger pieces of wood and was finally rewarded by a large, hot blaze.

"Anna, you and Iya stay by the fire," he called as he headed down the beach. Still shivering, Anna was more than happy to do so as she crouched close to the blaze, grateful for its warmth. She tucked a pelt around Iya and cuddled the little girl close.

Erik returned with several willows and a couple of stout poles. A few feet from the fire, he pounded the large poles upright into the sand, then strapped the willows across the posts with leather ties, forming a makeshift frame. Then he took two skins and lashed them across the top.

"That ought to do it," he said with a note of satisfaction in his voice. "It's not much but it should keep the rain off us."

Anna and Iya gratefully climbed inside and huddled together, still shivering.

Erik filled the coffeepot with fresh water, tossed in some coffee, and set it in the hot coals. He dug in his pack, found some of the dried meat, and handed a piece to each of the girls. Not until he had done this did he wrap himself in a pelt. He stared into the flames, chewed on a piece of venison, and tried to control his shivering as he waited anxiously for the coffee to cook.

When the aroma of the hot brew drifted up from the boiling pot, Erik pulled two cups from his pack. He filled one with the wonderful hot liquid and offered it to Anna. "Here, this will help warm you."

She accepted the gift without hesitation or complaint and took a sip of the hot drink. Closing her eyes, she relished the warm sensation as it washed down her throat. She wished she could drink it all but remembered Iya and offered the remaining coffee to her. She quickly drained it. Erik refilled

Anna's cup, then poured one for himself, and sat back to enjoy it.

This time, Anna quietly sipped the coffee while trying to study the big Norwegian without his knowing. Impressed by Erik's unselfish guardianship, she puzzled over what made him so different. *I have not known such a man before. He sacrifices and cares for us, even though he does not know us. Why?*

In such close quarters it was difficult to watch him, and Anna gave up her scrutiny and relaxed. As her body warmed, her worries and questions slipped away, and she was soon lulled to sleep by the heat of the fire, joining an already sleeping Iya.

Erik, too, finally gave in to exhaustion. The camp was quiet and the fire died down as they rested, and for a time, they were free from their worries and sorrows.

Several hours later, Anna rolled to her side, opened her eyes, and found Erik sitting cross-legged with his elbows propped on his knees, reading. He was so intent on his book, he seemed oblivious to his surroundings and completely unaware that Anna was watching him. The book looked very much like the one Father Ermelov had always carried with him, the one he had claimed held the words of God. He had called it a Bible. It seemed more precious to him than any other possession. Anna had never understood how a book could be of so much importance.

Erik glanced up and found her eyes on him. He returned her intense gaze, but said nothing and eventually turned back to his reading.

Anna rested her head on her arms and tried to recapture the peaceful world of sleep, but she was plagued by questions and remained awake. Finally unable to remain quiet any longer, she asked, "What you read?"

"My Bible. It used to belong to my mother."

"Father Ermelov had a Bible. Why you read?"

Erik cleared his throat and thought for a moment before answering. "Well, first off, it tells me everything I need to know about God: what he's like, how he feels about me, and how he wants me to live."

"You believe in this God?" Anna asked.

"Yes," Erik answered, meeting Anna's eyes. For a moment, he was silent, then looking back at his Bible, he said, "He is the God of all the world. I want to know him better, to understand him and his promises." He looked down at the book in his lap and gently closed it, then lovingly ran his hand across the leather cover and said, "This answers my questions. Here is where I find out why I even exist." He hesitated a moment. His voice tight with emotion, he added, "I learned about his son within these . . ."

Anna interrupted, "Father Ermelov say such things. I not believe this God loves." She turned her face away and lay her head on her arms, ending the discussion.

Erik stared at Anna and for a moment looked as though he would say more; instead he returned to his reading.

Chapter 9

*W*hile the storm battered the beach, the three travelers waited in their small shelter. When Anna awoke on the morning of the fifth day, she immediately knew something had changed. It was quiet. She peered out from beneath her pelts and squinted against the bright light of the sun. The wind had relented and a gentle breeze bent the beach grasses into graceful arcs. The angry storm clouds were gone, and in their place rested white pillows of moisture that left shadows on the beach as they moved across the sun. Steam rose from the wet beach, creating patches of shoreline fog. The sea was calm and sparkled in the sunlight. It was hard to imagine that only hours before it had been a dark churning threat. The song of a single bird echoed across the beach, and Anna took a deep breath and smiled. Once more, the world was a warm, inviting place. While cloistered in the tiny lean-to, she had almost forgotten this world of warmth and beauty.

Quietly, so as not to awaken her sleeping companions, Anna climbed from under her bedding and slipped away from camp. Thankful to be free of the cramped quarters, she stretched and took a long, deep breath, filling her lungs with fresh air, then slowly strolled down the beach. She lifted her face, warming it in the morning sunlight. "Mmm, I wish it could always be so nice," she sighed.

Her peaceful surroundings momentarily pushed aside unpleasant thoughts, and Anna was able to leave her sorrow behind. The waves washed ashore and reached out for her feet, tempting her to play. Unable to resist the teasing white foam, Anna dashed out of its reach. As the wave retreated back to the sea, she followed until it was met by another, then she raced back up the sand, just in front of it.

Spreading her arms wide, she lifted her face toward the sky and twirled around and around, enjoying the sensation of freedom. Finally she sprinted up the shoreline, hurdling clumps of grass and mounds of sand, forgetting for the moment that she was a woman in mourning. The little girl who used to dance across the beaches of her home emerged, free from adult burdens.

She danced and frolicked until she finally expended her energy, then stopped and stood gazing at the sea, wondering why the waves always marched ashore, one upon the other, never changing. She plopped down in the warm, soft sand, wrapped her arms about her knees, and closed her eyes. As she rested in the sun with the breeze washing over her, Anna decided it was good to be alive.

Her mother's kind face filled her thoughts. Instead of the pain her mother's memory usually generated, Anna felt a soft warmth and comfort as she remembered Luba. "I wish you were here," she whispered. A quiet chant rose from within Anna—words of hope from her childhood, learned while still young enough to sit in her mother's lap. Slowly Anna's voice grew louder and, carried upon the wind, drifted out across the great ocean. Anna wished her mother's voice would blend with her own, but it could never be. The song gradually died out, and Anna no longer felt content, but empty and alone as she stared out over the water. She felt cold and shivered.

"You have a real pretty voice," Erik said quietly.

Anna twisted about and found him standing behind her. Quickly she stood and faced him, furious that he had invaded her privacy. She clenched and unclenched her jaw. *He was watching me!* she thought and, remembering her childish play, wondered just how much he had seen. She tried to hide her anger and confusion with a mask of indifference.

"Nice day isn't it?" Erik said as he looked out across the waves. "Perfect weather for traveling. Hope it holds. I'd like

to do a little exploring before we leave. I won't be gone long."
He walked up the beach.

Anna hadn't said a word. Seething inside, she stared after him. *Why didn't I tell him what I thought of his spying?* she asked herself. *He had no right to sneak up and watch me!* Still, as she stared after him, she felt abandoned. She didn't like the feeling and turned back to her anger. "He always tells and never asks," she muttered. "It is clear he cares nothing of what I think." She headed back toward camp. "Go, I do not care what you do!" she said and kicked at the sand.

Iya was still half asleep. She stretched and yawned as she looked up at Anna, then blinked as her eyes adjusted to the bright morning sunlight. Grinning broadly, she said, "Good morning."

Anna looked at the sweet, trusting face of her younger sister, and her anger drained away. With a soft smile she responded, "Good morning, Iya. It is a good day to travel."

Iya nodded and stretched out on her bedding once more.

Anna started a small blaze in the fire pit, then retrieved Erik's frying pan from his bag. She had decided she would try his method of cooking this morning. She sliced large chunks of walrus into single servings and placed them in the pan. After adding more wood to the fire, she set the skillet in the hot coals as she had seen Erik do.

Some of Erik's bread would be good, she thought, wishing she knew how to make it. *Next time I will watch closely,* she decided. For now coffee would have to do. It had not looked too difficult to make. She filled the pot with fresh water, scooped two large handfuls of coffee grounds from the container, and dumped them into the pot. She looked at it for a moment, decided two handfuls weren't enough, and added another before setting the pot in the coals.

Anna returned her attention to the frying slabs of walrus. Taking the spatula as she had seen Erik do, she tried to slip it beneath the sizzling meat. But instead of easily sliding under the walrus, the spatula wouldn't budge. She pushed harder, forcing it under the baked-on food, then tried to flip the meat.

A large portion stuck to the pan while the rest slopped against the side and nearly fell to the ground. Anna carefully slid the charred meat back inside the pan, scraped the remainder from the bottom, and turned it. Burned and in pieces, it looked nothing like Erik's. She glanced at Iya and said hopefully, "Maybe it will taste better than it looks."

Iya wrinkled up her nose at the smell of the charred meat and shrugged her shoulders.

"It is not so easy. This cooking on a rock," Anna defended herself. The aroma of coffee was in the air, and she glanced into the pot to inspect the brew. It looked awfully black, a little like the walrus. Anna glanced about, expecting Erik's return, and was relieved when she did not see him. Breakfast wasn't turning out right, and she didn't know what to say about her effort. She turned her attention back to the over-cooked meal. The meat was blacker than ever, if that was possible, and was stuck even more solidly to the skillet. Anna decided she had better get the pan out of the flames and grabbed the handle, not thinking to protect her bare hand.

"Ouch!" she exclaimed, and quickly withdrew a blistered palm. She blew on the burn to cool it and washed it with the remainder of the fresh water. It stung, but she wrapped one of Erik's shirts about her hand and tried to ignore the pain as she pulled their charred breakfast from the fire.

Her hand throbbed and she stared at the pitiful, scorched meal. "This is not a good way to cook. Our way is better." The sound of sizzling coffee as it boiled over and spilled down the sides of the pot caught her attention. With Erik's shirt still wrapped about her hand for protection, Anna carefully removed it from the flames. Some of the coffee sloshed over the end of the spout and onto Erik's clothing. "Oh, no!" Anna exclaimed and quickly set the pot aside to examine the damage. A dark brown stain splattered the front of his shirt. Anna looked at Iya and said, "I have ruined it!" She jumped up and headed for the spring. Iya followed. "What have I done?" she murmured, her voice tense with fear. Anna rinsed and scrubbed at the stain, worrying aloud, "What will he say when he sees this?" She scrubbed some more, held it up, and inspected it. Most of it had come clean, but a small spot remained, so she dunked it back into the water and rubbed some more. Finally she pulled it from the stream, and after studying the shirt, asked, "Do you see any stain?"

Iya said, "No. It is clean."

Anna looked at the shirt again and, finally satisfied it held no evidence of her carelessness, returned to the fire. She lay the soggy garment across a piece of driftwood to dry. Frustrated and angry, she plopped down on a rock, leaned forward on her knees with her face resting in her hands, and scowled at the burnt meal.

Iya placed her arm about Anna's shoulder and said sweetly, "It is all right. I will eat it."

Anna glanced at Iya and tried to smile.

"Smells like breakfast," Erik said as he strode into camp. Seemingly unaware of the condition of the meal, he scooped out a chunk of the walrus and set it on his plate, poured himself a cup of very black coffee, and hunkered down next to the fire. He smiled and began to eat.

Anna watched and waited for his reprimand, but none came.

Gingerly, she filled a plate for Iya and herself, poured them each a cup of coffee, and settled down to join Erik. She eyed the burnt meal for a moment, then warily took a bite. The meat was dry and overcooked. It crumbled in her mouth as she bit down, making an awful crunching sound. Although she chewed slowly, she was unable to conceal the racket. It tasted awful and grated in her ears. She took a sip of coffee, hoping it would disguise the taste of the meat. Instead she had to fight the impulse to spit the bitter liquid from her mouth. It was too strong and held little resemblance to the coffee Erik had made.

Unbelievably Erik finished his meal. He stood and stretched. "Thanks for breakfast," he said as he went to rinse out his tin, still saying nothing about the disastrous meal.

Anna stared after him. *What kind of man is this?* she asked herself, amazed that he had eaten every bite and never said a thing about its poor quality. When he returned, he tucked his plate and cup back inside the pouch.

"I think I'll do some fishing while you and Iya hunt for berries and plants. I don't know how long it'll be before we put ashore again, so I figure we might as well stock up." He took his fishing pole and disappeared up the beach.

Anna wished she could learn to fish but quickly dismissed such a foolish idea. Women never hunted or fished; it had always been taboo and always would be. As long as there was a man to do such things, she would maintain her own place. She forced herself to finish the rest of her meal, reasoning that if Erik could eat it, so could she. Looking at Iya she said, "Hurry. We have much to do before Erik returns." She turned his wet shirt over and hoped it would dry quickly.

Iya pushed her meal around on her plate and said, "I am not hungry."

"I know it is bad, but you must eat."

Iya looked down at her food and frowned, but obediently placed a large piece of meat in her mouth. She closed her eyes tight, chewed slowly, and swallowed with a large gulp. She repeated this process several times. Finally, she held up her nearly empty plate and asked, "Finished now?"

Anna smiled and nodded as she took the tin and rinsed it, then placed it with the other utensils. "I think we should look over this part of the beach," Anna said as she handed Iya her basket and set out in the opposite direction Erik had gone.

Iya scampered ahead, her mind more on play than work, but she still scanned the beach for edible plants. "There are berries!" she suddenly exclaimed, pointing at a small patch of salmonberries growing on a protected patch of greenery.

"You pick those. I will keep looking."

Iya scurried across the sand toward her prize, and Anna continued to pick her way down the beach, all the while inspecting the cliffs, hoping to find a trail that led up to the bluffs. She could see grasses waving in the breeze above them and knew her chances of finding edible plants would be better there. Her mouth watered as she thought of wild celery and cucumbers.

She was a long way from camp when she found a remnant of netting entangled on a piece of driftwood. Carefully she removed it. She looked out at the ocean, then down the beach, and wondered where it could have come from. Finally, she shrugged her shoulders and decided that it must have come from the sea.

Thinking it might be of some use, she draped it over her shoulder and continued her search. As she walked down the beach, she scanned the expanse of sand, but found nothing more.

Disappointed, she was ready to return to help Iya when a dark object caught her eye. It looked about the size of a small seal, but was stretched out at an odd angle in the sand. She approached cautiously, uncertain what she would find.

As she drew closer, an uneasy feeling settled over her. She looked up the beach toward camp, but it was empty. She wished Erik were nearby. Driven on by her curiosity, she moved closer. It wasn't a seal.

A scream wrenched itself from her throat. A dead child looked up at her through empty sockets where her eyes had been. The birds and sand crabs had already begun to ravage the partially decomposed body. Anna's stomach lurched and she was unable to keep herself from retching.

She looked up and saw Iya racing down the beach toward her. "No!" she screamed as she ran to intercept the little girl. She grabbed hold of Iya and with her voice shaking, said, "No, Iya, you must not go down there!"

"Why? What is wrong?" she asked in a high-pitched voice.

Anna tried to control her shaking and forced herself to speak in a calm tone. "It is a girl." She stopped, choking back her horror. "She is dead."

This time, when she looked up, she found Erik hurrying down the beach toward them. Relief surged through her. Her need for someone to take charge, to ease her terror, temporarily replaced her need for independence.

"What's wrong?" he asked, as he reached the two girls.

"Girl . . . there . . . dead," Anna managed to choke out, as she pointed in the direction of the body.

Erik's face took on an ashen color. He looked at Anna as if for confirmation. All Anna could do was nod. Erik stroked his beard and glanced in the direction she had pointed, then slowly moved toward the dead child.

Anna and Iya clung to each other and watched. Erik stopped when he reached the body. He stood there for a moment, then did something surprising. He knelt down next to the child, and instead of looking away in horror or disgust, he reached out and gently brushed her hair back from her face. He stayed there for a moment staring at the lifeless little girl.

Taking long, slow breaths, he stood up and peered down the beach, as if searching for something. Slowly, he proceeded down the shoreline. Again he stopped, and Anna saw a shudder pass through his body as he gazed down at something in the sand. Erik moved up and down the beach, occasionally stopping, then moving on. Once, he stopped and bent to pick something up. He studied the object for a moment before heading back. His usual robust air was gone, his shoulders were no longer thrown back with their customary confidence and strength, and his eyes were filled with pain.

When he returned, he didn't say anything for a minute, then taking a long, ragged breath, he began, "It looks like the tsunami hit here too. I found three more bodies and wreckage from some homes. It doesn't look like there were any survivors."

He lifted his large callused hand and opened it slowly. "I found this." He held out a polished walrus tooth set in gold filigree on a piece of leather. "Looks like it belonged to one of the women. Why don't you keep it," he suggested as he handed the necklace to Anna.

Anna only stared at it, anguish washing over her. Then, as if awakening from a trance, she took the necklace and slipped it over her head. She felt as if she knew the woman who had worn it before her. These people were like her own. Blinking back her tears, she rubbed the polished ornament between her fingers and, without a word, turned and slowly shuffled back up the beach, away from the ravaged village.

She wandered aimlessly for a while as thoughts of her own people and their destruction assailed her. It was all so fresh. A sharp pain cut through her chest as though she had been pierced by a spear. But instead of slaying her, it only remained to torture her. She moaned softly while tears spilled down her cheeks. *I should have died with them,* she thought. *I wish I had.*

She looked at the black ocean and felt compelled to throw herself into the dark waves and allow the tide to drag her to the bottom. But even as she contemplated her death, she knew she could never leave Iya. She must remain.

Closing her eyes, she took a slow, deep breath, allowing herself to feel the breeze as it gently lifted her hair back from her face and raised goose bumps on her arms. She allowed the tranquility to soak into her and soothe her anguish.

Anna opened her eyes. As she did, she saw something completely unexpected. Erik and Iya were walking toward her, and Iya's hand was securely anchored within the large man's grasp.

Rage surged within her. *He is not one of us! Iya belongs to me!* She fought to control her anger, trying to appear calm as the two approached. Iya ran toward Anna with her arms outstretched. Anna knelt to accept the little girl's embrace and glared at Erik. His surprised expression providing some solace.

"Everything will be all right," Iya said to comfort her older sister. "Erik is a friend and will take care of us."

"We cannot trust him, Iya. Remember that."

Iya looked hurt and defiantly shook her head no.

Anna hadn't expected this traitorous behavior and anger welled up once again. Quickly, before she said something she would regret, she pushed Iya aside and strode off toward camp.

Erik caught up to her and placed himself in her path, forcing Anna to stop. "Look, I don't know what you said back there, but whatever it was, I can see it hurt Iya. You need to put your own feelings aside. That little girl is in pain. She doesn't need your anger."

He waited for some kind of response, but Anna turned her back and ignored him. His voice flat, he said, "I caught a couple of fish, but dropped them in the sand when I heard you yell. I'd better get them. They'll make a good lunch."

With his fists clenched at his sides and his back rigid, he trudged down the beach. Anna knew he was angry but decided she didn't care. Still, she was unable to put him from her mind, and as she considered his displeasure, she cringed.

Back at their camp, Anna poked at the coals, then added more wood until the fire reignited. Finding the water container empty, she decided to fill it and plodded down the trail to the spring. After returning, she poured a stream of fresh water into the coffeepot.

"I'd better do that this time," Erik said from behind her. Taking the jug, he said kindly, "Here, let me show you." Reluctantly, Anna handed him the pot and watched as he emptied it, then measured out a small amount of coffee into his hand and dumped it into the pot. After that he added the water slowly, trying not to stir up the grounds at the bottom, and set it in the hot coals. "See, that's all there is to it. You can make the next batch."

He smiled, and with no hint of his earlier disapproval, held up the two large fish he had caught. "Your people fillet fish differently. It seems a much better way—fewer bones. Could you show me how?" Erik asked as he offered her the salmon and a sharp knife.

After a moment's hesitation, Anna took the fish but reached into her pouch for her own knife. She slipped the blade expertly along the length of the fish, stripped away the bones in one piece, and with a half smile handed the limp meat back to Erik and said, "You do other."

Erik nodded and tried to imitate Anna's technique, but only managed to mangle the meat. Grinning sheepishly, he held up the butchered fish.

Iya stifled a giggle.

"I doubt I'll ever be able to learn your method," Erik said jokingly.

Anna tried not to smile and watched as he melted a small amount of fat in the frying pan before laying the salmon in the skillet. "Why you use fat?" she asked.

At first Erik looked puzzled. He glanced down at the pan, and considered her question before finally understanding. "Oh, the walrus fat. Well, I melt that first so the meat won't stick to the pan. It adds flavor too."

Anna nodded and watched.

"I thought we could leave at first light tomorrow," he said as he held the frying pan out over the flames. "If we eat now and get some sleep, we can be on our way early. What do you think?"

"You decide," Anna replied, unable to keep the resentment out of her voice.

"I've seen enough to know you have a lot of knowledge, and I'd like to know what you think."

"Women speak of things they know. I not know sea or hunt." She paused before continuing, "I make hides soft. I dry and keep food. I make good baskets." She stopped, suddenly embarrassed she had revealed so much about herself, then continued haltingly, "Not tell you about ocean."

"You are good with hides; I can see that by the quality of your tunic. It's very soft, and the stitching is fine. You can be proud of such fine work."

Anna blushed under his praise and quickly changed the subject. "I not find food. We go up?" she asked, pointing to the bluffs.

"There's a trail further up the beach," Erik responded. "How about we take a look after we eat? We'll have to hurry, though, if we intend to get enough sleep to leave in a few hours." He handed a piece of fish and a handful of berries to each of them.

After they had eaten, the three headed toward the trail. It was steep but not any worse than the one Anna and Iya had traveled at home. They made the climb easily and were soon above the cliffs. The wind was stronger on the bluffs and, even with the sun, Anna shivered. The land was mostly flat with a few small hills and blanketed with a variety of vegetation. The bushes were heavy with berries. The few stunted trees leaned away from the ever-present wind, looking ghost-like against the greenery.

Anna studied the foliage carefully and soon spotted something of interest. She fell to her knees at a cluster of sprawling bushes and began to dig about the roots of one of the plants. She quickly pulled it free and proudly displayed several small tubers hanging from the root base. "These good," she said, setting it aside and digging up another.

Erik joined her and dug up a similar plant. He held it up for Anna's inspection and with a sound of satisfaction in his voice, he asked, "Good?"

Anna nodded.

Erik resumed his digging.

Iya's tiny hands took the freshly dug tubers, shook the dirt from them, and piled them into one large mound.

"These remind me of the potatoes we used to grow back home," Erik said as he scooped up the roots and placed them in a sealskin pouch.

Anna didn't hear, for her mind had already moved on to something else. Her hands expertly popped small pods from a flowering bush. Anna worked swiftly and the small green pods quickly filled her basket.

Smiling, she looked at Erik and said, "These good," and popped one into her mouth. She motioned for Erik to do the same.

Suspiciously he turned it over in his hand. "Looks a lot like a pea." He sniffed it, hesitated a moment, and dropped it in his mouth. Uncertain what to expect, he chewed slowly. A smile washed over his face. "These are good. Really sweet."

Now able to understand some of what Erik said, Iya giggled and nodded in agreement as she tossed one into her mouth. She smiled as she contentedly chewed the sweet delicacy.

Brushing the dirt from his pants, Erik stood up. "I think we've got enough to hold us for a while. We'd better get back." Before moving on, however, he looked at Anna and added, "Thanks for your help."

Anna smiled and said, "We take these to camp, come back, pick berries." Her smile broadened, "I know much about gathering food."

Chapter 10

*A*fter a few hours' rest, Erik roused Anna and Iya. The three silently loaded the boat and pushed off into the unpredictable waters of the Pacific. The ocean was calm and the umiak moved swiftly through the swells. Anna took up her usual watch, enlisting Iya's help in looking for submerged rocks and floating debris. Erik sat with his back straight, his eyes trained on the horizon, and repeatedly plunged the wooden paddle into the water, pushing against the waves and propelling them ever closer to their destination.

As the sun climbed into the sky, Anna noticed Erik's growing weariness although he tried to conceal it and never complained. Several times her eyes moved to the spare paddle in the bottom of the boat as she considered the possibility of sharing the burden of rowing. For some time, she said nothing. Finally unable to keep her thoughts to herself, she said, "I watch you paddle. I can do." She hesitated, hoping Erik would ask for her help. He said nothing. She took a deep breath and asked, "You let me help?"

Erik let his oar slip inside the boat. He wiped the sweat from his brow with the back of his hand and studied Anna as he considered her suggestion. "You're awful small for this kind of work. It takes a lot of strength."

"I strong," Anna quickly assured him.

"That you are," he said as he stroked his beard thoughtfully, then almost to himself, added, "I could use the help." A little louder, he said, "I suppose we could give it a try. With two of us working, we can make better time. We'll need someone to keep watch."

"I watch!" Iya announced eagerly.

"You've got to keep a real close eye out and let us know if there's anything ahead. Do you think you can do that?"

Iya nodded.

"I guess you've got the job," Erik said, then took the paddle from the floor of the boat and handed it to Anna. "Be careful with this; it's the only spare we've got."

Anna looked at the paddle blankly. Now that it was in her hands, she felt uncertain how to use it. It no longer looked graceful but felt cumbersome and heavy.

Erik smiled. "First, just get the feel of it. Balance it, like this." He moved the weight of his paddle from one hand to the other. "It's not so heavy."

Anna turned the paddle over in her hands, feeling the weight of it as she had seen Erik do. It began to feel better.

"Here, let me show you. Push it deep into the water and always keep it flat against the waves." He moved through the motion slowly as he spoke.

Anna listened and tried to hold her tongue. After all, she had been watching him for days. It looked simple. Anna tried to imitate Erik's stroke, but her first few attempts were feeble, accomplishing little more than splashing water inside the boat. Keeping the flat side against the waves was harder than it looked, but Anna persisted, and was finally rewarded by a relatively strong, smooth stroke. She moved the paddle from one side of the boat to the other with relative ease and comfort. She liked her new role and quickly settled into the joint effort. They moved more rapidly through the water, and with two of them paddling, one was occasionally allowed the privilege of resting while the other kept them moving.

"You're doin' pretty darn good for such a little lady," Erik remarked after a while.

Anna appreciated the praise. Her back ached and her arms burned with the effort, but she gritted her teeth, determined not to complain. After all, this is what she had wanted. She continued to match Erik's strokes.

Iya sat proudly in the bow of the boat and, despite her age, proved to be a dependable sentry. Her eyes were sharp, and she quickly announced the presence of any obstacle. As she kept watch, she sang of happier times. Suddenly she stopped chanting and seemed deep in thought.

"Iya, what are you thinking?" Anna asked.

"Him," she answered, glancing at Erik. She turned and faced the stranger. "What place you from?"

"I'm from Minnesota."

"Minn-e-so-ta? What Minnesota?" Iya probed.

Erik thought for a moment before answering. "I don't know how to explain it to you. It's a long way from here. Much further than where we are going. It is many days' travel after you reach the mainland." He stroked his beard and a faraway look came into his eyes. "It's a good way from the sea, but there is a large lake near my home. Tall grasses grow for miles, and when the wind blows it looks a little like the ocean."

Iya smiled and nodded. "I see grass."

Erik returned her smile and continued, "There aren't many trees in the part of Minnesota where I grew up, and a person can see for miles in every direction." He stopped and scanned the shoreline.

"Tell more," Iya insisted.

Erik pushed hard on the paddle and stared out across the sea before continuing. "It's very hot and dry in the summer with big storms that light up the sky. The sun shines almost every day, even during the winter. Some winters are real cold, even colder than here. Most people live on farms where they grow all kinds of plants and raise cattle."

Iya looked at him with a puzzled expression and asked, "Grow plants? Why?"

"Well, food doesn't grow like it does here. If we don't plant what we need to eat, we go hungry."

Iya immediately asked, "What is cattle?"

"You know, cows." Erik sighed heavily. "Cows are like moose. Remember when I drew the picture in the sand?"

Iya nodded.

"Well, that's kind of like a cow."

Iya seemed satisfied and Erik continued, "We have mountains, too, but not like you have here. The mountains in Minnesota aren't so big." He took a deep breath and let it out slowly. "Used to be you hardly ever saw people unless you went into town, but things are changing. More folks are moving in all the time. The towns, or villages, as you would call them, are getting bigger. It's gotten too crowded for me." He stopped for a moment, deep in thought.

"We had a small farm just outside of town. But there wasn't much time for socializing. Too much work to be done. Oh, we went to church almost every Sunday and occasionally had a dance. And we had good friends—the kind of people you could always count on when there was a need. It was a good place to grow up." He stopped paddling. "Now that I think about it, your people and mine aren't really so different."

Anna had been listening, although she never broke her stroke. She wondered what this man was really all about. Why would he leave his home and his people? She twisted about and asked quietly, "You miss Minnesota?"

Erik didn't answer immediately. "Yeah, I guess I do. I remember the feeling of freedom I used to get when I'd stand out in a big field surrounded by nothing but open ground. I've always loved the prairie. When I was a boy I used to run through the deep grass, feeling like there were no boundaries in life. On a clear day you could see a long, long way.

"Sometimes when my mother would call me, I'd hide in the tall grass. She would always search, but I was usually too well hidden for her to find me. She'd act like she was getting really mad, and then I'd pop up and call out, 'Here I am!' She'd just shake her head and threaten to throttle me . . . but she never did."

Suddenly, Erik seemed uncomfortable. He cleared his throat and in a husky voice said, "There's no one left now. My parents both died from the pox six years ago. Never had a brother or sister." He stopped paddling and looked down at his hands as if he would find comfort there.

"I wrong. I think we not alike," Anna said gently.

"I was grown when my parents died."

"You have no one, like us."

Erik said no more but quietly resumed his paddling.

A heavy silence settled over the boat, and for many minutes no one spoke.

Suddenly Erik blurted out, "Look there!"

Anna and Iya both turned in the direction he was pointing. At first Anna could see nothing. Then water spouted into the air.

"A whale!" she exclaimed.

"I've never seen one up close before. How about getting a better look," Erik stated more than asked, as he turned the boat toward the animal.

Anna paddled hard trying to match Erik's quickened pace, although she was certain she didn't want a closer look. She had heard many frightening tales about the great whales. Trying to keep her voice from shaking, she said, "Not safe. Taboo for women to hunt whale."

Erik shrugged off her warning. "We're not hunting; we're just looking. I heard whales aren't the killers we've been led to believe they are. I'll be careful." Then as if Anna had said nothing, he went on, "I think we can overtake it if we work together." He fixed his eyes on the whale, and with his face flushed and his eyes alight, he paddled hard, closing the gap between them and the great beast.

Anna didn't share Erik's excitement but thought it would be useless to protest further. She had to admit to being a little curious.

The whale seemed in no hurry. It moved through the water in a slow, graceful dance. Slapping the waves with its broad tail, it would disappear below the surface and a few minutes later reappear, unconcerned by the approaching vessel.

Anna stopped paddling. "We move closer?" she asked, her voice trembling a little.

"Yes!" Iya shouted, straining to get a good look, her youthful curiosity overriding any caution.

Anna looked at Erik, certain this encounter was foolish, but she was unwilling to demand that he stop.

"I think it's all right. It doesn't seem upset by our presence and hasn't shown any signs of aggression. I don't think it's dangerous. In fact, I've heard these animals are really pretty gentle." With his eyes still trained on the beast, he pulled slowly on the oar and said, "We'll move real slow. I'd just like to get one good look."

Reluctantly, Anna returned her paddle to the water.

They were almost upon the whale when Erik set his paddle inside the boat. Anna did the same. Silently they drifted toward the beast and were soon so close any of them could have reached out and touched the huge creature.

It was bigger than Anna had thought, and her first instinct was to put as much distance between herself and the animal as possible. But she pushed aside her fear and allowed herself to enjoy the experience.

Its back was covered with patches of barnacles and displayed scars of previous encounters with unsuccessful hunters. It appeared content to let the curious onlookers travel alongside, seeming to know they were no threat. With unexpected grace the whale moved its great hulk slowly through the water, arching its body as it propelled itself through the sea.

Overwhelmed by the animal's awesome strength and size, Anna's fear slowly subsided. *It is not afraid; it does not threaten us.* Her pounding heart slowed to a steady rhythm as the whale's peaceful behavior affected her own tightly strung nerves. Close enough to touch the enormous mammal, Anna wished she had the courage to do so but kept her hands inside the boat.

"I've never seen anything like it," Erik whispered. "It's so big."

Iya sat with her eyes wide and her mouth slightly open. Without warning, she leaned out over the water and gingerly caressed the back of the whale. A subtle shudder moved through the animal. It made no attempt to retreat, but allowed Iya's dainty hand to slide gently across its back as it glided by.

"Iya, no!" Anna and Erik cried in unison.

Abruptly, Iya sat back, frightened by their sharp command.

With a sudden sweep of its tail, the whale dove out of sight and rocked the small boat perilously with its wake. They watched and waited for it to resurface, scanning the open sea.

Iya finally spotted it several hundred yards away. "There!" she cried.

"Well, it's gone," Erik said quietly.

They were disappointed but grateful they had been allowed to witness something so remarkable. For several minutes they said nothing, still stunned by what had taken place.

Anna was glad she hadn't been able to talk Erik out of what she had considered to be a wild and dangerous escapade. Her heart still pounded hard in her chest, and she felt that now she understood why the hunters loved the hunt. The experience had been exhilarating. A subtle sadness fell over her as she considered the whale. It was hardly the savage beast she had been told of or an adversary to be destroyed without cause. She would appreciate more the sacrifice paid next time she ate the flesh of such a magnificent creature.

"No one will believe what just happened!" Erik said, his voice still animated. "I can hardly believe Iya actually touched it!" He stopped short, turned to Iya and, with his brows knit together in a frown, said, "Which, by the way, reminds me; it was a foolish thing to do. You could have fallen in or tipped the boat over, or that whale could have thought it was in danger and killed us all. You've got to think before you do things."

Iya dropped her head and looked at her hands. "I not want do bad."

Her remorse softened Erik's ire. He smiled, then reached over and ruffled the little girl's hair. "You just scared me, that's all. What's done is done. It was my fault anyway. I'm the one who insisted on taking us so close."

Her voice tinged with fear, Anna said, "We drift far from shore. We go through channel?" She asked as she nodded toward a narrow strait just ahead of them.

"Yeah. Otherwise we'd have to go miles out of our way. It's a small passage, and some of the currents are tricky, but we can make it." Erik plunged his paddle back into the frigid sea and pushed them toward the waterway, putting the incident with the whale behind them.

A large island loomed ahead, looking as if it had just recently been thrust up out of the sea. It wore a crown of jagged snow-covered peaks, rising sharply from its base. A wall of ice reached right down to the sea.

"There's a big ice floe that comes down from those mountains. Giant chunks of ice break off the face of it and fall into the water. When I came through a couple of months ago, I saw pieces as big as houses sheer off and float out to sea. Once I got a little too close and the wake of one nearly swamped my boat. It's an unbelievable sight. There's still plenty of ice, so we'll have to watch closely."

As they approached the narrow strait, Erik became quiet and focused. He gripped his paddle and kept his eyes trained on the dangerous passage.

"I'm going to need both of you to watch for rocks. The depth of the water changes a lot here, and if we hit a rock it could rip right through the bottom of the boat. And big logs float through here. When the waves toss them about, they can be deadly. Anna, I want you up front, and Iya you sit in the middle. I'm counting on you to keep watch for me. I've got to keep all my attention on the currents and use them to get us through." He nodded in the direction of the confining strait and asked, "You ready?"

Anna and Iya glanced at each other, gripped the sides of the umiak, and turned their attention to scanning the water for hidden dangers.

Erik expertly maneuvered them through the dangerous channel, careful to keep them in the center of the main current.

"Watch out! Rocks," Anna called as she spotted and pointed to a submerged reef.

With the efficiency born of experience, Erik piloted them around the concealed hazard while manipulating the craft between the sheer cliffs that rose up on both sides. He had no time to relax, however, for another danger loomed ahead.

An outcropping narrowed his maneuvering space, allowing only enough room for the boat. The waves moved rapidly through the juncture, complicating matters. An error could mean death. Erik needed to slow the umiak to gain more control and make certain the sides of the boat didn't scrape against the protruding rocks. Just before the waves washed them through the tiny space, he placed his paddle flat against the current, slowing their progress, and they slipped safely through.

As they floated into the wider channel, Anna realized she had been holding her breath. She let out a sigh, then breathed in deeply, relieved that the dangerous spot was behind them. She considered Erik's ability; he was a skilled boatman. Anna felt a new sense of security and allowed herself to relax just a little.

The next few days were uneventful. Anna and Erik took shifts, sleeping and paddling. Iya slept much of the time. They were all weary and sun baked and had begun to feel they would never be free of the rolling sea.

"Our supplies are getting low," Erik said one morning as he took stock of what they had left. "We'll have to put in soon and restock. Better start looking for a beach." He scanned the shoreline.

Almost immediately, he became very still, and he stared hard at something in the water. "That's exactly what we need," he said as he pulled his paddle inside and slowly reached for his rifle.

"What is it?" Anna asked, her voice tense.

"A seal," Erik whispered, raising his hand to signal her to stop paddling. "That's good." He stood up slowly, raised the rifle to his shoulder, and braced his feet. Barely breathing, he waited for just the right moment. A lull in the waves steadied the boat, and Erik squeezed the trigger. A loud explosion rang out across the water, echoing as it bounced off the nearby shore. The seal jumped, then lay motionless, floating atop the waves as his blood stained the water a rusty red.

The noise of the gun had taken Anna and Iya by surprise, and for a moment they kept their hands over their ears. The men of her tribe had always used spears and lances; the sound of the gun frightened them.

Iya's chin quivered and her eyes filled with tears as she watched the lifeless seal float upon the waves.

Anna uncovered her ears and looked at the gun in Erik's hands. She knew of the use of rifles among outsiders, but she had never actually seen one used. She reached out and touched it, amazed that something could look so harmless and be so deadly. Killing that seal had been too easy.

Erik seemed unaware of her scrutiny and quietly returned the rifle to its proper place. "That should feed us for a while. Never did take much pleasure in killing, but I'm always thankful for God's provision." He paddled toward the dead animal. "We'll have to put in somewhere to butcher it."

"Why you kill?" Iya asked accusingly, wiping at her tears.

"We must eat," Anna answered for Erik. "Why do you cry? This is not different from the ones we have eaten before."

Iya sniffled and answered haltingly, "Not see before."

As they came alongside the seal, Erik reached out and pulled it close to the boat. Trying to hide what he was doing, he pierced a hole through the top of the seal's muzzle, threaded a piece of rope through the gash, and lashed the animal to the boat.

Iya continued to sniffle. Anna carefully made her way to her sister's side and sat next to her. Placing her arm about Iya's shoulders she asked in their native tongue, "Do you remember the story of the seal spirit?"

Iya shook her head no and, pointing at Erik, said, "Talk his words."

"Iya, this is a legend of our people. Outsiders do not understand."

"No," Iya said stubbornly. "Talk like Erik."

Anna sighed and began the story in English. "Once people live in land of ice. Young hunter need to bring food. His people hungry. Three days he wait by . . ." She hesitated as if searching for the right word. "He wait by hole in ice. He wait for seal. Finally seal come. Young hunter stand and raise spear to kill seal. But he cannot . . ." Again she stopped. "Throw?" she asked as she glanced at Erik. "Throw lance. He wait, know he must kill animal, but cannot. He drop spear and weep. His people hungry. He ashamed. Young hunter leave, but voice call out. Voice of seal."

Iya's eyes grew wide with amazement. "What seal say?"

Anna continued, "Seal say, 'Gods put me here for you. I give you life. My body help you live. I give to you.' Seal turn belly to hunter."

Iya's eyes grew wider.

"Man surprised. Think he dream. He splash face with water. But seal still there.

"Hunter must kill. No more fear. He stand, lift spear, and strike seal in heart. He chant song of thanksgiving. When he return to village, he not ashamed, but proud."

Anna stopped and squeezed Iya's shoulder. "Animals let us kill. If not so, we could not kill." She hesitated, "This seal just like others." She was quiet for a moment, then asked softly, "You understand?"

Iya wiped her nose and nodded, then leaned against Anna.

Anna glanced at Erik and thought she could see unshed tears in his eyes.

He quickly looked away and tightened the rope holding the dead seal.

Anna knew she should say nothing, but was unable to hold her tongue. "You know this story?" she asked quietly.

Erik cleared his throat and met Anna's look. "It just reminds me of something."

"What?"

"It made me think of what Jesus did for me, that's all."

"Jesus?" Anna asked, with a hint of accusation in her voice.

"Jesus Christ, the Son of God."

"I hear of Jesus," Anna said, her voice hard.

"Why are you angry?"

"Father Ermelov speak of this Jesus." She spat the name. "He is of most powerful God. God who destroy my people."

"Anna . . ." Erik began.

She cut him off. "Do not defend this God. I not hear!" She turned her back to Erik and paddled hard.

Erik clamped his mouth shut and said no more but picked up his own paddle and matched Anna's strokes.

Chapter 11

*A*s the sun sank below the edge of the sea, Anna thought about Erik's God and the one called Jesus. He seemed to know this God almost as one would a friend. *How can a man know God?* she asked herself. *And why would an ancient tale affect him?* Anna was confused.

Exhausted and sore from hours of rowing, she felt her endurance wane and searched carefully for a place to put ashore. When they found none, she stubbornly forced her strokes to match Erik's. Although mist hung above the water and the temperature was cool, sweat ran down Anna's temples. Finally, even her tenacity gave out. She had to concede. Too weary to continue, she laid her paddle aside.

Iya had curled up on the bottom of the boat and, with her hands tucked under her head, slept peacefully. Anna leaned against the side, rested her head on her arms, and tried to sleep, but thoughts of Erik filled her mind. He was unlike any other man she had known. *Is it his God that makes him so different?* she wondered.

She closed her eyes, breathed in the damp, salty air, and tried to remember what Father Ermelov had taught during his visits to their village. She had never been interested and had paid little attention. Now when she wished to know more, his words were no more than a jumble of confusing theology. "Oh, why didn't I listen?" she moaned. Finally, fatigue overcame the busyness of her mind, and the gentle rocking of the boat lulled her to sleep.

Erik continued paddling, his eyes trained on the nearby coastline. Gradually his strokes weakened and slowed, until he, too, succumbed to fatigue. Pulling his paddle from the water, he set it on the floor of the boat, rearranged his knapsack, and rested his head upon it. His eyes closed. Occasionally he forced them open to check their location, but after a while, his breathing slowed to a steady rhythm, and his eyes remained closed.

With its passengers asleep, the small craft floated aimlessly across the waves, now attended only by the stars that flickered in the dark canopy overhead.

A pesky sea gull squalling its irritation at the intruders awakened Erik the following morning. Disoriented, he rubbed his eyes and tried to rouse himself from the world of sleep. He glanced at his slumbering companions, then at the seal and remembered their need of a safe harbor. Fully awake now, he studied the shoreline and the sun to get his bearings. Then he returned to the task of paddling and searching for a place to beach the boat. Almost immediately he spotted a small inlet.

"Wake up!" Erik shouted. "We're putting ashore!"

Anna bolted awake.

Iya sat up slowly, stretched, and blinked her eyes as she peered about, looking a little confused.

Anna longed to set foot on solid ground. She quickly cleared her head and forced her sore, stiff muscles into action, paddling hard. Even one more minute in the cramped quarters seemed intolerable.

"What you find? Village?" Iya asked hopefully.

"Can't say for certain," Erik replied. "I don't see any sign of life. We'll just have to wait and see."

He continued his steady paddling, his eyes fixed on the bay. "Looks like this will be the safest approach," he said as he steered them past a large rock and headed the small craft straight into the cove. The surf picked the umiak up and carried it into the shallow waters. Erik and Anna jumped into the knee-deep surf and guided the boat onto the black sandy beach.

With the boat safely ashore, Anna pushed her hair out of her eyes and looked about. The beach was empty. There was no evidence of inhabitants. She felt a moment of disappointment that was quickly replaced by the joy of being on solid ground once more. It felt good to plant her feet upon a steady surface, one that did not roll beneath her.

Iya leapt out of the boat and scampered across the sand, throwing herself about in a jubilant dance. "Sand warm! Feel good!" she exclaimed.

Anna agreed; the warmth of the sand under her feet felt wonderful. Although she had grown accustomed to the swaying of the boat, she enjoyed the sense of security provided by the firm ground.

As she looked down the beach, the bright sun reflecting off the sand forced her to squint, bringing with it pain from her wind- and sunburned skin. Gingerly she touched her face. It felt dry and flaky. She sighed. She'd been careful to apply a protective coat of oil every day, but her face was still cracked and dried from the constant wind, salt water, and summer sun. She glanced up at the clear sky and longed for the familiar cloud cover with its accompanying moisture. Her much-loved sun only increased her discomfort. She remembered how she had complained about the damp weather to her mother. Luba had told her to accept what each day has to bring and be thankful for it. Her mother had been right. Anna wished she could tell her so.

The wind whipped her hair across her face, stinging her tender skin like a strap. Carefully she lifted it away from her face, but the breeze only tossed it back. She finally gave up.

Anna saw that Iya's skin was as damaged as her own. She quickly retrieved the pouch of rendered walrus fat and called to Iya, "Here, let me put some of this on you. It will soothe the pain." She knelt in the sand, carefully pulled Iya's hair away from her face, and gently applied the soothing balm to the little girl's skin. When she was finished, she asked, "Feel better?" Iya bobbed her head as she scanned the beach, her attention already on something else.

Anna held the oil up for Erik and asked, "You want? You worse than us."

"Take care of yourself first," Erik answered as he hauled the seal onto the beach.

Anna carefully spread the grease over her inflamed skin, then handed the pouch to Erik.

"This stuff smells terrible, but I'd hate to think how we'd feel without it," Erik said as he smoothed the salve over his face and arms.

After returning the oil to the boat, he dragged the seal further up the shore. Anna followed, intending to help with the butchering. Erik quickly skinned and gutted the animal while Anna watched, feeling useless as she waited for an invitation to help. Erik never asked.

As the minutes passed, her anger sprang to life, growing with each pass of his knife. Anna felt worthless as she watched him work but fumed silently.

Suddenly aware of Anna's presence, Erik looked up and asked, "Why don't you and Iya gather some wood. We'll roast a piece of this as soon as I'm done here."

Anna clenched her teeth and said nothing. *I should slaughter the animal! It is not for a man to do. He knows nothing of our ways!* she thought with disdain as she turned on her heel and took Iya to collect the wood.

As Anna and Iya worked, the occasional glint of Erik's knife caught Anna's attention. Her anger grew. After starting the fire, she approached him, determined to speak her mind. *He will give me my place!* she thought.

Standing directly in his line of vision, she spoke in a quiet but firm voice. "I good flesher and softener of hides. I clean skin." She met Erik's gaze, determined to have her way.

The sun was at Anna's back, forcing Erik to squint as he faced her. His eyes met hers and he held her stare, unperturbed by her demand. Without complaint, he accepted her decree.

"Sure. I'm almost done here. I'll cook up some of this while you get started."

Anna was ready for a fight, and when she found none, felt a little deflated. She let out a sigh, surprised she had won so easily. She wondered why Erik hadn't challenged her request and felt a little embarrassed by her anger as she sat quietly on a nearby log and watched while he finished. She hated to admit it, but he handled a knife with expertise. *He is skilled,* she thought, *wasting none of the flesh while still protecting the hide.*

As she watched Erik, she couldn't help comparing this tall, graceful man with Kinauquak. *They are so different. Kinauquak seemed always tense, ready to pounce. Erik is unhurried and calm, yet never slow or careless.*

Her throat felt tight as she thought of Kinauquak, but the pain was not so intense and he no longer seemed so near. A momentary sense of panic struck her. *Will I forget him?* she asked herself. Then her hand slipped to the small bulge in her stomach, and she knew he would never be forgotten.

After he finished, Erik plunged the blade into the sand, wiped the edge of it across his pant leg, and slipped the knife back into the sheath hanging from his belt.

"It's all yours," he said as he took a couple of meat chunks and headed to the fire. "After we eat, I'll slice the rest of it and hang it to dry. We could use a couple days' rest," he said as he glanced about. "This is as good a place as any."

Anna pulled a stone from her pouch. One side was rounded and the other was sharp, hewn to a fine edge for scraping away the sinews and tallow from the inside of a hide. Lifting the hide, she admired the sheen of the fur and the thickness of the seal's pelt. *This will make a fine coat,* she thought.

As she glanced back at Erik, feelings of admiration for the outsider emerged once more. She didn't welcome the emotions and scraped harder at the hide, trying to drive away the sensation, to push him from her mind. Nothing helped. His intense blue eyes plagued her. One moment they were gentle, the next filled with fire, always captivating and unreadable. Erik kept himself hidden. Anna wished she could see past the eyes, to the soul of the man, but Erik carefully guarded his feelings. *At times, he almost seems a boy, but always the man remains,* she thought.

After breaking for their meal, Erik and Anna both resumed their tasks and worked in companionable silence. Erik sliced the meat very thin and draped it over a makeshift rack while Anna continued to flesh the hide.

Erik placed the last slice of meat up to dry, nodded toward Iya, and said, "Looks like she's got the right idea."

Iya had curled up next to the fire and was sound asleep.

Anna nodded in agreement, stretched her back, and rubbed at the sore muscles in her arms. "Time I join her," she said and draped the partially fleshed hide over a log, then gratefully curled up next to the sleeping child.

Erik stretched out opposite them. He glanced across the flames at Anna and smiled at her before closing his eyes. Anna ignored his gesture of friendship, quickly looking away.

The burden of the trip had taken its toll, sapping the strength of all three travelers. They slept soundly the remainder of that day and through the night.

Late the following morning, Erik rose first and had a breakfast of mussels and dried berries ready for Anna and Iya when they awoke.

The three sat contentedly around the morning fire, enjoying their meal. *It seems so right, the three of us together,* Anna thought, nearly believing they were a family. She looked up and found Erik staring at her. She blushed under his gaze, and her heartbeat quickened. Immediately she looked away, hoping he hadn't noticed her reaction, and puzzled over why a simple look from him stirred such strong feelings within her. *He is only an outsider,* she reminded herself. She tried to focus on something practical and said, "Sealskin make good hide. Seal healthy. Gun not hurt pelt. If our hunters had such weapons, we always have full bellies." She hesitated before continuing, "You skin seal good, protect hide."

"Thank you. I consider that quite a compliment coming from you," Erik said, pleased by her praise.

"I work on pelt now," Anna said as she moved away from the campfire.

Iya followed. "You show me?" she asked.

"No. Very hard work. Not for little girls. You have to grow. I teach when time is right."

Iya frowned.

Anna stopped and caressed the child's cheek and said, "Later we search for berries, wild potatoes, and maybe find *putske.*"

A smile replaced Iya's frown, and she ran back to the campfire. She plopped herself down next to Erik and cuddled up next to the big man.

He emptied his coffee cup, then reached his long arm about the little girl, gave her a quick hug, and said, "I'm going to take a look around. Would you like to come along?"

Iya's smile broadened and she answered, "Yes," as she jumped to her feet.

"We're going to do a little exploring," Erik called to Anna.

She nodded her permission and quickly returned to her work.

Anna was so engrossed in her effort to produce a good quality pelt that she did not notice the passage of time. Not until the sun was high in the sky did she stop. Wiping the sweat from her brow, she stood and stretched her back. As she gulped down a cup of water, she glanced up the beach, but there was no sign of Erik or Iya. "They should be back by now," she said. The words sounded hushed on the empty shore. *They will come soon,* she thought as she returned to her work.

The day passed and evening came. Anna's back and arms ached from her work. She set aside the pelt and walked about for a few minutes to work out her stiffness. It was very late, and the sun had begun to set. *They have been gone too long,* she thought as she peered up the beach toward the cliffs. As twilight settled over the land, she could see no sign of them.

Fear struck a cold, sharp chord within her, but she tried to shrug it off, telling herself she was worrying about nothing, that Erik could take care of any situation.

She returned to her work but, unable to concentrate, finally gave up. She draped the hide over a piece of driftwood, thinking, *I will finish it tomorrow.*

She rekindled the fire and looked into the gloom as she melted fat in the frying pan. *What if they do not come back? What should I do?* she asked herself. She cut off slabs of seal and tossed them into the pan, then added the tubers to warm them.

With the coffee brewing in the coals, she huddled close to the fire and watched the sun sink into the sea. A feeling of foreboding choked her. As dusk settled all around, she tried to eat, but the food stuck in her throat. She set it aside, hoping she would share the meal with her companions later.

Unable to sit and wait, she paced back and forth. *What if they do not return? What should I do?* Anna's panic grew as the darkness deepened. *I cannot even look for them! I do not know where they have gone!* Then Anna thought she heard something and, suddenly alert, stopped her pacing and listened. Again she heard it. This time she recognized Iya's high voice as it filtered toward her out of the night. A sigh of relief escaped her. But as the sound of other voices, not those of Iya's or Erik's, reached her, she grew tense with uncertainty as she stared into the night and waited, wondering who approached their camp.

Iya stepped into the light of the fire wearing a smile, clearly not afraid. Erik followed, joined by five native men.

"Look what we found," he said jovially.

Iya's face was animated as she skipped toward Anna.

Unable to believe what she saw, Anna stood mute and waited for Erik's explanation. He seemed a little too jolly as he pointed to a stocky, middle-aged man and said, "This is Innokenti. He is the leader of the village."

The man pulled himself up to his full five-foot-six-inch height and, bowing his head slightly, said, "I Innokenti

Tungiyan." The others also bobbed their heads but said nothing.

Anna managed a small smile and returned a respectful bow.

"Looks like dinner is waiting for us. Please, sit." Erik said as he knelt down and poured a cup of hot coffee. He offered the dark brew to the tribal leader.

Innokenti accepted the coffee, looked at the other men, and motioned for them to sit. They all watched silently as Innokenti tasted the dark liquid and smiled as he downed it and returned the cup for a refill.

Anna carefully divided the meal and offered each guest a small serving of seal and potato tubers. She and Iya took their places outside the circle of men. Iya looked at her small portion and with pleading eyes, said, "I am hungry."

"Shh," Anna cautioned.

The visitors eyed their food greedily but waited until all had been served. Innokenti lifted his dish to thank the gods for their gift, then scooped a chunk of seal into his mouth. With the necessary proprieties out of the way, the native men wolfed down their meal.

Anna watched, astonished at how quickly the food disappeared. Something didn't seem right. She studied them and thought, *These men are more than hungry.*

With the edge off their hunger, the visitors sat back and belched in satisfaction.

Innokenti said, "Good." The others nodded in agreement.

"Wish I had more to offer you," Erik said as he refilled Innokenti's coffee cup.

Silence settled over the group.

Innokenti's eyes darted about as he surveyed Erik's belongings. He seemed uneasy and finally stood, nodded at Erik, and signaled for the others to follow him. Without a word, they disappeared into the darkness.

Anna stared after them, disturbed by their unusual behavior. An uneasy feeling settled in the pit of her stomach as Erik spoke.

"Their village is just over the hill. It might make a good home for you and Iya," he said as he stretched out on his bedding. "Tomorrow, we'll go and take a look." He yawned, rested his head in the crook of his arm, and closed his eyes, as if the issue were settled.

Anna said nothing. But as she stared into the dying embers of the fire, she knew she would be traveling no further with this man. The thought brought no pleasure. *Isn't this what we wanted?* she asked herself. *If so, why do I only feel anxiety?* Something was wrong.

"Anna, we live in village?" Iya asked in a small voice.

"I not know. Not time for talk. Time to sleep. We decide tomorrow."

Anna slept little and still felt edgy the following morning. She tried to push aside her uneasiness by focusing her attention on breakfast preparations, but nothing seemed to bring an end to her apprehension.

After breakfast they set out for the village on a winding trail that snaked up the cliff and down the other side into a cove. The small village sprawled out on a beach nearly identical to the one they had camped in.

Anna stood for a moment and surveyed it. There were several huts, but smoke rose from only a few and the village seemed somber. It took Anna only a minute to figure out why. There were no sounds of laughter or chatter . . . no children running and playing. It was too quiet. And although this was fishing season, the fish racks were empty; the smoke houses devoid of smoke. Something *was* wrong.

Anna tried to tell herself it had something to do with different customs, that she was worrying about nothing. But as they walked into the village it became more difficult to dismiss her doubts. The attitude of the people fueled her distress.

The villagers were unfriendly. Anna conceded that to these people they were outsiders, but it was still a very uncommon practice among the Aleuts. As she watched them, she decided, it was more indifference than hostility. Their faces looked hollow with dark circles beneath vacant-looking eyes. Most moved as if stripped of energy.

With each step, Anna became more ill at ease. She had to walk around a sightless elderly man who huddled near a crumbling hut. Her stomach tightened into knots. *He looks like he has been cast aside,* she thought, an unheard-of practice among her people. She fought the impulse to flee up the winding trail, over the cliffs, and back to the relative safety of their camp.

A young boy ran up and tried to speak to them but was quickly snatched away by his mother and reprimanded sharply for his indiscretion. Anna watched the two retreat. Iya clutched Anna's hand. She smiled down at the frightened child, trying to comfort her. Other children watched with bloated bellies and empty expressions. Anna knew what plagued these people. Starvation. *They will not let us stay,* she thought, finding some comfort in the fact.

Innokenti emerged from a nearby hut and approached them with short, quick strides. He seemed more robust than the others, but still had the sickly look of one who had not eaten enough for some time. He extended his hand in a sign of friendship and said, "Come, sit. We talk."

He led them back to his disheveled hut and motioned for them to sit but didn't offer any food or drink, which had always been the accepted custom of Anna's people. Anna thought over all that she had seen. *These people should have plenty. The sea always provides. Why do they go hungry?* She looked at Innokenti, wishing she could ask. An uncomfortable silence descended upon the group as they looked at one another and waited for someone to speak.

Erik finally ended the silence. "We've been traveling for many days. Thank you for your hospitality." Then, nodding in Anna and Iya's direction, he continued, "Their people were killed." He paused as his eyes met Anna's. Their eyes locked for a moment. He looked away before continuing, "I'm heading up to Cook Inlet and can't take them with me.

We've been searching for a place where they can stay." He received only blank stares. "A new home," he explained·

Innokenti's eyes turned cold and wary, his mouth settled into a hard line, and his air of friendship was replaced by one of mistrust and animosity.

Erik cleared his throat but held the other man's stare. "I was wondering if you could take them in. They're both hard workers, and Anna's a good flesher of hides. They will bring favor to your people."

Innokenti scowled at Erik. "My people hungry. We have no food for two more." He stood as if to leave.

Quickly Erik jumped to his feet, never taking his eyes from the other man's. "I can see you face hard times, but how can you turn your back on your own kind?" He stroked his beard and before Innokenti could interrupt, he continued, "I'll make a deal with you. You take the girls, and I'll give you the seal meat." With his eyes still trained on the village leader, Erik waited patiently.

Interest flickered in Innokenti's eyes as he considered the offer. Finally he nodded his head and said, "I talk to others." With no further comment, he turned and walked away.

Erik watched him go. "I guess that means we'll have to wait and see. Let's get back to camp." He headed back up the path with Anna and Iya close behind. They remained silent as they walked up the trail over the cliffs.

Anna was afraid. More·for Iya than herself. Her sense of peril grew as she considered their future, knowing life in this village would hold few pleasures. She mulled over the possibilities, and a dark foreboding laid hold of her. She did not want to stay.

The day dragged by. There was much to do, but work proved only a minor distraction as they waited. Erik prepared their noon meal, then called for Anna and Iya to join him.

Anna set aside the seal hide she was working on and glanced up. She wasn't hungry but forced herself to her feet and ambled toward the fire.

Iya glanced at Erik, tossed a stone into the surf, and scooted up the beach toward camp.

Erik dished out a stew made from the tubers and seal and said cheerfully, "Looks pretty good. I'm hungry. How about you?"

Anna nodded as she took her plate and sat on a nearby log.

Instead of the usual banter, they ate quietly, occasionally glancing at each other but unable to find anything to talk about. The scraping of spoons across the tin plates and an occasional crackle from the fire made the only sounds. The quiet grew so loud that it became unbearable.

Erik finally set aside his unfinished meal. "I know it's not a perfect situation here, but in time, I think they'll get back on their feet. One day it'll make a good home for you," he reasoned.

Anna glanced up at him, then looked out at the pounding surf. She wanted to tell him how she felt, that she didn't want to stay, that something was terribly wrong, that she was afraid. Instead, she turned her eyes to her plate and said nothing.

She could not ask him to continue to care for them. He had done more than she had expected already and she and Iya had been a burden far too long. They had no right to keep him from his own plans any longer. She couldn't expect more. She forced herself to finish her food and, as she gulped down the last mouthful, hoped her premonitions of peril were unfounded.

"Village bad," Iya spoke out. "They not nice."

"I think some of them had too much to drink last night, that's all," Erik tried to assuage her fears and, Anna thought, his own. "Some of the sailors along these islands sell hooch to the natives. They don't tolerate the stuff too well."

"If they take us, we stay," Anna said quietly, careful not to look up.

Erik glanced back toward the cliffs and dumped the remainder of his meal into the fire. Then, as if to convince himself more than anyone, he said, "Yeah, I'm sure everything will work out fine. Just wait and see."

The following morning, Innokenti approached the camp.

Anna stood with Iya tucked close to her. Her heart pounded hard in her chest, and she had to force herself to breathe slowly. She stood, stiff, unable to relax, and waited.

Erik looked calm as he stood and greeted the native.

Innokenti took Erik's hand briefly, then said curtly, "We think on your offer. We take woman and child, if you give food."

Anna slowly let out her breath. *So, it is to be.* She forced back her tears of alarm. *Stop being foolish. You knew this is how it would end.*

Half-heartedly, Erik answered, "That was the deal. The seal is over there." He pointed toward the drying seal meat.

Innokenti instructed his men to carry all they could back to the village.

As Anna watched the men gather the unexpected bounty, her dread grew. It was true. They would stay—Erik would go. She looked at the tall Norwegian, wanting to plead with him to take them with him. She could not. Instead, careful to keep her eyes averted, she said in a quiet, controlled voice, "Thank you for help."

Erik nodded stiffly.

Iya grasped what was happening and ran to her new friend. She hugged him tightly about the waist and cried, "You leave?"

Erik said nothing as he closed his arms about the little girl and held her tight.

She clung to him and between sobs said, "I miss you. Do not go."

Erik knelt down and gently wiped the tears from Iya's face. Unable to find his voice for a minute, he just looked at her, then finally said quietly, "I have to go." He stared at the child a moment longer, as if trying to imprint her image in his mind, then glanced at Anna. Without another word, he pushed Iya from him and loaded his supplies into the boat. He did not look back.

Anna and Iya watched as he pushed the umiak into the surf. Iya sniffled and wiped at her runny nose. Anna stared after him and blinked back her tears. Unconsciously she rubbed her fingers over the smooth surface of the walrus tooth that hung about her neck. Then, taking Iya's hand firmly in her own, she followed the men away from the beach.

Chapter 12

*E*rik paddled hard, battling to keep the umiak headed straight into the waves. If one hit him broadside he would capsize and lose all his gear.

Even as he moved away from the beach, he fought the impulse to turn around and retrieve his two companions. He had become attached to the girls in a way he had not thought possible. He glanced over his shoulder. The beach looked small, and the feeling he was leaving his family behind pulled at him. Erik turned forward to study the empty sea, straining to not look back. He plunged his paddle into the cold Pacific water and pushed forward toward an unknown destination.

This is how it should be, he thought. *Just me, God, and his creation.* He ignored the small voice that said, 'Anna and Iya are also part of God's creation. . . . A very important part.' "Life with me would be too hard for them," he argued. "They would never be happy." Then as if to convince himself that he had made the right decision, he said even louder, "I've always been a loner. Always will be. There's no reason to deny who I am. At last my life can return to normal." Except he couldn't recall what "normal" was.

As the hours passed, Erik felt lonely instead of enjoying his solitude. As he moved across the immense, empty sea, a feeling of isolation invaded his peace. The silence no longer brought tranquility. It was too quiet, too empty. He would even have welcomed the company of a cranky seabird. The shoreline had disappeared, hidden by a shroud of fog, and the distant pounding of the surf sounded muffled. He was alone; even God seemed far away.

What's wrong with me? he asked himself. *I've always been happy with my own company. Why this . . .* he searched for the right word, *loneliness?*

Erik stopped and tried to peer through the fog in the direction he thought the cove lay. His boat drifted aimlessly, but he didn't care. He thought of Anna and Iya, and a lump formed in his throat as he considered never seeing them again. Their not being a part of his life didn't seem possible. *There's no other choice,* he reminded himself. *They would never fit in. They'd always be outcasts.*

He continued to drift for several minutes. It seemed fitting, somehow, to have no direction, to be at the will of the ocean currents.

Erik brushed his hair off his face and took a deep breath. *This is silly,* he thought and tried to pull himself out of his melancholy state of mind. "They're going to be fine," he said. Grasping his paddle, he pushed against the waves and headed east.

The hours stretched by and, for a time, Erik regained some of his confidence and peace of mind. He concentrated on the future, his plans, and where he might go next. But he could not hold thoughts of Anna and Iya at bay indefinitely. Memories of the two girls rushed at him. He missed Iya's chatter, and her sweet face taunted him. Anna was ever before him, and as he considered her fierce pride and subtle beauty, a feeling of loss descended upon him. He was unable to discard it.

A dull ache settled in his chest, along with a vague sense that something was wrong, that Anna and Iya were in danger. As the distance grew between himself and his friends, so did his concern. He tried to tell himself it was just his imagination, that Anna and Iya were fine, but his uneasiness clung stubbornly.

Unable to ignore his apprehension any longer, he asked himself, *Could this be the Holy Spirit's prodding?* He reasoned with God. "I did what you asked. I took care of them. I found them a new home." But even as he excused his behavior, pictures of that home flooded his mind.

The truth stalked him like one of the sharks of the sea, but he refused to look at it. *Come on, Erik. Get a grip on yourself. You have no responsibility for those two. It's over and done with. They were part of your life for a while; now they're not.*

He paddled hard for a while, hoping pain and exhaustion would keep his mind occupied, but each stroke only served to remind him he was moving further away from the beach where he had left his friends.

The sun began to set, and Erik's energy was spent. He lay his paddle aside, leaned back, and gulped down some fresh water. As he did, a whale spouted and breached in the distance, then plunged back into the sea. Its tail rose straight into the air and, for a moment, seemed suspended as it quivered before disappearing beneath the waves.

Memories of an earlier encounter that he had shared with Anna and Iya assailed him. The excitement and joy of their unusual experience played through his mind. He remembered how Iya had reached out and touched the great beast, trusting he would not harm her, and Anna's look of shock as she watched the bold gesture. She had been so frightened. A small smile played across his face as he remembered the gift of that adventure.

Suddenly, his reflections were replaced by the same overpowering sense of anxiety that had hounded him earlier. Something was wrong. Anna and Iya were in some kind of trouble.

"All right, God!" he nearly shouted. "What's wrong? Why can't I stop thinking and worrying about them? Is something really wrong or is it just my imagination?" He hesitated and added, "Or my guilt?"

He could deny the truth no longer. He had betrayed them, let them down, and he had to go back. Fear gripped him as he saw the village for what it really was. *How could I have been so naive?* he asked himself. Aloud he answered, "I wasn't naive, just selfish. I knew what I was doing. I just didn't want to admit it. God, please forgive me. Keep them safe until I get there. Please don't let anything happen to them."

With renewed strength and a sense of purpose, he plunged his paddle into the water and turned back toward the beach. The moon was nearly full and provided enough light for Erik to navigate as he traveled toward the obscure beach, driven by a sense of urgency.

The adrenalin pumping through his body finally dwindled, leaving him spent. Erik stopped; he could push himself no further. *I will rest for just a few minutes,* he thought as he set his paddle inside the umiak and stretched his weary body out on the bottom of the boat. Exhausted, he was asleep in minutes.

The sun was high in the sky when Erik finally awakened. He felt sluggish and confused as he squinted into the bright morning light. Leaning over the side of the boat, he splashed his face with cold water, then, shivering, forced himself into a sitting position. He gazed about and downed a cup of water. Angry with himself for sleeping so long, he didn't take time to eat but forced his sore, stiff muscles back into service as he pushed his paddle in rhythmic strokes. His mind was clear now, and all he could think of was finding Anna and Iya soon.

The fog had lifted, and he searched the shoreline for familiar landmarks. *Everything looks so much alike,* he thought, his confidence waning. He glanced up at the heavens, and with a trust built on experience, said, "I need your help. You know where they are. Show me."

The hours passed, but the small bay's location remained a mystery. *If I don't find it in the next hour, I'll go back over all the coastline I've already covered,* he decided.

The sun beat down, scorching his already sunburned skin. Thirsty, he blinked up at the sky and stopped paddling. He gulped down two cups of fresh water and wiped the sweat from his brow, never taking his eyes off the shore. As he pushed the cap closed on the water jug, he saw what looked like a familiar portion of beach. He stood up and shaded his eyes, studying it more closely. "That might be it," he whispered.

Immediately, he picked up his paddle and moved closer. His heart pounded rapidly as he saw what looked like a woman sitting on the rocks. "This has to be it!" he cried as he sat forward and looked again to reassure himself that what he had seen was real. The figure of a small girl darted across the sand. "It's them," he whispered, breaking into a wide smile. His fatigue forgotten, he paddled swiftly toward the cove.

The two figures on the beach ran to the water's edge. The smaller of the two began jumping up and down, waving frantically as she entered the surf. Unable to contain her excitement as Erik drew closer, Iya continued to wave and cheer. She greeted him with a broad smile as the waves washed his boat into the shallow water. Erik eagerly jumped out and Iya catapulted into his arms, nearly knocking him back into the surf. She wrapped her arms tightly about the big man's neck, exclaiming, "You come back!"

Erik laughed and hugged her tight. "I sure have," he said, enjoying the feel of her in his arms, grateful she was safe.

Anna approached more cautiously. Instead of a smile, she wore a look of suspicion. "Why you return?"

"I was worried about you and couldn't get you off my mind." He looked down at the ground. "That's not entirely true. I knew this wasn't a good place to leave you, and I had to come back." Looking about, he asked, "Why are you down here on the beach?"

Anna's mouth hardened, and her eyes turned cold as she answered bitterly, "They take food. Force us to go. They care only about hooch."

"We watch. Hope you come back," Iya explained and hugged him again. "You did come."

"I never should have left you here. I'm sorry. There's nothing more I can say except I promise it won't happen again." He hesitated, still holding Iya close to him, and looked at Anna. "I want you to come with me. That is, if you still want to. This time we'll find some good people. We'll be very careful, and if you have any doubts, we'll just keep on looking. I promise."

Anna leveled a guarded look at Erik, then glanced back in the direction of the village. "We come with you," she said flatly.

Erik smiled. "Well, we'd better get moving." With Iya still in his arms, he waded into the water and deposited her in the umiak. Anna followed, allowing Erik to hoist her aboard.

With a quick look over his shoulder, Erik pulled himself over the side of the boat, pushed off with the paddle, and headed out to sea.

○○○○○○○○○○

"I knew I shouldn't have listened to you. At this rate, we'll never make Kenai before winter." Frank looked about and spit a wad of soggy tobacco into the nearby brush. "The leaves are already turnin' color, and I've been noticin' how cold it is at night too."

"Ah, stop your complainin'. I never made you come along. I don't remember twisting your arm," Jarvis snarled. "You can leave any time you want. I'm not stoppin' ya."

"Yeah, well, I don't feel like dyin' out here in this God-forsaken wilderness."

"What would you know about God?"

"I know enough," Frank defended. "My momma taught me."

"Yeah, I can see that," Jarvis smirked and sat on a log to rest a moment. He took his tobacco pouch from his pocket, expertly rolled a cigarette, and leaned his tall, slender frame against a tree. Nonchalantly he set the cigarette between his lips, struck a match, and lit it then took a long, hard drag on it. He leveled a cold gaze on Frank and said, "You're always whinin'. I'm sick of it. If you had any sense, you'd close your yap, or you could wake up one morning without a tongue."

Frank gaped at Jarvis, but said nothing as he plopped down in the dry leaves. He pulled out his knife and started whittling on a piece of birch. He whittled until the wood was no bigger than a toothpick before he said anything. His small eyes darted about nervously, and he licked his lips. "You know, just because you're smarter than me, don't give you any reason to talk down to me. I got feelings, too, you know."

"Yeah, don't we all," Jarvis answered, as smoke slowly streamed from his lips. "You ain't had it so bad."

"My life ain't been nothin to speak of. You know where my momma worked."

"At least you had a mother," Jarvis said, as he recalled his lonely childhood and settled into the familiar feeling of self-pity.

"That's what you call her, huh?"

Neither one spoke for a while. Jarvis flung his cigarette butt into the foliage and pushed himself up from the log. "Better get moving. We've got a long way to go."

"Well, what are we gonna do when winter sets in?" Frank asked as he scrubbed at his beard.

"Something will come up. You know my way. I believe in takin' advantage of every situation. Sooner or later, some sourdough will cross our path. I'm sure he'll want to help out two poor fellas down on their luck." He laughed mercilessly.

Frank didn't laugh. "Yeah? What are we gonna do about the snow?"

"If we get caught by the snow, we'll just find someone with a sled and take it off his hands."

Both men chuckled.

Jarvis pulled his hat snugly over his raven-black hair and headed east. Wheezing and grunting, Frank struggled to lift his rotund body off the ground and followed.

Chapter 13

*R*elief washed over Anna as they headed into the open water. Although she had no knowledge of where she and Iya would end up, and nothing about her future was clear, she was at peace. Everything seemed as it should be, at least for now. A small smile played across her lips as she glanced at Erik and Iya. She felt content. It seemed right to be together.

As the beach disappeared into the mist, she chose not to dwell on the uncertainty of life. Taking her place at the front of the boat, she picked up her paddle and, as the umiak cut through the waves, quickly returned to the rhythm of rowing.

Iya chattered incessantly, and her smile relayed her relief at having left the afflicted village behind. After a while, she stopped and asked, "I have water?"

Erik lifted the water jug and shook it. The splashing inside sounded hollow. "Not much left. Just take a sip," he said as he handed her the flask. "We'll have to ration it until we find a place to put in and refill our containers."

Iya nodded and was careful to take just one swallow.

Erik's face creased in concern. "We'll miss the seal meat. Until we have a chance to restock, everything will have to be used sparingly." A mischievous look crossed his face as he reached into his bag. Pulling out two containers he said, "I do still have my flour and sugar, so we can enjoy sourdough occasionally."

Anna smiled and Iya clapped her hands in delight.

With their growling stomachs and their thirst foremost in their minds, they scoured the shoreline looking for any safe harbor. It didn't take long before Erik spotted one and forged ashore.

When they had pulled the boat safely out of the surf, they went in search of fresh water. Anna was the first to spot the stream. "Here! I find," she called as she sprinted down a small hill. At the water's edge, she sprawled on the ground and scooped handfuls of the sweet water into her mouth then dipped her face into the cool stream. Erik and Iya were beside her almost immediately. Erik plunged his weather-worn face into the ice-cold water and drank his fill. Iya did the same, giggling and squealing as she splashed the water about.

With her thirst satisfied, Anna lay back into the grass along the bank and stared at the sky. She clasped her hands behind her head, took a deep breath, and said, "Taste so good."

Iya nodded, her eyes sparkling with pleasure as she plucked a late-blooming yellow poppy. She held the flower up to her face and touched it to her skin. "This beautiful."

Erik sat, leaning against a scraggly tree. He plucked a piece of tough grass and separated it into thin strips, then let his gaze fall upon Anna. He studied the petite young woman, taking in her thick, dark hair and lean, muscular body, momentarily forgetting to disguise his pleasure at watching her.

Anna cast a brief look in his direction, and he quickly averted his eyes. Abruptly he pushed himself to his feet. "I've got some fishing to do. Maybe you girls could round up some plants or berries," he said as he strode back toward the boat.

Anna hated to leave the tranquil spot but knew provisions were more important than rest. Besides, her empty stomach still rumbled. She pushed herself off the ground, pulled Iya up, and the two went in search of food.

"*Putske!*" Anna cried as she bent over and plucked a stock. It had been so long since she had enjoyed the tangy green plant. As a girl, she had spent many hours with her mother gathering the wild celery. As she broke several stems off close to the ground Luba seemed so near, but when Anna looked up, only Iya stood next to her. She quickly pushed aside the painful image of her mother and forced a smile as she said, "These good to eat. Also good to make poultice and medicine. Erik will like." After picking a large bunch of the wild celery, she searched for potato tubers.

"There," Anna said to Iya. "Plants with pink flowers."

Iya nodded and leapt in front of Anna in her hurry to be the first to dig the wild potatoes.

Anna frowned as she joined Iya. "Almost too late. Many dead plants. Some still live," she said as she pulled several small tubers from beneath the sprawling plant. "Enough for us. We go back now," Anna said and headed toward the beach. Along the way, they found some salmonberries and filled their baskets.

"Erik happy to see food," Iya said as she skipped down the trail ahead of Anna.

Erik was crouched next to the fire, frying a small salmon when the girls returned. Iya ran ahead and announced, "We find *putske* and potatoes and berries!" She held up her basket of berries.

"It looks like you had a pretty successful trip. I didn't do too bad myself. The fishing was good. We'll combine what we found and have quite a meal."

That evening they feasted. "What's this?" Erik asked as Anna served him some of the wild celery.

"*Putske.* It good. You try."

Cautiously Erik took a small bite. He chewed slowly and nodded his head in agreement. "Not bad. Kind of tangy."

"Very good plant," Anna explained. "Tasty to eat. Good medicine too. I will dry and save for sickness."

"What do you use it for?"

"Good for hurt throat or cough. Use for many things."

"I bet you know a lot about plants—which ones are good for medicine and which aren't," Erik said with respect.

"Mother teach many things," Anna answered a little sullenly, and gazed out over the landscape. She missed Luba. Would the hollow pain never end?

With their stores replenished, they continued their journey the next morning. The sea was calm. The swells gently rocked the boat and quietly lapped at its sides. Anna gazed over the water toward the distant shore and wondered what awaited them. Unable to keep her thoughts on the present, her mind filled with memories of her family. She felt empty and sad although she tried not to show it. She yearned to be part of a home, to belong somewhere. As she studied Iya she wondered, *What will there be for her? I am not enough.*

Iya looked up, met Anna's gaze, and grinned. Her smile showed off her large white teeth, lit up her face, and transformed her eyes into half-moons.

Anna smiled in return and longed for the naivete of childhood.

One day followed the next, blending into a steady, monotonous rhythm. The sea remained calm, and Anna found herself almost wishing a small storm would blow in to break the tediousness of the daily regimen. The constancy, however, brought with it a feeling of security. But even that could not be trusted. Anna knew complacency was dangerous, for the sea was never a safe place.

As if to remind her of its unpredictability, a dense fog settled about them. Anna felt smothered by the heavy white blanket. She had experienced fog before but never this thick on the water. On the safety of dry land, she could always find a refuge from the murky vapor. Here on the sea, she felt confused and lost. Not knowing what direction they were heading, she pulled her paddle from the water. Erik continued to row confidently, seeming to know their location.

Anna watched him for a while and finally asked, "How do you know way?"

"It's not easy. I have to stop depending on my eyes and use my ears. I keep the sound of the surf to my left," he answered matter-of-factly.

Anna listened and, sure enough, the muffled sound of waves against rocks echoed off the shore. Cautiously she returned her paddle to the water and once more matched Erik's strokes. She had confidence in him.

The weather began to change. The sea and the air around them grew colder, and Anna felt chilled much of the time. She worried about Iya, whose shivering increased despite the added protection of a sealskin coat. Erik seemed tense as darkness hung about them more hours each day. He spent time endlessly searching the shore, feeling the temperature of the water, and scanning the sky. "Is something wrong?" Anna asked more than once, but each time he assured her nothing was amiss.

She felt certain he was keeping something from her and found herself irritated with his unwillingness to trust her. *He must still think me unworthy or a child,* she thought, but she knew her feelings were unfounded. Hadn't he proved time and again that he trusted her good sense? Still, she wondered why he kept his worries to himself.

The further east they traveled, the more unfamiliar the shoreline became. Anna had known only the barren lands of the Aleutians. Here mountains thrust up from the sea and were draped with deep white pillows of snow. The shore proudly displayed forests of spruce and birch, and beneath the trees grew thickets of plants she had never seen. Anna wished she could explore and test the plants. *There is much good medicine here,* she thought.

Animals she never knew existed grazed upon the hillsides. As each was discovered for the first time, she asked Erik to name it. He patiently identified the animals for her. She came to know the caribou and moose and laughed at the antics of the fox as he pursued the hare.

This lush green scenery was something she had never known, and the pictures along the shoreline were captivating, always calling to her. She often found herself distracted, and had to be reminded to keep her eyes on the sea.

"I'm going to have to move us further into the channel if you can't keep your eyes on your work," Erik teased.

Anna laughed and made an exaggerated show of watching the waves. She knew Erik enjoyed the scenery as much as she did.

Despite his threat, he kept the boat only a few hundred feet off shore whenever possible. One morning they were rewarded by a close but safe encounter with a brown bear.

Iya saw it first and called, "Look! What is that?"

The huge animal stood on its hind legs and clawed at the bark of a spruce. Its body fat shook beneath its shimmering golden coat as it tore at the tree, unaware of its spectators.

Anna had never seen anything like it. The hairs on the back of her neck stood on end as she watched, fascinated by the magnificent creature. Its immense size and power sent shivers of fear through her body, and her heart beat fast as she whispered, "What is it?"

Erik answered in a hushed tone, "Grizzly. Foul-tempered devils. You wouldn't want to meet up with one."

Anna could not take her eyes off the animal.

Catching their scent on the wind, the bear dropped to all fours, lifted its head, and sniffed at the air. Anna sucked in her breath when the animal turned to look in their direction. It peered at them, trying to locate the source of the human scent, then nonchalantly turned and lumbered into the forest's cover.

Anna exhaled slowly and, with her voice a little unsteady, asked, "We see more?"

"Maybe. You never know. There are quite a few of them about. Just keep your distance. I've always given them a wide berth, and I've never had any trouble. But I always keep my rifle ready, just in case," Erik added as he affectionately patted his gun.

The weather grew even colder as they continued moving northeast, and Erik continued to push them as if pursued by some unseen enemy. An occasional squall kicked up but nothing bad enough to send them ashore. Anna decided she preferred the monotony of good weather. With each storm, they found themselves wet and shivering, wishing for the warmth of the summer sun or a fire. Still, each day brought new experiences, and Anna looked forward to what life sent her way. Her Aleutian home had always been unpredictable, but this country was even more so. Although Anna had never considered herself a traveler, she found she enjoyed facing new experiences. *Still,* she reminded herself, *along with the unknown comes greater danger.*

One day as she studied the shoreline, she realized this could become her home. She found the idea pleasant, so she asked, "Where we go?"

Erik stopped paddling, swept his hat off his head, and wiped his brow. "Well, I had planned on heading up to Cook Inlet." He glanced at the forbidding clouds that blanketed the sky. "But it doesn't look like the weather is going to hold. I don't think we can make it before winter sets in. It's getting pretty cold, and the snows could come any time. We'll have to find a place to spend the winter."

Shock swept through Anna. There would be no village home for her and Iya until spring? She looked at Erik, her feelings a jumble, and waited for him to explain further.

"I know this wasn't part of the plan, but I don't think we have any choice. It's too risky to try to go on. Winter's pretty unpredictable. We need to set up a place while there are still some berries to pick and plenty of fish in the rivers. As I remember, the hunting is good in this area. If we work together, we can put up a cache and build a cabin."

"We live here?" Iya asked as she pointed toward the beach.

"Well, not right here, but close by," Erik answered. "There's a small river I spent some time on last year. It can't be much further. There's plenty of timber for a cabin, and the fishing is great." He scanned the shoreline and under his breath said, "We'd better find it soon."

Anna heard his last comment and knew their situation could become desperate if they didn't locate Erik's river. She asked, "Are people at river?"

"No tribes that I know of. Once in a while a prospector wanders through." He thought for a moment and continued, "There's a tribe further up the coast. Good people, too, but I'm afraid if we try to make it, we'll be caught in the ice. The trees have already dropped most of their leaves, and the morning frost is getting heavy. I've noticed the animals are wearing heavier coats too. That's a sure sign of a hard winter."

"What is winter like?" Anna asked.

"Well, it's colder here than your home, but there's not as much wind. Once winter really sets in, there's no rain, only snow. Then it gets real cold. I've seen it so cold that a man's spit will freeze before it hits the ground."

Iya's eyes grew large, and she asked, "How you know winter come?"

Erik thought for a moment before answering, "First the wind blows cold down from the north. After that, the ground freezes up real hard and the rivers freeze solid. The ice gets so thick a man can walk across it."

"I walk on ice?" Iya asked as she reached out to touch the waves, causing the boat to rock dangerously.

"Whoa! Take it easy," Erik said steadying the umiak. "Sure. I'll take you out. It might be kind of tough for a little one, though. The snow gets pretty deep. We'll have to make you some snowshoes."

Anna remembered the time snow had piled up deep at her home and she had learned how to use snowshoes. She smiled as she recalled her first effort. As always, she had been a little cocky, certain there was nothing to it. She'd strapped the woven shoes to her mukluks and strutted across the snow. She didn't manage more than a couple of steps before she found herself face down in the cold white blanket. Embarrassed, she had needed help to right herself. She still blushed as she remembered how her family had laughed. Many nights around the evening fire they had chuckled over Anna's first attempt in snowshoes. But Anna had been determined to conquer the cumbersome shoes and, true to her nature, she did. She came to enjoy her occasional trips out into deep snow.

Erik's storytelling drew her back to the present. He talked of the local winters. "Some years even the sea freezes up solid. I've seen it so cold, a man's nose could freeze right off if he wasn't careful." A sour expression crossed his face as he went on, "You know, I don't mind the cold so much, but the dark gets to me. There are so few hours of daylight."

"Dark at beach," Iya said, proud to be able to add something to the conversation.

"Yeah, I think that's what I hate the most." His mind seemed to wander for a moment, then he said quietly, "Some years, it's just enough to survive." He rubbed his hands together. "Looks like it's going to be a cold one this year. One good thing is the animals grow heavier coats during a cold winter. If I set up a trap line, I ought to have some fine pelts come spring. Might even make enough to stake a claim somewhere."

Anna's head swam with information, and she found herself excited at the thought of spending a winter here. The long, dark months loomed ahead of her, but for some reason, they didn't seem so distasteful. In fact, she found the idea of spending more time with this strange man intriguing.

She remembered Kinauquak's baby. It would be born before they left in the spring. *How will Erik feel?* she worried, and pulled harder on her paddle. *I will not think about that now. There is much time before the snows melt,* she told herself.

They searched for the waterway, and with each passing day, Erik grew more weary, the lines of concern deepening on his face. The air took on a cold, sharp bite, and Anna often found Erik studying the clouds, as if looking for something.

The cold nights became intolerable. They needed to find shelter. Anna's worry deepened each time they went ashore in search of food; there were fewer berries, and the depth of the fallen leaves increased and their crackle grew sharper. *What will happen to us if we do not find the river?* she fretted.

A couple of days later, Anna and Iya were startled awake by Erik's shrill yell. "There it is! That's it!" He smiled happily and steered the boat toward the mouth of a river flowing into the channel.

"Anna, I'm going to need your help," he called to her, his voice sharp and tense. "It'll take both of us to move this boat upstream."

Anna positioned herself in the front of the umiak, alert and ready to follow Erik's instructions.

He shouted, "Now, when I say I want you to paddle, I mean it. You've got to give it all you have. We can only do this if we work together."

Anna nodded and held her paddle over the water.

Iya sat very still and rigid, gripping the sides of the umiak.

When Erik gave the order to paddle, Anna thrust hers deep into the water and pushed, forcing her muscles beyond what she had ever asked of them before. The water turned into a heavy chop where the creamy white tributary met the deep, shadowed ocean. She could feel the current pushing against the craft, trying to force them back into the sea. She gritted her teeth, lifted her paddle, and thrust it back into the water, fighting the strong surge.

It seemed like they fought the river for hours, but Anna knew it couldn't have been more than minutes. They slowly inched their way upstream until Erik called, "That's far enough." Pointing toward a small inlet, he said, "Steer for that sandy beach," and he turned the boat toward the shore.

Momentarily Anna felt the pressure against her paddle lessen as Erik dug in with his and pushed the boat toward the bank. Anna forced her weary muscles to obey her wishes once more, until the umiak floated into calm, shallow water and scraped along the rocky bottom. Anna finally felt the drag on her paddle relax. Erik leapt into the frigid water, and Anna followed him. Together they pulled the boat up into the tall grass that grew alongside it.

Her energy depleted, Anna dropped down into the deep grass and lay there panting. When her breathing slowed and the pain in her arms and back lessened, she sat up to survey her surroundings. It was a beautiful spot. She hugged her knees close to her, closed her eyes, and took a deep breath. The scent of spruce, alder, and birch greeted her.

She sighed, lay back down, and looked up through the branches of scraggly spruce and birch trees, standing so close they seemed to embrace. The wind blew across the tops of the trees, bending them gently and sending down a shower of leaves from the outstretched limbs of the birch. Anna made no move to avoid the flurry. She simply closed her eyes and allowed the leaves to cascade about her. One leaf landed on her face. She removed it and examined its delicate design, then reached out and stroked the smooth white bark of the birch tree's trunk. It felt cool and clean. She hoped there would be such trees growing near her home.

Erik examined the forest with a different eye. "These are strong, straight trees. They'll make a good cabin," he said as he patted a birch.

Iya sprinted through the leaves, kicking them up as she went, then, with her arms flung out from her sides, twirled about. She giggled and stopped, fighting to maintain her footing until her dizziness subsided. But she lost the challenge, plopped to the ground, and lay in the carpet of leaves, her arms extended above her head, and a smile of contentment on her face. She let out a big sigh and said, "It is nice here."

Anna smiled as she watched Iya's antics. Then slowly her smile faded as she thought of her mother and how much she would have liked it here. Tears filled her eyes as pictures of her family swept through her mind. *It still hurts so much,* she thought. *When will it stop? Please stop!* She fought to push the memories back into the hidden places of her mind, then composed herself. *I must remember. It is the only way I can hang on to them,* she decided.

Erik interrupted Anna's thoughts, unknowingly easing her pain.

"We need to build a temporary shelter and get a fire going. Iya, would you gather some wood while Anna and I work on the shelter?"

Iya jumped to her feet and went to search for wood.

"We can use spruce boughs for the roof," he told Anna as he cut off a low-hanging limb. "Could you cut some more of these while I look for larger branches for the frame?"

Anna nodded and quickly set to work, laying the cut boughs in a pile. Erik took his axe and chopped several large branches for the skeleton of the shelter. When he had enough, he hauled them back to the campsite.

After checking over the wood they had, Erik said, "Well, it looks like we're ready to put it together." He reached for one of the larger poles, and Anna bent to assist him. As they lifted the small log, Erik's hand covered Anna's. She sucked in her breath, taken off guard by the sudden contact.

Erik made no move to shift his hand as they hoisted the pole and stood it upright on the ground. They looked at each other. Erik was so close that Anna could feel his breath. For a moment, she was unaware of anything but his penetrating blue eyes. Finally, she blushed, looked away, and gently slipped her hand from beneath his.

His voice husky, Erik said, "Hold this for me while I pound it into the ground."

The moment passed quickly, leaving Anna's mind filled with questions. *Why does my stomach flutter at his touch? I am Kinauquak's. I carry his child.* She was unnerved by her feelings, and as she remembered his intense blue eyes, she couldn't deny that Erik had become more than just a traveling companion. She vowed he would never know of her feelings. They were of two worlds, and that is how they must remain.

They continued to work side by side, but there was no mention of what had passed between them. Soon they finished the shelter.

"Not bad," Erik said as he stepped back and examined their temporary residence. "It's not fancy, but it'll keep us dry until we can get the cabin finished." He glanced toward the river and said, "We'd better pull the boat further onto the shore. I'll build a rack for it later." As he headed toward the stream, he called over his shoulder, "I'll need your help."

Anna caught up to him. Because of his height, she had to take two steps for every one of his. She glanced up and said, "You walk too fast."

Erik countered, "No, you are too short."

Anna wished to debate the issue, but he grinned and went on, "Tomorrow we'll get started on the cabin. There's no time to lose; it's getting colder every day. We'll have to work harder than beavers to get it done before the first snow."

"Beavers?" Anna asked.

Erik chuckled, "Yeah, they're furry critters that live in ponds and streams. They use trees and limbs to build their homes and have a reputation for being hard workers. That's why I said we'll have to work as hard as beavers." Anna still looked puzzled. He shook his head and smiled. "Don't worry about it. You'll probably see lots of them before we leave in the spring."

A sudden gust of wind whipped Erik's hat off and carried it across the open field. He chased after it and, finally trapping it beneath his foot, stopped and put it back on his head. Grinning, he said, "No reason to worry about this old thing. All too soon I'll trade it in for a parka. Well, we'd better get to it."

After the boat had been hoisted further onto shore, Erik rubbed his hands together and said, "It's getting cold. I'm going to have to start wearing my gloves."

Anna nodded and said, "I make."

"Good, I'm sure they'll be the best pair I'll ever own," Erik said as he patted the boat. "Tomorrow I'll rub this down with some oil to keep it from cracking. It ought to last until spring." He shivered. "It's about time for a good hot fire."

After returning to camp, Anna heaped the leaves and small sticks Iya had gathered into a small pile and reached for her flints.

Erik stopped her. "No time for that tonight. I've been hoarding these," he said as he pulled a tin from his pouch, "so we've got plenty to see us through the winter. They'll make life a little easier."

Anna watched as he removed a small stick from the container. She had seen him use the fire sticks once before, when they had camped on the beach during the first storm. At the time she had been too frightened of him and too weary to care much about his strange ways, so she had said nothing. This time she was curious and watched closely.

"Here, let me show you," Erik said as he struck one of the matches against a rock. A small flame instantly flickered to life. Anna smiled, intrigued by the small miracle. Erik held the tiny fire to the leaves, and they quickly ignited.

"See how easy it is," he said as he added small pieces of wood to the fledgling fire.

Anna nodded and held out her hand. "I try?"

"Sure," Erik said as he handed her a match.

Anna examined the small stick of wood, rubbing the dark, smooth end.

"I covered them in wax," Erik explained, "to keep them dry."

Anna tentatively struck the match against the same rock Erik had, but nothing happened.

"You've got to hit it harder," Erik explained.

Anna nodded and tried again. This time the stick flared into a small, brilliant light. Taken by surprise, Anna dropped it, but quickly picked it up and watched the small flame until it burned down to her fingertips. "It is like the stars," she said softly.

Iya started jumping up and down. "I do it?"

Erik chuckled. "No, I don't think so. We'll wait until you grow some, then I'll teach you."

Iya frowned, then remembered all the wood she had gathered and proudly added some of it to the fire.

That evening, they feasted on berries and fish, then settled down for the night.

Anna looked up at the stars and stretched, thankful she was no longer cramped in the small boat. As the fire crackled and its heat warmed her face, she thought about how wonderful it felt to be warm and dry and on solid ground. She snuggled deeper into her bedding.

A fluttering sensation came from her abdomen. *The child grows. Soon I must tell Iya,* she thought, knowing her little sister would be pleased. But as she considered telling Erik, she was afraid.

She glanced back at the sky. *There is much time still,* she thought and cuddled up next to Iya.

Chapter 14

*E*rik nudged Anna with the toe of his boot. "Time to get up. There's lots to do before the snow falls."

Anna rolled over, peered up at Erik's cheerful face, and groaned. "Too early," she said as she buried her head beneath her blanket.

"Sorry, but if we don't get moving, we'll find ourselves camping in the snow. Not a pleasant thought."

Anna knew he was right and grudgingly sat up. She was still exhausted. As she leaned close to the fire to warm her hands, she wondered about her constant weariness. *The others are not so tired,* she thought as she glanced at Erik, who seemed to possess an endless supply of energy. She reached over and shook Iya.

"It looks like you're putting on a little weight," Erik said approvingly. He quickly added, "I mean, you were kind of skinny when I first met you. You're looking real good now," he finished lamely.

Thankful he had not guessed her condition, Anna smiled softly. She considered telling him the reason for her weight gain, but after a moment's consideration decided it was not yet time. "Good food," she said as she nudged Iya again.

Now fully awake, Anna lifted her arms and stretched as she stood. "I will be back," she said, and she set off for the river. The sights and smells of the forest washed over her. *It is beautiful here,* she thought, as she tried to soak it all in. The rushing sound of the river greeted her long before she stood on its bank. She knelt next to a quiet pool, bent over the water, and peered at her reflection. She studied the olive-complexioned woman who stared back at her from golden, almond-shaped eyes and liked what she saw: a woman, no longer a girl. *A woman about to have a baby,* she thought, warming at the idea. She slapped the water and the picture disappeared into quivering, ever-widening ripples.

This is a good place, she decided as she splashed cold water over her face and shivered. Steeling herself against the icy water, she dunked her hair into the river. The cold jolted her and she gasped, then quickly scrubbed and rinsed her hair before flinging it back out of the water. Her breathing didn't slow until she had squeezed out most of the excess moisture. Then she found a patch of morning sun, sat back, and combed her hair free of tangles.

Anna felt refreshed and lingered for a moment. She watched as the water washed over the shallows, tripped across rock beds, then slowed into large, deep pools. Finally it rushed on toward the sea.

Iya's greeting drew Anna out of her reverie. She looked up to find the little girl running toward her. Iya eyed the water suspiciously, then crouched along the shore and quickly rinsed her face. Shivering, she glanced at Anna and said, "It is cold!"

Anna smiled innocently, then as Iya turned away, she reached out, filled her cupped hand with the cold water, and playfully tossed it at Iya. The little girl squealed. With a bright smile and a look of mirthful revenge, she quickly reciprocated. One splash met another, and soon both were knee deep in the river, sloshing water at each other and laughing so hard they finally had to stop to catch their breath.

They were so involved in their play that they didn't notice Erik. But during a lull in their frolicking, he cleared his throat, just loud enough to catch their attention. The girls looked up at him in surprise, then surveyed each other's soaked condition. They said nothing, but looked meekly at the big man and waited to see what he had to say.

He stood along the bank with both hands planted squarely on his hips and a look of feigned annoyance on his face. "Look at you two," he said sternly. "You're both soaking wet and turning blue with the cold. Next thing you know, you'll be down sick." Unable to maintain his look of disapproval any longer, he let a small smile creep across his face, and he shook his head as an exasperated mother might when dealing with small children.

Anna and Iya glanced at each other. Then, as if they had planned it, they filled their hands with water and doused Erik before he had time to retreat.

Erik stepped back from the bank and sucked in his breath when the cold water hit him. A look of surprise spread across his face as he looked down at his drenched clothing.

Anna and Iya burst into peels of laughter. Erik tried to maintain a sense of authority and dignity in his wet condition, but finding it hopeless, joined in the gaiety.

Finally exhausted, the three waded ashore. Anna trudged up into the deep grass, suddenly aware that her wet condition made her bulging belly very conspicuous. She quickly turned away from Erik and asked, "What do we do today?"

"First I want you both next to the fire. You can dry off while you have your breakfast. After that, I was hoping you would pick some berries. Soon there won't be any left. I'm going to scout around for game."

Careful to keep her back to Erik, Anna took Iya's hand, and they went toward camp, leaving a wet trail behind. With a pelt wrapped about her shoulders for warmth, as well as to conceal her stomach, Anna stood with her back to the fire and gratefully enjoyed her breakfast. Iya did the same. Their early morning spree had given them both an appetite.

The cool air against their wet clothing sent shivers through both Anna and Iya. Anna tried hard to control her shaking, not wanting to give Erik any reason to berate her.

Erik said nothing, but a small smile played at the corner of his mouth as he sipped his coffee. After finishing his cup, he slipped his pouch over his shoulder, picked up his rifle, and said, "I won't be gone any longer than I have to. There should be plenty of game. With any luck we'll have meat for supper." He headed for the forest. Abruptly he stopped and looked back at the girls. "Don't wander too far. It's easy to get lost." With that, he turned and disappeared into the heavy brush.

Silently, Anna and Iya watched him go. Anna turned to warm the front of her tunic and let the pelt slide from her shoulders.

With their clothing only partially dry, Anna and Iya reluctantly left the warmth of the fire. There were berries to pick. Trying to ignore their discomfort, they each took a basket and went in search of the much-loved fruit. Anna moved cautiously through the underbrush as they explored, always aware of danger, and she marked their trail so they could find their way back. They soon found a large patch of berries.

Anna examined the fruit carefully. She had never seen these shiny red droplets that hung from weak, drooping vines. She plucked one and rolled it between her fingers. It was firm and smooth. It looked edible, but the only way to know for certain was to taste it. Anna took a small bite, bracing herself against bitterness, but was rewarded by a sweet juiciness. She smiled, popped the rest of it into her mouth, looked at Iya, and said, "Berries taste good."

Anna stripped the long green vines of their fruit, quickly filling her basket. Iya worked more slowly.

Anna found it hard to keep her mind on her labors. The forest was filled with smells and sounds she had never known. Squirrels' shrill voices filled the air as they ran about gathering stores for winter, scampering up trees, and disappearing into their winter burrows. The few birds that had not yet flown south flitted from tree to tree, calling to one another as they perched in the alders and birches.

The sun's rays stretched down through the trees, chasing away the forest shadows and illuminating the dust and insects that floated on the air. The wind whispered across the tops of the trees, sending down the last yellow leaves of the season.

Anna breathed deeply of the damp, musky fragrance that permeated the thicket, fighting her desire to run through the deep grass and romp among the sweet-smelling groves. Instead, she forced her hands to remain busy.

When she had finally filled her basket, she considered helping Iya with hers but decided she could stop for a moment and enjoy her surroundings. She glanced about at the evergreens and alders and wondered how the trees grew. Her senses brimmed with the fragrant scent of spruce mingled with the soft, sweet smell of her berries. *This is the most restful place I have ever known,* Anna decided. Somehow her troubles seemed smaller here in the forest. Almost anything could be possible. Maybe she could even find peace.

Anna pulled herself back from her daydreaming, and she helped Iya fill her basket. There were more berries than she had anticipated, and as she turned to tell Iya they would need to return to camp and empty their baskets, she thought she heard something. More precisely, she felt a presence.

The tranquility she had known only moments before fled. In its place she felt uncertainty and fear. Anna knew they were not alone. The hair on the back of her neck stood on end as she watched and listened. Fear gripped her, and her breathing became shallow and rapid.

Iya began to speak, but Anna shushed her. The little girl sensed her sister's anxiety and came closer. Anna strained to hear, but only the sounds of the forest greeted her. She peered into the thicket to see what hid there.

Without warning, an enormous brown bear rose to its back legs and towered above the bushes. No more than twenty-five feet from Anna, it glared menacingly in her direction.

Anna had never known such fear.

The bear's mouth opened, exposing large canine teeth, and its nose twitched as it sniffed the wind, trying to identify the intruders. Its small brown eyes searched, and its huge front paws clawed at the air. Again, it tested the breeze. Then its eyes met Anna's. For an endless moment they stared at each other. Neither moved. Anna held her breath. Her mind screamed, *Run!* But something held her steady.

Iya pushed closer to Anna.

The bear studied them. It snarled menacingly and dropped to the ground. Locking its front legs, it threw its weight forward and bounced twice, then blustered at Anna. It stood again, snarling and snapping at the air.

Anna forced herself to remain still, taking slow, shaky breaths. Her eyes never left those of her enemy. With her heart pounding in her chest, she gripped Iya close.

The bear threatened them twice more, then, as if bored with the whole thing, sniffed the air and lumbered off into the bushes.

Anna held her ground for several minutes, afraid to move, fearful that the bear was hiding in wait, ready to pounce at the slightest sign of weakness. Only after she was certain it had gone did she force herself to breathe deeply and relax. She crushed Iya to her, scooping the little girl into her arms, and allowed tears of relief to spill down her cheeks. Anna walked with shaky legs back to camp, still carrying Iya.

Every few minutes she glanced at the trail behind her to reassure herself that the animal had not followed. By the time she reached camp, she nearly collapsed, exhausted physically and emotionally. She forced herself to stay on her feet and build a fire. She pulled Iya close and huddled near the flames, watching the forest and wishing Erik would return.

It took some time before Anna's heart slowed to a normal pace. Although she finally managed to relax, she remained alert and watchful. Her mind played the scene over and over again. She wished it would stop. Then she remembered the baskets. She moaned. Overwrought by fear, she had forgotten them at the thicket.

Iya looked up when her sister moaned.

Her voice heavy, Anna told her, "We left the baskets." Wishing for another alternative, she added, "I must get them."

Iya shook her head no.

"I must go," Anna said as she set Iya away from her. "You stay close to the fire. I will be back." She hurried off after the forgotten baskets.

Anna crept soundlessly through the forest, listening for anything unusual, sniffing the wind, and watching for the great bear. Gratefully she located the baskets without any further confrontations. With one quick glance about the clearing, she snatched the berries up and raced back through the woods to the relative safety of camp.

The moment she saw Iya, she was sorry she had left her. The little girl's face was ashen gray and etched with fear. She had curled herself into a tight ball and backed tight against a tree. When she spotted Anna, relief spread across her face as she jumped to her feet, ran to her sister, and hugged her about the waist. As she did so, Anna realized Iya could no longer reach completely around her swollen waistline and remembered she would have to tell Erik soon.

"We are safe," she comforted Iya. "The bear is gone."

The sharp sound of a snapping twig followed by the crackling of leaves and brush came from the woods. Something was out there! Anna looked about for a weapon, and her eyes fell upon the shaman's spear. Just as she raised the weapon in the air, Erik emerged from the shadows.

He looked tired but content and carried a small animal across his shoulders. As he took in the fear written on Anna's face and the spear in her hand, his smile faded.

"What happened? What's wrong?" he asked. "You two look like you've seen a ghost."

Anna laughed with relief. "We thought we both be ghosts," she answered. "We pick berries and bear come. He look at us and beat ground, but not hurt us. Afraid he follow."

Erik slid the animal from his shoulders and glanced back into the woods. "I figured we'd be visited sooner or later. I just hoped it would be later, after the cabin was built." He sat on a stump next to the fire and thought for a moment before continuing. "I suppose if he'd wanted to cause trouble, he would have. You know, I've heard stories of Indians who talk to the bears. They say if the bear feels you're a friend, he won't attack. I don't know if I believe all that, but I tell you if I found myself in a tight situation, I'd try anything. Don't think we have anything to worry about. All the same, I'll feel better after the cabin is up. First thing tomorrow, we start."

The following morning they prepared the cabin site, and Erik began cutting timber. The next several days passed quickly with little time for thinking or rest.

Erik was good with an ax, felling one tree after another. Anna and Iya stripped away the limbs and heavy bark. The girls also gathered more berries and other edible plants and roots, always watchful for foraging bears.

After the trees were cut and stripped, Erik hauled them to the building site. To assemble them, he notched each, then stacked them one upon the other, pounding them together with wooden pegs. As the walls grew taller, it became difficult to hoist them into place. He angled a log at each end of the cabin wall and, with Anna's help, rolled the timbers up the incline and into position. It worked well, and they made four secure walls.

The roof was the next hurdle. First Erik built a steeply pitched frame, then he cut shakes from the remaining trees. He lay these across the frame, careful to overlap each, and notched them together to prevent rain or melted snow from seeping through.

Iya and Anna gathered moss and mud to fill the gaps between the logs, forming an airtight seal to keep out the cold winter wind.

Erik had left a four-foot gap at one end of the small cabin. Anna wondered why but, not wanting to appear foolish, didn't ask. Erik answered her question one afternoon when he asked her and Iya to gather stones from the riverbed.

Anna asked, "What for?"

With his arm stretched toward the gap, Erik answered, "They'll make a fine fireplace."

Anna considered what he had said for a moment, then as understanding dawned on her, she smiled and led Iya to the water. It took many trips to and from the riverbed. Each time Anna would stop to rest, she watched Erik expertly mortar the rocks with mud. Slowly a fine fireplace with a strong chimney took shape. Anna didn't mind the work, grateful for the assurance of warmth during the cold months that lay ahead.

Erik worked hard, spurred on by the ever-present threat of winter. As soon as he finished the fireplace, he immediately set to work fashioning a rough door of spruce poles hinged with strips of hide.

After hanging the door, he stepped back, removed his hat from his head, and wiped the sweat from his brow. "Not bad," he said examining his work.

Anna approached with a container and asked, "You like drink? Fresh water." With the jug tucked under her arm, she extended a cup of the cold liquid to him.

"Thanks," Erik said as he gratefully accepted and quickly drained the cup. "Ah, that tastes good." He held out the mug and asked, "A little more?" As he drank, he eyed the cabin critically. "It won't win a beauty contest, but it should keep out the cold. I'll have to fit the window after I get the cache up." He looked up at the gray sky. "By the looks of things, we don't have long to wait. I'd better get started on that cache if we're going to have any food stores. Once the cold weather hits, the animals will make short work of our labors." He stopped and thought for a moment. "Tomorrow I want to do some more hunting, but I'm going to need several poles for the cache. Could you and Iya cut the limbs for me while I'm gone?"

"We can," Anna answered as she turned and studied the cabin. A small smile settled across her lips as she remembered her secret. She remarked, "This is good house. It will keep us warm." She placed her hand over her stomach and thought of the child.

Erik looked at her quizzically and asked, "Is everything all right?"

Anna said, "Yes," then turned to gather boughs for the cabin floor. *I must tell him,* she thought. *Soon he will know even if I do not say.*

Erik retrieved his fishing pole and said, "I think I'll do some fishing. The river could freeze up any time, and we still don't have enough to see us through the winter."

Anna nodded, only half aware of what he had said, for a faint fluttering in her abdomen pushed away all other distractions. *It is the child! Kinauquak's and mine!* A blush spread across her face. She smiled again as she thought of the baby who was part of Kinauquak and part of her, who would carry on the heritage of her people.

Chapter 15

J'm sure glad that's done," Erik said as he stood back and studied the food cache. He turned to Anna and asked, "What do you think of it?"

Anna looked up at the odd little house on stilts and answered simply, "It is strong."

"I never liked having to climb a ladder to collect my dinner," Erik said. "But around these parts, we have no other choice."

"Why no choice?" Anna asked.

"Animals get hungry just like us. Once we get into winter, there'll be wolves, lynx, and other scavengers looking for a handout, and they won't ask. If we store our meat where they can get at it, they'll rob us blind."

Anna only nodded as she gazed at the new building. She had never seen one before. At the beach, they'd had no real predators and had never worried about food thievery.

A familiar thumping sound caught her attention. She glanced back at the cabin and found Iya hanging halfway out the new window. The shutter banged back and forth as she tottered. This was a new game Iya liked to play, and Anna had reprimanded her for it more than once. Out of patience, she called sharply, "Iya! Stop!"

Iya glanced up at Anna and quickly pushed herself back inside, allowing the slatted window to slam closed behind her. A moment later, she appeared at the door.

"Iya, I tell you many times not play on window."

"She's just being a little girl," Erik defended. "It's normal for kids to climb on things."

Anna glared at him. "I decide what Iya do."

Iya skipped to Erik's side and hugged his leg as she peered up at Anna.

Seeing she was outnumbered, Anna swallowed her reproach, turned on her heel, and headed for the river.

It was no small task to lay in a supply of firewood adequate for a long Alaskan winter. As the days grew shorter and colder, Erik cut and split wood from the earliest light until dark. Anna was impressed by his diligence. She'd met few men who worked so hard and did so cheerfully.

Anna and Iya stacked the cut wood, and Erik started to make a smokehouse. It was much easier to build than either the cabin or the cache and took only a couple of days to erect. It would provide months of mouth-watering smoked meats and fish.

Several times a week, Erik traveled into the surrounding countryside in search of meat. His assumption that the hunting would be good had been correct, and he rarely returned empty-handed.

One morning as he pulled on his boots, he said, "I don't think I'll do any more hunting until the weather turns cold. We've got plenty of game smoking already." He slipped on his coat. "We could use more fish, though. Before the river freezes, I figure I'd better do some extra fishing. Once it gets cold enough, I'll hunt some larger game that we can freeze. Smoked meat tastes good, but I sure do like a piece of fried caribou or moose on a cold winter night."

"We always smoke meat," Anna argued. "Not freeze it."

"Well, I guess it's time you learned something new," Erik countered with a grin. He stepped outside before Anna could respond.

As the nights grew longer, Erik used the hours to work with some of the spare wood. Anna watched, uncertain of what he was doing, but when she asked, he only smiled and said, "You will see."

One afternoon, with a look of satisfaction on his face, Erik pushed open the cabin door and deposited his wooden creation in the center of the room. He smiled and asked, "Well, what do you think?"

Anna examined the contraption and asked, "What is it?"

Erik quickly stepped around to the front of it and sat down, crossed his legs, then his arms, and leaned back, looking very smug. "It's a chair. You've never seen a chair?"

Anna only stared at him while Iya walked over to the piece of furniture, ran her hands over the smooth wood, and asked, "Can I sit?"

"Sure," Erik said hopping to his feet.

Iya quickly took his place and, with her feet dangling, sat back with a smile.

"I'd better make a smaller one for you," Erik said as he tweeked Iya's nose.

After that, one rustic chair followed another, until they each had one. Anna didn't find the seats very comfortable but tried to use them anyway, not wishing to dishonor Erik's efforts.

Last Erik made a large, sturdy table to join the other furniture, which took up residence in the center of their winter home. Anna appreciated the work space it provided, making it simpler to cook, but didn't understand the need to sit around a table to eat. However, since Erik seemed comfortable with this custom, Anna obliged him without complaint.

Next Erik designed a sturdy metal arm. He hinged its center and, after mortaring it into the stone fireplace, hung a cooking pot from it, which he gently pushed over the fire. "See, this way your food doesn't have to sit right in the hot coals. Things cook more slowly and don't burn." Anna studied the device with a puzzled look, while Erik continued, "The food will taste better."

A smile crept across Anna's face as she grasped the concept. "This is very good," she said and thought to herself, *Much better than a chair.*

Erik had brought many interesting ways with him. Some Anna found impressive, but she rarely doled out praise. She kept her thoughts to herself.

The task of preserving the fish and meat went primarily to Anna, with Iya as a willing helper. After filleting the game, she dried it in the sun, then hung it in the smokehouse. The smell of cooking meat floated in the air, making Anna's mouth water as she thought how good the salmon would taste during the long months of darkness.

The smell wafted across the meadow and into the forest. They all kept a close watch for would-be marauders who might be tempted by the aroma. Erik kept his rifle close and was unusually strict about Anna and Iya staying close to the cabin.

The furs generated by Erik's hunting would provide protection for the cold winter weather. Anna worked endlessly, fleshing and softening the hides.

One afternoon Iya begged, "Please, teach me."

"You are too little. This is hard," Anna tried to explain. But Iya continued to pester her until one day, against her better judgment, she laid her work aside and said with a sigh, "I will teach you."

Iya leaned close to Anna and watched as her older sister took the rounded side of the fleshing stone firmly in her hand, lay the sharp edge of it along the inside of the pelt, and in short, even strokes, scraped away the thin layer of fat and sinew. Anna explained each step as she went, then handed the little girl her own stone and said, "You try."

Gingerly, Iya mimicked what she had seen Anna do. But the fat clung stubbornly to the pelt. After several attempts, she dropped the hide and stone onto Anna's lap and said with a pout, "It does not work."

Anna patiently picked up the fleshing tool and hide and put them back into Iya's hands. "It will take time. Fleshing hides is not easy. You must not quit."

Iya just stared at her for a moment, then with renewed determination tried again. Eventually she conquered the difficult task and, to Anna's surprise, proved an adept pupil. After some practice, she worked alongside Anna and produced cleanly fleshed pelts.

Anna fashioned the fleshed and softened hides into tunics and parkas for the cold months ahead. In the winter, they wore fur against their skin for added warmth, and Anna took great pains to ensure they were well ventilated to prevent sweating. She fashioned boots from caribou hides and lined them with rabbit fur. At the top of each, she punched holes for lacings, so they could be cinched tight, preventing snow from getting inside and freezing the feet.

The last of the berries were harvested with no further interruptions by bears. Anna never forgot that meeting and always watched for unwelcome visitors. It was not yet cold enough to freeze the fruit, so she placed the berries in rendered fat where they would remain fresh. In the months to come, they would be a rare treat. She stored the tubers in the cache but knew they would lose their fresh flavor once they froze. It would be months before the three companions could enjoy the taste of fresh fruits or vegetables again.

The nearby beach had generously offered up a plentiful supply of seaweed. As always, Iya turned up her nose at the seagrass, but Anna was thankful to have it, knowing they would need it during the long winter. They had also found abundant mussels and clams. Some they steamed open and ate; others they smoked and preserved in oil for later use.

Anna felt a sense of accomplishment as she watched their stores mount up, confident that there would be plenty to eat and they would be warm and dry.

Iya, on the other hand, had grown weary of the labor. In their home on the beach, she, like the other children, had played most of the time and carried very little responsibility. One day as she helped Anna dig for clams, she sat on the rocky sand and pouted.

Anna noticed her disgruntled appearance and asked, "What is wrong, Iya?"

"I am tired," the child answered petulantly. "Too much work." She propped her chin in her hands. "No play. No children." Her eyes suddenly filled with tears.

Anna knew that she had asked much of the little girl. She stepped over the small rocks and slipped her arm around Iya's shoulders. Gently she said, "Iya, I know you miss friends. You play little and work hard. I am proud of you. But soon winter will come. We will have much time play games and tell stories."

Iya glanced up at Anna and pushed herself back to her feet, returning to the chore of scanning the beach for signs of clams.

The days grew even shorter, the frost thicker, and ice rimmed much of the river. An occasional piece broke free and tumbled downstream, only to become a part of the frozen waterway once more. The trees stood naked, reaching their empty limbs toward the sky as if to gather the last bit of fall sunshine. They appeared dead, but sap still flowed within.

Erik and Anna watched the sky, waiting for the first snowfall. They knew it would come soon, and tension grew as they waited. Anna found herself snapping at a whining Iya, while Erik withdrew and spent much of his time setting trap lines and hunting.

Although they had waited expectantly for winter, when it finally arrived, it took them by surprise.

One morning, after finishing a breakfast of grilled mussels and dried fruit, Erik drank the last of his coffee, then shrugged into his coat. Lifting his rifle from its rack, he walked toward the door. "I won't be long," he said as he reached for the latch. A blast of cold arctic air forced the door open and swept into the room.

Erik pulled his coat more tightly about himself, slipped his hood over his head, and looked at the bleak landscape. He peered up at the gray sky and said, "Looks like a cold day. There might even be some snow in these clouds." He pushed his way into the bitter cold and pulled the door shut behind him.

As the wooden latch dropped into place, it made a hollow sound, and Anna's stomach tightened in apprehension. She loosened the window clasp, lifted the shutter, and peeked out. As she watched Erik disappear into the woods, she shivered and glanced at the solid gray sky. The weather looked ominous, and she was afraid for Erik as he left the cabin.

The wind whipped through the open window, blowing Anna's hair about wildly and biting at her face. She leaned into the cold and forced the window shut. The room fell silent as she locked the storm out.

Anna rested her back against the wall, and a feeling of oppression settled over her. She shivered and clutched her cloak close and lit the oil lamp, hoping it would brighten the gloomy cabin. She set another log on the already-hot fire, trying to force the chill from the room.

Although she had waited anxiously for winter's arrival, Anna felt depressed. The reality that she would not hear birds singing or see bright flowers or take walks in the forest for many months—and that darkness would rule most of each day—overwhelmed her.

Restless, Anna moved about the cabin. She tidied up the room and rinsed the few dishes left from their morning meal. With nothing more to do, she turned to Iya and said, "Help me bring in wood."

They slipped their warm parkas over their heads, pulled their hoods tight about their faces, and stepped into their heavy winter boots. Iya was the first to the door. As she stepped out, she exclaimed, "Snow!"

Anna joined her. As she peered out to find large, soft flakes falling from the sky, she felt her depression lift. She pushed the door wide, almost laughing at the sight of snow. Winter had arrived! *I had forgotten how bright the snow is,* Anna thought and breathed a sigh of relief.

She followed Iya into the white shower. Tipping her head back, she allowed the soft wet flakes to fall upon her face. They felt cold and damp, and they quickly melted against her warm skin. She opened her mouth and caught one on her tongue. Exhilarated, she laughed and spread her arms wide as she twirled in slow circles.

Iya mimicked her, spinning more quickly until she became dizzy and staggered, nearly falling. Giggling, she sat on the ground and waited for the earth to stop pitching.

Anna forgot her earlier doubts about winter, pushing them aside in her excitement and joy at the fresh snow, the clean bite in the air, and the brightness, not darkness, that surrounded her.

Anna and Iya celebrated with a dance of thanksgiving then sat quietly among the trees and watched as the brilliant white snow piled up. After a while, the cold crept through their clothing, putting an end to their restful observations.

Abruptly Anna stood and said, "Today we will bathe." She retrieved Erik's metal bucket from where it hung just outside the cabin door and carried it to the river.

Dipping the pail into the partially frozen water, Anna half filled it and hauled it up the bank. She slowly shuffled back to the cabin, trying not to spill any.

Anna blushed as she remembered how Erik had taught them about his weekly custom of bathing. One evening after supper, he had said, "You know, among my people it is normal to bathe at least once a week." Anna had said nothing. He continued, "I know it's not customary for you to wash your bodies, but because you don't, you have an unusual odor."

"We do not smell bad. It is wrong to wash body. To remove oil from body is bad," she explained. She folded her arms across her chest and stated flatly, "We will not wash."

Erik had tried to be tactful and had already been more than patient with them. He refused to let another day go by without their bathing, so in a stern voice had said, "You will take a bath. Even if I have to strip you bare and do it myself." He had approached Anna menacingly as if to carry out his threat.

Anna had surrendered, and since that time, weekly baths had become a ritual. She had actually grown accustomed to them. Iya, however, still complained bitterly each time she had to bathe. Anna hoped she would not mind so much now that they could no longer wash in the river.

Anna set the bucket over the heat, and said firmly, "Erik is gone. We will bathe," making it clear that Iya had no choice.

After the water had heated, she stripped off Iya's clothing, dipped a cloth in the water, and washed the wiggling little girl. Iya shivered and grimaced at her.

Bracing herself, Anna wet Iya'a hair and washed it with soap. Iya weaved and dodged, trying to avoid Anna's new commitment to cleanliness, but in the end, she lost the battle and, despite her efforts, found herself clean.

Anna looked down the front of her soaked tunic. "Why you fight? You will not win," she said with a smirk. She toweled Iya dry, and patted the little girl's bare bottom as she trotted off to put on warm clothes.

After refilling the bucket with clean water, Anna slipped off her own clothing carefully to hide her bulging stomach and washed herself with lukewarm water. She still hadn't told Iya about the baby but knew she would soon have to.

The water had grown cool, and Anna couldn't keep from shivering as she washed. Finishing as quickly as possible, she donned a clean tunic and added another log to the fire in an attempt to ward off the cold. She sat down on the fur-covered floor near the fire, combed out her hair, then braided it into a thick plait. Iya's hair was next.

"You make mine like yours?" Iya asked as she plopped down on the floor in front of Anna.

"Yes," Anna said as she combed out the snarls and wove it. Iya's hair wasn't as thick as Anna's, but it still made a respectable braid.

Anna used the remaining bathwater to wash their clothing. She hung the clothes up to dry before the fire and, still feeling chilly, donned a cloak and sat close to the flames.

As the wind howled outside the cabin, she and Iya chanted an ancient tribal song, rocking and clapping their hands to the beat. A sudden gust of wind whistled down the chimney and blew smoke and ashes into the room. Startled, Iya scooted closer to Anna and glanced around with frightened eyes as the storm beat against the door and buffeted the cabin.

Iya shivered as she asked, "Is Erik safe?"

Anna watched the ceiling as a blast of wind threatened to strip the roofing away. She asked herself the same question but answered Iya confidently. "He is fine."

She opened the window a bit and peered out. What she found frightened her. The temperature had dropped sharply, and the snow no longer fell in soft flakes but was driven diagonally by the gale. It pelted the landscape and covered the grass and bushes as it drifted. The tree boughs already bent beneath its weight.

Anna tried not to worry, reassuring herself that Erik could take care of himself, but she couldn't keep her fear completely at bay. Half aloud she said, "Please come back." She paced about the cabin as she waited. Tiring, Iya cuddled up on her furs and slept. Occasionally Anna glanced at her and wished she, too, could find comfort in sleep. It was no use. She knew she would be unable to rest until Erik returned.

What can I do for him? she asked herself. *Something he would not expect.* She searched her mind for ideas. He had often talked of his mother's sourdough bread and how much he loved it. *That is it. I will make bread.* She smiled as she thought of how pleased Erik would be when he returned to the smell of baking bread.

After placing a pot of fish stew over the fire, she set to work. She knew where Erik kept the starter. She had some qualms about using any of their precious supply of flour and sugar, but the picture of Erik's pleasure when he found warm, fresh bread waiting for him prompted Anna to go ahead with her plan.

She tried to remember each step Erik had taken when he had made sourdough bread. She had watched him a few times and was certain it couldn't be too hard. It seemed simple.

She scooped out some of the starter and placed it in a pot then added a small amount of flour and water. Using the large wooden spoon Erik had crafted from an alder branch, she mixed the three ingredients thoroughly, scattering a fair amount of flour in the process. Finally she set the dough near the fire to rest. Erik had always waited a while before cooking the bread.

Anna's activity had awakened Iya who stood nearby to watch the process. "What do you make?" she asked.

"Bread," Anna answered with assurance.

Iya looked at the gooey mixture suspiciously but said nothing.

Anna knew it didn't look quite right but didn't know how to fix it, so she turned her attention to cleaning up the mess she had made and hoped for the best.

Iya pointed at Anna's face and laughed.

Puzzled, Anna asked, "Why do you laugh?"

Iya smothered her laughter and said, "You have a white face."

"Oh," Anna said and did her best to wipe away the flour.

Iya chuckled. "Still white."

Anna scrubbed at her face again. "Am I clean now?"

Iya nodded.

"Good," said Anna as she wiped her hands and reached to stir the stew. As she leaned over the pot, she felt the familiar fluttering and tiny jabs in her abdomen. She closed her eyes and lovingly rested her hand on her enlarged stomach. *This is a good time to tell Iya,* she thought. *Soon she will know the secret without my telling.*

She sat cross-legged on the floor next to the hearth, patted the ground next to her, and said, "Iya, come sit."

Eager to oblige, Iya skipped across the room and cuddled next to her older sister.

Anna took a deep breath and began, "Iya, I have a surprise. I know this for a long time, but I wait for right time to tell you." She hesitated, choosing her words carefully. "You know Kinauquak and I promised to each other. Yes?"

Iya nodded and with a puzzled look on her face waited for Anna to continue.

Anna's chin quivered and her voice shook a little as she said, "Kinauquak and I love each other." She swallowed past the lump in her throat. "We show our love. Now baby will come soon."

Iya looked up at Anna, still puzzled. But as what Anna had said began to make sense to her, she grinned. Gently she touched Anna's stomach and asked, "Baby? You have baby?"

"Yes," Anna nodded and smiled.

"How soon will it come?"

"When the snow melts, I think," Anna answered, and her eyes filled with tears as she thought of all that could have been. The familiar pain spread across her chest and settled in her throat. She could say no more.

Iya seemed to understand Anna's pain and silently rested her head on her sister's abdomen. After a few minutes she asked, "Do you still hurt when you remember?"

Anna nodded.

Iya nestled closer. "I miss Inoki. Mother. Father." Tears spilled down the little girl's cheeks. "Will hurt stop?"

Slowly Anna shook her head no. "It will always hurt. But one day not so much."

"Erik know of baby?" Iya asked.

"No. Do not tell. I will say when time is right." But she wondered if the time would ever be right. She was afraid of Erik's reaction. How would he feel about a child born beneath this roof, a native, another mouth to feed?

A sudden blast of wind shook the small cabin, reminding Anna that Erik was still out in the storm. She lifted the window latch. The wind was still strong, blowing the snow in a frenzied dance. The snow blinded her view. *He will come soon,* she told herself as she closed the window and went to check the simmering stew. It looked good and filled the room with a pleasant fishy aroma.

"I am hungry," Iya whined.

Anna pushed the pot back over the fire and said, "After I make bread, we will eat." Quietly she added, "Maybe Erik will be back." They both glanced toward the door, wishing it would open and a smiling Erik would fill the threshold. But it only rattled against the wind.

The bread dough had risen and spilled over the sides of the pot. *This looks wrong,* Anna thought as she dumped the sticky mess onto the table. She added more flour to the mixture, hoping that would help, then kneaded the dough for several minutes. It felt heavy and looked odd. Deciding more kneading would be useless, she placed the dough back in the pan and set it in the hot coals to cook. She sat and watched it for several minutes, but instead of rising into a smooth rounded loaf, it just sat flat and lifeless in the pan.

Something is *wrong,* Anna thought, but there was nothing she could do, so she allowed the bread to cook as long as she dared. When it looked as though it would burn, she removed it from the heat. After letting it cool slightly, she tipped it out onto the table, where it sat looking pathetic and overcooked. The heavy bread didn't even resemble Erik's loaves. Unwilling to waste even the worst food, she cut into it.

Just as she removed the first tough slice, the door blew open, and Erik hurried in. He quickly pushed the door closed behind him and shrugged off his coat. Removing his hood, he bent over to shake the frozen particles of snow and ice from his hair and beard. As he pulled off his gloves, he said, "What a storm! I was beginning to wonder if I'd make it back today."

He strode across the room to the fire and leaned close to the flames, holding out the palms of his hands to warm them.

"There is coffee," Anna said as she poured him a cup.

Erik accepted the hot beverage gratefully and, holding the cup between both his hands, sipped it slowly, allowing the hot brew to warm his insides. He smiled and said, "That's just what I needed. Thank you." He turned his back to the fire and his clothes began to warm; moisture rose from his body in a soft mist.

Iya giggled and pointed at the steam.

"I didn't dress warm enough and got wet. It's only thanks to God I'm even here. Something sure smells good." He peeked into the stew pot and asked, "Fish stew?"

Anna nodded.

He eyed the bread and added, "Looks like you've been busy."

Embarrassed by her failure, Anna ignored the comment and quietly set out the plates and utensils. Cradling the hot pan of stew in a heavy cloth, she placed it in the center of the table beside the sad-looking bread.

Erik refilled his empty cup and asked, "Anyone want some coffee?"

Anna and Iya both refused. "Boy, am I hungry," he said as he set the coffeepot back on the hearth and joined them for dinner.

Resting his elbows on the table, he bowed his head. "Lord, thank you for guiding me home safely and for taking care of the girls while I was away. Please bless Anna and Iya for all their hard work and for preparing such a fine meal. And thank you for loving us. Amen."

Anna had grown accustomed to Erik's ritual of praying before meals. She just wished he would stop bringing her name into it. Each time he did, her heart beat a little faster. She never felt right having him take her before his God. After all, she hated him and had decided she could trust in no one but herself. She wished Erik would stop his praying, but he seemed somehow connected . . . as if God were a part of the man, and she knew she couldn't ask him not to pray.

"Looks good," Erik said as he filled a bowl with stew for each of them.

Anna ladled the soup into her mouth and watched in amazement as he sawed two slices of bread from the loaf and, without the least bit of hesitation, took a bite. He chewed slowly and swallowed, then took another bite, never uttering a word of complaint or disappointment. After finishing his first slice, he tackled the stew and said, "Good."

Anna knew the bread was awful, but if Erik could stomach it, so could she. She cut herself a slice and reluctantly took a bite. It was hard and slightly burned tasting, but she forced herself to eat it, never saying a word about the poor quality.

Iya, on the other hand, wasn't concerned with sparing Anna's feelings, and as she bit into hers, complained, "This is hard. It taste bad." Theatrically, she set it aside and glowered at Anna.

Erik interceded. "There's a first time for everything. If we don't try, we won't learn. I think Anna did a good job for her first attempt. I figure the next time she makes bread, it'll be perfect." With that he dipped his second slice into his stew and devoured it.

Once more, Erik had managed to confuse Anna. *The bread is awful, yet he eats it. Why?* She had no answers, but her heart warmed toward him as she considered his kindness. No matter how much she fought her feelings of affection, his continued graciousness overruled her head, and she was unable to stifle the tenderness she felt when she thought of him.

She sat a little straighter in her chair and decided, *Next time he cooks, I will watch closer. One day I will make good bread for him.*

Erik leaned back in his chair and said, "Even in this awful storm, I managed to bring down a moose. He's a big one and should keep us in meat for some time. I quartered him but had to leave most of the meat hanging from a tree because I could only carry one portion. I'll have to go back for the rest tomorrow. He should be frozen solid by then. Well, I'd better get the hind quarter butchered before it freezes hard as a rock." He pushed himself away from the table.

"I will help," Anna said.

Erik nodded and helped her into her coat. Together they went to butcher the meat.

Chapter 16

*A*nna set aside her sewing and listened to the storm that raged outside. For two days they had been forced to stay inside their small cabin. But Anna didn't really mind. She'd grown accustomed to the winter onslaught and felt secure closed in against the storms. She glanced at Erik, who skillfully repaired a damaged trap.

"That's all for tonight," he said, sounding relieved as he set the trap aside. He pushed himself away from the table and got his Bible. After refilling his cup with coffee, he settled back into his chair and opened the small, worn book.

Almost immediately Iya was at his side. She leaned on the table and watched quietly as he read. Finally, unable to contain herself, she asked, "Read me a story?"

Erik looked up and smiled. "Which one will it be tonight?"

"Jonah and the great fish," Iya answered as she leaned against his arm.

"I've already read that one at least a half dozen times," Erik chuckled. "How about one you haven't heard?"

Iya nodded and Erik thumbed through the pages, stopping near the back of his Bible. He read, *"And Jesus, walking by the Sea of Galilee, saw two brothers, Simon called Peter, and Andrew his brother, casting a net into the sea . . ."*

Her face bright with interest, Iya watched Erik read. Sometimes she closed her eyes as if to visualize what he said, and occasionally she stopped him to ask a question.

Anna listened. The words intrigued her, but she was careful to conceal her interest. *It seems so real to him,* she thought. *His voice even softens when he speaks of Jesus. How can someone who lived so long ago affect him in such a way?* It made no sense to her.

The next day the weather broke clear and cold. Anna and Iya donned their parkas, braced themselves against the chill, and stomped into the fresh snow. Methodically, they packed down a new trail to the woodpile and cache. It was an endless job during the winter months, but Anna welcomed a reason to be outdoors. It gave her a break from the dark interior of the cabin.

Erik had been gone all morning when his "Hello!" echoed across the snow-covered meadow. He wore a broad grin as he approached with a long string of furs slung over his shoulder.

He held up the pelts and said, "Did pretty well. At this rate, I should make a good sum by spring."

Anna nodded and ran her hand over the satiny thick fur of a beaver. "These are good skins."

"Your handiwork will make them even better," Erik said.

Anna blushed, still unused to his praise.

"I should have enough to get me set up in Sitka."

Anna wished he wouldn't speak of leaving. Each time he mentioned spring and moving on, an empty feeling pulled at her.

Iya grinned up at Erik. "Can I have fur?" she asked.

Erik smiled mischievously and made a "Grr . . ." sound as he took a fox fur and rubbed it against the little girl's face.

Iya giggled and hugged him. "I want us always together," she said.

Immediately Erik's smile faded. He cleared his throat and his eyes darted across the dead-looking birch and poplar forest. "Well, a person can never tell what tomorrow might bring," he said, his eyes grim as he glanced at Anna. They both knew Iya wouldn't get her wish. Erik changed the subject. "My knife is getting dull and needs sharpening. Why don't you give me a hand, Iya."

Iya happily followed him inside and sat next to him as he took a sharpening stone and wet it. She leaned over the table and watched closely as he ran the knife over the stone. After a few minutes, Erik stopped and asked, "Would you like to try?"

Iya grinned and bobbed her head up and down, her eyes sparkling with anticipation.

He carefully put the handle of the knife in her palm, placed his large hand over hers, and circled the blade across the smooth flat rock. Iya grinned up at her blond friend, hugging him with her eyes.

That evening after supper, Iya crawled onto Erik's lap and asked, "Tell me of the outside."

"It's very different from your world. There's good and bad all rolled into one. San Francisco is the biggest city I've seen. It sits along the sea and has wooden docks with many boats tied up to them."

"Like the umiak?" Iya asked.

"Oh, much bigger. Bigger than this house."

Iya's eyes grew large and she said, "No," as she shook her head in disbelief.

"It's true," Erik countered.

"What are people like in this city?"

"Well, there are a lot of them. Hundreds. The streets are filled with people going here and there—some riding on horses, others in buggies."

"What are horses and buggies?"

Erik thought for a minute, "Well, a buggy is kind of like a boat, only it has wheels and a horse pulls it."

Iya looked at him quizzically. Erik lifted her off his lap, took a charred stick from the fire and, squatting down, drew a picture of a horse and buggy on the dirt floor. Iya's eyes lit up with understanding and she said, "I know now." Then she asked, "Are the people nice?"

Erik settled back into his chair as he answered, "Most are. But you have to be careful; there are some looking for trouble." He paused. "You don't have to worry about those types out here. Not many are willing to travel this far from home."

Anna watched their exchange with mixed feelings. The places Erik spoke of seemed unreal, like the stories from his black book. But, as she thought about what he said, she wished she could see a city. It sounded exciting.

She watched the joy on Iya's face, and her thoughts shifted to Erik's destined departure. *When he goes, it will be like losing our family again,* she thought. She wished she didn't care. Nothing could be done to change the future, so she pushed her dismal thoughts aside and tried to concentrate on Erik's account of the city called San Francisco.

○○○○○○○○○○○

One afternoon while Erik was out, Iya asked, "Anna, why do you not like Erik? He is good."

"I do like him," Anna answered. She stopped and thought for a moment before continuing. "I just do not trust him."

"Why not?"

Anna had nearly forgotten her reason and had to think for a moment. "He is from the outside. He worships a God I do not trust."

"I trust him. I think Erik is good. His God is good too," Iya insisted, her voice reflecting her loyalty to the man.

Wishing to put an end to their discussion, Anna set aside the skin she was working on and said, "Time to cook supper." She quickly crossed the room and busied herself with meal preparations.

Iya's words remained with her, however, and she wrestled with her doubts. *Why? Why do I not trust him?* she asked herself. *He has proven himself trustworthy many times.*

But Anna still blamed Erik's God for the death of her people, and when she looked at the man, she saw his God. The two were inseparable. She was bitter and had unknowingly hardened her heart, choking off her ability to believe in anyone.

A strong fluttering sensation interrupted her thoughts. She caressed her rounded belly. *This baby is already strong. It must be a boy. I know he will become a great hunter like his father.* She hummed a hunter's song. Remembering Erik, she thought, *I must tell him soon.* Her stomach tightened in apprehension as she considered doing so. She feared his reaction.

Erik pushed open the door and stepped inside.

Startled, Anna quickly dropped her hands to her sides and stopped humming.

He shrugged out of his coat and asked, "What were you singing?"

Anna blushed and stumbled over her words. "It is nothing. I like to sing. That is all." *I will tell him now,* she decided, and opened her mouth to do so when Iya stormed through the door.

"It snows more!" the little girl announced, shaking white crystals from her parka.

A new storm blew in, and the small group of travelers was trapped indoors once more.

When the skies cleared, Iya eagerly escaped to the outside. After she had been gone for a short time, Anna heard her yelling about something. She peeked out the door. Iya's face was bright with the cold and excitement as she exclaimed, "Watch!" She grinned and spit. Before her spittle reached the ground, it froze solid. Iya laughed and looked back at Anna expectantly.

Anna reacted appropriately, exclaiming how impressed she was with Iya's discovery and how cold it must be. To Iya's dismay she also said, "It is too cold. You come in now."

Frowning, Iya shuffled inside. She perked up when she saw Erik. "I remember when you told me how spit gets hard. I tried, and you are right."

Erik smiled. "It is pretty darned cold!" he said as he ate his last bite of caribou and pulled on his heavy parka. "I better check the trap line while the weather's clear. I'll be back in a couple of hours." Before Anna could reply, he slipped out the door.

After setting the cabin to rights, Anna and Iya hauled in a bucket of snow and scooped it into a large pot near the fire. As it melted, they added more. Anna waited to add more snow and thought she heard footsteps coming from outside. "Too soon to be Erik," she said, as her mind kicked around possible reasons for his early return. *Maybe he is hurt,* she thought. *Something might be wrong!* In two quick steps she crossed to the door and flung it open.

A man Anna had never seen before filled the doorway. His unshaven face peeked out from beneath a heavy fur parka hood. At first glance, he looked handsome, but as he leaned close to Anna and grinned, she looked into cruel ice-blue eyes and knew he was evil. His cold smile only emphasized his sinister appearance. As a shudder of fear and revulsion rippled through her, Anna thought, *He has the look of an eagle.*

"Afternoon," the stranger said as he tipped his head. "I was wonderin' if my partner and I could warm ourselves by your fire?"

Another man stepped from behind the first. He didn't bother to smile. His piggish eyes peered nervously out of a bloated face. A scraggly beard partially hid the man's double chin. Filthy, the men reeked of sweat and stale tobacco.

Anna's stomach rolled, and the air suddenly seemed depleted of oxygen. Instinctively she drew back and pushed against the door, trying to close it. The eagle-faced man easily pushed past her.

Feeling trapped, Anna stared at the intruders and did not know whether to flee or stand her ground. She decided that running would serve no purpose and stood by the open doorway, clenching her fists at her sides. Iya clung to her skirt. The piggish man shoved Anna into the center of the room and dragged Iya along. He turned a cruel grin, which revealed stained and missing teeth, on the little girl. "What's your name?" he asked as he reached out a gloved hand and patted her on the head.

Iya cringed beneath his touch, but said nothing. She stared back at him with large, frightened eyes.

He looked about the room and asked, "Hey, Jarvis, what're we gonna do now?"

The man with the cold blue eyes snapped, "Hold on. I haven't made up my mind yet." He glanced about the cabin. "Not bad. Maybe we'll stay."

Anna tried to slow her breathing and clutched Iya close to her. Swallowing hard, she threw back her shoulders, raised her chin, and leveled a cold gaze on the man named Jarvis. In her most intimidating voice, she said, "You leave. Now."

The men grinned at each other and, as if they had heard a good joke, threw their heads back and laughed.

"Pretty feisty, aren't ya?" the bigger man said as he lurched toward Anna and stroked her hair, pushing his face only inches from hers. Anna felt defiled by his touch and, as the stench of alcohol and tobacco assaulted her, she tried not to gag. He turned his pig eyes on her and smirked as he growled, "We'll leave when we're good and ready." Anna refused to yield and kept her eyes squarely on his, challenging his authority.

"Why, you cocky little half-breed. I'll teach you," he spat as he raised his hand to strike her.

"That's enough!" Jarvis ordered.

Anna felt faint with fear but threw her shoulders back further and tilted her chin even higher. "Erik will return soon," she said defiantly.

"Oh, is that so?" Jarvis scoffed and glanced at his partner. "Did you hear that, Frank? Her man is coming." They both laughed. He fixed his eyes on Anna and said coldly, "Well, we happen to know that's not so. We made certain he wouldn't bother nobody again. I wouldn't be expectin' no help from him." He plopped into a chair, leaned back, and casually crossed his feet on the table. "Fix us somethin' to eat," he demanded.

Anna glared back at him for a moment, then, realizing she couldn't fight him outright, turned back to the fire and stirred the pot of stew that hung simmering over the flames. Her mind groped for a solution, a way out. *What can I do? There must be something!* Furtively she searched for a weapon. There was nothing. Erik had the rifle, and her knife was in her pouch. She'd never be able to get to it. These men could easily overpower her. *The shaman's spear!* she thought, but quickly dismissed the idea. It had been stored in the cache.

Frank prowled about the cabin, searching through their belongings. What he found uninteresting he simply tossed aside. Not until he spotted Erik's collection of furs did his curiosity peek. He crossed the room and quickly rifled through the skins. He broke into a gruesome grin. "Looks like we hit it big this time," he announced as he held up a particularly nice fox pelt.

"Looks like pretty good stuff," Jarvis said from his chair as he dragged on a cigarette. "Maybe even good enough to get us a stake somewhere." He exhaled slowly. The smoke swirled about his head like an apparition.

"I thought you said we weren't settlin' nowhere till we find that Captain James," Frank said as he spit a wad of soggy tobacco on the floor. He turned back to inspect the rest of the furs.

"We'll find him, don't worry," Jarvis answered.

Anna dished out a plate of stew for each man. *Erik, please come home,* she pleaded to herself.

Frank wolfed down his meal, leaned back in his chair, patted his stomach, and belched. "Pretty good for a *half-breed,*" he said with contempt. "Maybe we'll just take you along. What do you think, Jarvis, should we take her with us?"

At first Jarvis didn't answer. Instead, he leveled a menacing gaze at Anna. Never taking his eyes from her, he answered slowly and deliberately, his voice ice-cold. "I was thinkin' maybe we'd stay, but goin' on and takin' them might not be such a bad idea. Luke can always use more girls this time of year, and he'd probably pay pretty good for this pair."

Anna stifled a shudder. She never looked away.

His mind made up, Jarvis suddenly barked, "You! Get your gear together!"

Anna jumped. She couldn't believe what she was hearing and stared back at him.

"Stop lookin' at me like an idiot. You and the girl get some supplies together. We're leavin'."

Anna set her jaw and glared at the man. "No. We will not go. You take what you want. You go," she said, trying to keep her voice from shaking.

Jarvis's face contorted in rage as he leapt from his chair, knocking it over in his haste. Before Anna could move, he had her arm in a tight grip and, with his face so close to hers she could feel his breath, he snarled, "You'll do *exactly* as I say. You hear me?"

Anna met his hard stare and jerked her arm free. She had no choice but to do as he demanded. She turned away, took her extra tunic from its hook and placed it inside a pouch. Then she added a cloak and some of Iya's clothing.

Jarvis turned his attention to the pelts. "Nice furs." Nodding toward Frank, he said, "We'll need the dogs and the sled." Frank didn't respond. Jarvis turned on him and bellowed, "Get the dogs!"

Frank looked like he was going to say something but thought better of it and tromped outside. A few minutes later, Anna heard what sounded like barking seals. Frank pushed the door open, and as he did, the clamor from the dogs filled the room. "The sled's ready to go," he announced. Anna peered over his shoulder and tried to get a look at what was making such a racket.

"Help me get these loaded!" Jarvis ordered irritably.

Still distracted by the yapping beasts, Anna didn't hear him. She had never seen dogs like this before. Most of them were large animals with thick, heavy coats. They yelped and snarled at each other, excited to be on the move. Iya pressed against Anna and stared fearfully at the group of impatient canines.

Oblivious to the dogs' yammering, Jarvis yelled at Anna, "Give us a hand!" and dumped an armload of furs onto the sled.

This time Jarvis's sharp voice penetrated Anna's preoccupation, and she grabbed some of the pelts, then warily edged around the barking animals. Jarvis took the skins from her and added them to the pile. They quickly loaded the furs, strapped them down tight, and tied on the additional supplies.

Anna furtively studied the edge of the forest, watching for Erik, hoping the men's threats were untrue. He had to be all right.

When the sled was ready, Jarvis took his place at the back of the sled, raised a whip in the air, and yelled "Hah!" The dogs, pulling and straining against the heavy load, set off across the white wilderness. Frank followed Anna and Iya on foot, occasionally prodding them with the butt of his gun.

Again, Anna scanned the dead-looking forest and the white, empty meadows, hoping to see Erik. *I must slow them down,* she thought and stumbled intentionally

Frank yanked her back onto her feet, jabbed her with his rifle, and barked, "Keep up, or we'll feed ya to the dogs." He snickered as Anna stumbled through the deep snow.

Iya gripped Anna's hand, and with her eyes full of terror, whispered, "I am afraid."

"Do not be scared," Anna reassured her. "Erik will come." She glanced about, wondering where he was and wishing she could believe her own words.

As they entered the woods, Frank muttered about something lying in the snow. Anna tried to catch what he was saying. Immediately her eyes were drawn to a figure sprawled against a snowbank. Frank swaggered up to it.

Shock swept through Anna, and for a moment, she was unable to move. In a choked voice, she exclaimed, "Erik! It is Erik!" His face looked pale against the blood-stained snow. He lay completely still. *He cannot be dead,* she thought. *No!*

For a moment Frank stood over the big Norwegian. He looked at him arrogantly and nudged him with the toe of his boot. When there was no response, he pushed harder. Still Erik didn't move.

"Well, there's your man for you," Frank smirked.

Anna felt sick. She choked down the bile that rose in her throat and blinked back forbidden tears. *They will not see my pain,* she told herself and clenched her teeth. *There will be time to grieve another day.* She glared at Frank and Jarvis. Her heart felt cold and empty. She loathed the two men.

Iya threw herself across the lifeless body of her friend and wailed, "No! Erik!"

Jarvis grabbed the little girl by the back of her parka, yanked her to her feet, and pushed her down the trail ahead of him.

Anna paused for a moment before stepping past Erik's inert body. A moan welled up from deep inside, but she choked it back. *He cannot be dead,* she thought, unable to accept what her eyes told her.

She moved on across the bleak terrain, leaving him beneath a leafless tree. Anna's mind emptied except for the picture of Erik lying in his own blood. Mechanically, she placed one foot in front of the other, barely aware of her surroundings or even the small hand clasped in hers. *Who would kill a man without cause?* she wondered. Her heart beat wildly as she realized she and Iya were at the mercy of such men.

They followed a path through the deep snow. Anna's legs began to burn from the effort, and her lungs stung from gulping in the cold air. She stopped to catch her breath, but Frank quickly pushed her on. "Get moving," he growled then called out to Jarvis, "Hey, how about letting me have a hand at the sled."

"Later," Jarvis called over his shoulder.

Anna glared at him, hatred her only emotion. *Why are they doing this?* she asked and vowed they would pay.

As they broke new trail, the going grew tougher. The temperature had warmed and Anna perspired in her heavy clothing. She wished she could stop to shed a layer. *They would only be amused at my discomfort,* she thought and decided to say nothing as she strained to keep up with Frank's relentless pace.

The hours passed and, certain she could go no further, Anna longed for rest. Finally, Jarvis called for Frank to stop. He sat on an exposed stump and lit a cigarette. Taking a long, slow drag, he swept his eagle-eyes over the landscape. "This looks like as good a place as any," he said. "You two, build us a fire," he ordered Anna and Iya.

Iya looked at Anna with fatigue-laden eyes, pleading for rest. Anna wished she could hold the child and cradle her to sleep. Instead, she took her hand and led her in search of firewood. She had no other choice. After they had a substantial fire going, Anna pulled Iya into her lap and rested near the blaze.

Jarvis exploded. "Dang lazy Indians! Get up off your backsides and make us something to eat!"

Iya's eyes filled with tears and her chin quivered. Anna stroked her cheek and through clenched teeth said in their native tongue, "We will do as they say now, but there will be a time when they will know our wrath." She pushed herself to her feet and pulled Iya up alongside her.

Jarvis saw to the dogs while Frank struggled with the tent. After the dogs were fed and settled, Jarvis carved out a seat in the snow next to the fire. He lay a pelt down to protect himself from the cold then sat and watched the others work. Taking a cigarette paper and a pouch from inside his coat, he expertly held the paper, tapped out a small amount of tobacco, rolled the tissue between his fingers, and licked its edge to secure it. Casually, he placed the cigarette between his lips and struck a match to light up. Turning his cold eyes on Anna, he dragged on his cigarette until it glowed bright red then demanded, "Where's my coffee?"

Barely able to hide her contempt, Anna poured him a cup. She handed it to him with slightly shaking hands. He took it without a word of thanks. Dismissing her, he glared into the fire. Anna turned back to the frying caribou and scooped out a chunk for each of them.

While they ate, the men seemed to forget their captives. Anna handed Iya a portion of meat, and they gratefully filled their empty stomachs. They looked at each other, but said nothing, afraid of attracting attention from the men.

It made no difference. Frank set his plate aside and glanced at Anna and Iya. "Luke ought to pay a good price, don't ya think?" he asked Jarvis.

"Yeah, as long as you keep your mitts off them."

"Ah, come on," Frank argued. "I won't touch the girl." He turned his gaze on Anna. "But it won't hurt none to spend some time with her."

Anna cringed inside and forced herself not to look away but was unable to swallow her food.

"Put your eyes back in your head! You keep your hands to yourself," Jarvis warned. "Damaged goods don't bring the money. You know Luke, he'll find any reason to lower the price. She's better lookin' than most, but she's still just a *siewash*. Not exactly top dollar."

Anna grimaced. She didn't know what offended her more, being treated like a piece of property or being called a *siewash*. She had heard the term before from outsiders, and it was never used to flatter. She glared at Jarvis and fought back biting words of contempt.

"We want to keep that man happy," Jarvis continued. "Besides, look at her. There's no way you'll touch her without a fight, and I don't want no bruises." He paused and thought for a minute. "Who knows, maybe Luke will sell you a piece of her—*after* he pays us. Until then, I'm warnin' you—keep your hands off, or you'll end up like that trapper we borrowed this sled from."

Frank grumbled something unintelligible and returned to his meal.

After supper, Frank and Jarvis crawled into the tent for the night. Anna and Iya, like the dogs, were left to fend for themselves. Anna studied the empty wilderness and considered fleeing. But she knew certain death awaited them in the vast frozen countryside. She dug a small alcove in the snow near the fire, lined it with furs from the sled, and burrowed inside with Iya. The heat from their bodies and the fading flames of the fire provided enough warmth to allow them to sleep.

Some time later, Anna was startled awake by a hand clasped roughly over her mouth. It cut off her breath. She looked into Frank's glazed eyes and wrenched his hand away. He threw himself on top of her and fumbled to find his way through her thick layers of clothing while seeking her mouth with his. Anna fought her attacker, flinging her head from side to side, trying to avoid his probing mouth. His foul-smelling breath choked her. She tried to break free, but his size overpowered her.

"Ah, come on," he hissed in her ear. "Relax. I'm not gonna hurt you." He smothered her mouth with his.

Instinctively Anna bit into his lip.

Frank let out a howl and reeled back in pain, his hand cupped over his mouth. He looked down at his bloody hand. His face twisted in a frenzied rage and he drew his arm back, then struck Anna full across the face with his fist.

Her head bounced against the snow. An explosion of bright light and sharp, penetrating pain seared her skull. The sound of a rifle shot echoed across the frozen plain, and Anna was suddenly free of Frank's weight.

Jarvis strode toward Frank, his gun leveled at the frightened man. "I ought to kill you," he snarled as he cuffed Frank hard across the jaw. "I told ya to leave her alone, and I meant it." Through clenched teeth he threatened, "If it happens again, you're dead." His eyes burned into Frank's for a long time before he turned and stormed back inside the tent.

Frank wiped his bruised and bleeding face with the back of his hand, glared at Anna, and stomped off.

Anna crawled back into the alcove, her eyes trained on the spot where Frank had disappeared into the woods. She shivered and cuddled close to her frightened sister. A small smile crept across her face as she thought of Frank's damaged lip. But it quickly faded as she rubbed her sore cheek and remembered Erik. *Why did you have to die?* she asked before closing her eyes and trying to shut out her present reality.

The following morning Anna heated the coffee while Jarvis grabbed some hardtack out of his knapsack. He tossed a piece to each of them. "This'll have to do for breakfast. We gotta get movin'."

Frank refused the dry biscuit and, shivering, clutched his coat tightly about himself. He dragged himself through his morning tasks, his face flushed and his eyes bright with fever. His bruised and swollen lip added to his grotesque appearance.

Jarvis growled, "What's with you? There's no time to waste if we plan to meet up with Enid James and do business with Luke."

Frank answered weakly, "I'm not feelin' so good, Jarvis."

"Ahh, you're fine. Come on, we gotta make tracks."

"No. I mean it. I'm sick."

"We're movin' on. Either you come with us or you're on your own," Jarvis said indifferently as he harnessed the dogs.

Anna watched the exchange and decided the two men deserved each other. *I have never known such cruel people,* she thought as she gingerly touched her swollen, bruised cheek.

Ignoring Frank's condition, Jarvis ordered the dogs to mush and headed across the snow. Anna and Iya followed. At first Frank just watched as they moved away, but finally he plodded along behind.

As the day progressed, the gap between the sled and Frank grew. Each time Anna looked back, he had fallen further behind. Stumbling along, he somehow managed to stay within sight of the sled.

At midday, Jarvis stopped to rest the dogs. Anna and Iya gratefully plopped down in the snow. Frank eventually stumbled into camp. His usual sallow complexion was now a pasty white, and beads of perspiration covered his forehead. His breath came in short gasps interrupted by fits of coughing.

Frank had been there only a few minutes when Jarvis prepared to move on. "I need to rest. Just wait a little longer," Frank pleaded.

Jarvis didn't even bother to look at his partner, but as he pushed off, said, "Don't have time to wait for loafers."

Anna shuddered at the heartless words. She and Iya were completely at this man's mercy. *We must escape,* she thought as she fell into step behind the sled. She looked about the desolate landscape and asked herself, *But to where?*

When Jarvis finally stopped to make camp, Frank was still with them. He fell into a heap in the snow, and lay there shivering, his body wracked by a hacking cough.

Anna loathed the sick man but was unwilling to be as inhumane as Jarvis and helped Frank into the tent, which she had set up. She lowered him onto a bed of furs where he remained, refusing to eat or drink. His fever rose and his condition steadily grew worse. There was nothing anyone could do for him.

After the evening meal, Anna and Iya made another fur-lined hollow in the snow and settled down for the night. They had no peace, however, as Frank's labored breathing and steady coughing rattled through the camp. Once a deep, gurgling cough was followed by a long silence. For a moment Anna thought Frank had died, but his shallow, rattling breaths resumed.

Jarvis glared into the fire.

Anna watched him through half-closed eyes and wondered if he would leave Frank behind.

Jarvis finally flicked his cigarette butt into the dwindling flames and reluctantly walked to the tent. Before disappearing inside, he glanced back at his prisoners. Anna pretended to be asleep.

Chapter 17

*E*rik struggled to free himself from the heavy darkness that held him captive. Only vaguely aware of the bitter cold, he blinked his eyes and squinted into the bright sunlight, attempting to bring the fuzzy image of a tree limb above him into focus. He ran his tongue across dry, cracked lips as he tried to grasp where he was and his eyes roamed over blurred images. Everything seemed odd and out of kilter. Gradually his vision cleared, and he realized he was lying against a snowbank somewhere along his trap line. *Why am I here?* he wondered as he tried to remember what had happened.

He rolled to his side and his skull exploded with pain. A moan escaped his lips as he grabbed his head in his hands and held very still until the throbbing eased. Gingerly he reached inside the hood of his parka and touched the side of his head. His hair felt damp and matted, and a large knot had raised beside a gash. He pulled his hand away. It was stained with blood. He looked down at the snow and it, too, had been tinted red.

As he pushed himself into a sitting position, a wave of pain and nausea washed over him, and the empty blackness threatened to envelop him again. He fought against it, knowing that if he gave in to its invitation, he would never leave the frozen wilderness but would instead, become food for hungry scavengers.

He hugged his heavy clothing more tightly about himself and thought, *It's too cold. I can't stay here much longer without freezing to death.* He staggered to his feet and through teeth gritted against pain said, "I've got to get back to the cabin." His head spun and he braced himself against a tree until the earth stopped its swaying. Slowly his mind cleared.

He looked over the white landscape. It seemed peaceful enough. The sky was clear, but the sun gave off little warmth. It glinted off something nearby, and he was surprised to find his rifle half buried in the snow. *Whoever hit me must have missed this,* he thought as he reached to pick it up. The sharp pain in his head jabbed at him as he grasped the gun and cautiously stood up.

He surveyed his surroundings, wondering who had hit him and why. Sled tracks and a set of prints made by someone wearing snowshoes led away toward the east. These were accompanied by two sets of smaller prints. Whoever had made them wore mukluks.

Anna! Iya! Erik's mind cried. Frantic, he scanned the horizon. It was empty—silent. *I've got to help them!* he thought. His first impulse was to set out after his friends. *Anything could happen to them,* he thought and lunged toward the trail. Several faltering steps later, common sense came to the fore and he stopped. He realized that if he hoped to help the sisters, he needed to gather some supplies and exchange his chilled clothing for something warmer.

Even as he envisioned Anna and Iya being brutalized by some unknown intruder, he forced himself to turn back toward the cabin. He ignored his throbbing head, driven by a sense of panic.

When he approached the cabin, he could see the door was ajar. He stopped and listened. It was still as death. He crept to the doorway and peered inside—empty. The room was nearly dark, but he could see that it had been ransacked and emptied of most of his furs and supplies.

As Erik stepped inside, he wasn't met by the usual blast of warm air. The embers in the hearth were dying and a pot of stew resting over the fire was cool. *Anna must have made this before* . . . Erik couldn't finish the thought. Shivering, he built a hot fire, set the stew and a pot of coffee on to cook, and stripped off his clothing. He slipped on two extra pairs of wool pants and a heavy shirt and waited for the coffee to cook. Impatient, he allowed it to perk for only a few minutes, then poured himself a cup of the steaming hot beverage. Holding his mug with both hands, he stood as close to the hearth as was safe and sipped.

His mind filled with questions and horrifying possibilities. He tried not to think of them and, instead, planned how he would find Anna and Iya and, hopefully, rescue them.

After downing a second cup of coffee and eating his fill of the hot stew, he finally felt his chills subside and his body temperature returned to near normal. Quickly he threw together a small pouch of food and extra ammunition, then slipped on several more layers of warm clothing. He slung his rifle over his shoulder and strode out the door; his only thought was to rescue his two friends. There was no time to lose.

As he set out across the stark countryside, his mind was again flooded by images of Anna and Iya under the control of their captors. Rage consumed him. With his face pale from loss of blood and set in angry determination, he held little resemblance to the kind Norwegian the two girls had come to know. He felt consumed by the need to find them.

Good thing the weather has held out, he thought as he glanced up at the sky. *It shouldn't be too hard to follow their trail. It looks like there are only two of them, one guiding the sled and the other seems to be in charge of Anna and Iya. At least I've only got two to contend with.* He set out after the small band.

Relentlessly he moved on, following the sled's tracks as it snaked through the forest and across the open fields of snow. The trail seemed to stretch out endlessly. As the hours passed, ice crystals formed on his mustache and beard. Carelessly he brushed them away. Weakness and fatigue pulled at him, but he refused to give in to his need for rest, determined to close the distance between himself and his enemies. He pushed forward, carried on by a power greater than himself.

As the miles passed, Erik's anger grew. Anna and Iya's tracks continued to follow the ruts made by the dogsled. "They haven't been able to rest!" Erik blustered as he followed the girl's prints. It was clear they had not been allowed to ride. *At least I know they're still alive as long as their tracks continue,* he told himself, trying to find some comfort in the continuing trail made by the mukluks.

His head throbbed and his stomach felt unsteady under the constant pain, but he refused to yield. He didn't stop to ponder the reason for his passion and fury, didn't recognize the love that prompted him to follow the seemingly endless trail through the wilderness. He only knew he couldn't abandon his two friends.

With each step he prayed, appealing to God for Anna and Iya's protection and seeking strength and wisdom for himself. When his legs felt like lead and he feared he could go no further he cried out to God, "Please, help me to go on!"

Uncertainty nagged at him. *Why did you let this happen? Haven't they been through enough?* he asked his Lord. *I don't understand,* he thought, then in the same breath, he cursed his lack of faith. But even as he argued with his heavenly Father, he knew he worshiped a Creator of great wisdom and power, a God of love, who does only what is best. His God sees the whole picture, not just a portion. Gradually his questions and challenges changed to *Not my will, but yours.* And, finally, grateful that the Ruler of the Universe was in control, he allowed himself to rest.

He dropped his pack from his back and painfully sat down. As he scanned the countryside, he pulled a piece of hardtack and a container of water from his pack and ate. He sat exhausted and fighting to continue when his mother's kind face came to mind. She had always been so wise.

He remembered the time his father had fallen from the barn roof while making repairs. His mother had remained calm even though his father lay unconscious. "Erik, you must run for the doctor," she had told him.

Erik remembered looking at her with disbelief and saying, "But, Momma, there is no horse! It is too far. What if I can't run fast enough?"

"You must trust God to carry you," she had replied. Leveling a look of total confidence upon her son, she had added, "You can do anything, as long as you go to the One who supplies." With that she had patted him on the cheek and said, "Now, go."

Erik smiled as he recalled how he had prayed the whole way and how fast his scrawny legs had carried him. He had never tired. God had saved his father that day and Erik had learned to trust in his heavenly Father.

Pulling himself back to the present, Erik felt stronger. He pushed himself back to his feet and continued on, knowing nothing was impossible.

Hours later, too exhausted to continue, he stopped to make camp. After building a fire, he hollowed out a small alcove in the snow and squeezed into it. He stared at the flames and wondered where Anna and Iya were.

He could not remember ever really hating anyone, but as his thoughts settled on his friends and the men who had taken them, he could find no other word to describe what he felt. He could see himself setting his sights on his enemy and squeezing the trigger. It felt good. He tried to jar the image from his mind; he had never thought himself capable of murder. But the sensation was intense. He didn't like it. Pulling his clothing tighter about himself, he curled into a tight ball and finally slept. His dreams were filled with jumbled pictures of his family and Anna and Iya. A great wave swept through his dreams and, feeling helpless, he watched as it began to engulf his two companions. Just as they were being swept away, he awoke to the winter's darkness, shivering and drenched with sweat. He had to find them!

Uncertain of the hour, he pushed himself up on one elbow and searched the horizon for any sign of morning light. The blackness was just beginning to lighten. He gathered his few belongings and, having eaten a piece of dried meat for breakfast, set out. A sharp, cold wind had kicked up during the night, and clouds scuttled across the sky.

Looks like a storm is coming. I'd better find them soon, he thought and hurried his pace. A couple of hours later, he came across an empty campsite. He knelt to feel the ashes. They were cold. He glanced out across the white landscape and asked, "God, where are they? Please help me! Show me what I must do." *I'd better find them soon,* he thought and hurried his pace.

Certain that he was closing the gap, Erik followed the sled tracks all day. Eventually exhaustion forced him to stop for the night. The sound of the wind and the lonely howl of a wolf were his only company.

Early the next morning, an unfamiliar sound carried through the forest, snapping his mind awake. Studying the terrain, Erik held his breath and listened for more.

The faint sound of voices came from a smattering of trees in the distance. Erik spotted a thin column of smoke rising into the air and his heart skipped a beat, then suddenly pounded hard in his chest. He had to stifle a cheer. He quietly dug through his bag for rifle shells. He loaded his pockets with them, gripped his gun as he crouched low to the ground, and moved slowly toward the smoke plume. A while later he caught sight of the camp. Lying flat against the snow, he crawled closer.

With no more than two hundred yards separating him from the encampment, he stopped and scanned the group. He spotted Anna and Iya and whispered a prayer of thanks. Both looked unhurt.

A surly looking man sat comfortably near the fire, spouting orders at Anna. Erik searched for his traveling partner, and when he couldn't find him, decided he must be in the tent. He watched the activity in the camp for a few minutes.

Iya huddled meekly near the fire. *She looks like a frightened fawn,* Erik thought as he watched her, his anger boiling to the surface. As a barrage of unreasonable demands came from the kidnapper, Erik thought how good it would feel to punish him with his fists. Anna's golden eyes flashed with anger as she silently did his bidding.

Erik crept closer. He stopped as a fit of coughing, followed by what sounded like a death rattle, came from the tent. His confidence grew now that he was assured there would be one less enemy to contend with.

The man resting by the fire tossed the remainder of his coffee into the snow, splashing a dark stain across it. He hollered at Anna, "Hey! *siewash.* This is cold, get me another cup!"

Erik watched the man's contemptible behavior and stroked the rifle trigger nervously. His loathing grew. Cautiously he raised the rifle to his shoulder, aimed his sights directly at the man's chest, and tried to squeeze the trigger. Everything within him cried, *Shoot him! He deserves no mercy!*

For a time he lay there, struggling to do what was easiest. Finally, he lowered his gun. As much as he wanted to, he knew it was wrong to shoot a man without warning. "I'd be no better than a criminal myself," he muttered, and crept another fifty yards. He waited for the right moment, rose to his feet, and with his rifle leveled at the man near the fire, shouted, "Don't move!"

Anna looked up, her face bright with relief, then Jarvis reached for his gun. "Erik!" she yelled.

"I see it," Erik said, never taking his eyes from Jarvis. His voice filled with contempt, he threatened, "Give me a reason. It would be a pleasure to put an end to you."

Glaring at Erik, Jarvis slowly returned his hand to his side.

Anna and Iya edged toward Erik.

"Stay put," he ordered the two girls, while he glared at their abductor. In a cold, hard voice he said, "Move away from your gun."

Jarvis stood his ground.

"Now!" Erik ordered, setting his rifle sights on the man.

"Okay. Okay. Don't get your dander up. I'm movin'." Jarvis jeered, as he stood and backed away.

"Keep moving until I tell you to stop."

Jarvis stepped another ten feet and asked insolently, "This far enough?"

"You'll back all the way to Sitka if I tell you to!" Erik snarled back. He quickly moved toward the fire and retrieved the man's weapon.

Another fit of coughing came from inside the tent. Erik nodded toward the canvas shelter and asked, "Who's inside?"

"Nobody. Just my partner."

"What's wrong with him?"

"Don't know," Jarvis answered coldly.

Erik glanced at Anna and Iya. He recoiled when he saw the dark black-and-blue splotch on Anna's cheek. He gritted his teeth as he thought of the man who had left the mark, and wished he could pummel whoever had done it. Not wanting to frighten the girls further, he asked as calmly as he could, "You two all right?"

They both nodded.

Erik turned his attention back to Jarvis. "I ought to kill you." He stared at him for a moment, then added, "But, it's your lucky day. All I want is what's mine." He lowered his gaze menacingly and added. "If I ever see you near my place again, I won't hesitate to put a bullet in your brain."

Jarvis snarled, "Don't worry. You won't see me. I've got more important things to do than mess with a couple of Indians and a miserable sourdough."

Erik ignored his derogatory remarks and, with his gun still trained on the man, asked Anna, "Do they have any other weapons?"

"A gun and knives," she answered.

"Where's the gun?"

"In there," Anna said, pointing toward the tent.

"Can you get it?"

Silently, Anna slipped inside the canvas structure and, a moment later, reappeared with the rifle.

"Wait a minute," Jarvis wailed. "You can't leave us without any weapons!"

"I can do what I want," Erik answered matter-of-factly. "Anna, you and Iya gather up your things and bring them over here." He turned back to Jarvis. "You can keep your knives. That'll do," he said as he inspected the sled. Keeping an eye on Jarvis, he sorted through the skins and supplies. As he filled a pack with furs, Anna's shrill voice echoed across the icy fields. "Erik!"

Erik looked up just in time to see Jarvis leap at him. Automatically he swung the butt of his gun about and struck his assailant across the jaw with the weapon, then quickly swung it back, hitting him hard along the cheekbone. A loud crack accompanied the second blow, and Jarvis stumbled and fell to the ground.

Erik's heart beat hard as he stood over the prostrate body of his enemy. His momentary surge of rage receded. He thought it would feel good to hurt this man, but he only felt empty. Crouching over Jarvis, Erik pressed his fingers to the man's throat, feeling for a pulse. "He's not dead, just unconscious," he said and stood up. "No telling how long he'll be out," he added, his voice weary as he returned to filling the packs. "Now's as good a time as any to head for home."

Anna handed him the few articles she had gathered and he added them to the two duffel bags. He tied the bundles with rope and slipped one over his shoulder. Glancing at Anna, he asked, "Do you think you could pull the other one?"

Anna quickly grasped the rope and hooked it around her arm.

Erik glanced down at Iya and with a smile asked, "Are you ready?"

Iya nodded, but didn't answer. Erik bent down to give her a hug, but instead of her usual affectionate response, she pulled away. Hurt and surprised, Erik asked, "Are you all right, Iya?"

Iya only nodded and went to stand next to Anna.

Erik was concerned by Iya's behavior, but this was not the place to deal with it. He stood up and glanced down at Jarvis once more, then turned and followed the trail he'd left in the snow. As another round of coughing came from the tent, Anna and Iya quietly fell into step beside him.

Soon the camp and cruel men lay behind Erik and his two companions. Silently, the threesome moved steadily toward home. Large white crystals fell from the clouds and floated to the ground. The wind gusted, whipping the flakes about, foretelling bad weather.

Erik finally broke the silence. "That's a bad bruise you've got. Did they do that?"

"It is nothing," Anna answered. "It does not hurt." She was quiet for a minute, then, her voice shaking, she said, "We thought you were dead. We saw you in the snow."

"They did their best to kill me but only managed to give me a huge headache," Erik answered.

Anna nodded, a small smile playing at the corners of her mouth. "I am happy you are alive."

"Me too!" Iya joined in. "They are bad, but you come. Anna told me you come."

Erik stopped and looked at his two friends. His voice sounded tight and tears filled his eyes as he said, "I was afraid I'd lost you." Embarrassed, he turned his attention to the threatening sky. "Probably wouldn't be a bad idea if we made camp. The wind is getting worse and it looks like a storm is going to come down on us at any time." He looked for a likely spot. "How about there in that little stand of trees? We can build a snow house and stay put until it passes."

Without another word, the three headed for the trees and quickly went to work. Packing and shaping snow into irregular shapes, then pressing the compacted snow together, they built three sturdy walls. With this done, Erik cut tree branches and laid them across the top, then all three covered this with snow, leaving a gap for smoke to escape. Next they searched for firewood, no easy task in the deep snow. Erik used some of the extra branches he'd cut for the roof.

Inside the shelter, they squeezed around a small fire, waited for the coffee to cook, and chewed on hardtack while some of the meat from their supplies roasted.

Anna studied Erik for several minutes and said, "You look bad. I will fix your cut."

"I'm fine. Just need a little sleep is all."

Anna ignored his protests and scooted around the fire until she was next to him. Resting on her knees, she gently pulled his parka back. Erik winced as his blood-matted hair pulled away with the hood. Anna gently moved Erik's hair aside and tenderly examined his head.

Her touch stirred feelings in Erik he had tried to deny. *I can't love a native girl,* he told himself. *It could never work.* Trying to think of something else, he asked, "How's it look?"

"It is bad, but you will live," Anna said playfully.

"Do you know why those men took you and Iya?"

"They talked of a man called Luke. He give money for us."

Erik said nothing, but his jaw tightened as he considered her words. He knew what would have happened if he hadn't found them.

"Need to clean cut," Anna said matter-of-factly as she gathered snow into a pan. She set it over the fire to melt, then rummaged through the bag until she found a piece of cloth to dip in the melted snow. With this she gently dabbed at his wound.

"This is a bad cut," she said as she rinsed out the cloth. The water turned crimson red. "This will hurt," she warned as she gently scrubbed. Erik clenched his teeth and, despite his efforts to not complain, was unable to stifle a moan.

Anna continued her ministries, ignoring Erik's discomfort until she was satisfied the gash was clean. Once more, she searched through the duffel bag for a clean cloth. Finding what she wanted, she ripped the fabric into narrow strips, which she tied together and wound snugly around Erik's head to protect the cut. "That will help. Tomorrow we will change the wrap."

Iya had said very little since Erik had rescued them. Much of the day, she had merely watched him with an unreadable expression in her eyes. It was this look that prompted Erik to ask, "Iya, is something wrong? You keep staring at me."

Iya hesitated before answering. "I thought I will never see you again. Thought you were a ghost." She smiled and added, "You are not." Her eyes filled with tears. "Now I watch you to know your face."

Erik's throat ached as he looked into the innocent eyes of the little girl. He knew one day soon he would have to leave her. He blinked back his tears, hoping she hadn't noticed and wished there was another way. There seemed to be no options.

He thought back to the time he had first met Anna and Iya. They had seemed so different then. He hadn't understood yet that people are people, no matter what their background or color. He never thought he would become fond of them. But he had been wrong about everything. He wished things could be different, but as he thought of the response of those from the outside, he knew they would never understand. Frustrated by his lack of choices, he forced his mind elsewhere.

"Time for us to get some sleep," he announced as he mussed Iya's hair and lay down next to her. "Anna, you look a little pale. Do you feel all right?"

"I am tired," she said with a sigh as she lay down.

Anna and Iya were soon asleep. Erik remained awake and alert, keeping the small opening in the roof clear and watching in case Jarvis had tracked them. After a while he convinced himself that it would be impossible for anyone to find them in the storm, and he joined his sleeping companions.

The storm swirled about the shelter during the night, and the wind howled at the entrance of their small haven. As snow piled near the doorway, the sounds of the storm became muffled and the room warmed. The fading fire cast misshapen shadows on the walls as the three travelers slept, oblivious to the storm that raged outside. The chaotic world beyond the walls of the shelter seemed distant and unreal as they huddled safely together.

Erik woke first. His head still throbbed. While Anna and Iya continued to sleep, he pushed the snow away from the opening and crawled into the morning sunlight. The storm had moved through quickly and except for the fresh powder covering the landscape, its passing would have been undiscernible.

He squinted against the brightness of the fresh white blanket that sparkled in the sun's light. Glancing about, he steeled himself against the pain in his head, then stood and stretched, gulping in the cold, crisp air. He felt better. As he took in the dazzling beauty of the Alaskan morning, he thought, *I don't care what anybody says, purchasing Alaska was the smartest thing Mr. Seward ever did.*

He looked inside at his sleeping companions and tried to decide whether to wake them or not. Until he had nearly lost them, he hadn't realized just how much he had taken Anna and Iya for granted. He looked forward to resuming their pleasant pattern of life and was anxious to return home. He wanted to pack and go. The sooner they made it back to the cabin, the better.

As he considered life with Anna and Iya, he warmed to the idea, then reminded himself, *They aren't my family. It's no use dwelling on the impossible. You can't let yourself care too much.* But he knew that he already did.

He crouched down and called to his companions. "Come on, you two, we've got lots of ground to cover."

Iya peered out with a quizzical look on her face and asked, "Ground to cover?"

Erik laughed and answered, "It's just an expression that means we have lots of traveling to do."

Iya smiled as she climbed from beneath her bedding and crawled into the bright sunlight. She stood for a moment with her face tilted into the sun as if to absorb its light and limited warmth, then with a mischievous look, placed her hands on her hips and barked, "Anna, wake up! We have ground to cover."

Anna moaned from beneath her bedding, lifted a corner and peeked out. She didn't smile, but buried her face beneath her furs a moment longer before forcing herself up.

Erik heated coffee and roasted more of the caribou while Anna and Iya added their sleeping gear to the packs. Anna's face was flushed and she stumbled more than once as she loaded her pack. Erik took it from her and tied the bundles.

"Breakfast is ready," he said, studying Anna closely.

Iya quickly plopped down and devoured her portion.

Anna moved listlessly toward the fire, refused any food, and only sipped at her coffee.

"Anna, are you feeling all right?" Erik asked, concerned by her behavior.

"My head pounds and I am tired is all," Anna answered weakly. "It is nothing."

Erik wasn't certain it was nothing and watched her for a moment longer before finally deciding to take her at her word.

"Well, we'd better get moving. We want to make it back before dark," he said as he hefted his load onto his back.

Checking his compass, Erik took the lead, and the three headed for home.

Chapter 18

*D*ark clouds had moved in and blotted out the sun. The break in the storm had been only a brief respite, and bad weather threatened to descend upon them once more. The idea of spending another night away from their cabin held little appeal for Erik, so he pushed on, picking up the pace, determined to make the cabin before the storm broke.

Iya trudged along beside him, chattering nonstop, her sullen mood of the day before long forgotten. Anna lagged behind. Several times Erik stopped to wait for her, each time asking if she was all right. Anna would only nod and wave him on, but as the hours passed his concern grew.

At midday, they stopped to rest and eat. Anna looked feverish and worn out. Erik offered her a drink of water, but she refused. Iya took the cup and held it out to her sister and, with concern etched across her face, said, "You need."

Anna tried to answer, but all that came out was a deep, raspy cough. Taking a long, shaky breath, she managed a small smile and took the cup with shaking hands and sipped the soothing liquid.

Erik's eyes never left Anna while he portioned out dried meat for each of them. He knew she was sick, but what could he do if she refused help? He didn't know much about doctoring. Anna turned up her nose at the proffered meat. "You must eat something," Erik encouraged. Too weak to argue, she took a small piece and nibbled on it. As a cough shook her again she held out her cup. Erik refilled it, and she quickly swallowed a mouthful to relieve her hacking.

"You look flushed," Erik said and reached out to feel Anna's forehead.

She deflected his hand. "I am fine," she said stubbornly in a croaking voice. "We go now." Unable to hide her weakness, Anna trembled as she pushed herself to her feet and headed in the direction of the cabin, forgetting her pack in the snow.

Erik took it, along with his own, and followed. Iya plowed through the snow alongside him. She no longer chattered, but instead kept her mouth in a tight line and silently watched Anna.

"Why does she have to be so stubborn all the time?" Erik asked. "She's sick and she knows it. Why won't she let me help?"

Iya looked up at him sharply, her eyes frightened, and asked, "Is she bad sick?"

"I don't know," Erik said, his voice grim. "I can't tell. She won't even let me check her temperature." Under his breath he added, "Darned stubborn woman."

"Elders of village say same. Anna is not like others. Always fight . . ." Iya stopped and searched for the right word. "Rule?"

"She certainly does that," Erik said.

"I hear story of her father. He from outside. Maybe that is why?"

"Who was her father?"

Iya thought for a minute. "Man from across the great sea, I think."

"You mean a Russian?"

"Yes. He did not stay with us."

That explains her looks, Erik thought as he followed the headstrong young woman. He was afraid for Anna. It was clear she was not well, but he had no way of knowing just how sick she was. She looked feverish, but Erik couldn't know how high her temperature was unless she let him check it. He felt frustrated and helpless as he trudged along.

Erik and Iya quickly overtook Anna. She moved sluggishly; her eyes seemed to stare at nothing. Erik watched her closely, slowing his own pace. *Why won't she let me help?* he asked himself, then aloud, said, "Let's stop and rest for a while."

Either unwilling to give in to her affliction or too sick to notice Erik's suggestion, Anna continued to plod through the snow. With each step she seemed to grow weaker. Finally she stopped. Another bout of coughing shook her body. She staggered and swayed, then sank to her knees.

Enough is enough, Erik thought as he dropped his trappings. "Mule-headed woman," he muttered under his breath, frustration masking his fear as he took two long strides and quickly closed the distance between them. Supporting her with one arm, he yanked the glove off his free hand with his teeth and lay his hand against her forehead. "My God, Anna! You're burning up!" he exclaimed.

Another coughing spasm was her only reply. Anna nearly toppled forward, but Erik caught her and gently lifted her slight frame, cradling her in his arms.

She leaned against him, unaware of his presence. The heat from her body radiated through her clothing. As he looked down at her feverish face, concern mingled with loving compassion flooded him. He gently caressed her bruised cheek and blinked back his tears. His voice tight, he choked, "We've got to get her back to the cabin."

Setting Anna down for a moment, Erik strapped the larger of the two packs onto his back and asked, "Iya, do you think you could drag the other one?"

Without a word, Iya took hold of the smaller pack, then in a small, frightened voice, asked, "Will Anna be all right?"

"I don't know, Iya. I just don't know," Erik said as he gently took the young woman in his arms and set off through the deep snow. As he fought his way through the seemingly endless wilderness, his mind was filled with questions and doubts. Memories of his mother's last days assailed him. He could still see her small, frail figure dwarfed by the over-stuffed feather bed. She hadn't seemed frightened by her impending death, only concerned for her son. Erik's eyes filled with tears as he remembered her last hours.

He had been sponging her face when she reached up and took his hand. Erik looked into her weary eyes, but emotion choked off any words. Weak, she spoke in a whisper. "Soon I will meet our Lord face to face. It will be wonderful." For a moment her eyes seemed to see beyond the small, dark room, and they suddenly glistened bright with hope. She turned her attention back to her son, caressing his cheek with her parchment dry hand. "Erik, do not grieve too long."

Afraid to face his mother's death, Erik had shushed her and said, "Here, let me get you some more laudanum."

"No. No more of that," she protested weakly. "I just want to look at you." For a moment she searched her son's face, her eyes full of pride and hope. A soft smile lingered as she feel into a peaceful sleep.

After his mother's death, Erik's father seemed to give up and soon yielded to the ravages of smallpox as well. Erik suddenly found himself alone. He had done everything he could, and it still hadn't been enough.

He looked down at Anna and was frightened. *I don't know what to do. I'm no doctor. What if she dies too?* It seemed everyone he cared for had been taken from him. Would Anna be taken as well?

"Get a hold of yourself," Erik chastised himself. "This isn't the same thing. She's going to be fine." He thought back to the days when he had been just a boy and how his Mother had cared for him when he was sick. Memories of her tender care filled his mind. She always knew what to do. He tried to remember every detail. His fears quieted as he realized he had been taught well and remembered that the greatest healer of all stood with him.

Erik's legs burned and his arms ached as he trudged through the snow. When he saw the cabin, he whispered a prayer of thanks.

"Hurry!" Iya called over her shoulder as she rushed ahead and pushed open the door.

Erik crossed the last few yards to the cabin. Iya quickly laid out a bed of soft furs and Erik gently settled Anna's small, limp form on the pallet. As he did so, his arm brushed against her swollen abdomen. Surprised, he studied Anna's shape and understood what he had been too busy, or unwilling, to see before. Anna was pregnant! There was no time to dwell on that, however, and he quickly pushed it to the back of his mind as he accepted another hide from Iya and covered Anna.

Once he was confident he had made Anna as comfortable as possible, Erik started a fire and tended it until heat radiated into the chilled room. It was so cold inside that ice had formed on the walls. Erik knew it would take a very hot fire to melt it and threw another large log into the flames.

Iya knelt next to her sister and wiped her brow. "She is so hot!" the little girl exclaimed in a panicky voice.

"Iya, stay back!" Erik blurted. Iya jerked back and looked at him, her expression hurt and confused.

More kindly, he explained, "I don't want you to catch what she has. I'm sorry for yelling, but you can't go near her until she's well." He knelt next to the young girl and gave her a squeeze to reassure her he wasn't angry, then turned and checked Anna. *She's hotter than ever,* he thought and prayed, *Dear God, help her! Show me what to do.* He wiped her face with a cool, damp cloth, then rested it across her hot forehead while he went to prepare a meal. He knew that if his stomach growled from emptiness, Iya's must as well.

After setting the coffeepot in the coals, he sawed off a frozen chunk of caribou and placed it in a pot of water, which he slid into place over the fire. The meat would make a good meal and the broth, he hoped, would help sustain Anna. He remembered when he had been ill, his mother had always kept him bundled up to keep off any chill and had fed him broth. It had always seemed to make him feel better.

Anna moaned and threw off her covers. "Hot. So hot," she mumbled.

"It's just your fever," Erik said as he knelt next to her and tucked the covers about her again. He took the warm cloth and rinsed it in cool water, then sponged her face again. "Here, this will cool you. Don't worry, you'll get well."

She seemed unaware of his presence.

The hours passed and Anna grew worse. Erik tried to get her to drink some broth, but she refused. When he offered water, she only choked on it. Her breathing became more shallow, and she wheezed as she struggled for air.

Iya sat in the far corner stitching a garment, but each time Erik glanced at her, the little girl's frightened eyes were trained on her sister.

Hour after hour Erik cared for Anna, rarely leaving her side. Even when he rested, his eyes seldom left her. Sipping a cup of coffee, he leaned his elbows on the table and watched as she fought for life. He was tired and his head ached. He had removed his cumbersome dressings and as he massaged his sore head, he brushed against his wound. He winced at the sharp, stabbing pain this brought.

Iya had been watching him and, in her most grown-up voice, said, "I will help you." She stood next to Erik and examined the cut on his head, then wet a cloth and wiped the wound clean. "That is better," she announced and patted his hand.

Erik closed his arm about the little girl and held her close. He didn't say anything. He couldn't. Each time he looked at her, he was reminded of his unavoidable betrayal: One day he would leave her. He couldn't bear to think of it.

Unaware of Erik's torment, Iya returned his embrace and with a smile said, "You do not take care of yourself."

"But you take good care of me," Erik croaked, his voice strained with emotion as he rubbed her back. "It's time you got some sleep. I'll stay up and watch Anna."

Iya shyly planted a kiss on Erik's cheek, crossed the room to her bed, and slipped beneath the covers. She watched her sister for a while, but finally her eyes grew heavy and she fell asleep.

Erik refilled his cup. He sipped and stared at the dark brown liquid with disdain. It had turned bitter. He drank it anyway, thankful that its strong bite would help to keep him awake.

Leaning forward on his knees, his cup in his hand, he watched Anna as she struggled to breathe. She had gotten no better. Erik felt helpless. Once more, memories of his parents' long, painful deaths traveled through his mind and, as he watched Anna's battle, he was afraid.

"God, where are you?" he asked. "How do I pray? I want her to live. I know you can do anything, that nothing is beyond your power. Please save her life," he ended with a moan.

He glanced up at the shelf where his Bible rested and knew it held the answers to his questions and the comfort he sought. But he didn't feel like reading it. He was angry with God. He felt betrayed. *Each time I care about someone, you snatch her away,* he thought. His eyes rested upon Iya for a moment and he wondered, *Will she be next?*

Then, almost against his will, God's quiet voice stole into his mind. *"I have always loved you, Erik. Have I ever failed to be there when you needed me?"* Erik tried to shut it out, but it came again, *"Am I not enough?"* Erik admitted that God had been an ever-present source of strength and comfort. He had never promised that life would be easy, only that he would share the burdens and trials Erik faced. The voice said, *"I will never leave you nor forsake you."*

Erik buried his face in his hands and sobbed, "God, I'm sorry for my lack of faith. Please forgive me. Sometimes it's just so hard." With resolve, he set his coffee aside, pushed himself to his feet, and went to the shelf for his Bible.

As he flipped through the pages, his eyes fell upon 2 Timothy 1:7. *"For God has not given us a spirit of fear, but of power and of love and of a sound mind."* He stared at the passage, trying to take it all in. His God was one of power and love, providing strength and steadiness in times of trial. The enemy was the author of fear. He turned to Philippians 4:6–7, which said, *"Be anxious for nothing, but in everything by prayer and supplication, with thanksgiving, let your re-*

quests be made known to God; and the peace of God, which surpasses all understanding, will guard your hearts and minds through Christ Jesus." Erik read and reread the verses and, finally, the peace he sought settled over him.

Tears rushed to Erik's eyes as he was overwhelmed by the knowledge that the God who created the universe was also a friend who cared about his life. God knew all things, the beginning and the end, and *only he* knew what was best.

Erik's thoughts returned to the baby Anna carried. His feelings were jumbled. He knew the natives had different ideas about relationships between men and women and weren't bound by the morality of his culture. They expressed love and affection openly. He had been offered the company of more than one native girl since coming to Alaska. *It makes no sense to hold what's right in her world against her,* he reasoned. *She has done no wrong.*

As he contemplated the child's reality, however, fear settled into the pit of his stomach. He didn't know when the baby would be born, but by the look of things, it would happen long before they would be established in a new village. *Anna will have to give birth to her baby out here, without a midwife or doctor,* Erik thought, and his heart beat faster as he realized what that might mean. He knew nothing about babies.

Almost immediately, he reminded himself who orchestrated these events. And with that knowledge, he felt comforted. God knew about the baby and Anna, and about his lack of education concerning women and, still, he had allowed this. God was in control. Erik looked up and, with trust, said, "Lord, I know my worrying about all this won't help, so I'm giving the whole thing to you. I know you have a plan."

Anna turned in her sleep and was jolted by another attack of coughing. Erik quickly slid to the floor and wiped the perspiration from her face and comforted her with words of encouragement. He looked at her, taking in the dark lashes against her flawless bronze skin and remembered the broad smile he'd grown accustomed to. His chest constricted in pain and a lump formed in his throat as he realized he loved this beautiful, strong-willed woman. "Please let her live," he prayed. Her death seemed too great a sorrow to bear.

As pictures of what her future would be like with a white husband flashed through his mind, Erik told himself that it would be impossible. It could never work. *I've seen how people treat the natives. If she lives, she'll never know how I feel,* he vowed. He stayed there through the night, sponging her face and praying for her recovery.

Two full days passed with no improvement.

On the morning of the third day, Erik woke to Iya's shout of, "Erik! Erik! I think she is better!"

Erik pushed himself up on his elbow. He had fallen asleep at Anna's side and confusion plagued him until he looked at Anna. Suddenly he was wide awake. She did look better. He touched her face. It felt cool. The fever had broken! Her breathing sounded easier too.

Erik grinned. "She *is* better!" he announced as he jumped to his feet and jubilantly lifted Iya into the air. She giggled as Erik twirled her about.

"Can I care for her now?" she asked innocently.

"Not yet, little one," Erik said as he stroked her hair. "But soon."

Anna's weak voice interrupted their merrymaking. "Thirsty," she croaked.

Erik immediately set Iya on her feet and dipped out a cool cup of water. Kneeling next to Anna, he cradled her head in his hand and held the cup to her dry, cracked lips. She gulped down the refreshing liquid.

"Not so fast," Erik said kindly. "Only a little at first. You've been pretty sick." To himself he prayed, *Thank you Father!* His voice husky, he said, "For a while there, I wasn't so sure you were going to make it."

Anna managed a weak smile and asked, "Iya?"

"She's fine. Just worried about you."

Iya smiled and waved from across the room. "Erik not let me come close," she explained.

Anna smiled back at her.

"Do you think you could handle some broth?" Erik asked.

Anna nodded weakly.

After warming some soup, he filled a cup, stooped down next to Anna, and gently slid his hand behind her shoulders. Lifting her slightly, he placed the cup to her lips.

She took a couple of sips. As she did, her eyes met Erik's. They were no longer filled with anger but with something he didn't understand. They held each other's gaze for a moment before Erik's discomfort forced him to look away.

He cleared his throat and asked, "How about a little more?"

Obediently Anna drank more of the broth. Exhausted by the effort, she lay back on her pallet and slept. Her breathing no longer labored, she rested quietly.

Gradually Anna regained her strength. Erik and Iya did all the chores until Anna insisted she be allowed to resume some of her daily tasks. Erik grudgingly relented.

One evening after dinner, he leaned back in his chair. He had been thinking about Anna and Iya's abduction when he said, "You must've gotten it from that fella in the tent."

"Gotten it?" Anna questioned.

"You know, your sickness."

Anna nodded in agreement and turned back to her sewing.

"He hurt Anna," Iya spoke up.

Anna flashed a look at Iya that told her to shush, but it was too late.

Erik leaned forward on the table, looked across at Anna, and asked, "What did he do to you?"

"He did not hurt me," Anna answered stiffly.

"That is not true," Iya said. "He did."

Erik looked at Anna and waited for an answer.

Anna reddened under Erik's gaze, and she finally repeated, "He did not hurt me. He," she hesitated, "he touched me. That is all. I do not want to talk of it," she added firmly and ferociously poked her needle back through the tough hide she was working on, making it clear the discussion was ended.

Erik forced himself to be still. He was angry and every part of him wished to lay hold of the man who had attacked Anna. He pushed himself away from the table and paced about the room.

Anna glanced at Erik, but said nothing more. Then, as if to change the subject, she playfully tweaked Iya's nose and said, "Time for you to sleep."

Iya frowned and pleaded to stay up a little longer. Anna merely smiled and shuffled her off to her bed, hugging the little girl tight before tucking her in.

"Would you sing me a song?" Iya asked.

Anna sat back on her heels. "Which song?"

Iya closed her eyes for a minute as she thought, then answered, "The song of spring that momma sang?"

"You remember that?"

"Yes," Iya whispered.

Anna clasped her hands in her lap, closed her eyes and, with her voice barely above a whisper, chanted a tune in her native tongue.

Erik relaxed and sat down. The words sounded strange to him, but the melody and elegant clarity of Anna's voice transported him to a place of beauty and peace. Iya joined in, her voice blending with Anna's. *I've never heard a sweeter sound,* Erik thought. Soon Iya's eyes were closed and only Anna's voice filled the cabin. Gradually the song faded and the room became quiet.

Erik wished she would continue, but instead asked, "What was that about?"

Anna turned a quizzical look upon him.

"The song, I mean."

"It speaks of sunshine and flowers, of the return of the birds. Melting snow and warmth. Life and death." She stopped and her eyes glistened. "My mother used to sing it when I was small."

Moved by Anna's grief, Erik cleared his throat and said gently, "It's beautiful. Your mother taught you well. I wish I understood the words." He paused for a moment, then thinking the time was right, he took a deep breath and continued uneasily, "There's something I've been wanting to talk to you about."

Anna never took her eyes from Erik as she waited for him to continue.

"Could you come and sit at the table?"

She crossed the room and joined him. "Is this serious?" she asked.

"Yes," Erik answered as he studied his hands, folding and unfolding them, uncertain how to begin.

Anna moistened her lips and sat very still.

"I know about the baby," he suddenly blurted out.

Anna sat back. Her eyes grew large as she stared into his. Unable to hold his gaze, she looked down at her lap. So quietly, Erik could barely hear her, she said, "It is Kinauquak's and mine."

"Why didn't you tell me?"

She looked up, her eyes angry and penetrating, and snapped, "Why should I tell you?"

"Well, I just think you should have, that's all. I mean, I'm responsible for you," Erik ended flatly.

"Do not worry about the baby. It is mine. I will care for it." Anna answered as she tilted her chin up, her eyes glinting with defiance. She sat straighter in her chair, her earlier gentle demeanor replaced by combativeness.

As usual I've said it all wrong. Now she's mad, Erik thought as he grasped for a way to salvage the conversation. Carefully, he continued, "I'm not upset about the baby. I was just worried, that's all. I understand about you and Kinauquak." His voice became gentle as he added, "I know you loved each other."

The challenge in Anna's eyes softened.

"When will it be born?" Erik asked quietly.

"When the snow melts."

"There are no villages nearby, and we will still be here," Erik said, knowing he was stating the obvious. When he received no response, he continued, a note of panic in his voice. "Who will help you?"

"I do not need help. I know how to have a baby."

Still uncertain, Erik continued, "But what if there's a problem? What if something goes wrong?"

"I helped my mother and others many times. I know what to do."

Realizing it would do no good to discuss the issue further, Erik just shook his head in frustration. He couldn't change the circumstances. "I'm tired," he finally said as he left the table and crawled into bed. He rolled over and stared at the wall as his mind filled with questions and fears. He closed his eyes and prayed, *Father, please take care of Anna and the baby. And show me how to help, not hurt.*

Chapter 19

I’ve got some work to do outside," Erik said as he shrugged into his coat. "I won't be long." He opened the door, looked out at the deep snow piled about the cabin and out-buildings, and said jovially, "Later we'll have to stomp down some of this snow. At this rate, it'll bury us by the end of the month." He closed the door and was gone.

As Anna watched him go, she asked Iya, "Do you think Erik is all right?"

Iya looked at her quizzically and asked, "Is something wrong?"

"No," Anna answered hesitantly, "he just seems different." She didn't tell Iya she was worried. Erik had been acting peculiar, spending hours working outdoors and often closing himself inside the cache as if trying to hide something. His behavior puzzled Anna but when she asked him about it, he was evasive, mumbling something about repairs. It made no sense to her. She was sure he wasn't telling her the truth, but after repeatedly asking what was going on and receiving no reasonable explanation, she decided he wanted privacy and stopped asking. She couldn't, however, keep herself from worrying.

Anna's belly had grown large and round, pushing tight against her tunic. She pulled at the garment and sighed, thinking she would have to fashion a larger one. Soon her present clothing would be unable to accommodate her ever-increasing girth.

The baby was active, and Anna was certain she carried a boy. *Such a busy, strong child must be a boy,* she reasoned. *One day he will be a great hunter.* She patted her abdomen affectionately. "Kinauquak would have been proud to have a son," she told the child, as if it were already in her arms.

Anna's short frame provided little room for the growing infant and as she examined her protruding belly, she wondered if she had miscalculated her date of confinement. *That would be good,* she thought as she pushed against the child, trying to dislodge him from beneath her rib cage where he often wedged himself and left Anna breathless.

One evening, as the three friends shared stories from their past, Iya's interest fell upon the unborn infant's activity. Intrigued by the rise and fall of Anna's stomach, she asked, "What does it feel like when the baby moves?"

Anna thought for a moment, searching for an appropriate description. Her eyes warm and bright, she stroked her abdomen and finally said, "It feels like life. I have known nothing like this before." She motioned for Iya to come and sit beside her. Iya made herself comfortable near her older sister and looked at her expectantly.

Anna took the child's hand and placed it on her rounded belly. Iya sat very still, her eyes wide with anticipation. Suddenly, Anna's stomach jumped beneath her hand and, as if she'd been burned, Iya quickly withdrew it. "It moved!" she exclaimed in a hushed voice and rested her hand on Anna's stomach once more. It didn't take long before the baby stirred again. This time, Iya didn't pull away, but her face lit up, telling of the joy she found in sharing the miracle that thrived within her sister. As Anna's stomach bounced again, Iya's expression turned to one of concern and she asked, "Does it hurt?"

Anna laughed. "No, it does not hurt."

Erik, who had been watching from a distance, moved closer, seeming as fascinated as the little girl.

Abruptly Iya turned to him and asked, "Do you want to feel the baby?"

Erik's face turned crimson and he stuttered, "That's all right; I don't need to."

Anna looked up shyly at Erik and said, "I do not mind."

Erik said nothing for a minute, fighting with himself over what to do. Finally he asked, "Are you sure?"

Anna nodded.

Hesitantly, he knelt on the floor next to her, fidgeted for a moment, then asked again, "You're sure you don't mind?"

Anna suddenly felt a little shy and wondered why. Pregnancy had never been something to hide but a thing to take joy in. She smiled, gently took Erik's hand, and placed it on the left side of her abdomen. His face turned red again as he glanced at Anna, then down at the floor. At first, nothing happened.

"Well, I guess it's gone to sleep," he said, sounding relieved and pulling his hand away.

"*He* has not. Wait. He will move again," Anna said as she replaced his hand.

Awkwardly Erik waited. Then he grinned. "It moved! It really did!" he announced. "How about that! I felt it!" He waited a moment longer. Again Anna's stomach bounced beneath his hand. "There he is again!" Reluctantly he removed his hand and sat on the floor next to Anna. "It's hard to believe there's another human being living inside you. It's a miracle. Only God could do something like that."

Anna frowned at the mention of God, but Erik didn't seem to notice her sour expression and went on enthusiastically, "Thank you for letting me feel it. I've never done anything like that before."

Moved by Erik's emotion, Anna forgot her irritation and declared, "I know he is a boy."

"Well, you can't be sure," Erik cautioned her.

"I know he is. Only a boy would be so strong. And he is a big baby," Anna said, her mind filled with thoughts of what kind of son he would be. She could see him as a young man, hunting the beasts of the sea as his father had done. He would be like Kinauquak. She would tell him of his father, his people, and where he came from.

A few days later, Anna awoke to the sound of the wind howling about the cabin. The shutters shook with each new blast, sending cold shivers of air under the door and along the window casing.

Erik was already up and had prepared a breakfast of fried caribou and sourdough pancakes. He whistled as he set the table, taking care that it was done just right.

Anna watched him and wondered why the extra prudence. However, the tantalizing aroma of frying meat quickly pushed aside her questions, and she stretched beneath her covers. "Mm, smells good," she said, with a dreamy smile on her face.

"Morning," Erik answered, almost too cheerfully.

Anna studied him for a minute as he went about his tasks. *What is different?* she asked. *Why do his spirits soar today?* Aloud, she asked, "Why are you so happy?"

"It's a special day," Erik answered.

"Why is this day special?"

Iya sat up, stifled a yawn, and listened to the banter between Erik and Anna.

"I know it won't mean anything to you, but according to my calendar, it's Christmas!" Erik answered as he flipped a pancake.

"Christmas? What is Christmas?" Iya asked.

"Well, Christmas is the day Christians celebrate Jesus' birth," Erik answered.

"I know Jesus. You read about him." Iya said as she climbed out from beneath her bedding.

"That's right. Jesus Christ is the son of God. He was born on this day, generations ago."

"I remember Father Ermelov talked of Jesus," Iya said as she moved closer to Erik. The caribou steaks caught her attention, and she said, "I am hungry."

"Breakfast is almost ready."

Anna's mood soured as she listened to Erik, and her anger and bitterness toward his God resurfaced. *I do not have to celebrate this Jesus' birth!* she fumed. Erik's joy was something she couldn't comprehend. *Why would a man's birth that took place so long ago cause so much excitement?* she wondered. None of it made sense to her.

She watched Erik and was reminded of the peace and steadiness that always seemed to be a part of him. *Is it his God?* she wondered, longing for the peace he seemed to possess.

"Come on, Anna. Get up. You too, Iya. I've got something for you. But not until you've eaten." Erik's urging cut into Anna's thoughts.

Grudgingly she crawled out of bed. Although she struggled to hang on to her foul mood, Erik's high spirits were contagious, and it slowly dissipated. Leisurely, she brushed out her hair, braided it, and with a smile, sat down at the table.

Iya was already eating, eager to see Erik's surprise. Anna ate slowly, purposely trying to hide her interest. She studied Erik. *He has been acting odd lately,* she thought and wondered if it had anything to do with his surprise.

The moment Iya finished, she jumped down from the table and, unable to control her curiosity, demanded, "Anna, hurry!"

Taking pity on her young sister, Anna finally pushed her plate aside with a smile. Iya fairly danced with anticipation.

Anna rose to clear the table, but Erik stopped her. "I'll take care of that," he said as he took her plate and swiftly cleared the table and washed the dishes.

Iya could stand the waiting no longer, and asked, "Can I see now?"

"All done," Erik said with a mischievous smile as he slipped on his coat. "I'll be right back." He walked out and closed the door behind him.

Anna and Iya glanced at each other, then back at the doorway. Iya's eyes were bright with anticipation. Anna's curiosity was acute, but she tried to maintain an appearance of indifference.

A few minutes later, Erik returned with a suspicious-looking bulge beneath his coat. He walked over to Iya and knelt in front of her. "I want you to close your eyes," he said in a teasing tone.

Iya promptly shut her eyes.

Erik pulled a doll from beneath his coat. "Keep your eyes closed and hold out your hands," he said. Iya promptly stuck her arms straight out in front of her, looking as if she might burst at any second. Erik gently placed the doll in the little girl's arms. "You can look now."

Iya peeked down at the bundle in her arms then stared at the toy. For several moments she didn't react as she gazed down at the gift. Suddenly she clutched the doll to her chest and hugged it as if it might escape. She held it away from her and examined it a moment before cuddling it again and rocking it gently. "She is beautiful!" she said, her voice quiet with wonder.

Anna's eyes filled with tears as she watched Iya's tender regard for the toy. She reached out and touched the babe, examining Erik's handiwork. He had fashioned the miniature little girl from hides, then stuffed her with soft pliable furs, using dyes from local berries to paint a sweet face with a winsome smile. Making it even finer, he had fashioned a parka nearly identical to Iya's. It was hard to believe Erik had done such excellent work.

"It is mine?" Iya asked. As she looked up at her big friend, her eyes filled with gratitude and joy.

Erik answered, "Who else would it belong to?"

Iya hugged the doll to her again.

Anna didn't understand what had prompted Erik to make such a wonderful gift and decided she didn't care. All that mattered was the joy it brought to Iya.

Iya held up her doll and said, "Look, Anna!"

Anna nodded and said, "She is beautiful."

Erik stood back and watched, a smile creasing his face. Then, remembering Anna, he said, "Now, I have something for you." He slipped outside again, leaving the door partially ajar. A moment later, he pushed it open and backed into the room, clutching something close to his chest. He turned about and, as if presenting a gift to a queen, held a wooden cradle out to Anna.

She stared blankly at the piece of furniture.

Erik moved closer and said. "It's for you."

"It is beautiful," Anna said hesitantly, then asked, "What is it for?"

A puzzled expression crossed Erik's face before he broke into a broad smile. "It's a cradle. You know, a bed for the baby."

He placed it on the floor and lined it with a pelt. "See, the baby sleeps in here," he said patting the soft fur. "If it cries, you rock it like this." He gently moved the bed back and forth.

Anna knelt next to the wooden cradle. She stroked the velvety smooth wood and slowly rocked it. Her eyes filled with tears as she realized Erik truly had accepted the baby and wasn't angry. In a shaky voice she said, "It is a fine bed. Thank you."

Erik stood up and, looking a little embarrassed, responded, "I'm glad you like your gifts. It was hard to think of something way out here. I didn't have much to work with and you made it awfully tough to do anything without getting caught."

Anna looked up at the tall Norwegian and asked, "Why do you give us gifts?"

Erik answered simply, "It's Christmas. It is the custom of my people to give gifts to the ones we care about at Christmas. It's a way of reminding us of God's gift of his son."

Anna and Iya looked at Erik, their faces blank. Anna understood the words, but not the meaning.

"Would you like to hear the story of Jesus' birth?"

Iya jumped to her feet. She clasped Erik's hand in hers and, with her precious doll tucked under her arm, cuddled in close to him and said, "Yes. Tell us the story."

Erik settled back in his chair and pulled Iya onto his lap.

"Long ago God promised to send a Messiah, a savior for his people. Well, these people waited a very long time for their king."

Iya's eyes were riveted on Erik, waiting expectantly. Anna listened suspiciously.

"One day an angel came to a young woman named Mary."

"I remember when you read about angels," Iya interrupted.

Erik smiled and continued, "Well, this angel told Mary that God had chosen her to bear his son. Mary wasn't afraid and believed the angel. She felt great honor at being asked to carry the son of God."

Anna felt uncomfortable and cleared her throat. She wished he would hurry and finish but didn't interrupt.

"When the time came for Mary to have her baby, she was in a town called Bethlehem."

"That is a funny name," Iya commented.

Erik nodded and continued, "There were many people in the city and there was no place for Mary and her husband, Joseph, to stay, so they had to sleep in a stable."

"Stable? What is a stable?" Iya asked.

"Well, this was a cave where the people kept their animals safe from bad weather," Erik explained, then went on with the story. "Soon after they got there, Mary had her baby. It was a boy just like the angel had said, and Mary named him Jesus as the angel had told her to. Soon people from all around came to worship the son of God because an angel had told them of his birth. Mary knew who Jesus was and wasn't surprised when they came. Even kings visited from far-off lands and brought gifts for the baby."

"Is a king like a chief?" Iya asked.

"Yes, just like a chief," Erik answered with a smile.

"Why did baby come?"

Erik stopped and thought for a moment. "In the beginning, when God made the people of the earth, they loved him very much and did all that he said. But one day, the evil one tempted them, and they disobeyed God. They were no longer pure and, as the years went by, they stopped listening to God. But God still loved the people, so he sent his son to speak to them and to save them from their sins."

"Sin is when people are bad," Iya announced.

"That's right. We all do bad things sometimes, don't we?" Iya nodded.

"Jesus came to take away our sins so we can have a home in heaven with him forever," Erik explained and glanced at Anna. She met his eyes, but looked back guardedly.

"Father Ermelov talked of Heaven. He said it is good," Iya explained.

"It is very good," Erik said, tearing his eyes from Anna's. "It's a place where we will be with God forever, and there will be no sadness or pain there, ever."

"How did Jesus take away sins?"

"Well, when he became a man he did many miracles, and everywhere he went he told people about God. Some of the religious men wanted to kill him."

"Why?" Iya asked indignantly.

"I think they were afraid Jesus' teachings would weaken the hold they had over the people. But Jesus wasn't afraid because he knew it was all part of God's plan. He taught for three years, and one day the leaders of the city captured him and nailed him to a wooden cross where they left him to die. But before he did, he took every sin anyone had ever done or ever would do upon himself—even the bad things you and I do."

Iya seemed to understand and asked, "How do I get to heaven?"

Erik smiled. "If you believe Jesus died for you and took away all your sins, he promises you will be with him in heaven one day. It is a gift from him."

"I do believe!" Iya announced.

Erik smiled and hugged her. "Then he is certainly saving you a place in heaven. It is your gift to keep. God never takes back something he has given."

Iya smiled, then turned to Anna and asked, "Do you believe?"

Anna didn't answer for a minute then said irritably. "I think it is a story like the one I tell about the seal."

"The story about the young hunter and the seal reminded me of Christ's sacrifice," Erik said kindly. "Do you believe your ancestors' story?"

Anna hesitated before answering, then said curtly, "That story was told by my people. It is not a lie."

Erik leveled a serious look upon Anna and said, "I believe your people are honest, Anna, and the story was a beautiful tale, but the seal only gave physical life to the people. Jesus gives spiritual life, life that never ends. Do you think God lies?"

Anna stared at him then glanced away as she mumbled, "I do not know your God."

Quietly Erik continued, "Anna, the only way you can see heaven is to know Jesus. Without him you will forever be separated from God. Please believe he loves you. That is why he died for you."

Iya nodded in agreement. "It is true, Anna. I know—I feel it here," she said as she placed her hand over her chest. Tears threatened to spill from her eyes as she looked at her sister. "Please, Anna, believe."

Anna didn't answer. Instead, she pulled on her parka, opened the door and said, "We need wood," then disappeared through the door.

Erik and Iya stared at the closed door as if to will Anna back and safely into God's grace.

Iya looked up at Erik and asked, "Why does she not believe?"

"It's hard for some people. The sorrows in their life pile up, and they hurt too much to trust anybody. Even God. We can pray she will know him someday," he said and hugged the little girl.

"I will pray," Iya said and looked back at the doorway.

Iya climbed down off Erik's lap and placed her new doll in the cradle. She gently rocked it while she hummed a sweet tune, then said, "I will name her Mary." She looked up at Erik and asked, "Will Anna's baby be like baby Jesus?"

"No," Erik answered. "Anna's baby will be a special person, but not God. Jesus is more than just a man; he is God."

Iya nodded, seeming content with his answer and returned to rocking the cradle. "Next Christmas, I will give you a present," she stated matter-of-factly.

Erik smiled. Blinking back his tears he thought, *You've already given me the best gift I could ever receive.* But as he glanced at the door, his smile faded.

Chapter 20

$\mathcal{T}$he weeks passed and the days gradually grew longer. Signs of spring began to emerge. Rain occasionally replaced the snowfall, and the temperature rarely dropped below zero. The sound of water dripping from the rooftop was a pleasant change from the constant howl of the icy wind. At times the heat of the fire provided more warmth than necessary, making the cabin stifling hot.

Each time Anna trekked outdoors, she watched for bare patches of earth, longing for the greenery she knew was hidden beneath the tiresome white carpet. Even more, she yearned for the first spring flower to push its way to the surface and proudly display its delicate finery.

One evening, Anna was unable to sleep. She felt hot and sticky and, although she pushed her covers aside, still felt smothered in the overwarm cabin. She tossed and turned. Finally, unable to lie quiet any longer, she slipped out of bed, carefully stepping over Iya's sleeping form. Cumbersome and heavy with her child, she stumbled as she groped her way through the darkness.

She found the wall and felt her way along the rough hewn beams until she came to the window. Quietly, she loosened the latch and propped the shutter open. Moonlight flooded the room, followed by a cold rush of air. Anna closed her eyes, allowing the cool breeze to wash over her face. She took a slow, deep breath, and enjoyed the icy sensation as the chilled air flowed into her lungs. Her breath misted as she exhaled.

Resting her arms on the sill, Anna peered at the moon. The large yellow sphere rested low in the sky, silhouetting the forest. A smattering of clouds drifted across its face, casting shadows over the snow. It was still and eerie. Anna imagined evil spirits among the shadows then chided herself for her foolishness and searched for peace within the quiet moonlit landscape. She closed her eyes to allow the stillness to quiet her nerves.

A noise from the cache disrupted the silence. Anna jumped and strained to see into the half-light. She listened and waited for it to come again. Anna was certain the sound had come from the cache, but she could not see anything. She continued to study the building and waited. A few minutes later, an animal emerged and leapt the few feet to the snow. Its body slung close to the ground, it lumbered away from the cache dragging something in its jaws. Fascinated, Anna watched for several moments before she realized it was escaping with a large portion of their meat.

"Erik! Erik!" she whispered sharply into the partially dark room.

Erik sat up immediately, blinked his eyes, and tried to clear his mind as he peered about the dark cabin. He finally found Anna silhouetted in the window.

"What is it? What's wrong?"

"Something is in the cache! It took meat!" Anna said urgently.

Erik jumped to his feet. He slipped one leg into his trousers while balancing precariously on the other. Stepping into his boots, he shrugged his coat on and disappeared out the door, rifle in hand.

Anna watched from the window as Erik approached the cache cautiously, his rifle cocked and ready. Snowdrifts were piled about the building, so Erik only had to climb a few rungs of the ladder to get inside, a blessing to him but an open invitation to cunning scavengers. Warily, he pulled the door open and peered inside, then glanced back toward the forest where the intruder had disappeared. He shook his head in disgust and tramped back to the cabin.

"Looks like a wolverine," Erik said as he set his rifle on its rack. "Ornery critters. They have a reputation for thievery. If I hadn't gotten careless about not stomping down the snow, we wouldn't have this problem. Now that he knows he can get in, he'll be back."

"It was my job to pack the snow," Anna apologized.

"No, it's my fault. You're in no condition to be tamping the snow. I just got too sure spring would take care of the problem." He slipped off his coat and hung it up. "There's nothing more I can do tonight. We might as well get some sleep," he said as he dropped onto his bed. He pulled off his boots but didn't bother to take off his trousers before climbing beneath the covers. Chilled by his brief trip into the cold night air, he shivered and burrowed deeper into his bedding.

Anna closed the window and returned to her pallet. No longer too warm, she pulled a fur over herself and tried to find a comfortable position. Lately, her bulging stomach and unceasing heartburn made it difficult to sleep. Still, Anna was thankful the baby thrived, and she often thought of its approaching arrival. She tried to imagine what her son would look like as she nestled beneath the covers and rested her head in the crook of her arm.

Erik rose early the following morning to investigate the damage done by their prowler. He returned to the cabin and announced that he was certain their visitor had been a wolverine. "He'll be back, if I know anything about those beasts," he said as he warmed his hands by the fire. "They almost always return. I'll set out a couple traps for him." His eyes sparkled with mischief and his lips turned up in a crooked smile as he added confidently, "He'll have the surprise of his life tonight. And I'll have a fine pelt to add to my collection."

The following morning, Anna awoke to the sound of the cabin door slamming. Erik stood just inside the doorway, muttering something about a no-good beast. He looked up and found Anna watching him. "That devil. He stole my bait and took off with more of our meat!" he complained indignantly. "Well, he won't outsmart me. Tonight, I'll be waiting for him."

Anna knew there was nothing she could say and held her tongue.

After supper that evening, Erik slipped into his boots, pulled on his parka and, with extra furs tucked under one arm and his rifle under the other, said good-night, then left the cabin.

○○○○○○○○○○○

Determined to catch the nighttime marauder, Erik trudged through the snow toward the cache. He stepped inside, making sure to leave the door unlatched, and sat propped against the far wall with his gun resting across his knees. There he waited, buried beneath the heavy furs.

The time passed interminably slow as Erik struggled to remain alert. After nodding off more than once, he stripped away the extra covers, hoping the cold would rouse him. Shivering, he thought, *I've got to stay awake.*

The moon was up and the woeful sound of wolves echoed in the distance. The hours passed and Erik began to wonder if the midnight visitor would return. He dozed off, and his chin bobbed on his chest.

A shuffling sound came from outside, followed by sniffing about the door. Erik was suddenly wide awake. Silently he cocked his rifle, raised it to his shoulder, and waited.

The door shuddered and jerked as something pushed against it.

Erik held his breath, frozen in position, his rifle aimed at the door.

A shiny black nose made its way around the door followed by the broad, banded face of a wolverine. Unaware of Erik, it inched into the room and peered about, searching for booty. It skulked toward a large slab of caribou, placed its forepaws on the meat, sunk long sharp teeth into the carcass, and began to drag it toward the door.

For a moment, Erik had a twinge of remorse. He couldn't help respecting the animal. It was strong, intelligent, and gutsy, all things Erik found admirable. But despite his feelings, he knew what he had to do. Applying a steady even pressure, he squeezed the trigger. A loud report reverberated across the silent countryside. The wolverine fell.

Erik pushed himself up from his cramped position and stretched his legs as he watched to make certain the animal had died. Cautiously he approached then picked up the lifeless creature and examined it. "You're a beauty, all right. Too bad you couldn't keep to yourself."

He carried the wolverine outside and left it near the cabin. *Tomorrow will be soon enough to skin it out,* he thought, sleep uppermost in his mind.

○ ○ ○ ○ ○ ○ ○ ○ ○ ○ ○

Anna heard the rifle shot and waited impatiently for Erik's return.

As Erik entered the cabin, he didn't need to say a word; his tired smile confirmed his success. "Well, that's the last of him," he stated proudly.

"Good," Anna said. "What did you do with it?"

"I left him outside. I'll skin him tomorrow." He yawned as he pulled off his boots. "I'm so tired," he said and crawled beneath his furs. He was asleep almost immediately.

Anna lay in the darkness and listened to his even breathing. The child within her stirred and she felt a sudden tight pressure stretch across her abdomen. As the tautness subsided, she thought, *Soon. He will be here soon.*

The smell of coffee roused Anna the following morning. She rolled to her side and looked about the cabin. The fire was hot and the coffee had already boiled and been set in the coals, but Erik was gone. Lack of sleep hadn't kept him in bed. Iya snoozed peacefully. Anna stretched and awkwardly pushed herself up off the floor.

She poured herself a cup of coffee and sat quietly sipping the hot liquid. A smile crept across her face as she remembered her first taste of the dark brew. She had never believed that she would actually enjoy the strong drink. That seemed a lifetime ago.

Erik will be hungry when he returns, she thought as she brushed her hair back. After combing it free of tangles and splashing her face with water, she set about preparing breakfast. She measured out flour and water and added fat and salt to it, then kneaded the mixture until it was blended.

The baby kicked her in the side, and she stopped to rest for a moment. As she placed her hand protectively on her swollen belly, she realized she could breath more easily. The baby had settled lower in her womb and felt heavy in her pelvis. As she turned back to her work, she took a deep breath and wished her son was already in her arms.

As she removed the last of the fried bread from the pan, Erik came through the door. "Mm, smells good," he said as he hung up his coat. He poured himself a cup of coffee and sat on a chair. "I'm beat and the day has only begun," he said as he leaned forward, placed his elbows on the table, and rubbed his face in his hands as if to scrub away his fatigue. "I don't feel like I got *any* sleep last night."

Anna placed the bread in front of him and called to Iya. "Time to get up, little girl."

Iya moaned softly, but didn't move.

"There will be no fried bread left," Anna teased.

Iya quickly sat up and said, "I am awake." She catapulted herself out of bed and hurried to the table, planting herself in the chair opposite Erik.

Anna joined them. She sipped her coffee and asked, "Did we lose a lot of meat?"

"Not too much. It could have been worse; wolverines can clean a man out. They're regular gluttons. But we've got enough left to last us until the spring thaw. After that, there will be plenty of fish again and there is always more than enough game."

Anna closed her eyes and tried to imagine the fields green with lush grasses decorated with fragrant flowers and warmed by a summer sun. "I cannot wait for spring. Will it be soon?"

Erik nodded. "Not long now. If these warm temperatures hold, the breakup should begin any time." He hesitated, "The days are getting longer. Did you notice?"

Anna nodded and sighed.

Iya crossed the room and pulled Erik's Bible from the shelf. She bounced into his lap and asked, "Will you read me story?"

"Well, I suppose I've got time for one. Which do you want to hear?"

"Jonah and the whale!"

"Are you sure you wouldn't like to learn a new one?"

Iya shook her head and looked up at Erik expectantly.

"Okay. Jonah it is," Erik said as he opened his Bible and began to read the account of the unwilling prophet.

Anna kept herself busy by clearing and washing the breakfast dishes. As usual, she acted as if she were not listening. Erik had often read stories aloud from his Bible, and Iya always seemed to soak in every word while Anna tried hard not to listen. Still, the words always drew her. She could not close them out. The story of the woman called Ruth was one she never tired of and, as she considered it, she thought, *I am like Ruth going to a new land. Maybe it will be a place of another God.* She considered the kind of woman Ruth had been and wished she could be such a woman. But she was afraid and knew she could never worship the outsider's God.

Erik finished the story as Anna sat down to do some sewing. Iya begged him to read another, but he pushed her gently from his lap and said, "There's nothing I'd rather do, but the work won't wait."

Iya pouted.

"Could you give me a hand?" Erik asked.

Iya's face brightened. "Yes!" she replied enthusiastically as she threw on her coat, slipped into her boots, and followed Erik out the door.

Anna pushed herself out of her chair and walked to the window. Quietly she opened it and watched the two. Iya followed the big man about, chattering all the while. He listened to everything the little girl said, careful to comment appropriately. It was good to see Iya so happy again.

As she watched the scene, Anna realized she didn't want winter to end. She wanted things to stay as they were. Spring meant they would be moving on and Erik would leave them. She wondered if Iya knew her friendship with the big Norwegian was to last only a short time longer, that soon she would have to say good-bye to her friend.

Slowly Anna closed the window and shuffled across the room. She picked up her sewing, but couldn't concentrate on it and finally set it aside.

She tried to imagine a bright future for her and Iya but was unable to shake the blanket of sorrow that had settled about her. With a sigh, she turned back to her stitching and wished the storms might continue.

he weather continued to improve. There had been no fresh snow for more than a week and a feeling of expectation hung in the air. Spring, with its turbulent breakup, was imminent, as was the arrival of Anna's baby. They all watched and waited.

One morning after Erik left to check his trap line, Anna felt stifled in the cabin and longed for a walk in the fresh air. She peeked outside to check the weather. The sky was gray but held no threat of rain or snow, and the air felt almost balmy.

She closed the door and took her boots to the table. Feeling awkward and clumsy, she struggled to pull them on. "Iya, would you like to take a walk? We will look in the woods for new grass. Maybe we will even find a flower."

A grin lit up Iya's face. "I would like to!" she exclaimed then looked dubiously at Anna's swollen belly. "Can you walk in the snow?" she asked.

Anna smiled, understanding Iya's doubts as she looked down at her stomach and patted it affectionately. "I am big and clumsy, but I think the baby needs fresh air."

A dull pain settled across her lower back, reaching around her sides and across her abdomen. Her stomach tightened for a moment before slowly relaxing as the pain dissipated. The sensation was familiar. Anna had been experiencing mild contractions for days, and although this one was sharper than the others, she wasn't alarmed. "I can do it," she said as she pulled her parka over her head.

Iya laid her doll in the cradle and took her parka from its hook. Before slipping it on, she asked, "You are sure?"

Anna nodded her head and stepped out through the door.

The snow was still fairly deep, but after the experience with the wolverine, Erik had been careful to keep it tamped down about the house and food cache. And with no fresh snow, his recent trips to the trap line had left a good path.

At first they walked in Erik's tracks, but soon Iya marched off in another direction, careful to lay a trail for Anna. She rushed ahead, whirled about, then ran back. Several times, she stiffened her body and fell backward into the snow. She would lie there giggling before repeating the stunt. One time, she grew quiet as she looked up at the gray sky and asked, "Will spring come soon?"

"Soon," Anna answered breathlessly as she trudged up to her sister. She stopped and breathed fresh air deeply. It no longer stung her lungs but was just cool enough to be invigorating.

Another contraction wrapped itself around Anna, this one stronger than the last. Trying not to show her discomfort, she waited for it to pass and decided it would be wise to return. She braced her lower back with her hands, trying to relieve the gnawing pressure that remained. *This is not the same as before,* she thought and smiled. It would not be long before Kinauquak's child was born.

"It is time to return," she said as she headed back the way they had come. Quieter now and no longer dashing about, Iya clasped Anna's hand in hers as she walked beside her. A strange sound carried across the forest. They both heard it and looked at each other.

"What is it?" Iya asked.

Anna waited a moment and listened. The noise grew louder. It sounded like cackling and came from the sky. Anna looked up to find a great flock of geese approaching from the south. She didn't speak for a minute as she watched the awesome sight of the great birds flying in formation. "The birds return!" Anna said with a lilt in her voice. "Spring will soon follow."

"Where do they go?" Iya asked.

"During the summer they live in the north."

The birds moved gracefully away from them. Anna wondered what it would be like where they were heading and felt an unfamiliar longing to see more of the world.

Iya interrupted Anna's thoughts. "Anna, do you know what it is like to have a baby?"

Anna smiled and answered. "I know it is hard. But it is what women do. It is a wonderful thing—only women can bring life into the world." She paused for a moment before continuing. "I helped bring other little ones when momma was called by women of the village. I know what to do."

Iya was quiet for a moment, then asked, "Can I help?"

Anna shook her head no. "This is not for little girls."

Iya's face was lined with concern. "Then who will help?"

"I am strong. I can do it," Anna answered as another contraction hit her. This one was more painful than the last. She breathed slowly and waited for it to pass.

"Are you all right?" Iya asked, the concern on her face deepened.

Anna waited for the pain to ease before answering. She took a deep breath and finally said, "Yes, I am fine. The baby is busy today, that is all." She moved slowly down the trail.

"Look!" Anna suddenly exclaimed and trudged ahead. "*Surah!*" She reached out for a dead-looking branch and stroked the soft, gray pods that clung to it.

Iya touched the fuzzy blooms. "Soft!" she said in a hush as she stroked her cheek with the plant's furry petals. "Can we take it home?"

Anna answered by breaking off the shoot along with two others. "We will surprise Erik," she said as she examined their prize. "This is a sure sign of spring. Soon there will be flowers too."

Once more the pain came, interrupting Anna's revelry. Just like the others, it began in the small of her back and grew stronger as it wrapped itself about her waist. *It has not been long since the last one,* Anna thought as she willed herself to not double over. The seconds passed slowly. This one was much worse than any previous. She breathed slowly, trying to remain relaxed as beads of perspiration appeared on her forehead. Finally the pain peaked and slowly subsided.

"We must go now," Anna said as she took Iya's hand and walked heavily toward the cabin. Twice more she was forced to stop. As a painful contraction ended, she smiled and said, "I think Kinauquak's baby will be born today."

Iya's eyes grew wide. She pulled on Anna's hand and said, "We must hurry."

"It is all right, Iya. The baby will not be born here. It will take many hours."

Erik had still not returned when Anna and Iya reached the cabin. Iya fussed over Anna, obviously uncertain what to do. Anna remained calm, confident that she was prepared for what lay ahead. She took the precious willows, stood them in a cup, and placed them ceremoniously on the table. She stood back to admire them. "Pretty. Erik will like these, I think," she said before putting coffee on to cook.

After this, she prepared a place where she could bear her child. In her village, she would have labored in a private hut, but here she would not be allowed that luxury. She gathered several pelts and spread them on the floor in the corner. Then she laid a special birthing blanket over these. Finally, she strung a line across the corner and draped skins over it.

Contractions came often now, forcing her to stop as they washed over her. When she had readied everything, Anna surveyed her work and realized there was one more thing she needed. She slipped into her cloak and went outside.

Iya followed. "Anna what are you doing?"

"I will need a strong branch when it is time for the baby," she answered as she scanned the ground.

"Why?"

Anticipating another contraction, Anna was distracted and had to stop. She bent down, gently placed her hands on

Iya's shoulders, and said kindly, "When it is time, there will be much pain."

Iya looked frightened.

"Do not be afraid. It is right to have pain. I will bite on the branch to ease my pain." Iya still looked scared, so Anna hugged her tightly and said, "I will be all right."

With Iya's help Anna finally found just the right limb. As she walked toward the cabin, she was hit by another painful spasm. She waited for it to pass before continuing on to the house.

The smell of coffee rushed out to greet them as they pushed open the door. Anna hung her cloak on its hook and sat heavily in a chair while Iya poured her a cup.

"Thank you," Anna said, taking the drink. She sipped the steaming liquid and tried to relax. As another pain jolted her, she closed her eyes and involuntarily tensed up with the discomfort. Once it passed, she said with satisfaction, "The pains grow stronger." She wished her mother were with her.

Iya looked worried and frightened. Anna ruffled her hair and smiled, trying to reassure the little girl.

With tears in her eyes, Iya asked, "Will it hurt bad?"

Anna believed in speaking the truth and answered, "Yes. But the gods make me strong. And the baby is strong." As she wiped the sweat from her brow, the sound of boots being stomped free of snow came from outside.

A cold breeze blew in as Erik opened the door. He looked tired but satisfied, and he hung his parka on its hook. "The traps did well today. Come spring we should have enough furs to pay for anything we need."

He glanced about the room, then at Anna and Iya. He looked concerned as he noticed the skins hanging in the corner. "What's that for?"

"Anna is having her baby!" Iya announced.

Erik turned to Anna. "Right now?"

"Yes. The baby will come today," Anna answered with confidence.

"Is there anything you need? Anything I can do?"

"Nothing," Anna answered calmly. Erik's concern touched her. It felt good to have him home.

Erik fidgeted with the fire. A minute later, he stood up and paced across the room. "What if you need help?" he finally asked.

"I will need no help to bear Kinauquak's son," Anna answered stubbornly.

Erik stared at her. She made no sense to him. As if to distract himself, he moved to light the lamps and restoke the fire. The flames shot up, and before long, the room was too warm.

Anna insisted on preparing the meal, claiming her pains were not so bad. After serving Iya and Erik bowls of soup, she joined them at the table but only sipped some water.

As Erik spooned soup into his mouth, he glanced at the twigs in the center of the table and asked, "Where did these come from?"

"We found them when we walked," Anna answered.

"Pussy willows, a sure sign of spring," Erik said quietly as he touched the soft pads.

"You call them pussy willows?" Anna asked.

"Yeah, see these soft petals? They feel like a cat's paw."

Anna gave him a blank stare.

"Pussy is another name for cat," Erik explained.

Anna nodded but was stopped from replying by another painful contraction. As soon as it passed, she stood and began to clear the table.

Erik intervened. "Enough's enough. No more work for you. You've got more than enough to do just having that baby. I want you to sit down."

Anna was tempted to argue but realized he was right and gratefully sank back into her chair. Solicitously Erik brought her a cup of coffee, which Anna only sipped. She was beginning to feel apprehensive and the coffee had lost its appeal.

Iya remained at the table; her eyes never left Anna. "Will it take a long time?" she asked, looking a little sleepy.

"I do not know," Anna answered. "Maybe many hours. You go to sleep. When the baby comes, I will wake you."

Iya nodded, slipped down from her chair, and snuggled into her bed. She tossed and turned for some time before finally falling asleep.

Although Anna's contractions had been increasing in strength and duration, she had maintained her sense of calm. But as one stronger than the others suddenly ripped through her, she shuddered, and before she could stop it, a moan escaped her lips.

Erik looked at her, his eyes filled with worry. Abruptly he rose from the table and refilled his cup.

As soon as the pain passed, Anna pushed herself up from the table. "I must rest now," she said and waddled across the room to her birthing bed.

Erik stoked the fire as he watched her painfully move. Restlessly he scanned the cabin for something to occupy his time. As his eyes fell upon his rifle he crossed the room, took it from its rack, and returned to his chair. He carefully disassembled it, placed the pieces on the table, and meticulously cleaned each one. Every few minutes he glanced at the curtained corner. Once Anna let out a sharp cry and in two long strides, Erik stood outside the fur partition.

"Anna, do you need me?" he asked gently. "Can I help?"

Anna hesitated a moment then in a tired voice said, "Yes. Can I have a drink of water?"

Erik filled a cup with fresh water and returned to the flimsy wall. Clearly out of his element, he asked in a tight voice, "May I come in?"

"Yes," Anna answered.

He peeked around the flap.

Anna sat against the corner, her face moist with sweat. She smiled weakly at Erik and gratefully accepted the water, saying, "I think it will not be long now."

Erik looked at the floor and asked hesitantly, "Do you need me?"

"No. Only woman," Anna answered stubbornly. Then as another contraction seized her, she said, "Please leave me now."

At first Erik didn't move. Finally, feeling helpless, he returned to the table. Instead of taking up his work, however, he bent his head over clasped hands and prayed.

Anna's pain intensified, and she knew it would be soon. She longed for her mother's gentle touch and brushed aside a tear as she thought of how different things might have been. Instead of cloistered in the corner of a cabin by herself, she should have been attended by capable women while Kinauquak waited with the men, anxious for the news of his son's arrival. Instead, he knew nothing of his child. He no longer even walked this earth.

Another contraction surged. *Momma!* Anna's mind screamed as she bit down on the stick. So much pain! Nothing existed outside her anguish. She tried to focus her attention on something else, but the contraction sawed through her. When she thought she could stand no more, it finally relented. Panting with exhaustion, she rolled to her side and tried to rest knowing another would soon grip her.

She stared at the wall and thought of her mother and of Kinauquak. *Kinauquak would be so proud of his son*, she thought. *If only he could have seen him.* A tear slipped from the corner of her eye and down her cheek. She felt so alone.

Another contraction began to build. Anna braced herself. Biting down on the stick, she forced herself not to cry out. *It will do no good,* she reasoned. *How long? How long will this agony go on?* she cried inwardly, wishing she could scream.

A strong need to push suddenly gripped her. She could not deny it. She grabbed hold of the chinking in the wall and squatted as the urge engulfed her. She bore down and tried to expel the child, then felt momentary relief. *Soon. He will be here soon,* Anna thought. She breathed in deeply and rested during the short respite, but was soon shaken by another contraction, then another and another. There seemed to be no end to the torture. *I am going to die,* she thought, as the all too familiar pressure began to build. She pushed, biting her stick, and groaned as she strained to bring forth the child. She waited. Again it came, and once more Anna pushed. She rested, and with one final push, delivered a plump, red infant into the world. She lifted the child from the birthing blanket and expertly laid it over her arm, patting it gently on the back. A wail rose from the baby's lips. Anna turned it over and swaddled the infant in a skin.

Erik asked, "Is everything all right?"

"Yes," Anna answered as she took her knife and sliced the cord that tied the child to her. She wiped her daughter's face clean as she gazed at her. A sudden outpouring of love overwhelmed her, and she realized she would never be free again. She would be forever tied to this child. She felt glad that it was so.

Anna tucked away the birthing blanket just as Iya called, "He is here!" and dashed inside the makeshift room. At first, she said nothing as she gazed down at the little brown bundle in Anna's arms. "He is beautiful."

"*She* is beautiful," Anna corrected.

Erik peeked around the draping. "Can I come in?"

"Yes, come and see," Anna said.

Iya jumped to her feet and announced, "It is a girl!"

Erik looked at Anna and asked, "Are you disappointed?"

Anna nuzzled the newborn, then held her up for Erik to see. "How could I be unhappy?" she asked

Erik looked inside the bundle. Heavy black hair framed the baby's round, golden face. She sucked on her small fist and had her eyes closed tight, not yet aware of her new surroundings.

"Do you want to hold her?" Anna asked.

"Me?" Erik responded with disbelief.

Anna nodded and held out her daughter.

Hesitantly, Erik moved closer. He clumsily took the little girl into his arms.

"Hold her head up, like this," Anna said, as she cupped the infant's head in her palm.

Feeling clumsy and stiff, Erik cuddled the newborn close to his chest. He stared at the little girl and whispered, "She's so tiny—a living miracle." The baby let out a small squeaky cry, and Erik immediately handed her back to Anna.

Anna settled back and suckled the infant at her breast.

Embarrassed, Erik turned and quickly retreated. Through the blanketed wall, he asked, "Would you like a cup of coffee? Are you hungry?"

"Coffee sounds good," Anna replied. "And I am hungry."

Iya came out a few minutes later, her face beaming. "Shh. She is asleep."

"Anna?" Erik asked.

"No. The baby," she answered, sounding a little annoyed, as if he ought to know babies sleep a lot.

Erik took a cup of coffee and a piece of fried bread from breakfast in to Anna.

She sat propped against the wall with the baby next to her, gazing at the little girl as if she couldn't believe she was real. "She is beautiful," she said.

"Yes she is," Erik agreed as he handed Anna the bread and set the coffee on the floor beside her.

Anna sampled her coffee, took a bite of the bread, and asked, "Will you sit with me?"

Erik folded his long legs beneath him and sat next to Anna. He watched the sleeping infant and asked, "What are you going to name her?"

"I have thought on that. My mother's name is right. She will be Luba. Her last name will be Kinauquak's—Omau."

"Luba Omau," Erik said, testing the sound of it. "That is a good name."

Anna glanced up at Erik but feeling awkward quickly looked away. Almost in a whisper she said, "That is not her whole name." She hesitated and lifted her eyes. "I think I will also call her Engstrom."

Erik met Anna's gaze. He was silent for a moment and finally choked out, "Engstrom? You mean after me?"

"Yes. You are the reason she is here. I know we could not have survived alone." Anna's eyes searched Erik's as she whispered, "I thank you, Erik Engstrom." She looked away and cleared her throat. "So, her name is Luba Engstrom Omau."

"That's an awful big name for someone so little, but I think it's a very good one," Erik said, his voice full of emotion.

Anna nodded and returned the half-finished coffee to Erik. "I need to sleep now."

"Good-night," Erik said as he left the enclosure. He blew out the lamp and crawled into his bed.

Iya had also returned to her bed and fallen asleep. Peace settled over the cabin.

Anna placed a thick layer of soft furs in the cradle Erik had given her and carefully laid Luba in the bed. She rocked it gently and marveled at the little girl who so recently had been hidden from her. She wondered if Kinauquak would have been pleased with a daughter. She was not certain he would be.

Exhaustion finally forced her to set her ponderings aside. Her last thought was of Erik. He would love any child, boy or girl.

Chapter 22

*L*uba whimpered and Anna quickly picked her up. She cradled the infant and crooned, "You are a good baby." Luba stopped fussing and turned her head, searching for the familiar voice. Her chocolate-brown eyes locked onto Anna's. Anna smiled down at the little girl and kissed her cheek.

Luba had quickly become part of the family and it seemed she had always been there. She rarely cried, but her disposition was far from mild. When she needed something, she wailed with zeal until someone took heed. For now, though, she was content, and as Anna gazed down at the little girl, life seemed nearly perfect.

Luba nuzzled her mother as Anna settled back in a chair to nurse her. The hungry baby closed her eyes, clenched her hands into tight little fists, and suckled greedily. Strong emotions washed over Anna as she watched the infant. Even the child's scent stirred something deep inside her. She had not realized how powerful a mother's love could be.

Kinauquak seemed so close, and Anna found herself thinking of him often. Each time she looked at Luba, she could see him. This child was part of him, all Anna had left of the young hunter.

Iya peeked from around the chair and stroked Luba's cheek. The infant swung her head about, searching for the intruder. Iya bent down and planted a kiss on her forehead. Startled, Luba waved her fists about wildly before returning to her mother's breast.

Iya asked, "Can I hold her?"

Anna grinned. "You hold Luba too much. She will always want her Iya."

Iya looked at her with pleading eyes.

"All right," Anna relented. "When she finishes."

It didn't take long before Anna resumed her daily tasks. Erik watched with concern, wishing she would do less, but he had learned it did little good to voice his opinion. Anna often did as she pleased.

Luba thrived. She quickly put on weight and began to watch the activities and people about her. Anna kept her in a pouch strapped across her chest while she worked and enjoyed having her child near.

"The way she's growing, she'll be walking before we leave," Erik quipped one day as he watched the baby. He was clearly taken with the latest addition to the household and often came indoors to check on her. He still made a hasty retreat at feeding time, however, embarrassed by the natural process of nourishing the youngster. Anna didn't understand his discomfort, but found it amusing.

Iya endlessly asked to care for Luba and, although Anna was a little uneasy at first, she found her young sister very capable. Carrying Luba about could be tiring, and Iya's help was a welcome relief. Iya seemed to feel no jealousy toward the new baby and always treated her with special care. Anna was thankful she had accepted Luba's presence so willingly.

Although Luba clearly captivated Erik, he never held her. Anna had asked him why and he had explained, "I just don't know much about babies. I'm afraid I'll hurt her. She's so tiny."

One evening after dinner, Anna decided to help him make the adjustment. When Luba began to fuss, she feigned weariness and asked, "Erik, would you get Luba?"

The big Norwegian looked at her blankly for a moment, then walked across the room to the cradle. For several moments, he stood towering above the chubby infant. Finally he stooped down and carefully picked her up. Very slowly he stood and balanced her in his arms as if she were a fragile piece of china as he returned to his chair.

Anna chuckled and said, "She not break."

Erik relaxed a little and sat back in his chair, cradling the little girl. Luba clasped her tiny hand about his finger, bringing a smile to Erik's face.

Anna smiled as she watched his insecurity slowly dissolve. Joy washed over her as she watched the interaction between them. How foolish she had been to fear that Erik would reject Luba. She should have known he would love her.

Later that night, Anna was awakened by something. Not knowing what had disturbed her, she checked Luba, but found her sound asleep with her thumb planted firmly in her mouth. She listened a moment longer and a sharp, cracking noise suddenly broke the stillness. Anna went to the window and peered out. There was no moon and the night was black. She could see nothing. Again a sharp, popping sound echoed through the forest. She waited and listened until it came again.

"Erik," she whispered across the dark room.

Erik groaned, rolled over, and buried his head beneath his covers.

"Erik," she whispered again, more sharply.

Erik pushed himself up on one elbow. "Is something wrong?"

"I do not know. Strange sounds come from the forest."

He climbed out of bed and groped his way to the window. Standing beside Anna, he scanned the darkness and listened, then muttered, "It's so pitch black, I can barely see."

Anna whispered, "Listen."

Erik waited quietly. When no sound came he said, "I don't hear anything. Are you sure you weren't dreaming?"

Anna opened her mouth to protest, but quickly shut it as the crackling came again. This time Erik heard it too.

He looked out the window, tipped his head, and listened closely. An eerie grinding sound floated out of the darkness, accompanied by a series of pops and snaps.

"It's the river!" Erik nearly shouted, forgetting to whisper. "The ice is breaking up!"

"It sound strange," Anna said. "Like angry spirits."

Erik grinned. "It's not spirits. Believe me. I've heard it before. Back in Minnesota the rivers used to freeze up tight during the winter. When the thaw begins they always make a terrible racket. It won't be long now until we'll be able to move on." He glanced at Anna and ran his hand through his hair. "Not long now," he repeated, his voice dropping off slightly as he went back to his bed. "First thing tomorrow, I'll go down and check," he said quietly.

Erik's outburst awakened Luba and she began to fuss. Thankful for the distraction, Anna cradled the baby in her arms and rocked her gently as she nursed her. "Not long now, Luba," she whispered Erik's words and stroked the baby's thick black hair. Her voice empty, she added, "Not long before we go." The thought of moving on brought with it a dull ache, and Anna suddenly felt lonely. With Luba cuddled next to her, she managed to fall into a fitful sleep.

Erik rose early the next morning and was back with a report on the river's condition before Anna had breakfast ready.

"Well, I was right. It's breaking up." He poured himself a cup of coffee and straddled a chair. "Don't know just how long it'll take before we'll be able to travel. If the weather stays warm, it should be soon."

Anna set the last of the berries and a plate of pancakes on the table and tried to sound cheerful as she said, "That is good. Soon we will go. This cabin grows too small." She looked about the room, brushed a strand of hair off her forehead and added, as if to convince herself, "It will feel good to travel again."

Erik speared two flapjacks and dropped them on his plate, but made no move to eat them.

"Will flowers bloom soon?" asked Iya as she worked her way beneath Erik's arm.

Erik forced a smile and said, "I betcha we'll be able to find some any day now."

Iya climbed up into his lap and hugged him about the neck. "Anna, can we look for flowers—today?" she asked.

Anna busied herself at the fire, keeping her back to the table, trying to hide her jumbled emotions. She had dreamed of spring, yearned for it, but now that it loomed before her, she wished she could stall its arrival. It meant flowers and warm, fresh air, but it also held unwelcome farewells. Without turning around, she quietly replied, "Not today, Iya."

Iya frowned but didn't argue.

Anna thought back over the last several months. They had been good ones. So much had happened. She cherished this home and the bond that had grown between Iya and Erik. She glanced at the man. *Admit it,* she thought. *You care for him.* She looked at the tall, handsome man who had become more than just her protector. He was family. The thought of remaining in some unknown village while he moved on into another world sent a searing pain through her chest. Hopelessness washed over her as she realized she had no choice but to live apart from him. *If only there were a way,* she lamented, knowing their two worlds could never meet.

"Well, I'd better get to that wood," Erik announced, his voice shocking Anna back to the present. "What we've got won't last us," he added as he scooted his chair away from the table and placed Iya on her feet.

Anna heard the door close but didn't turn around. She knew he had gone, but his presence remained. *He will always be with me,* she thought, and knew he was indelibly imprinted upon her heart where he would remain.

Iya skipped across the floor and knelt next to Luba. "Does she look like Momma?"

Anna settled her arm about Iya's shoulders and said, "Yes. She look like Momma." They both gazed down at the baby.

Iya finally said quietly, "Good. That will help me remember Momma."

Anna hugged her and said, "We will always remember."

The weather grew warmer. One day, Anna decided it was time for an outing. "Let us look for flowers," she suggested to Iya.

"Do you think we will find flowers today?" Iya asked and jumped to her feet, nearly dropping Luba in her excitement. After handing the baby to Anna, she quickly stepped into her boots, pulled on her coat, and bounced toward the door. "I am ready!" she announced as she waited anxiously for Anna to dress Luba. While Iya pranced, Anna slipped on a coat and strapped the baby securely into a backpack.

The snow was wet and packed. Much of it had melted, exposing patches of dead grass where small, green shoots emerged. While trying to decide the best route to take, Anna balanced Luba on her back, struggling to get the feel of the pack. It was the first time she had carried the infant in this fashion, and she felt a little unsure.

Iya ran ahead, excited to be out in the fresh air. Anna sighed and, unwilling to call her back, decided she should follow. The youngster twirled and skipped across the partially snow-covered meadow. Rather than keep her eyes on where she was going, Iya looked at everything all at once, glancing from one tree to another, looking for birds and animals.

Anna worried, certain Iya would take a tumble at any moment, but she never did.

The sun had brought the forest back to life. A few of the birds had returned and their songs echoed throughout the woods. They flitted from tree to tree, occasionally dropping to the ground and searching for bits of grass and twigs for their nests. Those without mates called in search of suitable partners.

A jubilant Iya squealed as she spotted a gray squirrel rummaging for tidbits on the forest floor. She took off after it, but it quickly scampered up a tree out of her reach. Iya stood at the base of the spruce, watching the small animal and hoping it would return. When it didn't, she moved off in search of something new.

"Iya. I want to look at the river," Anna called as she veered off and headed toward the waterway. Iya trotted alongside. Part of the time, she walked behind Anna and talked to Luba, trying to get a response from the baby.

Unexpectedly she announced in a piercing voice, "Anna! Luba smiled! She smiled!"

Anna jumped at Iya's shrill declaration. "Luba smiled?" she asked. "Oh, this pack," she muttered in disgust. "I wish I could see." She was tempted to stop and spend time playing with the baby, but her curiosity about the river's condition overrode her motherly instincts as she told herself there would be many opportunities to see Luba smile. She kept moving until she reached the riverbank.

Winter's icy grip had loosened its hold on the river as it had the rest of the land. The water was free of ice, except for a few small patches and, full from the melting snow, it rushed with a roar to the sea.

They would be leaving soon. *It might only be a few days,* Anna thought as the reality of their departure gripped her. Her stomach felt cold and her throat suddenly constricted. It was hard to breathe. *I should be happy,* Anna told herself. She squared her shoulders and tried to relax. But as she stared at a piece of spring ice floating downstream, all she could think of was Erik's leaving them. *Stop being silly,* she chided herself. *He is not leaving today. And when he goes, it will be right.* Deliberately she turned her back on the river. Trying to sound cheerful she said, "Now we will look for flowers." They went back toward the forest.

A small stand of birch stood apart from the rest of the trees and seemed to invite them to rest beneath the branches. Buds decorated the limbs and promised new spring growth. Patches of young, green shoots sprouted from the dead grass where the snow had melted. A single flower stood in the shadows.

Anna's eyes fell upon the delicate, blue star. She approached it slowly, as if it were a wild animal that might flee if she moved too quickly. She knelt next to it, trying to soak in its beauty. Oh, how she had missed the flowers. It had been so long. All of a sudden she was back on the bluffs overlooking the beach. There had been so many wildflowers there. Carefully she reached out and touched the fragile petals.

"Can I pick it?" Iya asked, as she crouched next to Anna. "It is very pretty."

Anna didn't answer right away. She blinked back her tears and answered quietly. "Yes, it is pretty, but do not pick it. It waits for its family to join it. Soon there will be many flowers. Then we can pick some and make the house pretty."

Even as she spoke, Anna was tempted to pluck the blossom. *It would be nice to look at a little longer,* she thought, but she couldn't bring herself to pick this first bloom. Abruptly she stood, afraid that if she waited a moment longer, she would take the delicate blossom.

Luba began to wail. Anna maneuvered the pack around to her side and carefully removed the howling infant. She sang softly and rocked her, but nothing would calm her.

"I think Luba is hungry," Anna said. "I will feed her here. If I do not, we will have to listen to her cry." She sat down on the damp grass, leaned against a tree, and nursed her daughter. Luba instantly quieted.

Iya's attention was still on the tiny blue flower. She examined it closely, and before Anna could say anything, pulled it from the ground, roots and all. Proudly she displayed her prize. "I will plant it near the cabin," she said. "When we leave, it will stay."

Anna resisted the urge to scold her. She knew the little girl had grown to love their winter home and hated to leave. *Maybe this will help,* she thought. "I will help you plant it at the house," she told her. Looking into Iya's expectant eyes she feared the plant might die, leaving Iya heartsick. "But it may be hard for the plant to live in new ground," she cautioned.

Iya ignored the warning and cupped her treasure protectively close to her.

Anna let the breeze caress her face. The creaking of the nearly bare limbs as they moved in the wind soothed her nerves, reminding her that it wouldn't be long before the rustling of leaves would accompany the breeze. Although the sun was bright, it gave little warmth and Anna shivered. She surveyed the patches of snow and grass and imagined what the area would look like in less than a month. Green bushes and flowers would emerge, followed by pesky insects and more birds whose songs would fill the forest.

I will miss this place, she thought.

Luba had fallen asleep. Careful not to waken her, Anna gently placed the baby in the pack and slipped it onto her back. "Time for us to go," she whispered to Iya. "If Erik comes back, he will worry."

Before pushing herself to her feet, Anna picked a stalk of the early spring grass. She ran her hands over its smooth broad leaf and smelled its fresh fragrance. *It is good that spring comes,* she thought as she placed the grass stem in her mouth. She chewed on it contentedly as they headed for home.

○○○○○○○○○○○

The winter storms didn't visit again and the river remained free of ice. It was time to leave. Erik seemed preoccupied and sullen as he made preparations for the journey. Anna wondered if he felt some sorrow at leaving but couldn't bring herself to ask, afraid of what he might say.

With Iya's help, she prepared food for the journey and gathered up the clothing while Erik worked on the umiak, making certain it was still seaworthy. He brought in his trap lines and banded the hides together.

"We did well this winter," he said as he tied up the last batch of pelts. "They're fine furs and should bring a good price." He looked at Anna and said, "You and Iya did a good job." Lifting up a bundle, he added, "I'll take these down to the boat." He stopped and, looking a little awkward, said,

"I'd like to give you some of the money when I trade them in."

"We did not help for money!" Anna snapped at him.

"I know you didn't. I just think you deserve something for all your hard work." He paused before heading toward the river, glanced at the smokehouse, and stroked his beard. "God has been more than generous. Smoked salmon will taste real good while we're traveling." Looking toward the river he said, "I'd like to be ready to go by tomorrow."

"We will be ready," Anna responded and, as she looked down at the baby, added, "Luba will be a good traveler." As she thought of the coming trip and the possible perils that lay ahead of them, fear welled up within her. Not wanting Erik to see her apprehension, she fought to dispel it. *Erik is a good boatman, and the umiak is strong,* she reasoned, trying to calm herself.

But Erik seemed to sense Anna's apprehension and said, "There's a village not too many days' travel from here. We shouldn't have to spend much time in the boat." He brushed his hair away from his forehead and gazed out toward the north. "The last time I came through, they seemed like good people. They live along the beach like your people did. It could be a good life for you, Iya, and Luba. There's even a trading post there," he added.

Anna only nodded her head, afraid to say anything for fear of giving away her true feelings. After composing herself, she talked of practical things. "There is much fish and meat, but no berries, and the flour is almost gone."

"Yeah, I know. We're getting low on supplies, but we can restock soon. I'd better get back to work," he said as he turned to leave.

That evening the cabin was unusually quiet. A heavy gloom had settled over the small home. Even little Luba was more subdued than usual. Anna cooked the last of the caribou and used a small portion of the flour for biscuits, making extra for the days ahead. Erik bounced Luba in his arms and nuzzled her soft round face. Iya merely watched the activity about her, saying nothing.

Before they ate, Erik bowed his head and prayed. "Heavenly Father, thank you for this food that you have provided. You have taken good care of us this winter and always made sure we had plenty to eat. Thank you for that and thank you for making Iya one of yours." He paused before continuing. "I'd also like to thank you for bringing little Luba to us." His voice faltered. "It's been a good year. I just ask that you would continue to watch over us and guide us in the days to come." He hesitated, "And God, I ask that you would help Anna to know how much you love her and draw her close. Amen," he finished abruptly.

He looked up and met Anna's gaze. She said nothing as she served the meal.

The next morning there was no time for misgivings or sorrow. There was too much to do. Erik began packing the umiak while Anna and Iya hauled the remainder of their belongings out to the boat.

They were ready to leave when Iya said, "Wait. I want to say good-bye to the flower." She rushed back to the cabin before Anna could stop her.

Anna handed Luba to Erik and followed. She had forgotten about the flower but was sure it must be dead. Iya would need comfort when she discovered its condition. But as she approached the cabin, she heard no wail of disappointment. Instead Anna found the little girl kneeling beside her beloved plant with a bright smile on her face.

Anna looked closer. There in the soft dirt beside the cabin stood the small spring flower. Anna found that it had grown and stood erect, reaching toward the spring sunshine, and instead of one blossom, it now held two.

"See, it has a family," Iya said. "It is not alone." She patted the ground near the plant. "Now we can leave."

Amazed, Anna stared at the little plant, but said nothing.

"Time to go." Iya announced and took Anna's hand. The two of them headed for the river.

Chapter 23

*E*rik paced along the riverbank, trying to quiet Luba. As Anna approached, he broke into a smile and happily handed the fussing baby back to her mother. Anna placed her child in the backpack and slipped it on.

"You all set?" Erik asked as he pushed the umiak partway into the river.

Quietly Iya asked, "Should we pray?"

Erik looked down at the little girl and smiled, then tied up the boat and knelt next to her. "Good thing you reminded me. I almost forgot." He glanced up at Anna before bowing his head. "Father, we place ourselves in your hands. We know you will never leave our side, and we trust you to protect and guide us. Thank you for loving us. Amen."

Before Anna could stop it, a quiet "amen" escaped her lips. She didn't know why she had said it and glanced up at Erik to see if he had noticed. She breathed a sigh of relief to find he seemed unaware of her slip.

After pushing the umiak back into the water, Erik lifted Iya and set her in the center of the craft. Anna followed, careful not to tip the small boat while awkwardly balancing the baby on her back.

"Are you sure we've got everything?" Erik asked as he scanned the bank. When there was no reply, he sloshed through the water and climbed into the rear of the boat. Planting the paddle in the soft gravel along the bank, he shoved off. The current quickly grabbed the umiak and Erik steered it into the deepest part of the river where there were fewer obstacles.

As they approached the open sea, the river widened and the water quieted, seeming almost tranquil. However, the underlying current was strong and swiftly swept them out into the ocean. Choppy waves rocked the boat where the two bodies of water met. Anna gripped the side, fearful that she and the baby might be thrown into the sea.

Luba, sensing Anna's anxiety, began to wail. Anna turned and crooned to the distraught youngster but was unable to raise her voice over her daughter's cries. All she could see was a flailing fist, and though she reached over her shoulder to try to calm Luba with her touch, she could barely reach her. She could do nothing until they were free of the rough water. So Luba cried.

"Sorry," Anna said as she looked at Erik and shrugged her shoulders helplessly.

"Don't worry. We'll be clear of this in a minute," Erik said as he worked to steady the boat.

Anna smiled, grateful that he wasn't annoyed, and wished she could shut out Luba's racket. She cupped her hands over her ears and sought relief as Luba's crying took on an even sharper, more demanding pitch.

Iya seemed unaffected by Luba's bawling. She held her chin high in the air as if trying to catch more of the breeze. "Do you smell it?" she asked.

"What?" Anna asked.

"The sea," Iya shouted over Luba's wailing. "The sea."

"Yes," Anna said and nodded her head knowingly. Even though they had taken short walks to the beach, she had missed the pungent odor of the ocean. It smelled like home. Pangs of homesickness swept over her. For a moment, the village and her people seemed so close, almost as if they had never perished. But, as quickly as it had come, the sensation passed, leaving Anna stunned and lonely.

"There's nothing like the ocean," Erik joined in. He closed his eyes and took a deep breath. "I didn't know I missed it until now."

The boat moved into calmer water and took on the steady rhythm of the waves. Glad to have something to do, Anna took Luba out of her pack and cuddled her close, shushing her as she rocked the infant. Luba continued to cry.

"This baby will not be happy until I feed her," Anna said as light-heartedly as she could manage. She settled down on the bottom of the boat to nurse her. Luba quieted immediately.

Erik blushed and kept his eyes on the open water ahead of them, careful not to look at Anna.

Still finding his embarrassment amusing, Anna grinned and chuckled softly.

"What's so funny?" Erik demanded.

"So, you do watch," Anna answered with a grin and glanced down at the baby.

"I was not. I heard you laugh." He stopped to gather his thoughts before continuing. "I just think it's a private thing," Erik defended himself. "Not something that ought to be done in front of a man."

Anna smiled sweetly and said, "Luba would have to wait a long time to eat if I waited until we were alone."

Iya giggled.

Erik struggled to suppress a smile and refocused his attention on the horizon.

The hours passed and the small group soon settled into the routine of ocean travel. Luba's presence did bring some complications, but Anna managed to keep her clean and fed. The infant proved to be a natural traveler and quickly adjusted to her new routine. The movement of the waves seemed to calm her, and she slept much of the time.

Iya gladly resumed her task of watching for debris.

Erik paddled hard much of the first couple of days, steadily moving in a northeasterly direction. He seldom rested, but exhaustion finally caught up with him and forced him to look for a beach.

He pulled his paddle into the boat and reached for the water jug.

Anna watched him with concern. He looked so tired. She wished she could help him more, but taking care of Luba occupied most of her time.

After gulping down a couple of mouthfuls of water, Erik shook the container. "We're running low." He studied the shoreline. "Watch for a place to put in," he instructed as he immersed his paddle back into the waves. He sighed and said, "I could sure use a good night's sleep."

Soon after that, Anna spotted a sandy spit reaching out from the coast. She pointed it out to Erik, who gratefully put ashore.

After a light meal, they settled down around the fire.

"My muscles aren't used to paddling anymore," Erik said as he rubbed at his stiff, aching arms. "I think I have a permanent crick in my back," he added with a wink as he stretched out on his bed. He fell asleep almost immediately.

Darkness settled over the land and the wolves sang to one another in the distance. Anna was the only one awake. She sat across the fire from Erik with her knees pulled up tight beneath her chin and her arms wrapped about her legs. Studying him across the dying embers, she wished she understood him better. *What does he think of me?* she wondered. *Does he think of me at all?* A dull ache settled in her chest; she wished he cared for her.

She watched his steady, even breathing. *He always seems at peace. My mind endlessly churns with questions and doubts.* She lay down upon her bedding and closed her eyes.

Rest eluded her. Thoughts of the journey ahead and the people they might find plagued her. What would they be like? Would they be good people? If they were, would she and the children be welcomed? Where would Erik go? The knowledge of their separation always remained in the back of her mind. It was a dark, heavy thing she tried to ignore, but it was always there, waiting like a demon to pounce upon her when she least expected it. She stared into the flickering embers and sighed as she tried to empty her mind. *I must rest,* she told herself, but it was nearly dawn before she fell into an uneasy sleep.

Anna was the last to awaken the following morning. Exhausted from worry and lack of sleep, she watched Erik through bleary eyes.

He grinned at her over the frying pan and said, "Just in time. This is nearly done."

Luba's happy chortle caught her attention. The infant lay content in Iya's lap, chewing on the handle of a cup and watching the activity about her.

Anna pushed herself upright and stretched. "Sorry I slept so late."

"By the looks of it, you needed the extra rest," Erik said as he slipped a piece of fish onto a plate. "You look a little peaked this morning."

She frowned at him as she brushed out her hair. Luba had recognized her mother's voice and whimpered, so Anna took her from Iya. Holding her at arm's length, she smiled into the round face and asked, "You hungry, little one?" Luba didn't quiet until Anna began to nurse her.

After breakfast was out of the way, Erik took the water jug and headed for the spring. "We'll be leaving as soon as we get everything packed," he called over his shoulder.

They quickly continued their journey east. Anna watched the shoreline for signs of life, and although the landscape held many pleasures, it remained empty of people.

The forests of spruce and aspen were thick with heavy underbrush. Tall, jagged peaks, still covered with snow, stretched up behind the dense forests, looking enticing and forbidding at the same time. The sea no longer stretched out endlessly. Another shoreline was visible to the south.

"What is that?" Anna asked, pointing to the opposite shore.

Erik studied the distant land mass. "I think it's Kodiak Island. We'll be in Cook Inlet soon. Shouldn't be too many more days until we see the village I was telling you about."

Anna nodded. The thought brought only uneasiness, so she turned her attention back to watching for debris. A short time later, she spotted something floating ahead of them but couldn't make out what it was. "Something is in the water up there," she said, pointing toward the object.

Erik followed the direction of her hand and carefully steered them around the obstacle. As they drew closer, they identified a floating chunk of ice. "I had hoped the waterways would be free of ice. If we hit a piece it could tear out the bottom of the boat. We'd better watch closely for it from now on."

They saw the shoreline to the south for several days, and when it finally disappeared, Anna felt a little uneasy. She had grown accustomed to being hedged in on both sides, and now an open expanse of water lay where the land had been. The openness seemed menacing. Ice continued to be a problem, but Iya had made a game out of searching for the frozen fragments. She wanted to be the first to find them and was always proud to point out her discoveries.

The days passed uneventfully and the weather remained cool. The color of the water had changed. No longer a bottomless black, its hue transformed with the tides and weather. One morning when the mist burned off, the vague contour of another coastline appeared.

"Are we in Cook Inlet now?" Anna asked.

"Yeah, I think so." Erik nodded in the direction of the hazy shore. "That ought to be the Kenai Peninsula." Soberly he added, "It won't be much further now."

As always, Erik kept the boat close to shore, occasionally putting in for rest and food. Fog became a problem, frequently closing in about them. It unsettled and disoriented Anna. But Erik always seemed to know which direction they were heading despite the fog.

One day as the dense moisture settled about them, Anna said, "I do not like the fog. I cannot tell up from down. Everything looks the same." She peered about, trying to penetrate the thick mist, and said, "I do not like it."

Erik nodded. "I'm not partial to it either. I hope it breaks soon."

When the sun did burn away the fog, however, they had to contend with its effect on their skin. Anna rubbed animal fat on herself and the little ones to protect them from the punishing glare of the unrelenting ball of fire. Anna shaded Luba with her body, but there was no relief for the rest of them. And although Erik used the salve liberally, his fair skin burned and blistered badly.

One morning, Erik suddenly tensed and strained forward on his seat. He stared hard at the shore. Saying nothing, he paddled hard, never taking his eyes from the beach.

Anna followed his gaze. "Is that smoke?" she asked.

Erik nodded. "Looks like that might be a village. Let's take a closer look."

He pulled hard on the paddle. Anna joined him and, together, they quickly closed the gap between themselves and the beach.

As they approached, a village became discernable in the landscape. Anna could see small houses made of wood and smaller buildings that looked like smokehouses. The people flocked to the water's edge.

"Is this the village you spoke of?" Anna asked.

"Sure looks like it."

The waves carried them toward the rocky shore. The villagers waded into the surf and pulled the boat onto a sandy section of the beach. Apparently happy to have visitors, they smiled and chattered in a tongue unfamiliar to Anna.

Erik recognized one of the men and leapt out of the boat to grasp his hand in a warm greeting. Smiling, they patted one another's backs and exchanged news of the past few months.

Anna stepped cautiously out of the umiak, for the moment forgotten. While balancing Luba on her back, she lifted Iya out and wished Erik would stop visiting and help. She took Luba out of her pack and stood back quietly, feeling strange and out of place.

Erik moved close to them and wrapped one arm around Iya's shoulders while resting his other hand on Anna's, and said, "I almost forgot. These are my friends Anna and Iya, and the baby is Luba."

The villagers all bobbed their heads in greeting and grinned at the newcomers. One woman walked up to Anna and motioned for her to follow.

Anna glanced at Erik for confirmation and, when he nodded and smiled, she cradled Luba against her shoulder, took Iya's hand, and followed the woman. The stranger didn't share Anna's tribal language, but could speak halting English.

"My name Affia," she said as they approached a small wooden hut. "You welcome stay my home."

Anna took Iya's hand in hers and followed the woman inside. The cabin was small and smelled musty, but light flowed in through a window. The room was neat and tidy, and Anna decided she liked it. It felt safe.

"You rest?" Affia asked.

Anna nodded and sank to the floor, cradling Luba. Iya sat, leaning against her sister's shoulder as if for protection.

Affia knelt in front of Anna and stroked Luba's hair. "Pretty baby," she said, her voice filled with longing.

"Her name is Luba," Anna said as she put the baby to her breast. She looked about and asked, "Do you have a baby?"

"My baby dead," Affia said quietly as she made up two beds on the floor.

It was not good to speak of the dead, so Anna turned back to Luba and said nothing more.

Affia motioned for Iya to rest. The little girl smiled shyly and lay down. The long journey and the excitement of the day had taken their toll, and she was soon asleep. After sharing a cup of tea with Affia, Anna joined Iya, keeping Luba cuddled next to her.

It feels good to be inside sturdy walls, she thought. *Like home.* Her mind filled with images of the cabin in the forest. In many ways it was a home to her, but the beach would forever be her true home. Before she could ponder such things, sleep swept over her.

If not for Luba's cries, Anna might have slept until evening. Groggy, she turned to answer the baby's wails. She wasn't there! Panicked at Luba's disappearance, Anna pushed herself up and looked for her child. Affia crossed the room with the squalling infant and, smiling, handed her to Anna.

"Thank you," Anna said as she cuddled the hungry infant. Affia returned to her work.

These are good people, Anna thought. She looked around the house and at the grass-covered hills outside the window and thought, *This is our new home.* She should have been happy, but sorrow strangled her joy. *What is wrong with me?* she asked. *This is what I want. A home and a people I can call my own.* Erik's face came to her mind and immediately she knew what suffocated her joy. Gaining this new family meant losing the one she longed for most.

Iya murmured, disrupting Anna's thoughts. She rubbed her eyes and glanced at Anna. She looked puzzled for a moment, then smiled and sat up. "Is this our home? Will we stay here?"

"If they say yes, we will stay." Anna answered. She looked at Affia and asked, "Where is Erik?"

"Erik?"

"The man we came with."

"He with men. Take furs." She offered Anna another cup of tea.

Anna accepted the warm liquid, took a sip, and asked, "What is this called?"

"Chia," Affia answered.

Erik poked his head through the doorway and, with a forced smile, said, "Something smells awful good."

Affia asked, "You eat?"

He grinned and nodded. Slipping off his hat, he sank to the floor next to Anna and accepted Affia's offer of tea. "Thank you." He tasted it. "This is good, very good."

Affia smiled and returned to her cooking.

"Did you and Iya get some sleep?"

Anna nodded and sighed. "Not enough. I am still tired. I feel like I will never have enough again."

"Yeah, I know. I'm pretty worn out myself. I've been down at the trading post and got a good price for the furs." He dug into his pocket. "Here," he said, as he held out a small bag of coins.

Anna looked at them and realized he wanted to pay her for the pelts. She shook her head no.

"Yes. You and Iya worked hard on those furs, and you'll need this to get yourselves set up. This will be a good home for you. The people are friendly and there's plenty of food. No one is going hungry here. They've got everything you'll need at the trading post. But you'll need money to buy it."

Anna felt hurt. *He does not understand,* she thought. *I never helped for money.*

Erik took her hand, pressed the bag of coins into it, and closed her fingers around it. "I won't take no for an answer."

Anna stared at the bag for a moment and finally dropped it into her pouch. Quietly she said, "Thank you."

Affia set out a grand meal for her visitors.

Iya stuffed herself full of fresh mussels and crab, saving her fried bread until last. Mumbling through a mouthful of food, she said, "I like these people. This is a very nice place to live." She turned her eyes toward Erik and asked, "You will stay too?"

Erik looked down at his plate and cleared his throat. "Uh, well . . ."

Anna fidgeted. She had known this moment would come and had dreaded it.

Erik stroked his beard. "I was talking to some of the other traders. There's a lot of Alaska I haven't explored yet and the trapping is real good on the other side of the peninsula. And gold has been found down south." He couldn't look at Iya. "I suppose I'll be traveling that way soon."

Iya's eyes filled with tears, and she clamped her mouth shut tight. Anna looked at him but said nothing.

"Iya, you knew I couldn't stay. I don't fit in here. A white man living among Indians?"

Iya's chin quivered and she turned away from her friend. Silently she gazed out the window as tears spilled down her cheeks.

Looking from Iya to Anna and back again, Erik awkwardly tried to explain, "A man could make enough money to get himself set up on a piece of land if he is lucky."

Anna nodded and quickly rose to wash her plate, hiding her own tears. With her back to Erik, she asked, "When will you leave?"

Erik sighed. "Well, it'll take a couple of hours to get myself set up. Then I guess I'll be on my way," he ended lamely.

"Oh," Anna said, her voice stiff and lifeless.

Trying to sound cheerful, Erik said, "Well, it looks like it will be pretty easy to make a new home here. The men told me Affia is on her own. Having you and the little ones to keep her company will be good for her."

"She is very kind," Anna answered cooly.

"Well, I'd better get moving. I have a lot to do," Erik said as he stood up. "Good meal. Thank you, Affia. He tipped his hat and disappeared out the door.

Anna choked back her grief as she followed Erik to the doorway. Her hand went to the necklace, and as she stroked the smooth walrus tooth, she remembered the day Erik had found it. Could it be true it had only been months ago? It seemed like a lifetime.

Chapter 24

*A*nna had known from the beginning that Erik would go, but she hadn't planned on loving him. She glared up at the sky and through clenched teeth, said, "You did this. It is your fault." Her outburst did nothing to soothe her; it merely intensified her sense of despair and emptiness. Fighting her tears, she slowly walked back inside.

Later that day Erik came back to the cabin. He stepped into the room but said nothing. Affia was the first to see him and asked politely, "You like chia?"

"No. No time. Thanks," he answered quietly.

Looking somber, Affia bowed slightly, and quietly left the cabin.

Iya sat on the floor with her legs drawn up close to her chest, resting her head on her knees. She rocked slowly back and forth while she chanted an ancient song, careful to keep her eyes from meeting Erik's. Her face looked lifeless and drained of the joy she had so recently rediscovered. Once more it was buried beneath the weight of her sorrow.

Anna poured herself a cup of tea. Before setting the pot back in the coals she asked, "Are you sure you do not want a cup?"

"Nah, don't feel much like it right now," Erik said soberly as he sat next to Iya. He looked tired. His brow was furrowed and he held his mouth in a tight grimace as he glanced at his hands. He seemed uncertain about what to say or do.

Anna tapped her finger against the edge of her cup. No one spoke. Only Luba was unaware of what was happening and cooed as she played happily in her cradle.

"Are you packed?" Anna finally asked, staring into her tea.

Erik cleared his throat. "Yeah, I've got everything ready to go. I just wanted to stop and say good-bye before I left."

Iya shot him a look of contempt.

Grief spread across his face. "Iya, I wish I didn't have to go. It hurts me too. I . . ."

Iya interrupted. "Then why do you leave? I thought you were my friend."

"I am your friend. I, I care about you very much . . ." Erik stumbled over his words. "It's just that we come from two different worlds. I can't stay in yours and you'd never be happy in mine."

"I would," Iya argued.

"No. I don't even have a home. I'm a drifter," Erik tried to explain, his voice weary. He glanced at Anna, unable to hide his guilt and pain. Setting his pack on the floor, he dug through it and pulled out his Bible. For a moment he let his eyes rest on it, then he ran his hand over the soft leather. "This belonged to my mother," he said to Iya. "I want you to have it."

Iya didn't respond. She kept her eyes trained on the floor in front of her.

Erik took her hands and placed the small book there.

Iya stared at the Bible for a moment before lifting her tear-stained face up to Erik. "I cannot read," she said. "Only *you* read stories."

Erik thought for a moment. "The man who runs the trading post is married to a woman who used to teach. Maybe she could read it to you. She might even teach you how to read," he added as he tried to smile.

Anna said softly, "Could you," she hesitated and glanced out the window. "Could you tell one more story before you go?"

Startled, Erik looked up at Anna and blinked away a sudden rush of tears. He cleared his throat and asked quietly, "What do you want to hear?"

Iya said nothing.

"The story of Ruth?" Anna asked.

Gently Erik took the Bible from Iya and opened it to the book of Ruth. He cleared his throat and self-consciously brushed at his moist eyes. His voice shook slightly as he began, *"Now it came to pass, in the days when the judges ruled, that there was a famine in the land. . . ."*

As he read about Ruth and her journey to a new land, a place with unfamiliar customs and strange ideas and a God Ruth had never known, Anna once more felt a bond with the woman who had lived so long ago.

"Then Naomi said to her daughter-in-law, 'Blessed be he of the LORD, who has not forsaken His kindness to the living and the dead!' And Naomi said to her, 'This man is a relation of ours, one of our close relatives.'"

Just as Boaz was to Ruth, you are my relation, Anna thought as she glanced at Erik. He was no longer the outsider she had met months before but family. Hope sprang to life as she considered how much like Boaz Erik was. Was it possible? Could he become her kinsman? Almost immediately reason told her no. *That was long ago. I am not Ruth. Erik is not Boaz. We are from different worlds. Two worlds that cannot blend.* But, as she remembered the sorrows, adventures, and joys they had shared, she wondered if they really were so different.

"So Boaz took Ruth and she became his wife," Erik continued. *"And when he went in to her, the LORD gave her conception, and she bore a son. . . ."*

Anna couldn't bear to hear more and abruptly interrupted Erik's narrative. "That is enough. I know the rest." She crossed the room and tended to Luba, even though the infant was content.

Erik slowly closed the Bible and returned it to Iya. Grudgingly he stood and fidgeted with his pack, unwilling to leave.

Iya stared at the Bible, and her eyes brimmed with tears.

Unexpectedly Erik scooped her up into his arms and held her close. Iya responded by clinging to his neck as if by doing so she could hold him there. Neither was able to speak through tears.

As Anna watched the exchange she wondered, *Why does he leave?*

Erik kissed Iya's cheek before reluctantly setting her down. Looking tormented, he wiped at his tears and forced a smile. "You take care of yourself and don't forget me, now."

Iya remained where he had set her, her shoulders drooping, and stared at the floor, unable to watch him go.

Erik turned and looked at Anna.

She focused her attention on Luba. She didn't want to say good-bye. Erik stood there watching her. His eyes filled with pain as he waited.

Anna cradled Luba against her shoulder and mindlessly patted her back. She knew he was waiting for her, waiting to say good-bye. Knowing it was useless to put it off, she finally lifted her eyes and looked into his steady gaze, searching for any sign of hope. Finding none, she took a ragged breath. She longed to tell him how she felt, but the words stuck in her throat. Mute, she waited for him to speak.

In a strained voice, Erik finally said, "Well, I guess it's time to go." He glanced at the floor, then back at Anna. "We've had quite a time, haven't we?"

Anna nodded, but remained silent. If she spoke she knew her sorrow would overflow, leaving her exposed and defenseless before him.

"Do you mind if I hold Luba for a minute?"

Anna handed the baby to him.

Erik held the little girl close. He lifted her up and studied her for a moment, as if trying to memorize her face, before returning her to Anna's arms.

He cleared his throat, "Anna, I'm going to miss you. I hope you find happiness here. I really do."

She thought, *You are my happiness,* but said nothing.

Erik hesitated and looked as if he wanted to say more, then without another word, hoisted his pack onto his shoulder, tipped his hat, and left the small house.

As Anna watched him go, every part of her longed to run after him; to stop him, to tell him she loved him. Instead, she stood motionless and whispered, "Please stay."

Iya stared at her sister with large, empty eyes.

Anna slumped to the floor and rocked the baby while chanting softly.

Crossing the room, Iya leaned on Anna's shoulder and asked, "Will we see him again?"

Anna didn't answer but continued her chant. The song grew quieter and gradually faded. Anna put her arm about Iya's waist and said, "I do not think he will return."

Affia rejoined them and quietly knelt next to her new friends, hugging and comforting them as if they were her own. For a long time they said nothing as they huddled together. Affia finally broke the silence and asked, "You love man?"

Anna blinked back her tears but couldn't find her voice and only nodded.

"Maybe he come back?"

Anna swallowed hard and answered, "No, he will not come back." Abruptly, she pushed herself up from the floor, set Luba in her cradle and rocked her. "We will live here now without him." She ran her hand across the smooth, cool wood of the cradle and wondered, *How can we live without him?*

The rocking lulled Luba to sleep. Anna wished she, too, could find comfort in slumber but knew it would be useless to try. Instead, she helped Affia prepare the midday meal.

As she scooped berries into a bowl Affia said, "After husband gone, I stay this house. Not move back to Mother's hut. Sometimes it lonely . . ." her voice trailed off and she seemed lost for a moment in another time and place. As if remembering where she was, she looked up at Anna and with a soft smile said, "I glad you stay."

Anna could only manage a small smile in return, her heart ached too much for more. She knew Affia missed her husband and child, and wondered what had happened to them. *Soon I will be more help,* she thought.

That afternoon, she worked on a summer tunic for Iya, hoping it would keep her mind off Erik. But the time passed slowly. Stiff and sore from sitting so long, Anna stood to stretch. Still feeling alone and empty, she stepped outside for some fresh air and was surprised to find that life had not stopped.

The little community flourished with life. A child cried out, and Anna turned to find his mother comforting him. Women chatted amiably as they cleaned shellfish and fleshed hides. An old man sat smoking a pipe while listening to the young men's tales of perilous hunts. He wore a knowing smile, for once he had been a brave hunter and had sought the whale and sea lion.

Anna studied the surrounding hills and decided a walk would feel good. She went back inside just as Iya awakened. "Would you like to help me cut grass for baskets?" she asked.

Groggy, Iya nodded her head and pushed herself upright.

Anna checked on Luba. As she stood over the infant, she was swept into the past. The village, her family, the wave—it all seemed like a distant, mystical dream. *She is all there is of Kinauquak,* Anna thought. He seemed so far away.

"I watch baby," Affia offered, cutting into Anna's thoughts.

Anna laid her hand on Affia's arm and, grateful for her kind support, thanked her.

Affia answered with a polite nod and patted Anna's hand.

Anna looked at Iya and asked, "Ready?" Iya nodded but didn't smile. Taking the little girl's hand, Anna led her out into the sunshine.

For a while they ambled through the village and met many of the local people. Each time they bowed their heads respectfully before moving on.

Rolling hills of deep grass decorated with blue and gold flowers bordered the village. Groves of trees stood like sentinels, watching over the small community. It looked so peaceful, so unlike Anna's turmoil. She wandered toward the alluring hills, hoping their tranquility would bring comfort.

For a short time the two sisters searched for the tough grasses of their island home, but were unable to find any. Tired, they sat atop a hill, surrounded by the fragrant field, and surveyed their surroundings. Anna took a long, deep breath and slowly let it out.

"It is beautiful here," she said approvingly as she gazed out at the sea. Her eyes swept over the village. "And these are good people. I think we will be happy here," she added, trying to disguise the emptiness she felt.

Iya stood and looked out over the vast ocean. Almost in a whisper she asked, "Does he not like us?"

Anna took Iya's hand and pulled the little girl close to her. "He likes us, Iya. He just cannot live our life and thought his was bad for us," she said and squeezed Iya tighter. They sat there for a long time, saying nothing.

Anna watched the waves sweep ashore as thoughts of the people she'd left behind and the lives they had shared washed over her. *They are only memories now.* Her eyes filled with tears. *Life must hold more,* she thought and sighed heavily.

Anna sat there for a long time before she noticed the sun lay low in the sky. She glanced down at Iya, who had fallen asleep. Shaking the little girl's shoulder, she said, "We must go. It is late."

They hurried back to Affia's hut. The smell of cooking fish greeted them. Anna fed a very hungry Luba. Although it had been hours since either of them had eaten, Anna and Iya had no appetite and ate very little. They settled into bed, hoping sleep, for a time, would cover their pain. But long after the others slept, Anna lay awake staring at the wall, unable to put her thoughts of Erik aside. She touched her necklace, felt its satiny coolness, and once more her thoughts returned to the day he had found it—the empty beach, the ravaged village, Erik's kindness. Now, more than ever, it seemed to symbolize all she had lost.

The room felt stifling hot so she slipped out of bed and opened the door. Remembering Erik's Bible, she felt compelled to hold it. *Maybe it will bring comfort,* she thought and fumbled through Iya's things in the darkness until her hands found the smooth leather cover. Taking it, she crossed to the fire and knelt in the dim light of the dying flames. At first she just stared at the book, wishing she could understand its secrets. She ran her hand over the old leather cover and flipped through the well-worn pages. She hugged it to her chest. Erik seemed so close. *Is this book what made him unafraid?* she wondered. *Or is it his God?*

Anna wanted to pray, but even as she considered speaking to God, the desire jolted her. She had never thought it possible that she would seek him. Gripping the Bible between her hands, she bowed her head and whispered a prayer. "You are the God of my mother. She was wise, always kind. Erik has been good to Iya and me. He, too, is wise." She hesitated, "I want to be like them. I want to know you." Tears spilled down her cheeks and she was unable to stop her sobs. "Can you take away my pain and give me peace?"

"Yes, he can," came a husky voice from behind her.

Anna jumped to her feet, whirled about, and peered into the dimness. The silhouette of a man stood near the door. She asked shakily, "Who is there?"

A figure emerged from the shadows, slowly illuminated by the dim light of the fire. It was Erik.

Anna stared at him, unable to believe what her eyes told her.

Slowly he moved toward her, and as he came close, he reached out and placed his hands on her shoulders. His eyes were filled with hope as he took a deep breath. "I had to come back," he said, looking into Anna's eyes as though searching for something.

Anna gazed back at him, unable to speak.

"I tried to leave. But as I paddled away from this place and you, I knew it was wrong. I couldn't leave without telling you . . ." He stopped as if looking for just the right words. "I know you think of me as an outsider and it's true. I come from a very different world and we are different, but I can't help," he swallowed hard, "I can't help loving you."

Anna sucked in her breath and stepped back.

Misunderstanding her reaction, Erik immediately apologized. "I'm sorry. I just had to tell you." His voice faltered. "I'll be on my way in the morning."

A smile spread across Anna's face as she stepped closer to Erik. She reached out and caressed his cheek. Her eyes never left his. Softly, she said, "Do not go."

Erik paused only a moment before enfolding her in his arms, crushing her to him, and holding her as though he were afraid she might suddenly disappear. Cradling her face in his hands, he gently kissed her forehead, each cheek, and finally touched his lips to hers.

Anna hesitated for a moment, then answered his kiss. She looked up into the face of the gentle Norwegian and wondered how she could have mistrusted him.

Erik's body shuddered as he held her close. "We almost lost each other," he whispered, the horror of what might have happened evident in his voice.

Anna drew back, placed her hands flat against Erik's chest, looked up at the big man, and said, "I want to know your God." She snuggled close to him. "My people are gone. You are my kinsman." She looked up into his eyes. "Where you go, I go. Your people will be my people . . . your God will be my God."

Anna's fears slipped away as she stood embraced by Erik. Finally she understood a God of love and possessed the peace he alone could give—the peace for which she had searched for so long.

ABOUT THE AUTHOR

*M*uch of Bonnie Leon's adult life has been spent as a homemaker and mother. She's dabbled in writing for years, but never set it in a place of priority in her life until an accident in 1991 left her unable to work. Little did she know at the time how important writing would become for her. Bonnie has never regretted the change in her life and thanks God for her family who has supported her through the difficult but exciting new direction her life has taken.

Bonnie and her husband, Greg, live in the small rural community of Glide, Oregon, with their three children—Paul, sixteen; Kristi, fourteen; and Sarah, twelve.

Although Bonnie spent her childhood in Washington State, her ancestors originated on the Aleutian Islands of Alaska. She grew up listening to fascinating and inspiring stories about Alaska and its people. Bonnie's mother, grandmother, and great-grandmother lived amid poverty and prejudice. But with the help of a loving God they grew up without the bitterness those conditions can bring. The stories of Alaska's early peoples is Bonnie's heritage—a heritage she wishes to pass on to others through her writing.

An excerpt from *Another Land,*
the sequel to *The Journey of Eleven Moons*:

*A*nna's feet had barely touched the wooden decking of the sturdy little clipper ship when the captain's orders to sail sent the crew into a frenzy of activity. They clambered over the riggings, pulling on lines and climbing up the masts to unfurl the sails. Each knew his duty.

The rush of activity fascinated Anna. She'd never seen anything like it. As the sails expanded and the ship moved beneath her feet, she smiled and turned her face to the wind. The air smelled good. She squeezed Iya's hand and hugged Luba close as she stifled an impulse to laugh. Her fears of the unknown momentarily faded as she delighted in being on the sea once more.

She took a slow, deep breath and looked up at Erik. His eyes were fastened on the swelling sails. He seemed unaware of anything but the billowing, white canvas that flapped in the wind. He was smiling, and his blue eyes sparkled with anticipation as he gripped the railing tightly, as if by doing so he might hurry the ship along.

Anna felt his excitement. At last, they were on their way.